Business Studies
Second Edition

Business Studies

Second Edition

DAVID NEEDHAM.

and

ROBERT DRANSFIELD

STANLEY
THORNES

First edition published in 1990 by:
McGraw-Hill Book Company

Second edition published in 1994 by:
Stanley Thornes (Publishers) Ltd
Ellenborough House
Wellington Street
CHELTENHAM
Glos. GL50 1YD
United Kingdom

A catalogue record for this book is available from the British Library.
ISBN 0 7487 1876 1

Typeset by TecSet Ltd, Wallington, Surrey
Printed and bound in Great Britain by Scotprint Ltd,
Musselburgh

Contents

Preface

Over recent years, business studies has established itself as one of the most popular A-level subjects. We believe that one of the reasons for this is an understanding that, no matter what profession the student eventually enters—whether as a nurse, teacher, surveyor or administrator—there is an increasing emphasis today on business skills, knowledge and practice. This book is intended as a comprehensive guide to business studies which will help students to understand many of the dynamic forces within the business environment.

Business studies involves finding out how organizations operate in a wide setting. Over recent years many organizations have not just measured their successes in terms of profits, but have also been proud to emphasize other corporate objectives such as concern for the environment, equal opportunities, not testing products on animals, etc. This represents a fundamental change in approach. Such increasing sensitivity towards issues that genuinely matter to their customers will help forward-thinking organizations to create a platform for social improvement. In this way we hope that, by responding to customer needs and other issues that concern them, organizations will play a role in developing the sort of society in which we would all like to live.

David Needham
Robert Dransfield

Introduction

As we move towards the era of the global village in a world of increasing change, new ideas, technologies and communication systems have transformed the business workplace. Our broad objective in researching and developing this, the second edition of *Business Studies*, has been to update the previous edition and to emphasize this world of change by using case analysis and other techniques to show how organizations respond and operate in such a dynamic world.

We have changed the structure of the book by increasing the number of chapters; this we have done by breaking down chapters early in the book into discrete units, which we feel provides a better introduction to business studies. We have also broken down the marketing area into 'Understanding customer needs' and 'Developing marketing strategies'; and, given the increasing contribution of small businesses to wealth creation, we have added a chapter on 'Small business enterprise'.

Apart from the last chapter, each chapter is made up of text, supported with case studies and a variety of activities including data response questions, essays and short-answer questions. As the reader works through the book, more assumptions are made about previous knowledge and greater emphasis is placed on integration. Chapter 24 contains a number of integrated case studies.

David Needham
Robert Dransfield

Acknowledgements

Given the nature of this book a large number of people from many organizations have made a valuable contribution to its development. Firstly, and most importantly, we would like to thank Anthea Coombs, Pat Church, Lavinia Porter from McGraw-Hill, as well as all of the other numerous editorial, production, sales and marketing staff who have made a direct input into this book. We would also like to thank the following: The University of Oxford Delegacy of Local Examinations, the University of Cambridge Local Examinations Syndicate and the AEB—for allowing us to use questions from part exam papers; *Management Accounting*, *Your Business*, *The Economist*, *The Independent*, *Business*, *Grantham Journal*, *Marketing Week*, *Personnel Today*, *Independent Grocer* and *Harrogate Advertiser*—for furnishing many of our case studies; Sherwoods Ltd, the Market Research Society (MRS), Procter & Gamble Information Service, J. N. Nichols (VIMTO) PLC, J. Sainsbury PLC, South Western Electricity PLC, Infocheck Credit Indemnity Ltd, Barclays Bank PLC, Shell Education Service, Understanding Industry, Young Enterprise, national statistical offices, Central Statistical Office, HMSO, the Department of Trade and Industry, Animal Rights Confederation, National Westminster Bank PLC, Concept Graphics, Clandrex Ltd and BP—for providing us with a vast array of materials; Rod Harris, Alastair Clelland, Val Charles, Peter Fletcher, John Day, David Hodgson, Mike Kirton, Marilyn Elliott, Aubrey Nokes, Sue Friery, Manjit Gill, Martin Coles, Jonathan Teesdale, Ram Singh, Kevin Fitzgerald, Jill Matthews, Ian White, Bryan Oakes and Laura Schuster—for providing help and support.

Finally, and it seems like we have said this many times (!), our thanks go to our families for their patience and understanding as well as the help of our teaching colleagues and the library staff at Darlington College of Technology and the Nottingham Trent University.

David Needham
Robert Dransfield

1

Introducing business organizations

In this book we set out to explore ways in which businesses and other organizations make decisions.

What is an organization?

An *organization* is a unit that is set up by people to pursue certain goals. Many organizations set down guiding principles which can be used to check how successful they are. Most organizations have the following features:

1. *A name*   This can range from the Church of England, the Girl Guides or Crystal Palace Football Club to Barclays Bank PLC, Mars or Virgin Airways.
2. *Objectives*   Objectives identify the direction/s in which you seek to move an organization. Every organization needs to have a clear idea of what it is seeking to achieve. By setting out a list of objectives, you make it possible to check how successful you are in moving in the right direction. (We will look at examples of organizational objectives in the following section.)
3. *Rules and regulations*   Some of these will be written down formally on paper. Other, informal, codes of practice are not written down but are recognized and responded to. Some of the rules will be imposed externally in laws laid down by the government; every school or college, for example, will have a set of rules governing safety in the school.
4. *Patterns and structures*   Organizations are *organized*—they have set ways of doing things. In the army, for example, there is a distinct organizational structure comprising a hierarchy according to rank. Other organizations are more democratic; there will be many decision-makers with similar status in, say, the Methodist Church.
5. *Posts and offices*   People within an organization will have different positions of responsibilities. In a football club, for example, there is a manager, trainer, coach, ticket seller, ground staff, etc.
6. *Chain of command*   In many organizations there will be a distinct chain of command, for example from archbishop to bishop to rector to curate, etc. The responsibility of each of these will be set out in official and unofficial codes.
7. *Power*   Officers will have varying levels of power vested in them. These powers will often be set out in a written contract. For example, in a sports team the manager may select the

team; the trainer may choose the training programme; the physiotherapist may set out a schedule for treating injuries; and so on.

8. *Records*   Organizations need to have systematic and well organized records—e.g. patients' records in a doctors' surgery. Nowadays many records are kept in computer files, but written records are also important. Most organizations will store records for several years.

 Task

Take an organization you know about and consider it in the light of each of the eight headings outlined above. To what extent is the behaviour of members of the organization governed by the features of the organization outlined above?

Classifying organizations by their objectives

Business organizations

We shall see in Chapter 5 that business organizations take several forms, ranging from small one-owner businesses to multinational corporations. Some businesses are concerned with making goods—we call these *industrial organizations*. Some are concerned with buying and selling—we call these *commercial organizations*. Some are concerned with banking and insurance—these are *financial organizations*.

Government organizations

Government organizations operate at both a local and a national level. They are accountable to representatives elected by citizens. They are concerned with running the country. Examples include the Department for Education and the county councils.

Public corporations

Public corporations are owned by the government on behalf of the people. An example is the British Broadcasting Corporation. They set out to produce goods and services to serve all the people of the country.

QUANGOS (quasi-autonomous non-government organizations)

These are unelected public bodies. They are run by boards of directors to manage a particular initiative. For example, local TECs (Training and Enterprise Councils) are responsible for providing training opportunities and schemes on behalf of local employers.

Economic interest groups

These are organizations representing groups of people with a shared interest. Examples are the Consumers' Association (representing consumers), the Confederation of British Industry (employers) and the Trades Union Congress (trade unionists).

Trade unions

Trade unions are an economic interest group. They are given a special status in law. They represent groups of employees in bargaining situations, both nationally and in individual plants.

Legal organizations

There are a number of legal organizations responsible for administering and supervising the legal process, for example the courts, the Monopolies Commission.

Political organizations

Many groups of people form themselves into political organizations. Some of these are highly organized (e.g. the Conservative Party); others are less organized, such as pressure groups campaigning on a particular issue, e.g. the destruction of the countryside.

Charities

Charitable organizations like OXFAM and the Spastics Society have a special status in law. In the past, charities were set up to provide for the helpless and the needy (the poor, the homeless). Nowadays many organizations have adopted charitable status in order to gain tax and other advantages (e.g. public schools).

Mutual help organizations

Some organizations have been set up so that members can help each other rather than to make a profit. Co-operatives are a good example—any surpluses may be shared among members. Some labour organizations work on this basis: members club together to provide support for the sick and needy.

International and multinational organizations

Many organizations now have a membership in several nations, either at a government or private level. Examples are the Red Cross/Red Crescent and the European Union. Business organizations may have tentacles in many countries (e.g. IBM, Marks and Spencer, Shell, Laura Ashley).

Developing corporate strategy

Every organization needs to have a clear idea of the direction in which it is going. This is the responsibility of strategic management.

○Case Study—Sun Valley Bakery

Figure 1.1

Sun Valley Bakery is a small bakery in the South of England. The business was set up in 1901 by Ebenezer Smith and was owned entirely by the Smith family until April 1989. At the start Ebenezer Smith had been the sole owner. In 1944 Ebenezer had retired to become a limited partner, forming a partnership with his daughter Jane and his son David. David and Jane concentrated on producing the traditional lines of Sun Valley Bakery—standard white and standard brown loaves. The bakery had done particularly well in the 1960s and 1970s, supplying loaves direct to shops selling fresh bread in the Oxford area. During the 1980s, however, sales had dropped, and David and Jane considered selling the bakery to a large bread manufacturer. However, David's son Noel was keen to take over the bakery and introduce some new ideas of his own. In April 1992 Noel Smith bought out his father's and aunt's stake in the company for a cash price of £0.5 million.

Noel immediately changed the organization of the business, which had previously been a partnership. Noel formed a private limited company and sold shares to three wealthy friends.

The next step was to diversify into wholemeal bread to take advantage of the current fashion for wholemeal products. Using capital obtained from the sale of shares, the company invested a further £0.5 million in updating the bakery ovens and purchasing two new delivery vans.

Figure 1.2 was produced by Noel Smith to show to his three major shareholders in December 1992. It shows the value of sales made by the bakery in 1991 and 1992. In March 1992 sales made by the bakery had been divided equally between white and brown loaves. However, with the introduction of wholemeal loaves the demand for bread from breadshops altered dramatically. The new demand pattern is illustrated by the sales breakdown for December 1992, shown in Fig. 1.3.

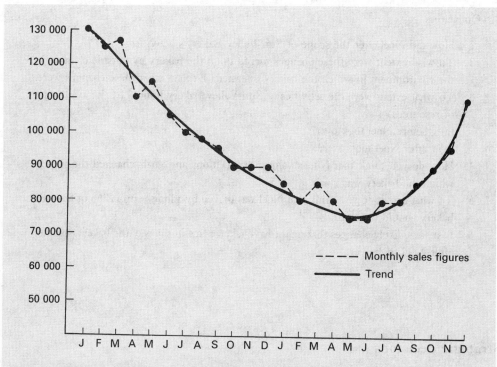

Figure 1.2 Change in value of sales made by Sun Valley Bakery, 1991–1992.

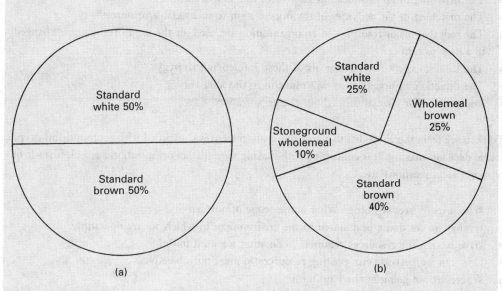

Figure 1.3 (a) Percentage of sales, March 1992, by value. (b) Percentage of sales, December 1992, by value.

Questions

1. How did Noel alter the scope of Sun Valley Bakery's activities?
2. To what extent were these changes forced upon the bakery by outside changes in the environment in which the bakery operated? Explain what these changes were.
3. To what extent were the activities of Sun Valley Bakery limited by the availability of resources
   (a) before Noel took over?
   (b) after Noel took over?
4. How do you think that Noel's values, expectations and goals changed the way in which the bakery was run?
5. To what extent do you think that Noel was driven by a long-term vision of how the bakery should develop?
6. List some likely changes that might have taken place in the way the bakery was run after Noel took over.

Strategic decisions

Strategic decisions are concerned with:

- The scope of an organization's activities
- The matching of an organization's activities to its environment
- The matching of the activities of the organization to its available resources
- The way that major resources in an organization are used, or the use of resources is changed to a new pattern
- The values, expectations and goals of those influencing strategy
- The direction an organization will move in in the long run
- Implications for change throughout the organization

You can see from the above list that strategic management is concerned with profound and deep-seated decision-making. It is concerned with making sure that an organization has a clear sense of purpose. Key questions are:

- What exactly are we doing? What is the scope of our activity?
- Is what we are doing best suited to the environment in which we are operating?
- Have we got the resources required to do what we want to do?
- How can we best use our existing resources to meet our objectives?
- Where are we going in the long term?

We return to look at strategic decision-making in more depth in Chapter 9.

Business aims

Businesses are set up for many different reasons. Profit may be an important motive, but it is certainly not the only one. Many people are prepared to take a cut in earnings in exchange for the satisfaction and freedom of working for themselves.

Businesses generally have a wide range of possible aims, including to:

- make as much profit as possible
- be the 'No. 1' product in a given market
- maximize sales
- grow quickly
- operate in a wide range of markets
- provide owners with a steady income
- provide the freedom for the owners to express themselves in the work they enjoy

Before we describe each of these aims in greater depth, it is necessary to introduce some simple theory.

Introduction to revenues and costs

In this introductory chapter we are setting out some of the important terms and concepts that are the basic building blocks of business studies. The terms 'revenue', 'costs' and of course 'profit' need to be included among these building blocks. These terms will be dealt with in greater depth later in the book.

Revenues are sums of money that flow into a business. *Money costs* are sums of money that are incurred in business activity.

Sales revenues

When an organization sells goods it receives sales revenues. For example, Sally has paid for a licence to sell ice creams at Wimbledon. She sells the ice creams from a small refrigerated truck. She sells only one type of ice cream, small blocks.

Sally sells the ice creams at 50p each. On the first day of the Wimbledon tennis championships, she sold 800 blocks of ice cream. We can therefore do some calculations on Sally's sales figures.

Total revenue

This is the total value of the products sold in a time period (in this case one day):

$$\text{Sally's total revenue} = 800 \times 50\text{p} = \pounds400$$

Figure 1.4

Average revenue

This is the average price of items sold. Sally sold all her blocks at the same price: 50p:

$$\text{Sally's average revenue} = \frac{\text{Total revenue}}{\text{Number of sales}} = \frac{£400}{800} = 50p$$

Costs

Sally incurs costs from running her business operation. One way of looking at these costs is to divide them into two elements:

- Fixed costs—which do not vary with the amount that Sally makes or sells
- Variable costs—which do vary with the amount that Sally makes or sells

Fixed costs

Sally has to buy a licence to trade at Wimbledon. The amount she pays is fixed whether she sells no ice cream or a million blocks that day. Sally has also paid for the hire of the refrigerated truck, and this too does not vary with the amount of ice cream she sells.

Variable costs

Sally buys her stocks of ice cream from a warehouse which is close to Wimbledon. She buys the ice cream at 25p a block. The more ice cream she is able to sell, the more blocks she can buy in and the more 25 pences she pays out. The cost of the ice cream therefore varies with sales (Fig. 1.5).

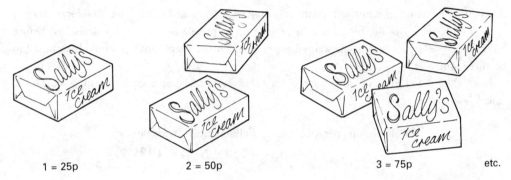

| 1 = 25p | 2 = 50p | 3 = 75p | etc. |

Figure 1.5

Total costs

This is the total cost incurred of producing goods over the time period:

$$\text{Total costs} = \text{fixed costs} + \text{variable costs}$$

For example, if Sally incurs £100 fixed costs and she buys 800 blocks of ice cream that cost her 25p each, then her total costs will be:

$$\text{Total costs} = £100 + (800 \times £0.25) = £300$$

Average cost

This is the average cost of each item produced. Sally's average cost per unit will be higher than the 25p she pays for each block of ice cream because she incurs some fixed costs as well:

$$\text{Average cost} = \frac{\text{Total costs}}{\text{Total number of units}} = \frac{£300}{800} = £0.375$$

Profit

A major aim for most businesses is to make a profit. Sally hopes that her sales revenue will be greater than the cost of buying the ice cream and the various fixed costs she has to pay:

$$\text{Profit} = \text{Total revenue} - \text{total cost}$$

So if she sells all 800 blocks of ice cream Sally's profit in the above example is:

$$\text{Profit} = £400 - £300 = £100$$

Breakeven

Accounting information is not just about recording what happened in the past. *Breakeven analysis* is useful for looking to the future and helping business people to make better decisions. Before Sally started selling ice cream, she wanted to know how many ice creams she would have to sell to be successful.

First, she needed to know how much money she would make on each ice cream sold. This is called *contribution per unit*:

$$\text{Contribution per ice cream} = \text{Selling price} - \text{variable costs}$$
$$= £0.50 - £0.25 = £0.25$$

So, for every ice cream sold, she would make a contribution of £0.25 towards paying her fixed costs.

Next, she needed to know how many of these 25 pences would be needed to pay her fixed costs:

$$\text{Breakeven point} = \frac{\text{Fixed costs}}{\text{Contribution}} = \frac{£100}{£0.25} = 400 \text{ ice creams}$$

More on business aims and motivations

On page 7 we listed a number of possible business aims. We will now look at these in greater detail.

Profit maximization

In the long run firms need to make a profit. People as a rule will tie their money up in a business only if they are satisfied with the return they get from it. This would suggest that profitability is a major business aim, although not necessarily the only one. The principle of profit maximization is illustrated in Fig. 1.6. A business has calculated the total cost of producing different outputs of a product and the total revenues that would result. Profit maximization will involve calculating the output that will achieve greatest total profit (i.e. the point Q on the profit-maximizing output axis at which the difference between total revenue and total cost is greatest). However, in the real world this process is a lot more complex than simply drawing up a diagram—it will involve a thorough programme of research, taking into account costings for different levels of outputs, the effects of charging different prices, calculations of potential sales and many other factors.

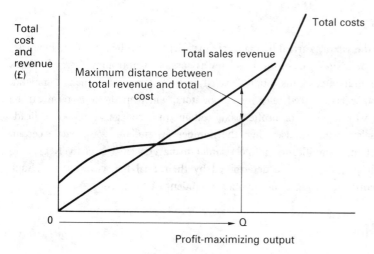

Figure 1.6 Profit maximization.

If we measured profit simply in money terms, then it would seem logical to assume that in the long term the rational business will seek to maximize the difference between its total revenue and its total cost. Accountants, for example, claim to be able to quickly weigh up the success of a business in terms of the financial profit—'the bottom line'. However, you will see in Chapter 15 that there are several ways in which accountants can calculate profits; indeed, this gives scope for what is called 'creative accounting'.

Market leadership

Many firms seek to be market leaders. They may want to sell more products than all rival brands combined, or simply to sell more than the next-best-selling brand. The most reliable indicator of market share is relative to other brands—that is, the ratio of a company's market share to that of its largest competitor:

$$\text{Relative market share} = \frac{\text{Market share of the company}}{\text{Market share of nearest competitor}}$$

A well-known study (by the Boston Consultancy Group) argued, on the basis of statistical information, that a ratio of 2 : 1 would give a 20 per cent cost advantage (i.e., you would be able to operate with costs 20 per cent lower than your nearest rival). If you dominate the market you can produce on a larger scale than your rivals. You can therefore spread your costs over a larger output. You can then produce more cheaply than rivals. Profits can then be ploughed back into research, advertising and further expansion to maintain market leadership.

Maximization of sales

In some large companies the salaries earned by managers may depend on the size of the business. Thus, their objective may be to make the business as large as possible. Controlling a large business concern might also give individuals satisfaction derived from the power at their command. Increased sales might also mean reduced sales for competitors, which in the long term can be seen as being consistent with a policy of profit maximization. In a college or school, a head-teacher's or principal's salary will increase when the number of students goes over a certain threshold. This is of particular significance as most senior managers will be relatively close to retirement age, and their pensions will be determined by their final few years' salary. Such managers have a big incentive to increase the number of students in their colleges.

Growth

Firms can benefit from growth. A firm that grows quickly will find it easier to attract investors and will be able to produce on a larger scale. However, one of the biggest mistakes that business people make in the early days is that of overtrading. Running a large business is very different from running a smaller one. Large businesses are managed differently and all sorts of problems arise from overtrading; for example, there might not be enough cash to pay bills in the short term; managing a large staff can be difficult; and so on.

Operating in a wide range of markets

Operating in several markets makes it possible to spread the risk. If one market fails, another may support the loss. However, opening into new markets also exposes a business to fresh risks. It may be better to operate in a small number of well-known markets than expose yourself to new risks.

Management by objectives

Most of us at some time have had the word 'satisfactory' written on our school report or profile. This indicates that we have managed to do enough to get by without making a great success of the task in hand. The theory of business *satisficing* is that managers in given situations set minimum standards which they feel will establish a reasonable level of performance. They will seek to establish obtainable objectives which can be measured (although some information may be imperfect).

'Management by objectives' (MBO) is a common business strategy which can be used to upgrade targets in the light of experience. It is a strategy that accommodates for the adjustment of objectives (see Fig. 1.7).

Peter Drucker was particularly influential in stressing the importance of MBO. He set out to find out how best to manage a business to make sure that profits are made and that the enterprise is successful over time. He felt that business objectives help management to explain, predict and control activities. The business should establish a number of objectives in a small number of general statements. These statements can then be tested in the light of business experience. It

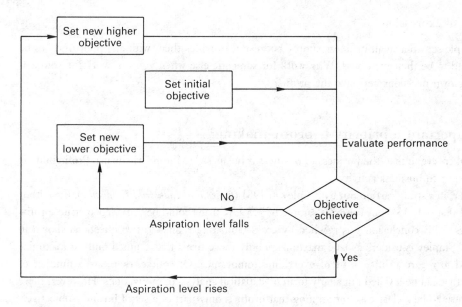

Figure 1.7 Management by objectives (MBO).

becomes possible to predict behaviour. The soundness of decisions can be examined while they are being made rather than by looking back on what has happened. Performance in the future can be improved in the light of previous *and current* experience.

Such objectives force the business to plan in detail what it is aiming at and to work out ways of achieving these aims. *Management* is the job of organizing resources to achieve satisfactory performance.

In concrete terms, Drucker listed eight areas in which performance objectives need to be set out:

- Market standing
- Innovation
- Productivity
- Physical and financial resources
- Profitability
- Manager performance and development
- Worker performance and attitude
- Public responsibility

We look at each of these areas in detail in this book. Managers need to have information available to them which enables them to measure their own performance and the performance of their organization.

Freedom of expression

Many people set up a small business simply because it provides them with an opportunity to be creative and to be their own boss. Why work for someone else when you can work for yourself, make your own decisions and take the profits?

How important a priority is profit-making?

Some thinkers argue that 'the business of business is business!' (Milton Friedman). Profitability is the chief spur to business activity.

However, in a study carried out by Shipley in 1981 (*Journal of Industrial Economics*), the author concluded that only 15.9 per cent of a sample of 728 UK firms could be regarded as 'true' profit-maximizers. This conclusion was reached by cross-tabulating replies to two questions shown in Table 1.1. Shipley considers as true maximizers only those firms that claimed both to maximize profits and to regard profits to be of overriding importance. Of course, there are a number of criticisms that can be levelled out at any form of statistical analysis of motivations. However, there would appear to be a clear case for arguing that profit is only part of a set of business objectives. (Perhaps students would like to carry out a similar survey in the 1990s. If so, please inform the authors of your findings.)

Table 1.1 Responses from a sample of 728 firms

	% of all respondents
1. Does your firm try to achieve:	
(a) Maximum profits?	47.7
(b) 'Satisfactory' profits?	52.3
2. Compared with your firm's other leading objectives, is the achievement of a target profit regarded as being:	
(a) Of little importance?	2.1
(b) Fairly important?	12.9
(c) Very important?	58.9
(d) Of overriding importance?	26.1
Those responding both 1(a) and 2(d)	15.9

Source: adapted from Shipley (1981).

The objectives of business firms are clearly of central importance to a course in business studies. We suggest that students carry out an applied piece of research, preferably by (a) talking to a small group of managers about their objectives, and (b) analysing the behaviour of a larger number of businesses.

Coalitions in goal formation

A managerial perspective of business objectives can be very narrow. Many business structures can be seen as being based on a coalition of interested groups. There are a number of internal groups within a business whose interests might be widely diverent—e.g. employees, managers, share-holders. At the same time, external interests will include those of consumers, governments, pressure groups and other producers. It is inevitable that goal formation will involve a balance of all these interests. Establishing business objectives will therefore involve a compromise between interested parties whose interest may conflict, for example over the distribution of company earnings between shareholders and employees.

The business environment

A *business* is a decision-making unit that sets out to produce a product in the form of a good or service (see Fig. 1.8). Any business today operates in a complex environment of changing forces that are interdependent (Fig. 1.9).

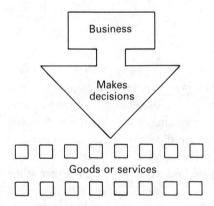

Figure 1.8 A business is a decision-making unit.

This dynamic web of factors forms the framework within which a business operates within a particular country. The web includes the social, economic, political, technical, legal, cultural and environmental systems in force, set in the context of historical influences and the pressures of the world economy and a competitive market.

No country is totally removed from external international influences. Countries today trade within global markets. While the business environment within a country retains a national flavour, because of its particular systems and history, it will nevertheless have to keep up with the demands of the world economy.

At the same time, businesses will need to recognize and respond to the regional flavour of their business environment. For example, patterns of buying behaviour may vary between Glasgow, Manchester and London.

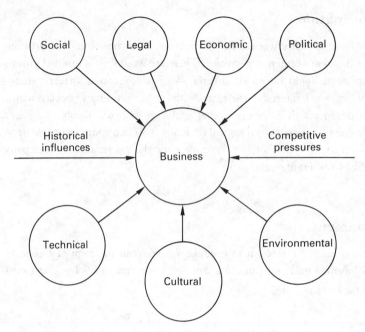

Figure 1.9 The dynamic web of factors affecting a business.

The business environment is therefore a highly complex web operating at a number of levels (Fig. 1.10). The decision-making process is therefore complex and dynamic. Change is the norm.

The three main groups operating within the business environment are individuals, business organizations and the state (Fig. 1.11). The activities of these three groups are constrained by limitations imposed by their environment. In turn, these groups help to create that environment.

While at first each individual action may seem to be independent, in reality it is a part of the environment in which it takes place. For example, the European Community (now the European Union) is setting out important aspects of the business environment within which companies wishing to trade in the Single Market will have to operate. These include:

- A legal framework
- Community-wide social policy
- Agreement on economic policy and trading arrangements
- Agreed technological standards
- A framework for political debate and political decision-making
- Shared commitments to the environment and limitations on pollution
- Processes for the exchange of ideas and inter-cultural links

Businesses need to be aware of these structures, frameworks and changes if they want to make the most of the Single Market.

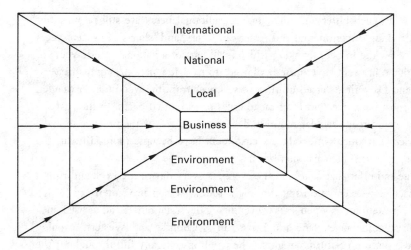

Figure 1.10 The many levels on which a business operates.

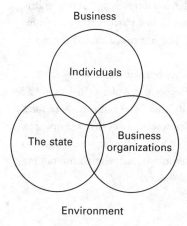

Figure 1.11 The groups operating within business.

Case Study—A business in its environment

Jane and Dave Partridge are the licencees of the Partridge Inn, a public house just outside Canterbury. They have owned the pub for the last thirty years. The pub is a free house, i.e. one that is not tied to a particular brewery. They are able to sell a range of beers and other drinks.

When they first started off, the Partridges had a group of regular customers. Today some of these regulars are still with them. Over the years, however, they have noticed a change in social attitudes to drinking. Nowadays there are more younger drinkers; in particular, there has been a rise in the number of young women. Thirty years ago the staple lines were English bitter and mild; today traditional beers are still popular but there is more drinking of continental and American lagers, and 'shorts'. In recent years there has been a decline in beer drinking which is all part of a national trend. Many of the smaller regional brewers have been swallowed up by a few national companies.

When Jane and Dave first started up they served beer from the wood (i.e. in wooden barrels); today most beers are sold from metal casks or as bottled beers. In the past the brewery lorries would make regular monthly deliveries; today it is the practice to make smaller deliveries at frequent intervals. As customers have become more affluent, the demand for pub entertainment has increased.

The Partridge Inn offers bar snacks in the evenings every day of the week and runs a restaurant service at weekends; during the 'high' tourist season in Canterbury (May–September) the restaurant is open every evening. The restaurant is advertised in a number of tourist guidebooks. Jane and Dave run a 'Country and Western' evening on Fridays and a disco on Saturday nights. Their pub is generally full throughout the spring and summer seasons.

Recently neighbours have complained about the noise coming from the pub at weekends. In addition, a petition was presented by residents complaining about traffic congestion in the streets around the pub. The local council has warned the Partridges that they will be taken to court if parking facilities are not improved and if the noise levels are not reduced.

The Partridges, for their part, feel strongly that taxes on beer in this country are too high. They point out that taxes on wine are much lower, particularly in other EC countries. They argue that it is taxes on beer and spirits that have reduced beer sales and forced them into new lines. They also feel that the new wine bars that are opening up in Canterbury present a threat to the traditional English pub. They argue that beer is the drink of ordinary working people. They say that a Labour government would not tax beer so highly and that this would revive the brewing industry.

Questions

1. Identify from this case study ways in which the business environment has (a) constrained and (b) encouraged business activity at the Partridge Inn. Consider in turn the social, legal, economic, political, technical, cultural and environmental factors.
2. To what extent have the changing activities at the Partridge Inn helped to change the business environment?
3. To what extent is the Partridge Inn exposed to competitive pressures?

Aspects of the business environment

As you read further in this book, you will develop an increasing understanding of how the business environment influences business activity.

In many cases the external environment will *encourage* business activity. The student needs then to explore the *opportunities* presented by that environment.

The external environment also *constrains* business activity. The student therefore needs to ask: How can we minimize these constraints, or even turn them into fresh opportunities?

The social environment

The social system consists of the fabric of ideas, attitudes and behaviour patterns that are involved in human relationships. For example, older people may have more conservative ideas about clothes and fashions than teenagers; these attitudes will affect the *buying patterns* of the two groups. Social systems can be viewed either at a *macro* level (i.e. studies of the structure and organization of large-scale systems such as national groupings, for example the buying behaviour of different age groups in Britain) or on a *micro* level (i.e. studies of small-scale groupings such as the buying behaviour of a small number of female members of the Royal Family).

Larger units can be seen as being made up of various sub-groups, e.g. the market for clothes, the market for fashion clothes, the market for skirts, the market for skirts made out of specific materials, the market for clothes bought by people in a particular income range.

The meanings and attitudes that influence social behaviour are formed and influenced by a range of economic, political, religious and other factors.

The legal environment

Every society is governed by a set of laws and codes established by the legal and political framework (Fig. 1.12). Local, national and international laws affect the running of organizations. Every organization, and all individuals working for one, must have a clear picture of their rights and responsibilities. For example, there are laws governing how many hours people can work, how safe working conditions need to be, the use of harmful substances in the workplace, etc. Many large organizations employ legal specialists whose job it is to be familiar with relevant laws and to communicate appropriate information to other members of the organization.

Common law is the term used to describe laws that have developed over hundreds of years through custom and practice. Their exact origin is unknown or uncertain, but they have become established by time and acceptance. For example, some footpaths existed before the first land records were ever kept; today these paths belong to the public and nobody can build on them, plough them up or fence them in.

Statute law is concerned with laws that have come into being as a result of Acts of Parliament. They can be altered or amended when they become dated or are no longer useful.

Every now and then new laws need to be passed to tidy up existing laws, for example governing how companies can operate in a changing world.

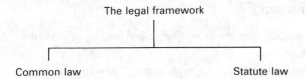

Figure 1.12 The legal framework.

Many statutory laws run to hundreds or even thousands of pages. It is therefore sensible for an organization to seek expert advice when introducing new or changing old practices.

The economic environment

The economic environment is a major influence on business activity. As we shall see in Chapter 22, Britain continues to experience periods of boom and slump. In a boom period unemployment starts to fall, more businesses start up, sales of goods expand, output increases and prices start to rise. This may continue for four or five years. Then sales of goods start to fall, output of goods is reduced, employees are laid off, wages rise only at a decreasing rate, prices start to tail off and the economy experiences a period of recession (Fig. 1.13).

The economic environment affects all businesses in many ways. For example:

1. The firm that has borrowed money finds that its interest repayments increase when interest rates rise.
2. The firm that wants to recruit more labour finds that its wage bill is pushed up in a boom period when wages are rising.

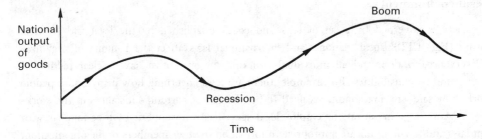

Figure 1.13 The economic environment.

The political environment

Politics is concerned with the organization and administration of public affairs. Major decisions are made by a number of political groups. These groups are chosen (elected) by a system of voting. Political groups that are given the power to make decisions (e.g. the government) have considerable influence in introducing new laws, raising taxes and spending substantial amounts of money.

In the United Kingdom, citizens are able to choose people to represent them at a number of levels.

At a local level they can vote for county, borough and parish councillors. *Local government* is concerned with running affairs in a given area. It has the responsibility for providing services such as local education and many welfare services. It is also responsible for such things as giving planning permission, and awarding contracts for refuse collection, running the local swimming baths, etc.

National government is responsible for all national public affairs. Under the British electoral system, the country is divided into 651 single-member constituencies. Representatives are elected to Parliament by the first-past-the-post (simple majority) method, which awards seats in the House of Commons to the candidates receiving the largest number of votes in each constituency (area that elects an MP). The boundaries of the constituencies are reviewed every 10–15 years to take account of population movements or other changes.

Under this system, the strongest party in the House of Commons may attain an absolute majority of seats with less than an absolute majority of votes. The system is generally considered to favour two-party competition, especially between parties whose support is concentrated geographically, and to discriminate against parties with support spread across the country; for example, the Liberal Democrats currently have a lot of support spread across the whole country, but only in parts of the West Country do they have a majority of the voters behind them in specific constituencies. The Labour Party is particularly popular in inner London, the North East and the North West. The Conservative Party has the bulk of the support in the South of England.

The party that wins most seats at a general election, or has the majority of members in the House of Commons, is usually invited by the Sovereign to form a government. The party with the next largest number of seats is officially recognized as 'Her Majesty's Opposition', which has its own leader (who is paid a salary from public funds) and its own 'shadow cabinet'. Members of both parties, plus any independent MPs who have been elected, support or oppose the government according to their party's or their own view of the policy being debated at any given time. Because the official Opposition is a minority party, it seldom succeeds in introducing or changing legislation; however, its policies or statements are important, since it is considered to be a potential government—and would become so if successful at the next general election.

European Community government

At a European level, electors can choose Euro-MPs (MEPs). The European Community is made up of 340 million people living in 12 member-states. Citizens choose an MEP to represent them. The United Kingdom has 87 MEPs in a Parliament of 567. The European Paraliament meets in Strasbourg. The MEPs discuss European matters and any laws that are being suggested or changed at a Community-wide level. They do not sit in country groups, but in groups of people with similar ideas.

The Community laws are made by ministers from the governments of each of the 12 countries. The Council of Ministers meets in Brussels. These ministers draft the new laws which will be discussed by the European Parliament. The Parliament can change the proposals for new laws if it does not like them. There is also a European Commission in Brussels made up of 17

Commissioners; their job is to monitor the need for changes in the laws and to identify ways of making sure the laws are kept. (From 1995 there may well be 16 European Union countries.)

The technical environment

Throughout history, society has experienced change. The industrial revolution, for example, changed people's lives radically. It brought great wealth to the mill and factory owners, but it also brought social upheaval by throwing thousands out of work from their traditional occupations.

Today the pace and the scope of change are as fast and as varied as ever. In this book we will be looking at a number of industries that have experienced rapid changes in technology, such as textiles and coal. We will also be looking at how major technological revolutions, e.g. the revolutions in information technology and food processing, have affected all industries and organizations.

The cultural environment

Culture arises from the traditions, beliefs and values of the community in which we live. It includes our religious beliefs, our attitudes towards alcohol, the food we eat and the importance we attach to family life. Cultural values can be very strong and can impose important constraints on business activity. For example, it would be unwise to try to sell products that are seen to insult religious sensitivities in particular countries; and it would be foolish to try to make people adopt working practices that are disapproved of by their cultural grouping. If business is to make best use of opportunities, then decision-makers need to understand the cultural framework in which they are operating.

The natural environment

Ecology is the relationship between living things and their environment. Over the years, a balance is created in the natural environment. However, rapid changes created by human development can threaten to upset this balance.

Human activity involves the use of resources. Some resources are replaceable; i.e. they are *renewable* resources. Other resources can only be used once; i.e., they are *non-renewable*. Some raw materials such as coal and oil take millions of years to form, yet they can be used up in seconds.

Recent major environmental concerns have focused on the problems created by acid rain and the destruction of the earth's protective ozone layer. The survival and growth of an industrial society requires a careful balance between industrial and ecological systems. Major decisions concerning the environment require careful collaboration between individuals, businesses and governments on an international scale. The ecological system is very much a prey to the social, political and economic systems. For example, substantial social changes will be required to achieve a major reduction in emissions of reactive hydrocarbons from the very wide range of sources involved.

Competitive pressures

Competition is one of the basic facts of business life. One bus company competes *directly* with another bus company, and *indirectly* with trains and other means of transport. Potential passengers may buy their own cars or decide to walk. Competition is always present in business. It should be seen as a threat. To be competitive means to get ahead of the competition.

Historical influences

Time is another basic fact of business life. Things change. The company that was the market leader ten years ago with very little competition may today be faced with many types of direct and indirect competition.

With the passage of time, social and cultural attitudes change, political and legal structures change, technology evolves, the economy goes through periods of boom and recession, and the environment is affected and affects business in many different ways.

The student therefore needs to give careful attention to the business *in its environment*. All those factors that influence the ways in which an organization can operate should be examined, and future changes anticipated.

Questions

Short-answer questions

1. What are the main features of an organization?
2. Describe three of the main concerns of strategic decision-making.
3. How would you work out (a) the total revenue of a firm producing a specific output? (b) the firm's average revenue at the same output?
4. List three variable and three fixed costs of a taxi business.
5. Why are fixed costs fixed?
6. If a business has fixed costs of £3000 and variable costs of £2 per unit, what will be its total cost of producing 6000 units?
7. If a business has variable costs of 50p a unit and fixed costs of £200 000, what will be its total cost of producing 100 000 units?
8. If a business has fixed costs of £10 000 and variable costs of 80p per unit, what will be its average cost when it produces 1000 units?
9. How do you calculate profit?
10. What is meant by contribution?
11. Explain the term 'breakeven'.
12. What is the difference between profit maximization and sales maximization?
13. How would you calculate the relative market share of a company?
14. Why might the principal of a college have a vested interest in increasing student numbers?
15. What advantages do firms gain from becoming the market leaders?
16. What is meant by 'management by objectives'? Why is it important to establish objectives?

17. What are the major environmental factors that constrain or encourage business activity?
18. What are the main three groupings operating within the business environment?
19. What is the difference between common law and statute law?
20. Explain the difference between direct and indirect competition.

Essays

1. The purpose of business is to make profits. Discuss this statement.
2. Explain in detail the main features of two organizations with which you are familiar. Compare and contrast aspects of these organizations.
3. Management is the job of organizing resources to achieve satisfactory performance; of producing an enterprise from material and human resources. Discuss this statement.
4. Do organizations need to make a profit? Discuss.
5. 'The business of business is business!' To what extent do you agree with this statement?
6. Any business that we set out to study operates in a complex environment of changing forces that are interdependent. Discuss this statement with reference to specific organizations.
7. To what extent is the environment in which a business operates an opportunity for, and to what extent is it a constraint on, business activity?
8. What is competititon? How does competition influence business activity?
9. Organizations are made up of groups and individuals with different interests and views. How can these different perspectives be accommodated in the organization of the organization?
10. What is an organization?

Data response questions

1   The cycling boom of the 1990s

Not since the Second World War have bicycles been as popular as they are today. From a postwar low in sales of 641 000 in 1970, demand has steadily grown so that today more bikes are sold than cars. In 1990 2.8 million bikes were sold, half as many again as in the 1930s. Today there are 15 million bikes in the United Kingdom compared with 22 million cars.

The growing popularity of cycling is based on health, environmental awareness, convenience and also image. Regular cycling can make you as fit as someone ten years younger. It is a highly efficient form of transport, using 50 times less energy than a car. It is also much quicker at getting you around a city (average speed 12 mph compared with a car's 6 mph).

Cycling is easier than ever before. Lightweight frames and up to 21 gears are taking the edge off hills. Puncture-resistant tyres have been developed. Modern fabrics offer rain-proofing without sweat.

The British Medical Association is among bodies advocating a switch to bikes and away from cars. A tenfold increase in cycling could cut car-borne emissions of carbon dioxide—the gas mainly responsible for global warming—by half. It would also save public money: a long-distance biking and walking trail, mile for mile, costs less than a thousandth of an extra lane on the M25.

However, in towns cycling can be a dangerous activity, and local authorities and the Department of Transport have made little provision for cycle ways. Also, it is becoming increasingly difficult to transport bikes on British Rail as the old guard's vans are removed on many routes.

1. You own a small firm producing bicycles which are sold throughout the United Kingdom. Which of the environmental factors hghlighted above would encourage you to expand production? Identify factors under the following headings: social, economic, legal, technical, political, cultural and environmental. What factors act as constraints on growth?
2. What factors would you need to take into consideration in devising a 'strategy' for growth?
3. What would be your main fixed and variable costs of production?

2   When growth slows down: Glaxo in the 1990s

When Paul Girolami became chief executive of Glaxo Holdings PLC in 1980, the first thing he did was to clean out the cupboards. At the time, the British drug giant sold everything from animal feed to vitamins. He sold off many of the none-core businesses until all that was left was prescription drugs. He increased research spending and launched *Zantac*, the blockbuster anti-ulcer compound. Glaxo's sales, profits and share price zoomed, transforming the company.

But now Glaxo faces a midlife crisis. It faces a number of problems, including patent challenges and pricing pressures, as new medical advances introduce competitive products.

Growth in the 1980s

After streamlining Glaxo, Paul Girolami turned it into a powerhouse by tripling research and development spending, decentralizing the organization and launching more new drugs in global-marketing blitzes. Sales grew from $1 billion in 1982 to $6 billion in 1992. It was a great strategy for the 1980s.

The changing nature of the market

The drug business has changed. Gone are the days when most patients obtained medicines by prescription. The market now is driven by large buyers—private health schemes, governments and even mail-order companies—which want to buy drugs at the lowest cost. Hospital groups and governments cap costs by setting out lists of drugs from which doctors can prescribe. To get their drugs listed, most pharmaceutical companies offer rebates, discounts and bulk sales. The bulk buyers usually go for the best deals. For example, California took Zantac off its list of prescribed drugs when it gained a better price from SmithKline Beecham for its rival anti-ulcer compound Tagamet.

Zantac contributes 44 per cent of Glaxo's sales and an estimated one-third of its profits. But cheaper products are now coming on to the market which are also effective in controlling ulcers. In mid-1994 a new version of Tagamet will be put on the market which will be priced 90 per cent below Zantac.

Zantac's patent runs out in 1995 and already two major rival companies are hoping to bring out drugs very similar to it. At the same time, medical researchers have come up with ways of curing ulcers outright. If this can be done, a drug like Zantac which keeps ulcers at bay will become redundant.

Moving out of prescription drugs

It seems likely that Glaxo may have to reverse Paul Girolami's strategy and move out of prescription drugs into over-the-counter drugs. There are a number of rumours linking Glaxo with existing companies that specialize in the consumer-marketing side of over-the-counter drugs.

What's new in Glaxo's pipeline?

It is expected that the growth of sales and profits at Glaxo will have slowed right down in the first half of 1993.

However, it's not all gloom and doom. Glaxo has a number of aces up its sleeves as a result of new products resulting from previous research and development programmes?

1. Imigran, an anti-migraine drug, is available in Europe and went on sale as Imitres in the United States in March 1993. Annual sales could hit $1 billion.
2. A promising anti-AIDS compound known as 3TC is undergoing clinical trials. Target launch date: 1996.
3. Ondansetron is in clinical studies for possible use against Alzheimer's disease. Target launch date: 1995.
4. A combination of Zantac and an anti-bacterial compound is under development as a possible ulcer cure. Target launch date: 1996.

1. Explain the significance of the following in the context of the case study:
   (a) Non-core businesses
   (b) Patent challenges
   (c) Pricing pressures
   (d) Streamlining
   (e) Global marketing
   (f) Strategy
2. What key factors do you think that Glaxo should consider in developing its strategic planning into the future?
3. In 1993 Paul Girolami resigned as chief executive of Glaxo holdings. Why might this have been necessary for the strategic development of the company?
4. List ways in which the case study highlights the influence of the business environment on a business organization. Explain the factors you identify.

3   Kettlewell Leisure Village

From summer 1993, Kettlewell Leisure Village ('KLV') has offered a unique combination of activities and facilities—all under one roof! It caters for the leisure and sporting needs of the people in Kettlewell and in the surrounding region (Fig. 1.14).

Figure 1.14

The village has a state-of-the-art leisure pool, laser arena, ice rink and nine-pin bowling centre. These are in addition to the usual facilities for tennis, squash and team sports. Complementing the facilities on site is a synthetic playing area and a 400 m athletics track.

Like most ventures in the tourism/leisure sector, KLV incurs significant fixed costs. Before the complex was started, its developers calculated that the venture would be viable only if visitors were willing to pay far in excess of the variable cost of their leisure activity (Table 1.2). With this commercial logic in mind, they have included a number of facilities to contribute additional revenues.

All visitors will be able to relax in the cafe or wine bar areas and enjoy the wide selection of food and beverages available. A post-match drink and meal can lead on to any remaining energy being spent in the disco. KLV can therefore be a centre for socializing, meeting friends and business contacts.

Companies can be catered for in many ways, from exhibition space and meeting rooms to a computerized golf centre and a health club.

The complex can also be a focus for entertainment; the main hall is able to seat up to 1700 people for concerts and exhibitions. Regional and national sporting tournaments are to be staged on a regular basis.

Table 1.2   KLV budgeted profit and loss account for one week

	£
Sales (3500 visitors × £8)	28 000
Expenses	
Maintenance costs of the buildings	500
Staff costs	6 900
Food and drinks	3 000
Wear and tear to inferior fittings/playing surfaces	500
Interest on capital	10 000
Heating and lighting	1 000
Business rates	500
Insurance of buildings	200
Marketing	500
Total expenses	23 100
Profit	4 900

1. Explain the following statements:
   'Most costs are fixed in the short term.'
   'All costs are variable in the long term.'
2. Identify which costs at KLV are variable and which are fixed on:
   (a) A day-to-day basis
   (b) A long-term basis
   Explain your reasoning for each item of cost.
3. Calculate the contribution each visitor makes to the fixed overheads of the complex.
4. Calculate the breakeven point for visitors per week.
5. To increase profits, KLV could allow off-peak discounts. With average cost per ticket working out at £6.60 (£23 100/3500), is there much scope for such a policy? Explain.

4   British sports cars: Lotus-eater

Frazer Nash, Austin Healey, Triumph and MG may have pulled into the pits long ago, but a clutch of small firms still carry the chequered flag of Britain's sports-car makers.

Lotus and TVR have led the way. Of the two firms, Lotus looked as if it had the best chance of surviving. Surely its giant parent, General Motors, had the money and expertise to succeed in the sports-car business. But on 15 June 1992 Lotus startled the motor industry by killing the Elan, its most popular model. The car was making heavy losses.

Perhaps Lotus's managers should have taken a look at their much smaller, independent rival TVR. This firm continues to make a profit selling a smaller number of cars. It sells to the same kinds of customers that Lotus was trying to woo with the Elan.

Lotus planned to produce 3000 of its £22 000 Elans each year. It ended up making only half that number. The firm's mistake was to apply GM's mass-production techniques to the Elan's tiny production runs. It spent six years developing the Elan and building a partly automated factory in which to make it. This led to fixed costs of £35 million per annum. Lotus stopped making the Elan after losing £13 million per annum.

Figure 1.15

The record at Lotus can be compared with the success of TVR, which sells just 700 cars per year and made a profit of £700 000 on sales of £15.4 million last year.

TVR's factory looks old-fashioned. There are no sophisticated machine tools to make its components. Such machinery can produce cheaeper parts, but only at far higher volumes than TVR needs. All this enables the firm to cut overheads to the bone. However, the firm has to use expensive materials that require little machine tooling; this increases its labour and material costs to £12 000 per car.

(*Source: The Economist*, 20 June 1992)

1. Calculate the variable cost per car for Lotus.
2. Calculate the fixed cost per year for TVR.
3. Draw a breakeven chart for both Lotus and TVR.
4. What is the breakeven point for each company?
5. How much profit would Lotus have made on the Elan if it had achieved sales of 3000 cars per year?
6. Why has TVR been more successful than Lotus?
7. Do you think survival for TVR is easy? Give your reasons.

5   Pinebeds Company

Table 1.3 gives the total cost schedule for Pinebeds, a small business making wooden beds.

1. Assuming that the firm is able to sell any quantity of beds at a price of £900,

   (a) Draw a diagram to illustrate the total cost and total revenue of producing different quantities of output.
   (b) How much output should the firm produce in order to maximize profits? Give five reasons why it might set this objective.
   (c) How much output should the firm produce in order to maximize revenue without making a loss? Give five reasons why it might set this objective.

Table 1.3 Costs of the Pinebeds Company

Output of beds per week	Total cost (£)
0	1200
1	2200
2	3000
3	3500
4	3700
5	4200
6	4900
7	5900
8	7200

(d) Assuming that the firm had originally set the target of producing five beds and selling them for £4500 in total, how might management react if it finds that customers are prepared to pay £2000 per bed?

Suggested reading

Barnes, S., *Essential Business Studies*. HarperCollins, 1992.
Bennett, R., *Organisational Behaviour*. Pitman, 1991.
Needham, D. and Dransfield, R., *Exploring Industry and Enterprise*. Cassell, 1989.
Palmer, A. and Worthington, I., *The Business and Marketing Environment*, McGraw-Hill Book Company Europe, 1992.

2

Interdependence and specialization

This chapter sets out to show how interdependence is a basic fact of business life and is therefore a key consideration in decision-making.

In all societies, goods and services are traded in the market-place.

Goods and services

A *good* is something that you can touch and see and which provides satisfaction for consumers. Cars, televisions, computers, bread, butter and wine are obvious examples of goods.

Goods can be categorized into *immediate-consumption goods* and *consumer durables*, which last for a period of time. A sandwich is an example of an immediate-consumption good; a microwave is a consumer durable—it is used for cooking over a period of time.

Services also provide satisfaction for consumers but the service itself is not a physical thing. You could not eat a service, or drive around in a service. It is something that is done for you (or for an organization)—a haircut, a college course, car insurance, banking, etc.

 Task

Categorize the goods and services shown in Fig. 2.1 under three headings: immediate-consumption goods, consumer durables and services.

The *market* is a general term used to include all buying, selling and the exchange of goods and services for money or credit. The *market-place* brings together consumers and producers (Fig. 2.2). *Consumers* are the general public and organizations who buy goods and services or who receive them free of charge. When I travel in a taxi I am consuming a service. When I eat an apple I am consuming a good. When I walk under a street lamp at night I am consuming a 'free' service (although I may pay for it indirectly through taxes).

Producers are individuals or organizations that supply goods or services to the market; for example, British Rail supplies train journeys, Mars produces chocolate bars, etc.

In the market-place, consumers are able to signal their preferences and choices by 'voting' with their money for certain goods and services. This week Brussel sprouts may be highly popular, so they will quickly sell out. The sellers realize that there is a healthy demand for sprouts, so tomorrow they may bring fresh stocks to the market and sell them at higher prices; and next

Figure 2.1 The market-place.

year farmers may grow more sprouts to meet the expected demand. At the same time, a particular type of tomato may not be selling well, so shops are left with stocks which go off. Consequently farmers next year will grow a smaller quantity of these tomatoes.

Every day millions of individual buying and selling decisions are made. When I go to buy a new shirt I am more concerned with my own buying decision than with the state of the market. However, my decision to buy one shirt rather than another has a tremendous impact if there are thousands of other consumers making decisions similar to my own. If we all want pink flowery shirts, then it will pay manufacturers to switch resources (such as labour, machinery and raw

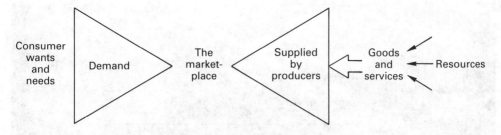

Figure 2.2 The market-place brings together consumers and producers.

materials) into making them. They may be able to make lots of them in a continuous production run at low cost and for high profit. If I am the only person who wants a pink flowery shirt, then I will struggle to find one, and I can expect it to be priced highly.

Needs and wants

The market is therefore an interdependent system that sets out to meet consumers' needs and wants. But what exactly are needs and wants? Are some needs and wants more important than others? These are some of the questions we shall begin to explore in this chapter and will take up again later in the book (see Chapters 4 and 11).

Some natural and man-made products are basic requirements for human survival. People require certain necessities, including items of food, shelter and clothing, in order to stay alive and healthy. However, it would be impossible to devise a generally accepted definition of an absolute standard of level of provision of goods and services that would meet every individual's needs. Needs vary according to a person's age, physical environment, health and many other factors.

At different times it has been argued that the old need less than the young, the low-born less than the high-born, the mentally ill less than the sane, the healthy less than the sick, the clerk less than the coalminer, and so on.

Perceptions of needs also seem to alter over time. For example, it is likely that many of the standards that are 'required' for survival by many modern Western citizens would have been regarded as extravagant luxuries in the no-so-distant past, including our current levels of heating in winter, a constant supply of hot water, electricity, soap and a wide variety of foodstuffs.

A distinction is usually made between needs and wants. Our *needs* make up our survival kit, while our *wants* are the desires we have for needs plus all our additional requirements. Most people strive for better conditions for themselves, their family and, frequently, their community, their nation and the whole world. They want better clothing, better living conditions, improved transport and many other products. Our wants are infinite. This is just as true of the relatively wealthy as it is of the poor.

In practice, it is impossible to draw the line at which absolute needs are met. Different measures have been produced at different times to define minimum levels of well-being below which people can be said to be living in poverty. Such measures produce an absolute standard

Figure 2.3 Dereliction in Manchester. (*Source*: David Rose, *The Independent*, 9 January 1989)

which can be called the *poverty line*. For example, in January 1989 the city council in Manchester published a report which found that a third of Manchester's 17 000 households were living in poverty (Fig. 2.3). The researchers defined poverty according to people's ability to buy 16 goods and services which are generally accepted as basic necessities of life. Those who were unable to afford three or more of these items, such as beds for everyone in the household, a warm waterproof coat, carpets in the living room and meat or fish every other day, were considered poor.

Another way of looking at poverty is to regard it in relative rather than absolute terms. A relative definition relates the living standards of the poor to the standards that dominate the society in which they live. For example, the poor might be defined as those whose incomes fall below, say, half the average income. Relative poverty is regarded as a real problem in modern society, in which people are all too aware of the lifestyles enjoyed by others and where advertising puts on public display a wide range of commodities associated with 'modern lifestyles'. However, relative definitions of poverty are also riddled with problems. For example, to adopt a strictly relative definition of poverty is to imply that the poor in Bangladesh are no worse off than the poor in Britain, which is clearly absurd (except, of course, for those experiencing abject poverty).

Ideally, a definition of poverty should incorporate both relative and absolute concepts. However, no generally agreed definition has been found. Clearly, though, poverty is a combination of being absolutely poor and relatively poor. A report published in 1991 (see Data response question 3 below) showed that pregnant teenagers have a high rate of miscarriage caused by inadequate diet resulting from poverty, and that mothers living on state benefit often go without food so their children will not starve. The Report claimed that the allowances provided to children and teenagers by the Department of Health and Social Security (DHSS) were insufficient and would allow only a poorly balanced diet, with insufficient food for energy and insufficient protein for growth.

Table 2.1 indicates the different pattern of food consumption for the rich and poor.

Table 2.1   Britain 1990: differences in vegetable and fruit consumption between rich and poor

	Ounces per person per week	
	Families with 3 children in richest income groups	Families with 3 children in poorest income groups
Fresh green vegetables	7.81	4.35
Other fresh vegetables	15.46	7.03
Processed vegetables	14.99	18.90
Potatoes	23.21	43.38
Fresh fruit	24.41	6.21
Other fruit/fruit products	15.22	2.23

Source: *Household Food Consumption and Expenditure 1990*. HMSO, 1991.

Scarce resources

In any society, resources will be scarce relative to the number of uses to which they could be put. A resource is a means of support. From the point of view of business studies, a resource can be regarded as any feature of our environment that helps to support our well-being.

There are two main types of resources:

- Physical or natural resources—e.g. soil, climate, water, minerals, forests and fisheries
- Human resources—people and their various skills

If we were to take stock of the world's existing bundle of resources, we would find that there are severe limitations to its ability to meet our infinite wants (Fig. 2.4).

Scarce resources can be broken down into four key ingredients: land, labour, capital and enterprise. Land includes all natural resources; labour includes all physical and mental effort; capital includes machinery and other items that go into further production; and enterprise is the art of combining the other three factors in the production process. These four types of production resource are termed the *factors of production*.

Scarcity can be seen as resulting from the lack of availability in resources, from people's insatiable wants or from a combination of the two. People have different views about how scarcity arises. For example, a famous quote from Mahatma Gandhi is: 'The earth has enough for every man's need but not for every man's greed.'

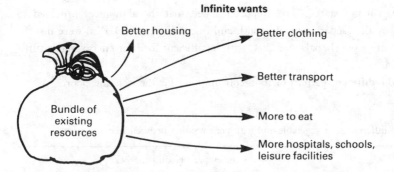

Figure 2.4 Infinite wants.

A society's strategies for using resources to produce finished products should consider long-term as well as short-term objectives. Some resources such as mineral reserves cannot be replaced; once they are finished with, new reserves cannot be created. At the same time, certain activities, such as the creation of acid rain, have been shown to destroy parts of the environment. Acid rain is an unwanted result of the emission of fumes into the atmosphere in the production of energy and other manufacturing processes. The chemicals created by this process have helped to destroy important timber, recreation and scenic resources in Europe and other parts of the world.

Opportunity costs

Businesses use up scarce resources. If society had all the land, labour, raw materials and other resources that it needed to make all the goods that people could possibly want, then we could produce goods without making sacrifices. However, resources are scarce, and therefore when we produce an item we are preventing the resources used to make it from going to produce something else. This is a major problem for any society. The real cost of using resources for a particular purpose is the next-best use to which they can be put.

We use the term *opportunity cost* to describe the next-best alternative which is given up in carrying out any particular activity. When referring to opportunity cost we need to be clear about whom these costs are related to. For example, if a new road is built the costs of this activity will appear to be quite different to the person whose house has to be knocked down to build the road, the person whose journey to work is shortened by the road, the firm that builds the road, and the taxpayer who contributes to financing the road-building.

Opportunity cost can be applied in all decision-making situations. The small child with only 20p to spend hesitates between a chocolate bar and a packet of sweets; the opportunity cost to the child of the chocolate bar that is chosen is the packet of sweets that is sacrificed. The same idea applies to production. A farmer decides to plant rape seed rather than sugar beet; the opportunity cost of the rape is the sugar beet that might have been grown instead. The cost to a country spending a high proportion of income on armaments is the lower standard of living than would be possible if resources were instead channelled into producing other types of goods.

ρCase Study—Alternative uses for scarce resources

The following extract appeared in the *Independent* (January 1989).

The swords, we are told, are being beaten into ploughshares. Seven weeks after Mikhail Gorbachev's historic address to the United Nations, announcing a cut of 500 000 men, or 10 per cent, in the Soviet army, the Soviet Union claims to have embarked upon the transfer of spending from military to civilian purposes, without which economic *perestroika* will remain just the words of its leader's countless speeches.

Over 200 military design offices are turning their hand to farm equipment. Between now and 1995, defence plants are supposed to supply 17.5 billion roubles (£7.5 bn) of food processing goods to the civilian economy, even tin cans and machines to make ice cream. The military sector is already starting to produce fridges, television sets and vacuum cleaners.

Questions

1. What does the article suggest is the opportunity cost to the Soviet economy of producing the consumer goods indicated?
2. Who will benefit from this alternative use of scarce resources? In each case state how they will benefit.
3. Who will lose out from this change in the use of scarce resources? How will they lose out?
4. Is it possible to evaluate whether the Soviet economy as a whole would be better off as a result of this change? What considerations would you have to bear in mind in attempting to answer this question?

Interdependence

Interdependence is one of the basic facts of business life. Business decision-making is part of a complex system of dynamic interrelationships. This means that the internal structure and functioning of an enterprise and the environment in which it exists will be in a continual state of flux. Some changes may be almost imperceptible, such as a gradual build-up of sales orders, while others, such as the arrival of a new managing director or the creation of the Single Market in the European Community in 1992 with the new opportunities for international sales coupled with the threat of increased competition, can have a dramatic impact.

An appreciation of the importance of interdependence is vital for effective business understanding. Enterprise involves not only the ability to come up with new ideas and to put them into practice, but also an awareness of changing business conditions, and the ability to respond with effective and positive measures in a changing climate.

The following examples illustrate some of the features of interdependence. The first one (Fig. 2.6) illustrates the interdependence between processes and employees in the production of

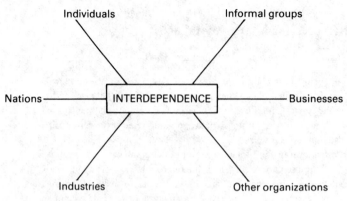

Figure 2.5 The web of interdependence.

chicken nuggets, while the second illustrates geographical interdependence in the production of a modern motor car.

1. Whole chickens arrive at the factory from the farms where the chickens have been reared. The chickens have already been killed and plucked. In the factory the chickens are sliced into the required segments: drumsticks, wings and breasts. These segments will then be either frozen and stored for future use, or passed along a conveyor belt to the mixing room where they will be prepared for their conversion to individual nuggets. Each nugget of chicken will then be inspected to check that it contains the correct proportion of meat before being passed to the next stage of the production line, where it will be dusted with flour. The nuggets will then be coated in batter, followed by bread crumbs. They will now pass along to be deep-fried before being frozen and packed ready for storage and final delivery to the retailer (Fig. 2.6).

    The production of chicken nuggets will have involved:

- The farmers who reared the chickens
- The manufacturer who processed and transported the chicken nuggets to the retailers
- The retailers who sell the nuggets to the consumers.

The nugget manufacturer employs a range of specialist employees, including:

- Management
- Cleaners
- Packers
- Lorry drivers
- Process operatives
- Supervisors
- Quality control inspectors
- Secretarial staff

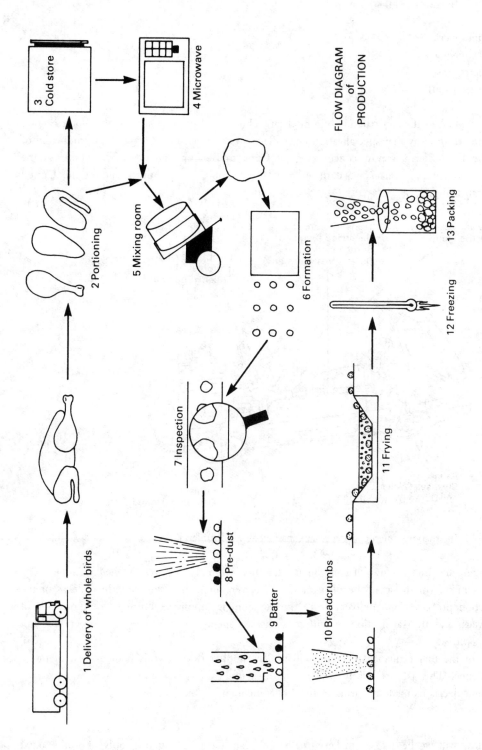

Figure 2.6 Interdependent processes in producing chicken nuggets.

- Wages clerks
- Sales people
- Electricians
- Canteen staff

2. If we look at the construction of a modern technological product such as the motor car, we can see the way that specialization takes place on an international level. The production of the Ford Sierra is now concentrated at Genk in Belgium, but the construction of the component parts takes place throughout the European Community and in the United States (Fig. 2.7).

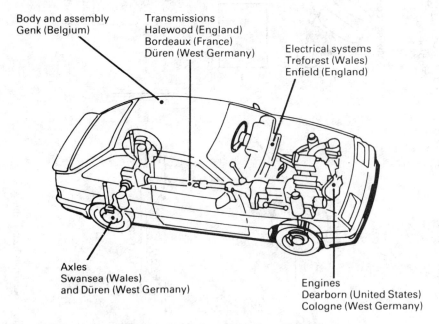

Body and assembly
Genk (Belgium)

Transmissions
Halewood (England)
Bordeaux (France)
Düren (West Germany)

Electrical systems
Treforest (Wales)
Enfield (England)

Axles
Swansea (Wales)
and Düren (West Germany)

Engines
Dearborn (United States)
Cologne (West Germany)

Figure 2.7 International interdependence in constructing a Ford Sierra.

Bringing together a range of components for final assembly requires detailed planning. The final assembler (in this case the plant at Genk) is very dependent on the effectiveness of the production processes and delivery from the component suppliers. The jobs of thousands of employees, and the satisfaction of end-consumers, depend on international co-operation and shared skills.

One of the major themes that you will notice running through this book is that of inter-dependence. This is particularly true in the area of business decision-making. Some of the important decisions made by firms in the 1990s include:

1. How will we be able to make sure that we can get an adequate supply of well trained employees?

2. How can we make sure that we have the technology required to make us competitive in a rapidly changing market?
3. How can we respond to changes in patterns of demand and supply in the Single Market?
4. How can we react to variations in international prices for basic commodities, raw materials and fuels?
5. How effective is our location in the light of the Channel Tunnel link?

Specialization

Specialization is fundamental to modern industrial societies. It occurs at a number of levels:

- Labour
- Equipment
- Plant and firm
- Industry
- Region (including national)

We have only to count up the large number of different workers, areas and types of plant and equipment that have contributed to the goods and services consumed every day by a typical family to realize how completely we depend on other people—on specialization—to satisfy our wants.

Specialization can be explained in terms of the *theory of comparative advantage*. This theory states that resources can be used in the most cost-effective way in those lines for which they are relatively the most efficient. For example, a tennis player might not only be good at her sport but also be a first-class accountant. However, she concentrates on her tennis and hires an accountant to do her bookwork because tennis is her most efficient area of specialism : it would take her a week to do all her paperwork and in that time she would lose £5000 in earnings, whereas it costs her only £800 to hire an accountant for the week's paperwork.

Specialization benefits everyone because, while the first-class specialists are concentrating on their best lines—playing rugby league for Britain, carrying out kidney transplants, designing wedding dresses for the Royal Family—the remainder of us can provide goods and services of an acceptably high quality even though there may be people who, given the time, could do the jobs even better. For example, at one time an author of this book worked on a production line producing electrical components—he was never particularly good at it, but was able to do a satisfactory job and earn a reasonable wage.

The advantages of specialization are that:

1. Resources can be concentrated into their most efficient uses—leaving other, less scarce, resources to concentrate on the other lines.
2. Factors of production become more effective if they concentrate on one set task. For example, the worker that specializes in the same task becomes faster and more accurate.
3. Specialization makes it possible to produce a greater output at lower unit costs.

4. Concentrations of specialists can lead to an increased sharing of skills and experience. This is as true for individuals as it is for the growing number of specialist companies in a particular region (who, for example, are able to pool resources to put on combined training courses for employees).
5. Specialization makes possible a higher standard of living. If individuals, groups and nations concentrate on their best lines and trade openly, then everyone should be better off. Surplus output can always be used to produce investment goods such as machinery which can lead to further increases in output.
6. Specialization means that one job can be done well rather than having a number of jobs done badly.

There are also a number of disadvantages:

1. Specialization can lead to a boring lack of variety. If one person repeats the same task over and over again, the work comes to have little meaning for him or her. If a particular region specializes in a narrow range of industries, choice of career and job opportunities may be felt by some residents of the region to be too limited.
2. Specialization can present a problem when one stage of production is dependent on the previous stage. If there are hold-ups and delays in the flow of production, this can be very frustrating. It can also be very annoying if another specialist fails to deliver goods for the quality and price that you expect.
3. Narrow specialism can make it difficult for factors of production to respond to change. Markets are continually in a dynamic state of change. This means that old skills and old industries will sometimes have to give way to new ones. This may be difficult when an individual, a group of workers or a whole region have become set in their ways.
4. Generalism is often more useful than narrow specialism. When flexibility is required—for example to rapidly ascertain whether a business can meet a new order quickly—it sometimes helps to have someone who can make a general audit of the various parts of the company to devise an overall strategy, rather than a specialist who is not prepared to look outside his or her own department.

Case Study—The division of labour in an eighteenth-century pin factory

Perhaps the most famous observation of the process of the division of labour was that done by Adam Smith in a pin factory and quoted in *The Wealth of Nations*:

> A workman not educated to this business (which the division of labour has rendered a distinct trade), nor acquainted with the use of the machinery employed in it (to the invention of which the same division of labour has probably given occasion), could scarce, perhaps, with his utmost industry, make one pin in a day, and certainly could not make twenty. But in the way in which this business is now carried on, not only is the whole work in a peculiar trade, but it is divided into a number of branches, of which the greater part are likewise peculiar trades. One man draws out the wire, another straights it, a third cuts it, a fourth

points it, a fifth grinds it at the top for receiving the head; to make the head requires two or three distinct operations; to put it on is a peculiar business, to whiten the pins is another; it is even a trade by itself to put them into the paper; and the important business of making a pin is, in this manner, divided into about eight distinct operations, which, in some manufactories, are all performed by distinct hands, though in others the same man will sometimes perform two or three of them. I have seen a small factory of this kind where ten men only were employed, and where some of them consequently performed two or three distinct operations. But though they were very poor, and therefore but indifferently accommodated with the necessary machinery, they could when they exerted themselves, make among them about twelve pounds of pins in a day. There are in a pound upwards of four thousand pins of middling size. Those ten persons, therefore, could make among them upwards of forty-eight thousand pins in a day. Each person, therefore, making a tenth part of forty-eight thousand pins, might be considered as making four thousand eight hundred pins a day. But if they had all wrought separately and independently, and without any of them having being educated to this particular business, they certainly could not each of them have made twenty, perhaps not one pin in a day; that is, certainly not the two hundred and fortieth, perhaps not the four thousand eight hundredth, part of what they are at present capable of performing, in consequence of a proper division and combination of their different operations.

Questions

1. Why are pins produced in large quantities? (Give at least four different reasons.)
2. What factors prohibit small-scale pin manufacture?
3. Why is it easy to use a process of division of labour in pin manufacture?
4. What problems might arise as a result of the division of labour in pin manufacture?
5. Adam Smith explained that in some factories distinct operations would be performed by distinct hands while in other factories the same employee would carry out two or three operations. How would you account for this difference?
6. What modern industries operate in a similar fashion to Adam Smith's pin factories? Do these industries have anything in common?
7. Using your own personal observation of a manufacturing plant employing a high level of specialization, what advantages and disadvantages immediately come to light? How could the difficulties you have noted be overcome?

Money

Money is anything that is generally accepted as a means of making a payment in a given area at a given time. We hear for example of cowrie shells being used as currency on South Sea Islands, and of cigarettes being used as a means of exchange in prisoner of war camps during the Second World War.

The advantages of using money are:

1. It makes specialization possible. For example, there is no need for a vet to build his own house, grow his own food and make his own clothes. Instead, he can concentrate on his

practice, because the money he earns can easily be exchanged for goods and services. In addition, he is able to save some of his money to make future purchases.

2. Money is often regarded as the most effective means of facilitating the process of satisfying consumer wants. Every consumer has his or her own set of preferences for goods and services. Using money as a measure of value makes it possible for thousands of different consumers to decide how they will best spend their disposable income.

3. Money makes it possible to create loans. Borrowers are able to buy goods and services when they want them instead of having to save up to make a cash payment. Credit is particularly important to businesses, and many business transactions are carried out on this basis.

Consensus or conflict?

We have seen that societies consist of individuals, groups and organizations that are mutually interdependent. The economic system is based on millions of individual decisions. Each decision will affect, and be affected by, many other individual decisions—decisions we all make every day.

For example, when a British firm decides to import computer systems from the United States, this will create extra revenue for the American company. The US computer manufacturer might then decide to employ extra labour and invest in new capital equipment. The extra employees taken on in America will then have more money, which they might decide to spend in local shops. Some of the goods they buy will have been made in the United States while others will be imported.

These buying decisions will then have further effects on production decisions, and so the process continues. At the same time, the decision of the British company not to buy an alternative computer system will have an impact on rival suppliers who may then have to make cutbacks.

Different people have different views about how members of a society should support each other. Some people argue that wherever possible members of a community should buy products from each other. Others argue that resources are used most effectively when people buy from the best sources, i.e. those that supply quality goods at the lowest prices.

In any society, certain values will be shared by all (or nearly all) of the members of that society, whereas other values will be exclusive to particular groups within the society. For example, most people would share the belief that a prosperous society is a good thing. However there would be considerable disagreement as to how prosperity should be achieved. There would even be disagreement as to what the word 'prosperity' means. The functioning of a society is therefore based upon conflict and consensus.

Conflict

Marxist thinkers (people whose ideas have been influenced by Karl Marx) believe that, while central values serve to keep society together, these values represent the values of the 'ruling classes'. Education and other systems encourage conformity. Marx (1818–83) argued that history develops in stages, determined by changes in the way people organize their lives. The move from

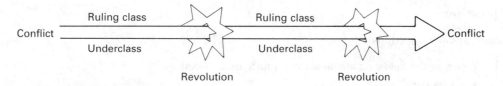

Figure 2.8 The conflict theory.

one stage to another is brought about through the struggle between different social classes which results in revolutions (Fig. 2.8).

Marx thought that the French revolution of 1789 marked the first change in modern Europe. It left behind the 'feudal stage', in which peasants were exploited by landlords. He believed that after the revolution society moved into a later, 'capitalist', stage of history: production shifted from the land to the city, from peasants to the urban working class (or 'proletariat'). Landlords were replaced by factory owners and investors ('bourgeoisie') as the leading class in society.

Marx stated that under capitalism employees are forced to sell their labour cheaply and thus lose control of the means of production (and of their working lives). He thought they could be freed through class struggles led by a revolutionary party which would rise up to defeat the bourgeoisie and take history into the next, 'socialist', stage, in which workers would gain control over the government and production.

This stage would eventually give way to the last historical stage: true communism. A 'communist' society would work according to the principle, 'from each according to his/her ability, to each according to his/her need'. The state would simply wither away.

Marx felt that the 'working class' is misled into being loyal and hard-working in a society in which it is exploited. The working class falsely accepts the ideology (ideas, values and justifications) of that society. He felt that a realization of this position would inevitably lead to conflict.

Consensus

In contrast, many other thinkers believe that society is based more on consensus—that is, on shared values. For most people the nation, and the local community, are units on which they can focus these shared values, which may include patriotism, loyalty, community spirit and obedience to the law. The American writer Talcott Parsons argued that 'fundamental values underpin the social system and without them it could not function'.

A synthesis (coming together) of the conflict and consensus views is presented by the idea of *pluralism*. A pluralist society is made up of many different groups—ethnic groups, religious groups, age groups, style and fashion groups, interest groups, etc. Members of these groups share many of the same and similar values with other groups, but some of their values are so fundamentally opposed (e.g. members of the local hunt and animal rights compaigners) that consensus is disturbed by periods of conflict. Embracing pluralism would entail members of these sub-groups recognizing and valuing their own interests and yet appreciating their similarities to and differences from other sub-groups.

Questions

Short-answer questions

1. Which of the following are goods and which are services?
   - A bicycle
   - Insurance
   - A carpet
   - Having your carpet layed for you
   - A taxi journey
   - Being waited on in a restaurant
   - Watching a film
   - A film projector
   - A computer
   - A photocopier
   - Having notes photocopied for you
   - A haircut
   - A hairdryer.

2. Give three examples of consumer durables and three examples of consumer non-durable items.

3. Explain the difference between goods and services.

4. What is 'the market'?

5. What factors are likely to determine whether buyers or sellers have more power in the market-place?

6. Define the terms
   (a) consumer
   (b) producer

7. What are
   (a) needs?
   (b) wants?

8. What is the 'poverty line'? Why is it difficult to determine?

9. Explain the difference between 'absolute' and 'relative' poverty.

10. Give three examples of
    (a) natural resources
    (b) human resources

11. Why are wants unlimited?

12. Describe the four main factors of production, giving examples of each.

13. Define the term 'opportunity cost' and give an example.

14. Explain the term 'interdependence'.

15. Describe three advantages and three disadvantages of specialization
    (a) to a business
    (b) to people working for a business

16. What is meant by 'comparative advantage'? How does comparative advantage encourage specialization?

17. Explain the term 'division of labour'. Show how division of labour enables a particular process or task to be carried out more effectively.
18. How does money make specialization possible?
19. What is meant by a conflict view of society? Give three examples of conflicts that may occur between members of an organization based on differences in power and interests?
20. Explain the terms
    (a) consensus
    (b) pluralism

Essays

1. Consider the opportunity cost:
    (a) to the school, or to the student, of buying this book.
    (b) to Virgin Airways of spending more on pilot's pay.
    (c) to the UK government of providing more funds for the research and development of a cure for AIDS.
    (d) to Arsenal Football Club for expenditure on building a new spectators' stand.
2. Do the advantages of specialization always outweigh the disadvantages?
3. The economic problem is that of infinite human wants with only a limited basket of resources with which to fulfil them. Discuss.
4. Business life is based on conflicting interests. Discuss.
5. Absolute definitions of poverty are more meaningful than relative ones. Discuss.
6. Use examples from industries with which you are familiar to show how specialization operates in the real world. Explain why such specialization occurs.
7. How can conflicts of interest be good for society, and good for business? Use examples to illustrate your answer.
8. People will always have needs and wants. Business has a role to play in satisfying these needs and wants. Discuss.
9. When resources are used effectively there is no sacrifice to be made by society! What arguments would you put forward to (a) support and (b) contradict this statement?
10. What are the main factors of production used by a business organization? Explain how a particular business organization converts factors of production into finished goods.

Data response questions

1 International interdependence in the car industry

In recent years the pattern of much of the multinational auto industry has been to disperse the various steps in the manufacture of the finished car into different regions and countries. This has made it possible for large car manufacturers to buy in parts from depressed regions or from less developed countries more cheaply than they could be made in the country in which the vehicles are finally assembled. A typical production system in the EC might see vehicle assembly in Britain of parts imported from Spain and Portugal. The company can switch its sources of parts between countries depending on where it can buy them most cheaply.

Having this ability to move production around gives a company considerable power. For example, it can use a practice which in the United States is called 'whipsawing'; by threatening to shut down a production unit or install new vehicle lines or models at another of its sites, the company can attempt to force unions into lowering their demands for increased wages or improved conditions.

However, spreading production is not without risk. For example, when Ford workers in the United Kingdom took industrial action in 1990, it was only a matter of weeks before Ford employees in Germany who were making parts for the assembly lines were laid off.

1. How can concentrating the production of particular car parts in one plant help to reduce cost of the end-product?
2. What factors would a car manufacturer take into account in deciding where to site various parts of the car production process?
3. How does car manufacturing illustrate some of the advantages of specialization to the producer? What are the possible disadvantages?
4. How can employees (a) benefit from and (b) lose out from such specialization?
5. What other examples can you list and explain to show international specialization in the production of particular products?

2   The arms trade

The arms trade is big business. In 1991 the world arms trade was worth an estimated £13 billion, of which the developing world paid out about £7 billion. Major arms include ships, aircraft, missiles and tanks as well as military equipment such as ammunition and vehicles.

The arms industry is a powerful interest group in the United Kingdom, and a major employer of people. In January 1993 the government estimated that 150 000 jobs in Britain are linked directly or indirectly to arms exports.

Arms companies have argued that, although developing new weapons systems is expensive, one way of keeping down the cost of each new tank or plane is for firms to produce large quantities, then sell the excess goods on the world market, giving their governments a twin benefit: cheaper defence and increased export earnings.

Arms sales have declined in recent years, (a) because of the end of the cold war, and (b) because world markets have become saturated with arms. The top five exporters of arms in 1991 were:

*   United States
*   Commonwealth of Independent States (formerly the Soviet Union)
*   Germany
*   China
*   United Kingdom

The top five importers are:

- India
- Israel
- Turkey
- Afghanistan
- Saudi Arabia

The arms trade is closely linked to famine. Every big famine in recent years has taken place in a war zone, such as Somalia and Mozambique. According to local reports, Soviet-made Ak-47 rifles could be bought in Somalia in 1993 for £54—the price of 1400 loaves of bread.

1. How can countries benefit from specializing in producing arms for exports?
2. How can (a) the government and (b) individuals benefit from the arms trade?
3. What is the opportunity cost of the arms trade?
4. What resource use issues are highlighted by the above report? (For example, are scarce resources being used in an effective way?)
5. How does this report indicate that the costs and benefits of the arms trade should not be measured simply in money terms?
6. How could you assess whether or not it is a good thing to have an arms industry?

3   A health diet?

In November 1992 the Ministry of Agriculture, Fisheries and Food produced a report stating that a healthy diet could be purchased for as little as £11.71 per person per week on average.

However, in another report, which contradicted the Ministry, the National Consumer Council stated that in order to conform to such a diet poor families would have to cut out meat almost entirely, double their consumption of breakfast cereals and eat five times as much wholemeal bread. Each person would have to eat eight slices of bread a day—five of which would be dry, the other three with thin scrapings of margarine.

The trend towards shopping in large superstores and away from shopping in high streets has increased the problems of poor people who generally cannot afford the fares to reach such stores. The cost of food in corner shops is at least 20 per cent higher than in supermarkets.

Women on low incomes with children cut down on their own food, living on tea and toast for days at a time, in order to give their children enough to eat, according to the National Consumer Council. A quarter of women on low incomes fall below deficiency levels for eight essential nutrients.

1. How would you go about developing a measure of absolute poverty?
2. What problems does the above report highlight in coming up with definitions of absolute poverty?
3. In January 1993 a packet of crisps, which would provide 100 calories of energy, cost 12p; a healthier choice—three small apples—would have cost 29p. What might have been the

opportunity cost to a poor person of choosing the apples? Why might he or she have gone for the crisps?

4. How might the government benefit from ensuring that all citizens had enough income to support a healthy diet?

5. If the government provided a safety net of income to ensure that all citizens had a healthy diet, would poverty still exist?

Suggested reading

Beardshaw, J., and Palfreman, D., *The Organisation in its Environment*, 4th edn. Pitman, 1990.
Fearns, P., *Business Studies: An Integrated Approach*, 3rd edn. Hodder & Stoughton, 1993.
Hollis, M., *The Business Environment*. Longman, 1993.
Old, J., and Shafto, T., *Introduction to Business Economics*. Stanley Thornes, 1990.

3

The changing industrial structure

During the 1990s a major source of debate has concerned Britain's changing industrial structure.

'Industry' refers to all the steps of manufacturing, distribution and servicing which go into the production and marketing of a company's product and other products of which they form a part.

Much of the talk in recent years has been about the decline of manufacturing in this country. We will look at this trend in detail in this chapter.

Typical of the criticism levelled at British industry was a report published in July 1993 by the Department of Trade and Industry which looked at the country's competitiveness. The report revealed that spending on research and development as a percentage of all national spending had fallen behind that in Japan, Germany, France and the United States. Although manufacturing productivity (output per employee) had risen sharply in the 1980s, there was still a gap with other advanced industrial economies. A major weakness was the 'low skills base' and the lower standards of overall educational attainment.

What is production?

The purpose of production is to add value to things so that they become goods or services that people want. Production involves a wide range of occupations, from acting, playing professional tennis or selling ice cream to running a laundry, growing crops to sell, working as a buyer for a textile business, making heavy engineering parts or acting as a paid child-minder. Each of these occupations is concerned with adding a bit more value to something to turn it into the product that is finally purchased by a consumer or group of consumers who derive satisfaction from it.

A wedding cake is made up of many ingredients—butter, eggs, flour, icing sugar, the heat of an oven, and of course many hours of skilled labour (Fig. 3.1). The end-product can clearly command a much higher price than the cost of the ingredients that went into its manufacture; i.e., value has been added in the production process.

Some people mistakenly associate production just with manufacturing. However, one of the most important trends in Britain in the twentieth century has been that of *de-industrialization*. While jobs in manufacturing have been disappearing, service industries such as tourism, catering, finance, banking and leisure pursuits have boomed.

Figure 3.2 illustrates this change by comparing the breakdown of employment by industrial sector between June 1959 and June 1988. During those 30 years manufacturing employment was

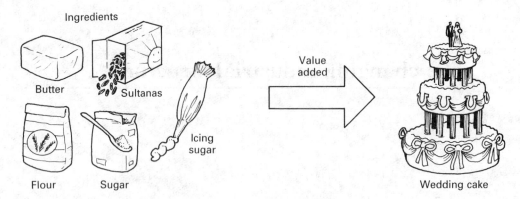

Figure 3.1 What is production?

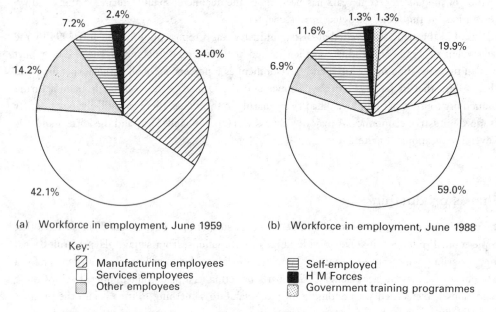

(a) Workforce in employment, June 1959   (b) Workforce in employment, June 1988

Key:
- ▨ Manufacturing employees
- ☐ Services employees
- ▥ Other employees
- ▤ Self-employed
- ■ H M Forces
- ▦ Government training programmes

Figure 3.2 The changing composition of the working population, June 1959–June 1988. (*Source*: Department of Employment)

increasingly squeezed out, to be replaced by service employment. We can also see a significant growth in self-employment, and reflecting the large increase in the number of small enterprises in the 1980s.

However, conditions in the labour market are constantly changing. It is important to bear in mind that the economic environment in which businesses operate is a very powerful influence on business activity. In the late 1980s and early 1990s, the British economy was in recession.

Task

Examine Table 3.1 before answering the questions that follow.

1. What major trends can you identify in the table? Look at figures showing:
    (a) the total number of people that were working.
    (b) numbers employed in services
    (c) numbers employed in manufacturing
    (d) numbers of self-employed people, numbers in the forces, numbers on government training schemes.
2. What does the table tell you about the process of de-industrialization in the four years covered?
3. What do you think would have been the most significant effects:
    (a) for employers?
    (b) for those in work?
    (c) for those leaving schools and colleges?

Of course, Table 3.1 concentrates on a relatively short period. You can find out about more recent trends by sending for a very important publication: The *Labour Market Quarterly Report* is available from the Department of Employment, Skills and Enterprise Network, Room W801, Moorfoot, Sheffield S1 4PQ.

As well as looking at short-term trends, it is always important to look at the longer term. For example, although unemployment was rising in the period covered in Table 3.1 it is important to note that the number of people in work in September 1992 was 1.3 million higher than in March 1983.

Divisions of production

Production is normally classified under three headings: primary, secondary and tertiary. *Primary industry* is concerned with taking out 'the gifts of nature', i.e. extracting natural resources. The *secondary sector* is concerned with constructing and making things. The *tertiary sector* is made up of services. There are two parts of this sector:

*   Commercial services concerned with trading activity
*   Direct services to people

Table 3.2 lists some examples of occupations that would fit into each category. You should add to this list.

Table 3.1   Workforce in employment in Britain, 1989–1992*

Quarter		Employees in employment				Self-employment	HM Forces	Work-related govt. training	Workforce in employment	Change on previous quarter (%)
		Manu-facturing	Services	Other	Total					
1989	Q2	5101	15 242	1799	22 143	3182	308	452	26 084	+107
	Q3	5108	15 304	1794	22 206	3192	308	456	26 162	+78
	Q4	5092	15 424	1788	22 304	3202	306	438	26 250	+88
1990	Q1	5081	15 470	1782	22 333	3212	306	423	26 274	+24
	Q2	5056	15 540	1769	22 365	3222	303	410	26 301	+27
	Q3	5021	15 529	1751	22 300	3183	303	397	26 183	−118
	Q4	4922	15 488	1719	22 129	3144	300	402	25 976	−207
1991	Q1	4818	15 416	1683	21 917	3105	298	390	25 710	−265
	Q2	4715	15 338	1647	21 700	3066	297	333	25 396	−314
	Q3	4645	15 292	1608	21 545	3028	297	318	25 189	−208
	Q4	4584	15 203	1557	21 344	2989	295	341	24 969	−220
1992	Q1	4534	15 286	1524	21 344	2951	293	352	24 940	−29
	Q2	4516	15 189	1493	21 207	2913	290	316	24 726	−214
	Q3	4388	14 964	1473	20 825	2901	284	306	24 317	−409

*Thousands, seasonally adjusted.
Source: Employment Department.

Table 3.2

| Primary | Secondary | Tertiary | |
		Commercial services	Direct services
Oil drilling	Oil refining	Retailing petrol	Hairdressing
Farming	Food processing	Transporting food	Police
Coal mining	Building work	Wholesaling	Chiropody
Forestry	Car manufacturing	Business insurance	Cinema

Structural changes in the economy

The economy can be seen to be made up of a number of component parts or 'sectors'. *Sectors* may be defined widely to include groups of industries (e.g. the energy industries), or narrowly to identify parts of industries (e.g. solar panel supply), depending on our purpose for making the definition.

In addition to commonly used broad classifications of sectors as primary, secondary and tertiary, the following are also important:

1. The *goods sector* is the primary and secondary sectors combined.
2. The *production sector*, or production industries, includes the secondary sector together with mining and quarrying from the primary sector. The term 'industry' is widely used to mean this sector, and an index (measure) of industrial production is drawn up on this basis.

Structural change refers to the changing relative significance of sectors within an economy (however the sectors are defined). It is a basic feature of the historical development of all societies. In advanced industrial societies structural change will need to be carried out at a rapid pace. People living in such societies, taken as a whole, will have more income to spend, and this will lead to a change in patterns of demand. This is illustrated by the boom in demand in the United Kingdom for 'recreation, entertainment and educational services'. (However, within this overall sector, while there was an increase in demand for television and video goods, real spending on books actually fell.)

Structural changes are initiated not only by changes in the demand for goods; changes in supply can also have a significant impact. Changes in the conditions of supply, such as improvements in technology, mean that some existing goods can be produced more cheaply, and that new varieties and variations of products will come to the market. Improvements in the processes involved in producing goods help to lower unit costs and hence prices. For example, the development of automated production lines and robotics in motor vehicle manufacture have helped to reduce the process costs of manufacture (for example by requiring less labour time per product) and have also added to the variety of gadgets and optional extras available in a motor car. Developments in information technology have created a whole new range of products such as video games and word processors.

Modern industrial societies such as the United Kingdom and the United States have been termed 'third wave societies'. The 'first wave' societies depend mainly on agriculture; the 'second wave' sees the transfer of domination to manufacture; finally, the 'third wave' sees a major switch in employment to the service occupations.

Table 3.1 records the switch of a large portion of the labour force in this country from manufacturing to the service industry between June 1959 and June 1988. A number of explanations have been put forward to account for this change.

De-industrialization

There has been a lot of talk about 'de-industrialization' in Britain in recent years. The term suggests empty factories and closed-down shipyards. The general feeling is that de-industrialization is a problem and not something to be welcomed.

The common-sense meaning of de-industrialization is a decline in the importance of industry within the economy. But how do we measure decline?

- Should we look at the numbers employed or the industrial output?
- Are we concerned with absolute decline or with relative decline compared with other sectors?

De-industrialization in the advanced industrialized countries in recent years has not been the result of falling industrial production. In fact, production has continued to increase. Today more products are produced, there is greater variety, and new models have replaced older ones. For example, there is no comparison between a computer today and one of 20 years ago; a modern car uses fuel more efficiently; and living standards have risen (see Table 3.3).

Table 3.3   Work time needed to pay for selected items*

	1971	1981	1986	1990
	(Hours and minutes)			
White sliced loaf	9	8	6	5
1lb rump steak	56	60	46	40
500 g butter	19	20	16	13
1 pt milk	5	4	4	3
1 dozen eggs	22	17	15	12
100 g coffee	22	20	21	14
1 pt beer	14	13	13	11
20 cigarettes	22	20	21	17
Motor car licence	40.31	27.11	25.39	17.55
Colour TV licence	19.27	13.12	14.37	12.32
1 l petrol	8	8	6	5

*For a married couple with only the husband working.
Source: Family Expenditure Survey, 1993.

However, as manufacturing has become better (not just in improving quality and efficiency, but also in responding to environmental concerns and other challenges), it has also become smaller. In every advanced nation, industry employs a smaller proportion of the workforce in 1994 than it did in 1984; in virtually every nation, it has also contributed a smaller proportion to the national output. Everywhere, the slack has been taken up by services. It was in the United States in 1959 that, for the first time, the service sector of a nation became larger in terms of GNP (i.e. gross national product = total output of a country) than the industrial sector. But by 1993 the service sector in every country was much bigger than the industrial sector, contributing 70 per cent of the GNP in the United States, Britain and France, 64 per cent in Italy, 60 per cent in Germany and 56 per cent in Japan. Between 1960 and 1993, the number of jobs in manufacturing in this country fell from almost two-fifth (38.4 per cent of the total) to less than a quarter (22 per cent).

While many of the traditional manufacturing industries such as coal, steel and shipbuilding have declined, however, others have grown, particularly those using advanced technological systems such as food processing, and the production of automated factory systems.

Much of the growth in jobs has been centred around particular localities which are sometimes referred to as 'growth poles'. Areas that were well known as growth areas in the late 1980s included the South East, the 'M4 Corridor', following the M4 from the Thames Valley through to south Wales, and the 'Cambridge Triangle', taking in boom towns such as Peterborough. There were a number of smaller pockets of growth dotted about in many parts of the United Kingdom, including towns such as Telford and Harrogate; in Scotland many jobs in the computer industry were created around Stirling in an area known as 'Silicon Glen'. However, in the early 1990s a period of recession was felt throughout Britain, including these growth areas. The first few months of 1993 saw a revivial in the UK economy. It remains to be seen whether the growth areas will pick up where they left off.

Commuting to work and home working have also become significant modern trends. Today employees are prepared to travel a long way to work by car and public transport. A report published by the Policy Studies Institute entitled *Britain's New Industrial Gypsies* says that weekly commuters, who come to the South East from as far north as Tyne and Wear, receive few time concessions from their bosses. This means that migrant workers have to leave home early on Monday and arrive back late on Friday, and so have less time to relax over a shortened weekend.

Factors leading to the decline of manufacturing

The decline of manufacturing is not a uniquely British phenomenon; the same pattern is typical of all major industrial countries. However, the British case stands out as being an early and extreme case of de-industrialization. As we have seen, the number of people employed in manufacturing has fallen since the early 1960s at an accelerating rate.

Whether or not this is seen as a problem depends on why such a change has taken place. There is considerable evidence that, as economies develop over time, gradual shifts take place between the primary, secondary and tertiary sectors. At early stages of development there is a shift away from agriculture towards industrial and service activities, as the relative importance of agricultural products (food in particular) declines in people's consumption and manufactured goods and services become more important. As incomes continue to rise, the share of manufacturing in output and employment tends to decline, and that of services tends to increase.

Two important causes of de-industrialization

There are many explanations of de-industrialization. Here are two important ones. (You can read more about the process in Industrialization and Development, Hewitt, Johnson and Wield, Oxford University Press, 1992.)

1. De-industrialization can result from change in the pattern of international specialization. A country that discovers a natural resource is likely to experience some de-industrialization. Production of this new sector will increase rapidly and the share of other sectors including manufacturing will be reduced. Can you think of an example? The obvious one was the discovery of North Sea oil. This changed Britain from being a net importer of oil to being a net exporter and saw a reduction in the share of manufacturing industry in output and employment. This type of de-industrialization is not necessarily bad. With the development of oil as an export, Britain did not need such a large manufacturing base.

2. De-industrialization can also be the result of a lack of competitiveness in manufacturing. It is this case that is really the major cause of concern. A country that is becoming less competitive in manufacturing will see its share of world exports of manufacturers decline and its imports increase. Declining employment in the manufacturing sector will not be offset by increased employment of labour in other sectors. The slow growth of domestic manufacturing will lead it to fall further behind its competitors as productivity increases lag, and a vicious circle of decline is set in motion, with rising unemployment and a deteriorating balance of payments.

Other explanations of de-industrialization

Stage of maturity

As we have already seen, some analysts regard the process of economic development over time as progressing from a stage of primary concentration of employment in agriculture, to the manufacturing sector and finally a domination of the service sector. The United Kingdom, as the world's oldest industrial nation, could reasonably be expected to be one of the most mature. With the growth of service sector employment, the labour force could be expected to transfer from manufacturing employment into services over a period of time.

The effect of low-wage competition

Another explanation put forward to account for de-industrialization is that the prices of UK manufactures have been undercut by cheap foreign products from low-wage economies. In particular, we have heard these arguments related to the textiles and electrical components industries. However, in low-wage countries output per head is usually low, and it is often in markets where Britain competes with high-wage economies that we have failed to be competitive.

Crowding out

An explanation for the decline of manufacturing that was particularly popular in the late 1970s and early 1980s was based on the notion that manufacturing was being 'crowded out' by the non-market public sector (i.e. services such as health and education, which are provided by the government free or at low prices to end-users). It was said that government taxed manufacturing and spent the tax revenues on government-provided services. Resources were therefore being taken away from manufacturing. However, this argument has lost some of its early popularity as the percentage of total national expenditure allocated to the non-market public sector fell in the late 1980s.

The high pound and high interest rates

Some people argue that the high cost of borrowing money (interest rates) combined with a high relative price of the pound in 1979/80, and more recently in 1986/92, had disastrous effects for the British manufacturing industry. Most businesses have to borrow to carry them forward from the time they buy in components, raw materials and stocks until they are able to sell finished goods. High interest rates can create crippling short-term debts. A high value to the pound means that British goods become relatively more expensive than competing foreign products. It is argued that a policy of high interest rates and high exchange rates have helped to seriously slim down Britain's manufacturing industry. Consumers have therefore had to resort to buying imported manufactures, which has seriously affected the balance of our payments with the rest of the world. (Details about why the government has periodically raised interest rates, and encouraged a high pound are given in Chapter 22.)

In 1991 Britain joined the European Community's Exchange Rate Mechanism (ERM). This made it difficult to reduce the value of the pound. Once we left the ERM in 1992 we were able to lower the value of the pound and to cut interest rates.

The North Sea

Some analysts see the importance to Britain of North Sea oil as having been a contributory cause of the decline in manufacturing. Because the United Kingdom was one of the few industrial economies to have been able to produce and export large quantities of oil, speculators in the 1980s tended to see the British pound as a potentially strong currency. The buying up of pounds as an investment gave the pound a relatively high value on international markets, particularly in the early 1980s. However, having a relatively strong pound made it more difficult to sell items such as manufactured goods on international markets.

Productivity

Until the middle of the 1980s, output per head in British manufacturing lagged well behind that of our international competitors. This made it difficult to compete in manufacturing. However, during the 1980s many of the old manufacturing jobs were shaken out of the economy. A slimmed-down manufacturing base has proved to be a more productive one. Government legislation has made it easier for employers to make people redundant. In addition, a large number of people are on part-time contracts. This means that in a recession it is easier to lay people off and to take them back on in a period of economic boom.

The growth of the service sector

There are three main reasons for the growth of the service sector of the economy.

1. As societies become richer, they choose to spend a higher proportion of their incomes on buying services rather than physical goods.
2. It has so far proved very much harder to wring additional productivity out of services than out of manufacturing. Greater productivity in a car plant means more robots on the production line: the product does not suffer—indeed, probably the reverse. However, if greater productivity in a school means fewer teachers in the classroom, the quality of education suffers immediately.
3. As countries become richer, they are able to 'export' their profits in the form of investments in other countries. It is evident that a number of countries have invested in manufacturing in developing industrial countries. The rewards are returned in profits, interest and dividends that can be spent on leisure services.

There is no sign at all that the shift of demand towards services will cease. Indeed, there is a powerful reason to expect it to accelerate, namely the ageing population in industrial societies. The proportion of people over 60 will continue to rise in every developed country for at least a generation. By 2020, more than 30 per cent of the population of Germany and Italy will be over 60. Older people are more likely to spend their income on health care, holidays and domestic services.

The countries that increase living standards most quickly in the future will be those that can improve the way they run the services. Services can be divided into four main groups: financial services and distribution tend to be in the private sector, whereas health and education tend to be in the public sector; and technology can be used to transform each of these areas. In financial services we will see, more than ever before, the development of paperless money. Financial services are also becoming increasingly tailored to the needs of individual customers. In distribution, the benefits of bulk retailing are likely to be grafted on to much wider swathes of the industry with resultant cost-cutting. In health, technological advances have led to people living longer; the focus of health care will now shift to raising the quality of care and fitness throughout people's lives. Education, too, will become a continuous process, involving people of all ages. Workers can expect to be retrained to take on completely different skills several times during their careers.

Giant trading and industrial/economic groupings

A recent major change to the international environment in which all businesses operate has been the development of gigantic regional groupings.

There are now three main powerful trading blocs:

- the North American Market (NAFTA - North American Free Trade Area)
- the European Community
- Japan and the Association of South-East Asian Nations (ASEAN)

The North American market is made up of the United States, Canada and Mexico.

The European Community is becoming increasingly integrated, both economically and politically. It currently includes 12 western European nations but is likely to be joined by others and an increasing number from the former Soviet bloc. It is possible that the European republics of the Commonweath of Independent States (CIS) will join this bloc to construct a Europe 'from the Atlantic to the Ural Mountains', as Charles de Gaulle put it in 1960. Currently the CIS has its own internal trading area, although this is fraught with problems.

Japan and ASEAN include, among other countries, Thailand, Indonesia and Malaysia, all of which are growing rapidly. Australia and New Zealand are also part of this group of Pacific-rim countries.

These blocs are for the most part still at an early stage of development, but they have the potential to be a very powerful influence on world trading relations. The new blocs are not restrictive, on the whole, to outside trading countries, although they do have certain restrictions on imports. However, each of the blocs is characterized by a very rapid increase in the development and use of new technology. These developments are of concern to countries outside the blocs which lag behind in technological development.

Questions

Short-answer questions

1. What is meant by
   (a) production?
   (b) value added?
2. Classify the following as primary, secondary and tertiary occupations:
   - Window cleaner
   - Cinema usherette
   - Computer programmer
   - Bus driver
   - Oil driller
   - Vegetable packer
   - Bricklayer
   - Cook
   - Teacher
   - Insurance broker
   - Steel erector
   - Bank manager
   - Fisher

- Firefighter
- Police officer
- Industrial chemist
- Welder.

3. Explain the difference between commercial and direct services. Use examples to illustrate the difference.
4. What is
   (a) the goods sector of the economy?
   (b) the production sector of the economy?
5. Define 'industry'.
6. What is meant by 'de-industrialization'?
7. What are 'first', 'second' and 'third wave' societies?
8. Explain two measures that can be used to indicate improvements in a countries manufacturing capacity.
9. What is a 'growth pole'?
10. Why has the service sector of the economy grown in importance in recent years?
11. List three major giant industrial/economic groupings.
12. How can productivity be measured?
13. What do you understand by the term 'crowding out' of manufacturing?
14. What is an industrial sector?
15. What is 'structural change' in an economy?
16. How can 'teleworking' reduce
    (a) business costs?
    (b) household costs?
17. What is the 'non-market public sector' of the economy?
18. What is a 'free trade area'?
19. Which of the following are in the service sector of the economy?
    - Entertainment
    - Coal
    - Hospitals
    - Bakeries
    - Shops
    - Offices
    - Leisure centres
    - Construction sites
20. How might an economy suffer from having a 'low-skills base'?

Essays

1. Why does the structure of industry change over time? Illustrate your answer by reference to an economy of your choice.
2. How would you account for the process of de-industrialization in the United Kingdom?
3. Explain how industrial activity adds value in the process of production.

4. In the 1990s population trends will reduce the number of young people entering the workforce. How might a firm respond to this situation?
5. Discuss the assertion that a 'third-wave' economy does not require a strong manufacturing base.
6. Why has the service sector risen to prominence in the United Kingdom and other Western economies?
7. Describe and discuss the structure of employment in the United Kingdom in the 1990s.
8. Industry creates value. Industrial activity also takes value away. Discuss.
9. What measures could be taken to make manufacturing a more significant contributor to the British economy in the 1990s?
10. Britain will never be competitive so long as the importance of manufacturing is ignored. Discuss.

Data response questions

1 Increasing numbers of women in the labour force

Britain is undergoing massive structural changes in employment with more women than men in employment in many regions (Table 3.4). The recession of the late 1980s and early 1990s cut a swathe through full-time job opportunities normally filled by men, while female part-time employment expanded.

Male-dominated work in manufacturing slumped to its lowest level for more than a century but the service sector held up. Female unemployment peaked at 9 per cent in 1986 and was down to

Table 3.4   Where women workers outnumber men (thousands)

County/region	Full-time men	Part-time men	All men	Full-time women	Part-time women	All women
Essex	218.9	24.2	243.1	123.6	123.3	246.9
Isle of Wight	17.7	2.7	20.4	9.4	11.6	21.0
East Sussex	90.0	14.4	104.4	61.4	59.3	120.7
West Sussex	116.6	14.8	131.4	73.3	64.1	137.4
Cornwall/ Scilly Isles	55.9	9.5	65.4	33.5	40.2	73.8
Devon	154.2	21.7	175.9	87.6	93.7	181.3
Hereford & Worcester	109.8	11.8	121.6	62.6	59.1	121.7
Merseyside	210.9	19.2	230.1	128.6	117.5	246.1
Mid-Glamorgan	70.1	4.8	74.8	41.4	35.8	77.3
Borders region (Scotland)	17.1	1.6	18.7	10.4	8.6	19.0
Lothian region (Scotland)	155.7	13.9	169.6	101.1	69.6	170.7

Source: 1991 Census of Employment; published in the *Employment Gazette*, April 1993.

5.6 per cent in early 1993, whereas male unemployment was 13.5 per cent in 1986 and had increased to 14.1 per cent at the start of 1993.

Researchers who provided the figures for Income Data Services reported that the trend was likely to continue among full-time male employees and that the economic recovery from 1993 onwards would further accelerate the shift towards a much larger part-time female workforce. Many companies in the early 1990s were replacing full-timers with part-timers, including Burton, BHS and British Airways.

In 1979 there were 13.1 million men in jobs and 9.4 million women; by January 1993 there were 10.682 million men in employment and 10.142 million women (4.637 million of whom were part-timers).

1. Summarize the major trends in male–female employment outlined in the case study.
2. What factors would you put forward to explain this trend?
3. Why are employers recruiting more part-timers?
4. What are the advantages of employing part-timers?
5. What are the disadvantages of increasing the number of part-timers
    (a) for the economy?
    (b) for individual businesses?
    (c) for families?
6. How have these trends continued into the mid- and late 1990s?
7. Summarize the regional trends in male–female employment shown in Table 3.4.

2   The development of the Information Society

Today microelectronics is used everywhere in modern technological societies—in factories, offices, shops and the home. The silicon chip microprocessor, with its low cost and extreme miniaturization, makes it possible to provide a brain and a memory to any piece of equipment humanly devised. The results appear in an enormous variety of microelectronic devices and gadgets.

Microelectronics has penetrated deeply into industry at every stage from design to packaging. Automation and robotization are changing industrial processes, and are cutting out dangerous, dirty and repetitive jobs, creating the need for new skills and making new demands on education and training.

There are some commentators who argue that information technology will create new products, new industries and new markets; that it will create economic growth; that some industries will be destroyed but new jobs will be created to take on the unemployed. There are others, however, who argue that the new technologies will destroy jobs and that the unemployed will not be taken up elsewhere.

Clearly, extensive automation in manufacturing is bound to cause redundancies, particularly among unskilled manual workers. If more labour is to be taken on in newer industries, it is essential that new markets for products be created. Markets for many goods in the affluent parts of the world are approaching saturation, so expansion can be created only if the populations of the developing regions can become mass markets for goods.

When agriculture experienced a similar revolution in technology, unemployed labour was taken up by manufacturing. Is it possible that those made redundant by manufacturing will find work in new service industries? Although service industries do require more labour than manufacturing, they too are experiencing an information technology revolution. For this reason, it is unlikely that they will be able to absorb all the excess labour.

It seems, therefore, that members of advanced industrial societies will need to spend more time on leisure activities and less in work. The inevitable results will be a later entry into the workforce, shorter hours, earlier retirement, periods off work for further education and retraining, etc.

1. List five types of job that are becoming less important as a result of the use of modern technology. Describe these changes.
2. List five types of job that are becoming more important as a result of the use of modern technology. Describe these changes.
3. Does the balance in this country currently seem to be towards the loss of jobs or the creation of new jobs as a result of technological change?
4. What measures can (a) individuals, and (b) the government take to deal with the destruction of employment by new technologies?

3 'The way ahead'?

In March 1993 Sir John Banham, former director-general of the CBI, outlined his solutions to Britain's industrial problems in a lecture to the Ernst & Young Yorkshire Fiscal Group. Read through his solutions, listed below, and identify points you agree and disagree with for a discussion with fellow students:

1. We must have a world-class primary, and particularly secondary, education system. First World social wages cannot be sustained with Second World education.
2. There needs to be greater emphasis on manufacturing and realistic expectations of the rewards that shareholders can expect if the pace of recovery is not to be constrained by a ballooning trade deficit.
3. Families and the nation will need to rely less on appreciation in housing values as a substitute for personal savings and investment.

By the year 2000, the United Kingdom must be a world-class provider of high-quality and cost-competitive products. This requires:

- Low inflation
- A thriving research community operating at the top edge of technology
- Continuous innovation to meet the requirements of world markets: UK manufacturers need to earn a universally respected reputation for responsiveness to consumer needs
- Commitment to sustained investment in world-class equipment and processes fully supported by banks, shareholders and the government
- Highly motivated, skilled and flexible people who are committed to continuous learning

- An internationally competitive infrastructure to support industry, i.e. first-class transport and communication systems
- An obsession with customer satisfaction
- A government committed to playing its part at home and within the EC to support industry in the same way that governments do in competitor countries

Suggested reading

Cook, G., *Business Studies Update*. Hidcote Press, published each year.
Crafts, N., *Can De-industrialisation Seriously Damage your Wealth?* Anforme Books, 1993.
Curwin, J., Goodkin, D., and Slater, R., *Business Studies in Context*. McGraw-Hill, 1989.
Stefanou, R., *Understanding Industry Now*, 3rd edn. Heinemann Educational, 1992.

4

Introducing business and economic systems

Systems theory

Systems theory is a helpful way of thinking about problems. You can use it for thinking about systems that are as different as the workings of a CD player, a set of accounts, a manufacturing operation or just the baking of a cake.

A *system* is a complex whole made from a set of connecting parts or things. A system processes inputs to produce outputs. In business studies systems can be simplified into three main 'black boxes', which are labelled Input, Process and Output (Fig. 4.1). In most industrial systems there will be several inputs, processes and even outputs.

Taking an everyday example that we are all familiar with, i.e. making soup, we can clearly see the three stages in Fig. 4.2.

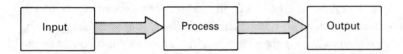

Figure 4.1 In most industrial systems there will be several inputs, processes and even outputs.

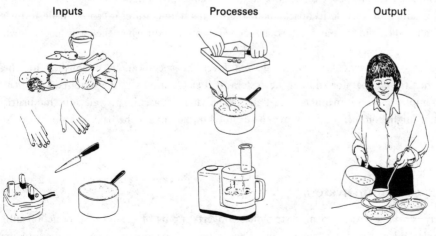

Figure 4.2

Boundaries

A production system is organized within defined boundaries. It will be fairly obvious when production is taking place. The inputs will flow through this system. Some of the resources used will be current resources, for example the ingredients and energy required to make soup. What actually goes into the production process will be filtered; there will be *barriers* that select what is to be used in producing a good or service. For example, quality control would (it is hoped) ensure that broken bottles were taken off the production line at a bottling plant. *Current resources* will combine with *elements* (or fixed assets) such as machinery (e.g. a production line) and buildings. Resources will flow from one element to another across links between the elements. For example, in making chocolate bars, chocolate will flow through a mixing element, through rollers, along dryers and so on.

At the end of the production line there will also be *output filters*. Some outputs will be filtered into different lines, e.g. when making different types of chocolate bars; others may be sub-standard and will flow into the reject line, or waste channel.

Such a system would be controlled and organized by a *user*. The user inputs are what are known as 'primary inputs' and 'secondary inputs'. The primary inputs are the settings (control parameters) that control the operations of the system, for example the speed of the line, the temperature, the quality standards, the hours worked. The secondary inputs are the current resources.

Closed and open systems

In an *open system* the output does not affect the inputs. In a *closed system* the output will directly affect the inputs. In order for a system to work automatically, feedback is needed. Imagine being blindfolded and then being told to walk along the edge of a cliff; it would be difficult, because our eye (and our other senses) normally provide constant feedback, enabling corrective action to be taken as needed. An electric heater without any form of feedback is said to be an open-ended control system; such a heater, once turned on, stays on even if the room is too hot. If a heat sensor (thermostat) is added to provide feedback about the room's temperature, it can be made to turn off automatically when the set temperature is reached and on again when the room cools down (Fig. 4.3).

If the contents of a particular product do not meet the specifications established for the *comparator*, then the comparator will tell the system to alter the inputs to the required specifica-tions. For example, in biscuit manufacture, if an output batch of biscuits proved to be too brittle the comparator might command more water to be added to the mix, or the baking temperature to be reduced.

The wider economic system

The economy can be seen as a giant system that converts inputs of factors of production into finished goods and services for customers. The factors of production are supplied to an

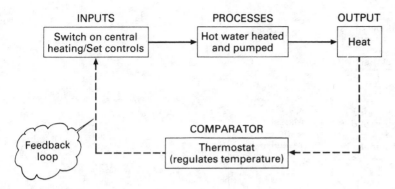

Figure 4.3 Example of a closed system.

appropriate market, e.g. the labour market. A business enterprise buys in factor services which it converts into finished goods and services to meet the needs and wants of consumers. If consumers are not happy with the finished goods that are available, they will not buy them—leaving business enterprises with unsold stocks. Businesses need to carry out market research and product research to find out:

- What people want
- How they can make that product to the consumers' requirements

The effective enterprise will then use the most appropriate inputs to make the most appropriate outputs to satisfy the end-consumer (see Fig. 4.4).

Designing systems to meet the needs of the market

Organizations are not just random collections of people, money and machines. These resources have little value unless they can be organized into systems which make sure that good products and services are made in a way that is valued by the final consumer or user.

The activities that create the value added in the production process are therefore just as important as the resources that go into the process. For this reason, an organization must focus on its *value activities* and the *linkages* between value activities (Fig. 4.5).

The value chain

Michael Porter (*Competitive Advantage: Creating and Sustaining Superior Performance*) has identified a series of activities that need to be done well if a business is to develop a competitive advantage. The *value chain* is concerned with organizing and linking a series of key activities. The end-user or consumer looks at value in terms of what a business is offering in relation to competitive offers. The value chain is therefore concerned with ensuring that a company organizes its activities to offer the best end-product.

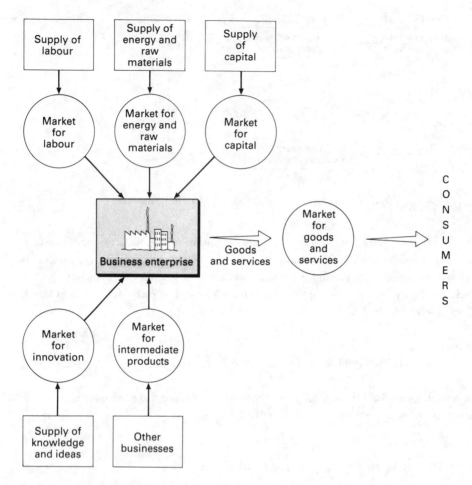

Figure 4.4 The conversion of inputs to outputs in the economy.

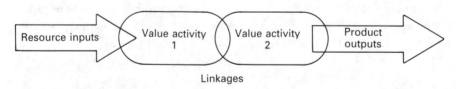

Figure 4.5 The importance of value activities.

The linkage between activities is a key ingredient in giving a business an edge. Many of these linkages will be with other businesses and organizations, e.g. suppliers, distributors.

Porter identifies a number of primary and support activities which lead to profitability (the end–margin) (see Fig. 4.6). There are five main *primary activities*:

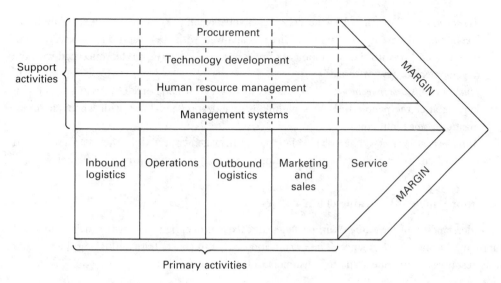

Figure 4.6 The value chain. (Adapted from M. E. Porter)

1. *Inbound logistics*   These activities deal with receiving, storing and distributing the inputs to the product. For example, in a food processing company this would involve bringing in supplies of vegetables, meat, etc. It would concern activities such as transporting the materials from farms and other suppliers, handling the raw materials and keeping a check on stock.

2. *Operations*   These transform raw materials into a final product. In a food processing operation this would include mixing and blending ingredients, cooking foods and packing and labelling them.

3. *Outbound logistics*   These activities relate to the storing and distributing of products to customers. Processed foods would need to be transported to and stored in warehouses before being delivered to shops and supermarkets.

4. *Marketing and sales*   These activities make consumers aware of products and make it easy for them to purchase goods and services. Market research would set out to find what types of processed food consumers want; advertising would make consumers aware of products; etc.

5. *Services*   These activities are concerned with improving and keeping up the value of a product, for example in the case of electrical goods installing equipment, repairing it and providing spare parts.

Each of these primary activities is linked to four *support activities*:

1. *Procurement*   This is the process involved in acquiring the various resource inputs, e.g. setting up systems to make orders, or make contacts. It will take place in many parts of the organization.

2. *Technology development*   All value activities involve technology even if it is just 'know-how'. Technological development may be directly involved with the product (e.g. research and development) or with the development of new processes; it may even be concerned with the development of raw materials.
3. *Human resource management*   This is concerned with a whole range of activities to do with looking after the people that work within an organization and those with whom the organization comes into contact.
4. *Management systems*   There is a wide range of management activities such as planning and financial control which are needed to support primary activities in many different ways.

The importance of the value chain

An understanding of the value chain provides an excellent overview on ways of maintaining and improving business performance. The organization needs to concentrate on making the best use of its resources to provide value to consumers. Therefore it needs to:

● Examine and improve all of its primary and support activities
● Examine and improve all linkages between primary and support activities

Many of these value activities and linkages occur inside an organization (internal); many others take place outside the organization (external). Organizations need to give equal emphasis to internal and external value activities and linkages.

Efficiency and effectiveness

It is important at this stage to draw a distinction between an 'efficient' and an 'effective' use of resources. Different organizations operate in different market-places. For some organizations it will be imperative to be able to compete on the basis of cost competitiveness; the emphasis will be on cost minimization. This situation requires an efficient use of resources. The key question will be *how well* resources have been used, regardless of the purpose for which they were used. An efficient organization might point to measures of efficiency such as profitability, maximum output per head from labour, machines being used to full capacity, etc.

An *effective* organization, by contrast, may be concerned to show that it is better than competitors, for example by sustaining and developing unique products. An organization that stresses effectiveness may concentrate on quality rather than quantity. The effective organization will seek to channel resources into those aspects of activities that emphasize its edge over competitors.

Business systems in a dynamic environment

Studies by the Tavistock Institute in the 1960s and 1970s looked at the business enterprise as an 'open socio-technical system'.

The system is 'open' because it obtains inputs from its environment and puts back outputs into its environment. The business system is therefore in a constant state of change because it is interacting across its boundaries with its environment.

The Tavistock group of writers therefore saw the primary task of management to be that of relating the total system to its environment by regulating interchanges at the boundary between the system and its environment.

A management that assumes that it is simply concerned with managing *within* the systems boundary of the enterprise is making a big mistake. Top management needs to be concerned with internal problems, but it also needs to be crucially concerned with environmental opportunities and demands. For example, managers in a school need to be aware of external pressures to change the curriculum, to manage its own funds, to changing attitudes in society, etc. Managers in a company need to understand changing environmental pressures, changing government policies, the impact of the Single European Market and so on.

In the 1990s environments are changing at an increasing rate and are becoming more and more complicated. Factors in the environment, over which the organization has no control or even no knowledge, may interact to cause substantial changes. A modern organization therefore needs to be able to cope with constant change. It needs to be as flexible as possible and to be informed about changes in the wider business environment.

The economic system: an introduction

We can look at the effect of the economy on organizations at a number of levels. Organizations may be as directly affected by local changes as by national or international ones; for example, the closure of the Swan Hunter shipyard in Sunderland hit local people harder than would the effects of a world recession. *Macroeconomics* is the study of large-scale economic changes that tend to affect the whole of the nation's economy. However, we should always remember that 'macro' trends affect different groups and individuals in different ways.

The national economy can be viewed as a systems model (see Fig. 4.7). Organizations use inputs such as labour and machinery to create goods and services. If the demand for goods is higher than the stock available, then organizations will employ more inputs to increase production. Prices may start to rise (scarcity) and unemployment to fall (more jobs). On the other hand, if supply is greater than demand, there will be unsold stock and companies may begin to discard workers, to invest less in new machinery and to reduce prices. This is a *simple model* of the economy.

A more complex model of the economy

The simple model of the economy illustrated in Fig. 4.7 shows that it is made up of two basic groups: business organizatons and households. Households supply labour and other factors of production to organizations (e.g. funds for investment). In return, households receive incomes for their services, which they then spend on the outputs produced by businesses. If the businesses supply products that households wish to purchase, this system works very well. Indeed, in a

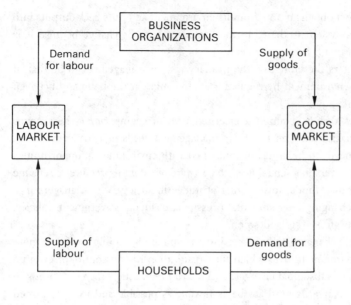

Figure 4.7 A simple systems model of a national economy.

market economy led by market-conscious business units, firms supply gods and services to the market. They employ labour and other factors. They also purchase capital items (e.g. machinery), raw materials and partly finished goods in the market-place. Although some goods will be temporarily unsold, new products will be developed to replace those that are outmoded.

In the real world, economies are more complex. We need to add governments and international transactions to our model. The government buys and sells goods; for example it buys armaments and health care in the market-place and it sells products and services such as the outputs of the nationalized industries. The government is the major purchaser of goods in the United Kingdom.

Trading between nations is also significant. Finished goods, partly finished goods, raw materials and foodstuffs are imported and exported. The service sector (e.g. financial services) also accounts for a considerable volume of trade.

We therefore need a more complex diagram to represent government activities and international trade. This is shown in Fig. 4.8.

Types of economic system

All societies must develop a system for dealing with three interrelated problems:

- What will be produced?
- How will it be produced?
- For whom will it be produced?

We can illustrate the wide differences in possible systems by looking at two imaginary island communities which are dependent on fishing and farming.

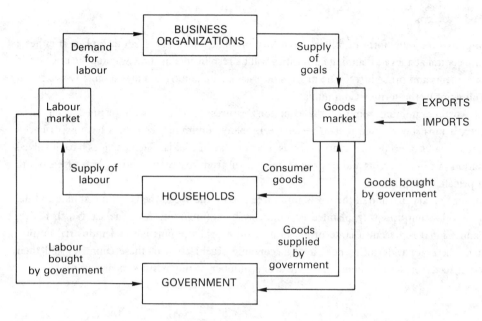

Figure 4.8 Labour and goods market in an open economy with government.

We shall call these two communities Sealand and Skyland. In Sealand all decisions are made by a small group of chieftains. The chieftains decide who will do the fishing and who will do the farming. They decide how many hours are to be put into each activity and how the necessary equipment will be made (e.g. the fishing boats, agricultural implements). They have also decided that everyone will receive an equal share of the produce—except for the chieftains, who will have a double portion of everything.

In Skyland there is no organizing group. Individuals are left to their own devices. They decide individually what to make and they trade or store their surpluses. They decide how to produce their equipment, and how long to spend at particular activities. They consume the bulk of their own produce, except for what they can exchange.

Make a list of eight strengths and eight weaknesses of each of the economic systems described. Devise a third system which you would regard as preferable to those of Sealand and Skyland. In what ways do you think that your system is preferable? Why might other people disagree with you? What would be the reasoning behind their objections?

In the past, the basic economic problems were solved by custom and tradition; for example, the way crops were grown and shared out was decided by folk tradition. In many parts of the world traditional economies are giving way to three major systems:

- The planned system
- The free-market system
- The mixed system

Within these three basic models, there will be a wide range of variations and differences.

Planned systems

Planning involves some form of official co-ordination of activities. This can take place at either a local or a centralized level. Planning authorities will be responsible in some way for the creation of targets, systems and procedures. The process or organized planning is most commonly associated with countries in the former Communist bloc.

It is worth examining some of the common features associated with planned economies. However, it must be stressed that in recent years many communist countries have experienced substantial phases of economic reform such as 'perestroika' in Russia. Such changes have involved a relaxation of price controls and of production control from the centre and a greater freedom to set up private enterprise.

In the customary division of the world into three parts—the West, the Communist bloc and the Third World—countries with planned economic systems (including Kampuchea, North Korea, Cuba and China) represent a large proportion of the world's population and industrial output. Although there are wide differences in the economic organization of these countries and their respective stages of development, there are also a number of important similarities:

1. The means of production are publicly owned. This takes the form of state, collective or co-operative ownership. However, decisions about their use can be made in a variety of ways, ranging from collective decision-making to decision-making by a small committee of people.
2. Planning is centralized and strategies to increase the quantity and/or quality of overall output are laid down by the planning authority.
3. There is a market for consumer goods (although consumers will not necessarily have the freedom to spend money in the way they would wish) and a market for labour. Wages are paid, and a large proportion of consumer goods are exchanged in the market, in transactions using some form of money.
4. Prices for all goods sold by the state are decided by planning authorities. They are not able to change spontaneously.
5. Nearly all decisions relating to capital formation will be made and controlled by planning authorities. Capital formation is the production of those goods and equipment that go into further production such as that of factory machinery.

The key feature of a planned, or *command*, economy is that it is planning committees that decide what will be produced, how it will be produced and how products will be distributed. Smaller groups such as factories and other business units submit their plans to a local committee. The local plans are then passed on for approval at the centre. The central organization may then decide which resources will be made available to each local area, which in turn will allocate resources to each factory, farm or other productive unit.

Productive units are often set production targets, and are then given a set quantity of resources and a time constraint to meet set targets.

Advantages of a planned economy

1. Effective long-term strategies can be developed taking into account the needs of the total system.
2. Planning can be carried out according to the collective needs and wants of each of the individual parts of a system.
3. Duplication of resources can be eliminated.
4. Resources and products can be shared out more equitably according to the dominant value system prevailing in that society.
5. Planning decisions can be made in a consistent manner.
6. The system can be shaped in such a way as to reflect the social and political wishes of a collective group of people.

Disadvantages of a planned economy

1. Heavy-handed planning and control may stifle individual enterprise.
2. The process of planning itself uses up scarce resources for administration and supervision.
3. The absence of the profit motive removes the spur to individual effort and enterprise. It is argued by some that people are more inclined to work harder and to make personal sacrifices if they can profit from doing so.
4. The process of communication between consumers and producers can become distorted so that the goods that are produced fall far short of consumer requirements. If planning decisions are made well in advance of consumption decisions, then by the time goods appear in the market-place tastes and fashions may have changed.
5. Where price controls are established unofficial black markets may develop, leading to bribery and corruption.

The free-market system

In a free market the decisions about what, how and for whom are made by consumers and producers; the government does not intervene. Consumers in effect 'vote' for a certain pattern of output by the way in which they distribute their spending between the alternatives on offer. How much they are prepared to pay is thus a reflection of the strength of consumer preferences. (Some people think that it does not always work quite like this; they think that producers often decide what they would like to make and then persuade consumers to follow their wishes through advertising.) If a product sells well firms will be inclined to produce it. The prices at which producers offer their goods for sale will depend on their production costs. The prices charged will thus reflect the relative scarcity of the various resources needed in order to produce that good for the market. If a product sells well firms will be inclined to produce it; if no one buys the product firms will stop making it, since under the market system firms seek to make profits from all the goods they sell. Producers are thus forced to pay attention to the wishes of consumers in order to survive.

The interests of consumers and producers conflict. Consumers want to pay low prices while producers would like to charge higher prices. The market serves to strike a balance, with prices settling at just those levels that match the strength of consumer preferences with the scarcity of resources. When prices change this acts as a signal for the patterns of production and consumption to alter. For example, when a new fashion style becomes popular, the producers are able to charge a higher price and to put more resources into producing more such garments, while for clothes that are no longer fashionable manufacturers may be forced to lower their price, put less resources into their production and eventually stop making them altogether.

Advantages of the free-market system

1. Production reflects the wishes of the consumer.
2. The system is flexible in the way it can respond to different conditions of demand and supply.
3. Individuals have greater freedom to make their own demand and supply decisions.
4. Scarce resources do not have to be wasted on administering and running (planning) the system.
5. It is argued that the free market will lead to larger, better-quality outputs at lower unit costs.

Disadvantages of the free-market system

1. The free-market system does not guarantee everyone what many would regard to be the minimum acceptable standard of living in a healthy society. The price mechanism, when it is freely operating, fails to provide a 'safety net' for citizens less able to compete, including the sick and the elderly.
2. There are some goods which by their very nature include elements of what is known as 'non-excludibility'. For example all ships using a particular seaway benefit from its lighthouse; all citizens (except for pacifists) could be seen to benefit from a national system of defence. If we take the example of bridges, it is immediately apparent why the price system could not always be effective as a means of provision. If people were made to pay to go over all bridges the traffic system would rapidly snarl up. (It is worth bearing in mind however, that when new roads were being built and road traffic was less common many toll bridges were used in this country.)
3. The free market can lead to great inequalities. Those with the means to purchase large quantities of goods can use their money to ensure that the goods and services *they* want are produced (hence taking away resources from other products). One way of looking at the opportunity cost to society of producing luxury goods (speedboats, expensive clothes) is to consider the inability of society to meet the needs of the less fortunate.
4. Resources may not be able to move as freely as a pure market theory would suggest. Regarding human resources (labour), people may be resistant to moving to new areas and away from their established roots; they may be reluctant to learn new skills which offer high pay packets if they feel that the job does not meet their needs for such factors as self-respect, pride in the job or the ability to work at one's own pace.

5. Many buying decisions are made by consumers with an imperfect knowledge of the market. Producers frequently change the details of their products including price, shape, size and packaging. This makes it very difficult for consumers to weigh up alternative purchases, and many buying decisions may be based on impressions rather than hard evidence. For example, a recent survey conducted by the authors revealed that, out of a sample of 400 shoppers, fewer than 10 per cent of them could remember the prices of five randomly selected commonly used items in their shopping basket.

6. In a free market many resources can be wasted through the high failure rate of new businesses. A lot of time and money is spent on setting up a new business. When it closes down after a few months, many of its resources may end up as little more than scrap.

The mixed economy

In the real world no economy relies exclusively on the free market, nor can we find examples of purely planned economies. A mixed economy combines elements of both the free market and planned systems; some decisions are made solely through the private sector while others are made by the government.

The United Kingdom is a good example of a mixed economy. Some parts of industry are owned and operated by the government but large chunks of the business world remain in private hands. The *public sector* is that part of the economy that is government-owned; the *private sector* is that part of the economy that is owned by private citizens.

Throughout much of the twentieth century, government spending in the United Kingdom has made up a significant percentage of all spending (see Figs. 4.9 and 4.10). However, during the 1980s significant steps were taken by the Conservative government to reduce the relative size of

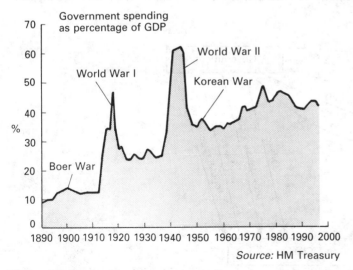

Source: HM Treasury

Figure 4.9 Changes in government spending as a percentage of national expenditure. (*Source*: HM Treasury) GDP = gross domestic product (the total value of a nation's output in a given region).

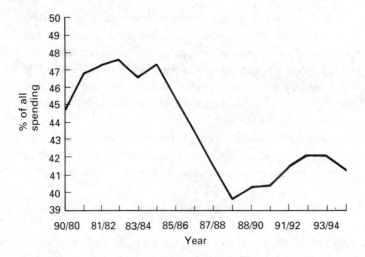

Figure 4.10 Government spending as a percentage of all spending, 1974–1994.

government spending. A major aim of the government since coming into office in May 1979 was the restoration of market forces throughout the economy.

In a mixed economy, one of the central issues of debate will be about the nature of the mix between private and public sectors.

Figure 4.11 illustrates some of the ways in which the activities of government, consumers and businesses are inextricably intertwined in a mixed economy. The government regulates the activities of producers and consumers, for example by setting out health and safety standards for the production of goods and by setting down legal requirements limiting the ways in which consumers can buy on hire purchase. The government sells goods and services that it produces to

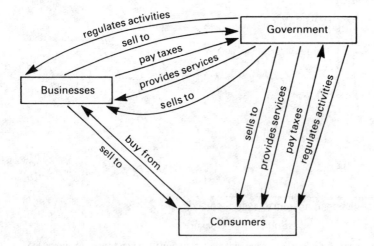

Figure 4.11 Links between businesses, consumers and government.

businesses and consumers *directly*, for example consultancy services to exporters, and of goods and services produced by nationalized industries. It also provides services to business and consumers *indirectly*—the disposal of waste, the provision of street lighting, the repairs to roads; these are paid for indirectly by taxes. Businesses sell goods and services to the government, to other businesses and to consumers; they also pay local and national taxes. Consumers buy goods and services from government and from businesses.

Questions

Short-answer questions

1. Explain the following terms in relation to systems theory:
   - Inputs
   - Processes
   - Filters
   - Boundaries
   - Primary inputs
   - Secondary inputs
2. What is the difference between an open and a closed system?
3. List three decisions that the national economic system makes.
4. What is a value chain?
5. Why is it important for businesses to have an understanding of what value means?
6. What is competitive advantage?
7. Why are linkages important in the value chain?
8. List the five main primary activities in the value chain.
9. What are the main support activities in the value chain?
10. Explain what is meant by (a) effectiveness and (b) efficiency in relation to organizational performance.
11. What is the concern of macroeconomics?
12. Draw a simple circular flow model of the economy.
13. Who makes the decisions in a mixed economy?
14. What is involved in the process of '*perestroika*'?
15. What are the principal features of a planned economy?
16. What is a market economy?
17. Which of the following are planned economies?
    - United States
    - Kampuchea
    - Russia
    - Lithuania
    - Germany
    - Uganda
    - China
    - Cuba

18. What is private enterprise?
19. How substantial is government expenditure as a percentage of all spending in this country today?
20. How can a central planning authority assess consumer needs and requirements?

Essays

1. There is no clearly charted route to the market economy.
    Discuss this assertion.
2. How does the economic system turn inputs into finished outputs?
3. Why does the government intervene in the economy? Illustrate your answer with examples.
4. What is the most effective way of allocating scarce resources?
5. How can an understanding of systems theory enable a manager to run an organization more effectively?
6. What is the value chain? How can a well organized value chain enable an organization to have an edge over its rivals.
7. Business systems operate within the context of a dynamic external environment. What are the implications of this for managers?
8. Planning leads to the most effective co-ordination of the use of resources. Discuss this statement.
9. There is no such thing as a 'free market'. Discuss.
10. Consumers know best how to spend their own money. There is therefore no need for a benevolent government! Discuss.

Data response questions

1   Recharging Russia's batteries

Study the article in Fig. 4.12 and answer the questions that follow.

1. What is meant in the article by 'lack of co-ordination'? Why is this seen to be a problem?
2. What conditions would be required for co-ordination to be effective?
3. In what ways might the process of co-ordination use up scarce resources?
4. Using the example of batteries, explain how the price mechanism might help to deal with the problem of co-ordination.
5. What problems might be introduced by introducing the price mechanism into this situation?

2   Problems of market reforms

As we move into the middle of the 1990s, more and more countries are moving towards some form of market economy. However, market economies differ enormously. Free-market principles often clash with local cultures.

Recharging Russia's batteries

O. MIKHAILOV

PRAVDA'S "Repair Shop" had a group of visitors from Kiev with an unusual request. They came straight from the counter of Home Radio, a shop which is forever throwing all sorts of batteries on the market.

· But is it? That's the point. This time (and we may safely add, many times before) there were no batteries in stock. Our visitors, ex-customers of Home Radio, were naturally annoyed and took the opportunity to exhibit their recently-acquired, but already silent transistor radios, portable tape-recorders and useless pocket-calculators.

● SHORTAGE

With our darkly muttering visitors still crowding around us, we telephoned the Ministry of Trade's Department for the Ukraine. They told us that every year shops in the Ukraine receive inadequate supplies of Krona, Uran and Yupiter batteries.

Inadequate? A mild word for an annual shortage of 60 million batteries! Shop assistants begin to complain that due to this lack, people are not buying transistor-operated equipment. Nobody wants to spend all their time running round shops in search of batteries.

Who is responsible for these drastic cuts? Customers reckon the Department of Trade is to blame: there has long been a dearth of batteries on the market.

The Department of Trade passes the buck to the Ministry of Electro-Technology. After all, the factories which systematically fail to manufacture adequate supplies of batteries, like the Yelets Factory of Batteries, the Klaipeda Dry-Cell Batteries Factory 'Sirius', and many others, come under this Ministry.

What's more, these shortages run into many millions of much-needed batteries. For their part, the factories explain their failure to meet demand by pointing to shortages of necessary materials.

The shortages of batteries for transistor-operated equipment are exacerbated by lack of proper coordination within trade departments. Millions of transistor radios, tape-recorders and other battery-operated articles often spend weeks sitting in storerooms and warehouses before being sent off to retail outlets.

During that time the elements deteriorate, so when they finally reach the customer there is not much life left in them. Sometimes they are no longer saleable merchandise. What a waste.

● ESSENTIAL

"It is the lack of coordination," complains L. Nikiforov, general manager of the Korolev factory in Kiev which manufactures Meridian transistor radios. "It is essential that regular supplies of batteries are ensured. Their production should be in conjunction with battery-operated equipment".

Thousands, even millions of people who have wasted their money buying expensive transistor-radios and tape-recorders which they can only use for a brief period, would like to ask the central Planning Office, the Ministry of Electro-Technology and the Ministry of Trade, when the problems of missing batteries will be solved.

Figure 4.12 Comments on 'co-ordination' in Russia. (*Source*: *Pravda*, English language edn, vol. 2, no. 4, 1988)

There is no clearly charted route to a free market. Eastern economies moving towards the market are doing so in many different ways. These countries, especially those of the former Soviet Union, have evolved different cultures based on communitarian values that stress security and fairness. It is unrealistic to expect them to quickly adapt to ideas based on competition for personal gain.

It does however seem likely that elements of the old system of central planning and one-party control—the 'old socialism'—will be reduced.

After 75 years of restraint, the Russian government has unleashed a frenzy of business deals as managers of failing state enterprises, ambitious young entrepreneurs and others have set up new enterprises. However, such developments clash with a strongly embedded 'socialist ethic'. The people in the Eastern bloc have grown accustomed to the security of guaranteed jobs, housing, medical care and other social benefits, and they are fearful of the risks and inequalities of capitalism. A 1991 poll found that most Russians reject the idea of a market economy, and another in 1992 found that only one in four Poles believes in free enterprise.

The great danger is that the inability of the new market structures to create visible benefits may result in a backlash in favour of the old communist system. Allowing prices to find their own levels has led to inflation rates of 2000 per cent or more while wages have hardly risen. High prices have brought an end to many of the old queues and have brought many new goods to shops. At the same time, however, millions of jobs have disappeared, old factories and workshops have closed down, and many people are now living at a subsistence level. Privatization still has a long way to go. Even in Poland, which has been at the forefront of change, only 25 per cent of state enterprises had been privatized by 1992.

A recent study estimated that the old communist bloc is likely to suffer a daunting period of deep economic recession, soaring inflation and high unemployment for several years to come. In Poland and Russia the governments are having to move back towards some centralized control by raising wages, increasing spending on welfare programmes, subsiding state companies and slowing the pace of reforms to stave off mass strikes and social unrest.

1. What do the following terms that appear above mean?
   (a) Market economy
   (b) Communitarian values
   (c) Central planning
   (d) Socialist ethic
2. Explain how the above example indicates that there is a clash between the socialist ethic and the move towards a market economy.
3. What other difficulties are there in moving towards a market economy?
4. What are the (a) short-term advantages and disadvantages and (b) long-term advantages and disadvantages in moving to a market economy?
5. What factors should be taken into consideration in deciding whether the advantages will outweigh the disadvantages in moving towards a market economy?

3   A new economic order?

It is arguable that both capitalism and communism are poor ways of managing the use of resources. Communism over-controls, capitalism under-controls. Communism suffers from scarcity, capitalism from overconsumption. Even the outrageously priced black markets produced by planned economies have their counterparts in capitalism—perfectly legal 'white markets' for outrageously priced luxury items which are restricted to the wealthy because most people cannot afford the prices.

Rather than regard the crisis of communism as an inevitable capitulation to capitalism, we can view it as a similar process to the transition Americans experienced during the Great Depression of the 1930s. The Depression occurred because of a severe failure in the market system, but it was cured by a variety of social welfare programmes which succeeded in stabilizing the American economy.

Russia lags behind the United States in its development by about fifty years, so it is now making a similar transition with many close parallels. Just as Franklin Roosevelt led Americans through a painful adjustment after the Great Depression, Mikhail Gorbachev provided and Boris Yeltsin is now providing the same charismatic but troubled leadership as Russia struggles through a similar transition. And, just as American did not abandon capitalism but instead corrected its flaws by adopting some elements of socialism, Russia seems likely to develop an advanced form of democratic, market socialism.

Opinion polls taken in 1991 showed that most citizens in the former Soviet Union favoured some form of democratic market socialism. In Poland the Democratic Left Alliance bases its appeal on the best features of socialism and capitalism. In China, too, a survey found that two-thirds of the population favoured a form of 'democratic socialism'.

This concept of a socially guided market economy offers a logical solution to the current crisis of communism because it could provide the advantages of the free market while retaining some sense of orderly control. Over time, the private sector in East Europe and Russia should grow from its present size to about 50–70 per cent of the economy. But these are socialist societies, so they should also ensure employment, medical care, housing and pensions to buffer their citizens from hardships of the market. It would also be best to maintain strategic control, perhaps through a regulation of state ownership over banking, utilities, transportation and other quasi-public industries. Perhaps the most crucial strategy would be to encourage some form of democratic economic governance in which workers, government, the public and managers share control of large organizations and key industries, offering a fresh application of socialist principles. Current examples of such practices include workers' councils, decision-making by democratically elected central bodies, employee share ownership plans, various types of privatization, joint stock companies, self-managed teams and other aspects of 'new socialism'.

(Based on an article by William Halal and Alexander Nikitin in *Business and the Contemporary World*, Autumn 1992)

1. Outline the key features of:
   (a) Capitalism.
   (b) Communism.
   (c) 'The Third Way' (i.e., the 'new socialism').
2. What have been the major obstacles facing Eastern European economies that are moving towards a freer market system?
3. Why do the writers of the above article suggest that a 'new socialism' is more appropriate for Russia and Poland than a free-market solution?
4. What features of the 'new socialism' outlined above are also features of the UK economic system?
5. Is either capitalism or communism an appropriate path for modern economies? What are the alternatives?

Suggested reading

Beardshaw, J., *Economics: A Students' Guide*. Pitman, 1992.
Harrison, B., *Economics*. Longman, 1991.
Johnson, G., and Scholes, K., *Exploring Corporate Strategy*, 3rd edn. Prentice-Hall, 1993.

5

Business organization in the private sector

Business organizations are found in both the private and the public sectors of the economy. The public sector is made up of organizations that are owned by the government for the people. The private sector is made up of organizations that are owned and run by private individuals to further their own interests (Fig. 5.1).

Private sector	Public sector
Owned by private individuals	Owned by the government for the people

Figure 5.1 The difference between the private and public sector.

Organization is required to turn ideas into activities which can be kept up over a period of time (Fig. 5.2). An entrepreneur needs to be able to identify business opportunities that will meet the wants and needs of consumers. Opportunties need to be converted into products that will be sold successfully for a long time. An organization needs to be formed with clearly established aims. It must have patterns and structures. To sum up, *a business organization needs to be organized to produce goods and services at a profit*.

Most large companies started off as small companies, usually owned and run by one person. The idea for the business may have come from a chance invention, copying an idea that had

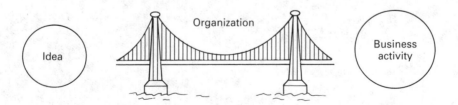

Figure 5.2 Business ideas are turned into activities but can be kept over a period of time.

worked somewhere else, spotting a gap in the market or in many other ways. The starting-point to this chapter is therefore the business idea and the creation of a small business.

The original business idea needs to be followed up by detailed business planning around which the business organization will function. A number of elements combine to create the business organization, i.e.:

- The form of organization (Will it be a sole trader, partnership or limited company?)
- The infrastructure, or pattern of authority within the organization
- The superstructure, or pattern of organizing employees into groups within the organization.

This chapter follows these elements through, as shown in Fig. 5.3.

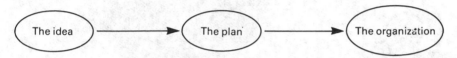

Figure 5.3 Putting business ideas into practice.

Case Study—Spotting a business opportunity

In Europe today, we have surpluses of butter, grain and milk because more of these products are being produced than customers can buy. But other agricultural products are in comparatively short supply.

Jonathan Newell studied agriculture at university and found out, through studying the relevant trade statistics, that not enough snails are being produced to meet demand. In particular, the demand is not being fully met in France. There is also a growing appetite for snails in this country.

In recent years, most snails coming into France have come from Eastern Europe. However, because of the Chernobyl disaster, these snails still have excessive amounts of radioactivity and have been banned in France at least until 1994.

Jonathan was convinced that if he could produce the product he could sell it to a ready market. He received a grant to do some more detailed marketing. He found that Britain imported over 100 000 snails per year in the late 1980s and that the figure was rising in the early 1990s.

He then set up a private company which he called 'Escargot Anglais' and he raised money by selling shares in the company to friends and relatives. The company had limited liability. This means that if it runs into difficulties Jonathan and the other shareholders will lose only the money they have actually put into the business. The idea of a limited company also appealed because limited companies must send a record of their accounts to Companies House every year. Jonathan felt that this would force him to keep records in an organized way.

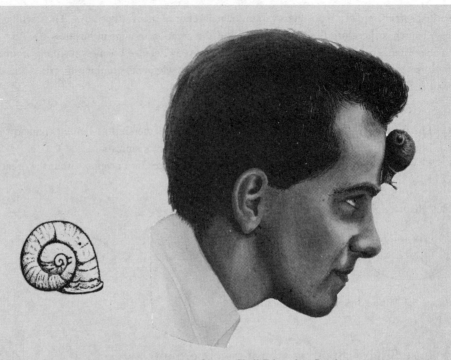

Figure 5.4 Spotting a business opportunity. (*Source*: Shell Education Service)

The next step was for 'Escargot Anglais' to hire a unit from the Kent Enterprise Agency in Ramsgate and to buy in a stock of 200 breeding snails from the Mediterranean. You will be glad to hear that edible snails are different from the ones you find in your garden. They grow more quickly and lay more eggs. They are also more tender.

Jonathan expects that his snails will produce an average of 10 clutches of eggs a year. Each clutch will hatch 60–70 snails. The eggs must be kept at a temperature of 21°C for about three weeks. It then takes between 100 and 120 days for the snails to build up to a marketable weight of 20–25 grammes.

The snails are kept in trays and are fed on animal feed. They can feed as soon as they start to move around.

Jonathan had been in business only a few months when the worst storm this century battered the Kent coast. Fortunately the snails survived, and since then Jonathan has bought 200 more snails from Europe. Normally, during December and January the snails are rested, but the remainder of the year they are expected to produce one clutch a month.

Questions

1. What is Jonathan's business idea?
2. Why is he taking a risk in setting out in business?

3. How can careful planning help him to reduce this risk?

4. What advantages will Jonathan gain from setting up in business?

5. What sorts of information would Jonathan require before setting up in business?

6. What evidence is given that Jonathan had researched and planned his business before setting up?

7. Apart from the ability to sell goods, what other criteria could be applied to measure the success of Escargot Anglais over a period of time?

8. What markets is Escargot Anglais trying to sell to? What factors influence the choice of markets?

9. What information would you need to know in order to evaluate Jonathan's business idea?

Business ideas

Where do business ideas come from?

Nearly everyone at some time or another thinks about setting up an enterprise of their own. You will hear people say things like 'Someone could make a fortune out of selling such and such', or 'If I had some money, I could make a business out of making this or that.'

Where does the idea to set up an enterprise come from?

Some people copy ideas that they have seen somewhere else (such as selling flowers at a busy railway station). Others spot a gap in the market—'Nobody round here runs a mobile disco service!' Others turn a hobby into a business—'I always enjoyed making wooden toys.' These are just some of the many ways in which people come up with business ideas.

Developing a business idea

With very few exceptions, every big company began as a small company, often with just one or two enterprising individuals at its head.

William Morris began by mending bicycles in a back street garage in Oxford, and went on to build up a major motor manufacturing company.

Michael Marks arrived in this country from Russia in the nineteenth century speaking very little English. He set up as a door-to-door hawker of buttons, needles, ribbons and other small items. He progressed to selling from market stalls, setting up in partnership with Tom Spencer. Today Marks and Spencer is the best known brand name in the United Kingdom.

Anita Roddick set up her own small shop in the 1960s to sell her preparations of cosmetics based on natural substances. Today the Body Shop can be found on most major high streets.

Developing a business idea usually requires a combination of careful planning and good luck. It also requires careful attention to detail in a number of key areas, including production, finance and marketing.

Business planning

An idea on its own does not create a business. What is required in addition is the ability to organize and plan. Businesses require inputs of time, information, raw materials, capital, labour and paperwork. These inputs need to be put together in an organized way. However, that is not the end of the story. In addition, a company needs to create a public image to market and sell its products; it needs to consider channels of distribution, packaging, display and the many other details involved in getting goods to the final customer. All of this requires detailed planning.

A *business plan* is one of the key ingredients of any successful business, no matter how big or well established. If you want to start a business, it is vital. It helps you anticipate problems and work out how to deal with them. It also gives essential information to the people whose support you need—particularly anyone lending you money.

Before setting out a business plan, it is necessary to carry out some preliminary research to find out:

- Whether people are prepared to buy the good or service
- What competition exists
- What premises and equipment are required
- Whether planning permission is necessary
- How much money/capital is needed
- The cost of borrowing money
- What grants and other forms of assistance are available

The contents of a business plan

A business plan should be clearly set out under the following headings:

1. *Contents page*   This is useful in any kind of report that is more than two or three pages long.
2. *The owner*   This section should give some information about the owner (or owners), including their educational background and what they have done. It should also contain the names and addresses of two referees.
3. *The business*   This should first contain the name and address of the business and then go on to give a detailed description of the product or service being offered, how and where it will be produced, who is likely to buy it, and in what quantities.
4. *The market*   This section will describe the market research that has been carried out and what it has revealed. It should give details of prospective customers—how many there are, and how much they would be prepared to pay. It should also give details of the competition.
5. *Advertising and promotion*   This should give information about how the business will be publicized to potential customers. It should give details of likely costs.
6. *Premises and equipment*   This section should show that the business has considered a range of locations and then chosen the best site. It should also give details of planning regulations (if appropriate). Costs of premises and the equipment needed should also be included.

7. *Business organization*   This should state whether the enterprise will take the form of sole trader, partnership, company or co-operative.

8. *Costings*   The business should give some indication of the cost of producing the product or service, and the prices it proposes to charge. It is then possible to make profit calculations.

9. *The finance*   This should give details of how the finance for the business is going to be raised. How much will come from savings? How much needs to be borrowed?

10. *Cash flow*   This should list all expected incomings and outgoings over the first year. Cash flow calculations are important, but at this stage can only be approximate.

11. *Expansion*   Finally, the business should give an indication of future plans. Does it want to keep on producing a steady output or is a dramatic expansion possible? Does it intend to add to its product range? What kind of new competition is likely to emerge, and how will the business deal with it?

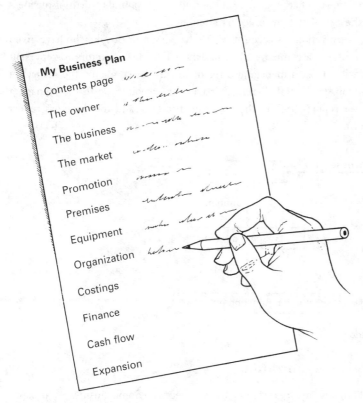

Figure 5.5 Drawing up a business plan.

Business structures

Formally constituted bodies are set up to achieve particular *objectives*, and are called *organizations*. A business is an example of an organization, and every business will need to have an organizational structure.

A business will need to adopt a basic form of organization from a range of alternatives that are commonly recognized. In the United Kingdom the most common forms are sole traders, partnerships and companies.

A business will also need to formulate an *internal structure*, which is a pattern for command, communication and relationships within the organization.

The prime objectives of business organizations will be established by those with the highest level of authority within a concern. For example, the directors of a major company may establish as a foremost objective that of making their company into a market leader through offering a quality service.

In order to attain this (or another) objective, it will be necessary to establish a *pattern of responsibility* within the organization. Individuals within the firm will be given varying levels of authority and responsibility. At one extreme of the spectrum of responsibility you will find the managing director of a multinational oil company handling millions of pounds worth of business each day, and at the other, the petrol station forecourt attendant.

Individual members of an organization are accountable to the person or people who have given them responsibility. For example, in a company shareholders will choose directors to represent their interests; the directors will choose a managing director to run the company; the managing director will in turn choose managerial staff. Senior managers are accountable to the managing director; the managing director reports back to the board of directors; and the directors report back to shareholders (Fig. 5.6).

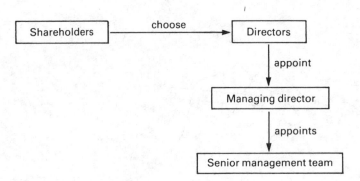

Figure 5.6 Company organization.

What makes an effective organization?

There is no set pattern that helps an organization to be effective. Some businesses prosper because they were 'at the right place at the right time', others because they are made up of the right blend of personalities. However, if an organization is going to be successful over a long period of time, it will need to combine most of the following ingredients:

1. *Unity of purpose*   All parts of the organization should be working towards a common aim. If some sectors of the organization are working in different directions, this can be very confusing and bad for morale.

2. *Effective leadership* Positions of authority and responsibility in an organization should be vested only in those who are capable of putting them into effect. Decisions can be implemented only if those in authority have the confidence and determination to see that they are carried out.

3. *Flexibility* An organization should not be too rigid. It should be able to alter course quickly if things are not going right, and to adapt to changing circumstances.

4. *Operational efficiency* This means that the operations that a company carries out must be studied, and the results of this analysis used to ensure that things are done in the best way possible. At one level this will involve studying each operation and function separately to see that time is not wasted, costs are kept down, work is done accurately and other aspects of a smooth operation are put into practice.

   At the same time, the whole functioning of the organization needs to be studied at a global level. It is important that the various parts of the organization work smoothly together and in the same direction. (This is called overall efficiency.)

5. *Interrelationships* Each member of an organization needs clearly to understand their rights and obligations with regards to other members. Lines of authority and communications need to be clearly defined and acted upon.

Forms of business organization

Before a business starts trading, a decision will have to be made about what legal form it will take, as this affects taxation and the accounting records that need to be kept.

There are various types of business organization and each of them is subject to different kinds of control. The United Kingdom has a mixed economy and this means that, although many businesses are privately owned, many organizations are run by the state (see Fig. 5.7).

The sole trader/sole proprietor

Although there may be other workers employed by the sole trader, he or she will be personally responsible for the financial liabilities of the company. The individual who is setting up the business may borrow some or all of the capital required to set it up and get it started.

Many small businesses are initially set up in the form of sole trader (also called 'sole proprietor'). This is because until the operation becomes established it is difficult to generate enough profit to support more than one owner.

Common examples of businesses that have the sole trader form are sign writers, graphic designers, plumbers, decorators, mobile hairdressers, window cleaners, bookkeepers and chiropodists. Common features of these businesses are that they do not require a lot of capital, they can be done effectively by one person, and they require flexibility (e.g. a willingness to work long and/or unusual hours).

There are a number of advantages to setting up as a sole trader:

1. There are no legal formalities to complete before commencing to trade.

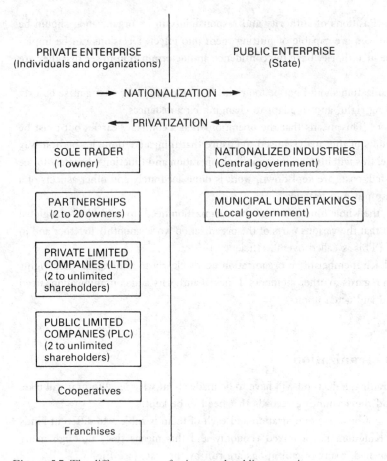

Figure 5.7 The different types of private and public enterprise.

2. There are no legal requirements governing the layout of the accounts.
3. Annual accounts do not have to be audited.
4. Decisions can be made quickly.
5. All profits belong to the sole owner.
6. The owner has the freedom to run the business in his or her own way.

However, there are also a number of disadvantages:

1. Capital is limited to the owner's savings, profits and the amount that he or she can borrow.
2. The owner has sole responsibility for debts and if necessary might have to sell personal possessions to meet business debts.
3. The responsibility for a range of separate tasks rests on the shoulders of the owner, e.g. paperwork, tax returns, management, dealing with suppliers and customers.
4. The success of the business will often depend on the owner's willingness to work long and/ or non-standard hours.

5. An unforeseen accident or illness may cripple the business at an important point in its development.

Case Study—The sole trader: Nursery Pieces

Marion Tate first became interested in producing wooden puzzles when she saw some for sale on a craft stall at a brass band concert. Marion had always been interested in the arts and in making things. She felt she could produce a similar product herself.

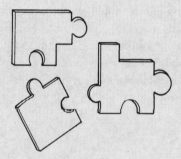

Figure 5.8

Initially she began to produce puzzles as a hobby and these attracted a great deal of interest from friends. She decided to produce a collection for a craft fair and they proved to be a 'hit'. Marion then decided to invest £700 on an electric band saw and spent a lot of her spare time purchasing a collection of three main animal puzzle designs to sell at craft fairs.

At the time Marion was working as an administrator at a 'special school' and was able to learn a lot about the sorts of colours that appeal to children.

Marion's decision to set up in business in a serious way was in many ways influenced by per personal circumstances. As a single parent, she needed some means of securing a steady income and yet be able to work flexible hours. Her daughter suffers from asthma and often has to take time off from school. This means that Marion is never sure when she will need to be at home to look after her child.

Marion decided to set up in business as a sole trader under the name 'Nursery Pieces'. Nursery Pieces is situated in a small workshop unit, from which Marion is able to carry out her manufacturing. (Sawing is a noisy process.) She concentrates her time on three main lines of woodworking: wooden clocks, personalized name jigsaws, and a range of 30 different animal jigsaw pictures. Only a small part of Marion's time needs to be spent at the workshop because sales, packaging, accounting and other activities can all be done from home.

The business provides Marion with a modest living, and gives her the flexibility and freedom needed to combine home and work. Running Nursery Pieces gives her a sense of achievement and satisfaction. Her time is her own (although she finds making puzzles addictive), she enjoys her work, and she feels that people respect her for what she does. Some have been known to remark that her work is better than that of many of the 'Big Name' firms.

Problems of running the business include the fact that after expenses are accounted for profits are very low. Nursery Pieces can sell as much as it makes, and for a substantial mark-up. However, a lot of Marion's time is taken up in making new business contacts, keeping the books up to date and packing and posting items. Marion felt that the business could really take off if she employed a few members of staff for production purposes. However, it would take at least three months to train them, and there would be no guarantee that they would stay with the business. There would also be a considerable risk in using Marion's house as security to raise a loan.

At times Marion feels that she would like the security of a steady job. She finds that cash flow is always a problem. A minimum order of wood (her basic raw material) costs £300, but the shops that are her customers may take several months to pay her for the puzzles supplied.

Questions

1. Do you think that the sole trader form is a suitable type of business organization for Nursery Pieces? Explain your reasoning.
2. What would be the main benefits and drawbacks to Marion Tate from such a form of organization?
3. What do you think are Marion Tate's main objectives in setting up in business?
4. Give ten examples of businesses that might suitably operate as sole traders. Explain why in each case.

The ordinary partnership

There may be two or more partners in a partnership. A sole trader will often take on a partner when there is too much work to be done by a single person or when extra skills are required. Many partnerships take advantage of a division of labour based on specialist skills or on the division of time so that partners will work different shifts. There are many professional businesses that take the partnership form, e.g. doctors, accountants, vets, solicitors.

A partnership agreement is usually set out in a legal document called a Deed of Partnership which is witnessed by a solicitor. However, it is possible to set up a partnership without any legal formalities, as the provisions of the Partnership Act 1890 will be taken as the partnership agreement. This Act set out a detailed framework to govern the affairs of partners in cases where a Deed of Partnership is not drawn up. For example, one of the provisions of this Act is that if a partnership ends the partners will be equally responsible for debts.

A Deed of Partnership will cover such issues as:

- How much capital each partner will contribute

- How profits and losses will be shared
- Rules for admitting or expelling partners
- Voting rights
- Termination of the partnership

A carefully worded and detailed Deed of Partnership will help to outline a clear working arrangement.

There are a number of advantages to setting up as a partnership:

1. Partners can raise more capital by pooling their resources than they could do by operating as sole traders.
2. Partners can share expertise and effort.
3. Partners can arrange to cover for each other, e.g. for holidays and lunch breaks.
4. Partners may be able to borrow more capital than if they sought individual loans.
5. A partnership, like a sole trader, has the advantage of secrecy in that it is not obliged to publish its accounts or have them audited.

The disadvantages of the ordinary partnership form are that:

1. Each partner is personally liable for all the firm's business debts.
2. Disagreements can arise between partners about the amount of work that each is doing, and how work should be done.
3. Partnerships can raise only limited amounts of capital compared with businesses that are organized as companies.
4. For most forms of ordinary partnership there is a legal maximum of 20 partners.

Limited liability

A legal protection known as limited liability exists to protect people who put money into a business but play no active part in running that business. Limited liability means that the maximum amount that a part-owner of a limited business can lose is the sum that person has invested in the business. The private possessions of such investors are safeguarded, as it is only their stake in the limited business that they stand to lose.

Limited partnerships

A limited partnership is one in which one or more of the partners has limited liability. A sleeping partner is one who provides capital but takes no part in the running of the business. There must always be at least one partner with unlimited liability. The greater the proportion of the firm's capital that is protected by limited liability, the bigger the risk that will be taken by those partners with unlimited liability. Limited partnerships are therefore fairly unusual. They might be found for example where a business owner has retired, passing on the day-to-day running of a business to a younger relative. The limited partnership also gives scope for an individual or company to invest in a partnership without having to run it.

Case Study—The partnership: Concept Graphics

Concept Graphics

Figure 5.9

Mike Pawson and Sue Wakefield had both worked in the publicity department of a printing company known as Lyne Printers, in Grantham. Mike had been the studio manager and Sue the chief designer. When Lyne Printers were taken over by a larger company, the publicity department was closed down and Sue and Mike were made redundant.

They then decided to set up their own business partnership called 'Concept Graphics'. They knew that there was a demand for good-quality artwork and that most of their existing clients would use their services. The main problem was finding premises, because the rent and rates of most of the properties in the town were too high. However, they were fortunate to find a small unit at the local Enterprise Agency and were offered a start-up grant by the local council.

In order to secure the grant and to obtain a loan from their bank, they produced a business plan giving details of their expected costs and sales revenues.

Mike and Sue set out a Deed of Partnership which they signed and had witnessed by a solicitor. This Agreement set out that they would jointly share the profits and losses of the business, contribute equal time and effort and so on.

Mke and Sue feel that a partnership is the best form of business structure for them. Mike's skill is in producing detailed technical illustrations (such as engineering drawings), whereas Sue concentrates more on book illustrations and cartoons. They are able to share out the work, and discuss the best ways of doing jobs. They take their holidays at different times, and if one of them is ill the other one can keep the business open. If one of them has to leave the studio, the other is available to meet callers and take phone messages. In this way they are able to maintain the goodwill of the business.

As a small business there are many little tasks that the partners must do themselves. These include making the coffee, tidying up and cleaning the office, doing the paper work and the accounts. In the spirit of the partnership, they choose to share each of these tasks.

Questions

1. Do you think that a partnership is a suitable form of business organization for Concept Graphics? Explain your reasoning.
2. What would be the main benefits and drawbacks to the two owners from such a form of organization?
3. Give six examples of businesses that might suitably operate as partnerships.
4. Choose two of these and explain in detail why a partnership might be a suitable form of organization for them.
5. If you were going to set up a doctors' partnership, what details would you think necessary to include in the Deed of Partnership?

Limited companies

Limited companies are the most common form of business organization. A limited company is a separate body in law from its shareholders and directors. The company may form contracts, sue and be sued in its own name. The shareholders are not liable for the company's debts except for the value of their shareholdings.

There are two types of limited company. *Public companies* have their shares traded on the main market of the Stock Exchange; *private companies* impose some restrictions on the trading in their shares.

To set up a limited company it is necessary to go through a number of legal procedures in order to gain recognition. This mainly involves the presentation of various records and documents to the Registrar of Companies. These documents are open to scrutiny by the general public.

All limited companies must present a *Memorandum of Association* and *Articles of Assocation* in order to receive a Certificate of Incorporation (Fig. 5.10). The Memorandum spells out the nature of the company when viewed from the outside. Someone reading the Memorandum would be able to get a general idea of what the company is and the business line it is concerned with. The Memorandum sets out:

- The name of the company
- The registered address of the company
- The objectives of the company, i.e. the types of activity it will engage in
- The capital of the company

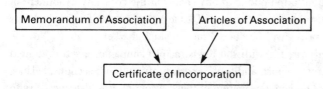

Figure 5.10 Documents required for corporate status.

Many companies will produce a fairly vague list of objectives in their Memorandum. This gives them the opportunity to alter their activities if market opportunities arise.

The Articles of Association set out the rules that govern the inside working of a company. These include:

- The rights attached to the holding of the various types of shares offered by the company
- The rules and procedures for issuing and transferring shares
- The procedures and timing of company meetings
- The details of how accounts will be kept and recorded
- The powers and responsibilities of the directors
- The details of how company officers will be appointed

Once a private company has lodged these documents and had them accepted, it will be granted a *Certificate of Incorporation* and can start to trade. The Certificate of Incorporation sets up the company as a legal body in its own right. The company (not the individual shareholders) enters into contracts and can sue or be sued in a court of law.

A public company must however take further steps before being granted a *Certificate of Trading*. The Memorandum of a public company must state that the company is to be a public company, and it must abide by a legally set minimum figure for allotted share capital. Before a trading certificate is granted, shares allotted must be paid up to at least 25 per cent of their nominal value plus the whole of any premiums payable.

The owners of limited companies are called shareholders because they each own a part of the business. *Private limited companies* can have from two to an unlimited number of shareholders and can expand by raising finance from new shareholders. However, their shares are not quoted on the Stock Exchange and they are not allowed to advertise the sale of shares publicly. There is also a danger of issuing too many shares and thus having to divide the profits between too large a number of shareholders. To warn creditors about the dangers of dealing with these companies, 'Limited' appears after their name.

Public limited companies have the opportunity to become larger than the other forms of private business organization. They are allowed to raise capital through the medium of the Stock Exchange which quotes their share prices, and this creates a breadth of financial possibilities. The initials 'PLC' (or 'plc') appear after the name of a public limited company.

Only two persons are needed to form a public limited company and there is no stated maximum of shareholders. The process of becoming a public company is in many ways similar to that of a private company.

Once a public company has received a Certificate of Incorporation it will issue a *prospectus*, which is an advertisement or invitation to the public to buy shares in the company. Allotment of shares then takes place and the Registrar of Companies will issue a trading certificate. Contracts can then be entered into and share prices will be quoted on the stock market.

All limited companies must, each year, file with the Registrar of Companies a set of audited accounts. These will include a directors' report, auditors' report, profit and loss account, balance sheet, source and application of funds and an explanation of these accounts. It is also necessary to file an annual return giving details of the directors, shareholders and other information required by law. All this information will be kept on file at Companies House and is open to inspection by members of the public.

There are a number of advantages to forming a limited company:

1. Shareholders have limited liability.
2. It is easier to raise capital through share issues.
3. It is often easier to raise finance from banks.
4. It is possible to operate on a larger scale.
5. It is possible to employ specialists.
6. Suppliers feel more confident about trading with legally established bodies.
7. Directors are not liable if they follow the rules.
8. It is easy to expand.
9. It is easier to pass the company down from one generation to another.
10. The company name is protected by law.
11. There are tax advantages associated with giving shares to employees.
12. Company pension schemes can give bigger benefits than those available to the self-employed.
13. Larger outputs can be produced at lower unit cost.

There are also a number of disadvantages associated with becoming a limited company:

1. Formation and running costs can be expensive.
2. Decisions can be slow and 'red tape' can be a problem.
3. There can be dis-economies in being too large.
4. Employees and shareholders are distanced from one another.
5. Affairs are public; e.g., accounts and annual returns must be audited.
6. Affairs are tightly regulated under various Companies Acts.
7. Heavy penalties are imposed if 'rules' are broken.

℘ Case Study—The private company: 'Clandrex Limited'

In 1976, under the name of David B Cleaning Services, a small business started providing a window and general cleaning service in a small Midlands town. Over the following years, as more companies contracted out their cleaning requirements to contract cleaners, this business expanded to meet the needs of the local community. It was and still is the largest window cleaning business in the town.

Contract cleaning is a very demanding business, with long unsociable hours; expansion of the business required obtaining contracts out of the immediate area. The nature of the work means that it is very labour-intensive, and management of a widely scattered labour force would create a great deal of work. It was therefore decided to target another sector of the cleaning market in order to expand.

Figure 5.11

A lot of experience had been gained by the firm in the use of cleaning chemicals, equipment and other materials. It was felt that this knowledge could be put to good use in providing cleaning requirements to commerce and industry.

Every business needs some form of cleaning equipment every day of its life, whether it be an industrial chemical in a factory or a roll of toilet paper in an office with one staff member. Most businesses at some stage or another will also need advice on how to get something clean, from a stain on a carpet to cleaning up a stone building.

David B Cleaning Services was a father-and-son partnership (David and Paul Bridle). In 1982 the two proprietors started a Sales Division. Working from home became impossible because of the quantity of materials they needed to store; they therefore bought a small industrial unit which also served as an office.

The owners felt that it would now be sensible to form a private limited company in which they would have a joint and equal shareholding. They felt that the provision of limited liability would be a valuable form of protection. It was quite possible that they would be dealing with a small number of major buyers; if a buyer failed to pay up this could cause serious cash flow problems and threaten the survival of the business.

With limited liability status shareholders stand to lose at most only their stake in the company. As a private limited company, therefore, the Bridles would have personal protection against market trends leading to a slump in demand for their products, or bad debts. Furthermore, being able to put 'Ltd' after their name would give the business status. Previously they had found that many larger companies were not prepared to deal with non-limited companies.

To become a private limited company you can either go to the trouble of carrying out all the necessary paperwork of registering as a company yourself, or you can simply buy a 'ready-made' company. There are a number of firms that make a living from setting up ready-to-run companies and then selling them off. These firms make out all the necessary documentation and registration including choosing a company name. David and Paul were able to cut out a lot of paperwork simply by buying a company that was ready to run under the name 'Clandrex Ltd', which was registered with the object of supplying cleaning materials.

Larger premises were obtained, and the company expanded to employ five full-time members of staff and several part-timers. The company was split into two divisions: Contract Cleaning/Window Cleaning and Sales.

Today Clandrex is one of the biggest distributors of Numatic vacuum cleaners in the United Kingdom. Machines are shipped all over the country—to hospitals, factories, offices and even private individuals. The company still supplies a range of cleaning chemicals, handcleaners and other janitorial products. Next to machines, the biggest line is paper products and cleaning cloths/wipers.

Questions

1. Do you think that a private limited company is a suitable form of business organization for Clandrex Ltd? Explain your reasoning.
2. What would be the main benefits and drawbacks to David and Paul Bridle from such a form of organization?
3. Give five examples of businesses that might suitably operate as private limited companies.
4. Choose two of these and explain in detail why a private limited company might be a suitable form of organization for them.
5. What extra work is involved in setting up and running a limited company which does not exist for the sole trader and partnership forms?

6.   What advantages and disadvantages might there be to allowing additional share-holders to become part-owners of Clandrex Ltd?

The co-operative

Although co-operatives are still a very small part of the private-sector economy, they underwent a rapid growth in the 1980s. In 1980 there were only 300 recognized co-operatives; two years later the numbers had expanded to 500, and in 1984 there were 900; by 1992 there were reckoned to be more than 2500 co-operatives, producing everything from shoes to bread and creating employment for around 30 000 people.

The basic idea behind the co-operative is that people work together and make decisions jointly.

Co-operatives occur most frequently in three main areas of business activity:

- Production
- Retailing
- Marketing

Producers' co-operatives

These involve people clubbing together to produce goods or services, for example a growers' co-operative producing vegetables, or a baby-sitting co-operative.

A workers' co-operative is a commonly found type of producers' co-operative. Its members will:

- Share responsibility for the success or failure of the business
- Work together
- Take decisions together
- Share profits among themselves

There are three basic forms of workers' co-operative:

1.   *Common ownership co-operatives*   These are owned and controlled by the workers. Each has one share in the business, which costs £1 and carries one vote. The shares do not pay dividends and any profits are retained in a bank or building society to pay overheads and wages. Shares in these co-operatives cannot be sold for personal gain.
2.   *Co-ownership co-operatives*   These are owned by the workers again through one share and one vote per worker. However, the shares are linked to the co-operative's profits and losses, so the value of the shares can rise and fall.
3.   *Community co-operatives*   These are owned and controlled by the workers, by non-working community members and sometimes by local organizations. This is ideal for a business that brings together local traders and members of the community.

All producers' co-operatives adhere to the principle of one person, one vote when it comes to decision-making. But some delegate day-to-day decisions to an apppointed manager. Many co-operatives operate an equal pay policy, with everyone receiving the same wages and conditions. A few do have pay differentials, but these are usually kept to a minimum.

Retail co-operatives

Nowadays, people tend to think of 'the Co-op' as just another supermarket chain. This is not the case, because co-ops see themselves as having an important role in serving the community.

The first co-op was set up by a group of weavers in Toad Lane, Rochdale, in 1844. At that time, most workers were paid low wages consisting partly of tokens which could be exchanged only in the company shop where prices were high.

Twenty-eight weavers, known as the 'Rochdale Pioneers', pooled money to buy foodstuffs at wholesale prices which were then sold cheaply to members. Profits were shared out among members in the form of a dividend, depending on how much each had bought. Since then, co-ops have spread and there are many retail co-ops in Britain.

To become a shareholder in a co-op you need only buy a £1 share; this entitles you to a vote at meetings and to elect the president and other officers of the local co-op society.

Retail co-operatives are organized on a regional basis. Over the years many of the smaller co-operatives have tended to be swallowed up by larger societies. The largest single retailing society is the CRS (Co-operative Retail Society), with its headquarters in Manchester. A small number of regional co-ops give stamps to shoppers. These stamps can be collected and stuck in books which can be used in payment for goods. However, many co-ops have stopped distributing their dividends in this way and simply use profits to improve their facilities and to make prices more competitive.

Some co-ops not only provide supermarket services, but also have their own bank, milk delivery service, funeral service and libraries and provide other benefits such as education courses for members.

In the later part of the nineteenth century the co-ops flourished and societies sprang up all over Britain. It was the co-ops that brought in some of the first supermarkets. However, in recent years they have had to face very severe competition from multiples like Tesco. In retaliation, many smaller co-operative societies have merged, and organizations like the CRS have established their own hypermarkets. (CRS hypermarkets trade under the name 'Leo'.)

Marketing co-operatives

Marketing co-operatives are set up to buy, distribute, sell and promote various products. Distribution is often a problem when there are large numbers of small producers. A co-operative organization will help to advise producers about production methods, collect produce, store produce, grade and pack, promote and sell.

Marketing co-operatives are frequently found in developing countries, where they play a major part in the distribution of agricultural products. Small famers will have a share in a marketing organization. The co-operative might hire advisers to suggest what sorts of products are best produced and by what methods. Co-operative members can then concentrate on production (to the specifications of the co-operative) without having to worry about the storage, transport and selling of their produce.

In Zimbabwe, for example, the government has supported the development of co-operatives. Government encouragement and assistance has enabled co-operative unions to construct and make operational over 50 warehouses and more than 200 distribution centres. Rural farmers who belong to co-operatives are able to get credit from the Agricultural Finance Corporation to buy seeds and fertilizers. The loan does not have to be repaid until after the harvest when they take their grain to the Grain Marketing Board. Without the co-operative, finding credit would be difficult, and the cost of seeds from private companies would be high. This way, farmers do not have to worry about the marketing process.

Franchising

Franchising is one of the most rapidly growing business forms in this country, although we still fall well behind the United States, where over half of all retail sales are made by franchise organizations. A franchise system operates on the basis that an entrepreneur (known as the *franchisor*) will have developed a particular business activity, such as producing fast food, manufacturing ice cream, producing cosmetics or unblocking drains. The franchisor will then sell the right to trade under the business name to other individuals—*franchisees*. The franchisee will have the sole right to trade under that name in a particular locality. Examples include Thorntons, Pizza Hut, The Body Shop, Kleeneze and Dayvilles (American ice cream).

Once an agreement has been made to sell a franchise, the franchisee will normally make an initial payment to the franchisor and in return will receive help and advice in setting up the business. The franchisor will often supply equipment and stocks of materials. For example, in the fast food business cooking equipment might be supplied, also menus, recipes, packaging and clothing.

Once the business is up and running, it is up to the franchisee to make a success of it. However, the element of risk is reduced if the business has been proven to be a success elsewhere and expert help and assistance is provided. A major advantage for the franchisor is that it does not have to risk its own capital and will take a regular share in the profits of franchised outlets.

The main disadvantage to franchisees is that, while it is their own business, they will at times feel beholden to the franchisor (for example, there might be an agreement that stocks have to be purchased from them), and a given share of the profits will have to be paid over. It might also be difficult to change methods from those recommended by the franchisor.

Case Study—A Tumbletots franchise

Nicky has taken out a franchise with 'Tumbletots'.

'Tumbletots' is a business, running exercise classes for toddlers aged one year upwards. When she started, Nicky had no business experience and no children of her own. She paid £8000 for the franchise which included the licence fee, equipment and training.

Questions

1. What are the benefits to Nicky of taking out a franchise rather than setting up her own independent business?
2. What are the benefits to the franchising company of selling the franchise to Nicky?

Figure 5.12 (*Source*: AEB)

3. How is Nicky taking a risk?
4. How could Nicky promote her business?
5. List six types of business that could suitably be organized as franchises.
6. Choose one of these types and explain why you think it lends itself to franchising.

Structures within organizations

Every organization will need to choose those business structures that most effectively help it to put its ideas into practice. There are a number of alternatives, each of which will suit different circumstances.

In the typical sole trader or partnership form of organization, it will be relatively easy to formulate policies and then put them into practice. This is because only a few people are involved in the decision-making process and the co-ordination of decisions will not be unduly complicated once procedures for consultation and the passage of information have been established.

In a larger organization, however, the process becomes more complex. While one person or group will make a decision, the responsibility for putting that decision into effect will frequently rest with another individual or group. An effective organization will need a well structured network of communication. Decisions will be communicated in one direction and reports and feedback on progress will be communicated in the reverse direction. The structure within the organization will be based upon the need for effective co-ordination between those responsible for giving and receiving instructions (Fig. 5.13).

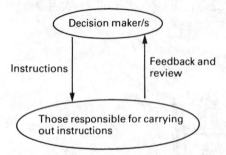

Figure 5.13 Co-ordinating the decision-making process.

Hierarchical structures and democratic structures

Some organizations are based on a distinct chain of command from senior to junior officials. Decisions are made at the top and passed down. Such organizations are usually based on clearly defined procedures and roles. Hierarchical structures tend to exist in situations that are fairly predictable (e.g. the civil service) and/or where it is necessary to be seen to be following carefully laid out rules (e.g. government departments, the police and armed forces).

Other organizations are based on more democratic lines. Decisions are made as a result of a consultation process involving various members of the organization. Ideas will be discussed and thought through collectively. *Democratic structures* tend to be found in situations where it is felt to be important for all members of an organization to understand what they are doing, where decisions require individual initiative, and where people need to work as a team.

A frequently quoted study of industrial structures is that carried out by Alvin Gouldner of a gypsum plant in the United States in 1954 (*Patterns of Industrial Bureaucracy*, 1954). The plant consisted of two parts, a gypsum mine and a factory making wallboards for which gypsum is an important ingredient. Gouldner found that there were significant differences in the ways in which the two units were structured. In the mine the hierarchy was less clearly defined, and the division of tasks and work areas were more loosely prescribed. Relationships between workers and supervisors were fairly informal and there was only a limited amount of reference to rules and procedures. For example, supervisors tended to issue general instructions, leaving it to the miners to decide how a job should be done. Carrying out a job involved collaboration between workmates, and jobs were rotated, with all miners being capable of doing a variety of jobs from repairing machinery to operating the coal-cutting machinery. Breaks were taken at irregular intervals. One miner summed up the situation: 'Down here we have no rules. We are our own bosses.'

In contrast, the factory was based far more on a hierarchical chain of command and on rules and procedures. There was a clear-cut division of labour, a set pattern to the working day, a formal relationship between officials and a distinct chain of offices.

Gouldner explained the difference in organizational structures in the following way. Work in the mine was far less predictable than in the factory. The amount of gypsum that could be cut would vary widely between different areas of the mine, and incidences such as 'cave-ins' could not be predicted. Miners needed to be able to make their own decisions 'on the spot', and to react quickly to changing circumstances. The problems they encountered did not follow a set pattern so that flexibility was important. In contrast, the production of wallboards in the factory followed a clearly set pattern which could be organized into a tight schedule of production.

The board of directors

The board of directors is the major executive body in a company. It is given authority by, and makes decision for, its shareholders.

The board of directors is essentially a committee. Normally, it will be made up of executive and non-executive directors. *Executive directors* are those that hold positions within a company, whereas *non-executive directors* will be engaged primarily in their own outside activities.

The executive directors will be involved in the day-to-day decision-making process of the business. They will be able to bring this expertise to board meetings. The accounts director, for example, will have first-hand experience of the company's figures and how they were achieved, and the marketing director will have been instrumental in steering marketing decisions.

Non-executive directors can bring to board meetings experience gained outside the company, perhaps from directing another company, or from academic experience, or experience of international trading relations.

It is only by ensuring a diverse blend of knowledge and skills on a board of directors that a company will benefit from a broad perspective of business trends. The boards of directors of major public companies are littered with the names of politicians, financiers and others with power and influence.

A board of directors will be responsible for:

- Appointing senior managers, including the managing director
- Deciding on how profits will be distributed
- Deciding on how to raise and spend capital
- Establishing the major policies of a company
- Ensuring that all legal requirements are complied with
- Ensuring that the company is successful

The board of directors will select a chairperson with the responsibility for acting as a 'figurehead' for the company. He or she will be responsible for chairing all board meetings and for making major public policy statements.

The board of directors will appoint a managing director with the responsibility for managing and steering a company on a day-to-day basis. The duty of the managing director is to put into practice the decisions that are made at board meetings. As a board member, the managing director will help to create policy, but his or her primary function will be to make sure that policies are carried out.

Case Study—A view of decision-making procedures in Britain and Japan.

> British managers are brought up in a tradition of debate. Put ten British managers, especially senior managers, around a table and there will never be agreement.

The 'British way' is that all the arguments are discussed and then the boss says do it this way. Everybody falls in or resigns. Jones compares it with a skier heading for the jump: the decision-making process is very fast and very efficient, provided nothing happens to throw the skier off-course.

In Japan it is different. The Japanese culture builds in a desire for consensus; Japanese managers actively seek it out. The purpose of a meeting is to iron out the differences and thereby reach consensus. On the surface it is a much slower decision-making process, and frustrating for British managers. But once a decision is taken, putting it into action is much faster because everyone is behind it. It is more like passing through a maze. A Japanese team will have explored every avenue. Although the decision-making process is slower and more convoluted, once agreed, the team understands all the options it rejected as well as the ones it is pursuing. Changing course is not a problem. This means that all operational decisions can be taken much faster.

(*Source*: Alun Jones, in *Personnel Today*,)

Questions

1. Do you think that the 'British way' or the 'Japanese way' as described above is more likely to require a hierarchical organizational structure? Explain your reasoning.
2. What are the main advantages and disadvantages of the 'British way' of management?
3. What are the main advantages and disadvantages of the 'Japanese way' of management?
4. In what circumstances would you expect (a) the 'British way' and (b) the 'Japanese way' to be more effective? Explain your reasoning.
5. What alternatives to these two methods can you think of? Explain the good and bad points of each.

The infrastructure of an organization

The infrastructure is the pattern of authority (and hence the line of communication) *within* an organization.

An important distinction is made in organizational theory between line and staff authority.

Line organization

Line organization is the typical structure of a hierarchical body. There will be direct communication links between superiors and subordinates. Each member of the organization will have a clear understanding of the chain of command within the organization and to whom he or she is responsible. This type of structure can be very effective because of its clarity. There are set rules and procedures which can be referred to. Figure 5.14 illustrates the way in which communication will flow down from top management in such an organization.

Line management is typically used to organize a firm's central activities such as the making and selling of products. In these areas there will be a clear hierarchical framework. Larger organizations will tend to have more rigid and bureaucratic structures than smaller ones. Although agreed and clear procedures will be necessary in such organizations, it will also be important to have an element of flexibility. Formal structures will frequently be subject to informal changes in the course of time as new situations arise.

Staff organization

Staff organization primarily services the various line departments of a company. Typical staff areas could include personnel, corporate affairs, data processing and office administration.

Staff departments typically cut across an organization providing a range of specialist services and consultancy skills. For example, any line department of a company might require specialist legal help from time to time, might want to have data processed or might need help with recruiting new staff. Figure 5.15 illustrates the way in which various staff areas can be made available to all line departments within an organization.

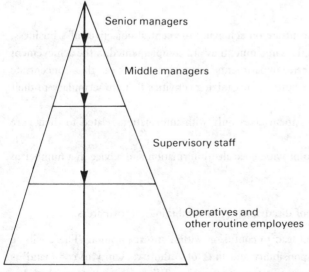

Figure 5.14 The downward flow of communication in line organization.

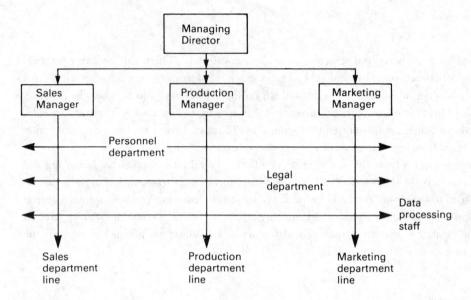

Figure 5.15 Combining line and staff organization.

Staff areas thus play an important role throughout an organization. However, a staff department itself might be organized on hierarchical lines. For example, the personnel department may have several tiers below the personnel manager.

Combined line and staff organization

Most medium and large business organizations will combine elements of line and staff organization. There will be a number of advantages to having this blend:

1. Line departments are able to concentrate on achieving the central objectives of a business, i.e. marketing, making, selling. At the same time, they are complemented in the achievement of these objectives by specialist service departments. Line departments can thus concentrate on their core function without the clutter of organizing activities that are secondary to their main purpose.
2. Line managers need to familiarize themselves only with information related to their core activity.
3. Staff groupings can be called in to provide specialist information and advice in a number of key areas.

However, there will also be a number of disadvantages to combining the two areas:

1. A major disadvantage is that it can lead to confusion within an organization. There will be less clarity over departmental responsibility and lines of authority. 'Unity of command' is often regarded to be the mark of an effective organization. Where there is more than one

centre of responsibility confusion can arise; one section can blame another for failure to carry out work effectively or for a breakdown in communication. Where department managers compete with each other to secure high-status work, or where they try to avoid less prestigious work, numerous problems can occur.

2. Often, line managers rise to a particular position through many years of hard work. This is particularly true in production departments, where it is not uncommon for managers to have worked their way up from the shop-floor. In contrast, many staff managers are 'academics' with a university background. Line managers may resent staff managers' rapid rise to managerial status, while staff managers may regard themselves to be better than those who have worked their way up. Such clashes can be detrimental to the smooth running of an organization.

3. Line managers may resent having to listen to the opinions of staff managers who may have different priorities from their own. For example, a corporate affairs or personnel manager might try to push a company into employing more youth trainees in order to project a certain image for a company within the community. In contrast, a production manager may be more concerned with using older, more experienced labour.

In order to overcome difficulties that may arise from combining line and staff organization, it is essential for a company to devise a clear strategy to co-ordinate staff and line groupings. This strategy will involve setting out the goals of the company and then deciding on the responsibilities of line and staff groupings. These responsibilities need to be set out in a clear statement of company policy. Some companies even have an 'organization and methods' department with the responsibility for clarifying such issues.

The superstructure of organizations

The superstructure of an organization is the way in which employees are grouped into various departments or sections. There are various ways of grouping employees depending on the needs and aims of a company.

The main methods of grouping employees are by:

- Function
- Product
- Process
- Geographical area
- Type of customer

We will also see later that a matrix structure can be used to combine grouping methods.

Grouping by function

This is probably the most important way of grouping employees in a company. Functional organization means that a company is divided into broad sectors, each with its own particular specialism or function—for example marketing, accounts, personnel (Fig. 5.16).

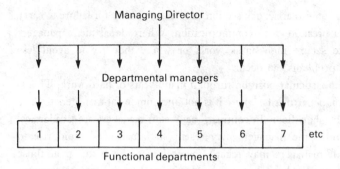

Figure 5.16 Grouping by function.

Every company will have its own way of structuring its functions. However, there are a number of common functional areas that will be typical of many large companies. These functions are referred to in outline here, and are dealt with in greater detail in specific chapters.

The company secretary and the legal department

By law it is necessary for every company to have a secretary. The company secretary is responsible for all the legal matters of the company. If paperwork is not done in the correct fashion, the company secretary can end up in court. He or she must fill in the documents that set up the company, including the Memorandum and Articles of Association, and must also keep the *share register*, which is a record of shareholders and any transfers in shareholding that take place.

The company secretary is regarded as a key link between the shareholders of a company and the directors. The secretary will handle correspondence to and from shareholders informing them of company meetings and other important matters. In some companies a registrar will be appointed as a subordinate to the company secretary with the responsibility of keeping the share register.

In some companies the secretary might also have other areas of responsibility such as that of office manager, or might offer specialist legal advice to other departments within a company.

The administration officer and administration department

Many large firms have a central office, or administration department, which is responsible for controlling the general paperwork of the firm. This department might handle the filing of materials and the company's mail, word-processing and data-handling facilities. The modern office is increasingly using computers and information technology.

In many companies each department will have its own clerical and support staff. However, it is common practice to have an office services manager, or administration officer, with the responsibility for co-ordinating office services and offering expert advice to departmental managers.

The work of the office manager will include:

- Taking responsibility for and organizing clerical training

- Advising departments on office layout, office equipment, working practices and staff development
- Co-ordinating the supply of office equipment and stationery
- Studying and analysing office practice within the company in order to develop an overall strategy for administration
- Ensuring the standardization of office practice, the layout of forms, invoices and other documents
- Providing and maintaining a communications system within a company including phones, mailing systems, computer hardware and other data-processing facilities
- Reporting to, and providing statistics for, the company board about the effectiveness of existing office practice

The information and computing manager and the IT department

In a modern company a large proportion of the staff may work directly with, or have access to, computer terminals. *Information technology (IT)* refers to the large and developing body of technologies and techniques by which information is obtained, processed and disseminated. The term therefore embraces computing, telecommunications and office developments. These three areas, which were initially distinct, are now seen as having more and more in common. They are progressively merging and blending together, while at the same time expanding to play an ever greater part in business activity.

The role of the information and computing function will be to promote effective exploitation of IT in a company and to provide the guidance, support and co-ordination necessary to accomplish this objective.

Information is vital to decision-making in both commerce and industry. The quality of any decision depends on the relevance, accuracy and timeliness of the information available. The main task for the information manager will therefore be to identify the decision-makers' information needs, to decide how best they can be met, and to develop the systems for meeting them.

Very rapid improvements in computing technology are providing opportunities for supporting businesses in ways that were not dreamed of a few years ago; for example, in many companies a computer work-station on the desks of all management and professional staff, as well as those of many support staff, seems likely by today.

The chief accountant and the accounts office

The chief accountant is responsible for supervising the accounts department. The accounts section must keep a detailed record of all money paid in and out and must present the final balance sheet, source and use of funds, the profit and loss acount and other financial records at regular intervals. Modern accounts are stored on computer files, and accounting procedures are greatly simplified by the use of computers.

Within the accounts department there will be two main sub-divisions:

1. The *financial accounting department* is responsible for keeping records of financial events as they occur. Accounts need to be kept of all money paid to or by a company, and records must be kept of all debtor and creditor transactions. The payment of wages will also require calculations involving deductions for national insurance, pensions and other factors.

    As well as keeping day-to-day records, the financial accounting department will also be responsible for producing periodic records such as the annual accounts and interim figures for discussion at meetings of directors.

2. The *management accounting department* has the responsibility for nudging the company in certain directions as a result of its analysis of figures for the present and predictions for the future. Management accountants will break down figures in order to extract information about a company's present performance and the sorts of improvements that can be made in the future. Using systems of budgetary control, it will set targets for achievement and limits for spending to the various parts of a business.

Within the accounts department, other sub-functions (i.e. functions within functions) might include a cashier's department and a wages department. The *cashiers department* will be concerned with handling all cash transactions as well as cheques and other payments through a bank account. These records will be kept in a cash book or on a computerized system.

The *wages department* will be responsible for supervising the payroll and calculating and paying wages. The data for these calculations will be generated by the works department or other department responsible for recording the amount of work carried out by employees.

The production department manager and the production department

The production manager is responsible for making sure that raw materials are provided and made into finished goods effectively. He or she must make sure that work is carried out smoothly, and must supervise procedures for making work more efficient and more enjoyable.

In a manufacturing company the production function may be split into five main sub-functions:

1. *The production and planning department* will set standards and targets for each section of the production process. The quantity and quality of products coming off a production line will be closely monitored.

2. *The purchasing department* will be responsible for providing the materials, components and equipment required to keep the production process running smoothly.

3. *The stores department* will be responsible for stocking all the necessary tools, spares, raw materials and equipment required to service the manufacturing process.

4. *The design and technical support department* will be responsible for researching new products or modifications to existing ones; for estimating costs of producing in different quantities and by using different methods; for designing and trying out new product processes and product types; and for developing prototypes through to the final product. It may also be responsible for arranging work study programmes and making suggestions as to how working practices can be improved.

5. *The works department* will be concerned with the actual manufacture of a product. This will encompass the maintenance of a production line and the carrying out of other necessary repairs. The works department may also have responsibility for quality control and inspection.

The marketing manager and the marketing department

The marketing department is responsible for identifying, anticipating and satisfying customer requirements profitably. Marketing and sales are sometimes combined in a single department, but there is an important distinction between the two. *Marketing* is concerned with getting the company to produce what the customer wants; *selling* tries to get the customer to want what the company has. The marketing department, then, will be concerned primarily with investigating consumers' needs and wants. This will involve carrying out market research to find out who comprises a particular market, what they want, where they want it, how they like it and at what price. In a manufacturing company there will be very close co-operation between the marketing and production planning departments, so that the wishes of consumers can be closely tied in with product development.

The sales manager and the sales department

The sales department is responsible for creating orders for a good or service. The size of this department will vary considerably, as will the way in which it operates. Some companies will employ a large sales force operating in the field on a regional basis. Sales representatives will visit businesses and other customers in order to secure orders for products. Other firms will sell their product by means of some form of advertising or other publicity and will employ only a small sales force. The sales manager will work from a central office-based location. Sales team meetings will be called from time to time to discuss strategy and to analyse performance.

The publicity manager and the publicity department

Publicity is closely allied to sales and marketing. The publicity department will be responsible for a number of areas which may include advertising, promotions and public relations.

The distribution manager and the distribution department

Distribution departments will generally be responsible for control over warehousing and dispatch as well as transport. The distribution manager will be responsible for making sure that goods are sent out on time, that orders are made up accurately and that transport is regularly maintained. The distribution manager will also be responsible for ensuring that the company employs the most cost-effective and reliable distribution channels.

The customer relations manager and the customer relations department

The goodwill of customers can be maintained only by an effective policy of customer care. The customer relations department will be concerned with handling customer complaints and feeding back suggestions and problems to other functional areas.

The personnel manager and the personnel department

The personnel function has three principal areas of responsibility:

1. It is responsible for recruiting, training, developing and deploying the people in a business.
2. It is responsible for ensuring that their terms and conditions of employment are appropriate, competitive and properly administered.
3. It is responsible for employee relations policy.

The overall objective of the personnel department will be to provide a highly productive, quality workforce.

Personnel provides a specialist service which facilitates the smooth running of a business's core functions. Personnel officers will be responsible for, or will help with, the interviewing of job candidates, the placement of job adverts and the assessment of staff needs and requirements.

The labour relations manager and the labour relations department

In addition to personnel officers, some companies employ specialists in the labour relations field. These officers will be responsible for industrial relations and the monitoring of employees perceptions of working conditions.

The health and safety officer

Every organization must pay close attention to health and safety regulations and laws.

Large companies will frequently employ an in-house advisory service on health matters. A wide range of guidance notes and pamphlets will be available from this department relating to clinical matters such as diabetes, hypertension and alcoholism. In a similar way, guidelines will be produced on safety performance and on the identification and correction of every unsafe act and condition before they can lead to accidents.

The community projects manager and the community projects department

A number of large companies in the United Kingdom work on the basis that their business can be successful only in a successful community. A community projects manager might be given the responsibility of running a department that handles a diversity of projects ranging from help for small businesses to an educational department or an environmental concern unit.

There are a number of clear advantages to organizing on a functional basis:

1. If groups of specialists are given control over specific work areas, this will prevent wasteful duplication within an organization. Invoices can be processed in a particular department, orders won by another and payment collected by a third. Provided clear guidelines are laid down to who does what, the organization's members will be clear about their responsibilities.
2. Specialists are able to work in a pool of like-minded people.
3. An organization is able to concentrate on its primary functions of production, marketing and finance.
4. Because each part of the organization is pursuing its primary function, it will contribute to the overall well-being of the total system.

Disadvantages are that:

1. Narrow specialism will restrict individuals' and departments' abilities to develop a global view of the total organization.
2. Individuals cannot move easily between departments.
3. Jealousies can arise between divisions, and departments may come to see themselves as having primary importance; they may come to block each other's initiatives.
4. As organizations become larger, communication channels may become slower or distorted, particularly between upper and lower levels.
5. Divisions may pull in opposite directions from one another. In many large organizations you will sometimes hear complaints such as 'This company is run by a bunch of accountants!' or 'Not enough attention is being paid to selling the goods.'

Grouping by product

When a large organization produces a range of different products, it might find it convenient to create an organizational structure based on product lines (Fig. 5.17). For example, a firm in the publishing industry might have a newspaper division, a magazine and periodicals division and a book publishing division. Each division will then contain a mixture of all the specialist ingredients required to enable it to work independently.

A great advantage of this form of structure is that divisions can concentrate on their own market areas. It also becomes possible to assess the profitability and effectiveness of each sector. At the same time, it is still possible to share expertise between divisions and to share services such as a combined transport fleet. By isolating the various parts of a business organization, it becomes possible to cut out loss-making divisions and to amalgamate divisions by merging them with similar divisions in other companies. It also becomes possible to generate competition within a company and to allow greater scope to create an internal promotion ladder.

Dairy group	Convenience foods group	Meat group	Grocery group
Northern Dairies	Park Cakes	Queens Drive	Fox's Biscuits
Dale Farm Dairies	Smith's Flour Mills	Hollands	Elkes Biscuits
Dale Farm Foods	Flecks	Trentham	Batchelors
NFT	Jeffs	Binghams	
Turners Decorating	Dale Farm Dairy Products	Bowyers	
	Riverside Bakeries	Witney Foods	
	Savoury Foods	Mayhew Foods	
	Fenland Foods	Nottingham Poultry	
	Lenton	Plymouth	
	Parrs	Dorset Foods	
	Gunstone		

Figure 5.17 Example of a divisional structure based on product lines. (*Source*: Northern Foods report to employees)

Grouping by process

Where the manufacture of a product requires a series of processes, departments will be set up to perform each process. To take the example of the publishing company, within each of the divisions departments will be responsible for carrying out stages of production—e.g. editing of copy, page layout and design, printing. Figure 5.18 illustrates the way in which process departments take the responsibility for each stage of production.

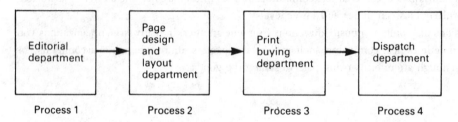

Figure 5.18 Grouping by process in a publishing company.

There are a number of clear advantages to organizing on a process basis:

1. Grouping by process makes it possible to set up teams of like-minded specialists.
2. It becomes easy to identify points in the production process at which things are going well or badly.
3. It is easy to introduce new technology at a given stage of production (i.e. a given process) and to familiarize the appropriate staff with new skills and working practices.

Disadvantages are that:

1. Process production will work effectively only if there is a steady flow from one stage to another. If one process gets out of step by producing too much or too little, problems will

occur as stocks pile up or run out. This situation might arise if, say, one group of process workers goes on strike or has a high absenteeism level.

2. Sections of employees may become too specialist and fail to communicate effectively with other sections.

3. It may become difficult to transfer employees from one process to another if there are too-rigid divisions between processes. Employees might prefer to stick with their existing work-group and with skills that they are familiar with.

Grouping by geographical area

Many companies will have branches spread throughout the country and sometimes overseas. Multiple retailing companies are a good example. A company like Marks and Spencer will have shops on every major high street in the United Kingdom. Groups of shops will be organized into a regional division which will have overall supervision of such features as training of staff and distribution policy. Figure 5.19 illustrates a company with six domestic divisions and two overseas divisions.

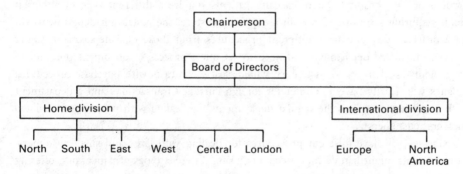

Figure 5.19 Grouping by geographical area.

There are a number of clear advantages to organizing on a geographical basis:

1. Setting up distinct regional divisions makes it possible to respond quickly to local needs, issues and problems. The organization thus becomes more sensitive to customers, employees and other groups. At the same time, it might be able to cut through a lot of red tape if the regional groups are allowed to make their own decisions.

2. Setting up national and regional divisions makes it possible to tailor the operation of an organization to local conditions. Differences would include those of language, law and custom. Local knowledge is best gained by hiring local specialists.

3. National governments will often look more kindly on multinational divisions that have a local head office and organization.

Disadvantages are that:

1. Having too many regional divisions can lead to a wasteful duplication of facilities and roles; too few divisions can lead to lack of co-ordination, gaps in communication and breakdowns.
2. Having an extensive regional structure requires the creation of a series of management positions. It is not always easy to recruit personnel of the required calibre to fill these positions.
3. Regional headquarters might take on a life of their own and start pulling in opposite directions to central policy-makers.
4. Although the local divisions will frequently have the best understanding of the situation 'on the ground', they might find themselves at loggerheads with central officials many thousands of miles away.

Grouping by type of customer

Organizations will often set up different structures to deal with different sets of customers. This is because they will often give some groups more time and attention than others. An obvious example would be in a hospital, where casualty patients require a different type of attention from patients requiring a routine X-ray. In a department store, the restaurant department will operate in a different way and have different procedures from those of a department selling underwear. The furniture department will need to set out a process of documentation and to make arrangements for delivery to customers, which clearly contrasts with purchase procedures for toys. Banks will usually have a counter for foreign currency transactions and a department dealing with enquiries, as well as the regular departments for dealing with private and business account holders (customers).

Many businesses will have different procedures for dealing with large and small customers. Separate departments might handle these accounts, using different types of paperwork, offering different rates of discount and treating customers in different ways.

The advantages of organizing in a pattern based on having different sets of customers are that:

1. Different types of customer can be dealt with by separate departments.
2. Customers will be more inclined to deal with a business that has departments concentrating on their particular needs.
3. It is easier to check on the performance of individual products.

Disadvantages are that:

1. Divisions may compete with each other for the use of company resources.
2. The structure may be costly to set up and will be cost-effective only if there is sufficient demand.
3. More administration and accounting services will be required.

Matrix structure

So far we have looked at the internal organization of a business as if there is a single pattern of organization. However, many large businesses combine two or more patterns in a matrix structure; for example, they might combine functional and geographical lines of command.

In a matrix structure each member of the organization will belong to two or more groups. This is illustrated in Fig. 5.20, where groups of employees are organized into regions (e.g. North and South) as well as functions (e.g. marketing or sales). In this example a particular group of workers (i.e. marketing section A) will be accountable to both the Northern manager and the marketing manager. Each member of the organization (below managerial level) will be accountable to two or more managers. Marketing, sales and other key functional managers will have a global responsiblity for their function within the organization, while divisional managers have responsibility for these functions on a divisional basis.

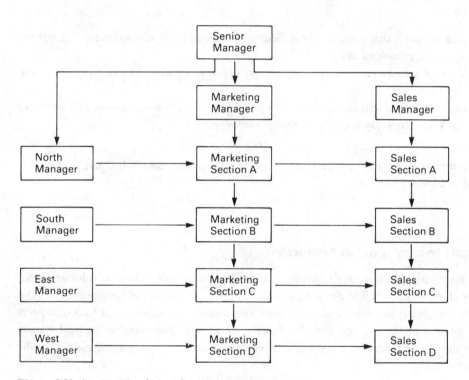

Figure 5.20 An example of part of a matrix structure.

Each divisional manager will be responsible for a specific project. In order to carry out this project, they will be able to call upon the full range of departments to collaborate in achieving project targets. Projects may be based on products, types of customer, geographical area or any other specific criteria. Inevitably, a matrix structure can be complicated, and it needs to be clearly laid out if it is going to be understood.

There are a number of advantages to be gained from implementing a matrix structure:

1. A matrix makes it possible to structure an organization in such a way as to focus on a number of aims at the same time, e.g. servicing different types of customers, servicing different regions, producing different types of product.
2. A matrix structure gives an organization extra flexibility to respond to new situations where there is an increase in demand for its resources.
3. The system makes it possible to draw groups from specific departments in the required numbers.
4. There can be cross-fertilization of ideas across departments, rather than having departments working in isolation.

Disadvantages are that:

1. A complex matrix structrure may be difficult to understand, and employees can lose sight of the major organizational aims.
2. This system will often require extra administrative resources, which can be costly in terms of time and money.
3. Because the system establishes more than one chain of command, this can lead to power struggles, contradictory orders and general confusion.

A matrix structure can be very effective. However, it must be clearly laid out, and clearly explained to all those involved.

The legal background to business

We look for security in the society in which we live. The legal system consists of rules supported by courts of justice on behalf of the state, and these provide an ordered environment. The rules determine how society is ordered and controlled. Governments are elected on the basis of support for their political philosophy and have the ability to change the framework of the legal system. Rules are therefore a product of the political process and change according to the morality of the ruling party.

In business we need laws to protect the majority against the practices of powerful bodies and individuals. For example, without rules governing employment protection, monopoly legislation, consumer protection and health and safety legislation (see Chapter 19), many would argue that our society would be an unsafe place to live in. The legal system provides a framework governing a wide range of business activities and the ways in which these activities affect the providers of finance, employees, customers and society in general; at the same time, this framework allows businesses to achieve their chosen objectives.

Broad areas of influence include:

1. *Laws relating to the constitution of businesses*   When people associate together to engage in a business or profession for profit, they are deemed to be in partnership under the Partnership Act 1890. As a result, each partner is separately liable for all of the debts of the business they engage in. If these people incorporate and create a separate legal 'person' which owns the business and is responsible for paying debts and fulfilling contracts, they then become members of a corporation that is carrying on in business on their behalf. Successive Companies Acts control the establishment, performance and functions of companies.

   For example, to register a company, the Registrar of Companies must be sent both a Memorandum and Articles of Association. The Memorandum describes factors that affect the outsider of the company such as features of the company's constitution and the objectives it was incorporated to achieve. The Articles contain rules governing shareholders' relationships with each other and with the company and which do not generally affect outsiders. Companies must have at least three kinds of officer: directors, a company secretary and auditors. Directors of a company must present the annual accounts and a report to members of the company (i.e. shareholders), and members have the right to dismiss directors. The word 'Limited' warns creditors that there is a limitation on the liability of members. It is an offence to use the word 'Limited' if the person(s) in business are not incorporated with limited liability.

2. *Consumer protection*   Organizations provide goods and services for consumers in return for payment. The legal system enables transactions to take place and provides a mechanism for resolving disputes. Laws attempt to overcome the inequality in bargaining power between large organizations and relatively small consumers. The need for such laws exists because of events such as poor-quality goods, misleading information, manufacturer's negligence, breach of contract and consumer safety. Legislation concerning business activities includes the Fair Trading Act 1973, which set up the Office of Fair Trading to keep a constant watch over monopolies and restrictive practices. In response, the Restrictive Practices Act 1976 ensures that traders who restrict competition by making agreements with other traders must register their agreements with the Office of Fair Trading; and the Competition Act 1980 allows the Director-General of Fair Trading to investigate businesses operating anti-competition policies restricting growth. Other areas of consumer protection refer to the poor quality of goods and services and to the provision of credit.

3. *Contract law*   Contract law consists of legal rules governing the enforcement of obligations between individuals arising from voluntary agreements. By making contracts, companies can buy raw materials and sell finished goods in relative safety as long as each side gives something of value.

4. *Law of torts*   The law of torts protects parties from each other's actions, particularly if a party suffers injury as a result of these actions—e.g. negligence.

5. *Employment law*   Under the Employment Protection Act 1978, employers are required to provide employees with the terms of their employment within 13 weeks of their employment commencing. These terms relate to holidays, pay, hours of work, job title, notice to terminate the contract and pensions. Of particular importance in recent years has been the Health and Safety at Work Act 1974, designed to maintain and improve standards of health, safety and welfare at work.

6. *The law of agency*   When organizations use outside specialists, the relationship of principal and agent is created. An agent is someone empowered to act on behalf of a principal in contractual relations with third parties. With this strong element of trust, clear legal guidelines are set to ensure the success of this relationship.

The potential list of areas covered by our legal system is almost endless. We could also mention the requirements of the legal system in relation to insurance, negotiable instruments, bankruptcy, data protection, financial services and the topical area of environmental law. With the prospect of considerable change in the near future since the 12 member-states of the European Union came together in the 'Single Market' in 1992, businesses cannot ignore the implications for areas such as quality, safety and common standards.

Questions

Short-answer questions

1. Who are the owners of a public limited company?
2. What is meant by 'chain of command' in an organization?
3. Distinguish between 'line' and 'staff' relationships as shown in an organization chart.
4. What are the important ingredients of an 'effective' organization?
5. What is meant by the private sector of the economy? Give examples of types of business organization that would form part of the private sector.
6. What is meant by limited liability? What protection is provided by limited liability?
7. How is an ordinary partnership set up and run? What advantages are provided by partnership forms of business organization compared with the sole trader form?
8. What steps need to be followed before a company can start to trade?
9. What advantages are available to public limited companies and not to private limited companies?
10. Who are the major decision-makers in a company?
11. What is meant by franchising? What types of business are most suited to this form of organizational structure?
12. How does the *direction* of decision-making vary between hierarchical and democratic structures?
13. What is meant by (a) line and (b) staff organization?
14. Illustrate how a company may group by function. Look at organizational charts from actual companies. Which company appears to have the most effective organizational structure? Why?
15. Describe the role within a company of
    (a) Executive directors
    (b) Non-executive directors
    (c) The company chairperson
    (d) The marketing director
    (e) The company secretary

(f)   The information and computing services manager

16. What is meant by grouping by process? Explain how this operates in a business with which you are familiar.

17. Draw a diagram to illustrate how a company might use a matrix structure.

18. What is meant by (a) contract law and (b) the law of torts?

19. Why is a legal framework essential to the smooth running of a business?

20. How does the Law of Agency operate?

Essays

1. Compare and contrast different forms of business organization in the private sector of the economy.

2. Every year approximately 50 000 businesses are started in the United Kingdom and in the same year over 10 000 fail. What do these statistics indicate to you?

3. What are the key ingredients of a business plan?

4. It is not enough just to have a good idea: you also need to have clear planning and organization. Discuss this statement.

5. What are the key features of an effective organization? Illustrate your answer by drawing on examples from the real world.

6. Two is always better than one. A partnership will always beat a sole trader. Discuss this assertion.

7. Franchising is the most rapidly growing form of business organization. What are the advantages and drawbacks of franchising?

8. What procedures need to be carried out to set up a company? What protection does company status provide?

9. Compare and contrast grouping by function, product, process and geographical area.

10. How might a company benefit from a matrix form of organization?

Data response questions

1 Selling shares in EuroTunnel

Eurotunnel is a private-sector company which is responsible for building and running the Channel Tunnel between England and France. The new link will join together road and railway systems between the United Kingdom and the Continent. The link should open in 1994. The advertisement shown in Fig. 5.21 was issued to advertise the sale of shares (units) in the company.

1. What do the letters PLC tell us about Eurotunnel?

2. What is meant by the 'private sector'?

3. What would be the price of one share in Eurotunnel?

4. How much did Eurotunnel PLC hope to raise from the share issue?

5. Why did Eurotunnel need to raise so much capital?

6. Who would buy the shares that were advertised?

EUROTUNNEL PLC

Offer for Sale

of 101,000,000 Units with New Warrants at a price of 350p per Unit

by

Robert Fleming & Co. Ltd   Morgan Grenfell & Co. Ltd   S. G. Warburg & Co. Ltd.

Figure 5.21

7. How might an investor benefit from buying shares in Eurotunnel PLC?
8. How were the merchant banks involved in the issue of the shares?

2   Growth comes to a halt at IBM

In 1980 IBM was valued on the stock markets as the largest corporation in the world. In the 1980s it was what US Steel had been at the beginning of the century and what Ford and General Motors had been in the boom of the 1950s.

IBM was founded in 1911 by an Ohio farm boy, Thomas Watson, a generation before the computer was invented. He had taken charge of the Computer–Tabulating–Recording Company, which produced a punchcard information system for the American population census of 1890.

The name IBM ((International Business Machines) came into being in 1924. By the 1930s IBM dominated the US market for clocking-on machines and punchcard tabulators.

In the 1950s the computer came on the scene. The first computer for public use was marketed in 1951 by a rival company. IBM saw the threat and hired experts to produce a series of computers which were supported by a superb sales force. By the 1960s and 1970s it had captured 80 per cent of the market.

The next innovation was the personal computer (PC). Computers now became household items. Today, anyone with a modern PC has more computing power than an industrial giant would have had in 1970. When in the 1980s IBM developed a PC it did so with a world beater.

Unfortunately, it bought the key chip for the computer from another company, Intel, and used software from a small company called Microsoft, both of which were able to sell to other companies. In the early 1980s IBM's sales were huge. However, IBM computers have been copied by many other companies. Today many IBM clone computers (produced by rivals) can do exactly the same operations as a genuine IBM. The result is that IBM sales have stagnated and IBM has made record losses.

1. Why was IBM such a successful company for most of this century?
2. What structural changes in the computing industry led to the fall in sales of IBM products?
3. Could IBM have done anything to prevent the collapse of sales?
4. What lessons can be drawn from the IBM case by other successful companies?
5. Who stands to gain and who to lose out from the demise of IBM?

3   Setting up and running a small business

A group of sixth-form students from the King's and Kesteven and Grantham Girls' schools set up their own company as a general studies exercise. The students set out to run the company for a year, using two hours of their time per week.

The first meeting of the students was concerned with brainstorming ideas for a company. Emphasis was placed on spotting a gap in the local market, copying an existing successful product or developing a new innovatory product based on existing skills within the group of 11 students.

A number of ideas were suggested, including:

- Running a stationery stall
- Buying and selling second-hand sports equipment
- Making gingerbread (Grantham is famous for gingerbread)
- Making neckscarves
- Hiring out a piece of land to learner-drivers

At the end of the day the group decided to investigate further the possibility of making gingerbread on the basis of a skills audit, because costs would be low, and the risks appeared to be minimal.

Market research
Market research involved finding out how much gingerbread could be sold in a week at different prices, where it would sell best, who would make up the target consumer group and what form the product should take (size, packaging, etc.).

Product research
Product research involved finding out alternative ways of making the product. Grantham gingerbread is a distinct product from ordinary gingerbread. Bakers had to be consulted, ingredients

purchased and trial runs carried out. The prototype products needed to be sampled as part of the initial market research.

Initial finance

The initial finace came from a £5 loan. However, because the gingerbread is very cheap to produce relative to the price determined by the market research, the loan was paid back within a few weeks. The company was then able to finance its expenditures out of income.

Forming a company organization

It soon became apparent that a company structure was required if all the functions of the company were to be carried out effectively. The following organizational structure was therefore formulated on the basis of making gingerbread:

1. *Managing director*: overall supervision of other functions
2. *Accountant*: responsible for money forecasts, recording all money in and out and keeping detailed records
3. *Secretary*: responsible for handling all paperwork
4. *Purchasing director*: responsible for purchasing and ensuring a smooth flow of equipment and ingredients to production
5. *Production director*: responsible for ensuring that products are made to agreed quality standards
6. *Marketing director*: responsible for finding out consumer preferences
7. *Sales director*: responsible for ensuring that products are sold

Early problems

It soon became obvious that the company would be unable to meet demand for the product. The first production run ran out in 2 minutes and 12 seconds. Gingerbread takes too long to cook, and takes up too much oven space to be produced in large batches, given the oven space available to the school company.

Looking for an alternative product

Given that the company felt that it should continue to concentrate on its existing skill area, it was decided to go for an alternative food product with greater value added potential which would not require oven space. A survey of alternative recipes came up with the idea of truffles, which simply require the heating up of chocolate for a few seconds.

The truffles proved to be an important 'bread and butter' line for the company because they are always popular and it is almost impossible to make mistakes in manufacture (Fig. 5.22).

Cash flow forecasting

One of the earliest stages in setting up the company was to prepare a cash flow forecast.

This involved calculating the likely income and expenditure of the company over a three-month period. It was necessary to work out the total expenditure and revenue each week in order to forecast future problems and anticipate future profits. The cash flow forecast was only

Figure 5.22 Members of Concept, Caroline Tomkins and Matthew Hollingsworth, producing truffles.

a rough-and-ready guide, but it indicated that, if sales matched market research predictions, income would always exceed expenditure. Using the cash flow predictions, it was possible to estimate total income, total expenditure, the break-even point of the company and profits.

The period of growth

Once the company had become established and had created a surplus of capital, it was decided to use the capital to diversify into new lines. The basis for further expansion needed to be based on the company's existing practices, i.e.:

- Detailed product research
- Detailed market research
- Accurate record-keeping
- Participative management

Research indicated the scope for establishing two new products: presentation glass apples (Grantham is the birthplace of Isaac Newton; the apples were bought at trade prices from a crystal manufacturer) and stationery (the stock was purchased from a wholesaler). Pricing for the new products was based on slightly undercutting competitors.

The company now chose a trading name, Concepts. It may seem unusual to have waited so long to choose a business name; however, it had been decided to wait until the full range of products was established before taking this step.

Concepts printed its own order forms, invoices and statements. The students made sure that stock was kept at a level that could be sold within a month, so as not to be burdened with unsold product. The company went on to make a very good profit.

1. What types of background research did the company have to undertake before going into the production of gingerbread?
2. What key questions would they have needed to answer before committing themselves to production?
3. Why was it essential for Concepts to prepare a cash flow chart?
4. What alternative sources of finance could Concepts have used in setting up the business?
5. What elements of running Concepts as a business would you regard to be
   (a) realistic?
   (b) unrealistic?
6. What problems did Concepts face which would be untypical of those faced by a small starter business?
7. What business ideas can you come up with for your own locality?
8. What steps would you need to take in creating a small school or college business?
9. What major weaknesses can you identify in the way in which Concepts set up and organized the business?

4   Smalley Excavators Ltd

Richard and Ann Smalley have built up Smalley Excavators into a business with an annual turnover of over £4 million.

Richard comes from a farming family, and it was his familiarity with agriculture and farm machinery, coupled with mechanical engineering talent, that enabled him to find a profitable niche in the market for his specialized form of excavator. Always inventive by nature, he had trained as an agricultural engineer before gaining experience with hydraulics at Lucas and Massey Ferguson, developing and testing hydraulic pumps.

In 1960 Richard started his first company, making a mechanical ditcher that sold for £69. A year later, while he and Ann were on honeymoon, he designed the first of his excavators. This was a hydraulic, portable grave digger, to which he later added wheels and 360° slewing, making it into a walking excavator. The usual practice of using four strong men to dig a grave was excessively labour-intensive, and the new product, launched in 1963 after a year's development, was an immediate success. He sold 50 all over the world in the first year.

Since then, he and Ann have always worked together. Today she is the publicity director with additional responsibility for equipment and transport purchasing. But 25 years ago she was a fully fledged working member of the production line, drilling holes and painting the finished units which were being turned out at a rate of four or five a week from their farm workshop. She was also sending out letters and typing invoices, preparing the publicity, and chasing around agricultural shows and exhibitions to boost sales.

Richard's early ideas proved to be effective. He had put a cab on an engine on a chassis. He knew that by pushing the load down into the feet, all the weight was going into the bucket and imparting a very substantial tearout force. It was an elementary principle of common-sense engineering that was very effective, and it is one that has been retained in his machines for a quarter of a century.

Richard continued developing two-wheeled excavators up to about 5 tonnes in weight. Ann says that, up to the size of small conventional excavators, the customer is not really interested in saving money. She realized that when the purchaser of their first machine walked away saying 'I can throw away my spade! I have always been a navvy but now I have an excavator.' In the boom days of the 1960s, the capital outlay on such a machine would be written down on the first contract and the operators didn't have to worry about saving money.

When the Smalleys began looking to other possibilities, the Waterway Authorities of England provided the biggest stimulus. The old canals were beginning to be used as leisure facilities and maintenance was essential. The authorities provided the boats, and Smalley mounted machines on them that could dredge and clear weed, working in shallow waterways under low, narrow bridges, unhindered by a counterweight tailswing.

At the same time, the firm started making peat excavators and more grave diggers. It was the peat machines that led the firm into producing low-ground-pressure crawler machines, which brought about the Smalley rubber-band type of track.

To a large extent, the Smalley success formula has been based on the flexibility of his designs. The units are all made from standard units produced by a variety of companies. These units can be mixed and matched to meet most customers' requirements without involving a lot of expensive specialized one-off production.

Another important ingredient in the formula is the Smalley's belief in personal contact with customers. The company has now spread its business over about ten different markets, and diversification is the name of the game.

1. Where did the original business idea come from?
2. What would have been the main problems in developing the idea into a finished product?
3. Could either Richard or Ann have run the business on their own?
4. Describe the most important stages in the growth of the business.
5. What were the key functional areas of the business?
6. What have been the main reasons for the success of the business?
7. What major problems can you possibly foresee for Smalley?

Suggested reading

Danks, S., *A First Course in Business Studies*. DP Publications Ltd, 1991.
Marcouse, I. with Lines, D., *Business Case Studies*. Longman, 1991.
Needham, D. and Dransfield, R., *Business Studies in Practice*, 2nd edn. McGraw-Hill, 1992.

6

Small business enterprise

Over recent years small businesses have re-established themselves as an important part of the social fabric of the UK economy. Statistical evidence supports the popular view that the 1980s were indeed the 'decade of the small firm', with small businesses accounting for a substantial and developing proportion of total employment within the United Kingdom.

In the past there was always a belief that large business with mass-production techniques and economies of scale would come to dominate the UK economy. Employment by a large business firm would represent security, opportunity and possibly a 'job for life'. However, an unfortunate feature of both of the recent recessions is that many jobs have been lost in large enterprises. This time the government and opposition both recognized the need to help small businesses, and many 'supply-side' measures were taken in the hope that a growing small business sector would create employment, wealth, competition and choice. Such measures included:

- Help and advice for small firms
- Government help with finance
- Increases in the VAT registration threshold
- Reduction in government regulations for small businesses
- Encouragement of entrepreneurial activity among the unemployed
- Professional advice and support

Unemployment has been a key factor in the small business revival. Redundancy, often with a golden handshake, has encouraged many to become entrepreneurs. Another factor has been the growth of the service sector. This sector has expanded rapidly over recent years and small firms have a competitive advantage in many service areas. One feature of the 1980s was that as businesses became 'leaner and fitter' they tended to subcontract out many of their activities to smaller enterprises. All of these developments have helped to create an 'enterprise culture' which has encouraged entrepreneurial activities and increased respect for the self-employed.

As the economy expanded in the 1980s the small business sector grew to more than a million enterprises. This was an increase of 70 per cent over a ten-year period to a point where they represented 17 per cent of the UK gross domestic product (GDP) and 35 per cent of private-sector employment by 1990.

Small businesses reflect opportunities for profit and recognition within society. Many people with imagination, courage and belief in what they are doing start their own businesses with a determination to use hard work, skills and creative talents in order to succeed. A word of warning, however: the small business sector is extremely dynamic. Although 380 000 small businesses started up in 1992, liquidations and bankruptcies were in excess of 62 000, and these figures do not reflect the businesses that simply withdrew from the market-place. It is estimated that one in three small businesses cease trading in their first three years of operation.

What is a small business enterprise?

There are many definitions of the term 'small business.' One is that it is a business 'which is independently operated and not dominant in its field of operations'. Clearly then, a small business has certain features which make it different from a large business. The problem is that small businesses come in so many shapes and sizes, from window cleaners to cafe owners and professional consultants, that trying to describe a small business with a fairly general definition becomes very difficult.

The first significant attempt to assess the small business sector was made under the chairmanship of J. E. Bolton. In 1971 the Bolton Report was published. This report indicated that a small business has three essential characteristics:

1. It is managed by its owner(s) in a very personalized way.
2. In economic terms it has a relatively small share of its market.
3. The owner is free from outside control in his or her principal decisions and the business is independent in that it does not form any part of a larger enterprise.

The Bolton Report also provided more specific measures of small business which were based upon the type of industry in which the business operated:

- *Manufacturing*: 200 employees or less
- *Construction*: 25 employees or less
- *Road transport*: 5 vehicles or less
- *Retailing*: £500 000 turnover p.a.
- *Miscellaneous services*: £500 000 turnover p.a.

(N.B.: The turnover levels for the last two categories refer to the 1971 figure and then relate them to today's prices.)

Why start a small business?

A small business owner is sometimes described as an 'entrepreneur'. The traditional definition of an entrepreneur is one who organizes, manages and assumes the risk of running a business in return for a form or reward, which we normally associate with profit. This definition is, however, a little bit flat, and if we develop the term further and call it 'entrepreneurial spirit', we tend to think of the creative elements of business in which individuals use their ideas to develop goods and services for customers. Peter Drucker emphasizes both creativity and innovation in his definition of an entrepreneur, whom he describes as someone who 'always searches for change, responds to it and exploits it as an opportunity'.

By defining the word 'entrepreneur' we can focus a little bit upon the sort of people who wish to start their own businesses and the motivations they might have for doing so. People have many different reasons for starting up on their own, and their motivations may be dependent upon a combination of personality characteristics. For example:

1. A lot of people start their own business because they *strive for achievement*. They may have tremendous energy and be willing to take risks in order to pursue their goals. For many such people, the measurement of their success is wealth.
2. The desire for *independence* is a frequently quoted motivation. Working in a large organization can be soul-destroying, particularly for those who are rarely consulted. Small business ownership provides an opportunity for individuals to make the decisions that determine their own futures.
3. Many people start their own businesses from a *hobby* which they particularly enjoy. Sometimes redundancy or changing circumstances push these types of people into the small business arena.
4. The desire to *exploit an opportunity*, having identified a gap in the market, encourages many individuals to start their own businesses. These opportunities may be based on an original product idea which they wish to pursue, or they could be based on an observation or simply on experience.
5. The *financial incentive* is often sufficient motivation for some people to go into business for themselves. A small business might provide a higher standard of living and an improved income. Sometimes a business can develop from a money-earning sideline. Many people feel that they are using their skills to earn money for somebody else—their employer—when they would prefer to set up their own businesses and earn money for themselves.
6. Sometimes people are pushed into starting their own business. *Lack of job security or disagreements with employers* may encourage some individuals to take the plunge.

In practice, small business owners are likely to have a range of motivations and to come from various backgrounds. Success will depend on how effectively they can implement their business proposals and on the commitment and other personal abilities of each individual.

$\wp$ Case Study—An enterprising couple looking for somewhere to live

Paul Kessling and Katrina Bryson are both graduates who are not short of either the skills or the confidence to succeed. Having taken heart from the government's praises about the value of free enterprise, they decided to create their own jobs, by starting a business that specialized in restoring floors. It was launched in October 1992 and shortly afterwards they were married.

Paul and Katrina were pleased with their first few month's trading. They felt that they had identified a gap in the market at a time when people were doing up houses rather than moving. With the growth of the green movement, more people seemed to be interested in renovating what they had got.

However, their confidence, success and energy has not been viewed favourably by mortgage lenders. Self-employed businesses normally have to present accounts for the previous three years to become eligible for a mortgage. The Kesslings' savings are with the Abbey National, which they hoped would look favourably on their mortgage application. However, the Abbey seems to feel that, although a big deposit shows effort and commitment, it will not pay the mortgage. As a last resort, they could try to persuade their parents to guarantee the mortgage; the problem with this is that it will risk their parents' houses if the business fails. Another alternative would be to look for combined residential and business premises.

Before forming the business Paul did a similar job for another firm for about 12 months. Though his take-home pay was less, the irony is that his chances of obtaining a mortgage would have been better!

Questions

1. From this short extract, why do you think that Paul and Katrina started their own business?
2. Identify the skills that you think they would probably be able to offer the business.
3. Explain why their application for a mortgage has not been viewed favourably by mortgage lenders. In your answer, comment on whether you feel that the mortgage lenders were right to treat Paul and Katrina in this way. What does your answer to this question tell you about the risks of running a small business?
4. Will many people who start their own businesses have to make similar sacrifices? Try to use examples known to you in your answer.
5. Was Paul right to start his own business, or should he have kept his job?

While it is extremely difficult to stereotype the traits of a small business owner, it is possible to think about some of the characteristics they will require (Fig. 6.1). For a small business to be successful in a competitive market-place, an entrepreneur must seek to use creative ideas in an effort to make his or her products better than those of the competitors. Many of the characteristics shown in the figure will help entrepreneurs both to develop and to implement their ideas.

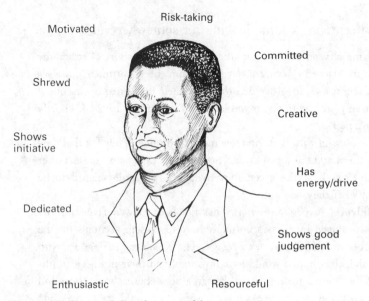

Figure 6.1 Characteristics of a successful entrepreneur.

Commitment is also an essential quality; for a business to succeed, particularly in the early stages, the business owner will have to put in long hours and to be determined and resourceful.

The first stage in setting up a business

The very first stage in starting a business is to think of a *good idea*. Small businesses are often viewed as a hotbed of creativity, where innovative products and new ideas abound. Many of the great entrepreneurs today came up with good ideas just a jew years ago—for example Anita Roddick at the Body Shop, Alan Sugar at Amstrad and Malcolm Walker and Peter Hinchcliffe at Iceland.

Whether the idea the entrepreneur intends to implement involves a good or a service, the output for the business should be thought of as a *product*. A good idea, however, should not just stop at the product; it might include selling products to new markets, or introducing better methods of doing business or new marketing methods. For example, Reader's Digest developed its range of products because of the direct marketing techniques used to communicate with customers.

There are varied sources of good ideas. For example:

1. *A unique creation* Developing a new invention may provide a unique opportunity in a market. Surprisingly, very few businesses start with inventions and only about 2 per cent of patents come from private individuals. N.B.: Although it is not possible to patent a business *idea*, the following apply:

(a) *Patents* relate to products, processes, mechanics and materials. In order to patent a product, it must be proved to be new, involve a unique step and/or be capable of industrial application.

(b) *Copyright* refers to printed matter, computer programs, artwork, etc. Protection is automatic and the © symbol may be used.

(c) *Registered designs* refer to the looks and style of a product.

(d) *Registered trade marks* relate to a symbol or word that identifies the products of a business.

2. *Copying*   Many entrepreneurs develop their idea from the others who have been successful with it in other parts of the country.

3. *Franchising*   This is a useful way of starting up under the name an established and well-known business, which allows the franchisee to use that business's reputation and expertise and provides many other benefits. Although the franchisee has to make regular payments to the franchisor, there are a considerable number of benefits. For example, the business format offered by the franchisor may include a well-known trade name, products, training, financial advice, operating systems, management control systems, centralized purchasing, national marketing and so on.

4. *Buying an existing business*   This is a fairly easy way of developing a business idea and cuts out many of the difficulties involved in the start-up process. When buying a business there will be immediate income. Market share will have been established and existing assets are available. Goodwill will also have been established. (N.B.: Management buy-outs (MBOs) are one way of buying an existing business.)

5. *Personal experience and skills*   Personal experience, skills or expertise may help entrepreneurs to develop their business ideas. For example, knowledge of an industry and contacts within that industry may help in the development of an idea. Alternatively, experience with arts and crafts or involvement wtih a hobby may provide a useful basis for setting up a business.

An important aspect of a business idea is the development of a product, or the ways in which it is presented, in a form that is different from that of competitors. By doing this a business can gain *differential advantages* over other businesses in the market and can also develop a *unique selling proposition* which will encourage consumers to give it their custom.

Peter Drucker identifies seven sources for innovative opportunity:

1. *The unexpected*   Unexpected successes or failures may provide important indications about opportunity.

2. *The incongruous*   This is the result of a difference between what everybody expects and what actually happens. Many business opportunities occur as a result of such a contradiction.

3. *Process need*   An identified need in the market for new products and processes will lead to opportunities for businesses.

4. *Industry and market structures*   Sometimes industries or markets change after a considerable period of stability. This can provide real opportunities for innovators with new ideas.

5. *Demographics* A study of the statistics of the population may reveal important changes within society which could become useful in helping to identify small business opportunities.

6. *Changes in perception* Trends, fashions and fads affect the ways in which consumers reported to products and provide a useful source of business opportunity. For example, a few years ago many of the smaller record labels developed quickly because they were able to respond more quickly to fashions in music.

7. *New knowledge* Many new products arise from discoveries and inventions.

⌕ Case Study—'From little acorns': the story of Jumpers

Mark and Linda Birkbeck started business in the early 1970s. They first operated a wholesale business providing sheepskin and lambswool products from their home in Kirkby Lonsdale. Mark visited customers up and down the country in his Morris Minor 1000 Traveller.

The business soon outgrew the home base and they moved it to a business site in Kirkby Lonsdale. They then ventured into retailing for the first time, and when their first Sheepskin Warehouse Shop opened in 1978 it proved to be immensely popular. In 1981 a partnership was formed between Mark and Linda Birkbeck, Ian Stewart and Adrian Johnson. By 1984 there were 12 Sheepskin Warehouse Shops in the north of England and this grew to 19 by 1987. In 1986 the partnership was incorporated under the name of Mark Birkbeck & Co. Ltd.

In the mid-1980s, as winters became warmer, the company anticipated a drop in popularity and changing trends for sheepskin products. They then moved into knitwear and produced a 'designer sheep sweater', which aimed to present a product to the public at an affordable price. As designer knitwear developed, visits were made to Germany to look at knitting techniques. The company later introduced new techniques of manufacture which became accepted throughout the knitwear industry. 'Picture' and 'handknitlook' designs were developed at affordable prices.

The success of the knitwear ranges prompted the decision to expand the retailing side of the business, and in 1987 Jumpers Ltd was formed. This was later bought out by its management (MBO) in March 1982. Franchising has been used to expand the company, and by 1992 107 shops had been opened.

In the niche market in which Jumpers has developed, there is no direct competition. Jumpers' products are naturally developed and are most appealing to women between the ages of 25 and 45 both for themselves and for members of their families. The company aims to combine the traditional decor of each shop with high standards and affordable prices.

While the recession affected retailing generally in the United Kingdom, Jumpers has been expanding both domestically and overseas in Canada and Japan. The story is one of a small business which has become large with rapid success.

Questions

1. What was Mark and Linda's first idea?
2. Describe how other ideas developed as the business got larger. Refer specifically in your answer to Peter Drucker's sources for innovative opportunity.
3. Comment on the different types of business organization that were used as the business developed. The business is still a private limited company; what would be the next stage of growth?
4. In your opinion, at what stage did the business cease to become regarded as a small business enterprise?
5. Explain why francising helped Jumpers to develop quickly.
6. What is an MBO? Why might Mark and Linda have left the business at this stage?
7. Explain the meaning of the following terms:
   (a) Niche marketing
   (b) Direct competition
   (c) Handknitlook
   (d) Changing trends

Analysing the opportunity

Having thought about an idea, the next step for a person intending to set up a small business is to analyse whether the business could be developed profitably. Small businesses are particularly vulnerable to a variety of unfavourable market conditions such as high interest rates, bank charges, government regulations and recession; these all make it difficult, no matter how brilliant an idea, for a small business to succeed. For example, in the early 1990s many small businesses failed because of circumstances beyond their control, even though their ideas were sound and were capable of development.

An analysis of the market the entrepreneur is about to enter provides a better undestanding of the market and its conditions. Small businesses operate in almost every market and so they face a variety of business environments, some of which might be favourable and others hostile.

Although industries differ, almost all industries will be influenced by both *national* and *local* conditions. There are many influences upon a national market that might affect a small business idea. For example, is that industry expanding, contracting or stable? Many pub landlords might provide, 'free of charge', some rather strong views on the state of their industry at this time! Is legislation planned for the industry in question? Is the economic environment favourable? What are the trends? Is there a lot of competition? Do articles about this industry ever appear in the media and if so what do they say? Even if a business is not intended for a national market-place, national influences will affect its success. It has been said that 'the only constant thing in life is change'. New organizations must try to develop a good understanding of changes in the national business environment. Earlier in this book we mentioned how *interdependence* influences the actions of a business. A new business should understand how such interdependent business influences could affect its operations and should develop a strategy that will respond with appropriate measures.

Having analysed the national situation, it will then be important to know about the industry at a local level. This might involve talking to others in similar businesses in the area and also to suppliers. Specific help may be provided by agencies and advisors. Market research is also very important (see Chapter 12).

Porter's model of the forces of industry competition can be used to analyse opportunities for a small business. This model identifies four factors outside the industry—entry, substitutes, buyers and suppliers—as well as one—rivalry—within the industry (see Fig. 6.2).

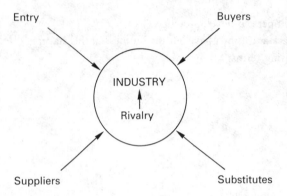

Figure 6.2 Porter's five forces of industry competition.

1. *Rivalry* within an industry may be friendly or fiercely competitive. It may take the form of marketing measures such as advertising, discounts, product changes, competitions, offers, etc.
2. It may be particularly difficult for a small firm to enter a market because of *barriers to entry*. These may include economies of scale and their effect upon unit costs. (N.B.: Small businesses may have higher unit costs than their larger competitors; see Chapter 14.) Established businesses may also have developed customer loyalty. Other barriers may include capital requirements and high distribution costs.
3. The *power of buyers* might influence the actions of a small business, particularly if it has only a few customers on which it depends.
4. The *power of suppliers* may also affect a small business, for example through a series of discounts and influences on marketing strategies. It is possible for small businesses to group together to reduce supplier power.
5. There is always a threat to small businesses from *substitute products*. We can all think of situations in our local high street where similar but not identical businesses have opened and taken away competition from other businesses. 'Indirect competition' provides other ways of meeting the same need, e.g. an Indian take-away competing with a chip shop. Industries with fewer sustitutes tend to be more stable.

Obtaining advice

There are a variety of sources of information and advice both for existing small businesses and for those people wishing to set up a small business. They include:

1. *Local enterprise agencies*   These are small advisory organizations which are funded from both private and public sources. For example, the main objective of Darlington Business Venture is to act as a source of advice to small businesses on almost any issue. Such advice frequently includes training and short courses.
2. *Small Firms Service*   The Small Firms Service used to operate within the Department of Employment. It provided information on a wide range of issues from supply to government legislation. It also provided opportunities to discuss plans. Since 1990 responsibility for this has been transfered to the Training and Enterprise Councils (TECS).
3. *Training and Enterprise Councils*   These were set up to improve the delivery of training and to provide other measures that could regenerate local economies. The 82 TECS have taken over the role of the Small Firms Service, and today most of their resources are directed at training.
4. *The Enterprise Initiative*   This is a package of advice, guidance and help launched by the Department of Trade and Industry. It is based on a number of consultancy services which small businesses can receive with a proportion of the costs paid.

Other organizations providing help and advice

Many other organizatons are prepared to offer advice and help for small businesses. For example, most *banks* have set up their own small business advisory services. NatWest claims to have a small business advisor in each of its 3000 branches. In its 'start-up guide' it says: 'When you have carefully weighed up the possibilities, why not come and talk to your local NatWest Small Business Advisor? He or she is there to help you with the procedure you need to go through to get into business, and to put you in touch with other people who provide free information and assistance for new business ventures.'

The *Rural Development Commission* has over 31 offices offering a wide range of advice to businesses operating in rural areas. *Local government* also offers advice to small firms, and their Economic Development Units may offer subsidized premises and planning controls.

Raising finance

Having investigated the idea, so that the small business person is confident that his or her proposals will be able to provide a product at a profit, the next stage is to consider carefully how much finance will be required to start and run the business. This should include:

1. *Start-up capital*   This encompasses start-up costs such as land and buildings, machinery, fixtures and fittings.

2. *Working capital*   This is the amount of money required to run the business. Most small businesses will not earn money straightaway, particularly if goods are sold on credit so that there will be a time delay before money is received in payment. In the early stages, therefore, finance will be required to be used as working capital.

It would be foolhardy to take the business proposal any further at this stage and incur heavy expenses if it is not possible to raise finance for the project. Seeking finance is an important part of starting the business. It will be almost certain that such funds will need to come from a variety of sources. (These sources are covered in Chapter 16).

Small business owners have to realize that setting up a business can involve considerable sacrifice and, when supplying finance from their own sources, can lead to a drop in living standards until the business starts to generate the targeted income. Many small businesses make the mistake of starting with too little income; this may make them difficult to run and extremely vulnerable to financial crisis. To make sure that proposals regarding their finances are accurate and allow for all contingencies, and in order to raise finance for the business proposal, the business owner should put together a *business plan* (see Chapter 5).

Case Study—Ark Geophysics Limited

For a number of years Richard Gleave, Kitty Hall and Andy McGrandle worked for companies involved in the processing and interpretation of geophysical software. Although they enjoyed the benefits of being involved in a high-tech industry, they felt that they were earning money for others and wanted to start their own business, which they felt would be more challenging, creative and stimulating. They clearly needed to satisfy a number of questions; for example:

- Where could they obtain business premises?
- What were their financial needs?
- What equipment would they need?
- Would there be enough work?
- What about the competition?

In order to answer these and many other questions, Richard, Kitty and Andy carefully researched their ideas and put together a *sensitivity analysis* to indicate the levels of risk they might face. They looked at their predicted sales, costs and overheads. They also looked at the capital expenditure that would be necessary before trading began. From their analysis, the indicators pointed towards the viability of their ideas.

Next, all of their ideas as well as financial forecasts and projections were incorporated into a *business plan*. The plan was taken to a number of banks, and they were suprised to find that they were getting different offers from each. The National Westminster Bank provided them with a package that included a loan and leasing facilities from Lombard North Central.

When Ark Geophysics Limited officially started trading, Richard, Kitty and Andy found that the financial predictions made in their business plan were accurate. Today Ark Geophysics is a successful private limited company with a developing reputation in the geophysics industry.

Questions

1. Why do you think that Richard, Kitty and Andy started their own business?
2. What was the purpose of carrying out a sensitivity analysis?
3. Explain the purpose of a business plan.

The business plan

The key to the success of a small business is the business plan. Many people with good ideas do not translate their ideas into a good business because they fail to plan properly (see Fig. 6.3).

Small business entrepreneurs will need to plan so that they will have a direction to follow. They will want to know:

- Where the business is likely to go
- How it is going to get there
- What resources are required
- Whether they are going to be able to meet their objectives

The plan will enable the *owner(s)* to check and monitor their business. Planning, therefore, provides both structure and direction. It can also be used to provide guidance for the *manage-*

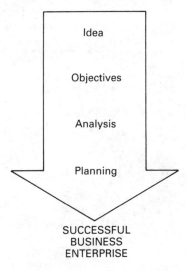

Figure 6.3 Using planning to create a successful business.

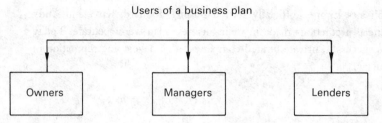

Figure 6.4 Users of a business plan.

ment of the business. Moreover, it can also be used to show others the direction the business is following. Support from people and organizations outside the business such as *lenders* will almost certainly be needed; they may supply the business with resources, including financial ones, but are unlikely to provide support for a business with no clear plans.

Business plans can be laid out according to a number of different formats and these will depend largely upon the nature of the business proposition and the intended users of the plan. Each business plan will be tailored to a specific business project.

Business plan outline

The business

- Name of business
- Address and location
- History or background
- Brief description of activities
- Proposed date for trading or start-up
- Legal identity—sole trader, partnership, company
- Objectives
- Professional advisors

Key personnel

- Names of directors and managers
- Background, experience, knowledge and expertise
- Relevant work and business experience
- Future personnel requirements
- Recruitment proposals

The nature of the business

- Description of product (including price)
- Patents, trademarks, copyrights, etc.
- Suppliers

- Proposed developments of product
- Market—size and potential
- Trends in the market-place
- Needs of customers
- Benefits offered to customers
- Description of competitors' strengths and weaknesses
- Unique features of product compared with competition
- Projected turnover—3 months, 6 months, 1 year, etc.
- Break-even analysis (see page 000)
- Production techniques
- Reasons why proposals are achievable

Marketing plan

- Marketing objectives
- Environment
- Market research
- Marketing methods
  — Product
  — Price
  — Distribution (place)
  — Promotion

Future

- Strengths, weaknesses, opportunities and threats (SWOT)
- Socioeconomic trends
- Technological trends
- Action plans
- Timetable of activities

Resources

- Premises, size and cost
- Machines
- Vehicles
- Equipment
- Overheads
- Materials
- Management salaries
- Labour costs

Financial analysis

- Start-up capital
- Working capital
- Grants
- Own resources
- Loans
- Assets available as security
- Cash flow forecast over three years
- Profit and loss forecast over three years
- Balance sheet

Other information

- Address of accountant
- Address of solicitor
- Insurance arrangements
- VAT registration
- Summary

Types of business organization

A small business can take a variety of forms (see Chapter 5). The choice will usually depend upon the objectives of the enterprise.

A *sole trader* (or *sole proprietor*) is the most common form of small business enterprise. The owner can trade under his or her own name and there is no legal separation between the assets and liabilities of the owner and those of the business. Sole traders do not, however, have limited liability, and this increases their risk.

Where two or more people set up in business together with the intention of sharing profits, then they are in *partnership*. Each partner then becomes 'jointly and severally liable' for any debts the business runs up. Many partnerships fail because of disagreements between the partners and a partnership agreement can prevent this.

A *limited company* is a legal body which has an identity that is different from that of the owners of the business. The owners, therefore, have limited liability. Although the directors may change from time to time, the company will continue to exist as a corporate body unless it is wound up.

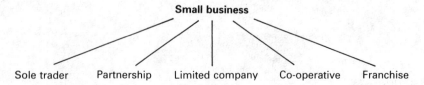

Figure 6.5 Forms of small business ownership.

A *co-operative* is a business enterprise in which the emphasis, management and running of the business are controlled by the people working for it. A registered co-operative has legal status and its members have limited liability.

Legal requirements

Rules and regulations introduced by both central and local authorities will influence the actions of small businesses. Such rules are deemed to be in the public interest and to benefit society as a whole. Frequently small business owners have to consult either their local enterprise centre or accountants, solicitors and tax consultants for advice. Small business owners will need to know how the law will affect their operations. Some of the main areas that influence small businesses include:

1. *Inland Revenue* A statement of income and expenditure must be submitted to the designated Inspector of Taxes.
2. *Value added tax* When total turnover rises above a certain level, the owner must notify the local Customs and Excise Office and register for VAT.
3. *Business names* Although sole traders and partnerships can trade under their own names, if a business name is used it must follow the procedures laid out by the Business Names Act 1985.
4. *Planning control* Where the use of premises is to be changed, the planning authority must be consulted.
5. *National insurance* Contributions to the Department of Social Security have to be made both for owners of the business and for their employers.
6. *Licences* These may be required for selling alcoholic products, operating as a driving instructor, providing credit services (Consumer Credit Act) and importing certain goods.
7. *Insurance* It is a legal requirement to have vehicle insurance and employers' liability insurance.
8. *Data Protection Act* A business will have to register if it keeps information about people on computer.
9. *Health and Safety Act* This places a duty on employers to ensure the health and safety of the workforce.
10. *Employment law* A small business should be aware of the law relating to areas such as redundancy, unfair dismissal, sex discrimination and union membership.
11. *Consumer protection* The small business must be aware of various consumer-related acts which are designed to protect consumers from faulty products, unfit food and misleading descriptions.

The purpose of this chapter has been to provide you with a brief insight into small business ownership. Although running a small enterprise can be both exciting and challenging, there is always considerable risk, and a lot of hard work is necessary to ensure that the business eventually achieves its objectives.

Questions

Short-answer questions

1. What is a small business?
2. Identify two advantages that a small business has over larger enterprises.
3. Name four reasons why people start their own businesses.
4. Describe the risks of starting a business.
5. Explain two features of a small business that are different from those of a larger business.
6. Provide two examples of occupations that are nearly always dominated by small businesses.
7. Name three sources of finance for a small business.
8. Identify four traits that a small business owner should have.
9. Give one example of someone who started a small business which has become successful and later developed into a very large and well-known business.
10. What is a patent and why might one be taken out?
11. Why is franchising a useful way to start a small business?
12. Why do many small businesses 'copy' other business ideas?
13. When buying an existing business it might be necessary to pay for goodwill. What is goodwill?
14. What is a unique selling proposition? Why should a good business idea have one?
15. Describe three of Peter Drucker's sources for innovative opportunity.
16. Name two interdependent influences that could affect the success of a small business.
17. List Porter's five forces of industry competition.
18. Name three sources of business advice.
19. Identify three groups that would use a business plan.
20. List four legal requirements of small businesses.

Essays

1. Every year approximately 50 000 businesses are started in the United Kingdom and in the same year over 10 000 fail. What do these statistics indicate to you? (*Source*: AEB)
2. Between 1980 and 1988 the number of self-employed people in the workforce of the United Kingdom increased from 2 million (8.4% of total employment) to 3 million (11.8% of total employment). Discuss the factors that might have led to this change. (*Source*: AEB)
3. What is a small business? What advantages would such an organization have over larger business units?
4. Ronald Todd is a skilled engineer working for a large company. Despite the security and the benefits he receives from his job, he would prefer to work for himself. What reasons might Ronald have for starting his own business? Comment on both the benefits and the pitfalls involved in starting one's own business.
5. Comment on the personal qualities required by a small business owner. Given the list you have made, does this mean that many will not succeed?
6. Describe where and how many entrepreneurs develop their business ideas.
7. Many good business propositions fail and bad business ideas succeed. Explain why.

8. With specific reference to Porter's forces of industry competition, analyse a business opportunity of your own choice.
9. Small businesses constantly require help and advice. Explain where this help and advice might come from.
10. Many rules and regulations make it difficult for small businesses to operate. With specific reference to at least two such rules, explain why this is so.

Data response questions

1 A task for the reader

Arrange an interview or a series of interviews with a locally based small business person. From the notes you take at this meeting, construct a case study which charts the development of the business. Make sure that:

(a) You choose your respondent wisely. He/she may be a family friend, relative or someone to whom you have written.
(b) You prepare a detailed list of questions for the meeting.
(c) You highlight important elements in the development of the business.

Whenever necessary use technical jargon. Make use of accounting information, analysis of market, reference to business issues, etc.

2 Sauces just like grandma's

Read the article on page 152 and answer the questions that follow.
1. Name two central government schemes that provide financial help for small firms.
2. Assume that Gramma's profit, after all costs and expenses are paid, is 6 per cent of sales. Equal quantities of each strength are sold at the following prices per jar:

Mild	£1.90
Medium	£2.10
Hot and spicy	£2.30
Very hot	£2.50

Calculate the annual profit before tax at the present capacity.
3. What information would Ms Alexander-Moore have needed to include in her business plan in order to obtain financial support from her bank?
4. Some reasons for choosing Gramma's distribution channels are given in the text. What other reasons might have made this choice a wise one?

Dounne Alexander-Moore's herbal pepper sauces sell at department stores and in supermarkets, yet until a year ago she was running her business from a kitchen in her flat in East London, and supporting herself and two teenage daughters on family credit.

Ms Alexander-Moore was determined to go into a business of her own when her marriage broke down. She started with a £3 000 bank loan, guaranteed by her former boss.

Her idea was to market the hot pepper sauces with which, she swears, her herbalist grandmother saved her life as a premature infant in Trinidad. She made the sauces on her home cooker, and bottled them as 'Gramma's Concentrated Pepper Sauces', designing the labels and packaging herself. She won orders from Harrods and six prestigious department stores.

As a black single parent living in a rented flat with no collateral to offer, she still found it difficult to persuade any bank to back her.

It took two years before she found a branch of NatWest Bank bold enough to finance her for expansion into the supermarkets.

'I went for department stores first, because they had prestige but would not order more than I could supply.'

From her London flat she could prepare just 500 jars a month.

Last January, production of Gramma's moved out to larger premises. One of Ms Alexander-Moore's daughters works for her full-time, the other part-time. Her mother, who had sacrificed her income to help the business start, is on the payroll too, and a brother-in-law is financial director.

Production capacity is now 100 000 jars a month, and Gramma's are on trial at a chain of major supermarket branches. The sauces come in four strengths, priced from £1.90 to £2.50.

(*Source*: adapted from *The Times*, 11 January 1991)

Figure 6.6 Financial struggle: Dounne Alexander-Moore had difficulty finding backing for her sauces (*Source*: AEB)

Suggested reading

Hingston, P., *The Greatest Little Business Book*, 5th edn. Hingston Associates, 1991.

Hubbard, R. T. and Hailes, W. D., *Small Business Management*, 4th edn. Delmar, 1988.

Stokes, D., *Small Business Management*. DP Publications Ltd, 1992.

7

Business organization in the public sector

By their nature, governments intervene on a regular basis in many areas of life, from imposing the tax on a packet of cigarettes to determining the appropriate sentence for mugging an old-age pensioner. However, since 1979 Britain has had a government that publicly claims to be against government intervention in industry.

The reality is that governments of all political persuasions have been intervening in industry for years, from Macmillan's decision in the 1950s to erect the Ravenscraig steelworks in Motherwell to the Thatcher government's repeated intervention in the aviation industry in preparation for British Airways' privatization.

Michael Heseltine, writing about the Conservative government in recent years, stated: 'This government, like all its predecessors for at least the last fifty years, is up to its neck in the business life of this country, stimulating one enterprise here, stifling another there and interfering everywhere.'

Working together

If societies work as groups of people co-operating together, they can seek common solutions to common problems. (It is worth noting that in a famous speech Margaret Thatcher claimed that there was no such thing as Society.)

We can illustrate the need for co-operation in the following way. Imagine that there are two cars heading for each other on a collision course. Each driver can veer to the left or the right. If both veer to the right or both veer to the left, a collision is avoided. Therefore there needs to be some form of co-ordination of the decisions of the two drivers if the worst possible situation is to be avoided.

Co-operation can be made effective by establishing *social institutions*, in this case rules and conventions about driving on the left or right-hand side of the road. The Highway Code 'codifies' UK driving rules and regulations. The co-operation that results from all UK drivers obeying the Highway Code leads to benefits for all.

If people concentrate on just looking after their own interests, this may be harmful to society as a whole. What is best for me alone might not be best for the whole community. Fisherfolk who consider no interests but their own may quickly deplete an essential national and international resource by overfishing so that fish stocks dwindle. Individuals who use aerosols to make their hair look nice may exacerbate the harmful effect on the ozone layer. And so on.

To achieve the benefits of co-operation, it is essential to have a referee or umpire who makes sure that all parties in society keep to rules that are of benefit to the whole community, thereby eliminating the need for national and international laws and governments.

Market failure

Markets working on their own are unlikely to create economic efficiency. There will be a tendency for too much of some goods to be produced and too little of others. In the extreme case of complete market failure, the market will fail to exist, so that certain goods will not be produced at all. The chief cause of market failure is the inability of individuals to work co-operatively on their own.

Causes of market failure include:

1. *Poor information*   Buyers and sellers are not clear about what goods are available in the market-place and at what prices.
2. *Externalities*   The act of producing some goods and services has knock-on harmful effects such as noise, waste, dereliction, etc. Externalities exist when the actions of consumers and producers also affect third parties. In a free market, how could we make people pay for the costs created by externalities?
3. *Public goods*   Public goods are goods for which, at any output, consumption by extra consumers does not reduce the quantity consumed by existing consumers. Examples of pure public goods include: the peace and security of a community; national defence; the law; air pollution control; fire protection; street lighting; weather forecasts and public television. If we take the example of peace and security, it would be very difficult to make people pay privately for a police service that everyone benefits from.
4. *Imperfect competition*   Competition in the market-place does not take place on equal terms between competitors. Some firms are much larger than others and are able to sell goods in bulk at low prices. Because of their size they are able to 'see off' competitors. Once they are in a position of power, they can start to exploit the consumers.
5. *Uncertainty*   In the market-place, consumers and producers may be unwilling to make products or to carry out transactions when they cannot see into the future.

The public purse

The government in all modern economies plays a key role in running and manipulating the economy. Nearly half of all government expenditure is on health and social security. To finance this expenditure, the government has available to it a very large chunk of national resources which are raised mainly through taxation (see Fig. 7.1).

The growth of public expenditure needs to be financed by increased taxation. Taxation in the United Kingdom as a percentage of national income (roughly, money earnt by all citizens) has

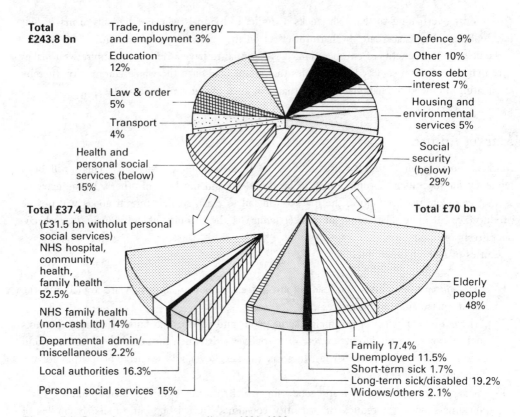

Figure 7.1 General government expenditure, 1991–1992.

risen from about one-third in 1955 to about one-half in the early 1990s. The Conservative government claims to be a tax-cutting government. Generally speaking, however, while it has reduced taxes on incomes (e.g. income tax) it has increased taxes on expenditure (e.g. VAT).

There are a number of reasons why the government plays such a prominent part in the economy:

1. Some goods and services are provided by the government because it is felt that all citizens are entitled to a share in the public provision of such items. For exampe, most people in the United Kingdom believe that all children should have some form of health care and education.
2. Some goods and services that everyone benefits from, if they are to be properly provided, can only be produced by the government. An example of this is the police force.
3. Some people believe that the government should try to reduce inequality. This might involve taxing some people at a higher rate than others and giving more benefits to those who are worse off. (Of course, there are others who believe that inequality is not a bad thing because it gives people a motive to try to better themselves; they would argue that the government should remove any obstacles that prevent people from bettering themselves by working harder.)

4. The government might also try to make the economic system run more smoothly. For example, it passes laws against monopolies and to protect consumers (see Chapter 11) and it takes measures against pollution and other anti-social practices (see Chapter 23).

Roles for the government

There are a number of possible roles for a government in the economy.

An allocative role

Given the existence of market failure, the government has a role to play to enable the effective use of resources. For example, it can subsidize certain activities which are poorly provided for by the market. There are other resources which the government might want to ration the use of; for example, if everyone wanted to visit Stonehenge at the summer solstice the monument might rapidly deteriorate from over-use. The government therefore limits access to the site on this day, and makes people pay a charge on other days, to restrict entry (as well as to raise revenue). Successive generations, therefore, will be able to benefit from the site. Everyone is better off in the long term. In this way, the government allocates some resources to maximize the benefits to the community.

A distributive role

The government helps to redistribute income and wealth in society by taking taxes from and giving benefits to citizens. Clearly, there are many views as to what social justice means. One of the famous sayings of Margaret Thatcher was 'Let all our children grow taller, yet may some grow taller than others.' Clearly, her view of social justice would be different from that of many other people.

The problem that faces society is to decide which particular distribution of incomes and welfare it prefers and then to consider alternative measures which will take it from its existing distribution to its most preferred.

A stabilization role

Economies periodically suffer from inflation, unemployment, lack of real growth, balance of payments problems, etc. The government will use economic politics to try to stabilize the economy; for example, it will try to cut down spending when prices are rising too quickly.

A regulatory role

The government administers a general system of law and justice which regulates the behaviour of individuals and organizations.

Public-sector involvement in UK industry

There are three major elements of public-sector involvement in industry:

- Direct state participation in industry through public corporations known as the nationalized industries and other Crown corporations
- Industries in which there is public-sector involvement together with private investment; for example, the government held a 39 per cent share in BP from before the Second World War until the late 1980s when shares were sold to the public
- Industries in which there is a public-sector involvement at local government level rather than at the level of national government.

A fourth group that can be identified by businesses that receive support from the government to establish new activities, such as research and development or product development in a particular field.

Public corporations

In the United Kingdom the government still owns a number of industries and businesses on behalf of the people. Most of these take the form of public corporations. In recent years, however, there has been a sustained period of privatization of government enterprises.

Privatization means the de-nationalization of state-controlled industries. We are all familiar with privatization such as the sale of the Electricity Boards, the Water Boards, British Telecom and British Gas (Fig. 7.2). However, privatization also includes the sale of council houses, the contracting out of local-authority-controlled services such as street cleaning and the introduction of private prisons.

A public corporation is set up by an Act of Parliament. Examples of public corporations include British Rail, British Coal and the Bank of England (1993). (At present there are extensive chunks of the railways and the coal industry that the government is preparing for privatization.)

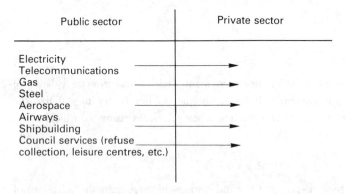

Figure 7.2 Examples of privatization.

Once a public corporation has been set up, the government appoints a chairperson to be responsible for the day-to-day running of the industry.

There are a number of reasons why public corporations have been set up:

1. *To avoid wasteful duplication*   In the nineteenth century, for example, there were railway lines between Leeds and Harrogate. This is wasteful. Imagine the problems caused by having three electricity companies operating in your town.

2. *To set up and run services that might not be profitable*   Would a private company supply post, electricity, gas and water to a small remote village if a lot of capital were needed to set up services that may not make a profit?

3. *To gain the benefits of large-scale production*   It may be more efficient to have one big firm producing a large amount of output than to have several smaller firms producing smaller amounts. When there is only one firm, the government as owner might be less inclined than a private firm to charge high prices.

4. *To protect employment*   The government might take into consideration the need to create and keep jobs rather than just considering financial profits.

5. *To control industries that are important to the country, such as coal, steel and the railways*   *Infrastructure* is the term used to describe the basic backbone of an economic system including the transport network, energy and water supplies. Some people argue that the government has an important responsibility for the supervision and maintenance of the infrastructure.

During the 1980s a number of public corporations were privatized and it is likely that this policy will continue into the mid-1990s. Privatization involves turning the public corporations into companies owned by shareholders.

There are a number of reasons for doing this, including the following:

1. Some people argue that state-run firms are not efficient because they do not have any real competition and do not risk going bankrupt, because the government will always pay off their debts.

2. It is argued that in a modern society as many people as possible should have shares in businesses. The idea is that everyone—not just the very rich—should become shareholders; people have therefore been encouraged to buy, in some cases, just a few hundred pounds' worth of shares in enterprises like British Telecom and British Gas.

Other people argue against privatization. They maintain that competition can be harmful in areas where standards need to be maintained, such as the National Health Service. Competition can lead to 'cutting corners' and to the deterioration of safety standards. There is also the strong argument that it is a nonsense to sell to the public shares in industries that are already owned by the people. Instead of an industry being owned by all citizens, it then becomes the property of shareholders.

When a public corporation is set up, an independent body is also formed to protect consumers' interests. Consumers can take their complaints to this body; for example, the Post Office Users'

National Council will take up complaints made by users of the Post Office about, e.g., the late delivery of letters.

The government keeps the power to make major decisions about how public corporations should run, for example whether to close down large sections of the railway network and whether to build new power stations. However, the chairperson and managers of the public corporation will decide on day-to-day issues such as wages and prices, timetables and industrial relations. The government does sometimes interfere even in these areas, leading to public argument and debate.

Whereas a limited company has to make an annual report to its shareholders, a public corporation must present its annual report to the appropriate government minister, who makes a verbal report to Parliament; at this time Members of Parliament will make criticisms or voice support for the way the corporation is being run. A committee of MPs has the job of studying the running of each public corporation and of reporting on its operation. For example, there is a select committee of MPs acting as a watchdog over British Coal.

Figure 7.3 highlights some of the differences between public corporations and private corporations.

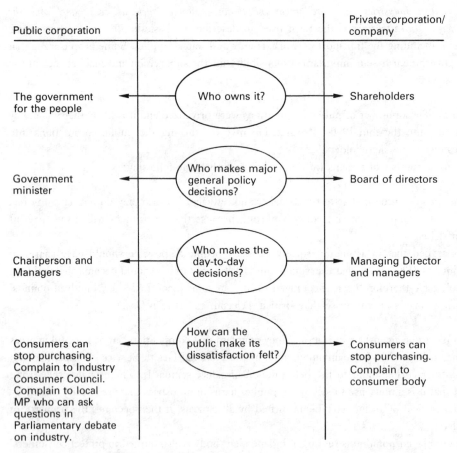

Figure 7.3 Some comparisons of public and private corporations.

Other central government enterprises

In addition to public corporations, the other two major areas of government control over economic activity occur where:

1. An activity is run by a government department.
2. An activity is run by a public company in which the government has a shareholding.

When an activity is run by a government department, a government minister has overall charge for the department. The department is staffed and run by civil servants. A typical example of this would be the Customs and Excise Department, which deals with the supervision and collection of some taxes.

The major criticisms of such a form of organization from the business point of view are that:

1. Decisions are made slowly because there are many links in the chain of command, usually wrapped up in rules and regulations.
2. The organization may appear to be inefficient because of lack of competition.
3. There is no external agency to protect the public's interest by checking on how the department runs. While in many cases there will be a mechanism for making complaints, it may be so complex as to be inaccessible to the ordinary person.

In recent years the government has reduced its shareholding in public companies as an extension of its policy of privatization.

Local government enterprises

In the UK certain services in local areas are supervised by locally elected councils. These councils usually run some forms of business organizations such as the municipal carparks, swimming baths, sports centres, bus services and toilets.

However, in the late 1980s council activities too have been subjected to the policy of privatization. Today many activities such as road cleaning and refuse disposal are contracted out to those firms that put in the lowest tender for a particular job. Council officials simply monitor the effectiveness with which the work is done, and can refuse to continue a contract if work fails to meet the required standards.

Local councils receive money from two main sources: a grant given to them by central government, and a local tax. Local councils often subsidize loss-making activities such as local parks which provide a benefit to the community.

Case Study—Presenting the arguments for and against privatization

In late 1989 the water industry was privatized. In 1990 the electricity supply industry was privatized. John Smith (the current leader of the Labour party) and Norman Tebbit (a former influential Conservative minister) were asked to give the views on the question, 'What, if any, advantages does the public gain from the privatization of natural monopolies like gas, water and electricity?'

What follows is in three parts:

- An introduction
- John Smith's views
- Norman Tebbit's views

Make notes on what you consider to be the key points made. Discuss the issue with other students. Which do you think is the stronger case?

Introduction

In an opinion poll by NOP in December 1986, 71 per cent of those polled wanted to keep the water and electricity supply services in state hands; only 21 per cent were in favour of privatizing them.

What is the objection to privatizing utilities? The most obvious is that industries that have no competitors, since the product they supply is unique and essential, are in such a strong monopoly position that they should be operated purely in the public interest. Take electricity. You can cook by gas, if you prefer, or coal, or even wood, but it is exceptionally difficult to operate a shaver or washing machine by gas and virtually impossible to light your house by gas.

The distribution (though not necessarily the generation) of electricity is a natural monopoly, and consumers are forced to pay whatever price the suppliers care to impose. Having no alternative supplier, they cannot withdraw their custom; and once the industry is privatized, why should their needs be rated above those of the electricity company's shareholders? The same considerations apply in the case of water. Water is an essential and irreplaceable commodity.

'The business of government', Nigel Lawson (a Conservative Chancellor of the Exchequer) famously said, 'is not the government of business.' However, most people would agree that the business of government is, above all, the happiness of the governed, and opinion polls have shown a dissatisfaction with the privatization of essential services.

John Smith's view

It was John Baker, the chief executive of National Power, who blew the gaff when he said to his staff: 'The job is not about shouldering national responsibilities but about meeting contracts, improving profitability, seeking out opportunities but exploiting them only if it pays to do so. Our task will not be to keep the lights on whatever the cost. It will probably pay us to ensure we never overstress our plant.'

I believe that the onus of proof must rest on the privatizers to persuade the rest of us that to hand over industries (such as electricity and water) that are essentially public services to profit-driven companies will not prejudice these services in the way Mr Baker describes.

The privatizers normally point to two influences which they claim will moderate the tendency to growth: the effect of competition, and the power of statutory control. Competition, it is said, will put control in the hands of the consumers who, by having the power not to buy a particular service from a particular company, can force it to keep up quality of service at a reasonable price. It is hard to see such a process at work in either a privatized electricity or water industry. Such limited competition as is envisaged in electricity is between the two privatized generating companies, National Power and Power Gen—one with 70 per cent of the action, the other with 30 per cent. Experts have argued that a duopoly (two firms in the market) is usually in unsatisfactory market structure. Firms tend to work together. They rarely compete in order to prevent price wars.

Consumers will not do business with the generating duopoly; they will buy electricity from a local electricity company which will have a regional monopoly. The household and the business consumer have no choice.

Can we rely on statutory obligations? In fact, the two generating companies will be removed from the statutory obligation that was previously imposed on the nationalized Central Electricity Generating Board.

In the case of water, there is no question of competition. The only source of water for a consumer will be the relevant privatized water company. It is intended to impose upon these companies standards of water quality as a necessary public protection. But these obligations may conflict with the profit motive, so that corners will be cut.

No wonder that public opinion is so hostile to the privatization of water. It is a precious national resource, crucial to the health and well-being of the whole population. It should be held on behalf of the public, rather than for private profit.

Why then carry on with privatizations? I can see three main reasons: first, political opposition to the public sector; second, to line the public purse by selling state assets; and finally, there is a momentum behind privatization supported by those who benefit from being managers of privatized companies, those who help to privatize the companies and those who benefit from the rising share prices in privatized concerns.

Norman Tebbit's views

A managerial failure in the South West Water Authority last year caused thousands of people to be supplied with toxic drinking water. It was not an act motivated by, or caused by, greed for profits or as a result of striving for higher earnings per share. The authority is a public body responsible not through a board of greedy, unscrupulous directors to shareholders, but through worthy public-spirited folk to the public they serve—in this case with poisoned water.

Had the water authorities been privatized before this particular affair, the opponents of privatization would have been very critical.

The fact is that most accidents, such as the one in Cornwall, arise from weak management, flabby direction, and in this case inadequate regulation of a monopoly. The latter is a characteristic of public-sector monopolies. It encourages a chronic lack of capital investment, misdirection of that which is made, consequent low or negative returns on capital, and poor output from the labour used.

I was once the minister to whom the nationalized British Telecom, which is in part a public utility, was responsible. I am now a director of the privatized company. As a government minister I had to receive BT's corporate plan. My officials, good able men, but not carrying executive responsibility, second-guessed the BT management. I had to third-guess them and then take the plan to the Treasury, where officials fourth-guessed us. The Chief Secretary to the Treasury then fifth-guessed us, with E Committee of the Cabinet ready with a sixth or seventh guess and the Cabinet a potentially eighth- or ninth-guesser. The process took months. Matters entirely outside of BT affected the outcome as well, such as the demands of other nationalized industries for capital investment or for subsidy to continue to produce poor-quality goods at prices too high to compete.

Eventually a plan for the year would be approved, sometimes after the year had already commenced. The management was frequently not properly rewarded for fear that it might lead to pay demands from other public-sector workers, the armed forces, civil servants, teachers, nurses, etc.

Contrast the scene with British Telecom today. The company can plan and carry out its capital investment programme without government battles. So long as it retains the approval of its shareholders and bankers, capital is available and a five-year rolling plan can be executed. If the company needs key people, it can recruit them without reference to the pay of generals or judges.

Yes, of course, the company is driven by the need to reward its owners: the shareholders. But it can do that only by serving its customers. Where there is competition, the customers are protected by that. Where there is not, the Director-General of the Office of Telecommunications is there to protect the consumer. Indeed, he is there also to ensure fair play between BT and its far smaller competitors.

Does the system work? If BT fails to meet complaints then the director of OFTEL [BT's regulatory body] can impose penalties which will be felt by shareholders.

Today, the Treasury, instead of financing the business, will receive billions of pounds in dividends, interest and tax.

Water and electricity are not different from other commodities because they are essentials of life. After all, food and clothing are far from inessential, and no one in their right mind suggests that public ownership of food production would give better consumer services than we receive in the street markets, small shops or supermarkets.

The utilities are different because final customer supply are largely natural monopolies. Monopolies require regulation to protect consumers.

Where regulation is needed to protect consumers against monopoly powers, it is more effective against the private than the public sector, because a private company maximizes returns to its shareholders.

Questions

1. Explain the following terms in the context of the views presented above:
   (a) Natural monopolies
   (b) Regulation
   (c) Returns to shareholders
   (d) Public-sector monopolies
   (e) Public-service obligation
   (f) Privatization
   (g) Duopoly
   (h) Improving profitability
   (i) Profit motive
   (j) Corporate plan
   (k) Capital investment programmes.
2. Outline five key arguments put forward by John Smith.
3. Outline five key arguments put forward by Norman Tebbit.
4. Highlight weaknesses in the arguments put forward by John Smith and Norman Tebbit.
5. How is it possible to measure the effectiveness of newly privatized companies?
6. What evidence can you uncover to highlight the effectiveness of the new water and electricity companies in recent years?

The declining importance of nationalized industries

One of the major criticisms of nationalized industries was that they used up a substantial part of national resources, which they did not utilize particularly well. In 1979 the combined turnover of the public corporations was £44 billion, which was nearly one-quarter of gross national output. Collectively, they employed nearly 2 million people and were responsible for 20 per cent of all investment in the economy. The argument was that money was being 'crowded out' of its best possible use, which in many cases would have been investment in the private sector. The critics felt that sluggish public-sector organizations were wasting resources and holding the country back.

Despite large-scale privatization, the turnover of public corporations was still nearly £40 billion in 1990 and they still accounted for 7.2 per cent of all investment. Corporations like British Rail and British Coal (due for part privatization in 1995 onwards) are major users of investment capital.

Figure 7.4 illustrates productivity growth in a number of industries between the early 1970s and the late 1980s. Study the measures of productivity and the performance of specific industries. What does the figure show? Does it give an accurate measure of performance? What are the major weaknesses in the figure?

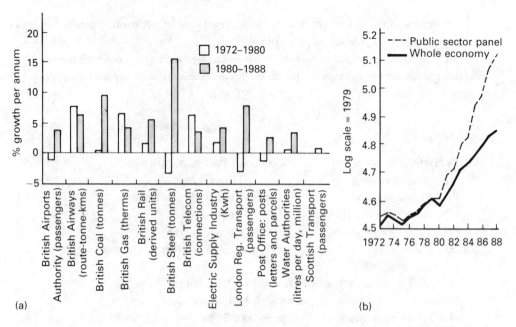

Figure 7.4 Focus: productivity growth of privatized industries, 1972–1980 and 1980–1988. (London Business School)

As we shall see in Chapter 11, public corporations in recent years have been increasingly expected to operate as if they were in the private sector.

Although nationalization was an important feature during the first half of the twentieth century (e.g. the creation of the Central Electricity Generating Board and the British Broadcasting Corporation in 1926), the bulk of nationalizations took place immediately after the Second World War under Labour governments; these included coal, transport, electricity generation, gas and iron and steel.

In 1948 the government set out that the nationalized industries were to meet the demand for their produce at a reasonable price which would enable them to break even over a number of years. In the years that followed there was a lot of criticism about the way in which targets were set for public corporations; for example, under the break-even policy it was possible to charge some customers who could be supplied cheaply (e.g. gas users in cities) the same price as other customers who were far more expensive to supply (e.g. gas consumers in remote areas).

In 1961 the government set more precise financial targets for public corporations. Taking into account conditions in the market, the government set targets as a rate of return on the assets employed in a specific industry. In 1967 even more stringent rules were set, whereby the cross-subsidization of one group of consumers by another was to be avoided. New investment was to be expected to yield a return equal to what the investment capital would earn in the private sector. It was however recognized that some activities of public corporations (e.g. supplying to rural areas and engaging in activities which were not profitable) were of a social rather than a commercial nature; these social contributions needed to be given a money value, and the goverment would provide a subsidy to meet these activities.

In 1979 the new Conservative government that came into power embraced a policy of privatization. The emphasis was therefore on cutting out unprofitable operations in order to make these industries attractive to prospective shareholders. Over the years, this has meant cutting down loss-making operations such as some steel works, coal mines and shipyards.

A large number of nationalized industries were privatized during the 1980s including electricity, British Telecom, British Gas, British Steel, British Aerospace, British Airways, British Shipbuilders, the National Bus Company, the British Airports Authority and the National Freight Corporation. During the 1990s it has become increasingly difficult to sell off the remaining nationalized industries, as the government is now left with a smaller number of substantial corporations which are significant employers, such as British Rail and British Coal, and which can be seen as more than just commercial organizations. In the Acts of Parliament that have privatized industries, the government has set up regulatory bodies such as OFTEL and OFGAS with the responsibility for checking that the privatized industries keep to established rules governing prices, competition and the quality of service offered. Today's remaining nationalized industries are expected to meet financial targets and to show a real rate of return on assets that indicates that resources are being used as effectively as if the capital were being employed by the private sector.

Public-sector organizations such as the National Health Service and the BBC have been broken down into a number of independent sections. Each section (e.g. fundholding GPs and hospitals) is expected to manage its own budget and to use resources efficiently.

The Citizen's Charter

In July 1991 John Major introduced his Citizen's Charter, which set out consumer rights as the 'central theme of public life' for the 1990s. The proposed consumer rights would extend throughout the National Health Service, education and transport to the privatized gas, water, electricity and telecommunications utilities.

Officials with responsibility for supervising public utilities (the utility regulators) have new powers, including the option to award compensation for reasonable complaints by consumers. This means clearer commitments to the quality of service, fixed appointment times and new means of seeing complaints through. There is a new charter standard for quality which entitles those who can prove they meet the high standards to use a 'chartermark'.

The social market

In the 1990s some of the free-market principles of the Conservative government have been toned down in recognition of the importance of the social market. Clearly, resources need to be used as effectively as possible. However, as we saw at the beginning of the chapter, market failures do occur. There are some services where the government needs to step in to provide for the essential needs of weaker members of the community, e.g. rural bus services, water to all households, etc. Some new and essential projects are very uncertain to start with and require the long-term vision that only government support can provide. There are investments in the infrastructure of the country (e.g. transport networks) which only the government has the resources and foresight to cater for. We need an effective public sector; however, it is still important to make calculations to cater for social welfare. The government needs to subsidize essential facilities and services. There is also a strong feeling among industrialists that the government needs to support growing industries, science, technology and research and development. Countries such as Japan and Germany benefit from a healthy industrial partnership between government and industry.

Questions

Short-answer questions

1. What is the public sector of the economy?
2. What is privatization?
3. List eight major industries that have been privatized since 1979.
4. How are consumers protected in a privatized industry?
5. What is 'market failure'?
6. What do you understand by the terms
    (a) externalities?
    (b) public goods?
    (c) imperfect competition?
7. What is
    (a) a monopoly?
    (b) a duopoly?
8. What is a public corporation?
9. Who (a) owns and (b) runs a public corporation?
10. What is
    (a) nationalization?
    (b) de-nationalization?
11. What is a government department? Give examples of government departments.
12. Name two sources of local government revenue.
13. Explain how the government has (a) an allocative role and (b) a distributive role in the use of resources in a country.
14. How is a public corporation set up?
15. How is an industry privatized?
16. How are privatized industries accountable?
17. Explain two arguments (a) in favour of nationalization, and (b) in favour of privatization of a particular industry.
18. Explain two arguments (a) against nationalization and (b) against de-nationalization of a particular industry.
19. What major criticisms can be levelled at the organization of government departments?
20. Describe three activities which were previously the responsibility of local councils and which during the 1980s and early 1990s have been put out to private tender.

Essays

1. 'The business of government is not the government of business' (Nigel Lawson). Discuss this assertion.
2. Outline the main arguments for and against the privatization of British Rail and/or British Coal.
3. There are some industries which by their very nature need to be in the government sector. Discuss.
4. What are the benefits to be gained by local authorities from putting out their services to tender with private-sector contractors?
5. Examine the view that markets cannot be relied upon to meet the needs of consumers; that market failure requires government intervention.
6. Explain how the government can perform the following roles:
    (a) To help allocate resources in society
    (b) To influence the distribution of resources
    (c) To help to stabilize the economy
    (d) To regulate business and social life
7. Why is the notion of an internal market a necessary part of the public sector today?
8. What are public-sector enterprises? How are they organized and run?
9. Industries and firms will always be more productive and more profitable in the private sector. Discuss.
10. When dealing with public-sector and private-sector monopolies, the consumer or user of the products has very little power. Discuss.

Data response questions

1 Creating an internal market at the BBC

In the early 1990s the BBC cut its workforce by 25 per cent to 23 000 by the end of 1993. The major cause of this was a government requirement that the BBC buy in a quarter of its programmes from outside producers. The new management at the BBC then created a system called 'Producer Choice'. The 23 000 staff have been divided up into 8500 'buyers' and 14 500 'sellers'. Since 1 April 1993, 'buyers' such as producers have had the option of shopping outside of the BBC for back-up services. 'Sellers'—studio managers, camera crews, technicians, librarians—are obliged to do enough 'business' with BBC producers to justify their jobs.

The producers are happy to be given more choice, but they are resentful of the way Producer Choice has been imposed on them from above. In a single stroke, Producer Choice has imposed financial accountability on BBC staff. It enables the BBC management to show the government that it has control of its costs, and it has forced BBC staff to think in a more market-orientated way, becoming competing 'business units'.

1. Explain the following terms in the context of the above paragraphs:
    (a) Buyers
    (b) Sellers
    (c) Internal market
    (d) Producer Choice
    (e) Financial accountability
2. Why do you think that Producer Choice has been introduced at the BBC?
3. What do you think are likely to be (a) the main advantages and (b) the main disadvantages of Producer Choice?
4. What do you think will be the main impact of the policy on:
    (a) programmes offered by the BBC?
    (b) the financial viability of the BBC?
    (c) the government's attitude to the BBC?
    (d) staff morale at the BBC?
5. How has the idea of the internal market been used in other parts of the public sector?

2 Warning British Gas

In May 1992 the OFGAS chairman (the regulator for British Gas affairs representing consumers and users) warned British Gas to cut its prices to domestic consumers or face court action. He claimed that British Gas had failed to honour an agreement made to reduce customers' bills. He demanded that 2p should be cut from each therm (the unit by which gas consumption is measured).

British Gas, however, indicated that it was reluctant to cut charges immediately, saying that it had honoured 'the spirit and the letter' of a formula controlling prices. The row followed hot on the heels of controversy over a 17.6 per cent pay rise for the company's chairman. Despite a fall in profits, his salary went up to £453 222 a year—an increase of £1252 a week—prompting a warning from the Prime Minister that company chairmen should show leadership on pay.

The OFGAS boss, Sir James McKinnon, stated that 'British Gas cannot get away with ripping off customers with its charges. A reduction is inevitable—to delay is totally unacceptable to us. People ought to get their money as soon as it becomes clear that they are entitled to it. If they do not do it now, we will enforce it,' Failure to reduce charges would leave the company open to action under the Gas Act.

1. Explain the following terms in the context of the above:
    (a) Chairman
    (b) OFGAS
    (c) Regulator
    (d) Gas Act
    (e) Court order
    (f) Gas consumption
2. Who is British Gas accountable to?
3. What restrictions are there on the ability of British Gas to raise prices?

4. How is British Gas in a powerful position in the market?
5. Why might British Gas feel justified in giving such a large salary to its chairman?
6. What arguments can be used (a) to support and (b) to contradict the Prime Minister's view that 'company chairmen should show leadership on pay'?
7. Should British Gas seek to maximize profits or to serve the wider community?

3 Involving the private sector in new roads

The Conservative government has been keen to involve the private sector in road schemes but has met little success. It has been able to attract private finance for estuary crossings, such as the QE II bridge from Thurrock to Dartford over the Thames and the second Severn crossing, only by giving contractors the old crossings on which they can charge tolls—a hidden subsidy.

In 1990 the government listed half a dozen schemes for which it hoped that private finance would be forthcoming, including a link between Chelmsford in Essex and the M25 and a link between the A1 and M1 at Scratchwood. However, private contractors were highly reluctant to become involved in such schemes. The only scheme where substantial progress has been made is the £500 million Birmingham northern relief road. Midlands Expressway has been granted a 53-year concession on the 26-mile road. It is hoped to be completed by the late 1990s without any public funds. Motorists using the relief road will be charged £1.50 per car and £3 per lorry at 1990 prices.

Generally contractors are reluctant to join such schemes. They say they require government grants to make the projects attractive.

1. Why do you think that the government wants the private sector to become involved in new road schemes?
2. Why do you think that the private sector appears to be reluctant to get involved in these schemes?
3. Why has the government found it easier to persuade the private sector to become involved in building estuary crossings?
4. Why do you think that a private-sector consortium is interested in building the Birmingham northern relief road?
5. Should the government subsidize road-building projects?
6. In many other European countries there are motorways on which motorists are charged a toll according to the distance they travel. Why do you think that it is difficult to persuade the private sector to become involved in such schemes in this country?

Suggested reading

Hurl, B., *Privatisation and the Public Sector*. Heinemann, 1988.
Lauton, A., and Rose, A., *Organisation and Management in the Public Sector*. Pitman, 1991.
Parker, D., *Privatisation and State Ownership*. Anforme, 1986.

8

The structure of organizations

Types of structure

All organizations have to work out a system for ongoing activities which are directed towards achieving given aims (Fig. 8.1). Regular activities such as deciding who will do what task, supervising the tasks and co-ordinating the various sectors of the organization are developed over time. Such regularities make up the organization's *structure*. Because activities can be organized in different ways, it is possible to have different structures. In this chapter we build on work begun in Chapters 3 and 4 exploring some of these possible structures. In doing so we draw on some important pieces of theory.

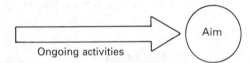

Figure 8.1 Business ongoing activities directed towards an aim.

Bureaucratic structures

Max Weber (1846–1920) set out a model of how a bureaucratic organization might operate which has served as a starting-point for the study of organizational society ever since.

Weber's model was developed at a time when large organizations were becoming increasingly important in industrial society. He argued that bureaucracies are the most functionally effective form of organization, although at times they operate in an 'inhuman way'.

Weber saw bureaucracies as representing the application of rational thought to practical problems in large industrial combines, in the civil service and in other important organizations (e.g. schools, churches, government departments). His model of bureaucracy was based on typical characteristics of such a form of organization (Fig. 8.2):

1. A set of offices (official positions) for the purpose of carrying out given organizational tasks, to be governed by a set of rules and procedures
2. A hierarchical structure of offices
3. Management based on office procedures, files, documents and office staff
4. The appointment of trained officials to take on roles within the bureaucracy

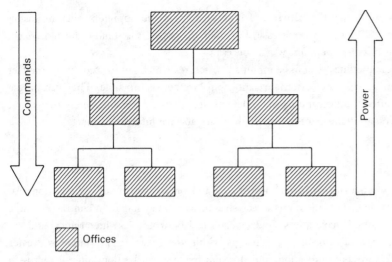

Figure 8.2 A bureaucratic structure.

Today, various forms of bureaucracy have become the dominant form of administration in political and economic systems in advanced industrial societies. Bureaucracy is the most rational form of social organization and dominates the structure of many business organizations.

The advantages of bureaucratic organization are that:

1. The application of a bureaucratic division of labour, combined with new technologies, has made possible massive increases in the production of goods and services.
2. Bureaucracy usually helps to create a predictable pattern for work cycles. People know what they are supposed to do, how they are supposed to do it and the extent of their responsibilities. Production targets can be set, and plans established to meet them.
3. Bureaucracy is often seen as being a 'fair' method of organization. Officials are appointed on the basis of qualifications, and the organization deals with individuals and groups with which it comes into contact on the basis of predetermined rules and procedures. Provided that officials stick to the rules, there should be no possibility of giving 'preferential treatment'.

However, a number of criticisms have been levelled at bureaucracies:

1. They are sometimes seen to be slow-moving, unimaginative organizations because of the way they stick to rules and procedures. Decisions may be arrived at slowly because they have to be processed through the 'right channels'.
2. Within a bureaucracy a displacement of goals might take place. Instead of bureaucrats focusing on the aims and purposes of the organization, they might become wrapped up in procedures. For example, a business might set itself the target of making a profit. In order to achieve this it will need to carry out a certain amount of documentary paperwork. However, if officials become engrossed in the paperwork and the procedures involved, insisting that orders are filled in using a certain method and processed by a certain

department, they might try the patience of both customers and suppliers, thereby losing business and profits. In the extreme case, bureaucratic procedures follow the old adage, 'The patient died but the operation was a success.'

3. Bureaucracies are sometimes seen to be inhuman structures which fail to account for the fact that many of their internal and external relationships are between people. They can have a depersonalizing effect, concentrating on relationships that are remote, anonymous and confined to rigorously defined topics rather than face-to-face informal contacts.

Organic structures

A basic distinction is often made between mechanistic and organic forms of organization. An example of the mechanistic form is the bureaucracy structure outlined above. In contrast, organic structures are less rule-bound, have a less rigid division of labour, are less hierarchical and are more open to the influence of informal relationships within the organization. There is greater emphasis on teamwork and communication, and decision-making can be done literally across a network. Teams can share power and responsibility. Figure 8.3 contrasts lines of communication and command in mechanistic and organic forms of organization.

Organic structures are most likely to occur in groups where there is a need to share common expertise and skills. Such a network may be found among high-level technicians or research workers in the oil or chemical industries. Alternatively, it may be found in an advertising agency, where one person's skill might be drawing, another's design and layout, a third's producing slogans and captions, and a fourth's finding the best media for getting a campaign across. In such a system, members of an organization are more likely to feel that their individual needs are being met. There is more of an opportunity for them to make an original contribution to decision-making and to feel that they are helping to shape organizational behaviour.

Organic approaches have also been successfully tried with manual workers. A frequently quoted example is that of Volvo's Kalmar plant, where assembly work has been broken down into 20 different functions. Each function is performed by a team of between 15 and 20 workers. The cars pass along from team to team on trolleys, allowing workers considerable freedom of movement. Teams work collaboratively, sharing work and ideas. They tackle problems together.

This process of organic team building is very important in a number of Japanese companies. For example, the tractor manufacturer Komatsu aims to create a group spirit in its workforce at its greenfield site in Newcastle. The company has tried to keep terms and conditions the same for

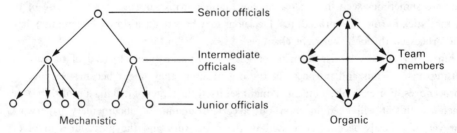

Figure 8.3 Mechanistic and organic organizational structures.

everybody. Everyone wears the same uniform, exercises in the morning, starts and finishes at the same time and is entitled to the same sick pay and pension schemes. The aim behind this is to create a feeling of commonality and commitment. Groups of workers are organized in quality circles, with joint responsibility for identifying problems and coming up with solutions.

Although mechanistic (bureaucratic) and organic systems are in some ways in competition with each other, they often appear side by side in different parts of the same company. Mechanistic systems are often best suited for the pursuit of clear goals in the stable conditions, such as producing a standard product for a market in which demand is constant. Organic systems are most effective where conditions of demand, competition, production and other factors cannot be readily predicted.

Theories of organizational structure

Systems theory

Systems theory is used to explore the ways in which different organizational structures respond to the types of change outlined above. In a rapidly changing technological society, it is likely that organizations will need to change their structures frequently.

Interaction theory

Interactionist theory is concerned with studying the human side of organizations and the way in which individuals and groups interact with each other. Interactionists explore the meanings and values that individuals attach to life in organizations. They scratch beneath the surface of organization charts, official rules and procedures to study real human relations. Interactionist studies of individuals in prisons, mental hospitals and other organizations have revealed that, in order to understand how individual members of an organization (e.g. inmates) feel about their position, it is often necessary to challenge official definitions of what is going on.

Conflict theory

Conflict theory is based on the premiss that there is an underlying conflict of interest in society between classes or groups. In capitalist societies, for example (e.g. the United Kingdom, the United States), there is a fundamental division between the owners of productive resources (e.g. factory owners, shareholders) and their employees.

Karl Marx (1818–83) and other conflict theorists believe that power is used by groups to further their own class interests. The basic power structure of society is therefore reflected in organizational structures. The purpose of most organizations is to organize the labour process.

At one level, this sort of analysis can lead to broad views of the world economy. For example, Wallerstein suggests that economic and social analysis should concern itself with the *capitalist world economy* rather than focusing narrowly on national societies. This view is based on the belief that the organization of capitalism is an international phenomenon.

Other studies of organizational conflict focus on relationships within industrial units. For example, the extreme fragmentation of the labour process in industrial and office work can be seen as one way of controlling the labour force because employees are no longer able to grasp the production process as a whole. Conflict theory is thus concerned with developing an analysis of power relations within organizations and of underlying conflicts of interest.

Organizational architecture

The term 'organizational architecture' refers to managers' more general views about their organizations and how they are structured. It focuses particularly on how traditional departments and more informal project teams can fit together, and on the role of work-teams.

Nowadays there is a lot of emphasis on the *work-team*. The idea is that business is really a series of projects carried out by small groups of people with complementary skills. This is a continuation of the movement away from the 'tall' or bureaucratic structure of organizations, which divides businesses into clearly defined functions such as finance and marketing (Fig. 8.4). In many companies today there is a movement to flatten out the organizational structure (Fig. 8.5).

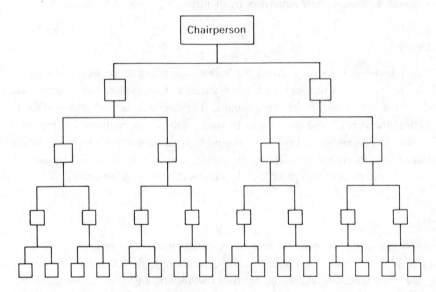

Figure 8.4 A tall organizational structure.

'Tall' organizations suffer from all of the problems of bureaucracy outlined on page 173-174. Giving independence to work-teams in 'flatter' organizations unleashes creativity and flexibility which are required in a dynamic world. Information technology provides instant access to information for all members of the modern work-team.

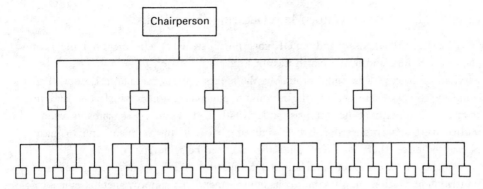

Figure 8.5 A flat organizational structure.

Total quality management

Total quality management (TQM) is a method of eliminating production faults through a philosophy of continuous improvement in every process of planning, production and service. It entails a continual raising of standards by management.

Some management consultants believe you can improve the performance and quality of a company through one all-embracing reorganization. However, the American originators of the TQM idea, W. Edwards Deming and Joseph Juran, insist that improving the quality of products and management is a never-ending process. They also maintain that the drive for quality control must come from the top of a company, and that management is responsible for 85 per cent of production faults.

Ironically, these ideas were at first ignored in the West but they were adopted in Japan. It was only the obvious success of Japanese companies that has forced Western managers to pay attention to them more recently.

Quality circles

An organization can attempt to motivate employees by developing special groups or teams called quality circles. Quality circles are typically small groups of seven or eight people who voluntarily meet on a regular basis to identify, investigate, analyse and resolve quality-related matters or other work-related arrangements using problem-solving techniques. Members tend to be from the same work area or to do similar work.

Quality circles have been particularly effective in Japanese industry, where they have been responsible for loyalty coupled with high productivity.

Case Study—Nissan Motor Manufacturing (UK) Ltd

On 1 February 1984, Nissan and the UK government signed an agreement to build a car plant near Sunderland in the North East of England.

Nissan's objective is to build, profitably, the highest-quality car sold in Europe. The company also wants to achieve the maximum possible customer satisfaction and to ensure the prosperity of the enterprise and its staff. To this end, Nissan aims to achieve mutual trust and co-operation between all employees in the company and to make Nissan the place where long-term job satisfaction can be achieved.

Nowadays, *kaizen* is a word much used in Sunderland. It is a Japanese term, the literal translation of which is simply 'continuous improvement'. The improvement is gained by slow and steady change, and once achieved it is maintained at that level until such time as the next step of improvement takes place.

During the 1950s Japanese industry made great efforts to improve the image of its product quality. These efforts were assisted by two prominent American specialists who visited Japan. In 1962 the first quality circles were formed. Currently Nissan in Japan has over 4000 quality circles. Throughout Japan there are over 10 million members of quality circles.

At Nissan's UK plant the *kaizen* programme has been developed as a replacement for periodic quality circle activity. It encourages constant quality awareness and is better suited to the needs and aspirations of the British workforce. *Kaizen* assumes the total involvement of all employees but recognizes that participation depends on individuals genuinely feeling part of the Nissan team. The company policy is that:

1. All staff have a valuable contribution to make as individuals, and this contribution can be most effective within a team environment.
2. *Kaizen* team activity helps to develop leadership and presentation skills as well as enabling people to understand, acknowledge and learn from others.
3. *Kaizen* is one way in which employees may participate in issues that affect their workplace.

The *kaizen* philosophy may be applied anywhere at any time. Everyone is encouraged to participate and, as members of a team, to learn how to analyse situations logically and factually and discuss issues meaningfully and efficiently. People who contribute to the activity include:

- *Leaders*, who receive special training in the *kaizen* process and then apply these skills to team activities
- *Members who participate in the activities*, often from the same work unit or area
- *Specialists*, who assist a team with a particular project

A steering committee develops the policies and guidelines under which the activity operates.

The *kaizen* process is designed to enable a team to move on from the stage of dealing with current problems or areas in need of improvement to the point where sources of concern are dealt with before they happen.

Questions

1. What advantages does the quality circle approach have over a bureaucratic form of organization?
2. How can the *kaizen* approach improve employee motivation?
3. What are the likely benefits to an organization of adopting the *kaizen* approach?
4. Why does Nissan want its employees to feel a part of the team?
5. Are there any weaknesses that you can see in the *kaizen* approach?

Fordist versus Japanese organizational structures

The term 'Fordism' has come to be associated with mass manufacturing organizations using high-volume output of standardized products with specialist machinery, and extensive stocks of spare parts, in a 'tall' organizational structure with clearly defined responsibilities and roles. In recent years such organizations have been characterized by poor productivity and have been replaced with 'leaner'-style, i.e. 'flatter' organizations. Japanese companies gain a competitive edge by using only the bare minimum of human and material resources, keeping minimum stocks, reducing trade union influence in the workplace and building work-teams with considerably devolved responsibilities.

Process re-engineering

'Process re-engineering' is a term used to describe ways of fundamentally changing the design of an organization. Tied in with the idea of the 'flat' organization, it calls for the overhaul of job descriptions (see Chapter 19), organizational structures and management systems. By involving people from all areas of an organization at an early stage, business objectives such as the launch of a new product will be achieved more quickly and at a lower cost by going through things one step at a time, for example designing, engineering and marketing.

Organizational 'culture'

Organizations are as individual as nations and societies. They have widely differing *cultures*, and these are reflected in their values, ideals and beliefs. The culture of an organization influences the way in which it operates, so it is necessary to understand the culture before deciding how people might contribute to the success or failure of the organization.

Put in simple terms, the culture of an organization can be defined as:

'The Way We Do Things Here!'

Organizational cultures determine the way in which things get done, for example:

- The way newcomers are welcomed to the organization
- Approaches to new technology?
- Approaches to work
- Attention to detail

Types of organizational culture

Cultures are built up over years by the dominant groups in an organization. We shall consider four main types (Fig. 8.6).

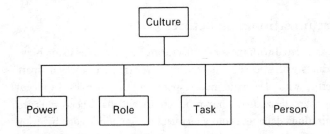

Figure 8.6 Types of organizational culture.

The power culture

Centralization of power is the key feature of this type of culture. It is frequently found in small entrepreneurial organizations where control rests with a single individual or a small group of individuals.

The structure of the power culture is best illustrated as a web (Fig. 8.7). There is a central power source and rays of influence spread out from that centre. In this type of organization the emphasis is on individuals rather than on group decision-making. Decisions can therefore be made quickly.

There is a weakness, however, in that, because the organization is autocratic, people may feel suppressed and demotivated by the lack of challenge. Size is also a problem; the 'web' can break if it tries to support too many activities.

The role culture

The role culture is typical of bureaucracies. An organization is arranged according to a set of functions that are determined by rules and procedures governing the way work should be carried

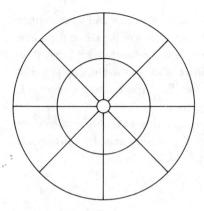

Figure 8.7 The web-shaped power culture.

out. The organization functions by logic and reason, and the simple diagram depicting this type of culture (Fig. 8.8) bears a resemblance to the temple of Apollo, the Greek god of reason.

In a role culture, power is hierarchical and is determined by the employee's position in the organization. Its strength lies in its 'pillars' or functions—e.g. the marketing department or the finance department. The interaction of these 'pillars' is determined by job descriptions and set communication procedures.

In this type of organization the job description is more important than the person who fills it, and performance over and above the role is not required. Position is the main source of power, and rules and procedures are the main source of influence.

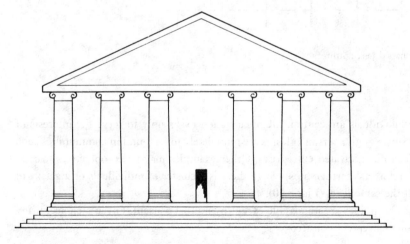

Figure 8.8 The shape of the role culture.

The task culture

A task culture is job- or project-orientated and places emphasis on completing a specific task. It is a team culture. It is the task that determines the way in which the work is organized, rather than individuals or the rules of the organization.

A task culture can be illustrated by a net of which some strands are thicker and stronger than others (Fig. 8.9). Much of the power and influence lies at the interstices of the net at the knots.

The *matrix* is a form of task culture. It brings together people and resources and is based on expertise rather than on position or personal power. The matrix relies on the unifying power of the group to complete a specific task. Teams are formed for specific purposes and are afterwards dispersed allowing the system to be flexible to short-term needs.

In a task culture employees have considerable freedom, and this flexibility makes them rewarding environments to work in. However, lack of formal authority and the considerable number of 'strands' can make management and control of the task culture difficult.

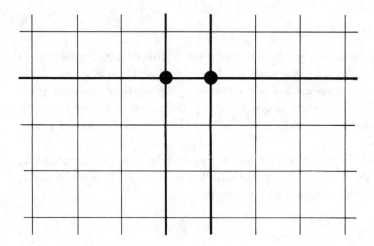

Figure 8.9 The net-shaped task culture.

The person culture

In a person culture individuals are central; the organization exists only to serve the interests of those within it. Nor surprisingly, person cultures are more likely to be found in communities such as *kibbutzim* than in profit-motivated enterprises. Other examples may be co-operatives, barristers' chambers and architects' partnerships, where there is a cluster of individuals or a galaxy of stars all operating at the same level (Fig. 8.10).

In a person culture hiearchies are impossible except by mutual consent. Given a choice, many people would opt for this type of culture.

Cultural changes

Most organizations start with power cultures. Then, as they mature and become less dependent upon the founder, they tend to become role cultures. When the role culture needs greater flexibility, there might be a further change towards a task culture to fit the requirements and needs of each part of the organization.

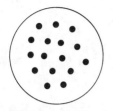

Figure 8.10 The person culture.

Stakeholders in an organization

In most organizations groups of individuals can be identified who have similar interests and shared expectations. We can call these groups *stakeholders*—for example managers, banks, shareholders, unions. When the BBC was restructured in the early 1990s it soon became apparent that there were a number of stakeholders with different views—the government, the managers of the corporation, employees' unions and programme-makers, among others.

Coalitions occur between stakeholders as a result of events. They may be formed between departments, geographical locations, different levels in the hierarchy or different age groups. For example, as a result of proposed cutbacks at the BBC, a coalition arose between programme makers and trade unionists worried about changes being imposed by managers.

Most individuals will belong to a number of coalitions. In order to have influence in decision-making, they will need to identify with the goals of these coalitions. Coalitions will exist both internally and externally to an organization.

Management

Managers have considerable power in an organization and we will look at these powers in greater depth in Chapter 9 on decision-making.

Henri Fayol was one of the first people to try to work out what managers should do and how they should do it. In 1916, after spending many years thinking about his job as a manager, he published a small book called *General Industrial Management*. In this book he identified five functions of management (Fig. 8.11):

- *Planning*—looking ahead and making provision for the future
- *Organizing*—making sure an organization has everything it needs and is managing its resources
- *Command*—directing and managing people
- *Co-ordination*—harmonizing activities to achieve successful results
- *Control*—making sure things happen the way they were planned

Power within an organization

Power in an organization can be acquired in a number of ways. The following are important sources of power:

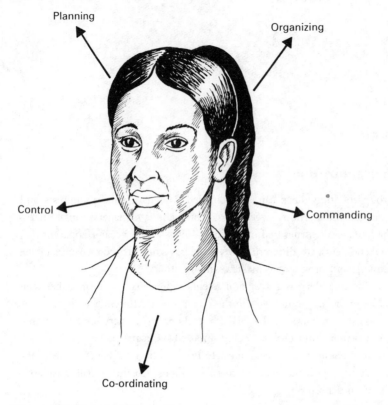

Planning

Organizing

Control

Commanding

Co-ordinating

Figure 8.11 The role of the manager.

1. *Hierarchy* Being at the top of an organization gives one considerable formal power. However, in many cases these powers do not exist when it comes to the crunch, e.g. in a dispute over wages and conditions.
2. *Influence* Having influence over others is very important. This can be gained through the personality of a leader (charismatic leadership) or alternatively, because of the way things are done. Influence can be enhanced by good communication skills and persuasive techniques.
3. *Control of key resources* Having access to key resources gives one considerable power. For example, in a business that depends on research and development, the R&D team has considerable powers; when labour is in short supply in a period of full employment, then trade unions are strong; accountants are usually regarded to have a lot of power in organization because of their control of the purse-strings.
4. *Knowledge/skills* Some individuals are indispensible, for example the star footballer in a team, or the employee that 'knows the ropes'.
5. *Control of the environment* Members of an organization that have the best understanding of the environment in which the organization is operating have considerable power. For example, members of the marketing department and the finance department often occupy this vantage point; other members of the organization are therefore dependent on their overall view.

6. *Exercising discretion*   Some members of organizations have power because the nature of their jobs allows them to exercise their discretion in making certain decisions.

Sources of power for external stakeholders

There are also many external stakeholders in an organization. Their power arises from a number of sources; for example:

1. *Resource dependence*   The organization may be dependent in many ways on the resources it needs, such as stocks and raw materials from a supplier, or loan capital from a bank. This power can be extensive; for example, a bank can demand repayment of a loan.
2. *Involvement in implementation*   Suppliers, distributors and other groups make an important contribution to the value chain (see page 71), and can be indispensable.
3. *Knowledge and skills*   Consultants and contractors may have knowledge and skills that are crucial to an organization's activities.
4. *Internal links*   External stakeholders such as members of the board of directors in some instances may play an important part in the decision-making processes of an organization.

Questions

Short-answer questions

1. List five features of a bureaucracy.
2. What organizations might be run effectively as bureaucracies?
3. What are the advantages of bureaucracy?
4. Draw a diagram to illustrate the difference between a mechanistic and an organic form of organization.
5. What are informal relationships within an organization?
6. Under what conditions are organic forms of organization most likely to exist?
7. What are (a) 'flat' and (b) 'tall' organizational structures?
8. What is total quality management?
9. Describe the organization of a quality circle.
10. What is *kaizen*?
11. Contrast a 'Fordist' with a Japanese organizational structure in the car industry.
12. Explain the term 'process re-engineering'.
13. What is a power culture?
14. Show how a power culture can be represented as a web.
15. Explain the term 'role culture'. Give examples.
16. What is a task culture?
17. What sorts of organization are most likely to be hierarchical?
18. What are the advantages and disadvantages of a person culture?
19. How do organizational cultures change over time?
20. Why might a bureaucracy be regarded as a 'fair' method or organization?

Essays

1. The 1990s model organization needs to be able to compete in the new global 'corporate Olympics'. It needs to be lean and fit. Explain and discuss this assertion.
2. What is meant by the 'culture' of an organization? Use examples to explain your answer.
3. Bureaucracy is the most efficient form of organization. Discuss.
4. Why are organizations becoming increasingly 'flat'?
5. Compare and contrast examples of mechanistic and organic organizational structures.
6. How can an organization benefit from involving its employees in decision-making processes?
7. What is the 'best' type of organizational culture?
8. How can quality circles help organizations to be more effective?
9. What is a work-team? How can work-teams contribute to organizational goals?
10. What is meant by organizational structure? Why do organizations have different structures?

Data response questions

1   Sir Philip Harris

On the early death of his father, Philip Harris decided to make a go of the three carpet shops that he had inherited from him. He expanded the business, adding shop after shop, and learned everything there was to know about the carpet business.

In the process, Harris revolutionized the selling of carpets. To cut costs, he virtually invented the computerized carpet-cutting machine. When an order is received, this machine reduces a huge roll of carpet to the customer's size in seconds.

In 1978 Harris Queensway became a public company. Harris owned most of the business and was a millionaire at 36. In 1988 he agreed to sell Harris Queensway for £450 million. This was just before a major recession. If he had held on to the company he would have lost out, as its value on the stock market tumbled.

After sailing his yacht round the Mediterranean for a year, Harris set up another business called Carpetland with just one shop in 1989. This company has continued to expand and in 1993 became a major public company. It remains to be seen whether he can build a successful carpet empire once again.

One commentator said: 'He is an intuitive business genius, but he ran Harris Queensway like a court, not like a public company. When a business grows you can't write all the cheques and you can't visit every shop every weekend. When you get big it's all about managing people, not about managing carpets.'

1. What benefits would be gained from becoming a public company?
2. Comment on the statement, 'When you get big it's all about managing people and not about managing carpets.'
3. What type of organizational culture does the above profile indicate results from Philip Harris's management style?

4. What are the advantages and disadvantages of this type of organizational culture for a public company?

5. What other forms of organizational culture might be appropriate for Carpetland?

2   A time of change at the BBC

John Birt took over as director general of the BBC in January 1993. He immediately promised to create an effective BBC which would clear away red tape, territorialism and confusion.

The BBC's television services had overspent by £38 million in 1992. Mr Birt therefore said that a priority was to appoint a new finance director. Key structural changes would include:

- Streamlining the operation to focus on aims and objectives, policy and performance
- The separation of programme production from commissioning and scheduling in television and radio, and the buying in of programmes from a range of sources
- The creation of separate resources, engineering and service departments to run the production side of the BBC.

So began the process of contracting out, reducing staff numbers, increasing productivity and rationalizing studios and properties.

John Birt prepared an all-embracing plan to take the BBC into a new world. Change was to be seen to be as important a part of the BBC's culture as was the aim to inform, educate and entertain. The architecture was created to highlight the progress, or lack of it, on a range of objectives. The emphasis that Birt wanted to make was that programmes are the supreme objective, but only if price and purpose is right.

The BBC has only recently begun to move from a culture of 'We know best; we are the best; we'll make it all ourselves; our size is our strength; what happens outside is their business.' Under Birt, the Corporation is coming to realize that it has much to learn from competitors and that size can be a weakness. In a document called *Extending Choice*, the new management team at the BBC has set out an agenda of distinctiveness, value for money and accountability.

The first two of these are generally accepted by most people. The concern comes over accountability. The BBC is criticized for seeming inattention to what the public wants and requires. For example, there is a complaint that it has been too highbrow, concentrating on a minority upmarket taste. Competitors resent the BBC being (as they see it) unfairly subsidized by the government.

Birt has set the standard he would like to see for the BBC. He wants it to be the 'best managed public institution in the UK'. This is necessary if the BBC is to be granted a new charter, and if it is to receive substantial moneys out of the licence fees that the public pays for television viewing.

However, the new regime at the BBC has been the subject of criticism. This was typified in a talk given by the broadcaster Mark Tully in July 1993. Tully claimed that an iron structure has been set in place in news and current affairs programming to restrict producers' freedom, and to ensure that they conform to what is known as 'Birtism'. He attacked the new 'internal market' accounting methods which put a greater premium on bureaucracy than creativity. Under this scheme, one part of the BBC must buy services from another at the full cost of the service (e.g. for using library services). Tully said: 'Accountants can easily argue that the whole management structure was too expensive, but it was that structure which preserved the independence of the various parts of the BBC and prevented the emergence of over-powerful director-generals.' He went on to argue that 'a broadcasting organization which depends so much on individual human talent needs to have some flexibility, perhaps even an element of chaos, to allow for experimenters and eccentrics.'

1. What do you think is meant by an 'effective' BBC?
2. What type of culture is Birt trying to create at the BBC?
3. How does this clash with the previous culture?
4. What new objectives has Birt tried to establish at the BBC?
5. What stakeholders in the BBC are identified in the above analysis?
6. What coalitions of stakeholders have arisen at the BBC?
7. What factors will determine who has the power and how much power they have at the BBC?
8. What difficulties is Birt likely to encounter in attempting to change the culture at the BBC?
9. Is it necessary to change the existing culture at the BBC?
10. How can the value chain at the BBC be best enhanced?
11. What is meant by creating an 'architecture for monitoring objectives' at the BBC?

Suggested reading

Dorton, I., and Smith, A., *A Student's Guide to Business Studies*. Hodder & Stoughton, 1992.
Griffin, R., and Ebert, R., *Business*, 3rd edn. Prentice-Hall, 1993.
Needham, D., and Dransfield, R., *Business and Finance*. Heinemann Educational, 1993.

9

Decision-makers and types of decision-making

Individuals, groups and organizations need to make new decisions continually. Decision-making is a central feature of business activity. This chapter sets out to explore some of the major types of business decision, and to look at some of the tools that are available to help in making business decisions.

Quantitive techniques frequently help the decision-making process. However, there are many activities and decisions that need to be taken which cannot be reduced to numbers. Sound judgement is therefore required in business decision-making, along with an ability to consider various alternatives and points of view.

Who are the decision-makers?

In the previous chapter we saw that there are many possible organizational structures. In most organizations there will be several layers of decision-making. In modern businesses it is important that all managers are able to take the initiative and make some decisions for themselves. For example, in a large oil company operating over a wide geographical area and producing in a variety of product markets, it is essential for decisions to be made quickly by managers 'on the ground' (Fig. 9.1). Decisions require the 'sounding out' of opinions from many specialists and generalists,

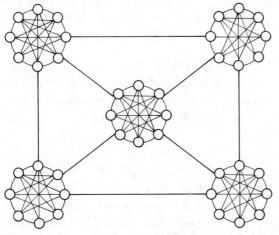

Figure 9.1 Networks of geographically dispersed decision-making units.

from researchers and computer programmers to maintenance operatives. The ability of individuals to make a contribution to the decision-making process depends very much on their ability to question existing views, to challenge the meaning of data and to ask relevant questions.

Employees who do what they are told are often valued. However, organizations will operate more effectively and produce the best long-term results when employees think for themselves and produce fresh ideas in changing situations. The petrol pump attendant is a decision-maker as well as the managing director of a company.

There are four groups of decision-makers within a company: shareholders, directors, managers and other employees. These groupings are not exclusive; for example, an employee might also be a shareholder (Fig. 9.2).

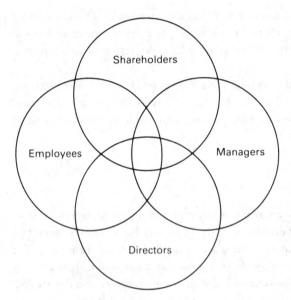

Figure 9.2 Decision-makers within a company.

Shareholders

Shareholders are part owners of a company. They elect the board of directors to represent them.

Shareholders have more influence in some companies than in others, and more in some countries than in others. For example, in Germany many of the major companies list only about 25 per cent of their ordinary shares for public trading; the ordinary shareholder therefore has very little power. In the United Kingdom most large companies list the majority of their ordinary shares. During the 1990s shareholders have become increasingly vociferous about how they would like to see companies run.

However, in some companies shareholders feel remote from policy-making decisions. The law requires a meeting of shareholders once a year, but because the Annual General Meeting involves complex procedures such as the presentation of the accounts, few shareholders feel fully in control at such meetings. Other companies, such as Shell UK, arrange informal meetings of shareholders at conference centres, where the everyday business of the company is explained; shareholders are given opportunities to ask questions and to discuss matters of interest or concern with senior company officials at a buffet reception.

Directors

Directors represent the interests of shareholders. Executive directors play managerial roles within the company, while non-executive directors add a breadth of experience to board meetings. Non-executive directors might also represent important shareholding interests, for example when a pension fund has a large shareholding in a company.

The role of the board is to make the important policy decisions and to make sure that they are carried out. The board will deal on its own with relationships with other companies, but takeovers and mergers will require the approval of the shareholders.

Managers

A manager leads and guides others in an organization. The task of the manager is to co-ordinate and direct work towards certain objectives. The manager will plan for anticipated or unanticipated changes.

Henry Mintzberg regards the most important part of managerial activity as that which is concerned with decision-making. He identifies four classes of decisions (Fig. 9.3), depending on the role that a manager is playing:

- Entrepreneur
- Disturbance handler
- Resource allocator
- Negotiator

As *entrepreneurs*, managers will make decisions about changing what is happening in an organization. They may have to introduce change and also to take part in deciding what actually is to be done. In principle they are acting voluntarily. For example, a sales manager might identify opportunities that would result from diversifying into new countries and new brands.

This is very different from the manager's role as a *disturbance handler*, where decisions have to be made because of events that are beyond the manager's control—for example, when an overseas country in which your company sells products suddenly raises import restrictions. The manager needs to have the skill to make an appropriate response to such a disturbance.

The *resource allocation* role of the manager is a key part of organizational management. Managers need to make decisions about how to allocate money, people, equipment, time and other resources. Mintzberg points out that in the resource allocation role the manager schedules time, programmes work and authorizes actions.

In the *negotiator's* role the manager has to negotiate with others, and in the process be able to make decisions about the commitment or organizational roles.

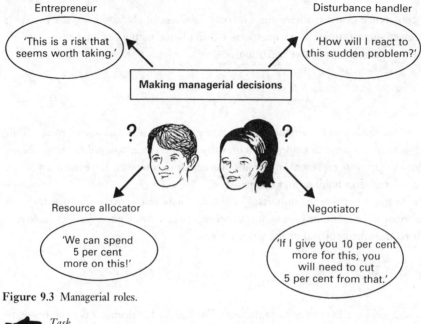

Figure 9.3 Managerial roles.

 Task

Joe Brown owns his own company producing shoes and handbags. Which of the decision-making roles outlined above is he exhibiting in each of the following examples?

1. Joe decides to branch out into producing football boots.
2. Joe decides that employees will spend less time on producing handbags and more producing shoes.
3. Joe bargains with the employees' trade union over a proposed pay settlement. The pay settlement will involve a reduction in capital expenditure.
4. Joe has to respond to a new government law limiting the number of hours that his employees can work.
5. Joe decides to purchase a rival outfit.
6. Joe decides to devote more time on making the company a success.

Employees

All employees will have a part to play in everyday decision-making. This may include the way that a work task is carried out, the way in which customers are treated and many other aspects of working life. Employees will normally report to a line manager.

Types of decision-making

Most classifications of types of decision are based upon the predictability of decisions. For example, Herbert Simon made an important distinction between programmed and non-programmed decisions.

Programmed decisions are straightforward, repetitive and routine, so that they can be dealt with by a formal pattern, e.g. the re-ordering of stock by a company. Non-programmed decisions are novel, unstructured and consequential. There is no cut-and-dried method for handling situations which have not arisen before.

Simon thought that these two types of decision were ends of a continuum, with all shades of grey lying in between.

Gilligan, Neale and Murray, in their book *Business Decision Making*, extend this analysis to identify three types of decision that managers might encounter depending on the degree of certainty or uncertainty associated with the outcome, the time period involved, the frequency with which decisions have to be made, the extent to which the subject is routine or non-routine and the implications of the decision for the organization:

1. *Short-term operating control decisions*   These are decisions that have to be frequently made involving short-term, predictable operations such as the ordering of new stock, the design of a production schedule or the preparation of a transport route for deliveries.
2. *Periodic control decisions*   These are made less frequently and are concerned with monitoring how effectively an organization is managing its resources. Such decisions might include the review of pricing strategies for certain products, the review of problems occurring in an ongoing company budget or the reappraisal of the way in which the sales force is being used. These decisions are concerned with checking for and rectifying problems concerned with meeting company objectives.
3. *Strategic decisions*   These are major decisions involving overall strategy. They will often require a considerable exercise of judgement by the person responsible for making this type of decision, because, although such decisions will require a considerable amount of analysis, important pieces of information will frequently be missing and so risk will be involved. Examples would include the development of a new product, investment in new plant or the development of a new marketing strategy.

Levels of decision-making

The structure of the decision-making process needs to be based on the types of decision that need to be made. The most obvious implication is that routine decisions are dealt with by routine procedures and that time and money are not wasted unnecessarily on them. There would be no point, for example, in a senior manager spending large amounts of time on a routine task that could be done by someone with less experience. By the same token, decisions requiring in-depth analysis and thought will require careful consideration by someone with a depth and breadth of experience.

Organizations therefore need to develop procedures for decision-making most suited to the nature of the environment in which they are operating. Gilligan, Neale and Murray recommend that, in broad terms,

> short-term operating and periodic control decisions should be made by junior and middle management who are involved in the day-to-day administration of the organisation, and not by the company's senior

management. The task of senior management is to concentrate upon non-routine, non-recurring, strategic decisions in which there is a high degree of uncertainty regarding the outcome and for which, as a consequence, a far greater element of judgement and creativity is required. In those organisations in which senior management does become embroiled in the day-to-day, straightforward operating decisions, the effectiveness and motivation of lower levels of management is likely to suffer, whilst at the same time, because of the preoccupation with short-term decisions, less time is available for long-term issues, with the result that the managerial focus switches from long-range strategic development of the company to short-range control.

Thus, insofar as it is possible to generalise, the primary concern of senior management should be with strategic decisions, whilst short-term operational decisions should be left in the hands of operating management. Middle management then acts as the meeting point between the two, taking as its focus the periodic control decisions.

Strategic decision-making

In recent years a very strong emphasis has been given in business studies to strategic decisions. Johnson and Scholes, in their key text *Exploring Corporate Strategy*, identify the following characteristics of strategy:

1. Strategic decisions are likely to be concerned with the *scope of an organization's activities*. For example, does the organization concentrate on one segment of the chocolate market, or does it concentrate on a wide variety of sweets, confectionery, ice creams, etc.? The decision about the scope of an organization's activities is vital, because it establishes the boundaries in which the organization operates.
2. Strategy is to do with the *matching of the activities of an organization to its environment*. For example, does an organization operate in a local, national or Europe-wide market? Clearly, this decision is of key importance in deciding a range of other matters, such as how the product is marketed, or what finance is required. An organization needs to weigh up the opportunities and threats presented by the environment in which it operates, for example the opportunity of increased sales, or the threat of increased competition in a wider market.
3. Strategy is concerned with a *matching of the organization's activities to its resource capability*. Clearly, the business needs to understand its resource limitations if it is to make the best use of opportunities. An organization that fails to invest in new technology may rapidly fall behind because of a capital resource deficiency.
4. Strategic decisions therefore have *major resource implications*. Decisions need to be made to ensure that the organization has the most appropriate resources to move forward. For example, in the late 1980s Mars moved into ice cream in order to compensate for the fall in sales of chocolate bars in the summer months. This required a considerable research programme and tooling the company up in new capital equipment.
5. Strategic decisions are likely to *affect operational decisions*. In the above example, when Mars moved into ice cream it needed to set in motion a whole new training programme for employees, as well as making changes to sales and distribution methods.

6. The strategy of an organization will be affected by the *values and expectations* of those who have power in the organization. Those groupings of stakeholders that have most influence in the organization will be able to shape the strategy according to their values and expectations. For example, an influential group of senior managers and directors may have a vision of their company expanding to dominate a market.
7. Strategic decisions are likely to affect the *long-term direction* of a company; they tend to involve thinking about where the organization is going in the longer period.
8. Strategic decisions are usually *complex*. This complexity arises because such decisions usually involve a high degree of uncertainty. They are likely to require an integrated approach involving all elements of the organization. They are also likely to require and involve major changes in the organization.

It is no wonder, therefore, that so much emphasis is placed on strategic decision-making. Strategic management is a highly complex process requiring a lot of information and the ability and foresight to consider many variables and possible scenarios in a dynamic business environment. It entails deciding on a strategy and planning how that strategy will be put into effect.

There are three main elements to strategic management:

1. Strategic *analysis* is concerned with understanding the strategic position of a company. (What is our scope of operation? How can we match our activities to our environment? How can we match our activities to our resource capability? etc.)
2. Strategic *choice* involves:
    (a) setting out a menu of strategic options;
    (b) evaluating strategic options provided by the menu;
    (c) selecting a strategy that is 'best' for the organization.
3. Strategic *implementation* involves putting the chosen strategy into action.

Figure 9.4 The tripartite strategy management process.

An open-systems decisions model

Many of the decisions that need to be made by individuals within organizations involve uncertainty. In a complex, dynamic society change is ever present. In such an environment it is helpful to develop an open-system approach to decision-making. A closed-systems approach would assume that organizations have clearly defined and unambiguous goals.

An open-systems approach dispenses with the notion that the effects of decisions can readily be computed and calculated and instead works on the premise that at best information will be imperfect. An open–systems model places emphasis on feedback, learning and adaptation together with the effects of this upon ends and means.

An open–systems approach can be used to show how the decision-making process can be made more flexible. The system can then adjust to changing circumstances and to changing perceptions and understanding of the meaning of available information.

Figure 9.5 illustrates one way in which an open-systems model might operate. The first stage involves the identification of the objectives to be pursued. These will rarely be clear-cut and therefore will be subject to review. Thus, it can be seen that setting objectives involves setting out courses of action that will be appropriate to the organization, and establishing measures for assessing their attainment.

The second stage, in the decision cycle is to outline some of the possible courses of action, and to evaluate them in various ways using available information. Evaluation processes will range from an inspired guess to a highly researched piece of analysis and assessment. For example, a marketing department might want to carry out a SWOT analysis of existing and/or potential products in order to identify strengths and weaknesses. (A *SWOT analysis* is an analysis of the Strengths, Weaknesses, Opportunities and Threats of a product or a particular course of action.)

The next stage in the decision-making cycle involves comparing the likely results of alternative courses of action with the desired level of performance. At this stage you have already established your performance objectives. You should now be asking questions such as, If we do X how close will we be to achieving our target?

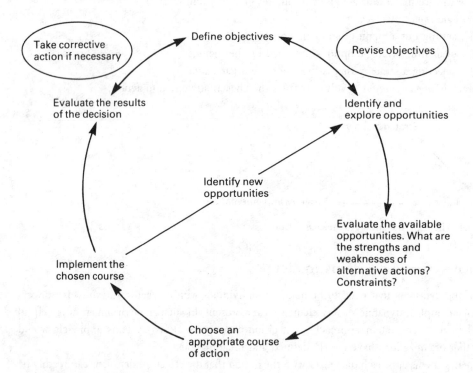

Figure 9.5 The decision cycle.

Provided there is a match, the decision-maker can then choose the most effective of the alternative courses of action that have been identified given the initial objectives. If a firm's objective is to achieve some measure of guaranteed success, it might choose a course of action that avoids risk. Alternatively it might be prepared to take a risk if the objective is to gamble on high returns.

If the chosen course of action does not look likely to meet the required objectives, the decision-maker should either reduce the target goal to manageable proportions or seek alternative courses of action to meet the original target.

Once the groundwork has been covered and all aspects of potential decisions have been 'kicked around', a decision can be made. The effects of the decision should then be clearly monitored. Putting the decision into practice may quickly lead to the identification of new opportunities. For example, once the early space programme had been implemented, researchers immediately became aware of fresh opportunities such as the Space Shuttle. These possibilities will help organizations to meet their objectives in new and different ways.

The results of decisions will need to be clearly appraised and evaluated to improve the decision-making process. Corrective action can be taken if necessary.

The decision-making cycle is an ongoing process. The open-ended nature of the process means that the quality of decisions should increase with time.

The open-systems approach highlights the importance of evaluation to decision-making. Results need to be continually fed back to decision-makers so that they can re-appraise decisions in the light of an increasing quantity and quality of information. Feedback can lead to adjustment. A simple illustration of how this can have beneficial effects is in the training of young cricketers using computer programs that simulate their bowling action. Programs have been developed which will play back to a bowler a picture of his action in bowling a cricket ball. The young cricketer is thereby provided with feedback on current performance, enabling him to take corrective action, to appraise his existing technique and to develop an understanding of new possibilities.

The nine-phase decision-making process

Ernest Archer studied over 2000 managers, executives and supervisors, as well as the research of major writers on organizations. He produced a decision-making framework which highlighted the decision-maker's need to monitor continually the environment in which decisions are made (Fig. 9.6). This necessitates obtaining feedback on any deviations from expected, acceptable, pre-planned or normal states.

1.   First, it is essential that managers have a clear idea of how things 'ought to be'.

The other eight stages involve the following tasks:

2.   *Define* the decision or problem to be tackled and clearly state the boundaries.
3.   *Specify* the objectives of the decision. What do you expect to achieve? What are the constraints?

4. *Diagnose* the problem or situation and analyse its causes.
5. *Develop* a range of alternative solutions and courses of action.
6. *Establish* criteria for weighing up alternatives.
7. *Appraise* the alternative solutions or courses of action.
8. *Choose* the best solution.
9. *Implement* the best solution or course of action.

In the modern business environment there are many factors that encourage the growth of group decision-making.

In the first place, the modern business environment is so complicated that effective decision-making now requires groups of minds working together to tackle problems and think things through.

Second, participative management has become increasingly fashionable in business circles. The encouragement of a wider number of people within an organization to think of themselves as managers and to become involved in decision-making means that a greater range of expertise can be drawn upon. At one time a large bank branch had just one person at the top—the bank manager; now you will find that there are several 'managers'.

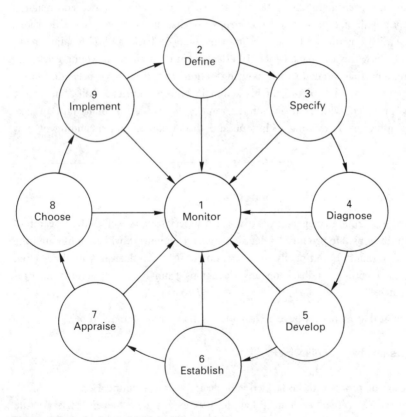

Figure 9.6 Archer's model of decision-making.

For any company, and particularly for those with wide geographical spreads and a range of product types, decentralization is essential. Most decisions, especially tactical ones, cannot be taken effectively at the centre, which may be miles—or continents—away: they have to be taken immediately, on the spot, by people who know all the circumstances.

One way of achieving this sharing of responsibility is to remove layers from the chain of authority, so that each division head reports directly to the managing director rather than to one of several assistant managing directors—who would themselves report to the top person. Another way is to create separate profit centres—sections of the overall business that are given the responsibility and resources (and guidance, where necessary) to run their own sections, as their own businesses.

In recent years this type of practice has become increasingly common in the public sector following on the success of decision-making operations in the private sector. Today we see a national policy of local management of schools, whereby each school is responsible for its own finances through group decision-making within the school. Doctors are also coming to be responsible for managing their own budgets, as are hospitals and other units in the National Health Service.

Finally, while in the nineteenth and early twentieth centuries it was not uncommon for businesses to be owned by one or a small number of owners who were also the decision-makers, nowadays it is far more common for businesses to be owned by shareholders who appoint a team of managers.

Factors influencing the way in which decisions are made

Decision-making is influenced by a number of important factors.

Personality

The personality of the decision-maker is a prime factor. Decisions are usually made by people. Even when they are made by machines, the machines will have first been programmed by people.

Decision-making requires a number of skills. Some decisions need a particular type of skill— e.g. the ability to follow a set pattern of rules—while others require a range of different skills, such as the ability to respond to novel and changing situations.

Some individuals may have the sorts of personality that are suited to analysing and evaluating various options but are hopeless at implementing a decision; others may have the strength to implement decisions but are ineffective at evaluating the results. Some people are cautious while others are rash. Different decisions require different types of decision-maker. We have all heard comments such as 'He can never make up his mind'; 'She comes up with ideas but never puts them into practice'; 'He won't listen to advice and just ploughs ahead without admitting that he has got it wrong.' These are all criticisms of attitudes to decision-making. Some decisions require caution while others require single-mindedness and still others, a combination of the two.

The ability to make a decision and to put it into effect will depend on intelligence and confidence. Different individuals have different abilities to cope with uncertainty, depending on such factors as status, which in turn depend on things like age, sex, education and social class.

Perception

An individual's perception of a situation will also have a major influence on how decisions are made. Given the same set of stimuli, different individuals will select what they regard to be important. The way that each perceives a situation will depend on his or her previous experience and understanding. For example, when an American 747 exploded in mid-air over the Scottish town of Lockerbie in December 1988, some of the residents thought that they were experiencing a major earthquake. This interpretation of events was on account of the wide media coverage of a catastrophic earthquake in Armenia the previous week which was still very much in the public imagination, and because they had no other way of explaining the widespread devastation. Other residents of the town, who had been able to locate an explosion in the sky, were immediately able to recognize that there had been an aircrash.

It has been suggested that there are four main ways in which perception influences the decision-making process:

1. Decision-makers are sometimes influenced by factors of which they are not conscious at the time. For example, when interviewing a candidate for a job you may feel that you like or dislike a particular person without being able to explain why. A particular decision might 'feel right' for no apparent reason.
2. When making abstract decisions, a decision-maker might simply be influenced by emotional factors; you might take a particular decision because it appeals to you, or because it makes you feel good.
3. When it is not clear what the exact nature of the problem is, you might make a decision on the basis of influences that are really irrelevant to the given issue. The novice gambler on horses doesn't always study the form card, but might instead select a horse on the basis of the horse's name, or the colours the jockey is wearing.
4. The comments and views of high-status individuals may be given more attention than those of low-status individuals. Status can be a key factor in influencing decision-making in group meetings.

Attitudes to risk

An individual's attitude to risk can have a bearing on decision-making. Studies have indicated that people who are more intelligent are likely to study and analyse a situation in some depth before making a decision whereas those with less intelligence are more inclined to 'hope for the best' (Scodel *et al.* 1959). Individuals who worry about failure are less likely to take big risks.

Values

An individual's values also influence the way he or she approaches decision-making.

Studies of managers indicate that there are two main sets of values that influence decision-making:

* The organization's goals—e.g. output maximization, profit maximization
* Personal goals—e.g. security, promotion, a high income

Different individuals will give different weightings to the relative importance of these two sets of goals. Some managers will be seen to be 'in it for themselves' whereas others will be viewed as 'company people'. However, it is often difficult to make a clear distinction. Someone that appears to be a 'good company person' may in fact be a shrewd 'go-getter'.

Decision-making by groups

Many business decisions will be made by groups, and managers will spend a large proportion of their time working directly or indirectly as a member of a team. A *group* can loosely be defined as a collection of people with a common purpose who communicate with each other over a period of time. Key elements of this definition are that:

1. Group members share a consensus of purpose.
2. There is interaction between group members.
3. There is a pattern of communication.

The definition also implies that there will be a system of rules and a group structure.

Group working

Whenever a group is required to make a decision, there will be three strands involved in moving from the start of the decision-making process to the finish, i.e. the final decision. These strands are illustrated in Fig. 9.7.

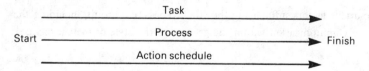

Figure 9.7 The decision-making process.

What is a task

The task is the content of the work. For example, the task of a management meeting may be to decide on the location of a new factory; the task of an interview may be to select the best candidate to take up a particular post. Thus, the task is the conversion of information and opinions from members into decisions or recommendations. In general terms, this covers *what* has to be done and *why*. Most groups give a lot of attention to the task.

Action schedule

The action schedule is concerned with how a group will be organized to do a given task. The schedule will cover such questions as who will fill the necessary roles, how progress will be checked and monitored, how it will be ensured that the group will keep to the time schedule. It will also deal with the procedures of decision-making—how to ensure that everyone gets a say, how conflict will be dealt with, etc. In general, the action schedule will cover the *where* and *how* of decision-making. Most groups will give some attention to their action schedule.

   For example, an action schedule for a meeting might set down when the meeting will take place, who will attend, who will run the meeting, how decisions would be voted on and other procedural matters.

Process

The process is the interaction that takes place between members of a group. It is about how people work together, their relationships and the feelings created by their behaviour within the group. It involves interpersonal skills such as listening to others and helping others to join in a discussion. It involves expressions of feelings and the giving and receiving of feedback. In general, it covers *who* does what and *when*. Many groups pay little attention to process.

These three threads of group working are all important in group decision-making. It will be obvious that a group that concentrates on its action schedule and its process entirely may have a wonderful time but is unlikely to achieve the task. It will not be long before morale will suffer and the group will disintegrate. In contrast, concentration purely on the task is likely to lead to arguments about how things should be organized, and inattention to group members' thoughts and feelings will lead to mishandled resources and to misunderstandings.

Factors affecting group effectiveness

There are a number of important factors influencing the effectiveness of a group, including the size of the group, the flow of communication within the group and the style of management.

The size of the group

There are a number of reasons why it is easier to make decisions within small (i.e. five or six people) rather than larger groups. The more people are drawn into the decision-making process, the more difficult it is to involve everyone, the more difficult to get everyone to agree, and the higher the level of dissatisfaction with the way the group operates. Individuals find it more difficult to identify with the group, and sub-groups start to form. In order to prevent a group from becoming fragmented, it is increasingly likely that a leader will need to take centralized control over decision-making as the size of the group grows.

Despite the disadvantages of large groups, there are also a number of clear advantages. A large group will be able to call upon a greater pool of skills, energy and resources. A further benefit is that, if a wide number of members of an organization feel that they are involved in the decision-making process, they may be more willing to implement policies.

Communication within the group

The main factors influencing the flow of communication within a group are the formal organization of the group, the informal organization and the means of communication employed.

Research carried out by Bavelas (1948) and Leavitt (1951) suggested that there are four main types of communication network (Fig. 9.8). The wheel and chain networks are typified by a centralization of the flow of information. Effective decision-making thus depends to a great extent on those in key central positions and on the quality of the communications channels to them.

Bavelas and Leavitt saw these centralized forms as exhibiting the following characteristics:

1. They are highly effective at making and carrying out straightforward, well structured, predictable activities.
2. Levels of satisfaction for group members are relatively low compared with those for members of less centralized groups.
3. The centralized form helps to strengthen the leadership position in such groups.
4. A stable structure rapidly emerges in the group.
5. The group becomes dependent on those with greatest access to relevant information.

In terms of our previous analysis, such a group structure lends itself to short-term operating control decisions.

In contrast, the circle network and the completely connected network lend themselves to a more open, decentralized form of decision-making. Members of these groups are mutually interdependent, and share the decision-making process. The group is not so dependent on key individuals, and levels of satisfaction are usually greater. Disadvantages are that, because responsibility is shared, there may not be an effective mechanism for pushing decisions through. There may be a lot of talk about action without the mechanism required to create action. Open networks may be more appropriate for periodic control and strategic decisions, where high-quality decisions need a substantial amount of discussion and shared analysis and evaluation. However, long-term and major policy decisions will also require leadership, perhaps in the form of a prominent individual who is able to say 'the buck stops here'.

Style of management

The way in which an organization is managed will have an important effect on how well its groups operate.

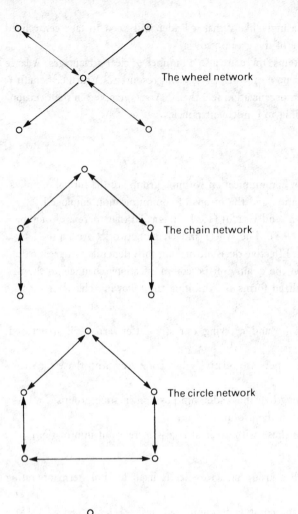

The wheel network

The chain network

The circle network

The completely
connected network

Key:

o   group members

←→ lines of communication

Figure 9.8 Types of communication network.

Studies of the characteristics of effective leadership have identified three main types of explanation of what influences the quality of leadership:

- Trait theories
- Style theories
- Contingency theories

It is important to bear in mind that no one theory has been effective in explaining all situations; each theory is good at explaining a number of examples, but poor at explaining others.

Trait theories

These theories are based on the argument that effective leadership rests with particular qualities which good leaders possess. The most commonly quoted personal traits are—intelligence, initiative and self-assurance.

Style theories

These theories are based on the belief that group members work harder under some styles of management than under others. The most commonly quoted contrasting styles are the authoritarian versus the democratic. In an authoritarian management structure the focus of power will be with the leader, who is responsible primarily for dispensing rewards and punishments; in a democratic management structure power will be shared more evenly. Studies tend to point out that in democratic structures individual group members will be more highly motivated. Such studies mention the positive factors of democratic styles by using such indicators as lower labour turnover, less conflict and greater job satisfaction.

However, it is important to point out that democratic styles are not always appropriate, for example when making a snap decision, or dealing with an emergency. Furthermore, some people prefer working with a structure; they like to know what it is they are expected to do.

Contingency theories

Contingency theories set out to account for the range of variables that may be relevant in a particular situation—the task, the nature of the work group or the position of the leader in the group.

Such theories can produce valuable insights and clues about appropriate management techniques in given situations. For example, Fiedler (1967) suggested that the appropriateness of using an authoritarian or democratic management style depends upon whether the situation facing management is 'favourable' or 'unfavourable'. A favourable situation would exist when:

1. The leader is popular and trusted by members of the group.
2. The task is well defined.
3. The power of the leader is high.

Fiedler felt that the first of these is the most significant. His findings led him to suggest that authoritarian approaches are most suitable in circumstances where (a) the task is well defined and the leader is strong and highly respected; or (b) the task is ambiguous and the leader is not in a strong position relative to the group. In the first case, decision-making will be effective because subordinates will support a respected leader. In the second case, leadership must assert itself and clarify its aims for the organization, or go under.

In contrast, where a task is ambiguous and the leader is well respected, the leader can afford to draw in the whole expertise of the group while still retaining power and authority.

The *'best fit' approach* can be used as an extension to Fiedler's work. It is based on the assumption that managers need to take account of four factors if they are to operate effectively:

- The leader
- The subordinates
- The task
- The environment

The *leader* will have a given set of views about how things should be done and what is important. The *subordinates* will have a given set of views about how they should be led and how things should be done. They will relate to tasks in different ways, and will have varying levels of commitment to group tasks. The *task* will vary in nature, complexity, time scale and importance. Finally, the *environment* will vary according to the nature of the group, the position of the manager within the group, what the group or organization is trying to achieve and the structure and technology of the organization.

The 'best fit' approach argues that there is no single best style of leadership. Different styles are appropriate to different circumstances. The best style in a given group will be the style that most closely matches up the requirements of leader, subordinate and task. The degree of fit can be measured on a scale running from 'tight' to 'flexible' (Fig. 9.9(a)). The three factors are then placed along the scale. In Fig. 9.9(b) we have a leader whose preferred management style is relatively authoritarian, working with a group whose members feel happier with a more flexible style, on a task which is fairly ambiguous. Because of this lack of fit, problems and difficulties are likely to arise. In the real world it is likely that either the three elements will move some way towards each other, or the job will not get done.

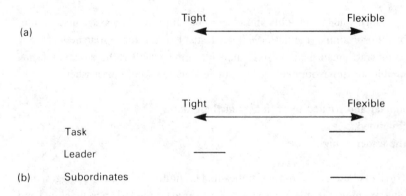

Figure 9.9 Degrees of fit in a fictional organization.

Group decision-making v. individual decision-making

Are groups more effective at making decisions than individuals?

The answer to this question depends on the context in which decisions need to be made. There are a number of important influences, including:

- The task in hand
- The time available to make a decision
- Whether or not a range of views is required
- The individuals involved
- The effectiveness of the communication process

See if you can list some other factors.

Generally speaking, the quality of decision-making in a group is likely to be higher because of the quantity and quality of data that can be drawn on.

In any group situation individuals will take on formal or informal roles. In a formal situation group meetings may involve officials such as a chairperson, a time-keeper and a secretary. In informal situations group members frequently take parts; for example, one person may try to force a decision on the group, another will oppose any new ideas, a third will act as peace-maker, and so on.

It has been suggested that the optimum group size is five people because:

1. The odd number will prevent an impasse.
2. A group that size is sufficiently large to avoid mistakes resulting from insufficient information, or the power of an individual with an entrenched view.
3. The group is small enough to involve everyone.

Gilligan, Neale and Murray have identified the following features that should lead to effective group performance:

1. The structure of the group and the status of group members should be stable and well formed.
2. The group should be large enough to fulfil the tasks, but not so large as to encourage the formation of sub-groups.
3. The group members should have the appropriate skills for the task.
4. The atmosphere should be informal and relaxed.
5. Objectives should be understood and accepted by group members.
6. Discussion should be encouraged and members should be willing to listen to each other.
7. Decisions should be reached by consensus.
8. The leader of the group should not dominate, nor should there be evidence of a struggle for power.
9. The group should operate with mild or moderate levels of stress.

10. Disagreements should not be overridden; instead, the reasons for disagreement should be examined and an attempt made to resolve them.
11. The allocation of tasks to members should be clear and accepted.
12. The group should act in a cohesive way.

Stages of small group development

We have found Fig. 9.10 (after Tuckman and Jensen) to be useful in helping students to think about how small groups can be most effective. The following stages are involved:

1. *Forming*   A number of individuals come together. They are simply that—a loose collection with no clear sense of purpose.
2. *Storming*   The group begins to exchange ideas, but there is as yet little structure to the group, and there are no clear plans to take the group forward.
3. *Norming*   The group begins to share ideas. Perhaps a leadership pattern begins to emerge, and the group starts to conform to a given set of ideas. Decisions begin to be formulated.
4. *Performing*   A clear organized pattern is established, based on mutual respect, the sharing of ideas and the drawing out of plans and proposals from all members of the team. Every member of the group is therefore able to make the best possible contribution to the group process.

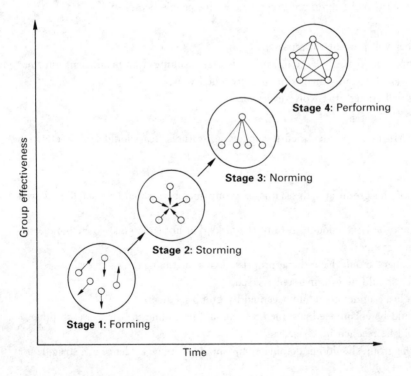

Figure 9.10 Stages of small group development. (*Source*: Tuckman and Jensen)

Developing a real team

Jon Katzenbach and Doug Smith, in their book *The Wisdom of Teams* (Harvard Business School Press, 1993), argue that there is a threshold that a group must cross before it becomes a team. They define a team as:

> A small number of people with complementary skills who are committed to a common purpose, performance goals and an approach for which they hold themselves accountable.

Katzenbach and Smith argue that managers need to be able to understand the ingredients of a team if they are to operate a successful organization. They set out a simple framework for the development of teams, and show a team performance curve (see Fig. 9.11).

1. *The working group*   This is a collection of individuals for whom there is no real opportunity or need to become a team. Each working group member produces something that helps the task to be completed without feeling a real part of the team. Being a part of the working group places no more demand on an individual than if he or she were working independently.
2. *The pseudo-team*   In this situation there is no joint benefit of being a part of the team. Indeed, each member's performance is worse than if working alone. This is because there is no focus, no common sense of purpose and no set of goals. The group members are confused as to what they should be doing or how they should be working together. At some stage in your life you are almost certain to work in a pseudo-team. It is very frustrating. Team members are 'feeling their way in the dark'. This may generate antagonism between members, and the team will quickly crumble.
3. *The potential team*   This is a collection of individuals with a clear performance need. They are seriously seeking to improve their impact on the group. In other words, they are aware

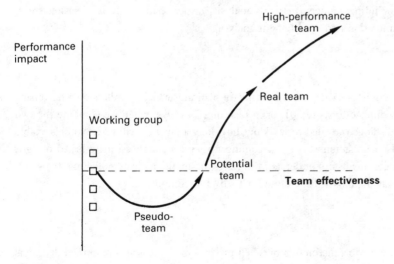

Figure 9.11 The performance curve.

that there is a need for something to be done in order to improve their performance and they want to do it. Unfortunately, however, they lack clarity about their aims as well as the discipline needed for a common working approach. Also, they will not have established the final criterion—mutual accountability. Many organizations are full of potential teams. This provides a real opportunity and a challenge for management.

4. *The real team*   It is worth repeating that a real team is 'a small number of people with complementary skills who are committed to a common purpose, performance goals, and an approach for which they hold themselves mutually accountable'.

5. *The high-performance team*   In addition to meeting the definition for a real team, this group will also be deeply committed—even beyond the team setup—to the personal growth and success of its members. It will significantly out-perform other teams.

The human side of decision-making

While a number of organization decisions can be programmed to follow set patterns (i.e. they can be made by reference to established procedures), there are many others that require an individual human input. Areas that spring to mind are consumer and personnel relations.

The human side of decision-making is affected by:

- Factors influencing the individual decision-maker
- Factors affecting group decision-making

Statistical and mathematical tools

There are many mathematical tools which can be used to aid decision-making. We shall look at some of these below including models, network analysis, critical path analysis, decision trees, linear programming, simulation and cost–benefit analysis.

Models

We use mathematical models every day—for example in planning which numbers on a dartboard to aim at and in what sequence to score 301; or in planning journeys, when we combine the two variables of speed and distance travelled to work out how long a journey will take. Models enable us to make more precise calculations than just coming up with a rough estimate based on 'gut feeling'. Today's manager needs to understand a range of mathematical modelling tools. Of course, many of these calculations will be done for us by the computer.

Types of model

Earlier in this chapter we made a distinction between programmed and unprogrammed decisions (see page 192). Highly structured situations lend themselves most readily to quantitative models.

1. *Quantitive models* involve clear logic patterns and precision, often at the expense of realism. Data are fed into a mathematical model and the output will be a fairly closed solution.
2. *Qualitative models* are more realistic but less neat than quantitive ones. The way this type of model operates is less clear-cut and unpredictable. (So too is the real world.)

Models are used mainly for quantitive decision-making. They can be employed at strategic, tactical and operational levels (see Fig. 9.12).

Strategic models
Planning organizational
  objectives
Policy planning
Choosing a plant location

Tactical models
Financial planning
Manpower planning
Designing plant layout

Operational models
Customer credit ratings
Media selection
Production scheduling
Quality control

Figure 9.12 Types of model.

Mathematical techniques can be summarized under four headings:

1. *Statistical decision theory* sets out to maximize outcomes of preferences of decision-makers.
2. *Mathematical programming* sets out to calculate the best solution with given conditions.
3. *Game theory* sets out to work out the best solution where several decision-makers or groups of decision-makers are involved.
4. *Multiple criteria decision-making* sets out to come up with the best solution where there are many criteria involved.

In developing a model, you need to:

1. Define and express quantitively the key variables involved in a decision.
2. Set out the main components and limits of a model in numbers.
3. Make sure that the problem can be tackled using mathematical tools.

The cost of the time taken to work out the problem in this way needs to be reasonable, i.e. cost-effective.

Network analysis

When co-ordinating a business project, it is important to map out the sequence of events that must be carried out. Activities need to be performed in a planned sequence—for instance, in building a house the walls would normally be assembled before the roof was put on; the layers of a

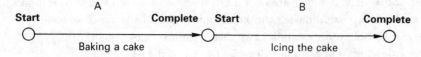

Figure 9.13 Network analysis.

sponge cake are made before the icing is put on; etc. These *events* can be linked in diagrammatic form as indicated in Fig. 9.13, where, before B can be started, A must be completed.

However, other activities do not have to take place in sequence; they can be carried out *simultaneously*. For example, the icing could be prepared at the same time as the cake is being baked. This is illustrated in Fig. 9.14, which shows that before you bake the cake and/or prepare the icing, you need to mix the ingredients for each—but the latter stages of production can be carried out simultaneously.

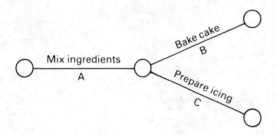

Figure 9.14 Simultaneous activities in network analysis.

Network analysis can be used to map out programmes of activities in such a way as to create the most effective planning.

 Task

Set out a network diagram to indicate the performance of the following activities:

Activity	Relationship to other activities
A	Must be done first
B	Can be started only when A is finished
C	Can be started only when A is finished
D	Requires completion of B
E	Requires completion of C and D
F	Completes project and must await completion of all other activities

A further important ingredient of constructing a network is the element of time, which will be a crucial element in project planning. Time needs to be incorporated into the diagram (see Fig. 9.15).

It now becomes possible to calculate the minimum amount of time required to carry out a particular project. Those activities that take the longest to complete in moving from one stage

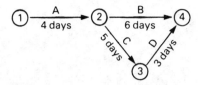

Figure 9.15 Introducing time to network analysis.

to the next in a project are described as 'critical' activities. The 'critical path' of a project is the path that these activities follow. It is essential that the activities are done well and that they are given priority if the project is not to fall behind. This can be illustrated by a simple diagram (Fig. 9.16). Activities A and B can be carried out simultaneously, as can C and D. However, activities A and C are the critical activities, in that if they fall behind in their execution the whole project will suffer.

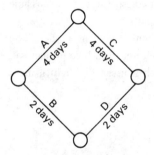

Figure 9.16 Establishing priorities in network analysis.

Critical path analysis and decision trees

Critical path analysis

The critical path is the sequence of key activities that determine the time needed to complete an activity. Think of an activity that you, or an organization that you are familiar with, have to carry out. Then:

1. List all the tasks that need to be carried out, how long each will take and in what order they must be done. (Are there some tasks that have to be finished before others can be begun, and if so which are they?)
2. Draw a network to show the links between each task, representing each with a circle, identifying it with a letter or number and connecting the circles using arrows to show the order in which the tasks must take place, pointing from left to right. (Write the time you estimate each task will take to finish above the arrow so that the time taken to complete a sequence can be calculated by adding the time required to complete tasks from beginning to end in the network.) In Fig. 9.17 tasks B, C and D can all be started at the same time, but E

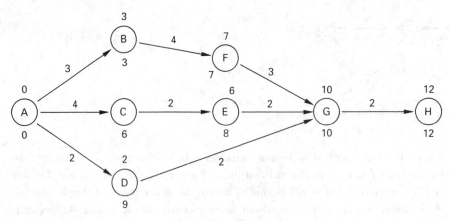

Figure 9.17 The critical path activity.

cannot start until C is finished, although work on E and F can be going on at the same time, and G can be started only when D, E and F have been finished; so the earliest possible completion time is 12 days—A, B, F, G, H being the longest path.

3. Work out the latest finishing times for each task and write them below the circles. The pathway that is the most urgent—the one where, if tasks are held up, the whole project will be pushed behind schedule—is known as the *critical path*, which you can highlight using a colour to indicate its route—i.e., A, B, F, G, H.

Decision trees

Decision trees can be used to decide on the best form of a range of strategic options (see Fig. 9.18). At the end of the tree are a number of different development opportunities.

The decision tree approach sets out to rank options by progressively eliminating the weaker ones. To do this, you need to work out a few key criteria that are required in future developments, e.g. growth, investment and/or diversification. In Fig. 9.18, if growth is an important business objective, then 1–4 will be ranked more highly than 5–8. At the second step, if another important criteria is low investment, then 3 and 4 would be ranked above 1 and 2. In a decision tree you will need to identify options and rank them at the same time. Clearly, such a process lends itself to the use of computer programs as aids to decision-making.

A major problem of decision trees is that they can tend to be a bit simplistic. At each stage you need to be able to rank and quantify options. If you put the wrong numbers in at any stage, the whole exercise becomes distorted. Decision trees are most effective when alternatives can be given clear numerical values. Be wary about using them when making decisions that cannot be clearly quantified.

Linear programming

Linear programming (LP) is a mathematical technique that can be used to determine the optimum allocation of scarce resources. There are two objectives: it aims to maximize profit or

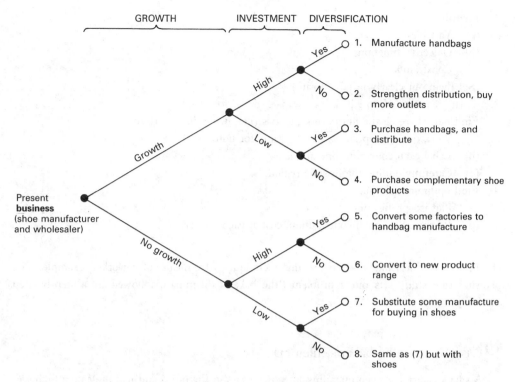

Figure 9.18 A simplified decision tree for a shoe manufacturer and wholesaler.

minimize costs while at the same time limiting various resources by short-term constraints. It is an effective method of making decisions about quantities of resources in the short term, as in the long term technology, price, production methods and other factors will alter the constraint limitations. Only in the short term and over limited ranges of output will the resources have linear relationships.

For a problem to be solved by linear programming, it is important to ensure that it meets all four points on the following checklist:

1. The problem must be able to be stated in numeric terms.
2. All factors involved in the problem must have linear relationships.
3. The problem must permit a choice or choices between alternative courses of action.
4. There must be at least one restriction on the factors involved. This may be a restriction on resources (e.g. a bakery can only bake bread for 72 hours in a week) or on particular characteristics (e.g. fertilizer used in a particular process must contain 15 per cent phosphates and 10 per cent nitrogen).

LP follows a strict procedure that makes problems easier to solve, in much the same way as a private detective approaches a case! The same procedure should be followed every time:

1. Identify
   (a) Variables
   (b) Objective function
   (c) Constraints
   (Set them out clearly in table form.)
2. Turn inequalities into equalities (swap $\leqslant$ or $\geqslant$ for $=$).
3. Find out where all the lines cross the axis (i.e. if $y = 0$, $x = 160$):
   (a) Work out appropriate scale (the same for both axes).
   (b) Label each constraint line and axis.
   (c) Carefully outline the feasible region.
4. Find optimum solution:
   (a) Plot iso-profit lines.
   (b) Work out the total contribution/cost at each corner.

The best way of learning how to use this technique is by means of a worked example. The following case study sets out a problem ('the baker's dilemma'), followed by a step-by-step solution.

Case Study—the baker's dilemma

A small bakery has been operating for a few years in Stamford and had built up a high reputation for its delicious wholemeal products. However, the recession and rising overheads has recently forced the owner to close his high street outlet. He has managed to negotiate with Tesco, the local supermarket, to sell his two most popular items. He has therefore decided to put all the bakery's resources into baking these two items. These are a wholemeal loaf, and sets of six wholemeal rolls. As the bakery's output is

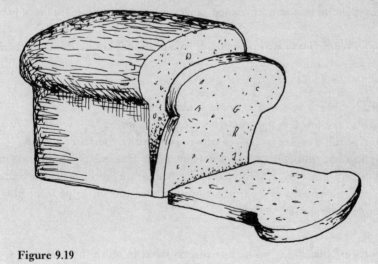

Figure 9.19

comparatively small, the supermarket will take all the bakery's weekly output, and no more than 1500 sets of rolls a week.

The owner has asked you to help him work out how much of each product he should produce to maximize his profits.

You tour the shop and interview the owner to gather the relevant information. He tells you that each loaf and each set of rolls makes a contribution of 30p towards costs. The capacity of his oven means that he can bake a loaf every 2 minutes and a set of rolls every 1 minute. He runs 10-hour shifts, seven nights a week.

There is also a large constraint on materials, as a specially ground high-quality wholemeal flour is used, and at present he can get only 600 kg a week. A loaf uses 200 g and a set of rolls uses 300 g.

In order to help him, you must set out the relevant information before you can solve the problem.

1. First, the variables in the case must be identified: loaves (L) and rolls (R).
2. Then the objective must be set out. This will be stated somewhere in the problem or in the questions. What is the required result or objective? This is most likely to be maximizing profit or contribution, or minimizing cost, time or some other appropriate measure. For instance, in the example above the objective is to *maximize the baker's profits*.
3. It is now necessary to state mathematically how these profits are made up. This is called the *objective function*:

$$0.3L + 0.3R = C$$

where C = contribution.
4. Next, all the constraints in the problem must be identified and expressed numerically. To do this set them out in a table form:

Constraints	L	R		Limits
Demand		R	<=	1500
Baking	$2L$	R	<=	4200 $(10 \times 60 \times 7)$
Materials	$0.2L$	$0.3R$	<=	600

5. Turn these three constraint *inequalities* into *equalities* to help plot them on a graph; i.e.,

$$2L + R = 4200$$

6. To find out where these constraint lines will cross the two axes, substitute 0 into each equation; i.e.,

$$2L + R = 4200$$
$$L = 0 \qquad R = 4200$$
$$L = 2100 \quad R = 0$$

7. Using the axis points, work out an appropriate scale. Use the same scale for both axes if possible.
8. Plot and label each line and axis on the graph (see Fig. 9.20).
9. Indicate by shading the side of each line that is 'out of bounds', i.e. the *unfeasible region*. Highlight or label each corner of the *feasible* region.

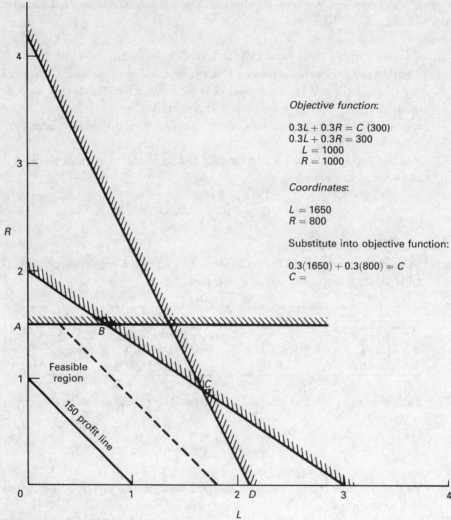

Objective function:

$0.3L + 0.3R = C \ (300)$
$0.3L + 0.3R = 300$
$L = 1000$
$R = 1000$

Coordinates:

$L = 1650$
$R = 800$

Substitute into objective function:

$0.3(1650) + 0.3(800) = C$
$C =$

Figure 9.20 Solution to baker's dilemma.

10. Find the optimum solution by using one of the following methods:

  (a) Plot *iso-profit lines*. Work out the *gradient* of the objective function by substituting any appropriate value for C. Then plot the line as in 6–8 above. Next, move parallel to this line to the furthest point on the edge of the feasible region. It will be an intersecting point between two or more constraint lines. The coordinates of this point are the optimum combination of the variables to maximize the baker's profits.

  (b) Another method is to substitute the coordinates of each corner of the feasible region into the objective function to find where the maximum profit lies. If the objective was to minimize cost, for instance, then the optimum point would be on the edge of the feasible region nearest to the origin, i.e. where the combination of necessary resources is smallest.

This procedure can be applied to all linear programming problems that meet the above checklist. The procedure considerably simplifies what seems at first a difficult problem.

With the advent of computers, similar problems can be solved with more than two variables. These would be very hard to solve graphically.

Once the graph has been drawn, a *sensitivity analysis* can be conducted. This involves carrying out exactly the same techniques as above, but all you do is change various aspects of the question to see what effect it will have on the solution. For instance, what effect will an increase in the contribution of rolls to 60p have on the optimum solution?

Simulation

Simulation is a useful technique for making decisions about something we all dislike—queues! It simulates the size of queues that form given different numbers of 'stations' or service points. It could apply to loading bays, shop assistants, counter clerks, docking bays, etc.

The advantage of such a method is that the effects on queues can be analysed without having the expense of actually carrying out the changes in real life until the conclusions have been made.

There are four factors that contribute to the formation of a queue:

- The pattern of arrivals
- The length of service time
- The number of service points available
- The queue discipline, i.e. first in, first out (FIFO), or last in, first out (LIFO)

All four of these factors must be known before the simulation technique can be used.

Simulation involves imitating the real-life situation of a queue. This is done by sampling the rate of arrivals and the service times. Random numbers are then used to simulate the fact that, over a short period of time, there is a randomness to the rate of arrivals and the service time. Hence it is sometimes called the *Monte Carlo method*.

The procedure is as follows:

1. Identify the problem.
2. Gather the information concerning the four factors listed above.
3. Allocate the random numbers and simulate the imaginary event.
4. Analyse the results.

⌕ Case Study—Sweet shop owner

A sweet shop owner wondered if the addition of another assistant would reduce his queues significantly. He took a sample one morning of the rate of arrivals..

Mins:	0	1	2	3	4	5	6
Nos:	6	15	23	24	16	10	8

The service time averaged out at 4 minutes per person. The following calculations could then be made. First, the frequencies (f) are turned into cumulative frequencies (cf), and these are then used to determine the range of random numbers that will represent each arrival interval. As you can see from Table 9.1, a larger range proportionally represents the more frequent intervals.

Table 9.1

Arrivals (min)	%f	%cf	Random nos.
0	6	6	01–06
1	15	21	07–21
2	23	44	22–44
3	24	68	45–68
4	16	84	69–84
5	10	94	85–94
6	6	100	95–00

The random numbers are taken from a random number table (Fig. 9.21). Each number in the table has an equal chance of appearing (1/100) as long as the numbers are read from the table in a systematic order, i.e. top to bottom or left to right. The random numbers (R nos.) are used to represent the random nature of people arriving at the shop (over a short period of time).

The shop opened at 9.00 am, and the first half-hour's activity is recorded in Table 9.2. The 'Queue' column increases as customers are kept waiting.

This table could then be drawn up with *two* servers to see if the queue would be eliminated. However, care would have to be taken by the owner to ensure that the two assistants were not idle for too long.

TABLE A

20	84	27	38	66	19	60	10	51	20
35	16	74	58	72	79	98	09	47	07
98	82	69	63	23	70	80	88	86	23
94	67	94	34	03	77	89	30	49	51
04	54	32	55	94	82	08	19	20	73
11	25	66	08	79	68	19	37	82	73
00	63	79	77	41	17	06	67	18	33
51	51	54	44	64	13	51	92	10	37
49	72	73	93	29	39	37	94	42	66
77	09	20	05	20	77	47	58	96	05

TABLE B

16	45	77	65	20	11	65	65	56	36
51	63	28	55	12	23	72	99	04	41
64	46	55	58	78	96	52	43	23	05
37	75	41	57	02	14	88	79	97	09
55	36	70	34	66	58	63	90	06	37
99	10	23	74	53	13	59	59	36	71
53	80	84	57	47	60	60	70	69	95
99	29	37	69	30	83	48	05	88	91
21	41	63	90	85	65	07	46	75	43
01	97	45	05	95	88	19	78	14	32

Figure 9.21 Random number tables. ⟶

Table 9.2

R (no.)	Mins	Arriv. time	Served at	Mins	Free at	Queue no.	Idle
20	1	9.01	9.01	4	9.05	0	1
35	2	9.03	9.06	4	9.10	3	0
98	6	9.09	9.10	4	9.14	1	0
94	5	9.14	9.14	4	9.18	0	0
04	0	9.14	9.18	4	9.22	4	0
11	1	9.15	9.22	4	9.26	7	0
00	6	9.21	9.26	4	9.30	3	0
51	3	9.24	9.30	4	9.29	6	0

Cost–benefit analysis

Cost–benefit analysis is normally associated with the evaluation of large-scale government-backed investment projects. The siting of an airport or the building of a new underground rail link are typical examples of projects for which cost–benefit analysis would be used.

However, cost–benefit analysis is a much more widely applicable technique than this. It could in fact be used to weigh up any policy decision, although it is not a magic solution to problem-solving.

Carrying out a cost–benefit analysis involves organizing all the relevant information involved in a particular decision in such a way as to focus on the key issues and to concentrate on the real choices to be made. It is an attempt to put a money value on all the costs and benefits of a particular decision—including intangible factors. Although it is often very difficult to measure intangibles in money terms, this is not always the case. Johnson and Scholes give an example of the expected costs and benefits of a particular decision and the basis on which the intangibles can be identified (see Table 9.3).

Table 9.3   The benefits and costs involved in constructing a new town centre carpark

	Bases of quantification
Costs	
1. Acquiring site	Already owned; market value known
2. Construction costs	Tenders obtained
3. Loss of amenity (gardens)	Known usage of gardens and notional entry charge (if privately owned)
4. Increased total transport costs	Differential between public and private (car) travel
Benefits	
1. Revenue	Demand and price forecasts
2. Reduced congestion in streets	Incremental increase in consumer spending due to easier access.

A local authority is considering whether to construct a new town centre carpark to be built on existing public gardens. The main costs and benefits are identified in the table.

Clearly, the basis on which costs and benefits are measured needs to be justified. Different people will have different views about the values given. For example, if the town centre is felt by some people to be 'spoilt' by the creation of the carpark, they may want to place a high value on the cost of losing the amenity (garden).

If you were going to do an analysis of building a new training centre for unemployed workers, you would have to find out who would benefit and who would lose out by its construction. You would then need to make measurements in money terms. One way of doing this would be to ask the people who would benefit how much they would be prepared to pay to see the project carried out. You could then ask someone who was going to lose out what was the minimum amount he or she would be prepared to accept as compensation for the project taking place. Then you would need to add up all the gains and all the losses. If the gains outweigh the losses, the project passes the test. (Clearly, you might want to eliminate from your research people who said 'I would not want the project to go ahead at any price!')

Although cost–benefit analysis is riddled with problems, when it comes to ascribing money values to costs and benefits it does at least force decision-makers to focus on the main issues and interest groups concerned in a decision. Weights can then be attached to the costs and benefits identified.

Information technology as a decision-making tool

The American business author Peter Drucker sees the late twentieth century as the dawning of the age of the information-based organization, the latest stage in the development of the modern corporation.

At the beginning of the century we saw the separation of management from the ownership of a company, as shareholders handed over responsibility for the running of a company to paid managers. This led to the growth of the command-and-control organization made up of departments and divisions. Now we are entering a third period of change, with the development of information-based organizations of knowledge specialists.

In this third phase, members of staff are freed from day-to-day administrative tasks by computers. Computers bring a large proportion of employees closer to the work of management; departmental hierarchies are broken down, creating a much flatter organizational structure with the opportunity to develop more skills. Networking of computer systems gives people access to many disciplines. When a company uses a number of personal computers, it is possible that some of the information on one of these may be useful to another user. Then, rather than continually swopping data on floppy disks, it is possible to connect the machines together using a *local area network*. This consists of a mixture of hardware and software which enables data to be transferred between the machines. Networking thus makes it possible for a range of experts to rapidly tap into each other's specialist skill areas while sitting at their own workstations. Such employees no longer need to work in the same building, and in fact can quite easily work from home. No longer is knowledge compartmentalized; instead, it becomes part of a pool of mutually shared information. Information technology saves time, cuts costs and makes companies more competitive. With new technology, the new organization is born.

However, we are still a long way from the widespread development of information-based organizations which are democratically structured. Rather than restructuring job design, many companies have tended to automate the existing organizational structure. Dramatic contrasts can be made between companies that have combined information technology with a more effective decision-making structure and those that have simply borrowed the new technology and retained their existing structure.

This point is illustrated by the *Management in the Nineties* programme report (Spring 1989) which includes a telling comparison of two organizations in the pensions business, each of which was responsible for managing an investment portfolio of £15 million. It showed how a new-model business compared with an older-style organization. The traditionally run business is represented by the division of a bank, employing 108 professional staff and 36 support staff. The newcomer, Battery March, a Boston-based financial investment management firm, handles a comparable business, but with 18 professional staff and 17 support staff.

From the outset, Battery March's founder operated on the principle that there was a better way of managing funds which would add value to the company's services. The operation was consciously organized to optimize the creative contribution of analysts and professionals with a strong emphasis on teamwork. It was a vision that depended on information technology.

Buying and selling stock directly, computer to computer, takes care of some routine clerical work. Technology is also used extensively to monitor stock and fund changes, select best options and so on, to enable staff to concentrate more on the creative aspects of the business. As a result, Battery March enjoys lower costs and a record for highly effective performance.

It is not just the younger companies like Battery March that are exploring the possibilities for innovative organization. Rank Xerox, for example, has dared to ask why all white-collar workers need to work in a central office. This company is one of the trail-blazers in the use of *networkers*, i.e. home-based specialist and professional workers contracted to the company but also working for other clients.

Computer-based simulations are important aids to decision-making. A computer simulation involves feeding in a range of relevant data to a program in order to simulate a real situation. The program can then be used for training purposes or to assist with real decisions, which can be as trivial as selecting winners in a horse race or as serious as trying to locate a fault in the operation of a rocket in a manned space launch.

Management information systems

A management information system (MIS) is a large, usually computerized, data-bank to which managers have access. It is made up of a number of files consisting of key data which are regularly updated.

A criticism of such systems in the past was that, while the data were extensive, they were not necessarily constructed in the way that best suited the user. The organization would put a lot of information into the system without thinking clearly about how it would be extracted. A newer approach involves manager-operated computers which are 'user-friendly' and with data that are 'needs-driven'. Managers can use the system to create their own models which are then built into the management system. This helps managers to think about the decisions they are making.

Decision support systems

Decision support systems (DSSs) involve managers using computer systems on a daily basis to support their decision-making. The DSS can be thought of as an extension of the manager's mind, exploring the consequences of alternative decisions.

Key features of a DSS are:

- A comprehensive data and model base
- A sophisticated software system for managing each decision
- A powerful command language to help decision-makers interact with both the data and the models.

The ingredients of a decision support system are shown in Fig. 9.22.

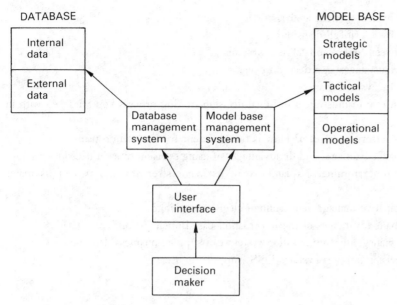

Figure 9.22 A decision support system.

Questions

Short-answer questions

1. Identify one decision that would be made by each of the following members of a small company:
   (a) Shareholder
   (b) Employee
   (c) Director
   (d) Manager
2. Why are information systems important to decision-making processes? Give three examples of how an information system can help in decision-making.
3. What is meant by middle management? What is the responsibility of middle management in a large company?
4. Study the decision-making process in a local company. Who are the decision-makers? How are decisions made? What is the structure of decision-making?
5. Distinguish between task, process and action schedule in a decision-making process.
6. Distinguish between programmed and non-programmed decisions. Give an example of each.
7. What is meant by:
   (a) chain network?
   (b) circle network?
   (c) completely interconnected network?

   Give an example of each from organizational situations with which you are familiar.

8. What is meant by cost–benefit analysis?
9. What is meant by a 'critical' decision?
10. Distinguish between 'open' and 'closed' systems.
11. Explain the various stages in a decision cycle.
12. What is meant by evaluation?
13. Draw a decision tree to illustrate a personal decision-making process you are faced with in the near future.
14. What is a high-performance team? How is this different from a pseudo-team?
15. What are the main advantages and disadvantages of using decision trees in decision-making?
16. What is linear programming? Explain two of its major strengths and two of its major weaknesses.
17. How can participative management facilitate decision-making?
18. What are the main advantages of the information-based organization?
19. Explain how a management information system can support business decision-making.
20. How does a decision support system (DSS) support its user?

Essays

1. Who are the decision-makers in a company? Explain.
2. Discuss the view that an effective and 'happy' organization is one that gives responsibility to *all* its employees.
3. Organizations need to develop procedures for decision-making that are most suited to the nature of the environment in which they are operating. Discuss.
4. What factors are likely to influence individual decision-making?
5. How can large groups work effectively together?
6. Show how the decision-making network needs to be tailored to
   (a) the size of the group
   (b) the nature of the decisions that need to be made.
7. How important is the 'leader' in the decision-making process?
8. What are the prerequisites of effective group collaboration?
9. How can decision-making techniques facilitate the decision-making process?
10. Large modern organizations cannot survive without systems that are based on modern information technology. Discuss this view.

Data response questions

1 Sequence of activities

The network shown in Fig. 9.23 sets out the sequence of activities for a project to be carried out. (The numbers indicate the number of days required to complete an activity.)

1. What is the critical path? What should be the total length of time required to complete the project?

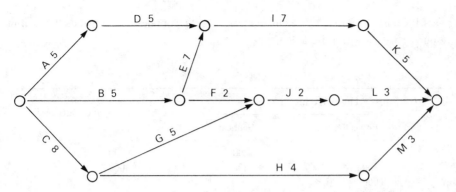

Figure 9.23 A sequence of activities.

2. Which of the activities indicated is the most crucial if the project is to be completed on time?
3. Imagine that a project planner has come up with a new network of activities whereby I would precede J, and K would be incorporated with H to take 8 days. Draw a new network.
4. Explain how project management can help decision-makers to plan new projects.

2   Sweet Tooth Ltd

A confectionery manufacturer makes two kinds of chocolate bar, A and B, each of which requires three stages of production: mixing, cooking and boxing. The number of minutes required to complete each process for a box of chocolate bars is as follows:

	Mixing	Cooking	Boxing
A	1.25	0.5	1.5
B	1.20	1.5	0.5

All the production equipment is available for eight hours each day. Accountants have calculated that the contribution on each box of A is £0.50 and on B is £1. The equipment may be used to produce A and B simultaneously. All production may be sold.

1. State the objective function, assuming the manufacturer wants to maximize contributions.
2. State all the constraints that are relevant to this production problem.
3. Graph the constraints, shading any unwanted regions, and determine the optimum production position.
4. What is the contribution generated by this optimum position?

3   The boatbuilder

A boatbuilder manufactures two types of vessel, a power boat and a family sailboat. The market is buoyant, and will consume all boats built at a contribution of £2700 per power boat and £3600 per sailing vessel. Construction is in three main areas, and the supplies and demands for each of the three resources are shown in Table 9.4.

Table 9.4

Resource	Hours required per boat		Boat unit hours available per month
	Power boat	Sailboat	
Boat assembly	600	1200	9000
Dry dock	300	300	3000
Engine shop	900	0	6300

1. Set up the equations of inequality for the problem.
2. Draw a graph identifying the various constraints.
3. Identify the optimum mix of boat types to be produced in order to maximize overall contribution.
4. What is the maximum contribution?

4 Competition in confectionery ice cream

The market for confectionery ice cream did not exist in 1989. By 1993 it was worth more than £150 million a year, and is one of the fastest growing areas in Britain's £770 million ice cream sector.

Created by Mars, which was first with its Mars ice cream bar in 1989, confectionery ice cream enables chocolate companies to balance the seasonal fluctuations in their business—sales boom in winter, only to fall away in the summer. However, Mars has been faced by strong competition in the field. Nestlé took over Lyons Maid and quickly entered the market. At the same time, the Walls part of the giant Unilever Group and producer of Magnum, Europe's best selling ice cream, teamed up with Cadbury's to produce ice cream versions of its chocolate lines.

Today, Mars is having difficulty in getting its Mars ice cream bars into retail outlets. Walls, which has more than 60 per cent of the impulse market (lollies bought from shops), and Nestlé's Lyons Maid (12 per cent) supply freezers free of charge to small retailers and corner shops on condition that they stock only *their* ice cream in the cabinet. Not only do they supply freezers to shops; they also maintain and service them. The shop just has to pay the electricity bill.

A leading expert has commented that if Mars had had access to freezers at an earlier date it could have made its position impenetrable. Now it is just another competitor in the field. Walls has spent more than £20 million on freezer cabinets over the past ten years.

Mars offers a range of well-known brands including Mars, Bounty, Twix and Snickers in ice cream form. Walls has Cadbury's Dairy Milk, and Nestlé sells its Milky Bar, Kit Kat and Aero.

Mars is understandably frustrated that it can't compete on equal terms in small shops.

1. How would Mars' move into confectionery ice cream have involved strategic decision-making?

2. How does the case indicate that there were some weaknesses in Mars' strategic thinking which has prevented the company from dominating the market?

3. What relative weaknesses does the case indicate in Mars' position compared with other competitors?

4. How have Walls and Nestlé's moves into this market involved strategic decision-making?

5. What lessons can be learnt from this case about strategic decision-making?

5   Nuclear power plant risks

Read the extract and answer the questions that follow.

CONCERN OVER RISK TO NUCLEAR POWER PLANTS

An air crash such as the one at Lockerbie could cause even greater devastation than the Chernobyl disaster if the wreckage hit a nuclear power station, according to Dr Raymond Seymour, a scientific adviser with Somerset County Council, Nicholas Schoon writes.

Dr Seymour disputes the official estimate of the chance of an aircraft directly hitting a nuclear power station as being once every 2 million years. Dr Seymour, a radiation expert, says the risk is 10 times higher. He has been assessing the risks in evidence to be presented later this month to the public inquiry into plans for a third nuclear power station at Hinkley Point in Somerset.

Much of the wreckage of the Pan Am Boeing 747 came down within 10 miles of the BNFL reactor at Chapelcross. If the bomb had detonated about a minute earlier the debris would have landed around the reactor. 'The effect of such a disaster could be far worse than Chernobyl and the chances of it happening at Hinkley Point are unacceptable,' he said yesterday.

In his evidence, given on behalf of a consortium of 23 local authorities opposing the Hinkley C reactor, he says the main risk comes from jets from the Royal Navy airbase at Yeovilton which fly to a practice bombing range in the Bristol Channel.

A spokesman for the CEGB, which wants to build Hinkley C, said the risks of aircraft impact had been assessed for the Sizewell inquiry. Even in the extremely unlikely event of an aircraft crashing into the power station, there was only a one in ten chance of this causing a big release of radioactivity, and a one in two chance of this leading to a meltdown.

Aircraft are not allowed within two miles horizontally of a nuclear power station or within 2000 feet vertically.

(*Source*: The Independent, January 1990)

1. Why might mathematical techniques be useful in:
   (a)   making siting decisions for nuclear reactors?
   (b)   calculating safety risks for nuclear reactors?
2. What do you think Dr Seymour meant by 'the chances of it happening at Hinkley Point are unacceptable'?
3. Why do you think that Dr Seymour's calculations differ from the official estimates?
4. What criteria do you think should be applied to the siting of nuclear reactors? Explain your reasoning.

Suggested reading

Drummond, H., *Effective Decision Making*, Kogan Page, 1991.

Fatseas, V. and Vog, T., *Quantitative Techniques for Managerial Decision Making*, Prentice-Hall, 1984.

Gilligan, C., Neale, B. and Murray, D., *Business Decision Making*. Prentice-Hall, 1983.

Johnson, G., and Scholes, K., *Exploring Corporate Strategy* 3rd Edition. Prentice-Hall, 1993

10

Using statistical and quantitative techniques

Every organization has to make decisions, and often such decisions are influenced by a host of both internal and external factors which can make decision-making very difficult. In such an uncertain world, therefore, organizations require information on which to base their decisions. Statistics fulfil this role by acting as a management tool, helping decision-makers to make estimates or comparisons of previous or current events so that decisions about the future can be made.

Much of the information that organizations have to deal with on a day-to-day basis involves figures and so is *quantitative* in nature. In order to understand the implications of figures, at any level, clearly some basic knowledge of statistics is required. Although decision-making calls for common sense, problem-solving skills and the ability to communicate, these will be enhanced by an ability to understand figures. No decision can lead to certain results—although something is likely, it might not happen. Statistics enable guidelines to be as precise as possible in an area of uncertainty. In undertaking this role, they are essentially a form of communication in business.

The word 'statistics' contains three fundamental elements: first, it can be used as a 'blanket' to describe a set of figures; second, it enables a mass of information to be presented according to a particular pattern; third, it provides a method of interpreting business data.

Information needs for simple problems

The first question any organization will need to ask is: What information do we need? Information should cover as many aspects of an organization's activities as possible. The more thorough and accurate the information, the more successful is decision-making likely to be; whereas misleading information may result in poor decisions. *Internal data* consist of information extracted from within an organization, whereas *external data* are found outside the business in the environment in which it operates (see Fig. 10.1).

If someone says that a certain type of motor car is best, he or she is making a *qualitative* comment about the vehicle. By looking at the specifications for the car and analysing details such as maximum power, torque, compression ratio and maximum speed, the *quantitative* details can be checked and a greater knowledge gained of the vehicle. Organizations are concerned with such precision and will wish to analyse issues in detail by gathering reliable quantitative information.

231

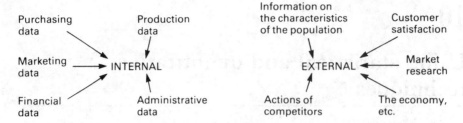

Figure 10.1 Some examples of internal and external data.

Before gathering information, a number of important questions need to be asked:

1. What are the precise objectives of the exercise? It is important to consider the aims of the exercise to ensure that time is not spent upon collecting information that might not be needed.
2. What units of measurement are to be used? If you are collecting information such as sales figures, will you require them in pounds, volume or both?
3. What degree of accuracy is required? To obtain a high degree of accuracy you will have to spend more time and effort gathering information. However, an investigation of a representative sample of the total may be just as revealing.
4. Is obtaining this information cost-effective? The whole point of the exercise—to collect information—must be that it is worth spending money to do so.

Each level of management will have different information needs. For example:

1. *Strategic-level* managers deal with policy decisions and matters concerning the future of the organization. They need carefully prepared and scientifically presented information, not only from within the business but also from outside sources.
2. *Tactical-level* managers tend to make decisions based upon strategic policy decisions. They will be concerned with analysing issues within the organization and will often require information relating to a particular time period.
3. *Organizational* decision-making involves dealing with grass-roots problems associated with the day-to-day running of an organization. The information required, although it need not be precise, may help to provide a solution to a practical problem.

Case Study—Information needs

Have you ever had that feeling that the information you are giving managers is not exactly what they wanted? Have you ever tried to find out what they do want? If you have, then you may well have researched—or at least approached—a state of despair! For years, no matter what variations and improvements I made to the information I gave to managers, I just never seemed able to satisfy their exact needs. I even went through the stage of believing it was some kind of plot to make management accountants feel inadequate.

Then one day I discovered—some people might say stumbled on—a solution to the problem of defining management's information needs. My 'amazing' discovery was that information is the raw material of decision-making and that, in order to know what information managers need, we have to know what decisions they take. This pretty obvious statement led to the development of a process which I have appropriately named 'decision information analysis'. This requires a careful analysis of the decisions that managers make and then, for each decision, assessing the information needed.

(*Source: Management Accounting*)

Questions

1. Explain why managers require information.
2. Why is it important to give managers the information that they want?
3. What solution is suggested by this case?

Collecting primary data

Primary data consist of information collected by an organization for its own purposes (see Chapter 12). Such information is therefore specific to an organization's needs and is collected solely for the purposes required. In organizing the collection of information, three important questions need to be asked:

1. Whom do you ask to get the information you require?
2. What questions do you need to ask?
3. What techniques do you use to obtain the right information?

Sampling

In obtaining information, the ideal situation would be to interview every member of the target group. This is known as a *census*. However, this could be both an extensive and a costly task. By *sampling*, you will be able to obtain conclusions by putting questions to a representative group which is reflective of a larger number of respondents. This can be done in a number of different ways.

Random sampling

With this method, the researcher chooses the size of the sample required and then picks the sample on a random basis. Respondents are drawn from a sampling frame in which each has an equal chance of being selected.

Systematic random sampling involves selecting items from the list at regular intervals after choosing a random starting-point. For example, if it is decided to select a sample of 200 names from 10 000, then every fiftieth name (10 000 divided by 200) should be selected, after a random start in the first 50. If number 15 is chosen as the starting-point (possibly by using a table of random numbers), then the sample would start: 15,...,65,...,115,...,165,...,215,...,265,...,315, etc.

Stratified random sampling takes into account the fact that some customers are more important than others. It therefore weights the sample on the basis of the importance of each group of customers in the market.

For example, if an organization has 5000 small users of products accounting for sales of £1 million, 4000 medium users accounting for £1 million, and 1000 large users accounting for sales of £2 million, a random sample of 200 would not be representative of the whole market. To make the sample more representative, you would need to allocate the large users $\frac{1}{2}$ the sample because they make up $\frac{1}{2}$ the sales, with $\frac{1}{4}$ of the sample allocated to medium users and $\frac{1}{4}$ to small users. The stratified random sample would then include 100 big users, 50 medium users and 50 small users, all randomly chosen from their respective categories.

Quota sampling

Although random sampling, if properly conducted, produces the best results, it can be expensive and time-consuming, and sometimes it is not possible to identify a random sample. In these situations quota sampling may be used. With this form of sampling, interviewers are given instructions as to the *number* of people to interview according to certain characteristics—such as sex, age, socioeconomic group and/or other demographic details.

Example

Imagine that you have been asked to obtain information on behalf of a company with four factories in different parts of the country. Table 10.1 shows a breakdown of the company's employees by age and sex. You are required to construct a quota sample of 5 per cent of the workforce to reflect fully the location, age and sex. As the total workforce is 1900, you are therefore required to interview 95 employees, or 1 in 20 of the total employees. You have to divide each number in the table by 20 and round it off to the nearest whole number (Table 10.2).

Table 10.1

		Under 40	Over 40
Sutton Coldfield	M	111	140
	F	89	32
Hull	M	240	80
	F	120	115
Camberley	M	148	120
	F	175	180
Darlington	M	105	60
	F	125	60

Table 10.2

		Under 40	Over 40
Sutton Coldfield	M	6	7
	F	4	2
Hull	M	12	4
	F	6	6
Camberley	M	7	6
	F	9	9
Darlington	M	5	3
	F	6	3
Total		55	40

If age and sex were no longer relevant to your survey, you would combine the classes and interview:

> 19 from Sutton Coldfield
> 28 from Hull
> 31 from Camberley
> 17 from Darlington
> 95

Cluster sampling

With cluster sampling, respondents are divided according to areas; but instead of selecting the areas at random, sampling is carried out in a few areas which are considered to be typical of the market in question. For example, you might divide a city such as Birmingham into 200 segments and then, because of the nature of the survey, sample only from those segments that contain a broad range of housing, one school, one church and a shopping centre, avoiding any segments that do not have these facilities.

Convenience sampling

This involves gathering information from anybody available for the interviewer to survey, no matter what their background.

Judgement sampling

This involves selection of respondents by the interviewer according to the interviewer's judgement that they seemed to be and/or looked representative of the group of customers in the market being researched.

Questionnaires

The design of the questionnaire is fundamental to the success of any survey. A badly constructed questionnaire can irritate the respondent and affect the quality of the input. It is important that the person answering the questions knows why he or she is being asked to do so and is happy to co-operate. A good questionnaire should obtain the information required and exclude anything that is unnecessary (see Chapter 12). For example:

1. The questions should be simple, unambiguous and easy to understand. If they are not, they will lead to inaccurate and incomplete responses.
2. The questions should be short, yet fully cover a given area of investigation. They should not ask for too much information.
3. Questions should be logically presented. If the questionnaire is confusing to follow and illogical in order, it will be difficult to complete and unclear in its purpose.
4. The questionnaire should not contain personal questions.

Designing a questionnaire requires considerable expertise. Questions should be brief, functional and provide the sort of information that is needed. The aim must be to obtain the maximum information possible with the greatest of ease. Testing questions on a pilot group is an essential step in questionnaire design, as no matter how carefully you try to anticipate the reactions of respondents to the survey, it is difficult to judge how they will react.

 Task

Prepare a questionnaire which identifies reactions to a local issue. Test it and then comment upon ways in which it could have been 'improved'.

A number of techniques can be used to obtain information:

1. *Direct observation*   This reduces the chance of dubious data being recorded and is considered to be the most accurate form of data collection. Though useful in determining customer patterns, it can be expensive.
2. *Postal questionnaires*   This is often not a very satisfactory method of obtaining data as responses to requests for information are usually not very high and often contain bias.
3. *Telephone interviewing*   Although this is a relatively cheap method of collecting information, depending upon the nature of the survey, results can be biased as not everybody has a telephone. Many respondents consider this method of collecting information to be intrusive.
4. *Face-to-face interviewing*   This will generally lead to more accurate and useful results being obtained. Sometimes it is possible to employ teams of interviewers who can then pool their results.

Collecting secondary data

Organizations prefer to collect primary data, as information collected for a specific purpose is likely to be more useful. However, time, cost and circumstances dictate that it is not always possible to do so, and secondary data, which is collected elsewhere by others, can sometimes be used instead (see Chapter 12). The problems associated with collecting secondary data are that the data might not present a complete picture; for example, the information could be out of date; there is little knowledge of how such data are collected; and the reasons for collection may not be known.

Sources of secondary data are numerous and wide-ranging (see Chapter 12). All published statistics are a form of secondary data, and a series of reference sources are useful for all organizations. Useful information may be picked up by looking at any of the following:

- Company reports
- Business publications such as *The Economist* and *Investors' Weekly*
- Newspapers such as the *Financial Times*
- Trade periodicals and professional magazines
- Reports from a variety of research agencies

Government statistics can often provide a base for further research and analysis. These are available from a number of sources:

1. *Central Statistical Office*   The CSO co-ordinates government statistics and is responsible for the *Monthly Digest of Statistics*, the *Annual Abstract of Statistics*, *Economic Trends* (monthly), *Financial Statistics* (monthly) and the annual *Blue Book on National Income and Expenditure*. For example, the *Monthly Digest of Statistics* will include information on population, employment, social services, law and order, agriculture, information on various industries, entertainments and weather.

2. *Department of Trade and Industry*   The DTI produces a range of publications, many of which are related to specialist areas such as its *Business in Europe* publications. It also publishes *British Industry*, which provides information about the volume of production in various industries as well as details of imports and exports.

3. *Department of Employment*   This department publishes *Employment News* and *Employment Gazette*. These contain details about unemployment rates, wage rates, overtime working, stoppages and retail prices. The following is an extract taken from a recent copy of *Employment News*:

You read *Employment News*, but you still need more information and analysis on

- The labour market
- Employment law
- Training and enterprise
- Health and safety
- Equal opportunities

Then you need to read *Employment Gazette*, the official monthly journal of the Department of Employment, with a unique 70-plus pages of labour market statistical tables.

 Task

Explain the importance of having information concerning two of the areas indicated in the above extract.

4. *Bank of England Quarterly Bulletin*   This analyses a vast amount of data on UK banks, the money supply, borrowing, monetary aggregates and economic indicators.
5. *Census information*   This can provide a range of demographic information which can be useful for marketing purposes.
6. The European Community has a Statistical Office which gathers statistics from member countries and publishes *Basic Statistics of the Community*. The United Nations also publishes statistics upon the world economy.
7. Libraries provide an abundance of useful material to be used for supplementing reports and ideas.

Presentation of data

Once statistical data have been obtained, they need to be broken down so that they can be presented in a way that emphasizes their significance. Information can be displayed in the form of a frequency distribution or table, as a chart or as a graph. The nature of the data collected and the circumstances for which they are needed will determine the way in which data are presented.

Frequency distribution and tables

As data come in, the likelihood is that they will not be in any kind of order. By introducing an order, we can begin to understand something of the values and concentrations of the values we have come across.

An *array* is a simple arrangement of figures into ascending or descending values. If the number of days' credit for 20 customers varied as follows:

        12   21   32   65   18   20   14   51   81   32
        31   45   16   51   71   40   24   32   18   33

we could arrange this in ascending order:

        12   14   16   18   18   20   21   24   31   32
        32   32   33   40   45   51   51   65   71   81

Tally marks are a quick and useful method of counting totals by displaying them in the form of matchsticks. After every four marks the fifth crosses out the previous four so that totals can be easily counted. The average age of a company's employees could be presented in tabular form as shown in Table 10.3.

Table 10.3

Age range	Tally marks	Number of employees
Under 20	II	2
21–30	JHT JHT I	11
31–40	JHT JHT II	12
41–50	JHT III	8
51–60	JHT	5
Over 60	III	3
Total employees		41

By grouping ages into bands, as shown in the table, we do not know the individual age of each employee, but we do know the age ranges. Within each band some measurements of a variable appear more than once, and as the table records how many times a value occurs, it is a *frequency distribution*. As groups have been used, it is a *grouped frequency distribution*.

 Task

The following number of machine breakdowns have occurred each hour over a 40-hour week:

8	15	43	12	51	2	4	19
4	18	39	56	12	23	27	28
11	2	5	25	18	51	19	50
12	5	6	29	16	57	19	33
24	37	18	3	12	6	60	39

Construct a grouped frequency distribution from these data using:

- Six class intervals of equal width
- Class intervals of ten

After data have been broken down, they can be organized into a *table*. A table is just a matrix, or rows and columns, demonstrating the relationship between two variables. In this way it summarizes information into a form that is clear and easy to read.

⌕ Case Study—European population forecasts

Table 10.4   Population forecasts ('000)

	1991	1995	2000	2005	2010	2015	2020
Austria	7 825	7 977	8 091	8 162	8 201	8 221	8 172[e]
Belgium	9 979	9 914	9 893	9 820	9 713	9 580	9 423
Denmark	5 146	5 192	5 233	5 224	5 172	5 095	5 019
Finland	5 029	5 078	5 096	. .	5 076	. .	4 984
France	56 627	57 061	57 883	58 451	58 766	58 821	58 664
Germany	79 113[b]	81 096	81 126	80 224	78 858	77 065	74 964
Greece	10 057[b]	10 110	10 335	10 448	10 554	10 571	10 594
Ireland	3 523	3 503	3 486	3 456	3 466	3 461	3 463
Italy	57 746	57 585	57 611	57 257	56 411	55 089	53 484
Luxemburg	390[c]	387	394	399	403	406	410
Netherlands	15 010	15 497	16 020	16 419	16 688	16 857	16 979
Norway	4 250	4 308	4 373	4 414	4 437	4 455	4 470
Portugal	9 859	10 491	10 577	10 639	10 703	10 612	10 460
Spain	38 960[b]	39 217	39 381	39 333	38 940	38 200	37 231
Sweden	8 644	8 795	8 950	. .	9 167	. .	9 507[d]
Switzerland	6 873	7 087	7 380	7 546	7 591	. .	7 533
Turkey	50 665[a]	62 732	70 440	79 420	. .	. .	. .
United Kingdom	57 486	58 240	59 039	59 599	59 966	60 306	60 674

Notes: [a]1985; [b]1990; [c]1992; [d]2025; [e]2030.
Sources: National statistical offices.

The following questions relate to Table 10.4.
1. What are the variables shown in Table 10.4?
2. Identify two countries that are forecast to experience a decline in population numbers.
3. Explain why a table is a useful method of making comparisons.
4. State one other method of showing this information.

Charts

Charts are eyecatching and enable information to be presented in a form that can be readily understood. A chart may seem to make information more meaningful.

A *pictogram* is a diagramatic form of display which uses pictures instead of numbers. The symbols used in a pictogram must be simple, and items represented by a symbol must be shown in a key (see Fig. 10.2).

In a *pie chart*, each slice represents a component's contribution to the total amount. The 360° of the circle is divided up in proportion to the figures obtained; in order to draw the segments accurately, a protractor is necessary to mark off the degrees. The following method can be used to convert each relative proportion to degrees:

Figure 10.2 Using illustrative material to represent figures.

$$\frac{\text{Proportion}}{\text{Total}} \times 360°$$

A company's export figures are as follows:

Exports	*Size (£m)*
USA	5
Europe	3
Australia	4
Canada	2
Others	6
Total exports	20

$$\text{Exports to the USA} = \frac{5}{20} \times 360° = 90°$$

$$\text{Exports to Europe} = \frac{3}{20} \times 360° = 54°$$

$$\text{Exports to Australia} = \frac{4}{20} \times 360° = 72°$$

$$\text{Exports to Canada} = \frac{2}{20} \times 360° = 36°$$

$$\text{Exports to others} = \frac{6}{20} \times 360° = 108°$$

The pie chart can then be presented as in Fig. 10.3

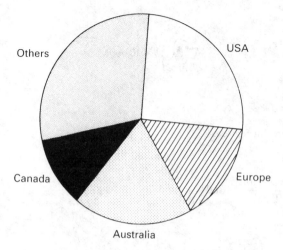

Figure 10.3 Illustrating export figures in a pie chart.

Although pie charts provide a simple form of display, they show only limited information, and it can be difficult to make accurate comparisons of segment sizes.

Case Study—Radio stations

In 1992 there were 156 radio stations in the United Kingdom. Figure 10.4 divides these into three groups:

- BBC national
- BBC local
- Independent local

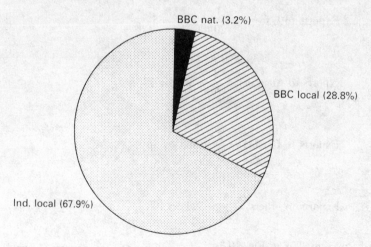

Figure 10.4 Number of radio stations in the United Kingdom, by percentage, in 1992.

Questions

1. What number of stations fall into each category?
2. The average daily listening of these radio stations is as follows:

   (a) BBC national: 89.1 minutes
   (b) BBC local: 13.5 minutes
   (c) Independent local: 59 minutes

   Draw a pie chart to reflect the percentage listening habits of each of the above categories of station.
3. Make a comparison between your own pie chart and the pie chart above and comment on the differences.
4. What use might this information be for a potential advertiser?

In *bar charts*, the areas of comparison are represented by bars which can be drawn either vertically or horizontally. The length of the bar indicates the relative importance of the data.

Suppose a company's production figures over the last five years are as shown in Table 10.5. Data could be shown in either of the ways depicted in Fig. 10.5.

Table 10.5

Year	Units produced
1989	4300
1990	4500
1991	3900
1992	4100
1993	4600

A *component bar chart* enables component areas to be subdivided. Individual component lengths represent actual figures (see Fig. 10.6(a)). With *percentage component bar charts*, individual component lengths represent the percentages that each component forms of the overall total; all bars will therefore be at the full height of 100 per cent (see Fig. 10.6(b)).

A company's sales of products A, B and C in value from 1992 to 1994 are as shown in Table 10.6. Component and percentage component bar charts drawn from the figures in the table are shown in Fig. 10.6.

 Task

Over the last four years the sales of three products for ASAP PLC have been as recorded in Table 10.7.

1. Prepare a percentage component bar chart from these figures.
2. Explain why bar charts are better for making comparisons than pie charts.

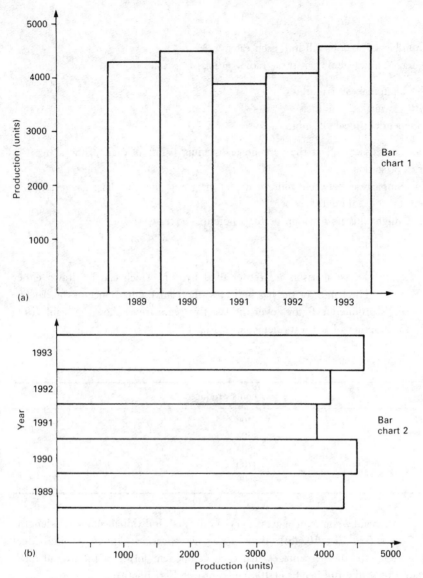

Figure 10.5 Two ways of illustrating a company's production figures from a bar chart.

Table 10.6

	1992		1993		1994	
	£	%	£	%	£	%
Product A	2200	36	2400	38	2500	37
Product B	800	13	700	11	800	12
Product C	3100	51	3200	51	3500	51
Total	6100	100	6300	100	6800	100

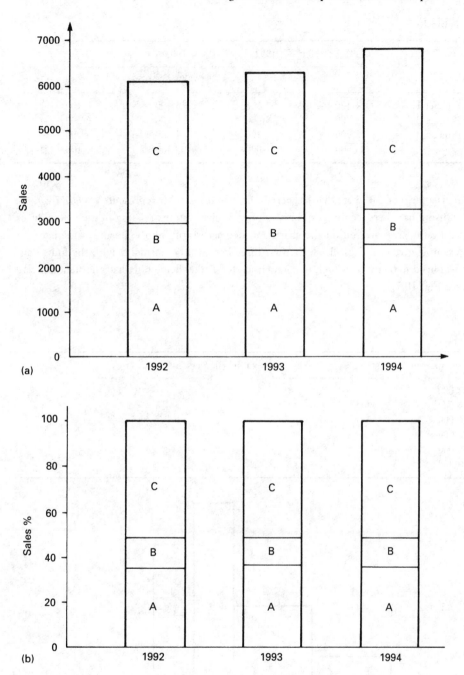

Figure 10.6 (a) A component bar chart; (b) a percentage component bar chart.

Table 10.7

	1991	1992	1993	1994
		(£'000)		
Product 1	4 100	4 500	4 400	2 100
Product 2	5 300	5 400	5 700	6 300
Product 3	2 200	4 100	4 300	4 700
	11 600	14 000	14 400	13 100

A *histogram* is a form of bar chart that has certain unique features. It represents *grouped frequency distributions* using bar chart techniques. The number of observations relating to each variable are represented by the area covered on the chart, and not necessarily by the height of the bar.

In the example given in Table 10.8, the first three bars will be normal height; the fourth and fifth bars will need to be twice as high to compensate for £1000 being only half the standard class interval (see Fig. 10.7).

Table 10.8

Sales per salesperson (units)	No. of salespersons
Up to 2 000	2
2000 to 4 000	5
4000 to 6 000	10
6000 to 7 000	10
7000 to 8 000	8
8000 to 10 000	2

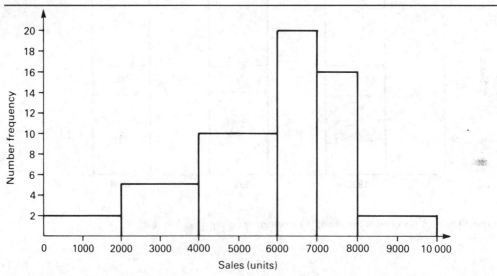

Figure 10.7 An example of a histogram.

Clearly, therefore, if the class intervals are different the height of each bar needs to be worked out. In many situations, however, it is more than likely that the class intervals of each bar will be the same and that this procedure will not be necessary, so that the histogram can be drawn straight from the frequency distribution. Histograms are a variation of a bar chart in which it is the area, and not necessarily the height, of the bar that represents the frequency.

Whereas a histogram is a stepped graph, it might be desirable to show information in the form of a single curve. Such a curve is known as a *frequency polygon*. It is drawn by constructing a histogram, marking off the mid-point of the top of each rectangle and then joining the mid-points with straight lines (see Fig. 10.8).

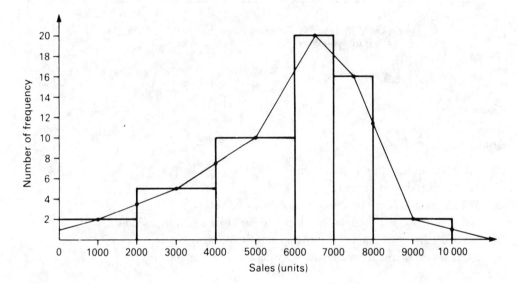

Figure 10.8 Frequency polygon and histogram.

The curve of a frequency polygon is extended at both ends so that it cuts the axis at points half a class interval beyond the outside limits of the end-classes. The area of the frequency polygon is exactly the same as that of a histogram, since the area lost as each rectangle is cut by the polygon has the same area as each triangle added. If the frequency polygon is smoothed out, it is known as a *frequency curve*.

℘ Case Study—Group sales area at Sainsbury's

Figure 10.9 compares the group sales area at Sainsbury's between 1988 and 1992. It can be seen that the group sales area increased by more than 40 per cent to 13.1 million square feet. Examine the chart and answer the questions that follow.

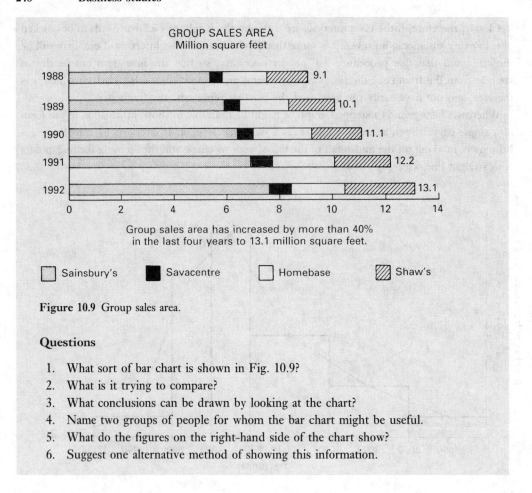

Figure 10.9 Group sales area.

Questions

1. What sort of bar chart is shown in Fig. 10.9?
2. What is it trying to compare?
3. What conclusions can be drawn by looking at the chart?
4. Name two groups of people for whom the bar chart might be useful.
5. What do the figures on the right-hand side of the chart show?
6. Suggest one alternative method of showing this information.

Gantt charts were named after Henry Gantt, a management scientist who lived during the early years of this century. They are a useful form of bar/line chart which compares *actual* progress with *forecast* progress. They can be used as a visual tool to indicate whether performances are on schedule (see Fig. 10.10).

A *spreadsheet* is a business tool which can be used for planning, budgeting and record-keeping (see Chapter 21). Many spreadsheets, such as Microsoft Works, appear as part of an integrated package of tools and devices for personal computers (PCs). Such spreadsheets frequently have *charting devices*, linked so that visual presentations can be made of spreadsheet data. These are specifically designed to make information easier to analyse and interpret and also to show a more dynamic way of analysing trends than by just using a table. The spreadsheet illustrated in Fig. 10.11 has been written on Microsoft Works.

Using the charting device, it is possible to show the production figures of just one department (Department A in Fig. 10.12(a), (b), (c)), or to compare the production figures of all three (Fig. 10.12(d)).

Month	Forecast	Actual	Percentage
1	300	240	80
2	350	350	100
3	400	440	110

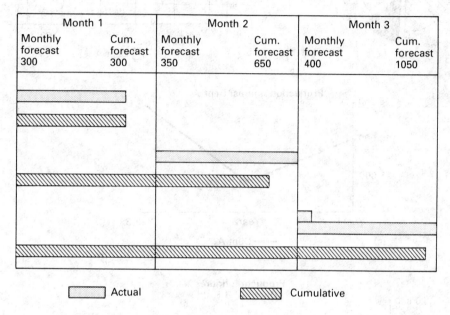

Figure 10.10 An example of a Gantt chart.

	Year 1	Year 2	Year 3
Dept A	10 000	4000	15 000
Dept B	12 000	5000	16 000
Dept C	15 000	6000	17 000

Figure 10.11 A simple spreadsheet showing the production figures of three departments over a three-year period.

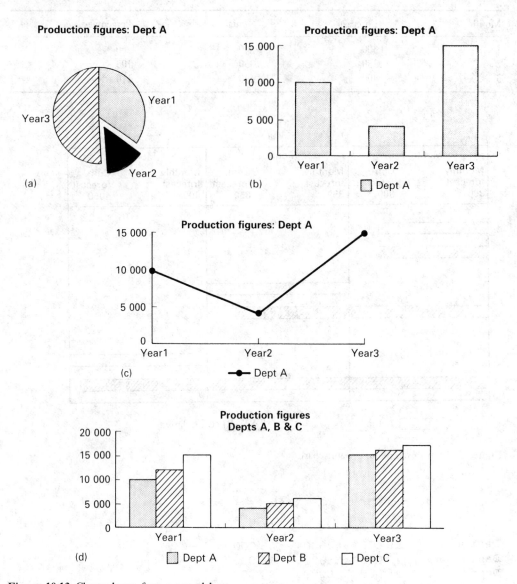

Figure 10.12 Charts drawn from a spreadsheet.

Graphs

Graphs show the relationship between two variables and can be presented in the form of either a straight line or a curve. Whereas frequency polygons show frequency distribution, the *ogive* is the name given to the curve when cumulative frequencies of a distribution are presented in the form of a graph. Figure 10.13 depicts a firm's sales totals over 40 weeks as shown in Table 10.9. Any point on the graph will not relate sales achievements directly to output in the same way as an ordinary graph, but it will indicate how many times the number of sales units (or less than that number) was achieved.

Table 10.9

Output (units)	No. of times sales realized (weeks)	Cumulative frequency
0–400	3	3
401–800	9	$3 + 9 = 12$
801–1200	13	$3 + 9 + 13 = 25$
1201–1600	11	$3 + 9 + 13 + 11 = 36$
1601–2000	$\underline{4}$	$3 + 9 + 13 + 11 + 4 = 40$
	40	

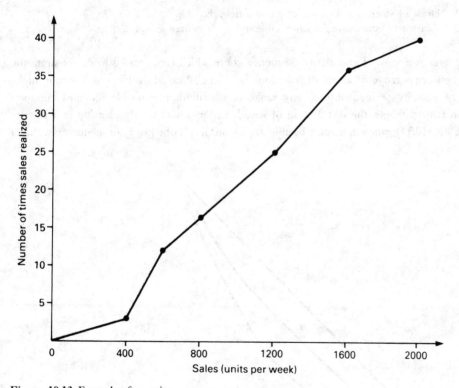

Figure 10.13 Example of an ogive.

 Task

You work for a building society in Barnstable and have been asked by your employer to present the following information in a graphical form as part of an exploration of your branch's activities to a group of fifth-formers in a local school:

Percentage of loans granted

House prices (£)	Buyers
Under 20 000	3
20 000–39 999	7
40 000–59 999	11
60 000–79 999	13
80 000–99 999	14
100 000–119 999	21
120 000–139 999	13
140 000–159 999	18
	100

1. Draw a histogram and frequency polygon from the table.
2. Construct a cumulative frequency table and use it to draw an ogive.

A *Lorenz curve* is a form of cumulative frequency curve which can be used to demonstrate the disparity between a range of actual distribution and a line of equal distribution, thereby highlighting the equality or inequality of any range of distribution. Probably its most common application is to highlight the distribution of wealth within a society. By glancing at a Lorenz curve (see Fig. 10.14), you will quickly be able to pick out levels of equality or inequality within a

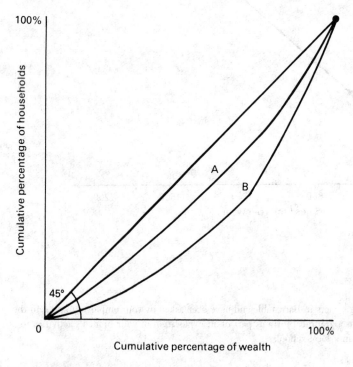

Figure 10.14 A Lorenz curve illustrating differences in the distribution of wealth in two countries.

society. If the distribution is completely even, this shows that wealth is spread evenly between members of a society (there is no concentration of wealth). If the distribution is uneven (a feature of most societies), then this will appear as a difference between the line showing the actual distribution of wealth and a line of equal distribution. In Fig. 10.14 we can quickly see that the distribution of wealth in country A is a lot more even than in country B.

It is possible to draw a Lorenz curve to show the relationship between the size of the firm and the output of an industry. In the example given in Table 10.10, the size of the firm is measured by the number of employees. In order to construct a Lorenz curve, these figures need to be broken down further. Table 10.11 includes a column that calculates each figure as a percentage of its column total, as well as a column that lists the cumulative total percentages; the cumulative total percentages are the figures required to construct the curve (see Fig. 10.15). If all firms were of equal size, then 25 per cent of output would have been produced by 25 per cent of the firms. The curve that would be expected to obtain if all firms were of equal size is therefore the line of equal distribution. The extent to which a Lorenz curve deviates away from the line of equal distribution reflects the degree of inequality. The Lorenz curve in Fig. 10.15 shows that, as we would expect, larger firms generate more output. By looking at the curve at its furthest point from the equal distribution line, we can see that 60 per cent of firms control 30 per cent of output, and so it is clearly not equally shared.

Table 10.10

No. of employees	No. of firms	Output (tonnes)
Under 50	50	3 000
50–99	80	12 000
100–199	120	21 000
200–299	135	48 000
300 and over	25	36 000
	400	120 000

Table 10.11

No. of firms			Output (tonnes)		
No.	%	Cumulative %	No.	%	Cumulative %
40	10	10	3 000	2.5	2.5
80	20	30	12 000	10	12.5
120	30	60	21 000	17.5	30
135	34	94	48 000	40	70
25	6	100	36 000	30	100
400	100		120 000	100	

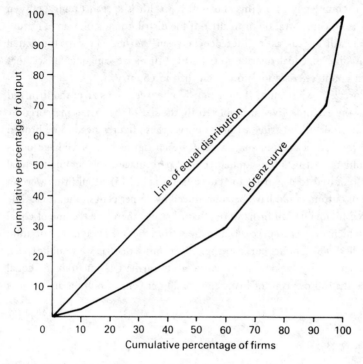

Figure 10.15 A Lorenz curve showing the distribution of production between firms.

 Task

A market research agency is undertaking a survey on behalf of a company concerned about falling sales in a town in Scotland. The company is particularly concerned about changes in the distribution of wealth caused by recent factory closures and increasing unemployment levels. After an extensive survey involving a carefully worded questionnaire, the agency has extracted the figures shown in Table 10.12 relating to the spread of wealth in the area.

Table 10.12

Wealth (£ per adult)	No. of people	Total wealth (£m)
Under 10 000	1200	9.5
10 000–49 999	1500	52.5
50 000–99 999	1300	97.0
100 000–149 999	400	50.0
Over 150 000	100	20.0
	4500	229.0

1. Construct a Lorenz curve.
2. Comment upon the distribution shown by the graph.

Central tendency

We have looked at information needs for simple problems, at the breaking down of data into frequency distributions and at how they can be represented diagrammatically. Having broken data down into a more manageable form, we need to be able to draw useful information from them, and a measure of central tendency provides one method of doing this.

Central tendency is a measure of middle values. When we talk about middle values, we normally think of an *average*. An average, as we know it, is an arithmetic mean, but two other measures of average or central tendency are the *median* and *mode*.

A company's production levels over 50 days were as follows:

```
5  6  2  6  5  2  6  4  6  5
5  6  4  5  3  5  6  5  6  5
6  5  3  3  2  4  3  2  3  5
4  3  5  2  1  5  2  5  1  4
5  4  4  4  5  3  5  2  4  5
```

From these levels we can derive the frequency distribution given in Table 10.13.

Table 10.13

Daily production levels (units)	Frequency	Level × frequency
1	2	2
2	7	14
3	7	21
4	10	40
5	16	80
6	8	48
	50	205

The mean is quite simply the total of a set of numbers, divided by the number of items. The mean of 6, 7, 14 and 5 would be:

$$\frac{6+7+14+5}{4} = \frac{32}{4} = 8$$

Therefore

$$\text{Arithmetic mean} = \frac{\text{Sum of observations}}{\text{Number of observations}}$$

In order to work out the mean of figures in the example, we could:

1. Add up all of the daily production levels and divide the total by 50 (see table). This can be time-consuming and prone to error.
2. Alternatively, we could use the frequency distribution table. By multiplying the value or daily production level by the frequency (f) with which it occurs, a similar total is achieved, which can then be divided by the number of days (see Table 10.13):

$$\text{Arithmetic mean} = \frac{205}{50} = 4.1 \text{ units per day}$$

Although the mean is the best-known of the averages and we often hear about it and see it in our everyday circumstances, it can be distorted by a few extreme values and also may result in an impractical figure, e.g. 1.35 workers.

The arithmetic mean is often written as $\bar{x}$ and its formula is shown as:

$$\bar{x} = \frac{\sum fx}{\sum f}$$

The *mode* refers to the value that occurs more frequently than any other. If the production level in units of four workers is 15, 12, 15 and 17, the mode will be 15 as that number has occurred more than any other value. If two or more frequencies occur the same number of times, there is clearly more than one mode and the distribution is *multi-modal*; where there is only one mode the distribution is *unimodal*.

Finding a mode in a grouped frequency distribution can be done only with approximate mathematical accuracy.

The figures given in Table 10.14 relate to value and frequency.

Table 10.14

Value		Frequency
At least	Less than	
10	20	5
20	30	12
30	40	18
40	50	10
50	60	4

The mode is approximated by:

$$L + \left[\frac{(F - F_m - 1) \times c}{2F - F_m - 1 - F_m + 1} \right]$$

where:

L = lower limit of modal class
$F_m - 1$ = frequency of class below modal class
F = frequency of modal class
$F_m + 1$ = frequency of class above modal class
c = class interval

Our estimate of the mode would therefore be:

$$\text{Mode} = 30 + \left[\frac{(18 - 12) \times 10}{(2 \times 18) - 12 - 10} \right]$$

$$\text{Mode} = 30 + \left[\frac{(6 \times 10)}{(36 - 22)} \right]$$

$$\text{Mode} = 30 + 4.28$$

$$\text{Mode} = 34.28$$

As we have emphasized, when calculated this way the mode is only an estimated figure and therefore is limited in use for further statistical processes.

The *median* is the middle number in a distribution or array of figures. When figures are arranged into either ascending or descending order, the median will be the one in the middle. For example, if data were ordered into an array containing 2, 7, 9, 12 and 15, 9 would be the number in the middle.

In our distribution of 50 days' production levels (see page 255), we have an even number of figures. If we are calculating the median for a frequency distribution, it is usual to accept the middle value as $(n + 1)/2$ if the total frequency (n) is an odd number, and as $n/2$ if the total frequency (n) is an even number. As we have 50 values, the median will be 50/2 and therefore the 25th number. The 25th number reflects a daily production level of four units in ascending order.

If data are incomplete, the median can still be calculated. If you do not have information about lower or upper salaries but know how many employees you have, you can still determine the median item. Also, as the median uses only one value in a distribution, it is not changed by distorted or extreme values.

Dispersion

Range

Although averages are important in providing us with information about the middle of a distribution, they do not tell us how other figures in the distribution are spread. Information might reveal the same mean, but the spread of some data might be tight while others might be well dispersed.

A *range* represents the difference between the highest and lowest values in a set of data. It is easy to find and provides information about a spread of figures:

Range = Highest value − lowest value

The problem with looking at a range is that it might be affected by one extreme value and it provides no indication of the spread between values. The range for 4, 4, 4, 4, 4 and 20 000 is 4 to 20 000. This is misleading in terms of both values and the spread between the extremes. This disadvantage can be overcome and extreme values can be ignored by slicing away the top and bottom quarters and then analysing what is left.

Whereas the median is the middle number of an array of figures and represents 50 per cent, a *quartile* represents a quarter or 25 per cent of a range. The lower or first quartile is the area below which 25 per cent of observations fall, and the upper or fourth quartile is the value above which 25 per cent of observations fall:

Inter-quartile range = Upper quartile − lower quartile

From this, conclusions can be drawn about the middle 50 per cent of data analysed.

We can extract the lower quartile, median, upper quartile and inter-quartile range from the following array of 20 numbers:

$$4 \quad 5 \quad 8 \quad 9 \quad 15 \quad 18 \quad 20 \quad 22 \quad 24 \quad 29$$
$$32 \quad 35 \quad 37 \quad 40 \quad 44 \quad 44 \quad 48 \quad 52 \quad 58 \quad 60$$

The lower quartile will be the value below which 25 per cent of the numbers will fall and therefore will be 25 per cent of 20 and the fifth value of 15. Using $n/2$, the median will be 20/2 giving the tenth value. This is 29. The upper quartile will be the value above which 25 per cent of the numbers fall. As there are 20 values in the array, it will be 75 per cent of 20 and the fifteenth value is 44. Whereas the range for this set of figures is 54 and extends from 4 to 60, the inter-quartile range will be the upper quartile of 44 less the lower quartile of 15 and will be 29.

Although the inter-quartile range, or *quartile deviation*, is easy to understand and is unaffected by extreme values, it might not be precise enough for a large sample. In these instances it could be necessary to use *deciles* or *percentiles*. Deciles relate the various tenths of a distribution. From our example, the first decile will be 10 per cent of 20 and the second value of 5; the second decile will be the fourth value of 9; and so on. Percentiles relate to hundredths of the way through a distribution. The 95th percentile of our values will be 95 per cent of the 20 values and so therefore will be the nineteenth value of 58.

Mean deviation

A measure of dispersion that further analyses a group of values and makes use of all observations is the mean deviation. This simply measures the average deviation of all values in a distribution from the actual mean. It averages the differences between the actual values in a distribution and the mean, while at the same time ignoring the negative signs of differences. For the figures of 5, 6, 13, 20 and 26, the arithmetic mean ($\bar{x}$) is:

$$\bar{x} = \frac{5 + 6 + 13 + 20 + 26}{5} = \frac{70}{5} = 14$$

The differences from the arithmetic mean are:

$$5 - 14, 6 - 14, 13 - 14, 20 - 14, 26 - 14$$

and these are:

$$-9, -8, -1, 6, 12$$

If we ignore the negative signs, we can find the mean deviation as follows:

$$\frac{9 + 8 + 1 + 6 + 12}{5} = \frac{36}{5} = 7.2$$

The mean deviation or average differences from the mean is therefore 7.2, and the more usual way of expressing this is:

$$\text{Mean deviation} = \frac{\sum |x - \bar{x}|}{n}$$

where $|x - \bar{x}|$ means the difference between the mean and the actual value but ignoring negative signs.

Variance and standard deviation

The major problem of all the methods of dispersion looked at so far is that they have limited uses in further analysing data. Having worked out a quartile or a decile, you know more about a distribution, but there are few further uses for this information. As the mean deviation ignores the plus and minus differences, it also has limited uses for further statistical processing. This is not the case for the variance and standard deviation, which have widespread use in statistical analysis and are considered the most important measures of dispersion.

Variance

Instead of ignoring the minuses in differences from the mean, the variance and standard deviation square the differences, and this process instantly eliminates the negative signs. When the squared differences have been averaged, a variance is created and the square root of this variance provides the standard deviation. This can be seen more clearly from an example.

If the output of a machine over five days were 4, 5, 5, 7 and 9 units, the arithmetic mean would be 6. The variance measures the extent of the dispersion around the mean by:

1. Calculating the difference between the number of units produced each day and the arithmetic mean: this is shown as $x - \bar{x}$.
2. Squaring the difference $(x - \bar{x})^2$.
3. Finding the average of the total of these squared differences. This is shown as $[\Sigma(x - \bar{x})^2]/n$, where n is the number of values (see Table 10.15).

Table 10.15

Outputs x	$x - \bar{x}$	$(x - \bar{x})^2$
4	−2	4
5	−1	1
5	−1	1
7	1	1
9	3	9
	0	16

The variance would be

$$\frac{16}{5} = 3.2 \text{ units}$$

Standard deviation

The standard deviation is the square root of the variance. In our example this will be:

$$\sqrt{3.2} = 1.79 \text{ units}$$

Thus we have an arithmetic mean of 6 units, a variance of 3.2 and a standard deviation of 1.79 units. By taking into consideration frequency (f) and denoting standard deviation as s, we can show its formula as follows:

$$s = \sqrt{\frac{\Sigma f (x - \bar{x})^2}{n}} \quad \text{or} \quad \sqrt{\frac{\Sigma f(x - \bar{x})^2}{\Sigma f}}$$

The example given in Table 10.16 takes into consideration frequency and has an arithmetic mean ($\bar{x}$) of 6. The standard deviation will be $\sqrt{1.4} = 1.18$.

Although it is sometimes difficult to understand the significance of the standard deviation, it can be said that the greater the dispersion, the larger the standard deviation. As all values in the distribution are taken into account, it is a comprehensive measure of dispersion capable of being developed further.

Table 10.16

Value x	Frequency f	$x - \bar{x}$	$(x - \bar{x})^2$	$f(x - \bar{x})^2$
4	4	−2	4	16
5	6	−1	1	6
6	9	0	0	0
7	8	1	1	8
8	3	2	4	12
	30			42

Distribution curves

Any frequency distribution may either be symmetrical or skewed. A *symmetrical* frequency curve will be divided into two equal halves so that the arithmetic mean, median and mode will all have the same value. Such distributions create a normal curve with a symmetrical bell shape and represent a continuous variable in frequency distribution (see Fig. 10.16).

The normal distribution curve represents all possible outcomes and the frequency with which they will take place. As the curve is symmetrical, 50 per cent of events will take place above the mean value and 50 per cent below the mean value (see Fig. 10.17). Therefore this can be used with measurements that follow a normal pattern of distribution to find probabilities of certain events taking place.

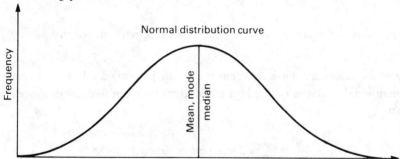

Figure 10.16 Normal distribution curve.

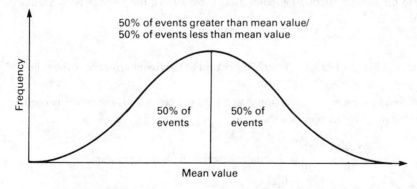

Figure 10.17 (50 per cent of events greater than mean value)/(50 per cent of events less than mean value).

Normal distribution tables can be used to find these probabilities, as they measure the area from the mean to a fixed number of standard deviations away from the mean. The letter Z represents the number of standard deviations a value is above or below the mean. It is calculated by:

$$Z = \frac{x - m}{s}$$

where:
Z = number of standard deviations above or below the mean
x = the value
m = the mean
s = the standard deviation

A frequency has a normal distribution, a mean of 50 and a standard deviation of 10. We can use this process to find out what proportion of the total frequencies will be:

- Above 30
- Above 60
- Below 45
- Below 75

To calculate the proportion of frequencies *above* a value, it must be remembered that:

1. Fifty per cent of the values are above the mean and so the proportion calculated as being between the mean and the value must be added to the 50 per cent. For frequencies above 30, we can see that:

$$Z = \frac{50 - 30}{10} = \frac{20}{10} = 2 \text{ standard deviations}$$

By referring to the normal distribution tables (see Table 10.17), the number of frequencies above 30 is therefore:
$$0.5 + 0.4772 = 0.9772 \text{ or } 97.72\%$$

The shaded area in Fig. 10.18 represents 97.72 per cent of the frequencies above the value of 30.

2. If the value is above the mean, the total proportion is 50 per cent minus the area between the value and the mean. With frequencies above 60,

$$Z = \frac{60 - 50}{10} = \frac{10}{10} = 1 \text{ standard deviation above the mean}$$

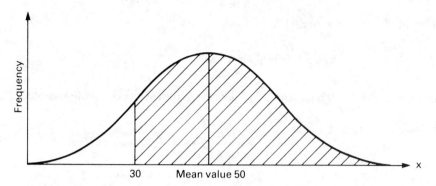

Figure 10.18 Frequencies above 30.

Table 10.17 Normal distribution tables

Z	0.00	0.01	0.02	0.03	0.04	0.05	0.06	0.07	0.08	0.09
0.0	0.0000	0.0040	0.0080	0.0120	0.0160	0.0199	0.0239	0.0279	0.0319	0.0359
0.1	0.0398	0.0438	0.0478	0.0517	0.0557	0.0596	0.0636	0.0675	0.0714	0.0753
0.2	0.0793	0.0832	0.0871	0.0910	0.0948	0.0987	0.1026	0.1064	0.1103	0.1141
0.3	0.1179	0.1217	0.1255	0.1293	0.1331	0.1368	0.1406	0.1443	0.1480	0.1517
0.4	0.1554	0.1591	0.1628	0.1664	0.1700	0.1736	0.1772	0.1808	0.1844	0.1879
0.5	0.1915	0.1950	0.1985	0.2019	0.2054	0.2088	0.2123	0.2157	0.2190	0.2224
0.6	0.2257	0.2291	0.2324	0.2357	0.2389	0.2422	0.2454	0.2486	0.2517	0.2549
0.7	0.2580	0.2611	0.2642	0.2673	0.2704	0.2734	0.2764	0.2794	0.2823	0.2852
0.8	0.2881	0.2910	0.2939	0.2967	0.2995	0.3023	0.3051	0.3078	0.3106	0.3133
0.9	0.3159	0.3186	0.3212	0.3238	0.3264	0.3289	0.3315	0.3340	0.3365	0.3389
1.0	0.3413	0.3438	0.3461	0.3485	0.3508	0.3531	0.3554	0.3577	0.3599	0.3621
1.1	0.3643	0.3665	0.3686	0.3708	0.3729	0.3749	0.3770	0.3790	0.3810	0.3830
1.2	0.3849	0.3869	0.3888	0.3907	0.3925	0.3944	0.3962	0.3980	0.3997	0.4015
1.3	0.4032	0.4049	0.4066	0.4082	0.4099	0.4115	0.4131	0.4147	0.4162	0.4177
1.4	0.4192	0.4207	0.4222	0.4236	0.4251	0.4265	0.4279	0.4292	0.4306	0.4319
1.5	0.4332	0.4345	0.4357	0.4370	0.4382	0.4394	0.4406	0.4418	0.4429	0.4441
1.6	0.4452	0.4463	0.4474	0.4484	0.4495	0.4505	0.4515	0.4525	0.4535	0.4545
1.7	0.4554	0.4564	0.4573	0.4582	0.4591	0.4599	0.4608	0.4616	0.4625	0.4633
1.8	0.4641	0.4649	0.4656	0.4664	0.4671	0.4678	0.4686	0.4693	0.4699	0.4706
1.9	0.4713	0.4719	0.4726	0.4732	0.4738	0.4744	0.4750	0.4756	0.4761	0.4767
2.0	0.4772	0.4778	0.4783	0.4788	0.4793	0.4798	0.4803	0.4808	0.4812	0.4817
2.1	0.4821	0.4826	0.4830	0.4834	0.4838	0.4842	0.4846	0.4850	0.4854	0.4857
2.2	0.4861	0.4864	0.4868	0.4871	0.4875	0.4878	0.4881	0.4884	0.4887	0.4890
2.3	0.4893	0.4896	0.4898	0.4901	0.4904	0.4906	0.4909	0.4911	0.4913	0.4916
2.4	0.4918	0.4920	0.4922	0.4925	0.4927	0.4929	0.4931	0.4932	0.4934	0.4936
2.5	0.4938	0.4940	0.4941	0.4943	0.4945	0.4946	0.4948	0.4949	0.4951	0.4952
2.6	0.4953	0.4955	0.4956	0.4957	0.4959	0.4960	0.4961	0.4962	0.4963	0.4964
2.7	0.4965	0.4966	0.4967	0.4968	0.4969	0.4970	0.4971	0.4972	0.4973	0.4974
2.8	0.4974	0.4975	0.4976	0.4977	0.4977	0.4978	0.4979	0.4979	0.4980	0.4981
2.9	0.4981	0.4982	0.4982	0.4983	0.4984	0.4984	0.4985	0.4985	0.4986	0.4986
3.0	0.4987	0.4987	0.4987	0.4988	0.4988	0.4989	0.4989	0.4989	0.4990	0.4990

The number of frequencies above 60 is therefore

$$0.5 - 0.3413 \text{ or } 15.87\%$$

The shaded area in Fig. 10.19 represents 15.87 per cent of the frequencies above the value of 60.

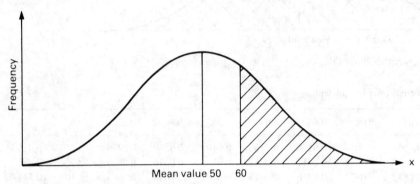

Figure 10.19 Frequencies above 60.

To calculate the proportion of frequencies *below* a certain value:

1. If the value is below the mean, the proportion is 50 per cent minus the area between the value and the mean. With frequencies below 45,

$$Z = \frac{50 - 45}{10} = \frac{5}{10} = 0.5 \text{ standard deviation below the mean}$$

The number of frequencies below 45 are therefore:

$$0.5 - 0.1915 = 0.3085 \text{ or } 30.85\%$$

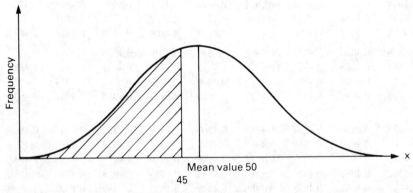

Figure 10.20 Frequencies below 45.

The shaded area in Fig. 10.20 represents 30.85 per cent of the frequencies below the value of 45.

2. If the value is above the mean, the proportion to be obtained is 50 per cent plus the area between the value and the mean. With frequencies below 75,

$$Z = \frac{75 - 50}{10} = \frac{25}{10} = 2.5 \text{ standard deviations above the mean}$$

The number of frequencies below 75 are therefore:

$$0.5 + 0.4938 = 0.9938 \text{ or } 99.38\%$$

The shaded area in Fig. 10.21 represents 99.38 per cent of the frequencies below the value of 75.

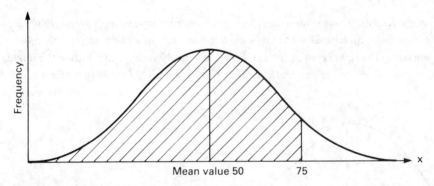

Figure 10.21 Frequencies below 75.

Binomial distribution

The name 'binomial' refers to another method of analysing probability from a distribution and relates to any situation where there are two possible alternatives. You might change your car, or you might not change your car: there are two possible courses of action. For any situation to fit the binomial pattern so that an experience can take place, one of the following must apply:

1. It must be an either/or situation with only two possible outcomes.
2. It must consist of a number of trials denoted by n.
3. It must have a known probability of success on each trial denoted by p.

Probability may be measured with some certainty. If a die is rolled, there is a 0.167 probability (i.e. one in six) that a 4 will turn up; when a coin is tossed, there is a 0.5 probability (one in two) that it will turn up heads. Probability may be measured from past experiences, from information such as weather records, analyses of machine breakdowns, faulty goods, working days lost, etc. It may also be estimated from surveys or a series of trials in the market.

If a sample contained five green products, two yellow products and three purple products, and if supplies were not replaced after having been taken, we can work out the probability of a customer picking out the two yellow products. On the first occasion the chances of picking out two yellow products are 2/10, so $p = 1/5$. As there is only one yellow left, the chances of picking that out are one in nine with only nine products remaining. By multiplying the two probabilities together, we can work out the chances of picking two yellow products:

$$\frac{1}{9} \times \frac{1}{5} = \frac{1}{45}$$

With a knowledge of probabilities, using the binomial to model a problem enables management to predict more precisely the outcomes of future events.

Skewness

Skewness is used to describe a non-symmetrical frequency distribution curve. A *positively skewed frequency distribution curve* will have a bias towards the left-hand side of a graph and will then have a long tail sloping out to the right (see Fig. 10.22). With a positively skewed distribution the mode will have a lower value than the median and the mean will have a higher value than the median.

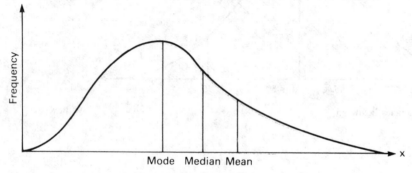

Figure 10.22 Positively skewed frequency distribution curve.

A *negatively skewed frequency distribution curve* will have a bias towards the right-hand side of the graph and will have a long tail sloping out towards the left (see Fig. 10.23). With a negatively skewed distribution the mode will have a higher value than the median and the mean will have a

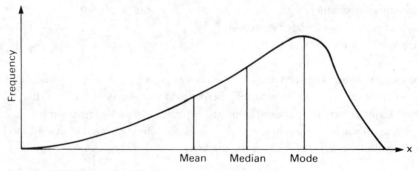

Figure 10.23 Negatively skewed frequency distribution curve.

⌕ Case Study—Statistical process control

Statistical process control (SPC) is a quality system which uses simple statistics to assist in the control of processes of manufacture. Any manufacturing process is the combination of the four M's—men, materials, machines and methods—which, together with the environment, affect output (Fig. 10.24).

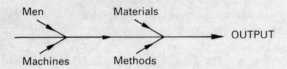

Figure 10.24 The manufacturing process.

With SPC, output is in statistical control only when the sole reason for variation is due to common causes and even these can be reduced. *Common causes* are inherent to the process and therefore are stable over time. These are always predictable and present. *Special causes* are not inherent to the process and are due to a few major causes. These are unpredictable and will recur if no action is taken.

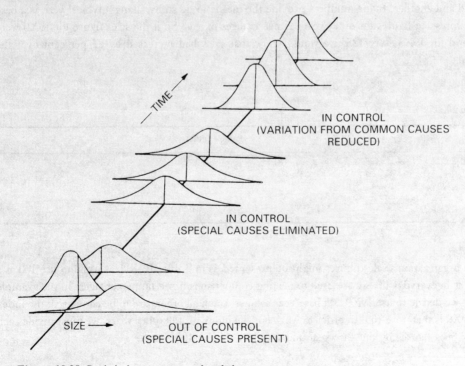

Figure 10.25 Statistical process control and the many causes.

The lower part of Fig. 10.25 shows that when special causes are present the distribution of products is skewed. When special causes are eliminated the distribution becomes normal, and when common causes are reduced more products are centred around the mean, median and mode. Statistical process control should be viewed as part of a never-ending search to improve product quality. A process is in statistical control when all of the points are within control limits and there are no abnormal patterns or trends present.

Questions

1. Explain how statistics can support manufacturing quality procedures.
2. Why do 'special causes' lead to skewed frequency distributions?
3. When is a process in statistical control?

Index numbers

It is sometimes difficult to make comparisons between sets of figures. Often the complexity, the relevance and the size of the units being measured can make direct comparisons meaningless. Instead of trying to make sense of complicated technical figures based upon a mass of information, it can be better to strive for a single figure which shows a direct comparison between one time period and another. Index numbers provide the means to do so by taking a typical year as a base and expressing figures for other years as percentages of this. So if the sales figure for 19X0 were 100 and for 19X3 were 125, we would know that sales had increased by 25 per cent over the period.

Table 10.18

Year	Sales ('000)
19X0	458
19X1	535
19X2	573
19X3	584

An organization's sales figures might be presented as in Table 10.18. It is usual to use 100 as a base, as in everyday life we are used to making comparisons based on percentages. In the example above we decide to use 19X0 as a base year against which all others are to be compared; the index for 19X0 is therefore 100. In order to work out the index for the other years, we must divide each year's sales figures by the base year and multiply this by 100:

$$\frac{\text{Figures for other years}}{\text{Base year's figures}} \times 100$$

$$\text{For 19X1 this will be} \frac{535}{458} \times 100 = 116.81$$

$$\text{For 19X2 this will be} \frac{573}{458} \times 100 = 125.11$$

$$\text{For 19X3 this will be} \frac{584}{458} \times 100 = 127.51$$

We can see from these figures that sales have increased by nearly 28 per cent from 19X0 to 19X3. We can also work out annual percentage increases from the index. Between 19X2 and 19X3 the index has risen by 2.4 points. By dividing this by the sales index figure for 19X2 and converting the result to a percentage, we can find the percentage increase in sales for 19X3:

$$\frac{2.4}{125.11} \times 100 = 1.92\% \text{ increase in sales}$$

Index numbers are often calculated to represent a wide variety of areas or items. We use an index number to compare retail prices between one year and another, and this Retail Price Index is used as an indicator of domestic price inflation. Domestic prices cover a host of commodities, and clearly more than one item is taken into consideration when putting this index together.

Table 10.19

Item	19X0	19X1
Bread	50p per loaf	55p per loaf
Cheese	130p per kg	125p per kg
Meat	160p per kg	180p per kg
Vegetables	40p per kg	50p per kg

We can produce a hypothetical example for country A, where the four commodities included in the retail price index are bread, cheese, meat and vegetables (Table 10.19). In the year 19X0 to 19X1, prices for bread, meat and vegetables went up but the price of cheese fell. We wish to produce a single index figure to reflect these changes, but the table gives no indication of how important each item is to the cost of living and also tries to compare different units. This can be overcome by *weighting* each item in proportion to its relative importance. By selecting a weight, the importance of each item and the units in which it appears are taken into consideration to produce a final figure which is directly comparable. The procedure for doing this is:

1. List all the items with their prices.
2. Select appropriate weights.
3. Multiply prices by their weights.

4. Add the weighted prices together.
5. Produce an index by comparing the total weighted prices from the base year to the other year.

In our example we allocate a weight of 80 to bread, 30 to meat and 10 to vegetables (Table 10.20). By using 19X0 as the base year and designating 100 to it, we can see that:

$$\frac{16\,550}{15\,700} \times 100 = 105.41$$

i.e., prices have risen during the year by 5.41 per cent.

Table 10.20   Weighted cost of living index

| Item | Weight | 19X0 | | 19X1 | |
		Price	Price × weight	Price	Price × weight
Bread	80	50	4 000	35	4 400
Cheese	50	130	6 500	125	6 250
Meat	30	160	4 800	180	5 400
Vegetables	10	40	400	50	500
Total			15 700		16 550

Probably the best known of all UK official statistics is the Consumer Price Index, which is generally accepted as the official measure of price inflation. This measures inflation in real terms rather than just monetary terms and has considerable ramifications for pay negotiation and settlements.

Although indices are traditionally associated with prices, they can also be used for a multitude of commercial purposes such as insurance and index-linked schemes. Perhaps their greatest advantage is that they are easy to understand and provide a common scale by which to compare different types of information.

$\wp$ Case Study—Internal purchasing power of the pound

The following questions relate to Table 10.21.

1. Compare the purchasing power of the pound between 1981 and 1991.
2. Explain how index numbers help to make such comparisons possible.

Table 10.21 Internal purchasing power of the pound (based on the Consumer Price Index)

Year in which purchasing power was 100p

	1981	1982	1983	1984	1985	1986	1987	1988	1989	1990	1991
1981	100	109	114	119	126	131	136	143	154	169	179
1982	92	100	105	110	116	120	125	132	142	155	164
1983	88	96	100	105	111	115	120	126	136	149	157
1984	84	91	95	100	106	110	114	120	129	141	150
1985	79	86	90	94	100	103	108	113	122	133	141
1986	76	83	87	91	97	100	104	109	118	129	137
1987	73	80	83	88	93	96	100	105	113	124	131
1988	70	76	79	83	88	92	95	100	108	118	125
1989	65	71	74	77	82	85	88	93	100	110	116
1990	59	64	67	71	75	78	81	85	91	100	106
1991	56	61	64	67	71	73	76	80	86	94	100

Note: To find the purchasing power of the pound in 1984, given that it was 100p in 1981, select the column headed 1981 and look at the 1984 row. The result is 84p.
Source: CSO.

Significance testing

Quite often, after a hypothesis is made and a decision taken and then implemented, at a later stage a random sample fails to support the original hypothesis. The difference could be attributed either to mistakes in the original hypothesis or to elements of chance distorting the sample. Significance tests are necessary to determine which of these two possibilities is more likely. If the difference is not properly explained as being due to chance, it is said to be *statistically significant*.

The purpose of significance testing is therefore to check that a hypothesis is correct unless results exceed certain limits. If a hypothesis is rejected, there is a possibility of a *type I error*. A type I error is the error of rejecting a hypothesis when it is in fact true. A sales manager might not be justified for admonishing staff for a sudden drop in sales. In the longer term the projected hypothesis on sales targets will be achieved, but fluctuations occasionally occur. On the other hand, a *type II error* is the error of not rejecting a hypothesis when it is in fact false. With this error sales might continue to fall so that targets are not met and action is not taken to correct this when in fact the hypothesis should have been rejected.

The *null hypothesis* is an assumption that there is no contradiction between expected results and actual results, and that if a difference occurs it is due to chance. The object of a significance test is to see whether or not the null hypothesis should be rejected. A null hypothesis is always tested at a specific level of significance. A 5 per cent level of significance is often used, and this creates a 95 per cent confidence level. If we expected 10 rejects from every sample of 100 objects and got 12, the null hypothesis would be that there is not any significant difference between the 10 and 12 rejects at a 5 per cent level of significance.

Data processing

Over recent years computers have proliferated in almost every business area so that, today, the role of the business statistician is significantly different. Whereas in the past statisticians were involved with manually compiling and presenting statistics, this role has largely been taken over by the computer which performs this type of calculation in a fraction of the time. Computers are:

- Substantially cheaper than they used to be
- Much faster than they were, and capable of multi-tasking operations
- Able to store and manipulate vast quantities of data
- Capable of using a wide variety of packages

Packages available to statisticians are either batch packages or interactive. Batch packages involve statistical information being entered as a complete task before the results are conveyed to the statistician for analysis. Interactive packages are more recent and involve information being entered as it is received so that, after each input, the computer updates its response. Statisticians can concentrate on analysis rather than preparation, while the tedium of work is performed by computers which process and attractively present information in a fraction of the time taken previously.

Questions

Short-answer questions

1. What is the difference between a qualitative statement and a quantitative statement?
2. Name two sources of external data
3. Using an example, explain how cluster sampling works.
4. Name four features of a good questionnaire.
5. Why are postal questionnaires often considered to be unsatisfactory?
6. Why might a business wish to use the *Monthly Digest of Statistics* published by CSO?
7. What is a grouped frequency distribution?
8. A business producing a range of products has total sales of £100 million in 19XX. For its annual report it wishes to present this information in diagrammatic form. State one method that might be used. (*Source:* AEB)
9. Why might a Lorenz curve be useful?
10. Define two measures of central tendency.
11. What is *one* main purpose of a pictogram? (*Source*: AEB)
12. What is meant by the terms
    (a) upper quartile?
    (b) lower quartile?
13. How does the formula for the variance differ from the formula for the standard deviation?
14. Name two features of a symmetrical frequency.
15. What types of probable statement can be made from a normal distribution?

16. Give two examples of a binomial problem.
17. Why will the mean have a higher value than the mode for a positively skewed frequency distribution curve?
18. Why are many index numbers weighted?
19. Distinguish between a type I and a type II error.
20. What is the difference between a batch package and an interactive package?

Essays

1. 'Businesses often present data for the use of customers, shareholders and other interested parties in the form of diagrams and charts. Sometimes this material is designed to hide as much as it reveals.'
   (a) Supporting your answer with examples and sketches, explain how a diagram or chart can be misleading.
   (b) Why might a business want to 'hide as much as it reveals' to interested parties?
   (*Source*: AEB)
2. Explain the differences between the quality of information required for a company's
   (a) strategic needs.
   (b) tactical needs.
   (c) organizational needs.
   What techniques would you employ to obtain information to satisfy each of these requirements?
3. Discuss why probability is an essential ingredient for business planning.
4. Make up an example to demonstrate each of the measures of central tendency and comment on the usefulness of each.
5. Statistically presented information is often criticized for being open to misinterpretation. Discuss.
6. Briefly describe four methods of presenting statistical information and justify the suitability of each for reporting to
   (a) directors.
   (b) company employees.
   (c) shareholders.
7. Explain what a statistician means by dispersion. In what circumstances might it be useful to use techniques that analyse the spread of data?
8. Explain why probabilities can be extracted from a normal distribution and describe the process for doing so.
9. Why are index numbers considered to be a useful statistical tool? Explain the purpose of weighting.
10. How does the standard deviation meet criticisms directed at the mean deviation? With reference to its formula, state how the standard deviation is calculated. What would be the significance of an increase in the size of a standard deviation?

Data response questions

1 Fletcher's Limited

The head of personnel at Fletcher's Ltd has John South's pay details for the last 25 weeks:

Payment	Frequency
£80–84.99	1
£85–89.99	1
£90–94.99	2
£95–99.99	3
£100–104.99	6
£105–109.99	4
£110–114.99	3
£115–119.99	2
£120–124.99	1
£125–129.99	1
£155–159.99	1

1. Determine John's mean weekly wage.
2. By constructing a cumulative frequency curve on graph paper, estimate the percentage of John's pay packets that have been in excess of his mean weekly wage.
3. The amount of redundancy pay (RP) that Fletcher's has negotiated with the Workers' Representative Council is calculated using the formula

$$RP = 2 \times \text{average wage} \times \text{number of years' service}$$

   Fletcher's interprets 'average wage' to be the median wage. Calculate the RP on this basis.
4. Why might the Workers' Representative Council propose the use of the mean wage rather than the median? (*Source*: Cambridge)

2 Expanding into Europe

The owner of a UK company selling coats, dresses and hats is considering expanding by setting up another shop in Europe.

1. What commercial information should the owner seek before making any decision?
2. The pie charts (Fig. 10.26) are taken from the company's reports and accounts for 19X6.
   (a) Discuss whether these pie charts satisfy the main principles one should always bear in mind when presenting data.
   (b) Show that the total sales in 19X6 were £45 million.
   (c) Calculate the percentage increase in the sales value of accessories between 19X1 and 19X6.

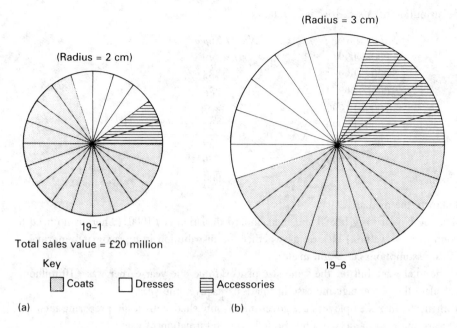

Figure 10.26 Analysis of sales by product.

(d) If total sales continue to increase by the same average amount over the next three years as they did in the five years 19X1 to 19X6, and sales of dresses increase by 40% in total over the next three years, what angle of a pie chart for 19X9 would represent the contribution to total sales by the dress department?

3. The managers of the three departments each claim that their product is 'doing best'.

(a) How could each manager use the pie charts in Fig. 10.26 to support his claim? (You are not required to undertake any calculations to answer this question.)

(b) Suggest an appropriate graphical method for displaying sales information. Give reasons for your answer. (*Source:* Cambridge)

3 Distributions of salaries

Three companies, A, B and C, have roughly the same number of employees, and the distributions of their salaries have the same modes. The distributions for A and B are approximately normal but that for B has half the standard deviation of that for A. The distribution for C is positively skewed, but with the same range as that for A.

1. Sketch the three distributions using the same axis for all three.
2. If you were an ambitious 'high-flyer', which company would you prefer to work for and why?

3. The distribution of A's salaries is as follows:

Salary range (£)	No. of employees
7 000–7 999	9
8 000–8 999	33
9 000–9 999	285
10 000–10 999	433
11 000–11 999	192
12 000–12 999	39
13 000–13 999	9
	1000

(a) Estimate the median salary.

(b) The mean salary is £10 500 and the standard deviation is £1000. (There is no need to confirm these values.) Determine whether the distribution is approximately normal. What assumptions have you made?

(c) If the total wage bill for the same size of workforce one year earlier was £10 million, calculate the percentage increase in total salaries over the year.

4. How might the firm's employees use government-published statistics in preparing their case for a salary increase? You may find the following information of use:

(a) Standard deviations from mean 0–1, 1–2, 2–3

(b) Percentage of area under normal curve 34 14 2 (*Source*: Cambridge)

4   Measures of dispersion

Study the figures below and answer the following questions.

$$
\begin{array}{ccccc}
5 & 12 & 24 & 23 & 4 \\
16 & 17 & 7 & 35 & 21 \\
43 & 19 & 42 & 27 & 60 \\
18 & 21 & 47 & 20 & 55 \\
2 & 44 & 18 & 19 & 5 \\
\end{array}
$$

1. Calculate:
    (a) The range
    (b) The mean
    (c) The median
    (d) The lower quartile
    (e) The upper quartile
    (f) The quartile deviation
    (g) The mean deviation
    (h) The standard deviation

2. Using examples, explain what is meant by a 'measure of dispersion'.

Suggested reading

Bancroft, G. and O'Sullivan, G., *Quantitative Methods for Accounting and Business Studies*, 3rd edn. McGraw-Hill, 1993

Clegg, F., *Simple Statistics*. Cambridge University Press, 1987

Gregory, D., Ward, H. and Bradshaw, A., *Statistics for Business*, 4th edn. McGraw-Hill, 1993.

Rowe, R. N., *A First Course in Business Mathematics and Statistics*. DP Publications Ltd, 1991.

11

The business in its environment

Competing influences on the businessperson

Entrepreneurs must try to achieve set organizational aims in the market-place in competition with other business enterprises. Businesses will compete for scarce resources and the sale of their products.

Business activity takes place against a background of many competing interests. These influences include:

1. Consumers
2. Suppliers
3. Other producers
4. Central government
5. Local government
6. Trade unions
7. Local residents

The effect of each of these influences is examined in other chapters, but it is worth looking at them in combination here. We will first consider the influences on the individual businessperson.

Peter Thompson is a window cleaner. He works a set round of private houses and small business premises. He feels that his *customers* remain loyal because of the quality service they receive. His prices vary from £3 to £6 for private houses; he charges £5 for shop fronts and between £5 and £10 for other business premises. His customers tend to stick with him, so he regards his prices as about right.

Peter's 'beat' covers an area around the town centre. He is able to carry his ladders, buckets and cleaning cloths around on his shoulder. Capital and material costs are very low. The ladder and bucket have lasted for over twenty years and water is free. The prices of detergents and cleaning cloths from *suppliers* do occasionally rise, and in the long term this has had a slight effect in pushing prices up.

Peter must always keep one eye on the *competition*. Window cleaners tend to have their own set 'patches' of houses, but there is always a certain amount of poaching. He needs to compete quite aggressively for the business of cleaning shop windows and he takes special care to do these well.

Peter must pay income tax to the *government*, the amount depending on his earnings. He has not registered to pay VAT because his turnover is not high enough.

Peter pays a local tax to the *council*, for which he benefits from a wide range of services including well maintained pathways and street lighting, which is a great benefit in the darker months of the year.

Being self-employed means that Peter has no need to join a *trade union*.

Going about his work, Peter must pay careful attention to the people with whom he comes into contact through his business, and to organizations within the *wider community*. His ladders and equipment need to be positioned safely, and he must avoid spilling water on to pavements, making them slippery. He has taken out a public liability insurance policy to cover himself against accidents for which he may be deemed responsible and which involve members of the public.

The individual business enterprise can be seen to be at the centre of a set of local, national and international influences and constraints (Fig. 11.1). In an interdependent world, a small change in any one factor that makes up the business environment will send out ripples affecting a number of others.

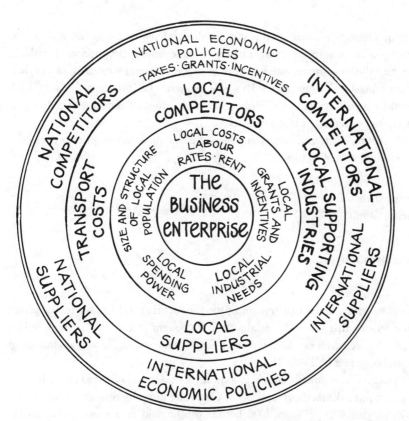

Figure 11.1 Influences on the business enterprise. (*Source*: Courtesy of Schools Industry Partnership)

For example:

1. An increase in local spending power might enable a firm to sell more of its products. Increased sales might make modernization of the plant worth while, in turn making it possible for the firm to gain a competitive edge in national and international markets.
2. A reduction in the number of local suppliers might force a firm to buy stocks from further afield, pushing up transport costs and reducing the enterprise's competitive edge.
3. An increase in the local population might increase both the local demand for an enterprise's product and the availability of the required labour force. These factors would help to enhance the enterprise's competitive edge.
4. National government decisions to tax profits may cut into the reserves being laid aside by a firm for modernization and expansion.

We shall now consider these influences in greater detail.

Consumers

A business needs to be constantly aware of the state of demand for its products. Its success depends on the ability of an enterprise to maintain a 'unique selling proposition' to which customers will respond. Business organizations need to work constantly towards identifying and satisfying consumer needs. Consumers need to be convinced that products are worthy of purchase. Success will be based on thorough research of a wide range of consumer needs. This research will then have to be translated into products.

The ability of producers to satisfy consumers in a market economy based on pricing decisions depends on two interrelated sets of factors:

*   Factors influencing demand
*   Factors influencing supply

Factors influencing demand

Price

The *demand* for a product means the actual amount of the product that will be bought at a given price. Common sense tells us that more of a product will be bought at a lower than at a higher price. For example, market research on the number of people who would use a new swimming pool produced the results shown in Table 11.1.

The demand for a product is commonly shown graphically by means of a *demand curve*. In Fig. 11.2 a stationer has drawn out a demand curve, DD, for correcting fluid. By reading off the graph, you can see that by charging 90p per item 2000 bottles will be sold in a month, whereas by charging 80p per bottle, 3000 will be sold in a month.

Table 11.1

Price for adults (£)	Demand per week (no. of people)
4.00	100
3.00	150
2.00	250
1.00	800
0.75	1200
0.50	1400
0.40	1500
0.30	1600

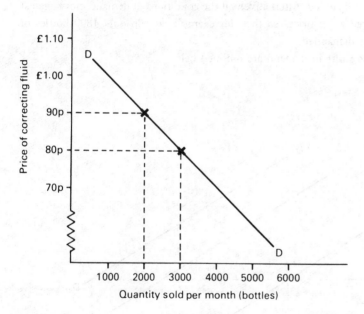

Figure 11.2 Demand for correcting fluid.

An individual demand curve can be likened to a snapshot taken at a particular moment in time showing how much of a product would be bought at different prices. At that moment, price is seen to be the only variable that can be altered which will influence the quantity purchased.

Most demand curves drawn from real situations will have a shape that is more of a squiggle than a straight line. However, the common factor of nearly all demand curves is that they slope down to the right, indicating that—the conditions of demand remaining the same—more units will be bought at a lower price than at a higher price. In this book, therefore, we will draw demand curves as if they are always straight lines.

Other factors

There are a number of other factors that influence the demand for a product in addition to price. If one of these factors alters, the *conditions of demand* are said to have changed. These factors include tastes, income, population, the price of substitute products and the price of complementary products.

Changes in one or a combination of these factors will cause shifts in the demand curve. The demand curve can shift either in a leftward or a rightward direction. A shift to the left indicates that smaller quantities are wanted than before at given prices; a shift to the right indicates that larger quantities are wanted than before at given prices.

These changes are illustrated in Fig. 11.3. The figure shows that in the original situation a quantity of 3000 would have been bought at 80p. When the conditions of demand move in favour of the product, more will be required at all prices so that, for example, at 80p 3700 bottles of correcting fluid would now be demanded. Alternatively, if the conditions of demand move against a product, less will be required at all prices so that, for example, at 80p only 1800 bottles of correcting fluid would now be demanded.

Factors that can cause these shifts in demand are outlined below.

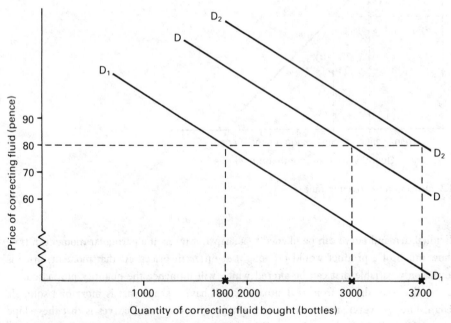

D – D shows the original demand curve
D_1 – D_1 shows a shift to the left in demand
D_2 – D_2 shows a shift to the right in demand

Figure 11.3 Shifts in the position of a demand curve.

Tastes

As time moves on, new products become more fashionable and popular while others go into decline. For example, the hot summer of 1989 provided an excellent climate for a fashion craze for Bermuda shorts. The effect on demand of tastes changing in favour of Bermuda shorts was to push the demand curve for the product to the right. Many firms started producing 'Bermudas', and many clothes shops sold them. With the passage of time, however, these shorts lost their popularity and their demand curve will have shifted to the left. Citizens' Band (CB) radios were very popular in the early 1980s, but by the late 1980s demand had dropped considerably.

A pronounced example of a rapid shift to the left in the demand curve for a product occurred in early December 1988, when the Junior Health Minister, Edwina Curry, pointed out a link between eggs and food poisoning. Overnight the demand for eggs crashed, huge stocks of eggs built up, and some producers went out of business.

Population

Population statistics can be very helpful for forecasting changes in demand. *Demographers* (people who compile population statistics), frequently make predictions about future population trends based on existing statistics. Predictions based on the size of the population in different age groups are particularly easy to chart because, once a child has been born, he or she will become steadily older.

Populations can be classified in a number of ways including by age, sex, locality, race, educational background—or even by the newspaper they read.

Demand forecasters will often analyse population statistics according to clusters of relevant factors, for example males in the 35–45-year-old age group living in Birmingham.

An increase in the relevant population will tend to move the demand curve for a product to the right. A decrease in the relevant population will tend to move the demand curve to the left.

Income

The more money people have, the easier it is for them to buy products. The amount of income that people have to spend on goods is known as their *disposable income*, i.e. their pay minus taxes and other deductions.

Average incomes tend to rise over time and this will lead to a general increase in the level of demand for goods. The demand for individual items, however, will be related more to changes in the incomes of different groups, such as teenagers (for teenage magazines and fashions), pensioners (for retirement homes, winter sun holidays) and others.

The demand for most products will rise as a result of an increase in incomes for the relevant population. This will lead to a shift in the demand curve to the right. Rising incomes will tend to result from improved job opportunities, and increases in the demand for goods.

Some products may become less popular as incomes rise. These are goods that come to be regarded as inferior when people's spending power increases. The consumer who was once happy to rent a flat, wear second-hand clothes and drive a second-hand low-powered car may switch to buying a house, wearing designer labels and driving a status-symbol car when his or her income increases sufficiently.

We can thus state the relationship between income and demand in the following way:

For most products demand will shift to the right when income increases, and to the left when income falls. In the case of inferior items, however, demand would shift to the left when incomes rise.

Inherited wealth

A number of studies have highlighted the level of inherited wealth that is coming the way of middle-aged households. Typical of these was a study by Morgan Grenfell in 1988, which pointed out that:

> about half the middle-aged households in the country will inherit property typically worth £35 000 ... As the proportion of elderly owner-occupiers rises, so will the proportion of middle-aged investors. By the end of the century property worth £9 billion (1986 prices) will be handed on each year. In south-east England granny will often leave her children a house worth £100 000.
>
> Most of the lucky legatees will be in their 40's or 50's. They will already have bought homes of their own, so they will sell their parent's home to a new generation of young house-buyers. Most of those who inherit their parent's home will have begun to plan for their own retirement.

The overall effect is that a sizeable number of middle-aged households inherit a considerable amount of wealth which is rapidly turned into spending power. An increase in inherited wealth in this way can have an important effect in raising the demand for products and thus shifting demand curves to the right.

The price of substitute products

The demand for products that have close substitutes will often be strongly influenced by the price of the substitutes. This would be the case, for example, with different brands of tinned fruit or different brands of petrol, because there are many different brand names to choose from.

The demand curve for a product is likely to shift to the right if a substitute product rises in price. The demand curve for a product is likely to shift to the left if a substitute product falls in price (assuming that other factors influencing demand do not alter at the same time).

The price of complementary products

Some products are used together so that the demand for one is linked to the price of another. An example of this might be a word processor and a floppy disk. If a particular brand of word processor were to rise in price, then users might switch new purchases to an alternative brand. This would also reduce the demand for the floppy disks that are compatible with the original brand of word processor.

Factors influencing supply

Price

The supply of a product is the amount that suppliers will wish to produce at a given price. Common sense tells us that more of a product will be supplied at a higher than at a lower price. For example, a survey of tomato growers' intentions in a particular farming district revealed that the acreages that would be committed to tomato production would vary with the price of tomatoes as shown in Table 11.2. (It should be borne in mind that quantities produced would depend on the acreage planted, but also on weather conditions and other variables.)

Table 11.2

Price of tomatoes (market price per lb)	Quantity of land committed to tomato production (acres)
15	800
20	2 400
25	4 400
30	10 000
35	14 000

The supply of a product can be shown graphically by means of a *supply curve*. In Fig. 11.4, a newspaper manufacturer has plotted the numbers of copies of papers that the company would be prepared to supply per day at different prices. By reading off the graph, you can see that at a price of 20p, 400 000 copies will be produced each day whereas at a price of 25p, 800 000 copies will be produced.

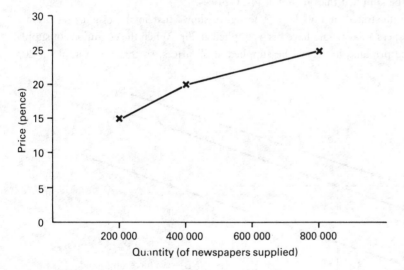

Figure 11.4 The supply curve of newspapers.

The individual supplier (e.g. the newspaper manufacturer) will be prepared to purchase more capital and equipment and to employ more factors of production the higher the price of the product. The risk becomes more attractive, and capital outlays (e.g. the cost of new equipment for an advanced printing process) can be recovered more quickly. In the market for national newspapers as a whole, more producers will be prepared to enter the market to supply at higher prices. More entrepreneurs will be prepared to risk capital if returns promise to be higher, and even the less efficient producers will anticipate an excess of revenue over costs.

An individual supply curve can be likened to a snapshot taken at a particular moment in time, showing how much of a product would be supplied at different prices. At that moment, price is seen to be the only variable that can be altered which will influence the quantity supplied.

Most supply curves drawn from real situations will have a shape that is more of a squiggle than a straight line. However, the common factor of nearly all supply curves is that they slope up to the right, indicating that—conditions of supply remaining the same—more units will be supplied at a higher price than at a lower price. In this book, therefore, we will draw supply curves as if they are always straight lines.

Other factors

There are a number of factors that influence the supply of a product in addition to prices. If one of these factors alters, the *conditions of supply* are said to have changed. These factors include the price of factors of production, the price of other commodities, technology and the changing objectives of producers.

Changes in one or a combination of these factors will cause shifts in the supply curve. The supply curve can shift in either a leftward or a rightward direction. A shift to the left indicates that smaller quantities will be supplied than before at given prices; a shift to the right indicates that larger quantities will be supplied than before at given prices.

These changes are illustrated in Fig. 11.5. The figure shows that in the original situation a quantity of 400 000 papers a day would have been supplied at 20p. When the conditions of supply move in favour of the product, more will be supplied at all prices, so that for example at 20p

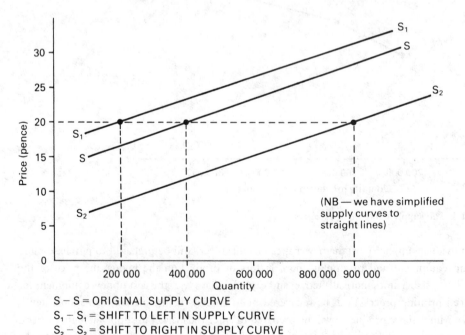

$S - S$ = ORIGINAL SUPPLY CURVE
$S_1 - S_1$ = SHIFT TO LEFT IN SUPPLY CURVE
$S_2 - S_2$ = SHIFT TO RIGHT IN SUPPLY CURVE

Figure 11.5 Shifts in the supply curve for newspapers.

900 000 newspapers will be supplied. Alternatively, if the conditions of supply move against a product, less will be supplied at all prices, so that for example at 20p only 200 000 newspapers will be supplied.

Factors that can cause these shifts in supply are outlined below.

Prices of factors of production

Production is based on the combination of factor inputs in order to produce outputs. If the cost of a factor input rises, then it will become more expensive to produce outputs. Factors of production will be used in the long term only if the value of their output is greater than the cost of their hire. As factor prices rise, fewer factors will be used in production, and hence the supply of a product will fall.

For example, let us assume that an agricultural crop requires three main inputs: land, labour and chemical fertilizer. If the cost of one or more of these inputs were to rise, then farmers might cut back on the acreage committed to this particular crop. Conversely, if the price of one or more factors of production were to fall, then supply conditions would move in favour of increased production and supply is likely to shift to the right.

Prices of other commodities

In a number of areas of production, it is possible to switch production from less profitable to more profitable lines. For example, many arable farmers have a certain degree of discretion over which crops to grow. A shipyard can choose whether to build tugs, oil rigs or bulk carriers. If a particular line becomes relatively more profitable, then scarce resources such as equipment, time and materials can be switched into producing it and away from producing other products. A rise in the price of carrots may therefore lead to a shift to the left of the supply curve for cabbages, and a fall in the price of carrots may lead to a shift to the right of the supply curve for cabbages.

Changes in the level of technology

An improvement in the level of technology means that more output can be produced with fewer resources. This means that the supply curve for a product will shift to the right. Modern technology based on computers and factory robots has enabled a wide range of producers to produce larger outputs at lower unit costs—for example in car production, newspapers, modern breweries and the processing of cheques by banks.

Producers' objectives

Business-owners have a wide range of objectives. To some, expansion may be seen as a goal in itself; the firm might therefore decide to produce more to gain a higher profile, to take a larger share of a market or simply because the owner enjoys the cut and thrust of business life.

The weather

One of the major factors influencing the supply of a number of goods and services is the weather. A number of services respond to changes in the weather, for example the appearance of umbrella-sellers at the entrances to underground stations in rainy weather! The supply of agricultural products depends very much on changing weather conditions.

The formation of a market price

A *market* is a situation in which goods can be bought, sold or exchanged. The essential requirements are buyers, sellers, goods and money.

In the market-place the forces of demand and supply will interact to create a market price.

To illustrate this point, we have drawn up a fictional daily demand and supply schedule for fish at a small fishing village (Table 11.3). When the price of fish is high, the owner of the only fishing boat will spend more time fishing than when prices are low. Conversely, consumers will want to purchase more fish at low than at high prices.

Table 11.3   Demand and supply in a daily fish market

Price of fish (p)	Quantity demanded	Quantity supplied
35	800	350
40	700	400
45	600	450
50	500	500
55	400	550
60	300	600

This information can then be plotted on a graph, as shown in Fig. 11.6. If you study this graph, you can see that there is only one price at which the wishes of consumers and the supplier coincides, i.e. 50p. At this price the quantity that will be bought and sold is 500.

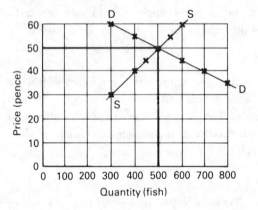

Figure 11.6 Graph showing demand and supply in a daily fish market.

We can see that the market provides a mechanism for automatically bringing the decisions of consumers and producers into line, even though the two groups have different motives. (The producer will want to sell at the highest price possible, and the consumer will want to purchase at the lowest price possible.)

We can see how the process of forming an equilibrium price comes about by considering two disequilibrium situations (see Fig. 11.7). If for example we consider the price of 60p, we will see

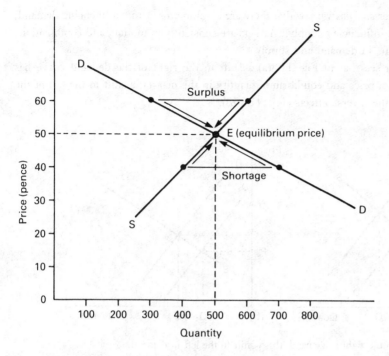

Figure 11.7 Creating the equilibrium price.

that at this price the owner of the fishing vessel would be prepared to work longer to supply 600 fish. However, at 60p consumers would be prepared to buy only 300 fish—leaving a surplus stock of 300 fish which would go to waste. In this situation, the owner of the fishing boat would lower prices and resort to working fewer hours.

Alternatively, if the price of fish was pitched at 40p, consumers would be prepared to buy 700 fish. However, the owner of the fishing boat would be prepared to work long enough to catch only 400. There would now be a shortage of fish—stocks would rapidly sell out and customers would try to bid up the price. This would make it worth while for the owner of the fishing boat to work longer hours.

The net effect is that at prices above 50p too much will be produced and so forces will interact to pull prices down to 50p. At prices below 50p too little will be produced, and so forces will interact to pull prices up to 50p. At 50p prices are just right and there is no tendency to change.

The above analysis is a simplification. In the real world markets do not always move smoothly towards equilibrium. Consumers and producers frequently lack important market information which would help them to respond promptly to changes.

Shifts in demand and supply

So far we have analysed market prices solely in terms of the relationship between price and demand and supply. This has been like taking a snapshot under the assumption that factors other than price do not alter.

However, in our earlier analysis we saw that there are a number of factors influencing demand, and a number of factors influencing supply. Markets are constantly in motion, and combinations of factors will cause shifts in demand and supply.

For example, we can see that in Fig. 11.8(a) a shift to the right of the demand curve has increased the equilibrium price and equilibrium quantity in the market; a shift to the left of the demand curve has had the reverse effects (Fig. 11.8(b)).

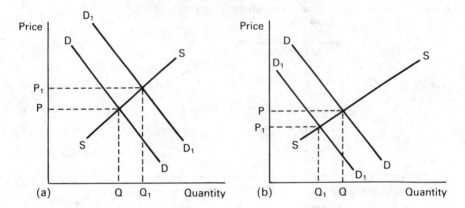

Figure 11.8 (a) A shift to the right in demand. (b) A shift to the left in demand.

In Fig. 11.9(a), we can see that a shift to the right of the supply curve has decreased the equilibrium price and increased the equilibrium quantity; conversely, in Fig. 11.9(b) a shift to the left of the supply curve has increased the equilibrium price and decreased the equilibrium quantity.

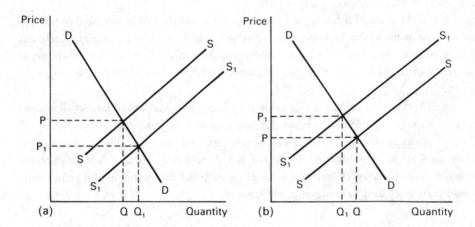

Figure 11.9 (a) A shift to the right in supply. (b) A shift to the left in supply.

Real-world situations will be complicated by the interaction of numerous demand and supply factors.

Review

Many students initially find it difficult to distinguish between factors causing movements up or down a demand or supply curve and factors causing shifts to the left or right of demand or supply curves.

The golden rule is that *movements along curves are caused solely by changes in the price of the item in question. Changes in factors other than price cause the whole curve to shift in position.*

State whether the following situations would lead in the first instance to:

(a)   A movement up the demand curve
(b)   A movement down the demand curve
(c)   A shift to the right of the demand curve
(d)   A shift to the left of the demand curve
(e)   A movement up the supply curve
(f)   A movement down the supply curve
(g)   A shift to the right of the supply curve
(h)   A shift to the left of the supply curve.

All situations relate to the demand and supply of British wine:

1.   Increased popularity of British wine.
2.   Improved technology involved in British wine manufacture.
3.   The falling price of British wine.
4.   A scare about safety standards in British wine production.
5.   A general increase in incomes.
6.   A fall in the relevant sector of the population.
7.   Falling wine prices.
8.   An increase in the price of a product that is produced on land similar to that used for growing vines.
9.   Excellent weather for wine growing and harvesting.
10.   An increase in European consumption of beer at the expense of wine.
11.   Removal of a government subsidy to wine producers.
12.   A general reduction in all price levels.

Of course, you need to bear in mind the dynamic nature of markets. For example, when there is an increase in demand this will be followed by an increase in price. This may then lead to an increase in supply, which may or may not help to modify the initial price increase. Markets will be constantly adjusting to a wide range of interdependent forces, such as changes in tastes, incomes, prices of complements/substitutes, etc.

Suppliers

Most firms are part of a chain of production. Many producers are therefore influenced by what goes on at the previous stage. In the late 1980s and early 1990s this is an important fact of life, particularly inasmuch as basic commodity prices such as those of fuels and metals have changed the costs of production for all producers. Because fuel is a basic cost of production for most products, changes in the price of fuel can lead to price rises and falls for thousands of products. In turn, such changes in prices have an effect on the wages and the standard of living of millions of citizens.

Competition from other producers

This is a major influence on business behaviour. A firm's prices and many other policies will be influenced by the level of competition it faces.

Direct competition exists when more than one business is producing similar products and appealing to the same group of people. Examples would include two firms manufacturing washing-up liquids, or two shops supplying children's clothes in the same stretch of the high street.

Even when a business produces a unique product with no direct competition, it must still consider *indirect competition*. Consumers can choose to spend their money on one product rather than another, quite different, product; for instance, if you feel that it is too expensive to go to the cinema, you might decide to go out for a pizza instead.

Firms compete with each other in many ways. Generally, competition is over product quality and performance. There can also be price competition; and in some product categories, such as petrol and oil, free gifts are important.

For shops, the sharpest competitive edges are created by 'location', opening hours and the friendliness and efficiency of service. Companies also compete on the effectiveness of their advertising. If it were possible to have two identical but competitive products, the one whose benefits were more powerfully projected in the advertising would outsell the other.

In reality, the most critical competitive factors any company has to cope with are the knowledge, intelligence, experience, scepticism and sometimes apathy of the prospective customer. No company that wants to stay successful ever takes the customer for granted. We are now living in a 'consumer society', with a market that is educated, aware and prepared to give and withdraw its custom as it decides. Keeping ahead of the customer is the greatest challenge a business faces.

The degree of competition faced by an enterprise will constantly change. The extent of this competition will depend to a great extent on the willingness and ability of consumers to transfer their purchase to substitute products. This will depend on the answers to a cluster of interrelated questions, including:

- Are substitutes available?
- Can consumers obtain them?
- Do consumers shop around?
- Do consumers know what is available?

- Can buyers switch to alternative sources of supply?
- Are the benefits of changing greater than the costs?

A number of market forms of competition are commonly recognized and are defined according to a number of key ingredients that influence the level of competition (see Fig. 11.10).

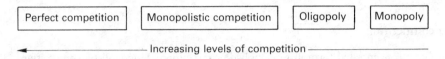

Figure 11.10 Degrees of competition.

Monopolies

A business that does not face direct competition is said to have a monopoly. It does not have outside pressure on it to be competitive. We must be careful, however, not to assume that monopolies are inefficient. Monopolies do not need to duplicate systems of administration, services and other processes. They can also put a lot of money into product development and research in order to keep up a long-term competitive edge.

In the real world there are unlikely to be many examples of pure monopolies because most manufactured goods can be copied. Some minerals are restricted to a few geographical areas; for example, a large concentration of world gold reserves are found in the former Soviet Union and southern Africa.

Oligopolies

Oligopoly exists when only a few producers or sellers dominate a market. Examples of products made and sold in markets with few firms are:

- National newspapers
- Petrol
- Breakfast cereals
- Beer
- Biscuits
- Chocolates and sweets
- Disposable nappies
- Washing powder
- Satellite television
- Contraceptives
- Pet food

There are no set rules as to the degree of competition that exists in such a market. Each producer will spend money on policies designed to create brand loyalty, such as advertising and promotion.

Each producer will attempt to differentiate its product from the others that are available. However, there is always a danger that open warfare with regard to pricing and other elements of competition will be to the disadvantage of all producers and sellers. The ability to make profits, and to plough profits into promotion, research and product development, is seen as being of crucial importance. Such markets will therefore be typified by lulls and surges in the extent of competitive practice.

Monopolistic competition

Oligopoly is in fact a concentrated form of monopolistic competition. Monopolistic competition exists where products or services are *in some way* differentiated from others; however, this differentiation can be eroded in the course of time because new firms have the freedom to enter the industry. Levels of profit in monopolistic markets will vary with the level of competition. The ability of firms to survive and prosper is in many ways dependent on their ability to keep innovating, to research and develop new product lines. Most products and services in this country are produced by monopolistic competitors, including hairdressers, insurance companies, book publishing companies, retailers and graphic designers.

Perfect competition

Perfect competition is a state that exists more in theory than in practice. In a perfectly competitive market there would be no differentiation of any sort—all products and prices would be identical. Consumers would have perfect knowledge of products, and there would be no sacrifice involved in buying from one outlet rather than another.

Although pure perfect competition does not exist, there are still some important lessons to be learned from the model. Pure competition ensures that no excess profits can be made in the long run (producers and sellers make just enough to stay in business) and that prices and hence costs are kept to the minimum consistent with a given scale of operation.

Central government

The central authorities set up a legal framework within which businesses operate. As we shall see later, there is a wide range of laws that constrain the activities of businesses. The government establishes the rules of the game. An example of this is the way the government has implemented anti-monopoly legislation to encourage competition between firms. For over forty years, the UK government has tried to prevent companies and traders from holding too large a share of the production or sale of a good or service. As a result, some mergers between companies have been stopped and the activities of a number of companies have been inquired into by a government committee. The Monopolies and Mergers Commission is the body that was set up to investigate cases involving monopoly situations referred to it by the government.

The main agency for carrying out government policy on competition is the Office of Fair Trading (OFT), which was set up in 1973. Under the Fair Trading Act, the Director General of this office was given powers to keep commercial practices in the United Kingdom under scrutiny and to collect information about them in order to uncover monopoly situations and practices that restrict freedom of business, trade and contract. The Director General can refer cases of suspected monopoly or malpractice to the Monopolies and Mergers Commission for investigation.

In February 1988, for example, the OFT discovered a web of glass supply cartels across the country when a West Midlands glass purchaser complained that he was 'tired of being ripped off'. (A *cartel* is a group of individual firms that make agreements which restrict competition.) The Director General assigned a team of three investigators to look into the industry. The team interviewed glass buyers and issued legal notices to companies suspected of operating cartels, compelling them to furnish details of agreements.

Among these agreements was one from Pilkington, which revealed that its executives had clandestinely met with other glass suppliers to agree on common price increases. Pilkington admitted to meeting several times with five other glass suppliers between 1978 and 1982. Their purpose was 'to agree the same percentage increase to each company's gross price tariffs and to certain other items normally charged as extras in orders for double glazing units, such as for the drilling of holes in double glazing units'.

This document was one of a catalogue of admissions from seven UK glass suppliers, which referred to 12 different cartels and named a total of 60 different companies.

In its recommendations, the Monopolies and Mergers Commission in recent years has tended to consider whether or not the benefits of a monopoly situation outweigh the costs. Concentration has not been seen as being a bad thing in itself. More important has been the ability of new firms to enter an industry, and the way in which firms established in concentrated markets have behaved. The 1980 Competition Act stressed that the Monopolies and Mergers Commission should be concerned more with the general competitive environment in an industry than with the level of concentration.

The government has powers to intervene in the case of takeovers of economic importance which raise public-interest issues. Under the provisions of the 1973 Fair Trading Act, a merger in which the gross assets taken over are worth at least £30 million, or which involves the creation or enhancement of a market share of at least 25 per cent, may be referred by the Secretary of State to the Monopolies and Mergers Commission. The Secretary of State for Trade and Industry has powers to prevent a merger or to impose conditions only if the Commission concludes that it would operate against the public interest.

In 1988 the White Paper, *DTI: The Department for Enterprise*, confirmed the government's policy that the main consideration in determining whether mergers should be referred to the Monopolies and Mergers Commission will be their potential effect on competition. Where competition is not affected, the government will not intervene, as for example when the Secretary of State allowed the acquisition of Matthew Brown by Scottish and Newcastle Breweries.

Competition policy is just one example of central government involvement in the creation of a business environment. Government activity is also writ large, as we shall see later in its economic policy-making, its purchases of goods and services, its business taxes and subsidies and a range of other interests and activities.

Local government

A small local business or a plant of a larger business must take into account local by-laws and rules. The local authorities are responsible for looking after the interests of local residents. Business activity is thus constrained by a wide range of local influences, including the protection of the local environment and planning permission specifications. An example of this might be a redevelopment project which can take place only if it fits in with the style of the existing architecture.

Local government taxes local businesses, provides a range of services including refuse collection, provides grants and other incentives and carries out a number of policies that affect business activity.

Trade unions

These can be looked on as both an internal and an external influence on the business. The local branch of a trade union can be seen as part of a larger national movement. Bargaining may take place between a group of employers and trade union representatives. Trade unions are dealt with in depth in Chapter 20.

Local residents

Local people may interact with a firm in a number of ways:

- As consumers
- As workers
- As shareholders
- As neighbours

In each of these situations the firm will have to take account of their interests.

Business in an international setting

Business activity takes place against a background of world trade; for example:

1. Many businesses based in the United Kingdom are owned by overseas shareholders or are offshoots of foreign companies.
2. Many UK firms buy raw materials and supplies from overseas.
3. Many UK firms face overseas competition.
4. Many UK firms sell their products or services overseas.
5. Many UK businesses have offshoots overseas and many foreign companies have UK shareholders.

In recent years we have become particularly aware of the impact of the world market on business life. In particular, in the 1990s we are highly aware of the repercussions for businesses of the creation of the European Single Market.

The European Union (EU) is the biggest free trade area in the world.

The European Union

Since joining the Community in 1973, the value of UK trade with the other 11 member-states has risen thirteen-fold (by 1993)—more than twice as fast as with the rest of the world. Eight of her EU partners are among the United Kingdom's top ten trading partners. In 1991 over 55 per cent of UK exports went to her EU partners. UK exports to Germany almost equal UK exports to Japan and the United States combined.

The Single Market

The end of 1992 saw the completion of the 'Single Market', which entails free movement of goods, services, people and capital, throughout the Community.

Benefits to EU citizens include:

- A wider choice of goods and services as barriers to trade are removed, and greater assurance about the quality and safety of imported products as clear guidelines become legally binding on businesses
- Easier travel, e.g. (hopefully) cheaper air fares, as competition increases
- More jobs as business opportunities grow (although unemployment is a major problem facing all EU member-states as we move into the twenty-first century)
- Wider recognition of qualifications, making it easier for people to live and work where they choose in the Community
- An end to routine customs controls at ports and airports and the freedom to bring back any good bought, duty-free and VAT-paid, in other EU countries for personal use.

A number of overseas countries, particularly Japan, have been attracted to invest in the United Kingdom in order to gain entrance to the Single Market.

The EU has been extended by joining together with the European Free Trade Association (EFTA), which is made up of Austria, Finland, Iceland, Liechtenstein, Norway, Sweden and Switzerland, to form the European Economic Area. This gives UK businesses a home market not of 55 million but of 375 million consumers. The resulting decrease in bureaucracy, e.g. by simplifying the paperwork required for trade, reduces business costs.

EU institutions

European Council

This is made up of EU heads of state or government. It usually meets twice a year to give overall direction to the Community's work.

Council of Ministers

This body decides on all the laws that establish EU policies. Each Council consists of government ministers from the 12 member-states, accountable to their own parliaments, representing national interests on the subjects under discussion—e.g. trade, fishing, sport. They take decision by unanimous agreement, qualified majority voting (where the number of votes depends on the population size of countries) or a simple majority vote, depending on what the subject is. On many important issues for national governments (e.g. taxes), decisions must be unanimous. Each member-state takes it in turn to hold the presidency of the Council, setting the agenda and chairing meetings for a six-month period.

European Commission

The Commission has three main tasks:

- To make proposals for Community laws
- To ensure that laws are carried out
- To manage EU policies such as the policy to ensure fair competition within the Community

There are 17 Commissioners, two from each of the larger countries and one from each of the smaller ones.

European Parliament

There are 567 Members of the European Parliament (MEPs). The number from each country is as follows:

Germany	99
France	87
UK	87
Italy	87
Spain	64
Netherlands	31
Portugal	25
Greece	25
Belgium	25
Denmark	16

Ireland   15
Luxembourg   6

MEPs are elected every five years. The next election will be in 1999. The Parliament is consulted on draft laws and may propose amendments. Along with the Council, it is responsible for setting the Community budget.

European Court of Justice (ECJ)

The Court interprets and adjudicates on Community law. There are 13 judges, one from each member-state and one extra to prevent deadlock. The Court is assisted by a Court of First Instance, which handles certain cases brought by individuals and organizations.

Court of Auditors

The Court of Auditors is responsible for auditing the Community's budget. It helps to prevent and to detect waste and fraud.

Making Community law

The procedure for making EU laws is complicated. Figure 11.11 gives a simplified version of what takes place.

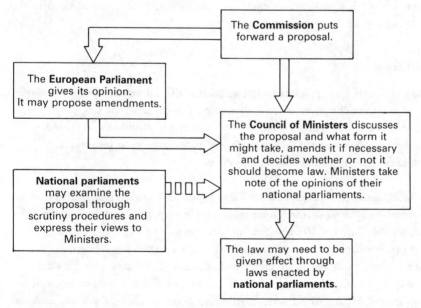

Figure 11.11 Making Community laws.

The Community budget

The Community's activities have to be financed by contributions from its member-countries (see Fig. 11.12). In 1992 the Community spent over £50 billion (about 3.5 per cent of total central government spending in all EU member-states). About half of the expenditure goes on supporting the Common Agricultural Policy (CAP) (mainly subsidies to farmers) and about a quarter goes to the poorer regions of the Community.

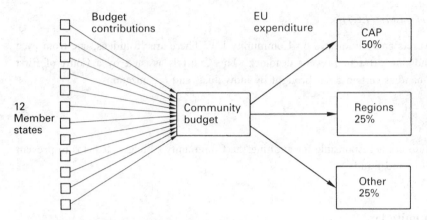

Figure 11.12 The Community budget.

All countries receive money as well as paying into EU funds. Countries with large farming communities and poorer regions benefit most from EU expenditure. Germany, France, the Netherlands and the United Kingdom are examples of countries that are *net contributors* to the budget (they pay in more than they take out).

The Maastricht Treaty

In 1991 the Maastricht Treaty was drawn up to strengthen the EC. However, different countries have different views about the objectives of the Community. For example, the UK Conservative government wants to create a more effective and efficient Community but to avoid centralization (government by a 'Brussels bureaucracy') or weakening of national political institutions.

The Maastricht Treaty contains the following objectives.

1. It will help build closer co-operation on foreign policy and justice/home affairs on an intergovernmental basis without the Commission and European Court having the roles they enjoy under the Treaty of Rome which initially created the EC.
2. It enshrines the principle of 'subsidiarity', limiting the Community's involvement in national affairs. In areas where both the Community and member-states have power to act, the Community will do so only if the objectives of the proposed action cannot be achieved sufficiently by an individual member-state. Furthermore, any action by the Community in any field must not go beyond what is necessary to achieve the Treaty's objectives.

Ultimately, if there is a dispute the European Court of Justice will judge whether EC action is necessary. This principle should ensure that:

(a)   the Community will not stray into areas where it is not needed;

(b)   where EC action is needed, it will go no further than is required.

3. The Treaty enables the European Court of Justice to clamp down on those that do not implement agreed EC rules.

4. It defines the scope for EC activity in such areas as education, training and health by setting out the sort of action the Community should take.

5. It enables EC action in other areas such as the environment, which affect all countries.

6. It makes the European Commission more accountable to the European Parliament.

7. It establishes new rights for EC citizens.

8. It provides for movement towards economic and monetary union.

The Maastricht Treaty establishes a new framework: the *European Union*. This is made up of three pillars of co-operation under the European Council (Fig. 11.13).

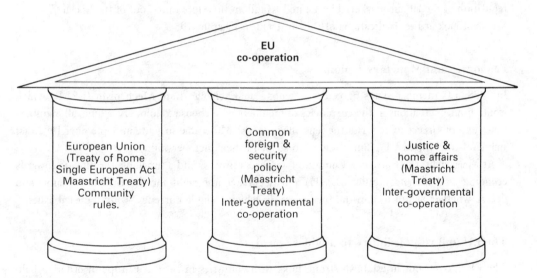

Figure 11.13 The European Union.

National parliaments will be encouraged to play a greater role in EC affairs through scrutiny of EC legislation. The European Parliament will be given new powers including the approval of the appointment of the European Commission, and will be able to carry out inquiries into the maladministration of EC laws, as well as having some say in EC law-making.

The European Court of Justice will have new powers to fine countries that do not comply with judgments. The Court of Auditors will now be required to provide a statement of assurance about the reliability of the Community's budget.

A new Committee of the Regions will advise the Commission and the Council of Ministers on regional policy.

A European Ombudsman will have powers to investigate maladministration in the European institutions.

The contentious Social Chapter

The Treaty of Rome enshrines the principles that member-countries will:

● Ensure that every citizen enjoys the freedom to take a job or set up in business anywhere in the Community
● Establish minimum standards for health and safety at work
● Ensure equal treatment for men and women in employment

At Maastricht, many governments wanted to expand the range of areas of social policy covered by EC legislation. The UK government would not agree to accept new laws that would increase regulation of the labour market. The United Kingdom therefore opted out of the Social Chapter. We shall look at the implications of this in detail in Chapter 19.

Economic and Monetary Union

In 1978, EC member-states agreed to establish an Exchange Rate Mechanism (ERM), which would limit fluctuations in the currencies of members who choose to join. Over time, all member-states except Greece joined. But the tensions in the ERM became so acute in September 1992 that Italy and the United Kingdom decided to suspend their membership.

At Maastricht, the European Community agreed a process and a timetable for moving towards economic and monetary union (EMU) and negotiated the right for the British Parliament to decide whether or not to join the final stage, in which a single currency would be established.

The EU and responsibility to a wider world

The EU has set out to establish strong links with countries in eastern Europe in order to help them in the process of moving towards market economies.

The Community also plays a role in helping developing countries; for example:

1. The EU food aid programme is the second biggest in the world.
2. The Community's agreement with 69 developing countries (the Lome Convention) provides technical aid and lower tariffs for their exports to the EU.

The problems of EU membership

Not all observers see the creation of the Single Market, or at least the implementation of it, as necessarily being beneficial to Britain. For example, a paper prepared by Henry Neuburger, economic adviser to the shadow industry secretary in 1988, stated that Britain stands to lose more from the internal market than any other member-country, and projected nearly 200 000 job losses, mainly in the Midlands. It warned that the industries most likely to be hit would be motors, office machinery, footwear, carpets and electrical household goods.

In March 1989 Sir John Hoskyns, who at the time headed the Institute of Directors, launched a withering attack on EC bureaucracy, saying that the then existing plans for 1992 would result in a 'collectivized, protectionist, over-regulated Utopia'. While acknowledging that the Single Market offered great potential and that it was important for it to succeed, he said that the warning signs of failure were clearly visible and that '1992' had the makings of a fiasco. While business prepared for a Europe without frontiers, the Single Market project itself was going wrong because of: shifting objectives, bad organization, the wrong people in positions of leadership, poor motivation, inadequate methods, weak management, personal politics and pilfering on a heroic scale. In 1995 the EU enlargement process will have included Norway, Sweden, Finland and Austria.

Export problems

Most UK exports now go to the European Community and to advanced industrial countries like the United States.

Today services make a significant contribution to UK trading with the rest of the world. Fortunately, the strength of demand for services is greater than that for manufactures, where there tends to be more competition. The United Kingdom tends to have a competitive advantage in a number of services based on years of experience in particular markets such as finance and tourism.

In 1991 invisible exports, i.e. exported services, were worth £32 billion. (This does not include interest and profit from overseas investments.) Services today tend to be more labour-intensive than secondary industries.

The United Kingdom also has a number of manufacturing industries that are world leaders, such as the chemical industry. Over a quarter of products (by value) are exported in the following product groups: chemicals, man-made fibres, mechanical engineering products, office machinery and data-processing equipment, transport equipment other than cars, and scientific instruments. It is also worth noting that the Japanese car giants, including Toyota and Nissan, are beginning to make a significant contribution to UK trade with the rest of the EC.

Whenever firms export goods, they must get the following right:

- Price
- Quality
- Delivery
- Presentation and promotion

The exporters must know their market. Information about overseas markets can be obtained from three main sources:

- Published market research, produced both in this country and abroad
- The government
- Banks

The government and banks play a major role in overseas trade because of their experience. They will help to organize finance, give advice, help with insurance and assist with foreign currency.

It is not surprising that some businesses are reluctant to engage in international trade. Problems include:

- *Uncertainty*—e.g. will you be paid, will exchange rates fluctuate, etc.
- *Language differences*, requiring translation on packaging, advertising materials, promotions, etc.
- *Differences in taste*
- *Paperwork*—the burden of extra documentation
- *Customs duties*, which in some instances will be levied, raising the price of exports in foreign markets
- *Extra transport and insurance costs*

Questions

Short-answer questions

1. List the external influences on the behaviour of a firm with which you are familiar. Give two examples of how these external influences have affected the behaviour of the business.
2. What is meant by the term
   (a) 'consumer'?
   (b) 'producer'?
3. What factors are likely to influence the demand for a branded chocolate bar?
4. What factors may shift the demand curve for commuter rail fares to the right?
5. What factors may shift the demand curve for a brand of washing powder to the left?
6. How can a knowledge of likely demographic changes help producers to predict the future pattern of demand for a product? Illustrate your answer with an example taken from the real world.
7. Does the demand for consumer goods always increase with rising incomes? Explain your answer with examples.
8. Give three examples of pairs of goods that can be seen to
   (a) complement each other.
   (b) act as substitutes for each other.
9. How is the demand curve for a product likely to be affected as a result of
   (a) a rise in price of a complementary good?
   (b) a fall in price of a substitute good?
   (c) a general fall in the relevant population?
10. Why does a typical supply curve slope upwards from left to right?
11. How are changes in the level of technology likely to affect the supply curve for a processed food, e.g. tinned peas? What other factors are likely to affect the position of the supply curve?

12. What is a monopoly? Give an example of a firm with a monopoly or near monopoly in the United Kingdom. Does being a monopoly affect the way in which a firm operates?
13. Are consumers likely to get a better service from a monopoly firm?
14. What is monopolistic competition?
15. Why is perfect competition unlikely to exist in the real world?
16. What is the role of the Director General of Fair Trading in competition policy?
17. In what ways can local authorities influence business activity?
18. Give an example of the way in which a local business has to take account of its local community.
19. In what ways is 'interdependence' a basic feature of business life?
20. What key changes were made by the Maastricht Treaty?

Essays

1. In what ways does business activity involve
   (a) competition for and
   (b) co-operation in the use of scarce resources?
2. Reconcile the following statements:
   (a) A decrease in demand leads to a decrease in price.
   (b) A decrease in price leads to a rise in the quantity demanded.
3. Explain how the demand for a particular product depends on a complex interdependence of factors.
4. How do the supply conditions for a product interact with demand to create a market price?
5. Markets that are dominated by a small number of firms will rarely be competitive. Discuss.
6. How does the UK government seek to make markets more competitive?
7. Mergers reduce competition and must always be against the public interest. Discuss.
8. Do the benefits to Britain of the Single Market outweigh the costs?
9. What major changes will be required for British businesses to succeed in the Single Market?
10. Supply is determined by price. Discuss.

Data response questions

1 Tabloid wars

The tabloid newspapers are never far from the spotlight of public attention. In recent years they have been faced by falling circulation figures. In the middle of July 1993, the *Sun* announced that it was going to cut its price from 25p to 20p (Fig. 11.14). In retaliation, the *Daily Mirror* announced that it would outdo this on one day only: on 12 July 1993, the price of the *Daily Mirror* was reduced to 10p.

Tabloid papers earn a large proportion of their revenue through the cover price rather than through advertising. This contrasts with broadsheets (*Independent*, *The Times*, etc.), where advertising is more important. When the *Mirror* was selling 5 million copies a day in the 1950s, it was calculated that it could make a profit without selling any advertising at all.

Figure 11.14

The *Sun* cut its price at an opportune time. The *Mirror* had been considerably weakened as a result of money lost to the newspaper through the dealings of its previous owner, Robert Maxwell. At the same time, another rival, the *Daily Star*, had been seriously weakened when the government banned advertising of sexually explicit phone lines which had provided the *Star* with a substantial income.

The newspaper industry is notorious for cut-throat competition. One of the favourite ploys of the tabloids is the 'spoil-up'. This involves finding out what a competitor is going to do and then copying its tactics on the same day. For example, when one paper comes up with an 'exclusive' interview setting out the detailed love life of a well known star, the other papers will produce their own exclusives, using old photographs and rewritten stories about that particular star.

Newspapers shadow each other's prices very closely. Newspapers are not as price-sensitive as other items such as groceries and petrol. Many readers show brand loyalty to a particular newspaper for long periods of time. (In the jargon of economics, demand is fairly *inelastic* in the short period.)

When the *Mirror* went up to 27p in the summer of 1992, the *Sun* did not follow but kept its price at 25p. In the first six months of 1993 *Mirror* sales fell by nearly 200 000 while the *Sun*'s dropped by only 70 000.

Since the 1970s, newspapers have competed through promotions such as big money prize bingo and sensational stories including tapes of alleged conversations involving the Royal Family.

It is a long time since a price-cutting strategy worked in the newspaper market. In November 1929 the *Daily Telegraph* halved its price to one penny (1*d.*) and within two months its sales had doubled to 200 000.

The Sun's offer

On 12 July 1993 the *Sun* set out its case in the following way:

> For just 20p, the Sun brings you the top stories, the big exclusives, the best pictures, the brightest package money can buy.
> We could say nasty things about our much-dearer rivals, but we won't. Judge for yourselves the incredible value the *Sun* gives you.

The Mirror's offer

On the same day, the *Mirror* stated:

> Today's the day we give our faithful family of readers a treat: your *Daily Mirror* for just TEN PENCE, the sort of offer we wouldn't—and couldn't—make every day…We've changed a lot when it comes to value—every day of the week there's a great centre section catering for readers whose needs have changed over the years. From Monday's bright Good Morning section, packed with interviews, previews, games and good reading, right through to Saturday's TV weekly—the best guide in Britain—we pack your week with fun and information…The *Sun* has always been the home of the dirty trick, cheap slur and total lie. And the *Sun*'s dark side has managed to offend and discredit the Royal Family, a hero soldier's widow and thousands of totally honest and decent football fans.

1. The owners of newspapers often put forward the argument that newspaper sales have fallen in recent years because of a fall in literacy, because people are watching too much television. What other factors might have led to a fall in newspaper sales at the same time?
2. What evidence is given above to indicate that tabloid newspapers operate in a highly competitive market situation?
3. What are the likely effects of a cut in the price of the *Sun* in the short run and the long run on
    (a) sales of the *Sun* newspaper?
    (b) sales of the *Daily Mirror* newspaper?
    (c) sales of tabloid newspapers?
    (d) sales of newspapers in general?
    (e) the cost of producing the *Sun* newspaper?
    (f) the profits of the *Sun* newspaper?
    (g) the costs of producing the *Daily Mirror*?
    (h) the profits of the *Daily Mirror*?
4. How can newspapers gain a competitive edge over rivals?

2 Selling abroad

Supersweets Ltd is a company based in the South of England. It produces chocolates and sweets. It is hoping to expand into the European Community to take advantage of the Single Market.

1. Apart from the United Kingdom, list 11 EC countries to which Supersweets Ltd could sell its products.
2. If Supersweets were also to sell to countries in the European Economic Area, what additional countries would be added to the 12 EC countries?
3. What is the Single Market?
4. How can Supersweets Ltd benefit from selling its goods in other countries?
5. (a) What problems might discourage Supersweets Ltd from selling goods in other countries?
    (b) How might these problems be overcome?

Suggested reading

Davies, H., *Managerial Economics for Business, Management and Accounting*, 2nd edn. Pitman, 1991.
Griffiths, A. and Wall, S., *Applied Economics*, 5th edn. Longman, 1993.
Harbury, C. and Lipsey, R., *An Introduction to the UK Economy*, 4th edn. Blackwell, 1993.
Needham, D. and Dransfield, R., *European Business Studies*. McGraw-Hill, 1994.

12

Understanding customer needs

Business analysts frequently consider issues that influence the success of a business organization. Its management, innovation and the setting and achieving of performance standards are frequently cited as being of importance. At the same time, however, authors of such studies tend to agree that good *marketing* is an equally vital factor in influencing business success.

So, what is marketing? Many people confuse marketing with advertising. In doing so they wrongly view it as a discrete activity rather than a strategic business process. Marketing involves everything that an organization has to make happen if customers are to be satisfied with its products. For this to be done effectively and successfully, an organization has, therefore, to discover and assess customer needs. The Chartered Institute of Marketing (CIM) defines marketing as:

> The anticipation, identification and fulfilment of a consumer need—at a profit

Meeting consumer needs involves developing strategies. It is this strategic process that lies at the heart of marketing. Such strategies are usually translated into a series of *marketing plans*, and these plans keep an organization in touch with its customers. Peters and Waterman define good marketing as 'being close to the customer'.

In today's competitive environment, marketing activities are influenced by a number of external factors. For example, market-places are constantly changing as buyers and sellers enter and leave the market and make decisions affecting purchase and supply. At the same time, buyers and sellers have the right, in most cases, to choose who they deal with, and they may be influenced by prices and other competitive activities. The following definition of marketing builds on the CIM definition to take into account competitive activities:

> Marketing is an essentially strategic function concerned with ensuring that a business satisfies consumer needs profitably and at the same time outperforms rival organizations.

To support marketing as a strategic process, organizations will use *marketing services* (Fig. 12.1). These services are the tools and tactics used by the marketing department. The marketing department will set out to identify the most appropriate marketing services to employ, for example advertising, public relations, promotional activities, sales literature.

So how does marketing affect the operations of a business? Marketing today is frequently viewed as a total business philosophy. It is a way of thinking about how an organization can satisfy the needs of its customers. In fact, it is frequently said that:

> Marketing is the generalship of business

Figure 12.1 The marketing process.

The belief is that, if organizations do not satisfy the needs of customers, they will not survive. It is therefore essential to match the production and development of goods and services with the identification and anticipation of customers' desires and requirements. This philosophy has been important for Japanese companies such as Sony and Honda for many years and today is becoming increasingly important for British companies. Customer needs and requirements are identified in every area of organizational activity, from the original idea and design right up until the final sale and then after-sales support.

The marketing orientation of a company can be contrasted with production and sales orientations. A *production-orientated* company holds the view that products will tend to find their own markets if they can be produced cheaply and to a good standard of quailty. Such companies spend relatively little time investigating consumers' wishes. As a result, they often come to grief because, although their products are good in a technical sense, they do not provide the benefits the consumers require.

A *sales-orientated* company holds the view that success depends on effective advertising, selling and promotion rather than on achieving a real difference between the product it is selling and those offered by its competitors. This philosophy will lead it to grief if consumers shop around and see through the selling strategy.

The real distinction between a marketing orientation and a sales orientation is that selling tries to get the customer to want what the company has; marketing on the other hand tries to get the company to produce what the customer wants.

⌕ Case Study—The carpentry business

Edward Sanson has recently moved his carpentry business from the East End of London to a small unit in Peterborough. In London Edward had been able to sell as much furniture as he could produce working from a small side-street workshop in an area renowned as a centre for the carpentry business. However, he had found operating costs to be a real problem. The rent and rates on his workshop premises were high, and because of competition from larger-scale furniture manufacturers he could make only a low margin of profit on sales.

Moving to Peterborough meant that Edward was able to reduce his overhead costs drastically and at the same time take on a larger unit. The unit was one of a number housing a range of different types of business set on an industrial estate four miles from central Peterborough. Edward was able quickly to build up a large stock of furniture and to store it in his unit. Unfortunately, however, he found that these stocks began to cramp his working space, and his order book remained very low.

Questions

1. What problems can you identify in Edward Sanson's business strategy?
2. What solutions would you employ to deal with this problem?
3. From first-hand observation of local businesses, try to identify enterprises that tend to have a production orientation or a sales orientation. What steps could their owners/managers take to remedy these problems?

The marketing environment

Today, organizations exist in a far more complex business environment than ever before and this increases the importance of the marketing function. Influences in the environment may be friendly or hostile and may pose many and varied threats and opportunities. The first step in the marketing process is to develop an understanding of this environment so that activities can be developed which enable the organization to deliver goods or services more effectively than its competitors. Such an understanding should underlie all decisions that are made.

One useful way of analysing an organization's external environment is by grouping external forces neatly into four areas, using a PEST analysis. These forces are the Political, Economic, Social and Technological environments (Fig. 12.2).

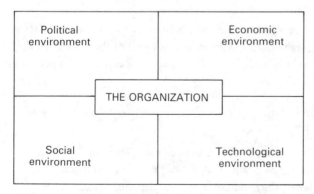

Figure 12.2 The wider business environment.

Political factors

Business conditions in every country are determined by the country's political system. For example, in some countries unfavourable political conditions or political instability may make it almost impossible for businesses to operate successfully. Governments may use taxation and legislation to influence business activities.

 Task

1. List four ways in which (a) taxation and (b) legislation affect business activities.
2. What changes in business taxation and legislation would you like to see? Discuss your answers.

Economic factors

Although the economic environment is influenced by domestic economic policies, it is also dependent upon world economic trends. For example, both domestic economic decisions and the world recession dramatically affected the UK business environment during the 1980s and early 1990s. All types of organization, no matter how successful, were in some way affected by such trends. Rates of economic growth, inflation, consumption patterns, income distribution and many other economic factors will determine the nature of products or services required by customers.

Social factors

Understanding the social environment involves a close analysis of the behaviour of society. Demographic changes such as population growth, movements and age distribution will be important, as will changes in cultural values and social trends such as family size and social behaviour.

Technological factors

In marketing goods and services, business organizations must become aware of new materials as well as developments in manufacturing techniques and business processes. At the same time, they have to look at the nature of their products and, in particular, at their cost-effectiveness and performance.

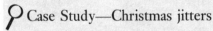 Case Study—Christmas jitters

Christmas came late for many companies in 1992. Executives were biting their nails in the hope that the Christmas sales surge would materialise. When it did come, the businesses that did well were those which adjusted to the changing nature of the business environment.

CBI reports indicated faltering consumer sales, and a Key Note/Gallup Survey indicated that a third of consumers expected to spend less on family and friends during the holiday period. To boost sales, many organizations joined in a pre-Christmas trade-war with price cuts, but this failed to persuade some retailers to take on large stocks. (A notable exception was the sale of Sega and Nintendo products, where sales surpassed expectations.)

A major factor in the sluggish pre-Christmas sales in 1992 was shifting consumer attitudes. Many customers were still spending the same amount of money on goods but had gone down-market, or else were buying at lower price-points or were looking for products with good brand assurance.

Running comparisons with previous years were difficult to make because of uncertainty over Sunday trading, and Key Note/Gallup reported increasing consumer resistance to Christmas on the high street starting in the middle of November.

The challenge to marketers for the Christmas of 1992 was to understand how the recession and the threat of redundancy had affected consumer markets and to adjust their strategies to keep their targets in sight.

Questions

1. What external factors influenced consumer markets in 1992?
2. Explain why it is important for marketers to understand how such factors affect their customers.

An organization can use the picture of its external environment created by the PEST analysis to help to identify marketing opportunities. Such opportunities will exist in the market-place.

A market exists when buyers and sellers come into contact.

In some markets the buyer and the seller may meet face-to-face; in others they may rarely meet and may simply contact each other by some form of external business communication such as phone or fax.

The market-place has a number of ingredients (Fig. 12.3). The key players are *buyers* and *sellers*. A transaction will involve:

- Communication
- An offer for sale
- Acceptance of the offer
- An exchange (usually goods or services for money or credit)

Among the factors in the market-place affecting an enterprise is that of *competition*. Competition occurs where two or more organizations act independently to try to sell their products to the same group of consumers. Some markets are signified by an abundance of products and services so that

Market-place

(Goods or services for money or credit)

Figure 12.3 The market-place.

consumers have a massive choice. In other markets there may be little competition (if any) and consumers may be able to make only a limited choice from the range of goods or services on offer.

Direct competition exists where organizations produce similar products which appeal to the same group of consumers. For example, the Ford Mondeo would be in direct competition with the Vauxhall Cavalier.

Even when an organization provides a unique end-product with no direct competition, it will still have to consider indirect competition. *Indirect competition* occurs where potential customers consider different ways of meeting the same needs. For example, instead of going on holiday to St Ives they might go to Majorca; instead of buying a newspaper they might buy a magazine.

 Task

Identify two examples of direct competition and two examples of indirect competition.

Customer behaviour

All business organizations, whether they are in the public sector or the private sector, have customers. Customers might sometimes be called clients or users. A customer can be either a person or an organization (Fig. 12.4). For most goods or services customers are expected to pay, but this is not always the case. For example, a customer in a supermarket is clearly the person buying goods from the shelves; at the same time, the supermarket is the customer of manufacturers and distributors; and you are the customer of the educational institution you attend.

It is the job of marketers to develop a close understanding of the needs of their customers. By doing so they can develop goods and services that meet these needs more precisely than do those of their competitors. The problem is that the process of buying a product is more complex than it might at first appear. Customers do not usually make purchases without thinking carefully about their requirements. Wherever there is choice decisions are involved, and these are influenced by constantly changing motives. The business that can understand why customers make decisions

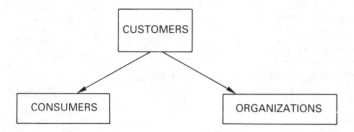

Figure 12.4 Types of customer.

such as who buys, what they buy and how they buy will, by catering more closely for customer needs, become potentially more profitable.

Consumer markets are made up of individuals who purchase items for personal or domestic consumption, usually from retailers. Their purchases may be *consumable* in nature, such as food, with a short shelf-life intended for immediate consumption, or they may be for *durable goods* with a longer life, such as televisions or video cassette recorders.

Organizational markets consist of buyers who purchase goods and services to use in the production of other goods and services. Some of these goods might require frequent purchase because they have a limited life, such as fuels, chemicals and stationery, while others would be more permanent in nature, such as buildings and machinery.

It is possible for some retailers to provide goods for both consumer and organizational markets; for example, a motor retailer may sell cars to private customers and commercial vehicles to businesses.

Consumers

If an organization hopes to match products with consumer needs, it must have detailed knowledge of consumer behaviour. Marketers will wish to know about the economic, social and cultural differences of their target group of customers as well as any reasons for changes in behaviour. This knowledge will help them to predict the answers to questions such as:

- What types of consumer can afford the products?
- What goods will they wish to purchase?
- How will they buy?
- Where will they buy?
- How often will they buy?
- What loyalty will they show?

There are many influences on consumer behaviour that affect purchasing patterns (Fig. 12.5), and it is important for marketers to understand fully how these influences affect individuals. For example, by identifying the need of working families to organize meals quickly without taking the time and effort of having to prepare them from scratch, marketers were able to develop the market for frozen ready-cooked meals.

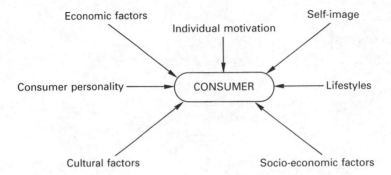

Figure 12.5 Influences on customer behaviour.

Case Study—Change and variety in the soup market

The soup market is one of the most stable grocery markets and is worth over £300 million. The two key sectors of the market are tinned and dried soups, which account for two-thirds and one-third of the market, respectively. The soup market is large and dynamic and has many varieties and ranges which are constantly adjusted to cater for changing consumer behaviour.

The dried soup sector was originally created to provide an alternative to popular tinned soups. In recent years innovation has been the key characteristic as new flavours, products and ideas have been introduced to reflect changes in consumer lifestyles and tastes.

For example, in the 1980s instant soups were launched, which could be made simply by adding boiling water. To add 'spice' to instant recipes, special varieties were introduced with ingredients such as croutons and noodles. Another new concept was the instant low-calorie soup in both wet and dry varieties. This was a direct response to the growing number of consumers wishing to follow a healthier lifestyle and concerned about gaining weight and improving their overall appearance.

In the late 1980s many consumers became aware of the issues surrounding the use of artificial ingredients. The soup market responded to these concerns with a reformulation of ingredients so as to eliminate artificial colours and ingredients. Wholesome, top-quality ingredients were introduced to match consumer expectations.

New ideas are currently the 'order of the day' in the soup market. Foreign travel has broadened consumer tastes. Exotic varieties of soup have had a big impact upon the market. Pre-prepared 'fresh' chilled soups, soups in jars and even soups aimed at young consumers have been launched. Another developing area is that of meat-free soups aimed at the growing number of vegetarians. The symbol of the Vegetarian Society is now prominently displayed on many soup labels.

The future success of businesses competing in the soup market will depend on how well they can respond to consumer preferences and tastes. In order to do this, they have to continue to show a good understanding of changes in consumer behaviour.

Questions

1. What aspects of consumer behaviour illustrated by this case study have changed over recent years?
2. How have such trends affected preferences for soups?
3. Explain why organizations in the soup market have to understand changing consumer behaviour

Economic factors

One group of factors affecting consumer behaviour concerns the economic determinants of consumer demand.

The most important of these factors is *real disposable incomes*, which are those incomes available to consumers for spending on goods and services. An increase in *real* incomes (i.e. after inflation has been taken into account) will generally increase the demand for goods and services.

A second economic determinant is the *relative price of a substitute product* whose purchase might be preferred or viewed as better value for money. A fall in the price of butter might switch some purchases away from butter substitutes such as Golden Crown.

The *size* and *structure of the population* will affect demand for various products. A baby boom will clearly stimulate demand for infant products such as disposable nappies.

Tastes, fashions and *habits* will act as a constant influence on the patterns of demand for goods and services. We have already seen how the market for soups has changed over recent years, but think of how the market for beverages or electronic goods has changed!

Finally, *government measures* in many areas, such as credit controls or safety, may influence the demand for goods and services.

 Task

How have the following markets been affected by changes in the economic determinants of consumer demand over the last year:

1. Fashion clothes?
2. Cars?
3. Albums?

Social factors

Society's influence on each consumer's motivations, self-image and personality will affect the ways in which they behave.

A provider of goods or services must be interested in what inspires a customer's *individual motivation* to purchase a particular commodity. In Chapter 19 we look at the work of Abraham Maslow in developing a hierarchical picture of human needs. As well as relating such needs to motivation and behaviour at work, it is also possible to use them to help us to understand consumer purchasing behaviour. Maslow identified five broad areas of human needs:

1. *Physiological needs* are concerned with acquiring food, shelter and clothing. These are the most basic of consumer needs.
2. *Safety and security needs* relate to well-being and the need for protection. Products that concern personal safety and protection fall into this category.
3. *Love needs* centre upon purchases that are linked to being part of society and to goods and services that provide us with an element of acceptance—for example socializing, or belonging to a football club.
4. *Esteem needs* stem from a desire for status and for a sense of achievement. Lavish lifestyle products and prestigious items fall into this category.
5. *Self-actualization needs* relate to products that allow individuals to develop fully and creatively.

The implications of Maslow's work are easy to perceive. Different products and services are related to different needs. By identifying where consumer needs lie, it is possible to develop goods and services to relate directly to them. For example, in Western societies many more products and services are related to higher needs than in poorer countries.

 Task

Identify two products that relate to each of the needs in Maslow's hierarchy.

Another theory that seeks to explain the behaviour of consumers is the *self-image theory*. Everybody has a self-image which reflects how we would like to view ourselves. There are various ways to maintain and enhance this image. An individual's choice of clothes, car, places to shop and food all reflect in some way that individual's perception of 'self'. By discovering how consumers wish to be perceived, organizations can develop goods and services that are consistent with the image sought. We can clearly think of many examples of image-orientated products where producers deliberately develop products to match a particular image.

 Task

What sort of image would you identify with

1. the Vauxhall Frontera?
2. real ale?
3. Coca-Cola?

The *personality* of the consumer is closely related to the self-image theory. As many customers have different types of personalities, it may be possible to divide up a market according to such stereotypes. Fashion products in particular tend to reflect the personality traits of customers.

Cultural factors

Culture encompasses standard patterns of behaviour and plays an important role in shaping our purchasing patterns. It stems from the traditions, beliefs and values of the community in which we live. For example, our attitudes towards alcohol, the food we eat and the relative importance of our families are all based upon our culture. Although a nation may be characterized by one dominant culture, there may be many sub-cultures within it—e.g. youth cultures, ethnic groups, senior citizens.

Socio-economic factors

Perhaps the most frequently used way of classifying customers into groups so that products can be accurately targeted at them is to use socio-economic groupings or *social stratification* (Table 12.1).

With social stratification, the assumption is that certain jobs have certain lifestyles attached. Whatever one may think of the correctness of socio-economic grouping, it does provide a reliable guide to the relationship between occupation and income and as such provides valuable information which can be used for marketing purposes. For example, members of each group are assumed to have certain priorities which will influence their needs. We would expect some members of groups A, B and possibly C1 to spend some of their income on private health and education, whereas members of groups D and E would spend more of their incomes on necessities.

Another socio-economic factor influencing purchasing patterns would be the lifestyle of the consumer. A *lifestyle* is a behaviour pattern adopted by a particular community or a sub-section of it. Marketers can deliberately target their products at those who enjoy such a lifestyle. For example, many products were deliberately targeted at the 'Yuppies' of the 1980s.

Table 12.1   A socio-economic classification

Socio-economic group	Social 'class'	Occupation types	Examples
A	Upper or upper-middle	High managerial Administrative Professional	Surgeon Director of a big company
B	Middle	Intermediate managerial Administrative Professional	Bank manager Headteacher Architect
C1	Lower-middle	Supervisory Junior managerial Junior administrative Clerical	Bank clerk Nurse Teacher
C2	Skilled working	Skilled manual workers	Joiner Welder Foreman
D	Working	Semi-skilled Unskilled	Driver Postman Porter
E	Lowest subsistence level	Low-paid Unemployed	Casual worker State pensioner

⌕ Case Study—Products to watch out for

One of the most interesting aspects of marketing is to watch for new products as and when they enter markets. The following products are all recent developments.

A scratch or a speck of dust on your compact disc (CD) can mean lost or misread data, and poor sound quality. The *Discwasher CD Hydrobath* minimizes this risk by cleaning all types of CDs automatically. Basically, it works like a washing machine complete with wash, dry cycles and suds! After filling a tub with a special cleaner, a CD is placed on to a rotor. As the disc spins, cleaning solution is pumped on to the underside where data are stored, dissolving and lifting off debris. Floppy disks can also be cleaned in this way.

The latest *personal computer activity centre* allows users to receive messages and to send or receive faxes. The AcerPAC is an IBM-compatible PC with built-in extras including a speakerphone, digital answering machine, fax modem, CD-ROM drive (which plays regular compact discs), an AM/FM receiver and alarm clock. The AcerPAC comes ready loaded with Windows and Microsoft business and reference software.

Moulinex is about to launch its *home controller*, which uses normal electricity lines to communicate commands such as 'on' and 'off'. The system will use specially designed plugs with built-in computer chips.

In America a healthy alternative to crisps is already on the market. Launched by Nabisco, these crisps are *baked* rather than fried in oil. As a result, they have only half the level of fat. Initially they have been sold in health food stores for roughly twice the price of conventional crisps.

Questions

1. Comment on the consumer needs that are met by each of the products mentioned in this study. In each case mention how their launch would be influenced by economic determinants of consumer demand, appeal to motivation, self-image, the personality of the consumer, culture, social stratification and lifestyle.
2. Briefly explain why a consideration of each of these factors is important before launching a new product.

Organizations

In the business market, organizations buy goods and services that are either used directly or indirectly in the production of *other* goods or services, or are stocked in order to be resold.

A complex manufactured product such as a motor car is made up of numerous parts obtained from many suppliers. What we tend to think of as a single product in fact represents the culmination of a process of assembly that has brought together around 12 000 parts, about half of which will have been bought in from other suppliers/producers. The organizations supplying such parts will also have suppliers from whom *they* will have purchased raw materials and components.

Perhaps the main difference between a consumer market and a business or organizational market lies in the total number of customers. A consumer market has a potential of 56 million domestic users; the total number of business organizations within the United Kingdom is fewer than 3 million. Furthermore, the likelihood is that the more specialized the product, the more limited will be its appeal.

The demand for organizational products is usually called *derived* because the amounts purchased are determined by the demand for the relevant goods and services that will be produced. Being dependent upon derived demand can have serious consequences for businesses, particularly during recession. Organizational markets are subject to *business cycles*, and the demand for industrial products may fluctuate widely as the pace of business activity changes. For example, businesses with organizational customers suffered badly during the recession of the early 1990s.

In organizational markets the smooth running of the purchasing function ensures that goods and services are provided by reliable suppliers. Over recent years many new business techniques have been introduced to this area; for example:

1. *'Just-in-time' production* involves having goods delivered just in time for their inclusion in the manufacturing process—rather than keeping large stocks of them in hand.
2. *Quality assurance* places great emphasis upon the seller to deliver goods of appropriate quality, so that the receiving organization is saved the time and trouble resulting from defects.
3. *British Stanard 5750* provides a framework that imposes specific requirements upon the quality of products provided by suppliers.
4. *Electronic data interchange* has the objective of speeding business transactions between suppliers and their customers. It achieves this by allowing data, messages or documents to be transferred directly from one company's computer on to another.

Companies supplying goods in organizational markets face constantly changing circumstances which are often called *contingency factors*. For example:

1. The supplier is usually expected to provide credit facilities for the customer.
2. There is always the risk of takeover by the customer.
3. Buyers may influence buying power over suppliers in areas such as discounts.
4. Buyers may deliberately delay payment for goods or services received.
5. There is always the risk of the supplier becoming too dependent on the buyer.

Organizational markets are sometimes described as being either vertical or horizontal. Where a supplier provides for only a few customers, the market is *vertical* in nature (see Fig. 12.6). Where there are many customers from different industries, the market will be *horizontal* (see Fig. 12.7).

Figure 12.6 A vertical market.

Figure 12.7 A horizontal market.

Market research

As we have seen, the first stage in the marketing process for any organization is to understand thoroughly the business environment in which it exists, its markets and its customers. To find out about each of these three areas, an organization needs *information*. Such information will help to reduce risks in decision-making. The whole success of the marketing process will then depend upon the quality of information gathered and on how this information is then used.

As a tool of management, the purpose of market research is to provide this information, thereby enabling business organizations to use precise techniques in order to plan ahead with certainty rather than rely on unsubstantiated guesswork and hunches.

The American Marketing Association uses the following simple definition of market research:

MARKET RESEARCH is the systematic gathering, recording and analysis of data about problems related to the marketing of goods and services.

This widely accepted definition can be broken down into each of its ingredients:

1. *Systematic:* undertaking research by using a clear method or system.
2. *Gathering:* collecting the appropriate information.
3. *Recording:* keeping clear and well organized records of information collected.
4. *Analysing:* making sense of information in order to draw out relevant trends and conclusions.
5. *Problems related to marketing:* finding the answers to questions relating to the successful delivery of products to the market-place.

No organization, particularly in the 1990s, exists in a static business environment. Circumstances constantly change. The market research function of any organization should be to attempt to assemble all the relevant information about the business environment, the market-place and the firm's customers. This is essential if an organization wishes to succeed with its business objectives. This process of market research should be an *on-going activity*, and a team of marketers should be constantly analysing information and feeding it through for use in planning and decision-making.

○ Case Study—The health food shop

Sarah Fullford is intending to open a health food shop in Darlo, a town in the North of England. She is convinced that over the next few years a transformation will take place in personal eating habits as more and more people come to appreciate the benefits of healthy eating.

Sarah wishes to open a shop that provides a dynamic approach to healthy foods. She wants it to be a self-service shop which has interesting product ranges and provides a daily sandwich service, a hot counter and also takes orders for office deliveries. The whole emphasis of her proposals is to provide something that is perceived by potential customers to be different from the current health foods market.

Questions

1. What questions should Sarah attempt to find the answers to before she invests in this proposition? (List your questions under the three headings of 'Business environment', 'Market' and 'Customers'.)
2. Explain briefly how the answers to such questions will help Sarah.

There are three broad areas in which market research can take place. First, existing organizations will have *internal information*, kept within their systems. Second, a lot of useful information may already have been published and will be obtainable as *external* or *secondary information*. The third source of information will not exist in any identifiable form and will have to be collected first-hand: this is *primary information*.

Internal information

A lot of the information that an organization will require will already be held within its various departments. Such information might include:

- Details of customers, such as average order size, methods of payment, credit periods, types of customer, new customers, old customers, profitability per customer, discounts
- Sales figures per customer/region, etc.
- Reports on competitors
- Information on opportunities not yet exploited
- Information on prospects
- Reviews of the business environment

It is essential that this information should not be placed in filing cabinets and left to become obsolete. Instead, it should be made available for those who might require it at short notice. Retrieval of this information is very important.

Today, a lot of information is held in *computer files*. Computers have revolutionized the ways in which information can be stored, retrieved and analysed. Vast quantities of information may also be stored in a significantly smaller area. *Databases* have now become a very important source of information for marketers.

Another important source of internal information is the *salesforce*. These members of staff might be working within the organization's buildings or outside the organization as sales representatives. As these people are close to the customers, they can act as the 'eyes and ears' of the market-place. For example, customers may frequently comment on the relative merits of various product lines or indicate to sales staff what changes they might like to see. This *feedback* can be extremely valuable and may influence product developments.

External information

Internal information will not provide all of the information an organization will need to know; for example, it will not indicate how the business is performing in relation to competitors. The next stage in the market research process is to collect information that has been already collected by somebody else. External information is more commonly called *secondary data* and can provide a broader dimension to data previously collected. This information may either be freely available through libraries or may be purchased from specialist organizations such as publishers and agencies.

External information will enhance an organization's existing knowledge. It will also help it to group together different types of customer according to various characteristics. For example:

1. *Domestic socio-economic data*   On page 319 we looked at social stratification. Such information may help to classify prospects by house type or lifestyle. An alternative to the classification we looked at is ACORN, which is an acronym for 'A Classification Of Residential Neighbourhoods'. This system divides the whole of the country into 50 different categories by post code. The classifications carry information such as types of housing within a post code area.
2. *Industrial classifications*   Business customers can be divided according to the nature of their activities. Certain types of organization will have predictable demands for their services.

External information may include the following.

Government statistics

The Central Statistical Office (CSO) co-ordinates the government's statistical service. Government departments prepare statistics which are submitted to the CSO, and these are then published in monthly and annual reports; in addition, Business Monitors are published quarterly to provide a range of information about various markets. Information on particular groups of industries is usually identified by the group's Standard Industrial Classification (SIC). As the SIC code is the government's way of classifying organizations and markets, it is frequently used in market research.

Another useful source of information, particularly for industries selling to consumer markets, is *census data*. A full census takes place every ten years, the last one having occurred in 1991. This information is published by the Office of Population Censuses and Surveys.

 Task

Explain why census information might be useful for a construction company.

Commercial research organizations

In today's dynamic business environment, the collecting of marketing information, compiling of reports and the selling of these reports to firms operating in those markets has become big business. There are many commercial research organizations which provide a range of services and operate either in specific markets or across a range of markets.

Mintel is a research organization which sells monthly journals on a variety of consumer markets. Reports are between 10 and 20 pages long and contain information such as market size, shares of competitors, projected growth, the amount spent on advertising of main brands, trends. *Euromonitor* operates in the same way as Mintel and broadens the availability of reports on various markets. Consumer market reports are also produced by research institutes. For example, the *Leatherhead Food Research Association* and the *Food Policy Research Unit* both publish information relating to the food sector.

A. C. Nielsen and *Retail Audits* collect details of retail sales from supermarkets and large chains and then sell the figures back to organizations in these markets. Such figures help manufacturers work out their share of the market, their recent successes and failures and the effects of any other recent strategies.

Panels

Panels are groups of consumers who record their purchases and/or media habits in a diary. Their diaries may then provide information about purchasing habits and this can be related to socio-economic groups, occupation, income, demographic details and neighbourhood. *Audits of Great Britain Ltd (AGB)* produces a variety of panel data. *Broadcasters Audience Research Board (BARB)* monitors the numbers of people watching TV programmes and stations at various times of the day.

Media information

A number of organizations provide information about the media. *Benn's Media Directory* provides details of TV stations, commercial radio stations, newspapers and magazines. *British Rate and Data (BRAD)* provides comprehensive coverage of virtually all media selling space, together with current rates. The *Advertisers' Annual* makes detailed comparisons of advertising agencies.

Company information

A range of information about companies can be used for secondary research. *Kompass* publishes two volumes of product and service company information listed by SIC code. *Extel* provides details and comparisons of the published accounts of all public companies and from many of the larger private companies. The annual publication *Who Owns Whom* gives details of the ownership of subsidiary companies.

Case Study—The market for tea

Tea is Britain's traditional drink; its use is ingrained upon our culture. As a nation, Britain imports approximately 22 per cent of the major tea growing countries' exports. Tea accounts for more than 43 per cent of everything we drink with the exception of tap water. The main organizations in the tea market are Lyons Tetley, Brooke Bond and Premier Brands. These firms compete not only in terms of taste, flavour and price but also in terms of packaging, convenience, innovation, value for money, quality and distribution.

The British consume an average of 3.56 cups per person per day, which adds up to some 178 million cups of tea daily. More than 80 per cent of the nation's inhabitants drink tea, and there are some 1 500 varieties and blends from which to choose. The information given in Figs 12.8, 12.9 and 12.10 was supplied on a specific date by several market research organizations.

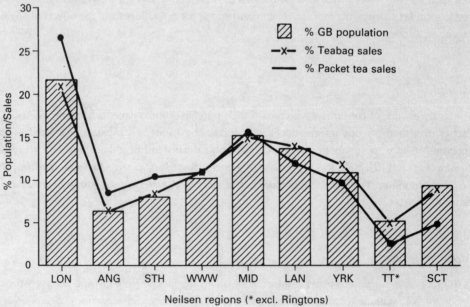

Figure 12.8 Regionality of total tea sales.

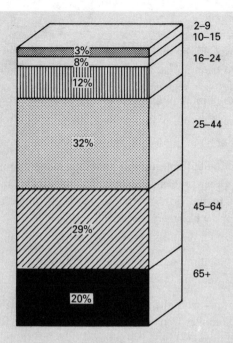

Figure 12.9 Age-group breakdown: teabag drinkers.

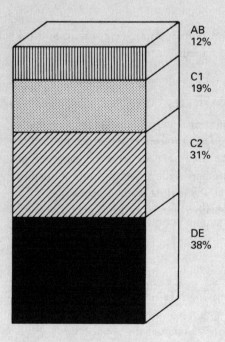

Figure 12.10 Social class breakdown: teabag drinkers.

Questions

1. Comment on the personality of teabag drinkers. In your profile, refer to groups of consumers (a) most and (b) least likely to use teabags.
2. Explain why, in your opinion, teabag sales vary regionally.
3. How might the information shown in Figs 12.8, 12.9 and 12.10 be used by tea producers?

Although secondary research will often save organizations considerable time and money, firms have to assess the degree of accuracy of such data. Other problems might be that the data are too old, or that they may not be specifically geared to the firm's particular needs. In order to overcome these problems, the firm may have to conduct primary research.

Primary information

Primary research involves the collection of data directly from the market. It is therefore 'straight from the horse's mouth'. Information a company compiles from its own research efforts, or for which a market research agency is specifically commissioned, is called *primary*.

Surveys

Surveys are the most common method used to collect primary data. Surveys are conducted with *respondents*, whose reactions to a range of issues are recorded in a *questionnaire*.

Case Study—The Market Research Society

The Market Research Society (MRS) is the professional body for market researchers. All of the members of the MRS operate within the Data Protection Act, which means that any personal data supplied in a survey will be used only for statistical purposes. In addition to the Data Protection Act, all MRS members abide by a strict Code of Conduct which ensures that the research is carried out to the highest possible standards.

The leaflet illustrated in Fig. 12.11 is representative of the sort that could be issued to survey respondents.

Questions

1. Give three reasons why an organization may wish to employ an agency to undertake primary market research.
2. Why may a researcher wish to talk to a cross-section of the population?
3. How important is confidentiality in a survey, and how does the Data Protection Act protect respondents?

market research

■ Why is market research important?

Market research is your opportunity to give your opinion on things that may affect you and your family. Manufacturers, retailers, service companies, political parties and the Government can only succeed if they please you, the customer, so they need to find out what you need and what you want. Your opinion can influence a wide range of products from pension plans to washing powder and also have a bearing on issues that affect the quality of your life.

It is the job of market researchers to ask questions - to find out what you, and people like you, think.

■ Why were you chosen?

For most research projects it is necessary to talk to a cross-section of the public-people from all walks of life and all ages. You have been asked to give your opinion as a representative of the population.

■ Why is it necessary to ask personal questions?

To make sure that we do achieve a cross-section of the population we do need to ask personal questions which may include details on occupation, income and age. This information is given in total confidence and is only asked to ensure that we have a representative sample of the population.

■ The replies are confidential so why do we ask for your name and address?

This is a safety mechanism mainly for your benefit. To check that this interview has been carried out fairly, and that the correct cross-section has been contacted, the Supervisor of the fieldwork company may contact you to confirm the accuracy of the interview. Nobody outside the fieldwork company will gain access to your name and address.

■ About The Market Research Society

The Market Research Society (MRS) is the professional body for market researchers, all MRS members have to operate under a Code of Conduct which includes certain guarantees for you, the interviewee. These guarantees state that you are entitled to remain anonymous if you wish, that you will suffer no adverse effects from being interviewed and that you may withdraw from the interview at any stage.

Answering questionnaires, in face-to-face interviews, via the post or on the telephone, gives you the opportunity to speak directly to those who can make the changes you want. As a safeguard for the public, the MRS has developed three schemes to check that you have been approached by authentic researchers and not by somebody trying to sell to you.

■ Interviewer Identity Card

Carried by up to 65,000 interviewers across the country, giving the interviewer's name, photograph and the company they work for.

■ Market Research Mark

For questionnaires sent out by post-this guarantees that the questionnaire is for research purposes only and that your name is not being added to a mailing list.

■ Freefone Market Research Society

The Freefone is available seven days a week, 9am-11pm by dialling 100 and asking for Freefone Market Research Society. You can then check whether the company carrying out the research (either by telephone or face-to-face) is recognised by The Market Research Society.

Figure 12.11 Market research.

4. What alternative methods of delivering questionnaires are identified in the leaflet reproduced in Fig. 12.11?

There are two types of survey: a census and a sample. A *census* involves questioning every customer in a market. Unless the market is very small, this is unlikely to be practicable.

Sampling

Taking a *sample* involves questioning a selection of respondents from the market. In order to ensure that the results of a sample survey are accurate, the market research process must attempt to identify a representative group of consumers. If the selection is fair and accurate, then information should be *statistically reliable*. If the sample is incomplete and does not accurately represent a group of consumers, the sample is said to be *biased*.

The various sampling techniques are dealt with at length in Chapter 10. At the heart of such techniques is the concept of the *standard error*. There are many ways of selecting samples from a very large population. Imagine that a large number of different samples of a given size are selected. What would we expect the variation to be in any estimate derived from the samples? For example, let us suppose that we want to find out the proportion of all adults who are men: we would expect it to be roughly just under half. The different samples will not give exactly the same estimate, but we would expect most of them to give roughly the right estimate—otherwise sampling would be of little value.

In fact, we know from sampling theory that the estimates given by a large number of samples fit into a standard pattern, called the *normal distribution*, a bell-shaped curve in which most of the sample estimates bunch together around the centre while some tail off in either direction, above and below the central estimate. It is possible to determine how sample estimates form themselves into a normal distribution by calculating the *standard error*: two-thirds of all the estimates would be within plus or minus one standard error of the average (central) estimate, 95 per cent within two standard errors and 99 per cent within three standard errors (see Fig. 12.12). Thus we know, by calculation based on sampling theory, the probability that the true proportion for the population lies within a certain range of the estimate given by our sample.

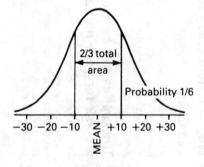

Figure 12.12 A normal distribution curve.

When carrying out market research it will usually be necessary to limit the cost of the research. Two important modifications are often made to limit the size of the sample:

- Clustering
- Stratification

A *cluster* is a sample made up of individuals with common characteristics. The existence of this characteristic simplifies the process of collecting data about the sample. A common form of clustering is based on geographical location. Samples are taken in stages. A sample is first selected from geographical areas (e.g. polling districts or census enumeration districts). Inevitably, the clustering technique will slightly increase the standard error of a sample, but the error can be calculated and is a small price to pay for the benefits of cost-effective survey work. Samples can be chosen so that interviewees all live within a small area.

Stratification involves deciding on what common characteristics will produce a representative sample. If your sample is going to represent a typical selection of individuals in a total population, it will be necessary to classify the common characteristics of the total group. Those individuals who will then be interviewed will need to match these characteristics.

Questionnaire

When the sampling issues have been decided, the market researcher must design a questionnaire.

A questionnaire is a systematic list of questions designed to obtain information from respondents about:

- Specific events
- Their attitudes
- Their values
- Their beliefs

The questionnaire design is probably the most crucial part of the survey. A badly designed questionnaire will lead to biased results and these could influence the decision-making process and ultimately affect profitability. For example, a badly designed questionnaire may lead to respondents misinterpreting questions.

In designing a questionnaire, the following points are important:

1. Questions should be simple, clear and unambiguous.
2. Questions should relate directly to information requirements so that issues can be addressed from the responses.
3. The questionnaire should not be too long or take too much of the respondent's time.
4. Personal questions should not be asked.
5. Questions should be arranged so that the respondent answers truthfully. They should not suggest or prompt the interviewee into making a preferred response.
6. Questions should have been tested, possibly using a series of trial interviews.

Another element to consider in questionnaire design is how to present questions to respondents and also how to record their responses. For example, questions in a questionnaire may be 'open' or 'closed'. *Open questions* allow the person answering to provide an opinion and may encourage them to talk at some length. *Closed questions* require an answer from a fixed list of responses which may simply be yes/no. Closed questionnaires can be answered more quickly and efficiently and their answers are easier to analyse.

In order to be able to quantify the various strengths of responses, some questionnaires have *rating scales*. Scales are a useful way of measuring attitudes or more subjective responses. A scale would offer a range of answers (see Fig. 12.13).

Do you like our new product ranges?				
(Tick one box)				
Very good	Good	Satisfactory	Poor	Very poor

Figure 12.13 A rating scale.

Prompt cards may be used to help respondents recall particular brands or items. For example, if

Asda	**01**
Tesco	**02**
Sainsbury's	**03**
Morrisons	**04**
Safeway	**05**

Figure 12.14 A prompt card.

respondents were asked where they did their shopping, a list of numbered supermarkets on a prompt card could be provided and the answers could be recorded as numbers (see Fig. 12.14).

Some questionnaires are designed so that respondents can concentrate on the questions of greatest relevance, and be able to skip over questions which do not relate to them. For example:

4. Have you shopped previously at this Centre?

☐ Yes   If yes go to question 5.

☐ No   If no go to question 6.

5. How often do you use this Centre?

☐ Every day

☐ Every week

☐ Every month

☐ Occasionally

6. Explain why you have not previously used this Centre.

Administering the questionnaire

There are three different ways of administering a questionnaire:

- With a personal interview
- By telephone
- Through the post

Personal interviews allow direct two-way communication to take place between the researcher and the respondent. Although such interviews are more expensive than postal or telephone surveys, they enable an experienced interviewer to gather more sensitive and detailed information.

Telephone interviews tend to be unpopular with the public as they are perceived to be intrusive and also are regarded as a selling device. They are, however, more appropriate for business surveys and can be a cost-effective way of analysing an organizational market.

Postal questionnaires are a useful way of reaching a closed market, particularly if a mailing list is available. They are easy to administer but tend to yield a poor response, which can often be as low as 10 per cent.

Case Study—A post-sales questionnaire

The questionnaire illustrated in Fig. 12.15 is given to customers at Sherwoods Ltd. After completion, customers are encouraged to post it back to the company using the Business Reply Service.

Questions

1. Broadly outline the purpose of the questionnaire.
2. Which questions are 'open' and which are 'closed'?
3. How might information extracted from the questionnaire in this instance (a) be analysed and (b) be used?

Sherwoods Limited

Sales, Service, Parts & Accessories
Approved Fleet Specialist, Master Hire Leasing, Motability, MasterFit, NetworkQ

Chesnut Street
Darlington
Co. Durham DL1 1RJ
Telephone 0325 466155
Fax 0325 381262

Dear Customer,

Thank you for your custom.

Our aim is to provide the highest levels of customer service and care together with modern facilities and friendly, professional staff, but we need your help.

By completing this questionnaire, you can help us to help you make your total motoring experience a pleasurable one.

Alasdair MacConachie
Chief Executive

1. Are the staff that you meet in the Reception generally helpful and courteous
   - 5 ☐ Very helpful and courteous
   - 0 ☐ Less helpful than they could be
   - 3 ☐ About right
   - 0 ☐ Unhelpful

2. Was the advance notice required for booking your car into our workshop acceptable? (How many days in advance did you have to book?)
   - 3 ☐ Yes
   - 1 ☐ No
   - ☐ Days

3. Were you given a satisfactory explanation for any work carried out?
   - 5 ☐ Yes
   - 0 ☐ Not really
   - ☐ No

4. Where relevant were you contacted about additional repairs completed?
   - 5 ☐ Yes
   - 0 ☐ No

5. Where work was not completed was this due to parts availability?
   - 2 ☐ Yes
   - 0 ☐ No

6. Was the quality of the repair or service up to the standard you expected?
   - 5 ☐ Yes
   - 0 ☐ No

7. Was your car returned to you in a satisfactory condition, free from grease marks, and clean?
   - 5 ☐ Yes
   - ☐ No

8. Was the service record book completed? (if applicable)
   - 5 ☐ Yes
   - 0 ☐ No

9. What is your opinion of the general level of efficiency in our Service Department?
   - 5 ☐ Excellent
   - 2 ☐ Satisfactory
   - 3 ☐ Good
   - 0 ☐ Poor

10. Do you feel that the service you receive is good value for money?
    - 5 ☐ Very good value
    - 4 ☐ Good value
    - 3 ☐ About right
    - 1 ☐ Too expensive
    - 0 ☐ Much too expensive

11. Do you plan to return to our Dealership for future service work?
    - 5 ☐ Yes
    - 0 ☐ No

MAX	ACT	%
50		

12. Date repairs carried out. _____

13. What is the thing you like MOST about our service? _____

14. What is the thing you like LEAST about our service? _____

YOUR ADDITIONAL COMMENTS:

_____

_____

Name _____

Address _____

_____

Tel. No. _____ Model _____ Reg. No. _____

THANK YOU FOR TAKING THE TROUBLE TO COMPLETE THE QUESTIONNAIRE.
PLEASE FOLD AND RETURN. POSTAGE IS PAID.

SV/WK/05

Registered in England No 1534622

Figure 12.15 Sherwood Limited (Vauxhall dealer) questionnaire.

Other primary research techniques

There are a variety of other ways of collecting information which may be used in the market research process. For example:

1. *Observation techniques* may be used to analyse how customers behave in buying situations. Information obtained by such methods may help with merchandising.
2. *Discussion groups* are a useful and inexpensive method of collecting qualitative information from customers. For example, product development at Vauxhall starts with the 'bubble-up' phase where the needs of targeted customers are communicated directly to designers through a series of *focus groups*, usually comprising about 20 customers each.
3. *Opinion polls* are often used to assess consumer awareness, opinions and attitudes. Questions are usually short and are designed to find out how consumers react to issues such as new products or changes in product image. Market research organizations such as Gallup are frequently used to collect such information.
4. *Electronic interviewing* is a market research technique which is based on an interactive system using the telecommunications network. A respondent need only be a television and telephone subscriber and can respond instantly with a range of answers to different forms of television advertising.

Organizing the data

When the market research process is complete, the business organization will have to decide what to do with the information. There are usually three stages involved:

* Sorting and storing the information
* Presenting the information
* Making sense of the information

Each of these stages has been transformed by the use of information technology. For example, *specialist software* has been introduced for market research purposes; this includes the Statistical Package for Social Sciences (SPSS) and Minitab. Use may also be made of information extracted from point-of-sale technology such as *bar code analysis. Electronic data processing (EDP)* is frequently used for summarizing the results from market research. Questionnaire answers can be numerically coded for data entry, which makes it easier to analyse the results.

Once statistical data have been extracted from surveys, they will need to be broken down and presented in such a way that their significance can be appreciated. Information may be displayed as text, tables, charts or graphs.

Finally, after the statistical analysis has taken place, market research information can be used as the basis for decision-making. The whole purpose of the process is to reduce risk-taking and to focus direction on the future so that strategic decisions and planning may be carried out with greater precision.

Uses of market research

There are a number of major uses of market research, including the following:

- Exploratory—to find out the nature of a problem
- Descriptive—to describe and explain what is happening
- Explanatory—to uncover possible reasons for what is happening
- Predictive—to predict what might happen

Exploratory research might involve an investigation of all types of data relating to, say, a production process to find out what is going wrong. This may involve interviewing the relevant members of staff and asking them to explain their perceptions of the problem.

Descriptive research is simply concerned with identifying what is happening and then identifying trends. For example, sales figures may be analysed over a particular period, or changes in the age structure of the population described.

Explanatory research will try to explain trends, sequences and other phenomena. This might involve looking at alternative hypotheses to uncover the assumptions on which they are based.

Predictive research is concerned with forecasting and other techniques used to look into the future.

Types of market research project

Table 12.2 lists the various types of market research project and briefly describes what each entails.

If the benefits of market research are to be reaped by an organization, the results and analysis of such research have to be made available for decision-makers to use. Market research should be viewed as an *agent of change*, enabling an organization to respond to the competitive world in which it exists.

Table 12.2

Project	What is involved
Attitude surveys	Carrying out surveys to find out how people feel about various products
Awareness tests	Carrying out research to find out whether people are aware of the existence of particular products and how informed they are
Product testing	Carrying out research to find out the reactions of samples of people to various products, wrappings for products, and other features of product presentation
Repeat awareness studies	Monitoring products at particular intervals to check on the public's ongoing perception of the product
Test marketing	Conducting trial sales of products in a specific area before making an introduction to the total market

Segmentation and positioning

Market research enables organizations to understand the operation of the markets in which they function. The 'total' market for a product is the total amount spent on the satisfaction of a need. Market research will reveal information about the various segments of each market as well as about the market as a whole.

Few organizations can serve all of their customers successfully by grouping all of their needs and wants together. Instead, they may focus or target their attention on different parts of the market-place. Within the total market, it is possible to group customers with similar characteristics into *market segments*, so that different strategies can be used with different sets of customers.

Supplying a single product to a whole market is sometimes said to be like using a blunderbuss, firing shots to pepper the whole market-place. It is also sometimes called *undifferentiated marketing* (see page 385). When it is not possible to satisfy all customer needs with a uniform product, the process of segmentation will help the organization to divide consumers into smaller segments consisting of buyers with similar characteristics, so that the marketing process becomes more like firing a rifle at a target than like using a blunderbuss. Marketing using segmentation becomes *differentiated* (see page 386).

Positioning takes the process of differentiation further. A positioning strategy would involve selecting a market segment and then creating a *differential advantage* over rivals in that segment. For example, it may be possible to position products up-market, mid-market or down-market.

Questions

Short-answer questions

1. What is meant by undifferentiated marketing?
2. Why are changes in the structure of the population of interest to producers? (*Source*: Cambridge)
3. Explain how primary and secondary sources can be utilized to construct market research.
4. Discuss those elements beyond a firm's immediate control which may influence its marketing decisions. (*Source*: AEB)
5. The manufacturer of a new breakfast cereal wants to find out the consumers' attitudes to this new innovative product. How would you go about devising
    (a) a random sample?
    (b) a non-random sample?
6. What do you consider to be the main differences between marketing the consumer market and marketing the organizational or business market?
7. What criteria would you employ for segmenting the following markets:
    (a) cars?
    (b) newspapers?
    (c) industrial machinery?
8. In matters of marketing research, state three sources of secondary data. (*Source*: AEB)

9. Explain how marketing strategy differs from marketing tactics.
10. Describe how a marketing-orientated company would differ from a sales-orientated company.
11. What is PEST analysis and why is it of use for marketers?
12. Explain the difference between direct competition and indirect competition.
13. How might the work of Abraham Maslow be of use to a marketer?
14. Give two reasons why the needs of a consumer in socio-economic group A would probably be different from the needs of a consumer in group C1.
15. Explain why demand for organizational products is usually *derived*.
16. What is the difference between a vertical organizational market and a horizontal organizational market?
17. Name three types of information held internally by a company which may be useful for market research purposes.
18. How might post codes be used by marketers?
19. What information is provided by a census?
20. How does a retail audit work?

Essays

1. How important is market research to the marketing and production strategies of a business?
2. Describe the statistical techniques that can be used in market research.
3. Explain why it is essential to have a clear picture of your target market.
4. Marketing is a dynamic function. Discuss.
5. What role should marketing play in decision-making processes?
6. No organization exists in a stable environment. Explain what is meant by this statement and examine the implications of the statement for the marketing process.
7. To what extent is a successful organization one that is close to its customers?
8. Identify a consumer product that has recently been launched. Discuss the business environment in which the launch took place, indicate the main competitors and identify the consumers at which it is targeted.
9. You have been involved with the development of a new engineering product. What considerations should take place before it is launched?
10. Marketing is a scientific business. Discuss.

Data response questions

1   Britain's industrial coal market

Read the passage and answer the questions that follow.

The first study of Britain's industrial coal market was published recently. Its co-author, Gerard McCloskey, says that the British Coal Corporation's (BCC) dominance will disappear before the year 2000. From its 6.5 m tonnes in 1989, representing 85 per cent of coal purchased by industrial customers, the report predicts that BCC's industrial sales will plummet to 1 m tonnes in the next ten years.

BCC's pricing policy comes in for examination in McCloskey's report. Some coal sold by BCC to paper mills, cement manufacturers and other large industrial users appears to be at a loss. Typically, large industrial customers pay between £32.50 and £35.00 a tonne before transportation costs. On the other hand, the two biggest electricity generating companies, Powergen and National Power, pay £39 to £43 a tonne.

The result is expected to be that BCC will lose a large part of its £300 m a year industrial market, but that its profitability will benefit.

The report also suggests that environmental pressures to reduce toxic emissions from coal burning will cause a decline in the market for coal.

(*Source*: adapted from *The Times*, 11 January 1991)

1. List four competitors of industrial coal produced by the British Coal Corporation (BCC).
2. In 1989, what was the total market in tonnes for coal sales to industry? Show your workings and state your answer correct to one decimal place.
3. The text suggests that a loss of market share will benefit BCC's profitability (para. 3). Explain how BCC might ensure that this happens.
4. What might be the impact on a coal mining community of the declining market for industrial coal?
5. Briefly describe how Powergen and National Power might react to the information contained in this article. (*Source*: AEB)

2 The market for daily newspapers

Figure 12.16 provides a recent analysis of positioning in the market for daily newspapers. Each of the newspapers is located in terms of the age and social class of its typical reader.

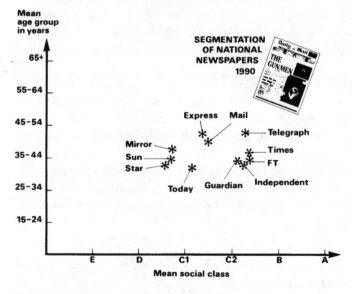

Figure 12.16 Position in the market for daily newspapers.

1. Can you identify three main segments in the market structure?
2. Can you spot any obvious market gaps?
3. What information about a potential market should a newspaper publisher try to discover before deciding on whether to publish a new paper?
4. Figure 12.16 indicates that socio–economic groups and age are important dimensions of segmentation. What other dimensions can you identify?
5. Most periodicals have to serve two markets, the reader and the advertiser. Can a newspaper effectively cater for both markets? Explain with examples.
6. Why do you think that there are no *daily* newspapers targeted at:
   (a) the 54+ age-group?
   (b) the 24-and-under age-group?
   (c) social class E?

(*Source*: Cambridge)

3 Savoury Snacks

Over the last ten years the savoury snack market in the United Kingdom has undergone a fourfold increase in value, from roughly £100 million to more than £400 million. The previous top flavours of Hula Hoops, Quavers and Discos are being seriously challenged by new contenders in the market whose innovation in shapes, flavours, textures and branding contribute significantly to the growth of the snacks industry.

The growth in the size of this market reflects the changes in snack eating habits. Snacks are today an integral part of children's diets, and adults nibble snacks with drinks more than they have ever done.

One of the main developments in the snacks market is that children who have grown up on snacks have now become adults who *still* consume snacks. This demand from an older generation has led to the introduction of more sophisticated snacks, such as Tortilla Chips, Kettle Chips and Indian Poppadoms. Snacks packaged with dips have also made a remarkable impact upon the market.

For children's products, shapes have had an enormous impact. Improved technology has meant that the shape and the texture of products have changed significantly. The ingredients of the products have also changed, with greater emphasis on healthy eating and the elimination of artificial colours and preservatives. Packaging has also changed; metallized film bags extend the shelf–life of products by up to 50 per cent.

In the snacks market, marketing has taken on a new meaning. Investment in product innovation and research into market needs has added considerable value to product portfolios. Competition will, however, continue to be fierce as many small independent companies enter this sector looking for a share of the growth.

1. Identify two market segments in the savoury snacks market. For each market segment, draw up a profile of a typical consumer.
2. Explain how the consumer has benefited from the growth of the savoury snacks market.

3. Have any groups/individuals been adversely affected by the growth of this market? Give reasons with your answer.
4. To what extent does this short report emphasize the various parts of the definition of marketing?

4 Television advertising revenue

According to Zenith Media, ITV and Channel 4 revenues suffered a nosedive at the end of 1992, down 7.1 per cent on their previous quarter. The fall is attributed to the recession and to a slide in profit contribution from advertisers with foreign 'parents', whose profits have been affected by the devaluation of the pound.

Another problem for these companies is that the cost of advertising on TV is expected to remain flat into the next century because of the rapid increase in the supply of TV airtime and the growth in competition as new channels come on-stream.

Zenith expects its advertising revenue to continue falling each year, from £1345 million in 1994 down to £1248 million in 2000 (1991 prices). C4's revenue will remain practically static over the next ten years. If the C5 licence is awarded, Zenith expects the service to attract only a nominal 8 per cent of total TV advertising. It is forecast that the ITV breakfast service GMTV will be sold at a 25 per cent discount to ITV, falling to 10 per cent after 1996. It is not expected to perform as well as TV-AM.

1. Comment generally on the changing business environment for television companies.
2. Identify three reasons why this business environment is undergoing so much change.
3. Suggest how further research might help these companies.

Suggested reading

Davies, E. and Davies, B. J., *Successful Marketing in a Week*. British Institute of Management/Hodder & Stoughton, 1992.
Hill, N., *Marketing for BTEC*. Business Education Publishers, 1989.
Lancaster, G. and Massingham, L., *Essentials of Marketing*. 2nd edn. McGraw-Hill, 1993.
Needham, D. and Dransfield, R., *Marketing – Everybody's Business*, 2nd edn. Heinemann, 1994.

13

Developing marketing strategies

In Chapter 12 we set out to understand the preliminary processes an organization has to go through in order to satisfy customer needs. This involved an understanding of the marketing environment (PEST), the nature of the market-place, customer behaviour, market segmentation and positioning. All of these activities are part of the *research* phase of a marketing plan; they are, therefore, concerned with preparation rather than implementation.

In this chapter we seek to broaden this understanding of the marketing process by looking at specific decisions that have to be taken about products that are already in the market-place. Such decisions will involve the successful combination of the ingredients of the marketing mix and will be fundamental to the practical operation of a marketing plan.

Marketing planning is often defined as 'anticipatory decision-making'. It involves planning today what has to be done tomorrow. This process of forward planning will help to:

- Focus the organization upon its business objectives (both marketing and corporate)
- Provide all parts of the organization with clear guidelines about what they are expected to achieve
- Co-ordinate the activities of various parts of the organization
- Provide a mechanism against which performance can be checked, modified and controlled

Marketing planning should be viewed as a continuous cycle (Fig. 13.1). Collecting and sorting information from the research process will help to develop plans and identify alternative courses of action. Plans can then be modified and controlled in the light of performance.

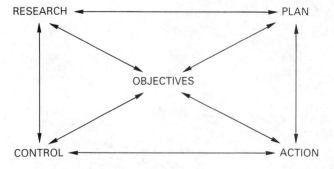

Figure 13.1 The marketing planning cycle.

342

Research

The research stage, largely covered in the previous chapter, is concerned primarily with diagnosis and prognosis. As a result of the research it has undertaken, an organization should be able to answer questions such as 'Where are we and why?' and 'Where are we going?'

Research is part of the *strategic audit* which finds out what has been achieved in the past and predicts what can be achieved in the future. One technique that is frequently used to match an organization's strengths and weaknesses with the external forces in the business environment is a *SWOT analysis*. SWOT stands for:

- Strengths
- Weaknesses
- Opportunities
- Threats

The *internal* audit element of the SWOT analysis are the organization's strengths and weaknesses; opportunities and threats reflect influences *external* to the organization which exist in the business environment (see Fig. 13.2). For example, a small business may have the following SWOT elements:

Strengths:	Good product
	Good relationship with customers
	Strong management team
Weaknesses:	Few economies of scale
	Liquidity problems
	Little experience of other markets
Opportunities:	New markets
	Changing tastes
	Diversification
Threats:	Actions of competitors
	Recession
	New legislation

SWOT analysis

Within the organization	In the environment
Strengths +	Opportunities +
Weakness −	Threats −

Figure 13.2 The planning balance sheet.

A SWOT analysis will help an organization to complete its strategic audit and place itself in a better position to compile its marketing plan and make decisions about the market-place.

The marketing plan

The marketing plan itself will comprise a number of plans drawn up by various parts of the organization. In this way it will match long-term corporate goals with shorter-term plans. At the centre of the marketing plan will be each of the ingredients of the marketing mix (see Fig. 13.3).

The *marketing mix* is often referred to as the '4Ps', i.e. Product, Price, Place and Promotion. To meet customers' needs, a business must develop the *products* to satisfy them, charge the right *price*, get the goods to the right *place* (i.e. ensure that the product is available when needed), and make the existence of the product known through *promotion* (see Fig. 13.4).

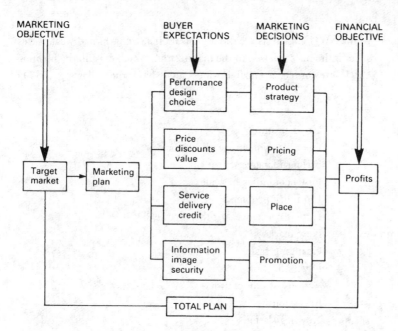

Figure 13.3 The planning process.

The marketing mix

Figure 13.4 The marketing mix.

Products

People buy goods and services for a wide variety of reasons. There are many characteristics of a product that can influence the decision to buy. Some of the most important features are:

1. *Function*   When you buy a new car, what will you want it to do? Will you want it above all to look good, to accelerate quickly or to last a long while? The function of a car might be radically different for a taxi driver and for someone looking for a vehicle for recreation purposes.
2. *Appearance*   For a number of products, the way they look is as important as what they do. This is as true for birthday cards and furniture as it is for handbags and hats.
3. *Status*   Consumers often associate certain products with a particular lifestyle. Advertisers often use this form of association to create an image for a product. Status symbols include items such as cars, jewellery and clothes and consumer durables such as washing machines and fridge-freezers.

Price

The price that is charged for a product is clearly an important determinant of the volume of sales made. However, it would be wrong to assume that organizations will set prices purely with the aim of maximizing profits or sales. The pricing policy that a business employs will vary with time and circumstances. For example, it is often the case that organizations will launch a new product at a lower price than what they intend to charge when the product becomes established.

An organization's pricing decision might also be aimed at finding a particular niche in the market. For example, if it wants to sell at the top end of the market it will charge a high price, at the bottom a low price, and so on.

Place

Roughly one-fifth of the cost of a product is spent on getting it to the consumer. Of course, the actual figure varies widely from product to product, but generally *distribution* is a very important and often underestimated element in the marketing mix. Distribution is a key feature in the trading process—i.e. getting the right product to the right place at the right time.

Promotion

The cost of promoting or advertising goods and services can represent a sizeable proportion of the overall cost of a product. However, through successful promotion an organization can increase its sales so that advertising and other costs are spread over a larger output. By selling more goods, firms can lower their selling prices, increase their profits or both.

Case Study—The Vimto vintage

Vimto was invented in Manchester 85 years ago as a tonic cordial by John Noel Nichols (grandfather of the present managing director John Nichols and financial director Simon Nichols). Since then it has grown to be a big brand name.

Vimto's core strengths are its unique flavour and its brand heritage. Vimto is a good healthy product with a unique fruit-based recipe which is, of course, secret. It is a natural drink in which there are no chemical additives or artificial flavours. Its strong brand heritage helps to conjure up an image of strength, reliability and tradition for a product that has been enjoyed by generations of users; parents and even grandparents remember the taste. At J.N. Nichols, the Vimto company, the emphasis is on developing a public perception of the firm as a small business with old-fashioned values.

Compared with giants like Coca-Cola, Schweppes and Britvic, J.N. Nichols is indeed a relatively small business. However, today the company is a multinational business in its own right with interests all over the world. Although the company has long since diversified, the flagship brand remains the Vimto portfolio.

The Vimto range is indeed vast: currently there are sparkling, diet, still and cordial varieties produced in a number of combination (Fig. 13.5). There are also a number of packaging options, including cans, bottles, PETs and RTDs in various sizes. Such a flexible range increases the product's appeal and versatility.

Figure 13.5 The Vimto vintage.

In addition to sales through supermarket chains, about 50 per cent of Vimto's sales are through the independent grocery sector. Support for independents includes a national salesforce plus plenty of promotions. Nationwide distribution is claimed to be 'second to none', thanks to a network of 50 franchise bottlers which allows independents easy access to products. The company invests heavily in brand support and advertising and is constantly investing in research and development.

Vimto is a good example of a well-known brand marketed successfully by a relatively small company with strategies that have earned considerable respect from many of its larger competitors.

Questions

1. Comment in general on the nature of the Vimto product portfolio. In your answer refer to the qualities that help to differentiate the brand from the products of competitors.
2. Identify at least two groups of consumers at which you feel this product is targeted.
3. Imagine that you are in the position of a brand manager: what factors would influence the decisions you would make when pricing this brand?
4. Explain briefly why distribution is particularly important for a relatively small competitor. In your answer refer to the distribution of Vimto.
5. List two benefits of investing in advertising and brand support for (a) the company and (b) the customer.

Product strategy

Probably the most important decision for any organization concerns the development of an effective product strategy. The product is the central point on which all marketing decisions have to be based. For example, product issues might include:

- When shall we launch this product?
- How are these products going to perform in the future?
- Which products require support?
- How can we help our products?

In solving product issues, organizations have to analyse what their products mean to the people who buy them. Customers buy goods and services for a wide variety of reasons and a number of factors influence their purchasing decisions. It is important for the marketer to consider what benefits its products provide for customers. For example, many products have clear tangible benefits, such as:

- Appearance
- Shape

- Colour
- Size
- Design
- Function

Sometimes the *intangible benefits* are not quite so obvious. These might include:

- Guarantees
- Servicing
- Customer care
- Repair service

It is important to remember that modern products have been extensively researched and developed in order to provide a range of benefits and dimensions designed to meet the needs of customers. Product dimensions include:

1. *Generic dimensions*   These are the key functional benefits of the product. For example, a microwave cooks or defrosts food; a doctor cares for patients.
2. *Sensual dimensions*   These include design, colour, taste, smell and texture.
3. *Extended dimensions*   These might include a wide range of associated services such as credit facilities, maintenance contracts and so on.

 Task

Using a product well known to you, identify the benefits and dimensions it offers.

As well as considering the benefits and dimensions provided by the physical nature of the product, the organization has to make product decisions about the depth and width of its product portfolio.

The *width* of a range refers to the number of different products made or sold by the firm, for example detergents, bleaches, washing-up liquids. The *depth* of a range concerns the number of different sizes or versions of each product on offer; for example, Smarties come in 'Fun Size', tubes and boxes.

The starting-point for any product is research and development. The aim of product research and development is to combine with market research to determine the changing preferences of consumers and come up with goods and services that will match the needs of tomorrow's customers. The design element is important here in that it involves developing products that serve these intended purposes and are also attractive to customers. Product researchers must also take into account production costs, ease of manufacture and projected selling price.

As one of the most important aspects of product development, an organization has to decide whether it wants its products to be proactive or reactive. *Proactive* products are those that take the lead in new product developments and are the first of a particular type to enter a market. Although proactive policies carry the greatest risk of failure, they also carry the greatest opportunity to develop large profit margins. *Reactive* products simply react to the strategies of other competitors; in doing so firms learn from the experience of those who have already tested the market.

In order for new products to gain market acceptance, it is important that customers perceive new products to have one or more advantages over the products of competitors. These advantages are sometimes called *Unique Selling Propositions* (USPs). These USPs might include a range of benefits and dimensions such as product performance, market advantages such as cost or volume, presentation, packaging and branding.

It is important for enterprises to try to encourage and develop a business environment in which sources of new product ideas are continually being put forward. New product ideas may come either from within the organization (see Fig. 13.6) or outside the organization (see Fig. 13.7).

Figure 13.6 Internal sources of new ideas.

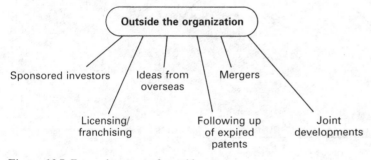

Figure 13.7 External sources of new ideas.

The *launch* is the most important day in the life of a product. This is the time when the product is finally exposed to the customer in the market-place. Sometimes considerable secrecy is associated with the launch; however, another technique is to leak a bit of information before the launch to whet the appetite of the market. Previews and exposures to the press are an important aspect of the launch.

The *product mix* covers the whole range of products produced by an organization. Managing the mix effectively through policies dealing with new product developments, segmentation, positioning and diversification is of fundamental importance for all organizations. The key to effective product strategies is to create a balance of products designed to meet a firm's objectives. There are three main tools that can be used to assist with the product planning process:

- The product life-cycle
- The Boston box
- Ansoff's product-market matrix

The product life-cycle

Markets are in a constant state of change. Over a period of time tastes and fashions will alter and the technology used to produce goods and services will be updated. As a result there will always be a demand for new products, and old lines will sooner or later become redundant.

The life of a product is the period over which it appeals to customers. We can all think of goods that everyone wanted at one time but have now gone out of fashion, obvious examples being hotpants and the beehive hairstyle.

The sales performance of any product rises from nought when the product is introduced to the market to a peak and then declines to nought again (see Fig. 13.8). A good example of a type of product that has had a short lifespan in recent years is computer game software. Each of these games was, at some stage, ahead of its competitors and achieved high sales, but as other games developed it lost popularity and was no longer in such great demand.

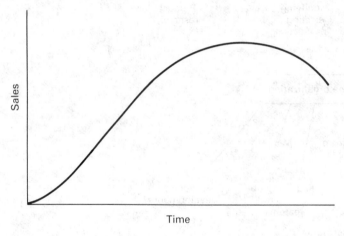

Figure 13.8 The product life-cycle.

The life-cycle of a product can be broken down into distinct stages. Sales grow slowly at the introductory stage, when a product is first launched into the market and there is only limited awareness of its existence. Sales then increase rapidly during the period of growth. It is during this stage that competitors enter the market and begin to promote their own products. This will eventually reduce the rate of growth of the product's sales. This is the period known as 'maturity', and it is shortly after this time that the market becomes saturated as too many businesses compete for customers. Organizations will compete in a variety of ways and some will drop out of the market. The product market finally declines to the point where the existing product becomes unprofitable (see Fig. 13.9).

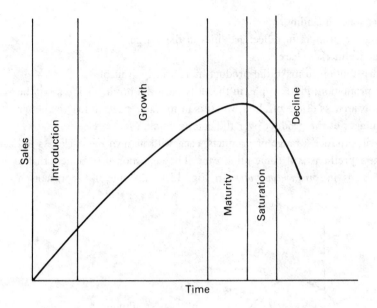

Figure 13.9 A more detailed breakdown of the product life-cycle.

The life-cycle of some products may last for hundreds of years while for others it may last only a few months. If a firm wants to prolong the life-cycle of a product or brand, it is essential to invest in its development. This can mean putting a lot of work into the product before it is launched. Once it is on the market, it may be necessary periodically to inject new life into the product (see Fig. 13.10).

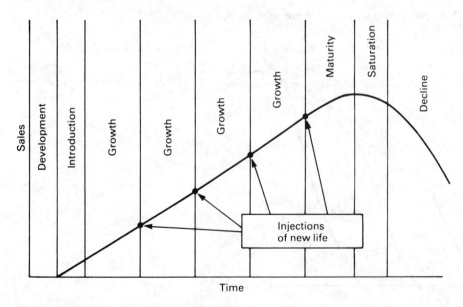

Figure 13.10 Injecting new life into a product.

This can be done in several ways, including:

1. Changing or modifying the product to reflect activities in the market.
2. Using pricing to influence market share.
3. Altering patterns of distribution to make the product more widely available.
4. Changing the style of promotion; for example, in the early part of a product's life it will be necessary to create an awareness of the product, whereas in the later stages it may be better to point out the advantages of the product over the competitors'.

Many large organizations will produce a range of products, each with its own life-cycle. As old products go into decline new products will come on-stream. The collection of products that a company produces is known as its *product portfolio*. In Fig. 13.11 the line T_1 represents a

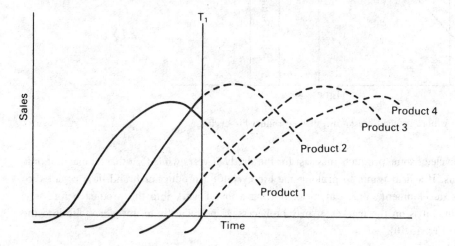

Figure 13.11 A portfolio of products at different stages in their life-cycles.

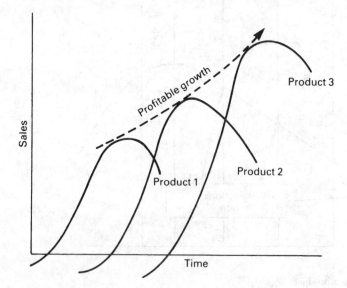

Figure 13.12 Planning for profitable growth.

particular moment in time. At that point, product 1 is in decline, product 2 is in saturation, product 3 is about to enter growth and product 4 is about to be launched. If the company is going to benefit from continuous growth, it will need to arrange its product portfolio in a well-timed way. This will be best achieved by the creation of appealing new products at regular intervals (see Fig. 13.12).

☌ Case Study—Fairy Liquid

In the late 1950s Procter & Gamble (P&G) set about the task of developing a new dishwashing liquid which would meet consumer needs. They wanted to develop a brand that would perform well and prove popular with consumers. More than 100 000 dishwashing tests on a range of formulations were carried out. Only those formulations that performed better than brands already on the market were retained for further development.

Figure 13.13 The Fairy Liquid line.

The next development criteria was that the product should not have harmful effects if used for anything other than the purpose intended by the manufacturer, such as on cookers or cars, or if drunk or used as a shampoo.

Research also took place into types of packaging. Metal cans, rigid plastic bottles and squeeze bottles were all contenders and were tested separately. At the same time, the testing of performance, mildness, perfume, colour and packaging was carried out among consumers, whose feedback would provide information that could be used for further improvements. The polyethylene squeeze-bottle was the type of container adopted for use.

The product was then test-marketed as the third member of the Fairy family, using the image associated with the other brands—a green colour and a 'mildness' platform. The test market was a success. Consumers liked the new product. At that time only 17 per cent of consumers used a washing-up *liquid*; the rest were still using powders or left-over pieces of soap.

In 1960 Fairy Liquid went on sale throughout the country following a launch held at the Savoy at which journalists were given the chance to wash up. One of the claims at the time was that a plate washed in Fairy Liquid could be gripped between finger and thumb, while one washed in a powder solution was too slippery and fell to the floor.

By the end of Fairy Liquid's first full year:

1. Six out of ten consumers in the country had bought a bottle.
2. The market for washing-up liquids had doubled.
3. Fairy Liquid was in number one spot in the market.

Fairy Liquid's theme song was:

> 'Now hands that do dishes can be soft as your face
> With mild, green Fairy Liquid'

The song was often the subject of jokes, sketches and cartoons and became part of the 1960s culture. The bottles also began to crop up all over the place—as the bodies of model rockets, windmill sails and protectors for prize leeks.

A number of developments kept the brand ahead of its rivals. Its advertising stressed its mildness—the mother-and-daughter commercials brought this out. Its economy was also stressed against cheaper liquids.

In 1981 the dishwashing market was relatively flat and uninteresting. Fairy Liquid had a market share of 27 per cent, about the same as its main competitor. Research indicated that consumers wanted a product that would last longer. The efficiency of the product was improved by 20 per cent, and Nanette Newman advertised Fairy Liquid for the first time. The message was that one bottle of Fairy would now last days longer than before. (The brand now lasted up to 5 days per 500 ml bottle longer than before, and about 11 days longer than its nearest rival.)

By 1984/5 Fairy Liquid sales were up by 5 million bottles a year and the market share was now 32 per cent. P&G wanted to build beyond this. To this end they introduced a line extension—a lemon-scented variety of Fairy Liquid. Advertising stressed both the differences and similarities between the two types and consumer research showed that consumers identified Fairy Liquid Lemon as the product with the nicest smell.

Fairy Liquid had gained another two market share points by 1978/8, and market research indicated the importance of targeting occasional users. The 'School' TV commercial was targeted at occasional users.

By the end of June 1988 Fairy Liquid was selling more than 100 million bottles a year. Consumer research indicated that consumers required still better economy, better grease removal and less mess on the bottle. A new performance booster and a rebalanced detergent system gave the brand a further 15 per cent 'mileage' boost and better grease handling.

So many changes had altered the nature of the product since it was first launched more than 30 years previously that in 1992 it was decided to replace the Fairy Liquid brand name with Fairy Excel. This new product has better economy, is better at grease removal and is kinder to hands, and testing has shown that consumers prefer the new dumpy bottle.

So what will the Fairy Excel of the future be like? The product has not remained static and has clearly been injected with plenty of support during its lifetime. One important fact, however, is that, if Fairy Excel hopes to maintain its present market share or develop it further, it will have to continue to monitor consumer needs and requirements as they change during the 1990s and beyond.

Questions

1. Was the launch of the original Fairy Liquid a proactive or reactive process? Provide an explanation to support the conclusion you reach.
2. What unique selling propositions did Fairy Liquid have at the time of its launch?
3. Comment on the length of the introductory phase of Fairy Liquid's product life-cycle.
4. What point of the product life-cycle had Fairy Liquid reached by 1981?
5. Summarize the actions taken by P&G over the next 11 years to inject life into the brand.
6. Imagine that you have been asked to work on the marketing plan for Fairy Excel:
   (a) As part of a strategic audit, draw up a short SWOT analysis of the brand.
   (b) Using your own ideas, suggest a further way of using line extensions to develop the brand. In your answer refer to both the current and proposed width and depth of the portfolio.

The Boston box

One of the main problems with the product life-cycle is actually knowing which stage your product has reached. To analyse this and other problems, the Boston Consulting Group from the United States developed a well-known product portfolio which relates market growth to market share (see Fig. 13.14).

The Boston box ties in closely with the product life-cycle. To see how this is so, we shall start with 'problem children' and then move in an anti-clockwise direction around the box.

Problem children are products that have just been launched. This is an appropriate name because many products fail to move beyond this phase. Sometimes such products are referred

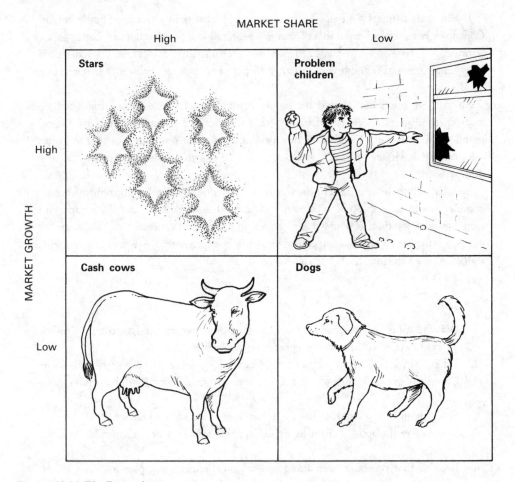

Figure 13.14 The Boston box.

to as 'question marks'. Is it possible to develop these products and turn them into the stars and cash cows of the future? It might be, but first they will require a lot of financial support and will represent a heavy financial commitment.

Stars are products that have successfully reached the growth stage in the life-cycle. Although these products too will require a lot of financial support, they will also provide high cash returns. On balance, they will provide a neutral cash flow and are good 'prospects' for the future.

Cash cows have reached the maturity stage in their product life-cycle and are now 'yielders'. They have a high market share in markets that are no longer rapidly expanding. Because the market is relatively static, they require few fresh injections of capital; for example, advertising and promotion may be required to inject a little fresh life from time to time. However, the net effect is of a positive cash flow. Cash generated by the cash cows may be used to help the problem children.

Dogs are products in decline. These have a low market share in a low growing or declining market. As they begin to generate a negative cash flow, they will usually be disposed of.

Task

Using your own experience of a product portfolio provided by an organization, identify its

- Problem children
- Stars
- Cash cows
- Dogs

In each case, explain what evidence you have to draw the conclusions you make.

In order to maintain an effective portfolio development, it is important to have a balance of products at any one time. An organization will require a number of cash cows to provide its 'bread and butter'. At the same time, it is important to develop the cash cows of the future by investing in the problem children. Fortunately, the stars should pay their own way. It is also important to identify the dogs and cut them out.

Products in the top half of the Boston box are in the earlier stages of the product life-cycle and so are in high-growth markets. Those in the lower half of the box are in the later stages and so are in markets where growth will have slowed down or even stopped.

Ansoff's product–market matrix

This theory was developed by H. Igor Ansoff. It looks not just at the management of a product portfolio but also more widely at market developments and opportunities. Ansoff's matrix matches existing and new product strategies with existing and new markets (see Fig. 13.15). In this way, his matrix suggests five alternative marketing strategies which hinge upon whether the product is new or existing and whether the market is new or existing.

1. *Consolidation* implies a positive and active defence of existing products in existing markets.

Product Market	Existing products		New products
Existing markets	Consolidation	Market Penetration	Product development
New markets	Market development		Diversification

Figure 13.15 Ansoff's product–market matrix.

2. *Market penetration* suggests a further penetration of existing markets with existing products (see Fairy Liquid case study). This will involve a strategy of increasing market share within existing segments and markets.
3. *Product development* involves developing new products for existing markets.
4. *Market development* entails using existing products and finding new markets for them. These new markets will be identified by better customer targeting, market research and further segmentation.
5. *Diversification* will lead to a movement away from core activities. This might involve some form of integration of production into related activities.

Price

The *Oxford English Dictionary* defines price as the 'sum or consideration or sacrifice for which a thing may be bought or attained.' This will have different meanings for different groups of people. For example, for a seller price is a key selling point and a key factor in determining revenue and profit, whereas for a buyer price may simply be an unwelcome cost.

The importance of price will vary from one market to another and between different market segments. For example, in low-cost non-fashion markets price can be critical; in contrast, in fashion markets price may be a relatively minor element of the marketing mix.

Objectives

In order to develop pricing strategies, organizations need to be clear about their pricing objectives. These might include the following:

1. *Maximizing profits*   A key assumption for many business theories is that profit maximization is the most important pricing target. While it is true that unless businesses can make profits in the long run their futures will be uncertain, studies of actual business behaviour reveal a wide range of alternative strategies to short-term profit maximization.
2. *Competitive pricing*   Pricing decisions may be based on the prices charged by competitors. A competitive price is one that provides a competitive edge in the market-place.
3. *Maximizing sales*   Prices may be set at a level that will maximize sales, and thereby take a larger share of the market, rather than profits.
4. *Cost-plus pricing*   Some organizations have an objective or target of how much profit they would like to make over their costs; for example, they might work out their cost per unit and add 20 per cent for profits to calculate price.
5. *'Satisficing'*   H. A. Simon put forward the view that businesses might want to 'satisfice', that is to achieve given targets for market share and profits from sales that might not maximize profits but instead would inflate boardroom egos. This can be the case when the managers of a company are clearly different from the owners. Provided that the managers can produce sufficient profits to keep the shareholders satisfied, a proportion of the profits can be diverted to provide more perks for managers and larger departments.

'Satisficing' policies are most likely to be associated with industries where there is only a limited degree of competition. They are fairly common in many organizations, ranging from schools to oil companies. Managers will readily produce a long list of achievements which do not always relate to a profit margin at the bottom line. In large organizations it is often difficult to relate activities to financial statistics, and managers with the ability to make a lot of noise can give the impression of being effective.

6. *Other short-term objectives*   In the short term a business may also have other pricing policies. For example, it may well sell new promotional items at a low price to introduce them to the market. Also, it might adopt a low-price policy in order to destroy the market share of rivals, or to prevent new firms from entering the market. A firm might also set a price that will give it a particular position in the market; i.e. it would be a *positioning* decision. For example, a high price might be selected by a firm that wanted to project an 'up-market' image.

Factors affecting pricing decisions

There are a number of important factors to consider before arriving at a pricing decision concerning a new product, including the following:

Costs

Many enterprises relate prices to cost in the following way. They first calculate fixed costs such as rent, interest repayments and salaries. To these they will add variable costs; these are costs that increase with the level of output (see Chapter 17 and Fig. 13.16).

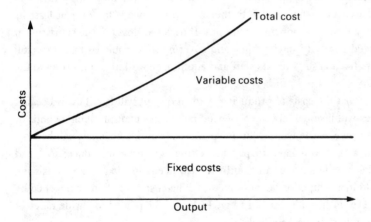

Figure 13.16 Components of total cost.

A break-even chart can show the relationship between costs, profits and revenues at different levels of output. Using this information, an enterprise can then establish a revenue target. The revenue target will coincide with a given level of output; it will establish the price charged per unit. In Fig. 13.17 the revenue line crosses the fixed cost line at A. At this point the business

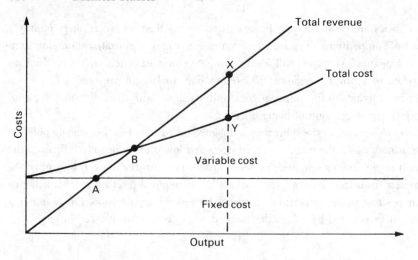

Figure 13.17 Establishing a revenue target from a break–even chart.

would be just covering its fixed costs. As output increases the revenue line rises to the point B, at which total revenue covers total cost (comprising fixed and variable costs).

Above point B (i.e. to the right of it) the firm moves into a profit position. Point X represents the chosen target revenue and the line XY indicates the profit margin.

The amount of sales that the firm makes will depend, among other things, on the price charged. If prices are too low, the revenue line will be less steep and revenues may not cover costs; or profit margins may be too low. If prices are too high, the revenue line could be very short.

Pricing policies are therefore crucial to the success of a business. In the long run a firm will continue in business if it can cover its total costs. In the short run it needs to cover at least its variable costs if it is going to be worth producing an output. If it closed down in the short run, it will still need to cover its fixed costs. By staying open and covering its variable costs, it may still be able to pay off some of its fixed costs, keep its staff and equipment working, and preserve the good name of the business.

In the long term it is likely that the costs of producing units of output will fall. This is because as time progresses businesses will become more experienced in all aspects of producing goods or services. Technology will improve, waste will be cut down and distributive channels will become more effective. In addition, a firm will have to pay its setting up costs only once; tool and equipment costs therefore become less important until the firm needs to modernize its existing lines. When products are sold in a competitive environment, falling costs will often be matched by falling prices. This type of relationship, illustrated in Fig. 13.18, can be related to a wide range of products, from personal computers to package holidays.

Price sensitivity

A measure known as the *elasticity of demand* is used to calculate the way in which the quantity demanded of a product will alter as price changes. Some products are highly sensitive to price changes so that demand is said to be *elastic*; the demand for a product with many competitors,

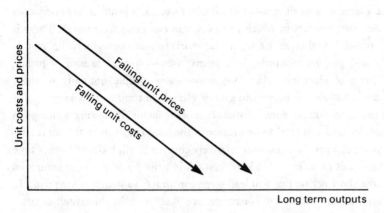

Figure 13.18 Falling costs and falling prices.

such as a brand of marmalade, is likely to be highly elastic. In contrast, a product with little competition such as a distinctive luxury motor car may face an *inelastic* demand curve over a range of prices.

There are a number of factors influencing elasticity, including the following:

1. It matters whether a good is a necessity or a luxury. Necessities by definition will be needed by purchasers. These include basic items of food, shelter and clothing. When the price of a necessity increases consumers will be reluctant to reduce their purchases; in contrast, it is easier to give up or postpone the purchase of a luxury item. Of course, with the passage of time individuals' perceptions of what is a necessity or a luxury will alter; today, for example, many people regard central heating in winter to be a necessity in colder climates. If consumers perceive an item to be necessary, they will continue to purchase more or less the same quantity as the price increases. For example, the demand for petrol is seen to be highly inelastic over a considerable price range.

2. There may be many substitutes for a product or just a few. Goods and services offered by a large number of competitors tend to experience elastic demand conditions. Examples would include brands of fish fingers, tabloid newspapers and various tinned groceries. Inelastic demand would be most likely to occur where there is little competition, such as when there is only one service station on a long stretch of motorway.

3. There is a variable proportion of household income that may be spent on an individual product. If only a small proportion of a household's income is spent on a product, then demand is more likely to be inelastic. The reason for this is that, if a household spends only a small fraction of its income on an item, e.g. salt, shoe polish, mustard, then a rise in the price of the item will hardly be felt. In contrast, however, items that comprise a sizeable proportion of total expenditure, e.g. heating, a new motor car, will have a more dramatic impact when their prices change. The items comprising small fractions of income will tend to have inelastic demand curves over a particular price range, whereas items making up large fractions of income will tend to have greater elasticity.

4. A product may have a large or a small number of different uses. If a product has many uses there will be many different markets in which price changes can exert their effect. There is therefore a greater possibility that in some of the markets substitutes may be readily available. Electricity and gas, for example, have many uses—cooking, heating, lighting, etc. A rise in the price of electricity therefore might cause people not only to make economies in these areas but also to substitute gas for electric heating and cooking.

5. The length of the time period under consideration is another factor. Following a change in price, the elasticity of demand will tend to be greater in the long run than in the short run. For example, if the price of a product becomes relatively cheaper it will take consumers time to adjust to this change. Let us assume that kiwi fruit fall in price by 50 per cent compared with other fruits. In the short period this will lead some consumers to switch to kiwi fruit. In the longer term an even greater number of consumers are likely to make the switch as tastes alter and awareness increases.

6. If the price of durable items increases, consumers are likely to try and extend the lifespan of that product. This applies to a whole host of consumer durables and factory machinery; for example, you might make your existing car last one year longer before trading it in. This is impossible with non-durable items such as cream cakes, eggs and bread.

Consumers' responses to price changes are an important ingredient of price determination. Businesses have more scope for charging high prices in markets where consumers are insensitive to price increases (i.e. where demand is inelastic).

In Fig. 13.19 a firm has a choice of charging a high price, A, or a lower price, B. The demand curve for the product is relatively steep, indicating an inelastic demand for the product. The total

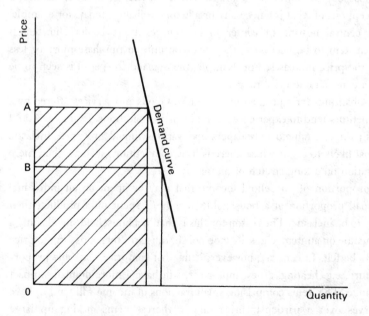

Figure 13.19 Comparing revenues at different prices (demand–inelastic).

revenue accruing to the firm is calculated by the formula:

$$\text{Total revenue} = \text{Quantity sold} \times \text{price}$$

The shaded area represents total revenue at price A. Quite clearly, this is larger than the rectangle under price B, so the firm will gain most revenue from charging the higher price.

In contrast, if consumers are sensitive to price changes the firms might adopt a low-price strategy. In Fig. 13.20 the demand curve is relatively flat and the firm gains greatest revenue from charging price B rather than price A. (Readers should note, however, that costs are an important

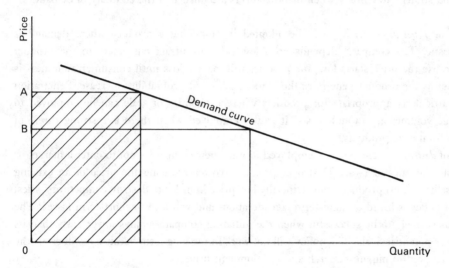

Figure 13.20 Comparing revenues at different prices (demand-elastic).

factor in determining price and output. If the extra costs of expanding output exceed extra revenues, it may pay to produce a smaller output even when demand is elastic.)

Price elasticity is measured by dividing the percentage increase or decrease in the quantity demanded (or sales) resulting from a change in price by the percentage change in price:

$$\text{Price elasticity of demand} = \frac{\%\ \text{change in quantity demanded of A}}{\%\ \text{change in price of A}}$$

'Elastic' markets are those in which the change in quantity demanded is a higher percentage than the percentage change in price. Conversely, 'inelastic' markets are those in which the change in quantity demanded is a lower percentage than the percentage change in price.

The problem is that in the real world it is very difficult to apply theory to the making of price decisions. For one thing, firms rarely possess the empirical data (i.e. realistic figures showing how much would be demanded at different prices) required to construct actual demand or revenue curves for their products, and often are unable to distinguish costs sufficiently clearly to construct cost curves. Second, the goals that firms set themselves are rarely easy to build into theories such as 'profit maximization'.

A policy of *skimming pricing* may be adopted in launching a new product where demand is relatively inelastic because there are few competitors in the market and consumers have little knowledge of the product. Using this policy, firms will set a high price in order to capitalize on the fact that there are people prepared to pay a high price for the new product. Once the first segment of consumers is saturated, the manufacturer will lower prices in order to tap fresh segments of the market. The process continues until a large section of the total market is catered for. By operating in this way, the business removes the risk of underpricing a product. This might also be a good strategy to employ when manufacturers are unsure of the elasticity of demand for their product.

A policy of *penetration pricing* may be adopted in launching a product where demand is relatively elastic. The company depends on a low price to attract customers to the product initially. Because the price starts low, the product will make a loss until consumer awareness is increased; but as the product penetrates the market, sales and profitability increase. Penetration pricing is particularly appropriate for products where economies of scale can be employed to produce large volumes at low unit costs. It is also employed when there is a strong threat of competition from rival products.

A policy of *destroyer pricing* may be employed to warn new companies not to enter a market or to undermine the sales of rivals. Destroyer pricing involves reducing the price of an existing product or selling a new product at an artificially low price in order to destroy competitors' sales. This type of policy is based on long-term considerations and will lead to short-term losses. The strategy is most likely to be successful when the initiating company enjoys lower costs than its competitors or potential rivals. The policy will not work in the long term because it will erode the profit base required to initiate research and development projects.

A policy of *promotional pricing* may be used from time to time to inject fresh life into an existing product or to generate interest in a new product, for example, reducing prices to increase sales in the short-term. Again, it is a short-term policy and will not match long-term revenue targets.

Customers' perceptions of price

Customers generally have views about what constitutes value for money. If prices are thought to be too high they might consider that they are not getting their money's worth. If prices are considered too low, they will begin to question the quality and value of a product. (There is the story of the very expensive designer coat reduced to £20 in a department store window; nobody bought the coat because they thought that there must be something wrong with it.)

Figure 13.21 shows that the product costs A to produce. The business cannot sell the product for less than B without quality being questioned. Competing products are selling for prices between C and D, and the maximum chargeable price would be E. If the product is not very exciting, the business will need to pitch its price between B and D; if, however, the product is a market leader and has some novel features, then it can pitch the price between C and E.

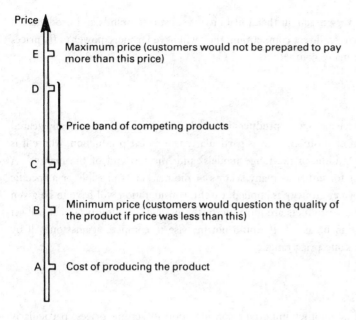

Figure 13.21 Price bands.

Competition

The nature and extent of competition is often an important influence on price. If a product is faced by *direct competition* then it will compete against other highly similar products in the market-place. This will often constrain pricing decisions so that price-setting will need to be kept closely in line with rivals' actions. In contrast, when a product is faced by *indirect competition* (i.e. competition with products in different sectors of the market), there will be more scope to vary price. This opens up the possibility for a number of strategies. For example, a firm might choose a high-price strategy to give a product 'quality' feel. In contrast, it might charge a low price so that consumers see the product as a 'bargain'.

Because price is only one factor that gives a product a competitive edge, it is not always necessary to charge the lowest price in the market. For example, Shell stresses the point that price is considerably less important than other factors. In a recent annual report it stated that: 'The Company's marketing strategy is based on establishing a differentiation between Shell and its competitors through quality in its facilities, products and services.' This policy is based on the belief that customers are more interested in performance and reliability—'You can be sure of Shell!'

Although there is only a relatively small number of companies operating the petrol sales market, there is intense competition. Price competition frequently does occur in this sector although often it proves to be self-defeating. (For example, if all producers were to lower prices by 10 per cent, the total increase in the volume of sales would inevitably be much less than 10 per cent.) Competing petrol companies have therefore more commonly resorted to non-price competition, including longer opening hours, free gifts and extending the range of services offered.

Price competition depends very much on the availability of substitute brands and products. In situations where producers have no direct competition, they will have far more power to fix prices than in areas where there are many competitors.

Product range

A number of companies produce a range of products in which each product is specifically geared to a particular market segment or position. This is particularly true in car production, where it is common practice to refer to 'middle-of-the-range models' and 'the top end of the market'. A manufacturer will aim to cater for either as many sectors of the market as possible or a specific market segment. When the former strategy is applied, careful consideration will have to be given to the product range. When new products are introduced, the price of existing products will set boundaries on the price that can be asked. It would not be wise to compete against oneself by producing two models in the same price range.

Distribution costs

The cost of distribution will be another important consideration in setting prices, particularly when producers use outside transport, wholesaling and retailing services. Each of these services will want to take its own profit margins and these need to be considered in terms of the price strategy.

Until 1967 manufacturers were able to control the prices at which their goods were resold. The 1967 Resale Price Maintenance Act stopped this practice. This means that the retail price of items can vary considerably. The implication for producers is that, if retail outlets compete extensively with each other, inefficient units will be forced out of the market. As a result, producers might be faced with fewer sales outlets. Some producers control retail prices by owning their own selling outlets, for example breweries, shoe manufacturers and some bakeries.

Pricing policies

There are two main types of pricing decision:

- Setting a price for a completely new product
- Setting a price for an existing product

The only time a firm genuinely has complete freedom in setting prices is before it has committed itself to developing and marketing a new product (see pages 348–349 above). Once the product has left the drawing board, a whole host of influences will affect the pricing decision. Some of the influences will be internal and others will be external to the business.

Internal influences on price include:

- The objectives of the business (e.g. profit maximization, satisficing)
- The pattern of direct and indirect costs

- Existing prices of similar and other products produced internally by the company
- Existing ideas about price-setting in the company
- The firm's knowledge of the market
- Pressures from feedback from salespeople and other members of the organization
- Levels of research and development and the pace of new product development

External influences on price include:

- The strength and behaviour of competitors
- The attitudes and influences of other groups involved in the chain of production and distribution (e.g. what size margin do distributors want, and how much power do they have?)
- Pressure from suppliers of raw materials and components used in the product
- Elasticity of demand for the product
- Motivations of customers
- Existing and anticipated government policies
- General conditions in different markets

Because there are so many variables involved in pricing decisions, and because information available to a firm at any one time will be imperfect, it will be necessary to select certain 'critical' factors to help make pricing decisions.

Pricing strategies

Having looked at factors affecting pricing decisions and influences on pricing, we can now look in greater detail at the four main pricing strategies:

- Cost-plus pricing
- Contribution pricing
- Competitive pricing
- Customer-value pricing

Cost-plus pricing

Information about costs is often easier to collect than information about other variables such as revenues. Firms will often, therefore, choose to make pricing decisions based on adding a margin to unit cost. (The unit cost is the average cost of each item produced; e.g., if a firm produces 1000 units at a total cost of 2000, the unit cost will be £2.) Talk to many small business owners, and they will tell you that they cost out each hour worked and then add a margin for profits.

The process of cost-plus pricing can best be illustrated in relation to large firms where economies of scale can be spread over a sizeable output. As we have seen, large firms are often characterized by flat-bottomed average cost curves where average cost is constant over a large range of output. It is a relatively simple calculation to add a fixed margin, e.g. 10 per cent, to average cost. The firm is therefore able to select an output to produce and to set a price that will be 10 per cent higher than unit costs of production (see Fig. 13.22).

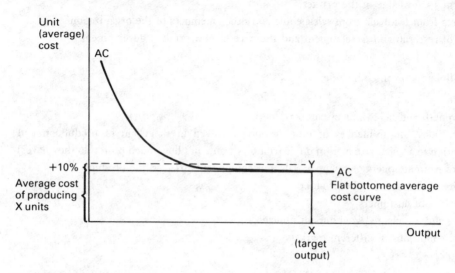

Figure 13.22 Cost-plus pricing.

The dangers of applying this pricing method are that if the price is too high sales may fall considerably short of expectations and if the price is too low then potential revenue is sacrificed.

If a firm applies average cost pricing too rigidly, this can cause problems in the market-place. If demand is lower than expected, for example, average costs may be slightly higher (bearing in mind that, although we talk about flat-bottomed curves, they will inevitably have a slight downward slope). In this situation the company accountant may press for price increases. This will make it even more difficult to make sales.

Conversely, if demand is higher than expected, average costs may fall slightly, leading to a demand for a price reduction. This may result in a loss of potential revenue.

Contribution pricing

Contribution pricing involves separating out the different products that make up a company's portfolio, in order to charge individual prices appropriate to a product's share in total costs.

As we have already seen (page 359), two broad categories of costs can be identified:

- Direct costs, which vary directly with the level of output
- Indirect costs, which have to be paid irrespective of the level of output

Contribution is the sum remaining after the direct costs of producing individual products have been subtracted from revenues. When the contributions of all the individual products that a firm produces have been added together, this should more than cover the firm's indirect costs.

There are strong arguments in favour of contribution pricing because of the ways it separates out individual products and analyses them in terms of their individual ability to cover their own direct costs. A new product may be brought 'on-stream' because it can be shown that it will more than cover its direct costs and make a contribution towards the company's total indirect costs.

In contrast, if we analysed individual products in terms of the relationship between total revenue and total cost for the products, calculations might show a loss. For example, if two products used the same distribution facilities, it would not make sense to expect both products to cover their own distribution costs individually. Contribution pricing enables a more rational analysis of individual products. Prices can be set in relation to each product's own direct costs (see Fig. 13.23).

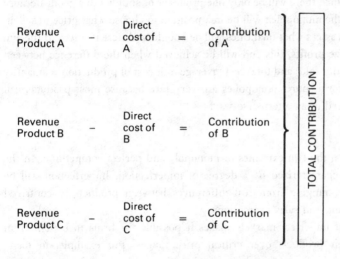

TOTAL CONTRIBUTION – TOTAL INDIRECT COSTS = PROFITS

Figure 13.23 Contribution pricing.

Competitive pricing

An important 'critical factor' in making price decisions may be that of competition. An organization may feel that it needs to tie its own price strategy to that prevailing in the market. This may mean that there are frequent price changes in highly competitive markets. Alternatively, some form of price leadership may prevail whereby a market leader tends to establish different prices for other, often smaller, companies. In more established markets set prices may come to dominate and the firms that constitute the market may be reluctant to 'rock the boat'. An individual firm may try to insulate itself against price sensitivity for its product by differentiating it from rivals.

Markets are sometimes classified according to the level of competition that applies.

Perfect markets

A perfect market would consist of firms producing identical products. Consumers would have perfect knowledge of the market, and of the prices charged by each firm. Firms would each control only a very small section of the market and there would be many buyers and sellers. Of course, such a market exists only in theory. However, the conditions show us that in such a highly competitive situation firms would have to take their price from the market (they would be *price-takers*). If an individual firm tried to raise prices, sales would fall to zero because of perfect consumer knowledge. Because competition would be so intense, the market price would be set at such a level that producers would make the bare minimum of profit required to keep them in production. As a result, producers could not lower prices because this would push their profits below the bare minimum required.

Monopoly markets

A monopoly market is one in which there will be only one producer or supplier of a good. Because of the absence of competition, the monopolist will be in a position to choose what price to sell at. The monopolist will then try to assess what quantities will be bought at different prices. If the aim of the monopolist is to maximize profits, this end will be achieved when the difference between the total revenue (price × quantity sold) and total cost (average unit cost of production × quantity sold) is greatest. In the real world, pure monopolies are very rare because most products can eventually be copied or produced in an alternative way.

Imperfect markets

An *imperfect market* lies between the two extremes of monopoly and perfect competition. In the 'real world' most markets are characterized by a degree of imperfection. Imperfection will be based on a number of factors, ranging from real differences between products to contrived differences created by advertising and sales promotions.

The widespread existence of imperfect markets makes it possible for firms to benefit from degrees of inelasticity for their products over critical price ranges. For example, in many imperfect markets it is possible for firms to make more than the required minimum of profit, at least in the short term. In the long term new firms will be attracted into the market and excess profits will be competed away.

Oligopolies

One type of imperfect market is the oligopoly. This is the name given to a market dominated by a small number of organizations. For example, the car and petrol markets are dominated by a handful of producers.

An enterprise's policy in an oligopoly market depends on how it thinks its competitors will react to its decisions. The outcome of the firm's policy depends on other firm's reactions. When one firm cuts its prices others may feel obliged to follow suit; when it raises the price, it needs to consider whether or not others will follow. The danger of such price warfare often leads to price agreements between competing oligopolists. Price leadership may be vested in a dominant firm.

The demand curve for competing oligopolists' goods is said to be 'kinked' (see Fig. 13.24). If they raise prices, demand will be elastic because consumers will switch to rival products; if they lower prices, demand will be inelastic because competitors will follow suit. Revenue is therefore lost by moving away from the prevailing market price.

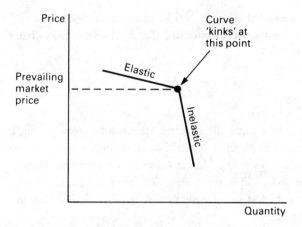

Figure 13.24 A kinked demand curve.

In the real world, however, oligopolistic markets are frequently highly competitive. Individual oligopolists apply a mix of non-price and price competition strategies to gain a long-term advantage in particular markets. Large *conglomerates* (i.e. large companies producing a range of often quite different products) are able to channel excess profits from markets in which they have near-monopoly positions to other markets where they are fighting for an increased share of sales.

The *theory of games* is sometimes used to try and explain the behaviour of firms in oligopolistic markets. A 'game' situation is said to exist when there are a number of players (firms) with a conflict of interests and with limited rewards to be shared out between them. For individual players to make decisions, they will need to be aware of how others will respond and what effect this will have on the eventual outcome. This situation will arise because oligopoly markets are based on uncertainty and interdependence.

The theory of games sets out two possible scenarios:

1. *Pure conflict*   This is likely to exist when the gain made by one firm will directly lead to losses by others. This will remove the incentive for firms to co-operate.
2. *A mixture of conflict and co-operation*   This is most likely to exist if firms can benefit by increasing total market share through co-operation. However, conflict might arise because individual firms might attempt to gain for themselves the biggest share of the increased total market.

These scenarios can and frequently do exist in many markets. Oligopolists will normally be engaged in activities directed towards protecting and increasing their market share. Periods of outright conflict are interspersed with periods of co-operation. In the real world there will usually be several oligopolists, many different game strategies, and variations in which strategies can be practised. Game theory provides us with a useful insight into the interdependence of oligopolistic strategies and the ways in which organizations have to think to predict how their rivals will react to their actions. Large corporations keep an eagle eye on the policies of rivals, and constantly discuss and evaluate ways in which competitors will react to their strategies.

From time to time, oligopolists are suspected of collusion. In many countries formal and informal price-fixing and other forms of restrictive practice are illegal. However price-fixing agreements do occasionally come to light.

Customer-value pricing

This method can be a very effective way of maximizing revenue. As we have already seen, a customer's valuation of a product is influenced by price. Certain price bands are acceptable to consumers, and prices need to be set within this range. Market research is essential to establish and monitor consumer's perceptions of price. This type of pricing involves reacting to the intensity of demand for a product, so that high demand leads to high prices and weak demand to low prices, even though unit costs are similar.

When a firm can split up the market in which it operates into different sections, it can carry out a policy of *price discrimination*. This involves selling at high prices in sections of the market where demand is intense (where price is inelastic) and at relatively low prices where demand is elastic. For example, slight modifications to products may allow high and low price strategies for different groups of consumers. Many cars have additional extras and customers can be provided with the opportunity to purchase either cheaper or more expensive versions. It may also be possible to discriminate according to time. Prices can vary according to different times of the day—as for example with telephone calls or the 'happy hour'. This type of pricing involves constantly monitoring customer perceptions to provide them with products that they regard as value for money.

ρ Case Study—Pricing policy

The information given in Fig. 13.25 was produced in a booklet called *Starting Your Own Business*. Read the information provided before answering the questions.

One of the crucial problems you have is to find the right price. It's full of pitfalls—what seems like common sense may not be the best thing to do. Try this two-step process:

Step 1
If your business is going to provide a service, calculate your service charge on a weekly, daily or even hourly basis; e.g. weekly service charge: all the costs of running a business divided by 46 (the number of weeks in a year, less an allowance for holidays and sickness time).

This calculation will show you the amount that the business has to charge out weekly in order to cover its costs, i.e. break even.

If you divide this figure by the number of working days in a week you will have calculated the daily charge, and this figure divided by the number of *working hours* in a day gives you the true hourly rate for the business, i.e. the amount per hour the business will have to charge to break even. Don't forget to review your calculations regularly, taking into account how well the business is doing.

Your business however may be involved in manufacturing, in which case you will need to calculate the unit cost of the product. In a one-product firm, this will be calculated as follows:

Unit cost of product: all your fixed costs and all your variable costs (e.g. raw materials and sub-contract labour) divided by the number of units made in the period.

In this calculation, you will need to make an assumption about how many units your business can make *and sell* in any one period. The resulting calculation will show you the amount the business needs to charge for each unit to cover its costs, i.e. break even, *assuming that the business sells the expected number of units*.

Step 2
The price you set

You'll always need a *mark-up* on your basic cost. That's your profit—you need it to help your business grow and prosper. The ideal price is the highest that the largest number of customers will pay. One guideline to use is 'the going rate'—what your competitors charge for similar things. Or you could simply add a figure to your costs, say 50%. Bear in mind:

- People will pay more for better quality and better service.
- Low prices can make customers suspect low quality and poor service.
- Economies of scale cost a lot of money—you have to spend more to achieve them.
- If your price is too low, you have to work harder to get the same amount of return. Selling one expensive thing once in a while can be better than dozens of cheap things all the time.

Remember:

(a) The most important rule of pricing is—never undercharge.
(b) When you are small, think small. Don't get seduced by economies of scale, especially if you have to spend everything you have and borrow up to the hilt to do it. Charge more; it's dangerous to risk everything being cheap.

Figure 13.25 Advice on pricing policies for small businesses (*Source*: Barclays Bank Information and Advisory Services)

Questions

1. In terms of the pricing theories that you have just examined, what type of pricing policy is being recommended by the article?
2. What advantages and disadvantages can you point out in such a policy?
3. What alternative policies could you suggest?
4. Would they be more (or less) effective than the ones suggested?

Place

As we have seen, the main objective of a firm's distribution policy is to make sure that products are where they are wanted at the time they are wanted. This will entail having a network of distribution links often involving intermediaries linked by a communications system. The total cost of distribution should be kept as low as possible in relation to output. The real cost of distribution is made up of all distribution-related costs including the obvious ones of transport and warehousing.

The process of distribution is not just concerned with physically moving goods from manufacturers to consumers. It is also concerned with: choosing from available channels, deciding whether to use one channel or several and whether to sell direct to consumers or to go through intermediaries, and deciding how much spending to allocate to distribution and how much financial involvement to make in the existing channels.

Successful development of sales might require quite a large involvement by the manufacturer in the process of distribution. Close contact with intermediaries might enable manufacturers to promote the image they would like to convey.

Intermediaries such as wholesalers, transport companies and retailers may be more effective than the manufacturer at providing goods in the right place for consumers (see Fig. 13.26). They will expect a reward for their services, the margin being the difference between the price at which they take on products and the price for which they sell them. The profits on distribution will frequently need to be shared between several intermediaries, and this all adds on to the end price.

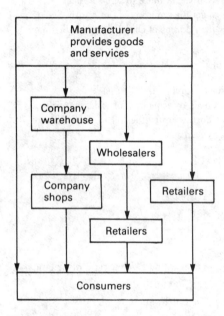

Figure 13.26 Alternative channels of distribution.

The total cost of distribution is made up of five ingredients:

- Facilities
- Inventory
- Transport
- Communications
- Unitization

Decisions about *facilities* include where to locate warehouses, the size of the warehouses and how many to have. The more warehouses a company has, the higher will be its overheads and the number of staff employed. However, this will need to be traded off against a reduction in transport costs.

Decisions about *inventories* include how much stock to hold and which items to stock up on. The higher the level of inventories, the greater will be the costs of insurance, deterioration and theft. However, this will need to be traded off against the ability of the well-stocked company to fill orders quickly and hence to keep customers.

Decisions about *transport* relate to the type of transport to be adopted, whether to own or lease the vehicles, how to plan delivery and so on. Once again, trade-offs need to be made in relation to speed, reliability, effectiveness in different weather conditions, etc.

Decisions about *communications* relate to the communications system to be employed, the procedures to be adopted for processing documents and how much emphasis to be placed on the quality of service. A good communications system is essential in any company.

Decisions about *unitization* relate to the way in which goods are packaged and assembled for handling. Considerations pertain to the size of loads, reductions in breakages, reductions in manpower employed, etc. Raw sugar, for example, would not need to be packaged and could be transported in bulk by lorry or ship; however, once the sugar has been refined, decisions need to be made about the size, shape and materials used in making the individual bags of sugar. Decisions about the unitization of the bags will be based on factors such as strength and cost of materials. The bags will then need to be transported in larger units such as boxes. Decisions about size and shape will be based on such factors as ease of handling and storage, and minimization of breakages and damage.

Channels of distribution

The channel of distribution is the route that a product follows from the manufacturer to the consumer. Market research will often reveal the channels of distribution used by competitors. Modern commerce involves thousands of different channels and methods of distribution including newspapers, mail order, computer link-ups and television, as well as more traditional routes.

The traditional way of distributing goods from a manufacturer to a market is through a small number of wholesalers who then sell the goods to a large number of retailers. In this way, a wholesaler is a go-between who buys in bulk from manufacturers and breaks the bulk down into small units for retailers. Wholesalers often provide a variety of services which benefit both manufacturers and retailers, such as warehousing, credit, transport and packaging. However, the existence of wholesalers adds to the selling price, and wholesalers cannot be expected to concentrate on any one manufacturer's goods.

If a manufacturer sells to a retailer directly, it can exert firmer control over its sales and the manufacturer and retailer can work together on sales promotion schemes. Selling direct to retailers involves a larger salesforce and increased transport charges when sending smaller consignments. If circumstances allow, it can be possible for manufacturers to sell directly to consumers, particularly if the product is a high-cost one and has a good reputation within the market.

Retailers are in direct contact with consumers and therefore are often in the best position to understand individual consumers' desires. An efficient system of retailing is essential if the types of commodities made by producers are to relate closely to consumer's desires. A *retailer* is the outlet through which goods are sold to the consumers; it may exist in a variety of different forms.

○ Case Study—Distribution at Toyota

Toyota has awarded the distribution business for its UK plants, worth £15 million per year, to two Japanese-led groups. The £15 million will pay for just-in-time (JIT) transport and warehousing facilities of car parts for Toyota factories at Shotton in North Wales and Burnaston in Derbyshire. The JIT system requires parts to be delivered to a factory just as they are needed on the production line, which minimizes storage costs.

The two winning bidders will soon find out what transport, storage or logistics management they will be responsible for providing. It is thought that Toyota will prefer a single logistics manager of the parts supply chain.

Toyota has yet to decide whether to site a warehouse close to the factories. It says that a warehouse would not fit in with its view of how JIT deliveries should work, but that the special circumstances of taking deliveries from all over Europe may mean modifying this view.

Of the 160 suppliers expected to be delivering to Burnaston and Shotton, about 70 will be based on the Continent. Most of the rest will be from the United Kingdom and a smaller number from Japan. Most of the car components will eventually come from the United Kingdom and continental suppliers. In the early stages of production about 60 per cent (in value) will be UK and continental imports; but by mid-1995 this is planned to increase to 80 per cent.

Having decided upon the contractors, Toyota must now turn its attention to distribution to its dealers throughout Europe. Space for a railhead has been incorporated into the factory near Derby and the company is still deciding whether to use rail for some of this distribution, particularly to continental Europe. The company is talking to British Rail, but any plan is unlikely to come to fruition until the Channel Tunnel is fully operational.

Questions

1. Explain how important the process of distribution is for a new car plant such as Toyota.
2. Why does siting a warehouse near to the new factories not fit in with the principles of JIT?
3. What action has Toyota taken to develop facilities for its dealers in Europe?
4. Explain why distribution is sometimes referred to as *logistics management*.

Promotion

Promotion is the business of communicating with others. Today this exchange of information takes place through sophisticated media and is carefully targeted to achieve maximum effect. An efficient network of communications is essential for successful promotional activity.

The *promotional mix* comprises all of the marketing and promotional communication methods used to achieve the objectives of the marketing mix. These methods are either non-controllable or controllable. *Non-controllable* methods are messages that take place on the basis of personal recommendations, word-of-mouth or a consumer's perception of a product or service. *Controllable* methods are those that are carefully targeted at achieving certain objectives through some form of campaign. Controllable methods pertain to four main areas:

1. *Advertisements*   These are messages sent via the media to inform or influence the people who receive them.
2. *Sales promotions*   These are a range of promotional techniques designed to increase sales, such as free samples and competitions.
3. *Personal selling*   This involves using the promotional mix to make sales and emphasizes the importance of selling.
4. *Publicity*   This is not identifiable with the sale of a particular product; its key component is public relations.

Promotional requirements will vary according to the size of the market; demographic dispersion and market segmentation. The more precisely an organization can define its particular market segment, the better the targeting of the promotional mix.

In order to achieve promotional objectives, the mnemonic of AIDA is frequently used:

A :   Customer's *attention* is captured and they are made *aware* of the product.
I :   The *impact* of the promotion is designed to stimulate their *interest*.
D: They are persuaded that they are *deprived* because they do not have the product, and this helps to stimulate a *desire* for the product.
A: The final *action* involves the purchase of the product.

The promotional mix must be used to match the various stages of the product life-cycle; for example, consumer awareness must be developed during the introductory stage. As the product experiences growth, promotional injects into the cycle must be made from time to time. As the brand reaches maturity, its heritage must be emphasized in order to sustain consumer loyalty.

Advertising

Advertisements are messages intended to inform or influence the people who receive them. An advertiser pays for a message in order to sell a good or a service, to seek support and participation or simply to provide information. Most adverts, however, are not just there to inform the public. For example, you do not see a soap powder advert that simply provides *information* about the powder; the advert goes further to provide a *persuasive message*.

A persuasive message is one that promises a desirable and believable benefit to the people to whom it is addressed. For example, persuasive adverts might:

1. Show a famous personality using the product, such as John Barnes and Lucozade.

2. Compare one product with another product.
3. Use sex appeal.

Many organizations aim to develop strong brand images through advertising—e.g. 'Frosties' or 'Marathon'. If consumers can be led to associate a brand name with a product, then the organization will be in a better position to make more sales and to encourage loyalty to the brand.

 Task

> Identify a current advertising campaign. At which groups is the promotion targeted? Comment upon the persuasive nature of the campaign and on what you feel it hopes to achieve.

For advertising to be effective, it must: reach the right audience; be attractive and appealing to the reader or viewer; and cost little in relation to the extra sales made.

1. *Reaching the right audience*   Advertising needs to be geared towards the right target audience. This will involve selecting appropriate media and particular areas of the media. For example, if you want to reach socio-economic group B, you will need to research the media slots that are most likely to reach group B. Test marketing may be employed to gauge the reception that a sample of the population gives to a selected product or promotion. For example, when a new biscuit is being prepared for a market 'launch', members of the public may be tested to find out what they think of various possible presentations of the product. Perhaps several different labels will be prepared for the product. A selected audience of consumers might then be asked to watch a TV screen while the labels are flashed in front of them. They will then be asked to fill in a questionnaire saying which labels they remember and which they liked best. Market research thus makes possible the design and preparation of adverts and other promotional techniques that will have maximum impact. The remainder of the recipe for success depends on the flair with which the advertising campaign is constructed and projected.
2. *Being attractive and appealing to the reader or viewer*   The starting-point in any campaign is to employ a team of specialists from an advertising agency.
3. *Costing little in relation to the extra sales made*   The extra sales made as a result of an advertising campaign should bring in far more revenue than the cost of the advertising. As a result, advertising will be effective only if consumers respond to the message.

DAGMAR is a mnemonic which is frequently used to assess how well promotional money is spent. It stands for:

Defining Advertising Goals for Measured Advertising Results

To plan an advertising campaign, an advertiser will consult an advertising agency. The agency will then act as the link between the advertiser and the consumer, creating, developing and implementing an advertising campaign on behalf of the client. Some agencies will offer all kinds of advertising services, while others may specialize in buying media or in particular types of creative work.

The team of experts in an agency services clients who are known as *accounts*. An account executive will supervise the work of the client and, together with the account director, will attempt to meet the objectives of the campaign. The account group will comprise representatives from various departments within the agency (see Fig. 13.27).

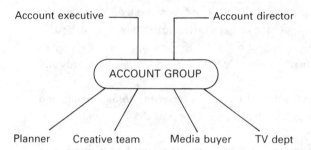

Figure 13.27 The account group.

The planner will assist the account executive, timetable the activities and assess the reactions of the public to the campaign. The creative team will consist of an art director, who will develop and create 'rough' drawings or visuals for a copy writer, who produces words known as copy. Ideas are discussed with the client. The message may be a combination of words, symbols, gimmicks, colours and sounds. For example, buzz words or straplines such as 'Once driven, forever smitten' may be used. Sometimes a character may be used to help consumers identify with the brand. Good artwork and effective use of colour can also help to create a distinctive identity.

A key element in advertising is media selection. Media selection will depend on the target audience—that is, the number of potential customers the advertiser may wish to reach (*coverage*) as well as the number of times the advertiser wishes the message to be transmitted (*frequency*).

⌕ Case Study—Beer battle at the carnival

At the world famous Rio carnival, there is more at stake than just samba, choreography, costume and song. Recent carnivals have become a glitter-clad battleground for Brazil's two largest beer producers.

Brazil's 6 billion litre annual beer market is hotly contested by two companies—Antarctica and Brahma—each of which claims to produce the best-selling brand. In fact, Brahma is Brazil's biggest brewer, with 35.4 per cent of the market for its main seller, Brahma Chopp; but Antarctica's Blue Label is hot on its heels with 33 per cent.

Brahma was the first company to spot the real potential of the carnival. One of its factories lies alongside the Sambadrome where the official parade takes place. Their marketing director decided to exploit this opportunity. The company was given a box in exchange for land. The box and, of course, the brand name were the focus of attention of the television cameras beaming the scene live to 40 million viewers. Brahma's marketing director feels that 'Carnival means happiness and parties, when everyone forgets recession and misery and has a good time. That's what we want our beer to be associated with.'

The idea proved to be such a success that Antarctica is copying it. They readily admit that they are copying the Brahma idea and are working hard to improve it.

Over the Carnival period in 1993 the two companies spent £575 000 sponsoring rival samba schools, street bands and carnival balls. They also rented boxes in the Sambadrome to which they invited international stars. Brahma is now one of Brazil's biggest spenders on advertising with an annual budget of $25 million, recruiting singer–songwriter Tom Jobim and splashing 'Number One Beer' across buses, billboards and magazines.

Not to be outdone, Antarctica has increased its advertising spend to $25 million and has run a campaign under the slogan 'Antarctica, the Best and the First and there is nothing more to be said.'

In 1993, for the two days of parades, Brahma's box played host to a number of politicians, film stars and leading society figures. Little more than 200 metres away, the Antarctica box offered a night-long banquet, playing host to actress Liza Minelli, film-maker Franco Zeffirelli and Canadian model Linda Evangelista. Meanwhile, Brahma was dropping rumours about the appearance there of Kevin Costner and Richard Gere.

Both firms felt that they were getting value for money by being associated with an event that everybody will talk about!

Questions

1. Explain why the core values generated by the Rio carnival might be useful for a brand of beer. To what extent are these values (a) similar to and (b) different from the core values generated by Coca Cola advertisements?
2. Identify a campaign known to you where two or more competitors use a similar approach to advertising—e.g. lager one-liners, or humour in the market for tea.
3. Comment briefly on the two straplines 'Number One Beer' and 'Antarctica, the Best and the First and there is nothing more to be said'. What are these straplines attempting to communicate?
4. Using two examples known to you, explain why famous names are frequently used in advertising campaigns.

Controls over advertising

Advertisers cannot say anything they like when preparing an advert and they must keep within the law. For example, the Trades Description Act lays down that goods advertised for sale must be as they are described. The advertising industry also has its own code of practice.

The *British code of advertising practice* is a voluntary agreement by firms in the advertising industry to keep their adverts within certain standards. For example, when advertising slimming aids, the advertiser must state that these should be taken in addition to a balanced diet. This covers newspapers, magazines, cinema adverts, leaflets, brochures, posters and commercials, but not TV and radio adverts.

The *Advertising Standards Authority (ASA)* is an independent body which exercises control over all advertising except that on radio and television. The Authority draws up its own codes which it uses to ensure that advertisements are 'legal, decent, honest and truthful'. For example, you might have seen an advert which appears in newspapers and magazines, part of which looks like Fig. 13.28. The advert goes on to say that if you have any complaints about adverts you should write to the ASA, which will take up your complaint. If the ASA feels that an advert is indecent or untrue, it will ask the advertising agency that produced it to change it.

A number of other agencies are involved with consumer protection issues, part of which may include looking at misleading adverts—for example the Independent Television Commission, the Office of Fair Trading, consumer groups, the Chartered Institute of Marketing and other professional bodies.

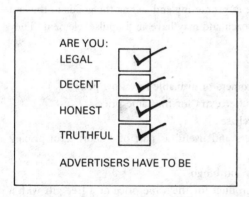

Figure 13.28 Advert for the Advertising Standards Authority.

Sales promotions

These are a series of techniques used to encourage customers to make a purchase. They tend to be used to complement advertising, personal selling and public relations and might include point-of-sale materials, competitions, demonstrations and exhibitions. Whereas advertising is more of a long-term communication process which builds and develops a brand, sales promotions are frequently used as a short-term inducement used to encourage customers to react quickly.

Sales promotions can be divided into those techniques that push stocks into the distribution system and those that assist in selling products to the end-user.

Promotions into the pipeline

Promotions into the pipeline help to sell goods into the distribution system. Although many distributors may be impressed by materials designed to encourage final consumers to make a sale, many will undoubtedly be influenced by techniques addressed at themselves. Sales promotions of this type may include:

- *Dealer loaders*, such as a free case with every so many bought; 13 of something for the price of 12 is known as a 'baker's dozen'
- *Point of sale (POS)* materials, such as special displays, posters and racks
- *Dealer competitions* with attractive prizes
- *Staff training* if the handling or the servicing of the product requires special expertise, such as cars
- *Sale or return*, which can be used to encourage a dealer to stock an untried product
- *Promotional gifts* such as bottles of spirits, clocks, watches, etc.

Promotions out of the pipeline

Promotions out of the pipeline will assist the trade in promoting and selling the goods to the end user. Such promotions will require a creative approach and may have an 'impulse' element. They may include:

- *Free sample or trial packs*, either given to customers or available for a low price.
- *Bonus packs*—beer and lager cans frequently offer extra for the same price
- *Coupon offers* such as money off the next purchase
- *Price reductions*, always popular with customers and useful as part of a short-term pricing strategy
- *Competitions* such as scratch cards, free draws and bingo
- *Premium offers*, which may provide an extra product for the same price or a free gift with a pack

 Task

Identify and then analyse the effectiveness of at least two sales promotions that you have recently come across.

Personal selling

This involves a seller using persuasive communication techniques in order to convince the buyer of the need to purchase the goods or services on offer. The objective of this element of the promotional mix, therefore, is to make a sale, and this represents the culmination of all of the marketing activities that have taken place beforehand.

The role of personal selling will vary from business to business. For some organizations the high cost of salaries, commissions, travel expenses and hotels can make it a very expensive process. In organizational markets the purpose of a salesforce is to *push* products into markets, whereas in consumer goods markets advertising tends to *pull* products into the distribution network.

The sequence of events used in the personal selling process is often described as the *five P's*:

1. *Preparation*   Sales staff should be well trained and familiar with the products they are selling. Equally important, however, is a good knowledge of the customers, the competition and the market.
2. *Prospecting*   This process involves identifying prospects or potential customers before selling takes place.
3. *Pre-approach*   This involves learning about the customers, finding out about their past history of transactions and generally trying to identify and ascertain their general needs and aspirations.
4. *Presentation*   This involves active use of selling skills using AIDA (see page 377). The process will start with *probing* in order to identify customers' needs and will finish with *buying signals* which can be used to complete a sale.
5. *Post-sale support*   It is always important to follow up a sale and this will help to create repeat business.

Sales staff act as an information link between suppliers and their customers. Because they are constantly meeting customers or clients, they have a boundary role which is not just that of selling but also of interpreting the needs and requirements of customers (see Fig. 13.29).

Figure 13.29 The link between customers and suppliers.

Public relations

The purpose of public relations (PR) is to provide an external environment for an organization in which it can do well. The PR process includes all of the actions of and communications from the organization. By reacting to a range of social, political, economic, local and environmental forces, an organization can build a positive image which may influence a variety of groups such as shareholders, local residents, employees and special interest groups. Building *goodwill* in this way requires sound organizational behaviour and the communication of such behaviour to a range of different groups.

Whereas the objectives of all of the other areas of the promotional mix are essentially short-term, public relations is a long-term process which sends messages to outside bodies and attempts to build and develop a reputation and an image.

According to Frank Jefkins, PR involves a transfer process which helps to convert the negative feelings of an organization's many publics into positive ones. By identifying *unfavourable* feeling of bodies external to an organization, the company can then use PR to create a more *favourable* environment by reducing negative perceptions and building positive ones (see Fig. 13.30).

Negative		Positive
hostility	⟶	sympathy
prejudice	⟶	acceptance
apathy	⟶	interest
ignorance	⟶	knowledge

Figure 13.30 The PR transfer process.

Public relations activities may include:

- Hospitality at sporting events
- Press releases
- Press conferences
- Visits and open days
- Event sponsorship
- Corporate videotapes
- Magazines, publicity, education services

Public relations activities should help to create a favourable environment in which the organization can operate. It can provide information, build confidence and help to develop an image.

Case Study—PR by Post

To help transform inexperienced entrepreneurs into public relations professionals, Holder Swan has launched 'PR by Post', a 10-part do-it-yourself course. The partnership, based in north London, has extensive PR experience in the travel and leisure industries.

Sylvia Holder views the course she has set up with Lyndsay Swan as particularly attractive for those who are too far from London to make a trip to a seminar. Much initial interest, she believes, will come from overseas, where she feels that many people are influenced by London's leading role in public relations.

For a fee of £350 plus VAT, those signing up for the course receive study notes, media lists and the PR manual. By means of practical projects, specialists in such fields as national newspapers and photography guide the course members through the basic public relations skills including writing press releases and brochures.

According to Sylvia Holder, 'If you're bright enough to run your own business, you're bright enough to do your own PR. This has been proved time and time again by delegates at our courses who have frequently beaten us at our own game and achieved extensive publicity'. She insists that the course involves more than just sitting down with a book. The course helps business people to learn the basics without making a big commitment of time, and at a fraction of the cost.

Questions

1. Explain why business organizations require public relations.
2. What does 'PR by Post' hope to do?
3. With reference to the organization at which you work or attend, identify two PR activities and explain their purpose.

Using the marketing mix

As we have seen, the marketing mix comprises a range of techniques which can form the basis of a marketing plan specifically geared to meet corporate objectives. Whenever objectives change, the blend of ingredients has to be altered. No two mixes will ever be the same, and each will represent a unique way of developing a strategy from the available resources.

Undifferentiated marketing

Undifferentiated marketing involves offering a single marketing mix to the whole market. This is not always likely to be successful because, as we have seen, markets are made up of different types of buyers with different wants and needs (see Fig. 13.31).

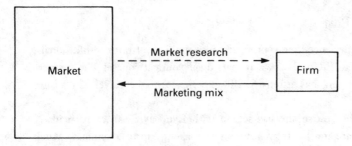

Figure 13.31 Undifferentiated marketing.

Differentiated marketing

Differentiated marketing is the strategy of attacking the market by tailoring separate products and marketing strategies to different sectors of the market (see Fig. 13.32). Different mixes will be involved for each sector of the market. For example, the car market might be divided into an economy segment (buyers looking for a cheap form of transportation), a luxury segment, a sporting-orientated segment, and so on. The marketer will develop different strategies for each of these segments.

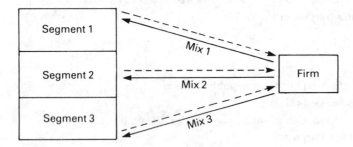

Figure 13.32 Differentiated marketing.

Concentrated marketing

Concentrated marketing is often the best strategy for the smaller organization. This involves choosing to compete in one segment and developing the best mix for this sub-market (see Fig. 13.33). Jaguar, for example, concentrates on the luxury segment of the car market.

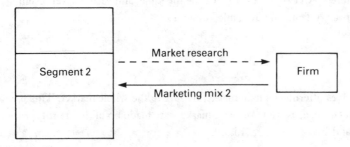

Figure 13.33 Concentrated marketing.

Action

Implementing the marketing plan will involve getting individuals and departments to develop their own action plans. Within their plans will be a series of time limits, deadlines, sales forecasts, budgets and quotas.

The test of consistency attempts to see whether strategic choices or plans made by managers are (a) feasible and (b) achievable. The question is, having drawn up a marketing plan, is it possible to put it into practice? This will help to identify whether the organization has the resources to achieve objectives, the extent to which its strategies deal with threats, and the overall implications of the strategic decisions made by the plan.

Control

Not all plans progress in the way intended. It is important to assess how far a plan has progressed and whether or not strategic decisions are actually working. Events must be monitored against the plan and used as a basis for feedback and managerial action. For example, corrective action might be required if predicted events fail to materialize (see Fig. 13.34).

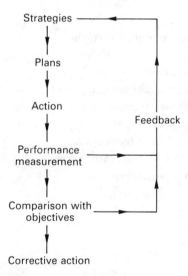

Figure 13.34 Monitoring events and taking corrective action.

Planning is fundamental to the marketing process. The purpose of planning is to develop a competitive advantage so that the organization can outperform competitors in the same industry. It is a key process which ensures that a company's actions are focused on stated goals and objectives.

Questions

Short-answer questions

1. Give two reasons why a company might sell, for a limited period, part of its product range at a loss. (*Source*: AEB)
2. Give two examples of non-price competition. (*Source*: AEB)
3. What is the purpose of the Advertising Standards Authority?
4. How does the government attempt to prevent misleading advertising? (*Source*: AEB)
5. Give three reasons, which are within the control of the firm, for a loss in market share. (*Source*: AEB)
6. What might be the objectives of a local newspaper publisher in introducing a free paper in addition to its existing publication? (*Source*: Cambridge)
7. What is meant by a policy of penetration pricing?
8. How might the manufacturer of a new chocolate bar decide to market the product? (*Source*: Cambridge)
9. A furniture manufacturer is concerned about a reduction in sales of its existing product range. What action should it take? (*Source*: AEB)
10. Explain what is meant by the 'place' element in the marketing mix.
11. Identify two intangible product benefits.
12. What are the generic dimensions of a product?
13. Explain the difference between the depth and the width of a product portfolio.
14. Provide two examples of proactive products.
15. According to the Boston Consulting Group, what is a cash cow?
16. Identify two situations in which an organization might wish to use skimming pricing.
17. Why is a reduction in price unlikely to benefit a firm whose products are price-inelastic? (*Source*: AEB)
18. Briefly explain the difference between cost-plus pricing and contribution pricing.
19. At what point on an oligopolist's demand curve will firms tend to set their prices?
20. Why might a firm's long-term pricing policy differ from its short-term one? (*Source*: AEB)

Essays

1. Why might a firm wish to:
   (a) change the position of a product in a particular market?
   (b) relaunch an existing product?
   Explain your answer by using actual examples.
2. Why does the emphasis on different elements of the marketing mix vary between products?
3. To what extent are costs a determinant of price?
4. How could a knowledge of price elasticity help an organization to make pricing decisions?
5. Describe the part played by the marketing function in business.
6. A good product does not require marketing. Discuss.
7. (a) Why might firms possess a range of products at different stages in their product life-cycle?

(b) Why is it that some firms find it difficult to achieve such a portfolio?   (*Source*: AEB)
8. Marketing is essentially a process of planning. Explain what is meant by this statement.
9. Examine the connection between the product life-cycle and the Boston box. Explain how each helps with the management of the product portfolio.
10. Imagine that you are in the position of a brand manager of a product portfolio which is well known to you. Explain what you would do to manage the portfolio effectively over the next decade.

Data response questions

1   Hot Air Products Ltd

Hot Air Products Ltd makes a wide range of industrial and domestic dryers, including a very successful domestic hair dryer.

  Read the memos reproduced in Fig. 13.35 and answer the following questions.

1. Prepare information for the managing director to present to the board. She has asked you to calculate the following (show all your workings):

   (a)   The number of hair dryers the company will produce at full capacity.
   (b)   Their percentage share of the total market, if all these units are sold.
   (c)   The retail price of hair dryers considered likely to capture this share of the market.

HOT AIR PRODUCTS LTD

INTERNAL MEMORANDUM

To: Marketing Manager   Date: 19.9.91
From: Managing Director   Ref: RL/PS/7/1

Subject: Market Share Targets 1992/93

To exploit our competitive advantage in the domestic hair dryer market, the Board is considering ways of increasing our market share. Please prepare relevant research data for the Board Meeting on 30th November.

Figure 13.35a Hot Air Product memos

HOT AIR PRODUCTS LTD

INTERNAL MEMORANDUM

To: Managing Director   Date: 29.9.91
From: Marketing Manager   Ref: JA/LM/3/1

Subject: Your memo dated 19.9.91 (RL/PS/7/1)

Data on domestic hair dryers indicate the following:

   i) The total annual market in the UK is 800,000 units and
      this is likely to remain static for a number of years;
  ii) We have a 10% share of the total market at a retail
      price of £20 per unit. We are among the market leaders;
 iii) This product is likely to show a price elasticity of −4;
  iv) The estimated advertising elasticity is 0.8. Our
      present advertising expenditure is £80,000 per year;
   v) Our output of domestic hair dryers can be increased by
      20% without increases in plant or manpower;
  vi) Variable costs per unit will remain unchanged.

Figure 13.35b Hot Air Product memos (*continued*)

      (d) The estimated advertising expenditure to attract this increased market share.
  (e)   The increase or decrease in sales revenue that would result from selling all the units produced at full capacity at the new retail price.

2. Outline three additional pieces of information that would assist the board in deciding whether to attempt to expand their market share for hair dryers.
3. Discuss the value of the concept of elasticity in determining pricing policy. (*Source*: AEB)

2   Launching a new product

The product manager of a large manufacturing firm supplied the following information on 32 new product ideas examined over a period of two years. These ideas led to the full development and successful launch of only one new product (see Table 13.1).

He commented on the fact that new product development is becoming increasingly difficult to achieve because of:

- Growing social and governmental constraints
- Costliness of new product development
- Capital shortage
- Shorter life-spans of successful products

Table 13.1 Estimated cost of finding one successful new product (starting with 32 new ideas)

Stage	No. of ideas	Pass rate	Cost per product idea (£)	Cost of each stage (£)
1. Idea screening	32	1 in 4	500	16 000
2. Concept test	8	1 in 2	10 000	80 000
3. Product development	4	1 in 2	100 000	400 000
4. Test marketing	2	1 in 2	250 000	500 000
5. National launch	1	1 in 1	2 500 000	2 500 000

1. Of the 32 ideas that were considered, how many passed the concept testing stage?
2. What was the total cost of developing and launching one successful product?
3. Discuss two sources of new product ideas.
4. Comment on each of the reasons put forward to explain why new product development is becoming increasingly difficult.
5. Give three reasons why new products often fail to win acceptance in the market.
   (*Source*: AEB)

3   The Suntrap Hotel

The cost accounts for the Suntrap Hotel for the period 1 January 1985 to 31 December 1985 are shown in Table 13.2.

Table 13.2 Cost accounts for the Suntrap Hotel, 1985*

	Total number of room/nights let	Revenue per room per night (£)	Variable cost per room/per night (£)
April	160	8	6
May	180	10	6
June	220	12	7
July	280	15	8
August	340	15	8
September	170	10	6

*Total annual semi-variable and fixed costs are £1440.

In the past the hotel has had a season of six months per annum from 1 April to 30 September. In an effort to increase profits, the proprietor is considering extending his 1987 season to cover the period from 1 March to 31 October. Market research suggests that in both March and October he can expect to sell 100 room nights at £7. Variable costs are estimated to be £6 per night, and annual semi-variable and fixed costs are expected to rise by £100.

1. What is the difference between a fixed cost and a variable cost?
2. Calculate the profits for 1985.
3. What effect would the plan have on the proprietor's overall profits?
4. If he were to have opened during March and October in 1985, what is the minimum that he would have had to charge during those months per room per night, if he were to break even during those months?
5. Give four examples of alternative ways for the proprietor to increase profits. (*Source*: AEB)

4   Advertising and sales promotion

Figure 13.36 (a)–(c) illustrates the effects of advertising and sales promotion on the volume of sales of a product, and the effects of skimming and penetration pricing strategies on the prices charged for a product. Study the diagrams and answer the questions that follow.

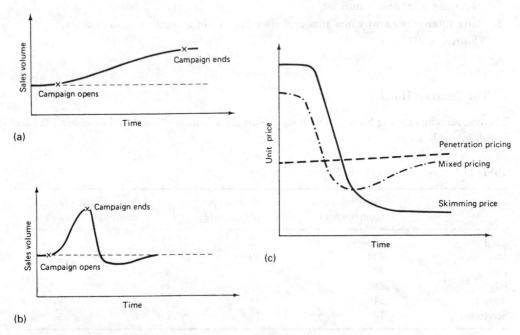

Figure 13.36 (a) Advertising—effects on sales volume. (b) Sales promotion—effects on sales volume. (c) Skim and penetration pricing. (*Source*: adapted from *Mastering Marketing* by D. Foster, Macmillan)

1. Distinguish between advertising and sales promotion, and with reference to parts (a) and (b) comment on the different effects advertising and sales promotion are expected to have on sales.

2. What is the combined effect that advertising and sales promotion are likely to have on sales? Plotting time on one axis and sales volume on the other, produce a diagram to illustrate this effect.

3. With reference to part (c) choose either penetration or skimming pricing strategy. Explain its nature and the circumstances in which it may be used.

4. How might the product life-cycle influence a firm's pricing and promotional strategies?

5. State and explain three influences (other than the product life-cycle) on the marketing mix for a particular product. (*Source*: AEB)

5   Continuing popularity of the Mini

Read the extract and answer the questions that follow.

After 31 years the Mini keeps on growing

THE French adore them and the Japanese simply cannot get enough. After 31 years in production, the evergreen Mini has become one of Britain's biggest export earners.

Rover yesterday disclosed that output of the little car is at its highest for five years with 1,000 rolling off the assembly lines at the company's Longbridge plant in Birmingham every week.

Most of the demand is coming from abroad where the Mini has become a cult car. It is the best-selling imported car in Japan, with more than 10,400 sold there this year.

Rover sales staff, sensing a trend, pandered to the demand by introducing a new version of the Mini Cooper, the rally car which enjoyed huge success in the 1960s. Now the Cooper accounts for four out of ten of worldwide sales of Minis and the car is commanding premium prices when the rest of the market is having to discount.

The enormous success of the Mini after more than three decades is baffling Rover executives, who were going to axe the model six years ago. But Sir Graham Day decided to keep the car running when he took over as chairman in 1986 because, he said, it was 'a nice little earner'. How much the Mini is earning has not been revealed by Rover, but export sales could be worth about £180 million, according to industry estimates.

Rover said: 'Foreign markets love the Mini. In France, women love the car with special paint jobs as a chic runabout. That is why the Mini Cooper is so popular.'

Its original design is little changed, although its engine has been cleaned up to meet modern environmental emission laws. More than five million have now been built, and the Mini sits alongside the Volkswagen Beetle and Citroen 2CV as one of the most readily identified cars in the world.

(*Source*: adapted from *The Times*, 22 December 1990)

1. What proportion of total Mini production is sold in Japan?

2. Explain why 'the car is commanding premium prices when the rest of the market is having to discount' (para. 4).

3. Identify and discuss the product extension strategies that resulted in the growth in sales of the Mini.

4. What two methods might a government use to protect the car industry from foreign competition?

5. What financial justification could Sir Graham Day have had for reversing the decision to take the car out of production? (*Source*: AEB)

Suggested reading

Chisnall, P., *Marketing: A Behavioural Analysis*. McGraw-Hill, 1985.

Jefkins, F., *A First Course in Marketing*, DPP 1989.

Morden, A. R., *Elements of Marketing*. DPP, 1989.

Needham, D. and Dransfield. R., *Marketing – Everybody's Business* , 2nd Edn. Heinemann, 1994.

14

Production

Throughout the world people are involved in identifying opportunities to create goods or provide services to match the needs and wants of consumers. The process of providing goods and services to satisfy such needs is known as *production*.

Any activities associated with production are *wealth-creating*. A simple example of wealth creation would be the production of this book. The difference between all of the costs of production and the price of the finished book represents the wealth that has been created. The contributions of all of those involved in its development have 'added value' to this process and have helped to create that wealth.

Production involves all occupations in the primary, secondary and tertiary areas because everyone in each occupation (a) helps to add a bit more value to something the user benefits from, (b) improves the welfare of our society and (c) provides us with the standard of living to which we have become accustomed. For example:

1. *Primary production* This is the earliest stage in the production process and is concerned with extracting the gifts of nature. Examples of primary activity would include tree felling, fishing and agriculture.
2. *Secondary production* This is the second stage in the production process. It involves processes that transform raw materials from the primary stage into finished or part-finished products, through either construction or manufacture.
3. *Tertiary production* This includes the productive activities of the service sector of the economy. It comprises *commercial services* which facilitate business activities, such as banking and insurance, and also *direct services*, which are of benefit to individual members of the community, e.g. policing, teaching and nursing.

Modern societies such as the United Kingdom are said to be in their 'third wave of development'. In their first wave most occupations were based on agriculture; the second wave was dominated by manufacturing industry; while in the third wave the service sector has become increasingly important. A society in which production takes place is therefore one based on the process of creating value—through both paid and unpaid activities—in the primary, manufacturing and service sectors.

Wealth creation provides the goods and services we need. Almost everything we see around us has been provided through a series of wealth-creating activities, which add value at every stage to transform inputs into outputs. The management of this process is known as production or operations management. This is a key function in every organization, because without it the firm's objectives cannot be achieved (see Fig. 14.1).

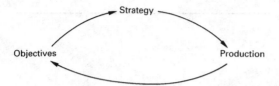

Figure 14.1 Meeting objectives through the production of goods and services.

Organizations depend upon the management abilities of their production/operations teams to carry out the production function. Many would argue that this function is the most difficult to understand and perform. Production/operations usually employs the largest amount of capital, assets, labour and other factors, and it is important that a company has a proven strategy for dealing with production problems as and when they arise.

We can therefore say that an operations manager must be concerned with the following issues:

- Costs of production
- The condition of the means of production (machinery, etc.)
- Keeping production going
- Health and safety
- Keeping employees motivated
- Keeping up-to-date with technology
- Satisfying the requirements of customers
- Maximizing the use of plant
- Minimizing the waste of materials

Clearly, supervising production involves the use of a diversity of skills to control a range of resources in a variety of areas which may all be interdependent.

We can try to break down the function into five broad areas shown in Fig. 14.2, although in practice there will be considerable overlap.

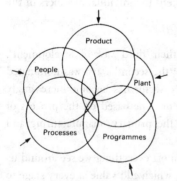

Figure 14.2 The five broad areas of production.

$\mathcal{P}$ Case Study—Manufacturing myths

'Manufacturing' stirs up some powerful emotions in the United Kingdom, conjuring up names such as Stephenson, Baird and Whittle. Many commentators today refer to the erosion of our manufacturing base as the cause of all of our economic ills. But is this really the case?

Britain's share of manufactures has declined from 20 per cent in the early 1950s to less than 8 per cent today; at the same time, the world's trade in manufactures has grown massively. Much of Britain's share has been taken over by countries such as Japan and Korea; in addition, the recovery of Germany and France in the 1960s and 1970s saw those countries regaining shares lost in the immediate postwar period.

However, it should be remembered that the 20 per cent share of the world market enjoyed by Britain in the 1950s comprised mainly exports to the Commonwealth and Irish Republic; today the top four markets for British goods are the United States, Germany, France and the Netherlands, and penetrating these markets is much more difficult.

Another myth is that the UK is dependent upon manufacturing exports to pay for its essential imports such as food and raw materials. In the early 1950s the imports of such goods accounted for 60 per cent of all imports, but by the late 1980s only 14 per cent fell into such categories. Today the export of UK manufactures pays mainly for the import of non-essential goods. Spending patterns have changed over the years, and Britain has a high propensity to import manufactured goods, which largely accounts for the balance of payments deficits over recent years.

In the past, large companies such as ICI manufactured goods in the United Kingdom and then exported them overseas. Increasingly, today many large UK companies locate manufacturing facilities overseas; although such manufactures are not being made in Britain, these operations create foreign currency earnings which flow back and help to improve the health of the UK economy.

The UK export record is not as poor as we tend to think, either: 20 per cent of gross domestic product is in exported goods, compared with less than 20 per cent of Japan's GDP and 10 per cent of the US GDP.

The British manufacturing base is not, therefore, as weak as many seem to think. Furthermore, it is a mistake to emphasize the distinction between goods and services. Service industries, too, create wealth and earn foreign currency. The successful development of the UK economy depends on the development of business in general, and not just on manufacturing.

Questions

1. Explain why it is confusing to say that Britain's share of world manufactures has dropped from 20 to 8 per cent over the last 40 years?

2. Using examples, describe the sort of imported goods we tend to buy today. Are these sorts of goods essentials?
3. Manufacturing clearly has an important role to play in the UK economy, but to what extent? Why is the development of business in general and not just manufacturing important for the UK economy?

The product

In an ideal world, a customer's needs would be spotlighted by marketers who would then communicate this information to product developers. Too often in the past, marketing information was ignored and products were developed because production costs appeared to be low. Scant regard was paid to the demands of the market. Instead of looking at appearance, performance, quality, safety and durability, producers concentrated their efforts on what they considered to be an efficient use of materials, skills and processes. Their approach was clearly *product-led* rather than *market-led*. Today, however, it is rarely possible for organizations to ignore the wishes of consumers.

⌕ Case Study—Product-led or market-led

Examine an electrical product that you have bought in the last three years and that you use at least once a week (e.g. hairdrier, CD player).

Questions

1. List five features of this product that you feel would appeal to consumers and would encourage them to buy it.
2. How would you rate the product (relative to similar products and in terms of value for money) in
   (a) appearance?
   (b) special features?
   (c) safety?
   (d) durability and planned obsolescence?
3. What qualities and features could have improved the appearance and performance of this product?
4. Do you feel that this product is:
   (a) market-led?
   (b) product-led?
   (c) an effective combination of the two?
5. Discuss your response with someone else who has also undertaken this exercise.

Research

No matter what the source of product ideas, it is important to undertake some form of research in order to develop a new product successfully. Research is the systematic search for facts and information which will help to solve problems. *Market research* tries to anticipate the needs of potential and existing customers by means of a thorough understanding of behaviour patterns and the consumer environment. *Product research* then takes this further: it uses the knowledge of consumer needs to develop new products or make changes to existing ones. Distinguishing between the different characteristic of consumers to develop a product to appeal to a particular group in a specific market segment is known as *differentiation*.

Product developments may occur in a variety of ways:

1. *Chance ideas*   These may develop from discussions with colleagues, suggestions schemes or brainstorming sessions.
2. *Market gap analysis*   An organization's existing range may have a number of gaps that need to be investigated and filled. Gap analysis will identify under-exploited market segments so that products can be directed at them.
3. *Attempts to use idle resources*   Organizations will seek to maximize the use of their resources. Unoccupied plant, unused machinery and idle cash reserves need to be put to work. By producing a new product, the firm might be able to mobilize its excess capacity. For example, a magazine publisher may need to use its printing press for only a few days in the month to produce a magazine; the plant could be used more effectively by producing additional titles or taking smaller jobs for paying customers.
4. *Attempts to spread the risk through product diversification*   If a range of products is too narrow it can present a real danger, particularly in a rapidly changing market. This is true in the production of fashion items such as clothes, where demand for styles may last for only a few months.
5. *Desire to gain prestige*   Producing a good-quality 'flagship' commodity may improve the image of the whole product range.

Design

A new design is one for which the details are different from earlier products intended for the same use. Customers should be able to identify features of the new product that are different from and better than those of competing products. For most major projects, a *design team* is established which is led by a design manager. The team will remain with the project throughout its development.

The purpose of *computer-aided engineering* is to use computers to solve engineering problems. Design engineers, particularly in high-technology industries, have used computers to model design mathematically and to solve design problems for many years. Computers have made it possible to create sophisticated designs with a considerable saving in time and effort.

Computer-aided design (CAD) refers to the application of a computer to solve design problems. A CAD system will consist of a computer, a workstation and a graphics board with a magnetic pen which enables the operator to touch symbols and select options so that a design can be made up. This technique can be used to draw:

- Two-dimensional engineering drawings
- Design layouts
- Three-dimensional views and models
- Electronic printed circuit board design layouts
- Architectural drawings

CAD has completely transformed the role of the designer. Developments in artificial intelligence, mathematical modelling and many other technological areas represent fundamental changes in the ways in which the needs of consumers can be satisfied.

Stages in product development

There are a number of stages that can be identified in the preparation for launching a new product (see Fig. 14.3). As new ideas and product developments go through successive stages, unsuccessful ones are eliminated.

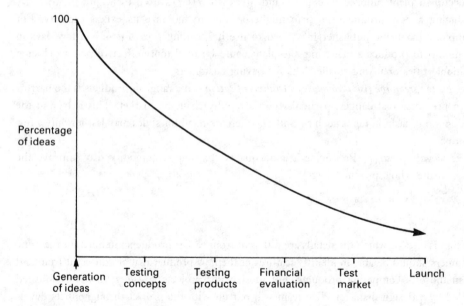

Figure 14.3 Stages in launching a new product.

Testing a concept

This will involve trying to make sure that product designs will succeed in the market-place. The following questions will need to be asked:

- What benefits does this product offer?
- How will it appeal to the consumer?
- Does the product meet the needs of the market?
- How could the idea be improved?
- How long would demand last for such a product?

Testing the product

This will involve developing a model or prototype and then trying to see if it matches consumer needs. The objective at this stage is to understand areas such as:

- Quality, performance and safety
- Ensuring that the product works efficiently
- Ensuring that the product is aesthetically sound and that its appearance is pleasing to consumers
- How to produce it economically
- Planned obsolescence (so that the product will need replacing after a given period of time)
- The ingredients of the marketing mix (see Chapter 13)

In certain cases it may be worth while for a company to apply for a *patent*, which is a legal protection giving the firm the exclusive right to produce and sell a given item.

Financial evaluation

The financial evaluation of a new product's potential is essential for assessing whether or not it will ultimately generate profits. Techniques of investment appraisal, and cost–volume–profit predictions using costing techniques, are essential at this stage. Predictions of sales, investments, costs and selling prices have to be made. A major difficulty at this stage is the reliability of data. Prediction always carries an element of risk.

Test market

A test market involves setting up a market situation that is as near to the real market as possible. Through this situation, the new product can be given a 'dry run' and the experience gained used to reduce the risks of the full launch. A test market also measures consumer behaviour in a real situation and provides valuable information which can be used to develop the marketing mix.

When a Japanese manufacturer wants to find out about changing consumer tastes and fashions, it will sometimes open a shop or restaurant where new product and service ideas can be tested and consumer responses monitored. Called 'antenna' shops because they are used both to 'broadcast' ideas from the manufacturer and to 'receive' ideas from consumers, they are concentrated in the fashionable districts of Tokyo and a few other major cities.

For Nissui, Japan's largest fishery company, the problem was that fish was becoming unfashionable among young Japanese, many of whom thought it smelly and unappealing. To counteract this trend, Nissui developed new fish products for modern tastes such as frozen tempura and fresh frozen oysters. Spicy red chilli peppers were added to liven up canned fish, and ranges of fish *hors d'oeuvre* garnished with mustard relishes were launched. To taste-test its new ranges and to explore how the Japanese could be wooed back, the company opened up a number of 'antenna' restaurants, flying in fresh fish from around the world to try and start new food fashions.

The launch

The launch is the time when the product is presented to the market and is exposed to the ultimate critical test. Ideally, the launch will create an awareness of the product, followed by an interest in it and then a desire to purchase.

Value analysis

The objective of value analysis is to satisfy the customer as economically as possible. Value analysis involves examining all of the elements of the marketing mix in order to eliminate any unnecessary or wasteful expenditure.

For example, if designers were left free to operate without cost control guidelines, they would undoubtedly produce components of a higher quality than those required for a specific task. This could be costly, would fail to satisfy the manufacturer's objectives and would not be regarded as value for money by the purchaser.

A value analysis team will be made up of experienced personnel with the specialist knowledge to be able to contribute to cost-cutting decisions. Such a team might include, for example:

- A designer—for knowledge of the product
- A member of the sales team—for knowledge of the market
- A production engineer—for knowledge of the production processes
- A member of the work-study staff—for experience of efficient working procedures
- An accountant—for knowledge of cost analysis
- A buyer—for knowledge of sources of supply

The objective of this exercise would be to ensure that the product is manufactured economically and provides the customer with real value for money.

Product life-cycle

Constant changes in the market-place will determine the success or failure of a product. In the same way that marketing managers are interested in changing tastes and fashions and their impact on a product's sales performance, designers will wish to base their plans on what they expect a product's life-span to be. Life-cycles for different products might vary considerably in length. Designers must keep in touch so that the right product can be put forward, tested and developed at precisely the right time (see Chapter 13).

The plant

In order to manufacture a product or provide a service, some sort of plant or base is necessary. Often the plant accounts for the larger proportion of a company's fixed assets and can involve a massive capital commitment. The location, size, capacity, design, layout, performance of equipment and safety of the plant are all of fundamental importance to the production manager.

The location of the organization

The location of the organization will undoubtedly have a major effect on its performance. The problems of location are long-term, and clearly, decisions taken today have implications for tomorrow. For many smaller businesses, the problem is not so much one of location but of finding a site. For example, an owner who lives in one area may not wish to set up a business away from that locality. The local area may provide the entire market for a small local business such as that of a plumber, electrician or fast food retailer. In contrast, large companies may have the world as their market, and numerous factors when taken together are capable of influencing any decision that is taken.

Whatever the type of business, the aim will be to locate in an area where the difference between benefits and costs is maximized. Important considerations will be the minimizing of unit costs and maximizing of outputs from given quantities of resources. Some of the important factors influencing the choice of location are considered below.

Transport costs

In situations where raw materials or finished goods are bulky, the transport costs are more significant. If the output of an industry is more expensive to transport than its input, it is a *bulk-increasing industry*, and is more likely to locate near to the market (see Fig. 14.4). For example, brewing tends to take place close to the market because of the expense of transporting the finished product.

On the other hand, if the raw materials are bulky and expensive to transport and the industry is a *bulk-decreasing industry*, it would be beneficial to locate near to raw materials (see Fig. 14.4). For example, historically the steel industry has located near to sources of coal, iron ore and limestone.

In practice, decisions are not as clear-cut as theory would indicate. Markets tend to be spread out and raw materials tend to come from a number of suppliers. The type of industry, the spread of the market, the availability of raw materials and their influence upon the costs of transport all have to be weighed against each other.

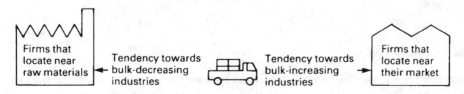

Figure 14.4 Location and product 'weight changing'.

Case Study—Location in the retailing industry

It has been said that only three things matter in retailing; location, location and location. If a shop is sited in the right position, the belief is that the business cannot help but succeed.

The question is, how do retailers choose the right site? In the past they often tended to listen to chartered surveyors, who advised on the availability and suitability of each site in terms of physical resources. This was often a hit-and-miss affair. Today, however, reatilers are using a growing mass of demographic information to select prime sites.

One market research company, Pinpoint, has recently launched a service called Site Optimizer which uses a range of market research information to find the optimal location for a store. Pinpoint uses census information, cross-referenced with data from CSO regional reports, family expenditure surveys and trade association figures. Details of regional population breakdown by age, sex, nature of household ownership and car ownership help retailers to develop sophisticated models of local economies and their spending patterns.

Grocery chains such as Tesco and J. Sainsbury have developed highly sophisticated models of local spending and demographic patterns and intensively research these wherever they locate stores. Tesco claims that its assessments of store turnover are usually accurate to within 5 per cent.

Kevin Threlfall, chairman and managing director of T & S stores, which runs 583 convenience stores in Britain, swears by a very simple method of assessing a store's viability. He counts the passers-by during a five-minute period at the busiest time of the week, invariably between 11 am and 1 pm on a Friday or Saturday: 100 passing would then equate to a turnover of about £10 000 a week and 200 would equate to about £20 000. As a rule of thumb, he feels that though not very scientific it is pretty accurate.

Questions

1. How important is location for a small retailer? In your answer comment on one retailer which you feel has a bad location and one which you feel has a good location.
2. What is demographic information, and how might this be used to influence location?
3. Comment on the approach to location of T & S stores. Why do you think their approach works?

Integration with group companies

A large organization will wish to locate a factory where its work can be integrated with the work of other units in the same group. The ease with which it can integrate will influence its location.

Labour / housing

Labour and skills are more readily available in some areas than in others. Providing labour with incentives to move can be expensive and has had little success. Variations in house costs may also inhibit the mobility of labour. Often organizations will find it easier to move work to the workers than to try to encourage workers to move to the work.

Amenities

There are five standard amenities to be considered: gas, electricity, water, waste disposal and drainage. For example, certain industries use considerable reserves of water such as for food preparation, metal plating and paper making; their use of water could exert considerable pressures on a local system. In the same way, the disposal of waste can be an expensive business. An assessment must be made of all these requirements, as underestimating the cost of amenities can be costly.

Land

Land costs will vary from area to area. In some circumstances the geology of the area needs to be considered, e.g. whether the land can support heavy buildings and plant. Climate may also affect the manufacturing process; for example, the Mars confectionery company occasionally has to shut down its Mars Bar production line in a very hot summer—it would not be wise to produce such a product in very high temperatures. Local regulations may also affect certain types of activity and may need to be checked. Moreover, it would be unwise to build a factory that used up all the land available on a given site with no room for expansion. A large employer will also require parking spaces and have investigated access to land, etc.

Regional advantages

Locating in an area that contains similar businesses, suppliers and markets may be a considerable advantage. Local research facilities and commercial expertise may be of some use.

Safety requirements

Certain types of industry may be considered to be a danger or a nuisance to the local environment, e.g. nuclear power stations, munitions factories or chemical plants. Locating such plants away from high-density population levels may be considered desirable.

Communications

Accessibility of ports, airports and motorways has become an increasingly important factor over recent years. A good infrastructure will encourage industry to move to a region.

Government influences

High levels of unemployment in certain areas of the country are likely to be a feature of the 1990s. Governments look towards balanced economic and regional growth and provide incentives for organizations to move to identified areas.

Case Study—High Tech Operations Limited

High Tech Operations Limited is a firm in the electrical components industry which is in the process of reviewing its present location at site D (see Fig. 14.5). A, B and C are three possible alternative locations for an electrical components factory.

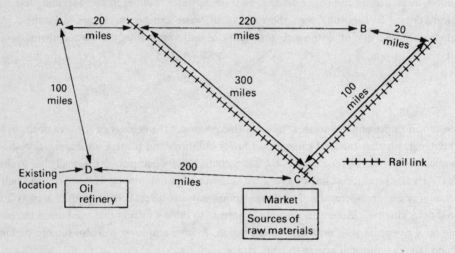

Figure 14.5 Alternative locations for an electrical components firm.

The management at High Tech understands the need to take many factors into consideration when deciding on the most appropriate location. These factors include:

- Cost of transporting finished goods to the market
- Cost of transporting raw materials and oil supplies to the plant
- Grants and other inducements available from the government
- Labour costs
- Removal costs

The firm will locate its plant at the point where all of these costs are minimized. Production costs are constant wherever the factory is located. The High Tech management needs to compare the costs involved, and then provide a recommendation. This can be done by calculating the costs of providing electrical components at each of the three alternative locations and comparing these with the costs of staying at the existing location. The preferred location will be the one with the lowest costs.

The market for components exists at location C, and locations A and B are eligible for government grants. For each 1000 electrical components:

1. Transporting oil costs £2 per mile by road and 50p per mile by rail.
2. Transporting raw materials from C costs £4 per mile by road and 70p per mile by rail.
3. Labour costs are £1300 at A, £1400 at B, £1300 at C and £1500 at D.
4. Transporting finished goods to the market at C costs £5 per mile by road and £1 per mile by rail.
5. Removal costs would be spread over 10 years and would be £1000 per 1000 units per annum.
6. Government grants reduce costs by 20 per cent.

Work out the costs by copying out and filling in the table shown in Fig. 14.6.

	A	B	C	D
	£	£	£	£
Oil transport costs				
Raw material transport costs				
Labour costs				
Finished goods transport costs				
Removal costs				
Effects of government grants				
Total cost per 1000 units				

Figure 14.6

Questions

1. Find the lowest-cost location.
2. Production is forecast at 492 000 units for the next year. How much would moving to the lowest-cost location save in the first 12 months?
3. What additional information do you think would help the firm in making a locational decision?
4. What factors are likely to alter, and thereby upset the calculations you have made?

Wherever a factory locates, there will be certain limiting factors to the choice of site. For example, a chemical plant needs to be near vast sources of water; a large engineering workshop will need to be close to its labour force; and an ice cream seller needs to be close to customers. Choosing a site means taking a number of relevant factors into consideration and attempting to weigh them in relation to each other. Sometimes a ranking technique which gives appropriate weights to relevant factors can be helpful. Under this technique, factors affecting location are assigned weights relative to their importance and each location is examined and ranked in terms of the factors;

when ranks have been multiplied by the weighting factor and the scores totalled, the desirability of locations can be compared.

An example of such a comparison is given in Fig. 14.7. The rank attached to the relative importance of each locational factor for each location appears in the top left-hand corner of each cell, and the rank multiplied by the weight appears underneath the diagonal. Location D is shown as the most desirable location using this method.

Factor	Weight	Possible location			
		A	B	C	D
Transport	7	1 / 7	2 / 14	3 / 21	4 / 28
Integration with group	2	4 / 8	3 / 6	1 / 2	2 / 4
Amenities	4	1 / 4	2 / 8	3 / 12	4 / 16
Land	2	1 / 2	3 / 6	2 / 4	4 / 8
Regional advantages	3	2 / 6	3 / 9	1 / 3	4 / 12
Communications	6	4 / 24	2 / 12	3 / 18	1 / 6
Government grants	2	1 / 2	2 / 4	3 / 6	4 / 8
Totals		53	59	66	82

Figure 14.7 Possible factory location by rank and weight. (N.B.: for each criteria the most favourable location is given a ranking of 4.)

The size of the organization

Organizations will often generate many operational benefits if they produce goods in large volumes. Whereas bridges and submarines will never be mass-produced, the vast majority of everyday consumer goods can be. The scale or size of production is usually measured by the number of units produced over a period of time. If the scale of production increases, average unit costs over most production ranges are likely to fall because the firm will benefit from *economies of scale* (the advantages gained from becoming larger). All businesses will aim for the scale of production that suits their line of work best, and this will be achieved when unit costs are at their lowest for the output produced. Beyond this point a firm will start to find that inefficiencies push average costs up, and *diseconomies of scale* set in (i.e. the disadvantages of growing too large).

If output increases faster than the rate of inputs, average unit costs will be falling and a firm is said to be benefiting from increasing returns to scale. Beyond the point at which average unit costs are at their lowest, the increase in output will be less than the increase in input, so that average unit costs are pushed up and the firm is suffering from decreasing returns to scale (see Fig. 14.8).

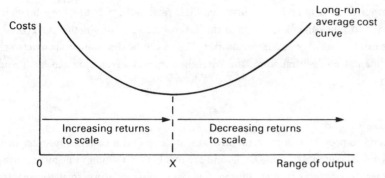

Figure 14.8 Returns to scale.

If, as the organization becomes larger, it manages to organize its production more efficiently, it is benefiting from *internal* economies of scale. If the firm is a member of an industry that is growing, benefits will be felt outside the individual organization, i.e. by all the firms in an industry, and these are known as *external* economies of scale.

Internal economies

Technical economies

Large organizations use techniques and equipment that cannot be adopted by small-scale producers. For example, a firm might have four machines each producing 1000 units per week at a unit cost of £2; as the firm becomes larger these could be replaced by one machine that can produce 5000 units per week at the lower unit cost of £1.75. If small firms tried to use such specialized machinery their costs would be excessive, and the machines might become obsolete before the end of their physical life. (The economic lifespan of a machine may be shorter than its physical life because demand for the goods produced by the machine can diminish before the machine wears out.) An essential by-product of higher-tech operations is that processes are simplified and standardized so that cost reductions can be made in other areas, e.g. labour.

Labour and managerial economies

In larger organizations highly skilled workers can be employed in jobs that fully utilize their specialized skills, whereas in a small business unit they may have to be 'Jacks of all trades'. The division of labour possible in a larger organization therefore avoids the time-wasting element caused by the constant need to switch from one type of job to another. In the same way, a larger firm can employ a number of highly specialized members on its management team, such as accountants, marketing managers and personnel managers, in the hope that the improved quality of work and of decisions made by this more qualified workforce will reduce overall unit costs.

Commercial economies

Larger organizations obtain considerable benefits in the commercial world. They can gain enormously by devoting more resources to market research and the development of new products. Raw materials can be purchased in bulk so that large discounts and extended credit periods can be negotiated. Larger firms may be able to organize their retail outlets or to have a financial stake in their suppliers, and thus can collect profit at the various stages of production. Overheads such as rent and rates can be spread over a larger output. Goods can be distributed via a network of warehouses rather than at one central store, and carefully targeted advertising can be spread over a wider market-place.

Financial economies

As larger companies tend to present a more secure investment, they find it easier to raise finance, are frequently treated more favourably by the banks and are in a better position to negotiate loans with preferential interest rates; for example, during the last recession many small businesses complained at the treatment they were receiving from the banks. A further financial advantage to large firms is their ability to raise capital by issuing new shares on the Stock Exchange.

Risk-bearing economies

As well as having a financial stake in suppliers and outlets, a larger firm may have the opportunity to diversify by investing in a variety of new operations in order to spread risks. By spending more on research and development and producing a wider product range, a business covers itself against any loss of business in certain areas.

External economies

In many industries the reduction of average unit costs and the benefits of internal economies of scale will depend upon the ability of a company to increase the length of production runs, introduce mass production and standardization techniques and increase the output capacity of the industry as a whole. This could lead to the following external economies of scale.

Concentration

A concentration of special benefits builds up as firms within an industry concentrate in a particular area. These benefits may include: a skilled workforce, the reputation of an area for high-quality work, local college courses tailored to the needs of that particular industry, and better social amenities.

Information

Larger industries often set up information services designed to benefit all producers in that industry, such as the Motor Industry Research Association.

Disintegration

Firms producing components or supplying specialist machinery might well be attracted to areas of specialized industries, along with firms that are able to help with maintenance and processes.

$\mathcal{P}$ Case Study—Sumners Shoes

Over recent years Sumners Shoes has developed through a massive expansion programme to become one of the largest shoe factories in the North West. The figures
shown in Table 14.1 have been extracted from their financial statements.

Table 14.1

	1990	1991	1992	1993
Yearly output ('000)	300	450	525	615
Number of machines	8	9	11	12
Number of employees	175	182	190	197
Number of products	14	27	38	51
Cost of manufacture per unit (£)	4.95	4.47	4.25	3.76

Questions

1. Examine the figures carefully. What economies of scale have taken place? Describe
   how they will have helped Sumners Shoes.
2. What other information can you extract from the table (e.g. output per machine,
   labour productivity)? What do these figures tell you about the growth taking place
   in the company?
3. What other benefits not shown by the table will Sumners Shoes obtain as it
   becomes larger?

Organizations can obtain the benefits of economies of scale through a gradual build-up of their
business, through acquiring assets, developing products and/or expanding sales. *Organic growth*
of this kind, however, is often a slow process. A quicker and more dynamic form of growth is
through mergers or takeovers, which involve the *integration* of a number of business units under a
single umbrella organization. In addition to enjoying the benefits of being larger, the new
organization will have a larger market share, will probably be more competitive in export markets
and, depending on the type of merger, could be in a position to control raw material supplies or
the sales of the finished product.

A *horizontal merger* takes place when two firms producing goods of a similar type at the same
stage of production join together. A *vertical merger* takes place when two firms producing goods of
a similar type at different stages of production join together; *backward vertical integration* involves
the takeover of a supplier, and *forward vertical integration* involves joining with a firm at a later
stage of production. Fig. 14.9 illustrates the way in which a car manufacturer may integrate
horizontally and vertically.

It is common practice today for organizations in industries that are only loosely connected to
join together in order to maximize risk-bearing economies. For example, a firm producing

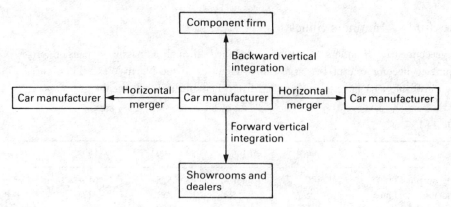

Figure 14.9 Forms of integration.

toothpaste may join together with a soap manufacturer in order to benefit from similar channels of distribution.

 Task

Study the financial pages of newspapers and professional business magazines and make a list of some of the recent mergers and acquisitions of larger companies. Find out about the main trading activities of the companies involved and comment on whether the mergers were horizontal, vertical or lateral. What motivations would you expect to lie behind each merger?

One of the dangers that companies face when they become large is that the optimum size for the business could be exceeded. Large organizations are considerably more difficult to manage, and these inefficiencies are known as *diseconomies of scale*. They include:

1. *Human relations*   Larger numbers of employees are always more difficult to organize. It can be difficult to communicate information, and instructions that need to be passed down long chains of command reduce the personal contact between decision-makers and staff. This can lead to a low level of morale, lack of motivation and ultimately industrial relations problems. Larger organizations tend to have more industrial disputes than smaller organizations.

2. *Decisions and co-ordination*   The sheer scale of production may limit the management's ability to respond to change and make good decisions. With a large hierarchy, both the quality of the information reaching the decision-maker and the quality of the instructions passed on could be affected. Difficulties arising from discussions could involve considerable paperwork and many meetings.

3. *External diseconomies*   In recent years many consumers have become more discerning about both the quality of products they purchase and the activities of certain organizations. Public displeasure can ultimately lead to some form of consumer boycott. For example, some consumers boycotted tuna fish unless it was 'dolphin-friendly'. Consumers sometimes form groups to represent their interests such as CAMRA, the CAMpaign for Real Ale.

Not only is the existence of small businesses necessary because of diseconomies of scale; they also obtain many separate and vital economic advantages. Small businesses have the flexibility to respond quickly to market opportunities. Small firms often specialize and so contribute towards divisions of labour within the wider productive process. Relations with both employers and customers tend to be good and, although specialists may not be employed on a full-time basis, consultants may be called in.

Clearly, some industries will suit a larger-scale organization better than others. A business needs to look carefully at the effects of size upon its cost structure before deciding on the most appropriate scale. There may be little scope for economies of scale because of limited demand (the small corner shop, for example, may cater for a very local demand); or the product may be highly specialized, as in the case of the market for 'customized' motor bikes.

Case Study—Better not bigger in Italy

Italian towns do not bristle with chain stores and businesses, the equivalent of W. H. Smith, Woolworths and NatWest. Chains do not exist in Italy; nor, with a few exceptions do conglomerates.

Italians seem to have a distrust of large institutions, and so family businesses remain the backbone of the Italian economy. Such businesses grow rich by doing things well, and 'better not bigger' is their preferred route to wealth.

What is surprising is that loose networks of small businesses in Italy seem to manage to produce better goods more cheaply than their European counterparts. They do not have to deal with the bureaucratic requirements found in Britain and seem to respond more quickly to consumer needs.

There are clearly lessons to be learned from the Italian experience. Rich societies will be prepared to pay more for products that are tailored for their requirements. Businesses can be small and wealthy as long as they are good at what they are doing.

Questions

1. Explain how a small business might be better able to respond to customer needs than a large business.
2. Why do you think that many Italians distrust large institutions?
3. Give an example of a small business which you think operates well. Using your example, state whether you think that a larger business could improve upon the product provided.

Design and layout of plant and equipment

The design of a plant and the positioning of equipment should enable it to function efficiently. Although designing the layout is normally a work-study problem, it needs to be carried out with specialist engineers who are concerned with factors such as the structure of the plant, power availability, maintenance requirements and so on.

Plant layout tends to follow one of a number of basic designs:

1. *Product or line layout*   Plant is laid out according to the requirements of the product in a line of production. Products 'flow' from one machine or stage to another. Control is simplified as paper work, material handling and inspection procedures are reduced (see Fig. 14.10).

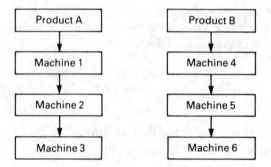

Figure 14.10 Product layout.

2. *Function or process layout*   All operations of the same type are performed in the same area; for example, spot welding may be in one location, riveting in another and stapling in another. It is rather like the provision of a typing pool or centralized print service. Although this system is flexible, considerable pre-production planning is necessary to ensure that machines are neither overloaded nor idle (see Fig. 14.11).

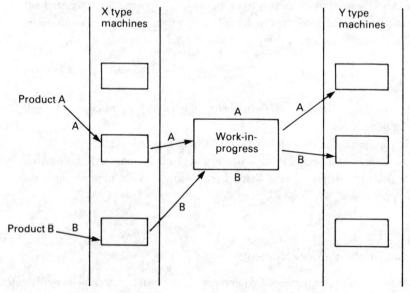

Figure 14.11 Process layout.

3. *Layout by fixed position*   Operations are performed with the material or part-finished good returning to a fixed position after each process (see Fig. 14.12).

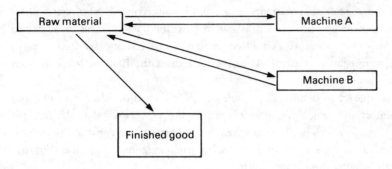

Figure 14.12 Fixed position layout.

Whatever techniques are used in setting up a layout, the aim must be to maximize flexibility and ease of co-ordination so that process time and costs will be minimized.

Case Study—The hypermarket

You have been given the responsibility of planning the entrance layout of a large hypermarket and have been asked to draw up a chart suggesting locations for the following:

- A bay of trolleys
- A tobacco kiosk
- A facility for selling newspapers and magazines
- A chemist
- A photograph developing service
- A key-cutting service
- Toilets
- A building society counter

Design a suitable arrangement to avoid congestion and justify your decisions. In what way is this typical of the types of problem encountered by operations managers? What should you aim for and what should you avoid?

Performance, maintenance and safety of the plant

The justification for expenditure on new equipment is that it contributes towards the quality of goods and services being provided. Before equipment is bought, the general effects upon the organization have to be evaluated, and standard capital appraisal techniques have to be applied to find out if such changes will be worth while.

Maintenance of plant and equipment is essential for the efficient provision of goods and services. If the size of the organization warrants it, a typical maintenance department will be able to call on the services of specialists such as electricians and joiners. The maintenance department will work to a plan to ensure that all equipment is checked and serviced in turn. The effectiveness of a maintenance department can be judged on the basis of freedom from emergencies.

It is the duty of any employer to remove all possible causes of accidents. Accidents can cause time to be lost by the unfortunate employee, other employees and supervisory staff. An accident can damage equipment, interfere with production schedules and lead to compensation payments. Employers need to anticipate circumstances likely to lead to such accidents, to try and eliminate hazards and to train staff in good production practices.

The process

In looking at the production process, we have to distinguish between goods and services. Whereas goods provide a tangible product, services are a benefit of an intangible nature received by the customer. The important distinction between the two at operations level is that a service cannot be stored, as production and consumption take place at the same time. Many services, however, do come with a physical element; for example, when you open a bank account you are kept informed of your bank balance by means of statements.

There are three main types of process: job, batch and flow production. The operation of each type of production will depend upon the stage of a company's development, the nature of the work and the conditions necessary for working.

Many organizations start with job production and, as they develop and become larger, move to batch production and finish up with flow production. It is, however, rare to find any factory where only one type of production is carried out. Certain items tend to be produced individually under job production conditions, others in batches and others in a flow. Production is *intermittent* when it involves changing operations from one product to another, and *continuous* if the product emerges as a continuous stream.

Job production

Job, or 'make complete', production is the manufacture of single individual items by either one operative or a team of operatives. Ships and bridges are built this way. It is possible for a number of identical units to be produced in parallel under job production—for example, several ships of the same type. Smaller jobs can also be seen as a form of job production, e.g. writing this book, hand-knitting a sweater, rewiring a house. Job production is unique in that the project is considered to be a single operation which requires the complete attention of the operative before he or she passes on to the next job.

The benefits of job production are:

1. The job is a unique product which exactly matches the requirements of the customer, often from as early as the design stage. It will therefore tend to be specific to a customer's order and not in anticipation of a sale. For example, someone doing a customized spray job on a motorcycle will first discuss with a customer the sort of design he or she would like. A detailed sketch will then be produced on a piece of paper. Once the sketch has been approved, the back of the sketch will be traced on to the relevant piece of the motorbike. The background work will then be sprayed on with an airbrush before the fine detail is painted on. Finally, the finished work is handed over to the customer, who will pay for a unique product.
2. As the work is concentrated on a specific unit, supervision and inspection of work are relatively simple.
3. Specifications for the job can change during the course of production, depending on the customer's inspection, to meet his or her changing needs. For example, when a printing firm is asked to produce a catalogue for a grocery chain, it is relatively simple to change the prices of some of the goods described in the catalogue.
4. Working on a single unit job, coping with a variety of tasks and being part of a small team working towards the same aim provides employees with a greater sense of purpose.

There are however a number of problems:

1. Labour, plant and machinery need to be versatile in order to adjust to a range of relatively specialized tasks associated with the same job. Trying to provide the right type of tools, equipment and labour to cope with such a range of specialized operations may be expensive.
2. Because job production is unique, costing is based on uncertain predictions of future costs and not on the experience of past events; for example, the Channel Tunnel project cost twice as much as originally forecast.
3. Unit costs tend to be high; for example, there will be fewer economies such as bulk purchasing and the division of labour.

Batch production

The term 'batch' refers to a specific group of components which go through a production process together. As one batch finishes, the next one starts.

For example, on Monday machine A produces a type 1 engine part, on Tuesday it produces a type 2 engine part, on Wednesday a type 3 engine part, and so on. All engine parts will then go forward to the final assembly of different categories of engine parts.

Batches are continually processed through each machine before moving on to the next operation. This method is sometimes referred to as 'intermittent' production, as different types of job are held as work-in-progress between the various stages of production.

The benefits of batch production are:

1. It is particularly suitable for a wide range of nearly similar goods which can use the same machinery on different settings.
2. It economizes on the range of machinery needed and reduces the need for a flexible workforce.
3. Units can respond quickly to customer orders by moving buffer stocks or work-in-progress or partly completed goods through the final production stages.
4. It makes possible economies of scale in techniques of production, bulk purchasing and areas of organization.
5. It makes costing easy and provides a better information service for management.

Problems associated with batch production include:

1. There are considerable organizational difficulties associated with batch production; for example, sequencing batches from one job to another to avoid building up excessive or idle stocks of work-in-progress is difficult in terms of routing and scheduling.
2. There is a time lag between an initial investment in material and its eventual transfer into cash upon the sale of a product.
3. The time spent by staff on problems of paperwork, stock control and effective plant utilization can be lengthy.
4. Part of a batch has to be held waiting until the rest is completed before moving on to another stage.

Flow production

Batch production is described as 'intermittent' production and is characterized by irregularity. If the rest period in batch production disappeared, it would then become flow production. Flow production is therefore a continuous process of parts passing on from one stage to another until completion. Units are worked on in each operation and then passed straight on to the next work stage without waiting for the batch to be completed. To make sure that the production line can work smoothly, each operation must be of equal length and there should be no movements or leakages from the line, e.g. hold-ups to work-in-progress.

For flow production to be successful, there needs to be a continuity of demand. If demand is varied this will lead to a constant overstocking of finished goods (or periodic shortages, if the flow is kept at a low level). Apart from minor differences, all flow products need to be standardized as flow lines cannot deal with variations in the product.

Achieving a smooth flow of production requires considerable pre-production planning to ensure that raw materials are purchased and delivered on time, that sufficient labour is employed, that inspection procedures fit in with the process and that all operations take the required time.

For example, we will assume that a production level of 800 units per hour is required and that there are three stages in the process, requiring the use of machine A for stage 1, which can process 200 units per hour, machine B for stage 2, which can process 100 units per hour, and machine C for stage 3, which can process 400 units per hour. How can a balanced flow be established? (See Fig. 14.13.)

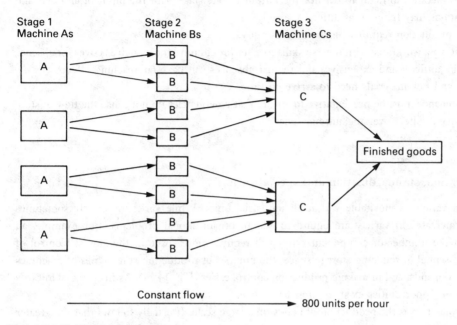

Figure 14.13 Flows in production.

 Task

Carefully consider the traffic situation within your local town or city. Try to identify roads or traffic areas that are processed by:

- Batch
- Flow

1. What factors influence the ways in which traffic is processed?
2. How could situations be improved?

The benefits of flow production are:

1. Labour costs will tend to be reduced as comprehensive planning and often investment will generate economies in both the type and the numbers of those employed.
2. Deviations in the line can be quickly identified.
3. As there is no rest between operations, work-in progress levels can be kept low.
4. The need for storage space is minimal as there is no waiting period between processes.
5. The physical handling of items is reduced.
6. Investments in raw materials are more quickly converted into sales.
7. As material and line requirements are easy to assess, weaknesses are highlighted and control is more effective.

There are, however, a number of problems:

1. It is sometimes difficult to balance the output of one stage with the input of another, and operations may function at different speeds.
2. Flow production requires constant work-study.
3. Providing a workforce with diverse skills to cater for circumstances such as cover for absence may be difficult and expensive, and regular absences can have far-reaching effects.
4. Parts and raw materials need to arrive on time.
5. Maintenance must be preventative to ensure that emergencies do not cause the flow to stop.
6. If demand falters overstocking may occur.

Simplification, standardization and specialization

Production variety is inevitable within all industrial units. While variety is clearly sometimes desirable, increases in variety are bound to add to organizational problems. For example, an increase in the number of component types will require more space in the stores. Control of variety is essential in reducing storage space, the number of production runs, types of machines and production aids, and in making production control easier (Fig. 14.14). As firms move towards specialization, opportunities exist for *mass production*.

Mass production is the production of goods on a large scale. It usually follows that the greater the volume of mass production, the greater the benefits of economies of scale as the firm moves towards its lowest unit cost size. It is often assumed that mass production will affect quality. However this is rarely the case. With mass production, quality will be more uniform and will depend not on the scale of production but on the skill of the managers.

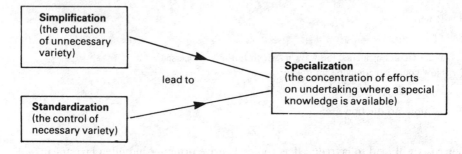

Figure 14.14 Simplification, standardization and specialization.

$\mathcal{P}$ Case Study—The birth of mass production

A new era began when in 1913 Henry Ford opened up a moving final assembly plant at his car factory in Michigan. This development represented the birth of mass production with the Model T Ford.

Henry Ford's ambition was to manufacture the simplest car possible in large numbers at low cost. His aim was to create mass consumption by making cars available for everybody; to achieve this he had to create mass production. As a result of both this and other developments, Ford guided the evolution of car manufacture from the primitive methods of the early 1900s towards some of the advanced techniques we see today.

In the early days Ford workers built cars in the same way as everybody else. They started with the chassis. Helpers and stock runners brought parts to mechanics who assembled the car while it was left standing in one place. Later cars were assembled on stands which could be moved from one team of workers to another. This speeded up production a little, but cars were still largely hand-made.

The production of interchangeable parts in quantity was introduced by Eli Whitney in 1798 when the US government gave him a rush order for 10 000 muskets. Instead of making these weapons by hand, Whitney built machines that duplicated parts so accurately that assembling them into muskets was comparatively simple.

A second antecedent of mass production was the development of conveyors, an invention of Oliver Evans in 1738, who used them in his automatic grain mill. This technique was developed further in the 1860s when Chicago meatpackers hung hog carcasses from an overhead rail. The carcasses were carried past a series of workers who each performed a single operation on the carcass.

The principle of dividing work to multiply output was given a boost by Elihu Root, one of the great production geniuses. While working for Samuel Colt, Root proceeded to accelerate the production of six-shooters by further dividing steps in manufacture and inventing machines to perform each step. Another great innovator whose methods led towards mass production was Frederick Winslow Taylor, a contemporary of Ford, who was the original efficiency expert.

Mass production as we know it today was the result of Henry Ford's combining into a single manufacturing process the principles of Whitney, Evans, Root and Taylor and then refining them. For example, he made extensive use of interchangeable parts and experimented with different types of conveyors in order to gain maximum efficiency. By breaking each manufacturing operation into various parts, he multiplied the production of products often by a factor of four.

Questions

1. What is mass production?
2. Comment on the methods Henry Ford used to introduce mass production.
3. Name (a) two advantages and (b) two disadvantages of mass production.

CADCAM and CIM

Over recent years, considerable developments in technology have taken place in production industries. In addition to computer-aided design, developments have taken place in machine tools, many of which are now controlled numerically (numerical control—NC) or controlled numerically by computer (computer numerical control—CNC). Other developments have taken place in robotics. CADCAM (computer-aided design/computer-aided manufacturing) exists where data from the CAD system is used to drive machines and has therefore become involved in manufacturing processes.

A more recent development in this process is called computer-integrated manufacture (CIM). This process goes further, as not only is the product designed on a CAD system, but it also orders materials, drives CNC machine tools and has its own control system which provides data for purchasing, accounts, sales and other functions.

The production planning and control department

All organizations will make plans that are designed to fulfil their corporate function. These plans will differ according to (a) the levels of operation and (b) the time period.

Much of production planning and control will be concerned with the company's plans for the future and will need to be carefully co-ordinated with marketing policy, for example in areas such as product life-cycles.

In the near future, however, production planning and control will look at immediate concerns such as:

- How do we meet that order?
- How close is the job to completion?
- Can it be completed on time?
- Do we need to use more labour?

In order to try to cope with these problems, the department will have to organize itself in such a way as to gain the most from its materials, labour and plant. The production controller has one of the most difficult jobs in any organization. He or she needs to understand fully the organization of production processes and costing and administrative procedures and will need to use complex mathematical techniques to solve problems.

The programme

Programming is essentially concerned with timetabling the vast resources used by the production department. Much of its success will depend on the abilities of the production planning and control department, whose staff will set dates and timetables for the delivery of finished products and will allocate production services accordingly. Delivery timetables will generate further timetables in areas such as purchasing, stock control and quality control.

Purchasing

Procuring materials is a key management function for any type of business. The importance of its role can be appreciated when one takes into account that an average manufacturing company spends about half of its income on supplies of raw materials and services.

The purchasing department will aim to provide the company with a steady flow of materials and services while at the same time ensuring a continuity of supplies. It will aim to obtain the best value for money and will try to provide the best service for a low cost. The use of value analysis often makes it possible for considerable savings to be made, though a particular danger is that quality could be sacrificed to cost considerations. A successful purchasing department will keep its costs down, produce a fast stock turnover, reduce obsolescence, ensure a continuity of supplies and reduce lead times (the interval between the realization of a need and its ultimate fulfilment upon delivery). For example, *just-in-time* (JIT) is a system that relates purchasing decisions and stock levels to current production needs. It involves working with the lowest possible stock levels, but at the same time making sure that materials are available when required, that they are of good quality and that they are fit for the purpose intended.

Expert systems have recently been developed for the purchasing function. These systems can:

- Analyse a problem (e.g. economic ordering levels)
- Explain a process (e.g. documentation)
- Make a choice (e.g. from a selection of suppliers)

Stock control

In an ideal world, in which businesses know demand well in advance and suppliers always meet delivery dates, there would be little need for stocks. In practice, demands vary and suppliers are often late, so stocks act as a protection against unpredictable events.

Organizations hold stocks in a variety of forms:

- Raw materials
- Work-in-progress
- Finished goods
- Consumables
- Plant and machinery spares

The aim of any stock control system is to provide stocks that cater for uncertainties but are at minimum levels, thereby ensuring that costs are kept low while, at the same time, not affecting the service to customers.

Clearly, balancing stocks at the right levels is of fundamental importance to the business. The keeping of insufficient or excessive stocks can have harmful effects. High stocks will represent money lying idle when it could be put to better use, whereas low stocks could result in the business not being able to take on and meet orders. Table 14.2 illustrates the disadvantages of having the 'wrong' stock levels.

Table 14.2

Problems of low stocks	Problems of high stocks
1. It may be difficult to satisfy consumer demands.	1. There is an increased risk of a stock item becoming obsolete.
2. It can lead to a loss of business.	
3. It can lead to a loss of goodwill.	2. The risk of stock losses is increased.
4. Ordering needs to be frequent and handling costs are higher.	3. The costs of storage are high
	4. Stocks can tie up a company's working capital..

Buffer stocks can be built up as a preventative measure against stocks running out owing to unexpected variations in demand. A minimum level will be set below which it will be hoped that stocks will not fall, although this may depend upon the lead time between placing an order and its receipt.

Figure 14.15 illustrates an ideal situation in which stocks never fall below the set minimum level or go above the set maximum level. Stocks are replenished just at the point at which the minimum stock level is about to be breached. (It is worth noting that in the example, should the replacement stock not arrive on time, the firm will at least be tided over by the buffer stock.) In reality, delivery times, re-order quantities and rates of usage will vary, and either a continuous or periodic review system will monitor and control the levels.

At regular intervals stock is counted and accurately recorded so that trading results can be calculated. The physical counting of stock can be time-consuming, and it is inevitable that inaccuracies will creep in. After stock is counted it is checked against records so that discrepancies can be investigated.

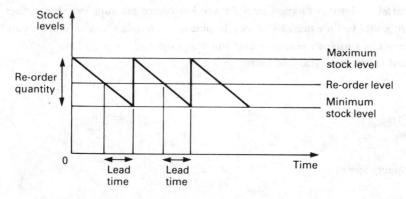

Figure 14.15 Managing stock levels.

Case Study—Computers in distribution

We have seen an enormous number of changes take place in distribution networks in recent years. The value of consumer goods distributed to the market has increased, retailing and distribution organizations have grown in average size, and there has been a net decline in the number of wholesale and retail outlets. New technology has facilitated these changes by making the process more efficient and enabling better methods of selling to take place. The computer can deal with thousands of details in a systematic manner. With broad product ranges and continually changing lines, the distributor needs to be continually updated with information such as:

- What stock is moving
- What stock is not moving
- Different brands
- Past sales
- Present sales

Complex information systems make it possible for management to be given the quality of information they need so that they have the flexibility to become involved with broader aspects of the business organization.

Questions

1. What is a distribution network?
2. How has new technology helped changes to take place in distribution?
3. Why does information technology have particular importance for the area of stocks?
4. In what ways are the benefits of information technology carried through to the consumer?

Quality

Those of us who enjoy listening to music would undoubtedly prefer to listen to the best possible system, although, unfortunately, few of us can afford to do so. In the same way, often when we purchase a good we are aware that better models of the item exist, but we are prepared to forfeit quality in the interest of saving money. Clearly, quality, reliability and cost should be seen as interrelated and often competing threads of production and consumption decisions.

Quality relates to the individual characteristics of each product or service that enable it to satisfy customers. The basic objective of any control system is to satisfy the customer as cheaply as possible with a product that can be delivered on time. Although quality control was seen in the past as a form of inspection, today it is seen as a system that tries to co-ordinate groups in an organization to improve quality at a cost-effective level (see Fig. 14.16). In doing so, they will look at:

- *Design quality*: the degree to which features within a design satisfy customers
- *Product manufacture quality*: the success of a manufacturing process in matching design specifications

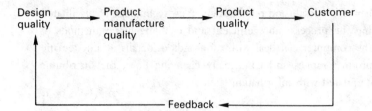

Figure 14.16 Ensuring quality control.

- *Product quality*: the degree to which the finished good or service satisfies the wishes of customers

There are five essential stages in the quality process:

- Setting the quality required by the customer
- Planning to achieve the required quality, e.g. by selection of the right materials, costs of prevention such as maintenance, shop-floor quality control and the training of operators
- Monitoring the manufacturing process
- Correcting any problems such as scrap
- Providing long-term planning

The essential requirement of any system is feedback, so that any sources of faults can be corrected.

Over recent years, many organizations have adopted a much broader approach to quality under the guise of *quality assurance*. With this approach, deliveries are expected to be of an appropriate quality and the operations of the organization providing the good or service are designed in such a way as to *assure* that that quality is achieved. The idea is that this approach makes sure an organization gets the quality right first time and thus avoids problems arising from failure.

BS 5750 was developed by the British Standards Institution to provide a framework within which organizations can be certified as having comprehensive quality management.

Quality circles, i.e. groups of workers at the workplace, are set up to identify problems and try to present solutions to quality issues. Another modern idea is the *zero-defects approach*, which aims to get workers to develop a commitment to flawless working. All such approaches are designed to eliminate problems and thereby ensure that quality is achieved.

Some organizations interpret quality more widely and talk about *total quality management* or the *total product*. Quality is considered not only in the finished product but also in other areas of the organization—so that quality becomes everybody's business, from the most junior member of staff to the most senior member of the management team. In this way an organization develops a framework enabling quality to be achieved at all levels, thus creating a genuine competitive advantage over rivals.

ρ Case Study—Quality control at Black & Decker

Study the information in Fig. 14.17 which is produced by Black & Decker for suppliers of Black & Decker equipment.

Preventative Quality Control

If the supply of poor quality is to be prevented then the procedures previously referred to must be enhanced by a joint Black & Decker/Supplier programme which:

- Involves suppliers at the earliest possible stage in new product design. Black & Decker is committed to listening constructively to supplier comments and expects suppliers to take this first step to avoid future quality problems.

- Will use all existing techniques and develop new ones to ensure that any new design of component when produced will consistently meet the requirements as specified — quality, supply, price.

- Requires the suppliers to submit samples of a new part only after a representative number of components have been measured (where appropriate using three dimensional equipment) and a process capability study has been completed.

- Requires the supplier, once in production, to use techniques to provide parts with a continuously improving level of uniformity. If 100% automatic process control is not feasible then Statistical Process Control will be the most appropriate technique and it is expected that all suppliers will introduce SPC as quickly as possible. Black & Decker is committed to the provision of all possible assistance.

Business will cease with all suppliers who do not comply with the above requirements after a reasonable period.

Figure 14.17 Information on quality control at Black & Decker.

Questions

1. Explain what is meant by 'preventative quality control'.
2. Why does Black & Decker involve suppliers in new product design?
3. Why does Black & Decker indicate that 'business will cease with all suppliers who do not comply with the above requirements'? How will (a) Black & Decker, (b) the suppliers and (c) the customer benefit from this policy?
4. To what extent do you feel that quality control is an issue that companies wish to air in public?

The people

The success of the production process depends upon people. Just as with other resources, the abilities of any labour force will vary and will depend on such elements as training, background and experience. Management will always be looking to obtain the most from employees, yet at the same time will want to nurture employees as a valuable resource. As the bulk of this resource will be employed in the production process, senior production staff need to be involved with policy decisions involving employees who fall within their responsibility. Not only work-study techniques are important, but also personnel administration concerning areas such as employment, industrial relations, staff welfare and so on.

Organization and methods (*O&M*) (quite commonly called *work-study*) has developed as a managerial science to help managers use their labour forces more effectively. Its primary concern is to analyse efficiency in order to maximize the use of resources. By looking at ways in which activities are carried out by human and material resources, O&M tries to ensure that the techniques used create the maximum possible benefits for the organization. Its objectives are:

- To reduce costs by establishing the most cost-effective ways of doing a job
- To standardize such methods
- To establish a time pattern
- To install such methods as standard working practices

Work-study, therefore, entails a study not only of methods, but also of measurement in order to achieve higher productivity.

Method-study involves examining both existing and proposed methods of undertaking a job, in order to determine how to do the job more easily and therefore increase output. The steps are shown in Fig. 14.18.

Work measurement, or *time study*, is the establishment of techniques to time activities so that they can be carried out with a defined level of performance—e.g. to improve worker motivation,

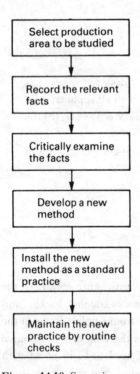

Figure 14.18 Stages in a method study.

create incentives and improve future performance. The steps are shown in Fig. 14.19. After a method study and work measurement process have been carried out, management must decide what changes, if any, will need to be made.

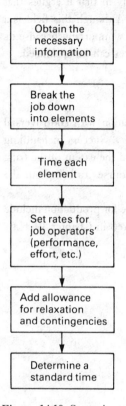

Figure 14.19 Stages in a time study/work measurement.

One feature of work study is the understanding of *ergonomics*. Ergonomics is the study of behaviour in the working environment. It looks at the relationship of workers to machines and tries to understand how these relationships can affect performance. For example, with regard to the working environment it will be concerned with issues such as:

- Is it too hot/cold?
- Are noise levels too high?
- How will lighting arrangements affect operations?

In the relationship of operator to machine, it will look at issues such as:

- Are all machine performance indicators visible to the operator?
- Is the operator likely to be given too much information to handle effectively?
- Are the controls within easy reach?

- Are seats provided?
- Are seats of the right dimensions?

In some ways ergonomics works in the opposite direction to work-study in that it argues that workplaces should be designed around the capabilities of the operator. Although this field is a complex one because it involves the analysis of human behaviour, it is very important, because its purpose is to produce a better working environment so that performances can be optimized.

Human relations

Work-study can make its practitioners unpopular because of its association with controversial areas such as bonus payments, incentives, redeployment and redundancy. Success in handling such an exercise will clearly depend upon the abilities of management and the extent of the trust between managers and workers. Some organizations run appreciation courses to bring out the benefits of work-study.

Other areas of human relations policy that have fundamental importance for production include conditions at work, safety, education and training. These areas are covered in Chapter 19.

Questions

Short-answer questions

1. In what ways are primary, secondary and tertiary production:
    (a)   different?
    (b)   similar?
2. List the three aims of a production strategy.
3. Name the five Ps of production.
4. List two appraisal techniques used for the financial evaluation of new products.
5. Explain the importance of value analysis.
6. Name two factors that limit the mobility of labour. (*Source*: AEB)
7. Distinguish between 'product orientation' and 'market orientation'. (*Source*: AEB)
8. Distinguish between vertical and horizontal integration. (*Source*: AEB)
9. Explain the difference between internal and external economies of scale.
10. Distinguish between organic growth and integration.
11. Explain what is meant by a process layout.
12   Describe three differences between (a) job production, (b) batch production and (c) flow production.
13. Why do simplification and standardization lead to specialization?
14. What is meant by the term 'mass production'?
15. What is meant by CADCAM?
16. Name three day-to-day problems faced by a production controller.
17. Give four reasons why a manufacturing company might choose to hold stocks of raw materials. (*Source*: AEB)

18. Distinguish between method-study and work measurement.
19. Give one advantage and one disadvantage to a manufacturing firm for the introduction of an incentive bonus scheme. (*Source*: AEB)
20. What is quality assurance?

Essays

1. (a) Why are changes in the structure of the population of interest to producers?
   (b) In what ways will these changes be viewed by:
       (i) builders of old people's residences?
       (ii) manufacturers of school uniforms?
   (c) Distinguish between the production system that might be used in producing (i) white shirts and (ii) school ties. (*Source*: Cambridge)
2. Discuss how systems of wage payments may sometimes conflict with quality standards. (*Source*: Cambridge)
3. (a) Do entrepreneurs always aim to minimize average costs when deciding on a location for a new factory?
   (b) Identify other factors that might influence the decision and explain difficulties that are likely to arise in reaching a decision. (*Source*: Cambridge)
4. (a) Differentiate between work measurement and method-study.
   (b) What do you consider to be the main problems likely to be caused by the introduction of a work-study unit to a manufacturing firm?
   (c) Discuss the usefulness of data collected by the work-study team and suggest to whom it should be made available. (*Source*: Cambridge)
5. To what extent is the availability of such facilities as good restaurants, schools and golf courses a more important locational factor for modern hi-tech industries than any of the conventional factors? (*Source*: AEB)
6. How far do the marketing and production functions have to compromise their objectives in order to accommodate each other (*Source*: AEB)
7. It has been asserted that management is the process of getting things done through people. How can managers improve the productivity of their manpower without additional expenditure on capital equipment? (*Source*: Oxford)
8. 'Fitting the person to the job' or 'fitting the job to the person' are two of the major approaches employed by the ergonomist. What are the main concerns of the ergonomist in ensuring that a working environment is conducive to efficient manufacturing? (*Source*: Oxford)
9. Discuss the considerations that influence a firm in deciding between growth by internal or exernal expansion. Present a reasoned case for the criteria you feel the government should use in deciding whether or not some merger is against the public interest. (*Source*: Oxford)

10. The nature of any company is influenced by:
    (a) the nature of the product.
    (b) the manufacturing process.

(c)   the market forces in its field.

What criteria is a manufacturer likely to take account of in reconciling the different priorities arising from each of these areas? (*Source*: Oxford)

Data response questions

1   Micro Tech PLC

Micro Tech PLC is a progressive and very profitable UK engineering company producing high-technology equipment for the aerospace industry. Its biggest customer is the military, which takes over 80 per cent, by value, of Micro Tech's products.

An important factor in the firm's success is its ability to modify quickly its standard products to meet a customer's special needs. It can do this by virtue of a very competent design department, well equipped with up-to-date computer-aided design (CAD) facilities.

The company employs over 500 skilled and well-trained personnel in the manufacturing processes in which it is engaged. Labour turnover is very active and there are plenty of alternative employment opportunities for Micro Tech's employees. Replacement and recruitment are a headache to the company, and the performance of the personnel department is beginning to assume a position of key importance in the company's operations. The company is facing growing competition from a number of American firms and there is evidence of government support for these companies. At the same time, there has been a change of UK government, and the new chancellor is clearly concerned to make savings and cut back on government expenditure. This is bound to affect the economic environment in which Micro Tech is operating.

Increased overseas competition and the new UK government's expected austerity measures were the main subjects of Micro Tech's last board meeting. The board decided that the company must diversify its range of products and extend its market opportunities. Such a policy would involve the company in a significant re-equipment programme, and there is considerable doubt concerning the company's capacity to finance such an investment programme from within its own resources.

1. As Micro Tech's personnel manager, how would you set about tackling the company's labour turnover and recruitment problems?
2. Identify the characteristics of the CAD which make the facilities so important for the particular needs of Micro Tech.
3. What are the main mechanisms available to the UK government to shape the environment within which companies such as Micro Tech operate?
4. What financial alternatives are available to the board which might facilitate a capital investment programme and allow Micro Tech to diversify its range of products? On what basis might Micro Tech choose among these alternatives? Make your assumptions clear. (*Source*: Oxford)

2   Assembly-line operation

You are to design a simple assembly line in a group of four to produce the model shown in Fig. 14.20.

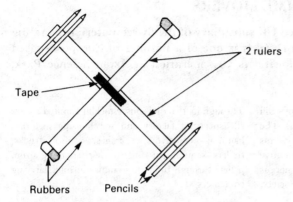

Figure 14.20 Product design layout.

1. Carefully consider a workplace layout for the operation.
2. Have a dummy production run lasting five minutes.
3. Describe how you could improve the location of equipment.
4. Compete in a 10-minute production run with another group and discuss your results.
5. Comment on areas such as quality, method study, work measurement and ergonomics.

3   Cost, quality and reliability

Compare two items with which you are familiar which attempt to serve the same function for the user or customer. Show for each how cost, quality and reliability are related. Suggested items are:

- A small car versus a luxury car
- A stereo record system versus a compact disc player
- A biro versus a high-quality pen

4   Stocklin Limited

Read the article, 'Prime Movers', on page 434 and answer the questions that follow.

1. What is meant by the term 'a wholly owned subsidiary'?
2. Consider three reasons why Walter Stocklin AG decided to locate its UK operation at Aston Science Park.
3. Why is it important to the success of Stocklin Limited that its equipment 'conforms to European and UK standards' (line 31)?

4. Explain two advantages and two disadvantages to 'companies such as Nationwide Building Society . . .' (lines 5 and 6) of centralizing and automating their document stores. (*Source* AEB)

PRIME MOVERS

Stocklin Limited is the wholly owned UK subsidiary of the Swiss materials handling specialist company, Walter Stocklin AG. It is one of a number of European-based organizations that has chosen to locate its UK operation at Aston Science Park, Birmingham.

Two years ago, under the direction of Bill Strickland, Stocklin Limited was formed. The company has installed materials handling systems across a wide range of manufacturing, distributive and service industries including numerous companies such as Nationwide Building Society, Walkers Crisps, and Proctor and Gamble.

Stocklin Limited works in close collaboration with another Swiss company which also has its UK headquarters at Aston Science Park. In fact, Bill Strickland reports that the decision to start-up from Aston was largely influenced by the presence of Sprecher + Schuh Automation Limited—specialists in complementary computer control and software for warehouse applications.

'There were also a number of other factors that we considered important to Stocklin', explains Bill Strickland. 'We appreciate the range of facilities offered by Aston—and the big city environment with its tradition of engineering means that we can draw on a specialist engineering labour pool.'

Through its two divisions, Stocklin Limited covers all aspects of factory and warehousing materials handling—conveyors, cranes, lift trucks, trailers—equipment for moving anything from pallets through fluids to granules in bulk carrying containers.

The company specialises in designing complete warehousing systems. However, all Stocklin equipment will interface with that of other suppliers—and conforms to European and UK standards.

Increasingly Stocklin Limited is being commissioned to install systems in banks and building societies, to store property deeds, stocks and share certificates and wills for clients. 'Many such institutions are centralizing their deed stores—which can amount to some 6 million items under one roof. Such facilities need to be fully automated—and that means total accuracy. Without that assurance you could end up with complete chaos!' Bill Strickland points out.

(*Source*; adapted from *Aston Science Park 'Venture'*, Vol. 2, no. 6, Autumn 1990)

Suggested reading

Harrison, M., *Advanced Manufacturing Technology Management*. Pitman, 1990.

Muhlemann, A., Oakland, J. and Lockyer, K., *Production and Operations Management*, 6th edn. Pitman, 1992.

Scarbrough, H. and Corbett, J. M., *Technology and Organisation*. Stanley Thornes, 1992.

15

An introduction to the accounting process

In Chapter 1 we saw that all organizations will have a range of aims and objectives. Although this range might be broad, the successful achievement of such objectives will frequently depend upon one overriding financial objective: its success in terms of profits—'the bottom line'. Entrepreneurs require compensation for taking business risks. They need a return on their investments to justify the time and effort of running, or at least contributing to the running of an enterprise.

For example, contrast the following two extracts which appeared in the press during the summer of 1993:

Bosch, the German electrical and car components group, is to shed a further 11 000 jobs this year. The privately owned group saw pre-tax profits in 1992 slide by 29 per cent. Bosch have engaged in a series of cost cuts over a 3 to 5 years period. They aim to make savings with job cuts and increased efficiency. They believe that by reducing costs they can save existing plants and jobs.

Smith New Court doubled its profits last year. Michael Marks, the group chief executive, said that profits had been earned across a range of deals. Proceeds would be used as 'working capital' to be handed out to existing businesses where and when they are needed.

Both extracts show that, as a result of changes in profitability, important decisions about the future of each business have been made.

Setting up an accounting system

In order to measure profitability and performance, an organization will have to set up an accounting system. Accounting acts as an information system by processing business data so that interested parties can be provided with the means to understand how well or badly a business is performing.

For example, the advert shown in Fig. 15.1 was placed by South Western Electricity PLC in the national press. It is a summary of the company's financial performance for the year ended March 1993 in the form of financial highlights. This sort of presentation enables a wide number of interested parties to appreciate the peformance of the business. This information was recorded, collated, analysed and presented by the accounts department at South Western Electricity.

SOUTH WESTERN ELECTRICITY plc

ANOTHER YEAR OF PROGRESS

Results for the year ended 31 March 1993

	1993	1992	%
Turnover	£892.0m	£847.1m	+5.3%
Profit before tax	£101.1m	£83.0m	+21.8%
Earnings per share	63.1p	50.6p	+24.7%
Total dividend per share	20.0p	17.4p	+14.9%

"These results show the benefit of concentrating our resources on our electricity business: we have improved our profit margins and further strengthened our balance sheet. We continue to achieve both enhanced customer service and improved operating cost efficiency as the necessary response to our changing environment.

Progress has also been made in the careful and selective expansion of the Group's operating base through the development of businesses related to our existing strengths. I am particularly pleased by our successful entry into the gas supply market and by the progress made by our investments in electricity generation projects."

John Seed
Chief Executive

Copies of the Annual Report will be posted to shareholders on 9th July. Others who would like a copy should contact: Investor Relations, South Western Electricity plc, 800 Park Avenue, Aztec West, Almondsbury, Bristol BS12 4SE. Tel: 0454 201101

Figure 15.1 Providing financial information. (*Source*: SWEB)

Business data are the inputs for an accounting system. The output is financial information (see Fig. 15.2). Financial information can then be fed to those who require such information for record-keeping and decision-making purposes.

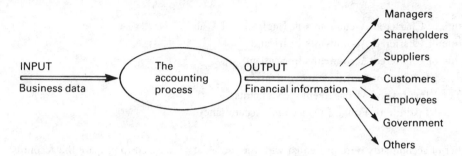

Figure 15.2 The importance of the accounting process.

For example, *managers* need information in order to run the business efficiently and constantly improve their decision-making capabilities. *Shareholders* need to assess the performances of managers and to know how much profit or income they can take from the business. *Suppliers* need to know about the company's ability to pay its debts, and *customers* wish to ensure that their supplies are secure. Any *provider of finance* for the business (bank/debenture holder, etc.) will need to know about the company's ability to make repayments. The *Department of Inland Revenue* needs information about profitability in order to make an accurate tax assessment. *Employees* have a right to know how well a company is performing and how secure their futures are. *Financial advisers and brokers* need to know about company performances so that they can advise clients accurately.

The process of accounting can be divided into two broad areas:

1. *Financial accounting* This is concerned primarily with the accuracy of the record-keeping process. A financial accountant will ensure that an organization's accounts bear a 'true and fair' view of a business's activities and that they comply with the provisions of the Companies Acts. Financial accountants provide statements called *final accounts* which are handed to shareholders who will then know how well the directors or 'stewards' have performed on their behalf. From final accounts, ratios and other figures can be extracted which can provide fairly precise indicators of an organization's performance. Such knowledge will help to influence the decisions that have to be made.
2. *Management accounting* Though financial accounting is important, it deals with the past and views the organization as a whole. Management accounting is concerned with providing information for managers so that they can plan, control and make decisions about future activities. It involves guiding an organization in a particular direction so that it can achieve its objectives. Business operations can be closely monitored to ensure that processes, products, departments and operations are managed efficiently.

Accounting standards

The accounting profession is represented by six major accounting bodies. For somebody to call him- or herself a qualified accountant, he or she must have passed examinations to have become a full member of one of these professional bodies:

- Institute of Chartered Accountants in England and Wales
- Institute of Chartered Accountants in Ireland
- Institute of Chartered Accountants in Scotland
- Chartered Institute of Certified Accountants
- Chartered Institute of Management Accountants
- Chartered Institute of Public Finance and Accountancy

If a number of accountants were presented with the same data and asked to prepare the accounts of an organization, they might well come up with different figures or arrive at different conclusions. This is because estimates have to be made about future events, and this involves an element of opinion or guesswork. For example, in calculating depreciation—how an asset loses its value over time—estimates have to be made for the useful life of each asset, and different accountants will have different estimates of an asset's lifetime.

In the 1960s the accounting profession came under pressure to impose standard procedures upon its members to avoid inconsistencies between the accounts of companies and to improve the quality and usefulness of financial statements.

An example of varying practice occurred in 1967 when AEI was taken over by GEC. AEI had forecast a profit for that year of £10 million, but when the figures were published they showed a loss of £4.5 million. At the time it was argued that such diversity of practice brought the accountancy profession into disrepute. Financial accountants try to ensure that a company's accounts bear a 'true and fair' view of business activities. The question is, can they do this? In recent years many questionable practices have come to light in accounting statements, and often frauds have failed to be discovered by the audit. Although auditors probe the inner depths of a company's affairs, they frequently deal just with totals, each of which reflect millions of financial transactions. Detecting a fraud can be almost impossible.

The 1970s saw the introduction of a number of accounting standards. In 1970 the first Statement of Standard Accounting Practice (SSAP) was introduced with the aim of limiting the ability of accountants to use diverse accounting procedures. SSAPs were created by the Accounting Standards Committee, a sub-committee of the Consultative Committee of Accounting Bodies which links the six major accounting bodies. Members of the professional bodies are expected to observe accounting standards while undertaking responsibilities in connection with financial statements.

For example, the second SSAP refers to the four fundamental concepts that should underlie financial accounts (see Fig. 15.3).

1. *The going concern concept* This assumes that the business will persist with its business activities in the foreseeable future; therefore the accountant will not assume that there is

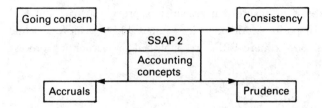

Figure 15.3 The fundamental concepts of accounting practice.

a desire to cut back on business operations or an intention to liquidate. The significance of this concept is that goods should be valued not at their break-up value but at their net book value, based on the estimation of the cost of the depreciation provision.

2. *The accruals or matching concept*   This recognizes that revenues and costs are incurred when their liability is taken on and not as money is received or paid. Thus, at the end of a trading period all transactions relating to that period will appear in the accounts whether payments have been made or not. Revenues and profits earned in that period are 'matched' with the costs and expenses associated with these business activities.

3. *The consistency concept*   This concept indicates that the accounting treatment of similar items should be consistently applied with each accounting period and from one period to the next. For example, later in this chapter we refer to the various ways in which stocks can be valued using methods such as LIFO, FIFO and cumulative weighted average. This concept indicates that, once a business has selected its stock valuation method, it should stick to it.

4. *The concept of prudence or conservatism*   This maintains that businesses should not lay claim to profits unless they are sure that they have been earned. Accountants will therefore tend to underestimate profits and overstate losses; as a result, profits are included in accounts only if it is certain that they have been made.

In the 1980s criticisms were voiced about the Accounting Standards Committee; for example:

- A general failure to respond to emerging issues
- A lack of timeliness in setting standards
- Doubts over the independence of the standard-setters
- Concern over the flexibility of their pronouncements

On 1 August 1990 the Accounting Standards Board took over from the Accounting Standards Committee. Unlike the ASC, which was a joint committee of the six major accounting bodies, the new Board is independent of the professional institutes and can set accounting standards in its own right. All accounting standards (SSAPs) now come under the authority of the ASB and are subject to independent scrutiny and change. In September 1991 the ASB set out its first *Financial Reporting Standard (FRS)*, FRS 1, on cash flow statements. Since then several other FRSs have been published. The creation of the Accounting Standards Board is a progressive step designed to produce a better world of accounting.

The purpose of SSAPs and FRSs is to ensure that accountants provide a 'true and fair' presentation of a company's financial position. Although it is impossible to achieve absolute uniformity in the accounting profession, as more FRSs are published the accounting process will gain greater credibility.

The recording process and its influence on final accounts

The recording of business transactions provides accounting information. Records of transactions are taken by bookkeepers who initially record transactions in day books, the journal or a cash book before transferring them to a series of ledgers (see Fig. 15.4).

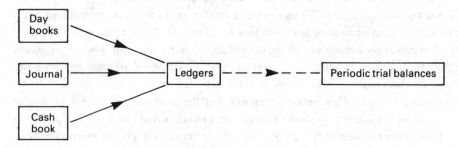

Figure 15.4 Stages in the recording process.

Auditors will require information from these books in order to draw up final accounts at regular intervals. These final accounts can be used to assess performance. Information is taken from the ledger and compiled in the form of a list of balances called the *trial balance*. The use of information technology in business has meant that today integrated software packages contain the books of first entry, and these are linked to a system that updates all records whenever a transaction takes place.

In this chapter we are concerned with the implications of recorded entries for the final accounts. The double-entry system is the backbone of accounting, providing information for ledgers and then the final accounts.

The double-entry system assumes that all entries into an accounting system reflect a process of exchange. It takes into consideration the fact that every transaction involves two parts and both of these are recorded in the books of account. For example, if we buy equipment for cash, we lose cash but gain equipment. We must therefore record both the loss in cash and the gain in equipment. In the ledger two records are made for each transaction and, as we will see, the dual element in this process is carried through to the final accounts.

Final accounts are made up of four types of account:

- A balance sheet
- A trading account
- A profit and loss account
- An appropriation account

Balance sheet

A balance sheet is a statement of what a firm owns and owes on a particular date. We will first look at how a balance sheet appears in a horizontal format and then show how business transactions have a dual effect upon it. A horizontal balance sheet has two sides, an assets side and a liabilities side. In Fig. 15.5 we have set out a fictional balance sheet for A. Sole Trader.

(Assets side)			(Liabilities side)		
FIXED ASSETS			Capital as at 1/1/94		23 000
Freehold premises		35 000	*add* Profit for the year		7 000
Fixtures & fittings		4 000			30 000
Motor vehicles		1 500	*less* Drawings		4 100
		40 500	Capital as at 31/12/94		25 900
CURRENT ASSETS			LONG-TERM LIABILITIES		
Stock of goods	4000		Loan		20 000
Debtors	1500				
Prepayments	500		CURRENT LIABILITIES		
Bank	1000		Creditors	1500	
Cash	400	7 400	Accrued costs	500	2 000
		£47 900			£47 900

Figure 15.5 The balance sheet of A. Sole Trader as at 31/12/94.

The balance sheet is a clear statement of liabilities, assets and the capital of a business at a particular moment in time (normally, the end of an accounting period). As you can see, a horizontal balance sheet is divided into two halves with assets shown on one side and capital and liabilities on the other. The accounting process ensures that the total value of one half will equal the total value of the other half. The following equation always applies to balance sheets:

$$\text{CAPITAL} + \text{LIABILITIES} = \text{ASSETS}$$

We can now look at each part of the balance sheet in more detail.

In business accounts we always treat the business owner (or owners, in the case of partnerships and companies) as a separate legal entity to the business itself. The capital provided by the owner/s is therefore deemed to be owed by the business to the owners. The balance sheet therefore keeps an updated record of the amount owed by the business to the owner/s.

During a year's trading, the owner's capital will be increased by inflows of *profits* and decreased by outflows of *drawings* (money/assets taken out of the business for personal use). Having taken these into consideration, a new capital figure will exist at the end of the year.

Other liabilities are classified as current liabilities or long-term liabilities, depending on their duration.

Current liabilities

Current liabilities are debts of the business which need to be paid in a fairly short period of time (normally within one year). Creditors are normally suppliers of goods on trade credit for which the business has been invoiced but has not yet provided payment. *Accrued charges* are bills, often for expenses, that are outstanding at the end of an accounting period. They must be included in the accounts as they are a debt, often for a service that has been provided, e.g. gas or electricity. Other short-term liabilities could include a bank overdraft, short-term loans and any taxes owed to the Department of Inland Revenue.

Long-term liabilities

A long-term liability is sometimes called a 'deferred liability' as it is not due for payment until some time in the future; by convention, this means longer than one year in a set of accounts. Examples would include long-term loans, e.g. bank loans, mortgages (loans secured against a freehold property) and debentures. Debentures are sometimes issued by companies at fixed rates of interest which have to be repaid on a specific date in the future. Those who hold debentures are therefore lenders of money.

Assets

Assets are items that are *owned by* a business and money and other items that are *owed to* the business. The asset side of the balance sheet will normally be set out in what is called an inverse order of liquidity. This means that items that are difficult to convert to cash quickly (i.e. are *illiquid*) appear at the top of the list. By examining the order in which they are listed, you can gauge the ease with which successive assets can be converted to cash until you come to the most liquid asset of all, cash.

A useful way of classifying assets is to use two classes:

1. Fixed assets
   (a) Tangible fixed assets
   (b) Intangible fixed assets
   (c) Investments (long-term)
2. Current assets

Fixed assets

The simple distinction is that all fixed assets must have a lifespan of more than one year. (Therefore all current assets will have a lifespan of less than one year.) A *tangible fixed asset* is one that can be touched and seen, e.g. machinery, buildings, vehicles. An *intangible fixed asset* is one that does not have a physical existence and therefore cannot be touched. For example, the 'goodwill' of a business is an intangible fixed asset. Over a period of time a business builds up a client base and a reputation; this is a real asset to the business and can be valued when the business transfers ownership. (The *goodwill* of a business will normally appear in the books only if the business is taken over or transferred to new owners.)

Investments are also counted as fixed assets. A company might invest in the shares of another company or purchase *debentures*. These are investments that are usually made with a view to retaining the assets for more than 12 months.

Fixed assets might be held for a number of years, but they will eventually wear out. The accounts of a business try to recognize this gradual erosion of value, and *depreciation* is written off against profits so that the value of fixed assets should be at their net book value after depreciation has been accounted for.

Current assets

Current assets are sometimes called 'circulating assets' because the form they take is constantly changing. A business will hold stocks of finished goods in readiness to satisfy the demands of the market. When a credit transaction takes place stocks will be reduced and the company will incur debtors. Debtors will have bought goods on credit and therefore will owe the company money. After a reasonable credit period, payment will be expected. After this inflow, payments will be made on further stocks. Thus, the firm has a cash cycle (see Fig. 15.6).

Current assets might include short-term investments; although these may be in the form of stocks and shares in other businesses, it would be the company's intention to sell them in the near future. They could also include prepayments; these are sums paid for goods or services that have not yet been received, e.g. business rates paid in advance.

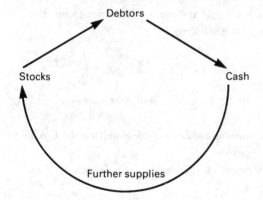

Figure 15.6 The cash cycle.

N.B.: Stocks are normally valued at cost based upon the particular system used (LIFO, FIFO, etc.). However, if the net realizable value (NRV) of stocks is less than their cost, stocks will be valued at NRV rather than at cost (see page 463).

Case Study—CWS plans huge asset disposal

The Co-operative Wholesale Society (CWS), Europe's biggest co-op, is planning to sell up to £100 million of assets in the next 18 months in a crackdown on its borrowing, which rose to £361 million over 1992/3. CWS has been forced to dip into reserves to maintain its annual dividend and also had to rescue the Greater Nottingham Society which had got into trouble. Trading profits at CWS were stable at £50.5 million in the year. However, it shouldered about £100 million of extra debt when it absorbed the Nottingham Society and the interest bill grew by £9.1 million to £34.5 million.

David Skinner, the new chief executive, said that, with debt at 75 per cent of shareholder's funds, the position was now 'uncomfortable'. He plans to cut the debt by selling from £50 million to £100 million of assets and by lifting trading profits.

CWS, with annual sales of £3.3 billion, has widespread food production, distribution and retailing operations. It is also the country's biggest funeral director and owns the Co-operative Insurance Society. Among the CWS assets likely to be sold are shirt factories, farms, printing works, packaging works, safety footwear factories and a substantial property portfolio. CWS's attempt to sell its Scottish dairies business to the Scottish Milk Marketing Board was blocked on monopolies grounds. But so far it has raised cash by selling a southern dairy business, a laundry, its vehicle leasing arm and other assets. CWS loans are syndicated to co-operative banks across Europe.

CWS is carefully watching the American group Costco's plans to set up large UK warehouse stores offering discounted merchandise to shoppers paying annual subscriptions, and has not ruled out following suit. Despite the many difficulties facing the group, David Skinner feels that CWS is still in good shape.

Questions

1. Explain how CWS's balance sheet will be affected when assets are sold and borrowings are reduced.
2. How would the saving of the Greater Nottingham Society have affected the CWS balance sheet?
3. Why is the position of debt at 75 per cent of shareholders' funds described as 'uncomfortable'?
4. Describe why a smaller, leaner CWS might be a better investment.

We can now try to understand the implications of the double-entry system for the balance sheet. Assume that A. Box sets up a business on 1 January by putting £25 000 into a business bank account. The business then owes A. Box the amount he had invested, but, at the same time, it will have received £25 000. Both the asset side and the liability side of the balance sheet will have an entry:

Balance sheet of A. Box as at 1 January

	£		£
Bank	25 000	Capital	25 000
	£25 000		£25 000

On 2 January the business purchases a motor vehicle for £5000 by cheque. This transaction involves a transfer from one asset to another:

Balance sheet of A. Box as at 2 January

	£		£
Motor vehicles	5 000	Capital	25 000
Bank	20 000		
	£25 000		£25 000

On 3 January the business purchases stocks for resale for £15 000 on credit. Therefore liabilities increase as creditors are created and assets increase as stocks are now owned:

Balance sheet of A. Box as at 3 January

	£		£
Motor vehicles	5 000	Capital	25 000
Stocks	15 000	Creditors	15 000
Bank	20 000		
	£40 000		£40 000

On 4 January stocks valued at £10 000 are sold for £13 000 on credit. Clearly there is a profit element here. Stocks will decrease by the value sold (not by the sale price), i.e. by £10 000, but debtors will now have been created and so liabilities will be increased by £13 000. Assets have, therefore, increased by £3000 in total. The profit element of £3000 made on the sale of the stock items will be added to capital and as a result liabilities will also rise:

Balance sheet of A. Box as at 4 January

	£		£
Motor vehicles	5 000	Capital	25 000
Stocks	5 000	*add* profits	3 000
Debtors	13 000	Creditors	15 000
Bank	20 000		
	£43 000		£43 000

On 5 January A. Box's business pays the creditors off and the debtors all pay up. Both liabilities and assets will decrease when the creditors are paid. One asset disappears and another increases when the debtors pay up:

Balance sheet of A. Box as at 5 January

	£		£
Motor vehicles	5 000	Capital	28 000
Stocks	5 000		
Bank $\left(\begin{array}{c} 20\ 000 \\ 15\ 000\ (-) \\ 13\ 000\ (+) \end{array} \right) = 18\ 000$			
	£28 000		£28 000

On 6 January A. Box's business pays rent, rates and electricity totalling £1000 by cheque. As we will see in the profit and loss account, business expenses are deducted from the gross profit to leave the final, or net, profit. In this example, expenses will be treated as a negative item and carried forward from the profit and loss account by reducing capital by £1000 and bank by £1000:

Balance sheet of A. Box as at 6 January

	£		£
Motor vehicles	5 000	Capital	27 000
Stocks	5 000		
Bank	17 000		
	£27 000		£27 000

We could continue this process and record many more transactions. It is important for you to appreciate that all business transactions affect the balance sheet in some way or other. Because of the double-entry system, transactions will influence both sides of a horizontal balance sheet.

   Although it is common practice to use horizontal balance sheets for demonstration purposes, the majority of businesses today present their balance sheets in vertical form. Vertical balance sheets are often thought to be easier to interpret; for example, working capital or net current assets can be identified at a glance (see Fig. 15.7).

Profitability statement

The trading account, profit and loss account and appropriation account are, more often than not, linked together in a profitability statement, which compares a company's income with outgoings over an accounting period. If a balance sheet is a snapshot, these accounts are like a video which has recorded how the business has performed over a period of time.

	£	£	£
FIXED ASSETS AT NET BOOK VALUE			
Freehold premises			45 000
Machinery			6 000
Fixtures and fittings			3 000
Motor vehicles			5 000
			59 000
CURRENT ASSETS			
Stocks		14 000	
Debtors		3 000	
Prepayments		500	
Cash		100	
		17 600	
LESS CURRENT LIABILITIES			
Bank overdraft	1 300		
Creditors	1 200		
Accrued costs	100		
Taxation payable	1 000	3 600	
NET CURRENT ASSETS (WORKING CAP)			14 000
			73 000
LESS LONG-TERM LIABILITIES			
Debentures			18 000
			55 000
Financed by:			
SHARE CAPITAL			
Ordinary shares			20 000
Preference shares			20 000
			40 000
Reserves			15 000
			55 000

Trading account

The trading account shows the gross profit made over an accounting period. *Gross profit* is the difference between the value of sales and the cost of purchases or the production costs of manufactured goods:

SALES – COST OF SALES = GROSS PROFIT

Cost of sales is found by applying the following:

OPENING STOCKS + COST OF PURCHASES – CLOSING STOCKS = COST OF SALES

(In a manufacturing company the *cost of purchases* is the cost of production.) The *opening stock* is effectively a purchase as it will be sold in the current period, but the *closing stock* must be deducted from purchases as it will be sold next year.

Profit and loss account

The profit and loss account shows the net profit of the business:

GROSS PROFIT + INCOME FROM SOURCES OTHER THAN SALES − BUSINESS EXPENSES = NET PROFIT

Income from sources other than sales might include any rents received, commissions received, discounts received, profits on the sale of assets, etc. A full list of *business expenses* would be too numerous to mention; however, some of the more important ones would be salaries of staff and directors, travelling costs, marketing costs, discounts to customers, electricity, rates and bad debts. (Debts are written off as 'bad' if a debtor has failed to make a payment, interest payments, etc.)

Appropriation account

The appropriation account is the section of the profit and loss account detailing how profit is shared between the owners. From this section the Inland Revenue will require its statutory levy in the form of corporation tax on a company's profits. Also in this section, companies set aside funds for reserves. Reserves are set up either as capital reserves from the balance sheet or as revenue reserves from the appropriation account. Revenue reserves represent tied-up, retained profits which are unlikely to be distributed. Retained profits generally increase from year to year as most companies do not distribute all of their profits as dividends. A full appropriation account would include:

NET PROFIT − CORPORATION TAX

− DIVIDENDS TO SHAREHOLDERS

− ANY TRANSFER TO A RESERVE

+ BALANCE OF PROFIT FROM THE PREVIOUS YEAR

The final balance from the appropriation account is then transferred to the balance sheet as the retained profit carried forward. Remember the four stages:

- Tax
- Dividends
- Reserves
- Last year's balance

In Fig. 15.8, which shows a complete profit and loss account, we can see how these four stages are combined.

	£'000	£'000	£'000
Sales			2300
less Cost of sales			
Opening stock		150	
Purchases		1700	
		1850	
less Closing stock		200	
			1650
Gross profit			650
add Profit on disposal of plant			50
			700
less Overheads			
Wages and salaries		250	
Sundry expenses		105	
Light and heat		5	
Depreciation—buildings	12		
—plant	8	20	
Debenture interest		4	
Bad debts		2	
Advertising and distribution		4	
			390
Net profit			310
less Corporation tax			108
Profit after taxation			202
less Dividends—preference shares		18	
—ordinary shares		20	38
			164
less Transfer to general reserve			64
			100
add Retained profit brought forward			40
Retained profit carried forward			140

Figure 15.8 Makemore Limited: Profit and loss account for the year ending 31/12/94.

Cash flow statements

The profit and loss account provides information that matches sales and costs, and a balance sheet is a static statement showing a business's financial position at a point in time. Neither of these shows how a business has used its funds and cash.

Funds flow statements (1975–92)

In 1975 the tenth Statement of Standard Accounting Practice (SSAP) was issued, requiring a business with an annual turnover of £25 000 or more to provide a statement to fill this gap as part of its final accounts. This was called a *funds flow statement*.

Funds flow statements were prepared through a process of comparison. If a company's balance sheet figures for two successive years were listed in two adjacent columns, then the changes during the year could be seen clearly. Differences between the two years could then be listed and grouped together either as sources or as applications of funds. The example below shows how an increase in stocks was financed:

B Nice Balance sheets

	£ 31/12/90	£ 31/12/91	£ Comparison
Premises	3 000	3 000	0
Stocks	8 000	10 000	+2000
Bank	3 000	3 000	0
	£14 000	£16 000	
Capital	14 000	14 000	0
Creditors		2 000	+2000
	£14 000	£16 000	

Clearly, this increase in stocks was financed through the credit provided by suppliers, and this could be shown in the form of a statement:

B Nice Funds flow statement from 31/12/90 to 31/12/91

	£
Sources of funds—creditors	2000
Applications of funds—increasing stocks	2000

Another way of presenting this sort of statement was to have a section that analysed *working capital* changes. The reason for this was to enable managers to exert a firmer grip on these changes. The change in working capital between the two balance sheets would then equal the difference between the source and application of funds (see Fig. 15.9).

Cash flow statements (1992–)

As we saw earlier in this chapter, when the Accounting Standards Board took over from the Accounting Standards Committee, this heralded a new era in standard-setting. In September 1991 the ASB set out the first Financial Reporting Standard (FRS1), which has replaced SSAP 10 for all accounting periods ending on or after 23 March 1992.

The problem with funds flow statements were that:

1. Companies drew up their statements in different ways.
2. They were difficult to use to compare one business with another.

	£ 31/12/90	£ 31/12/91	£ Comparison
Fixed assets	450	550	+100
Long-term investments	500	450	−50
Current assets – Current liabilities	150	200	+50
	£1100	£1200	
Capital	360	400	+40
Profits	300	500	+200
Loans	440	300	−140
	£1100	£1200	

Figure 15.9 (a) T. Chest Co., Limited—balance sheets.

Sources of funds		
Capital	40	
Profits	200	
Sale of investments	50	290
Applications of funds		
Fixed assets	100	
Loan repayment	140	240
Increase in working capital		50

Figure 15.9 (b) T. Chest Co. Limited—funds flow statement from 31/12/90 to 31/12/91.

3. They looked at funds or profit rather than at cash.
4. The meaning of funds was not very clear.

Cash flow statements, which FRS1 has required must replace funds flow statements, provide more information on the connection between liquidity and profitability. They also actually record the cash flow generated by an organization over its financial year. The statements, therefore, assist in emphasizing to investors the risks they are undertaking. For example, the aims of cash flow statements are to assist users to:

1. Assess how well an organization can generate positive cash flows in the future.
2. Evaluate whether an organization can meet future commitments such as dividends, interest payments, etc.
3. Identify the differences between profits and cash flows.
4. Assess the effects on finances of any major financial decisions made during an accounting period.

The cash flow statement should list the inflows and outflows of cash and cash equivalents for the period under the following standard headings:

- Operating activities
- Returns on investments and servicing of finance

- Taxation
- Investing activities
- Financing

For example, the cash flow statement in Fig. 15.10 for Workmore Ltd. focuses on something with which all business managers can identify—the need for a steady cash flow. The bottom line in the statement indicates the change in cash and cash equivalents. The cash flow statement explains this movement by placing all cash flows into five categories. (Note that in this statement we have adopted the more usual convention of putting outflows of cash in parentheses, rather than using a minus sign.)

The idea is that a user can see at a glance the extent to which, for example, cash from operations has paid for various activities over the accounting period. In the example:

1. There is an inflow from operating activities.
2. Investments also provide an inflow.
3. Taxation has been paid.
4. There is an outflow from investing activities.
5. Financing has provided an inflow.
6. Over the period there has been an increase in cash and cash equivalents.

	£'000	£'000
Net cash inflow from operating activities		6900
Returns on investments and servicing of finance		
Interest received	3000	
Interest paid	(50)	
Dividends paid	(2500)	
Net cash inflow from returns on investments and servicing of finance		450
Taxation		
Corporation tax paid		(3000)
Investing activities		
Purchase of intangible fixed assets	(70)	
Purchase of tangible fixed assets	(700)	
Receipts from sale of fixed assets	500	
Net cash outflow from investing activities		(270)
Net cash inflow before financing		4080
Issue of ordinary capital	200	
Repurchase of debenture loan	(150)	
Expenses paid with share issue	(2)	
Net cash inflow from financing		48
Increase in cash and cash equivalents		4128

Figure 15.10 Workmore Ltd—Cash flow statement for the year ended 31 March 1994.

The advantage of cash flow accounting is that it directs attention towards cash flow. Many external parties such as creditors are more interested in a company's ability to pay than in profitability. Cash flow statements help managers with decision-making and can better satisfy the needs of all users.

Other new accounting standards

FRS 2 has superseded SSAP 14, *Group accounts*. The objective of this FRS has been to indicate the way in which parent undertakings provide financial information about the activities of their subsidiary groups by preparing consolidated financial statements. Such statements are intended to present financial information about a parent undertaking and its subsidiary as a single economic entry, showing the resources of that entity and the results achieved with those resources.

FRS 3, *Reporting financial performance*, has introduced changes to the format of the profit and loss account and supersedes SSAP 6. Changes introduced by this FRS include a layered format for the profit and loss account to highlight a number of components of financial performance. These include:

- Results of continuing operations
- Results of discontinued operations
- Profits or losses on the sale or termination of an operation
- Extraordinary items

The interpretation of accounts

Under the Companies Acts, all limited liability companies are required to file copies of their accounts with their annual return to the Registrar of Companies. The Acts specify the information that should be contained in the balance sheet and profit and loss accounts and indicate that these accounts must provide a true and fair view of the affairs of the company for the period concerned. Additional information required with the accounts includes:

- Details of subsidiaries
- Group accounts if there is a group of companies
- A directors' report which has to contain certain information
- An auditor's report

Shareholders and debenture holders receive copies of these accounts and notice of the company's general meetings.

A company's accounts are a useful source of information about the conditions of that business. Final accounts can be carefully analysed, often by using ratios, to make comparisons between one year and another.

Earlier in this chapter we mentioned a number of people who need to receive accounting information. It is important that these groups fully understand the feedback they gain from a company's final accounts. The accounts can be analysed to look at:

- Profitability
- Liquidity
- Asset usage
- Capital structure

We are going to examine each of these areas and consider the usefulness of the information that can be extracted from them.

Profitability

The profitability of a company could be assessed on the basis of the profits the company is making on sales and on the general profitability of the investment made in the company.

Gross profit to sales

$$\frac{\text{Gross profit}}{\text{Sales}} \times 100$$

This will indicate the percentage gross profit made on sales. It is sometimes called *profit percentage*. Changes in this percentage might reflect increases in the cost of raw materials, stock losses, changes in pricing policy, etc.

Net profit to sales

$$\frac{\text{Net profit}}{\text{Sales}} \times 100$$

This indicates final profit as a percentage of sales. If the gross profit percentage is consistent, any changes in net profit percentage could indicate an increase in overheads as a proportion of sales and a need to make economies.

Return on capital employed (ROCE)

$$\frac{\text{Net profit}}{\text{Capital employed}} \times 100$$

where capital employed = net assets before deduction of long-term debt.

Capital employed is usually taken at the beginning of the year, as this is the capital that generated the profit during the year to follow. The best way to think about the percentage return is to compare it with other investments. For example, if you invest £100 with a building society and receive £5 a year in interest (before tax), then you can see that you are getting a return on your capital of 5 per cent. This is a good measure of how effective your investment is. ROCE is therefore a quick and useful way of calculating the effectiveness of an investment in the business: it relates profitability to other investments.

Return on equity capital

$$\frac{\text{Profit after tax and preference dividend}}{\text{Ordinary share capital and reserves}}$$

This is an alternative way of calculating ROCE and relates profit after taxes have been paid and preference dividends distributed to the ordinary shareholder's equity.

Earnings per share (EPS)

$$\frac{\text{Profit after payment of tax and preference dividends}}{\text{Number of ordinary shares}}$$

This indicates the amount that each share is earning. It provides the ordinary shareholder with information about the earning capacity of each share. EPS can be contrasted with dividends per share. EPS shows total earnings, but some of these earnings will be utilized as retained profit and will not be distributed as dividends to shareholders.

Price/earnings (P/E) ratio

$$\frac{\text{Market price per share}}{\text{Earnings per share (EPS)}}$$

This is a comparison of the current market value of a share with the earnings per share. These ratios vary from company to company and from industry to industry. Companies with a higher status tend to have higher market prices and higher P/E ratios. Retail stores tend to have ratio averages of about 10, whereas property companies tend to have averages in the region of 35. From this it is possible to estimate how long it would take the earnings from an investment to pay back that investment.

Dividend yield

$$\frac{\text{Dividend per share}}{\text{Market price per share}} \times 100$$

This relates the shareholder's dividends to the market price of the shares. If the percentage yield is poor, the investor might consider alternative uses for the investment. This could depend on interest rates, the future prospects of the company and changes in the prices of shares, among other factors.

Case Study—Unigate PLC

Examine the 1991/2 accounts for Unigate PLC shown in Table 15.1

Table 15.1 Unigate PLC Accounts 1992

	1992	1991
Turnover	£1894m	£2142m
Operating profit	£91.3m	£87.3m
Profit after taxation	£63.7m	£51.6m
Earnings per share	27.3p	22.3p
Dividends per share	15.3p	15.3p

Questions

1. What is another word for 'turnover'?
2. Comment on the changes in profitability and turnover over the two years. Use figures to support your analysis.
3. Explain the difference between earnings per share and dividends per share.

Liquidity

This refers to the ability of a firm to convert its short-term or current assets into cash to cover payments as and when they arise. Stocks are the least liquid of the current assets because they must first be sold (probably on credit) and the customer provided with a credit period. As a result, there is a time lapse before stocks are converted to cash. It is the responsibility of the company to ensure that it can meet debts likely to arise in the near future. Current liabilities are items that have to be paid for in the short period.

Current or working capital ratio

This is the ratio of current assets to current liabilities.

Clearly, some current assets are more liquid than others, and the time factor involved in transferring them to cash is something an experienced manager should be able to estimate. A prudent ratio is sometimes said to be 2:1. This might not necessarily be the case if stocks form the bulk of the value of the current assets. Companies have to be aware that bank overdrafts are repayable on demand and that figures extracted from a balance sheet might reflect the position of the current assets and liabilities at that time but not over the whole year. In practice, most businesses operate with a ratio slightly lower than 2:1.

Acid-test ratio / quick ratio / liquidity ratio

This is the ratio of current assets *less* stocks to current liabilities.

This ratio assesses how well a business can meet its current liabilities without stocks. It ignores stocks because they are the least liquid current asset. A prudent ratio is 1:1, although some businesses operate with a lower quick ratio of 0.5:1.

Debt collection period

This is calculated by the formula

$$\frac{\text{Debtors}}{\text{Average daily sales}}$$

where average daily sales are calculated by dividing sales by 365.

The normally accepted level of debt period is about 60 days. It may be possible to improve liquidity by reducing the debt collection period. Customers who are late in paying their debts are receiving free finance for their businesses. This ratio indicates the average number of days of credit received by customers before they provide a payment.

Period of credit taken from suppliers

This is calculated by the formula

$$\frac{\text{Creditors}}{\text{Average daily purchases}}$$

Just as liquidity can be analysed by looking at the debt collection period, it could also be beneficial to look at the average period of credit taken from suppliers.

Example

The final accounts of Cavity Contractors at the end of its first two years' trading are illustrated in Fig. 15.11. The company is concerned about whether liquidity has improved during its second year.

Increases in both the company's current and quick ratios have improved the company's liquidity during the year. A deterioration has taken place in the debt collection period, as the number of days' credit allowed to customers has increased from 41 to 68. Cavity Contractors is also now taking longer to pay suppliers, and this has increased from 65 to 86 days.

	Profit and loss account	
	Year 1	Year 2
	£	£
Sales	18 500	18 900
less Cost of sales	11 200	10 100
	7 300	8 800
less Overheads	5 000	5 200
Net profit	2 300	3 600
less Dividends	300	400
	2 000	3 200
add Retained profit brought forward	—	2 000
Retained profit carried forward	2 000	5 200

	Balance sheets			
		Year 1		Year 2
	£	£	£	£
FIXED ASSETS		14 100		16 000
CURRENT ASSETS				
Stocks	2 500		3 000	
Debtors	2 100		3 500	
Bank	400		200	
	5 000		6 700	
less CURRENT LIABILITIES				
Creditors	2 000		2 400	
Net current assets		3 000		4 300
		17 100		20 300
Financed by:				
Ordinary shares		15 100		15 100
Reserves		2 000		5 200
		17 100		20 300

	Liquidity ratios	
	Year 1	Year 2
1. Current ratio	2.5	2.8
2. Quick ratio	1.25	1.5
3. Debt collection period	41 days	68 days
4. Period of credit taken from suppliers	65 days	86 days
(N.B.: Purchases taken as cost of sales figure)		

Figure 15.11 Cavity Contractors—final accounts at the end of first two years' trading.

Asset usage

Asset usage ratios make it possible to assess the efficiency of certain areas of business activity. Use of these ratios assists, for example, in the analysis of stock turnover and enables comparisons with other industries and previous periods to be made. They are also useful tools in analysing the efficiency of asset handling.

Stock turnover

This can be calculated by using the formula:

$$\frac{\text{Cost of sales}}{\text{Average stock}}$$

where

$$\text{Average stock} = \frac{\text{Opening stock} + \text{closing stock}}{2}$$

Stock turnover is the average length of time an item of stock is held in stores before it is used or sold. The adequacy of this ratio depends upon the type of industry a particular business is in; for example, a greengrocer would expect a much higher stock turnover than a furniture business. Many firms hold smaller stock levels today than in the past. They operate a 'just-in-time' system (i.e. keeping just enough stock to meet current demand) and consequently have a higher stock turnover.

Asset utilization

This is calculated by the formula

$$\frac{\text{Sales}}{\text{Fixed assets}}$$

This ratio indicates how effectively fixed assets are being used to generate sales. It is really an efficiency ratio designed to show how well managers are using fixed assets in the running of the business. The level of the ratio will depend upon the type of business concerned.

Capital structure

Companies are financed by share capital, loans and other sources. The return on these investments is in the form of dividends or interest payments. Both investors and suppliers of loan finance will wish to ensure that their incomes are maintained and that the future of their money looks secure.

Gearing

This is calculated by the formula

$$\frac{\text{Prior-charge capital (long-term loans and preference shares)}}{\text{Equity (ordinary shares plus reserves)}}$$

Gearing makes a direct comparison between the long-term capital in a business provided by ordinary shareholders and that provided in the form of long-term loans and preference shares. Using the above formula, we can say that a company is:

- Low-geared if the gearing is less than 100 per cent
- High-geared if the gearing is more than 100 per cent

If a high-geared company wishes to raise extra finance, it may find it difficult to raise a loan. Lenders like to see shareholders provide a large proportion of a company's capital. Shareholders might prefer a company to be low-geared, because if it took on further loans it would mean that the profit allocation would be reduced because of the necessity to make interest payments. The advantage of using debt capital is that interest rates are fixed, loans do not carry voting rights, interest payments attract tax relief, and the reward to debt holders is generally lower than that required by shareholders. Gearing levels vary from firm to firm and from country to country. If a company has a stable background, higher gearing is safer.

Interest cover

This is calculated by:

$$\frac{\text{Profit before interest and tax}}{\text{Interest paid in the year}}$$

This refers to the risk of gearing. If the ratio is less than 1, a company has not earned enough to cover interest charges. A ratio of 3 would provide the minimum level of safety required.

Dangers of using ratios

There are a number of dangers to using ratios. First, it is difficult to make comparisons between the accounts of two firms in the same industry; they may vary so considerably in size and structure that any such comparisons become unrealistic—for example, they may have different techniques of asset valuation. Second, ratios can be criticized for oversimplifying business activity. They can often cloud events with generalizations so that any conclusions become unrealistic. There are many positive factors within businesses that are completely ignored by an analysis of final accounts—good-quality staff, good location, etc. Another problem with accounting statements is that comparisons made with the past could easily be distorted by inflation; for the same reason, it is often unwise to use this year's accounts to predict next year's business activity.

Accounting policies

Irrespective of the limitations placed on auditors by accounting standards, they still have the flexibility to adopt certain accounting policies and it is, therefore, usual for companies to attach a note of the accounting policies they use to their financial statements. Three elements normally mentioned in these statements are policies on:

- Inflation accounting
- Stock valuation
- Depreciation

As items portrayed in final accounts might vary according to accounting policies in these three areas, it becomes evident why these statements are made.

Inflation accounting

The section entitled 'Accounting policies' which appeared in a recent Annual Report for ICI began: 'The accounts have been prepared under the historical cost convention and in accordance with the Companies Act 1985.' The term 'historical cost' indicates that ICI records assets taken into the business at entry cost and that these are then reduced in book value over each period through depreciation. Many would argue that this method:

1. bases measurements on actual costs;
2. is easy to understand by accountants and users;
3. relates to documentary evidence, e.g. invoices;
4. is the system recognized for tax assessment; etc.

However, a number of criticisms can be levelled at the historical cost valuation method. The major criticism is that this method can severely undervalue assets during periods of inflation. Over a number of years this would mean that it would be difficult to compare financial statements. In an inflationary period profits can be overstated, and they would not include adequate provision for the replacement of fixed assets at higher prices. The analysis of a company's performance would be distorted. The company would find itself paying excess dividends or making over-generous pay settlements.

The accounting profession has taken measures to overcome these problems. Various techniques have been applied in recent years to minimize these difficulties, including:

- Current purchasing power (CPP)
- Current cost accounting (CCA)

Accounting standards have been introduced and then withdrawn for both of these techniques; for example, in June 1985 SSAP 16, entitled *Current cost accounting*, was suspended because many companies did not comply to it. At the moment, neither technique has a mandatory status.

Current purchasing power

Current purchasing power was a system that translated the amounts extracted from historical accounts into inflation-adjusted units calculated by reference to price indices. (A price index is a measure of average prices; see Chapter 10.) Because this system used as its base historical cost figures, it retained many of the advantages of the historical cost method.

Under this system company assets are given values that reflect how much the original expenditure on them would be worth at current prices. However, this is clearly an unrealistic calculation because price indices cover average baskets of goods, and the price of individual items may vary widely from the average.

Current cost accounting

Current cost accounting involves making four adjustments to historical cost figures in order to counteract the distortions of inflation:

1. *Cost of sales adjustment*   The opening and closing stock are restated at the average price for the year.
2. *Depreciation adjustment*   Fixed assets are revalued in terms of the price index so that they reflect their current cost of replacement.
3. *Monetary working capital adjustment*   Average figures for current assets and current liabilities are calculated for the year in terms of a price index; for example, you should calculate the average annual figure for debtors and creditors.
4. *The gearing adjustment*   Companies gain by borrowing in times of inflation, and therefore an adjustment needs to be made to account for the benefits of borrowing.

The problems of presenting accounting information that allows for inflation are still being discovered. Inflation fell to under 3 per cent in the mid-1980s, rose almost to double figures in 1989 and has since fallen to below 2 per cent. Accounting for inflation is clearly a problem, but only in periods of high inflation.

Stock valuation

Controlling everyday stocks is nearly always a headache. A business has to balance the danger of running out of stock with that of overstocking. Business activities are continuous, but accounting statements must be drawn up on a particular date. Stocktaking therefore has to take place in such a way that:

1. the quantity of stock held on the balance sheet date is verified;
2. a monetary amount can then be allocated to each stock unit.

Stock valuation has a direct influence upon profits:

	£	£	£	£
	High valuation		Low valuation	
Sales		5000		5000
less Cost of sales				
Opening stock	2000		2000	
add purchases	4000		4000	
	6000		6000	
less Closing stock	5000		3000	
		1000		3000
		£4000		£2000

Including a higher stock valuation in the accounts has an obvious implication for the profit declared, as higher stock valuations will lead to higher profits (see table).

The prudence concept rules out the use of selling prices in stock valuation, as profits should be recognized only when they are actually made and after the goods are sold. SSAP 9 indicates that stocks should be valued either at their cost or at their net realizable value—whichever is lower. Net realizable value is the selling price of stocks *less* the costs incurred in getting them ready for sale and selling them.

Stock item	£ Cost	£ NRV	£ Lower of cost/NRV
No. 1	15	17	15
No. 2	21	18	18
	£36	£35	£33

It would be wrong to state stocks at £36 (column 1) in the balance sheet, as the cost total would be ignoring a loss on item no. 2. The prudent valuation would be £33, which values item no. 2 at the lower of cost or NRV.

A major problem of stock valuation is allocating the purchase cost. A business will continually purchase items, and newer items will often be mixed with older items in a bin. Accountants are not concerned with physically identifying the older items so that they are always used first. However, they are concerned with developing a pricing technique that allocates a cost to each component in the stores.

Three of the principal methods of stock valuation are:

- FIFO (first in, first out).
- LIFO (last in, first out).
- Cumulative weighted average cost (AvCo).

We will look at each of these methods in turn and relate them to the following transactions:

- January: balance 100 units at cost of £2.90 each
- February: received 100 units at £3.00 each
- March: issued 80 units
- April: received 70 units at £3.80 each
- May: issued 50 units

FIFO

The FIFO, or first in, first out, method of stock valuation, as the name implies, makes the assumption that stocks are issued in the order in which they were delivered, so that the stocks that have been held the longest will be issued first. This means that issues are priced at the cost of the earlier stocks while the stock remaining will be priced at a level nearer the replacement cost. FIFO provides a slightly higher valuation than some of the other methods we shall illustrate (see Fig. 15.12).

Date 1990	Receipt and price	Issue and price	Running stock valuation (£)
Jan		Balance	100 at 2.90 = 290
			100 units 290
Feb	100 at £3.00		100 at 2.90 = 290
			100 at 3.00 = 300
			200 units 590
Mar		80 at £2.90	20 at 2.90 = 58
			100 at 3.00 = 300
			120 units 358
Apr	70 at £3.80		20 at 2.90 = 58
			100 at 3.00 = 300
			70 at 3.80 = 266
			190 units 624
May		20 at £2.90	70 at 3.00 = 210
		30 at £3.00	70 at 3.80 = 266
			140 units 476

Figure 15.12 The FIFO method of stock valuation.

The final valuation using FIFO is 140 units at £476.

LIFO

The LIFO, or last in, last out, method of stock valuation assumes that recent deliveries are issued before the earlier ones. This means that stock issued is close to the replacement price while remaining stock is kept at the older and probably lower price. The tendency with this method is to undervalue stocks in relation to current market values (Fig. 15.13).

Date 1990	Receipt and price	Issue and price	Running stock valuation (£)	
Jan		Balance	100 at 2.90 = 290	
			100 units 290	
Feb	100 at £3.00		100 at 2.90 = 290	
			100 at 3.00 = 300	
			200 units 590	
Mar		80 at £3.00	100 at 2.90 = 290	
			20 at 3.00 = 60	
			120 units 350	
Apr	70 at £3.80		100 at 2.90 = 290	
			20 at 3.00 = 60	
			70 at 3.80 = 266	
			190 units 616	
May		50 at £3.80	100 at 2.90 = 290	
			20 at 3.00 = 60	
			20 at 3.80 = 60	
			140 units 426	

Figure 15.13 The LIFO method of stock valuation.

The final valuation using LIFO is 140 units at £426.

Cumulative weighted average pricing

With cumulative weighted average pricing (AvCo), every time a new consignment arrives the average cost of stock is calculated. Each unit is assumed to have been purchased at the average price of all the components (Fig. 15.14). The average unit cost of stock is a weighted average price and is calculated in the following way:

$$\frac{\text{Existing stock value} + \text{value of latest purchase}}{\text{Number of units then in stock}}$$

The final valuation using AvCo is 140 units at £456.40. (This falls between FIFO and LIFO stock valuations.)

Date	Receipts	Issues	Weighted average unit cost ($£$)	Number of stock units	Running stock valuation ($£$)
Jan		Balance	2.90	100	290.00
Feb	100 at £3.00		2.95	200	590.00
Mar		80	2.95	120	354.00
Apr	70 at £3.80		3.26	190	619.40
May		50	3.26	140	456.40

Figure 15.14 The AVCO method of stock valuation.

The recent ICI report comments on stock valuation by saying that 'Finished goods are stated at the lower of cost or net realizable value, raw materials and other stocks at the lower of cost or replacement price; the first in, first out or an average cost of valuation is used.'

Depreciation

Fixed assets are acquired in order to earn profits. Although their lives are not limited to a single accounting period, they will not last for ever. Most companies have expectations about the lifetime of their assets. They will wish to show a true asset value in the balance sheet and to charge the cost of its declining value to the profit and loss account.

SSAP 12 defines depreciation as 'the measure of the wearing out, consumption or other reduction in the useful economic life of a fixed asset, whether arising from use, time or obsolescence through technological or market changes'.

There are a number of different methods of depreciation, and of these the most common are:

- Straight-line method
- Reducing balance method
- Machine hour method
- Sum-of-the-digits method

Straight-line method

The most frequently used method is the straight-line or *equal instalment method*, which charges an equal amount of depreciation to each accounting period for the life of an asset. The instalment is calculated by:

$$\frac{\text{Cost of asset} - \text{residual value}}{\text{Expected useful life of asset}}$$

For example, a machine expected to last five years costs £20 000; at the end of that time its residual value will be £5000:

$$\text{Depreciation charge} = \frac{\pounds 20\,000 - \pounds 5000}{5 \text{ years}} = \pounds 3000$$

	Year 1 ($\pounds$)	Year 2 ($\pounds$)	Year 3 ($\pounds$)	Year 4 ($\pounds$)	Year 5 ($\pounds$)
Cost	20 000	20 000	20 000	20 000	20 000
Accumulated depreciation	3 000	6 000	9 000	12 000	15 000
Net book value	17 000	14 000	11 000	8 000	5 000

Reducing balance method

The reducing balance method calculates the depreciation charge as a fixed percentage of net book value from the previous period. This method allocates higher depreciation costs to the earlier years of an asset. It can be argued that this system is more realistic, as it caters for the increased expense of repairs and running costs as machinery becomes older.

For example, a machine is purchased by a business for $\pounds 20\,000$ and its expected useful life is three years. The business anticipates a residual value of $\pounds 4320$ and thus wishes to depreciate it at 40 per cent (see Fig. 15.15).

($\pounds$)	($\pounds$)	Accumulated depreciation
Machine at cost	20 000	
Depreciation year 1	8 000	8 000
Net book value	12 000	
Depreciation year 2	4 800	12 800
Net book value	7 200	
Depreciation year 3	2 880	15 680
Residual value	$\pounds 4\,320$	

Figure 15.15

Machine hour method

The machine hour method relates depreciation to use rather than time; therefore depreciation is calculated on the basis of the number of hours a machine has been worked. The depreciation charge per hour is calculated by:

$$\frac{\text{Cost of asset} - \text{residual value}}{\text{Estimated life of asset in machine hours}}$$

For example, a machine is purchased for $\pounds 34\,000$ with an estimated useful life of 10 000 machine hours and a residual value of $\pounds 4000$. The rate of depreciation would be:

$$\frac{34\,000 - 4\,000}{10\,000} = \pounds3 \text{ per machine hour}$$

Therefore, if the machine was used for 2000 hours in year 1, 3000 hours in year 2 and 1000 hours in year 3, depreciation would be charged in the following way:

	Depreciation charge (£)	Accumulated depreciation (£)	Cost of asset (£)	Net book value (£)
Year 1: 2000 × £3	6000	6 000	34 000	28 000
Year 2: 3000 × £3	9000	15 000	34 000	19 000
Year 3: 1000 × £3	3000	18 000	34 000	16 000

Sum-of-the-digits method

The sum-of-the-digits method is similar to the reducing balance method in that higher levels of depreciation are charged in earlier years. However, it uses digits rather than percentages as a simplified way of working out the depreciation charge. Digits are allocated in a descending order to each year of the life of an asset and a charge is worked out for each digit used. For example, a machine is purchased for £15 000 and is expected to last for three years, after which it will be sold for £3000:

Year 1	3 digits
Year 2	2 digits
Year 3	1 digit
Sum of the digits =	6

A weighted charge is then calculated as follows:

$$\frac{\text{Cost of asset} - \text{residual value}}{\text{Sum of the digits}}$$

$$\frac{15\,000 - 3000}{6} = \pounds2000 \text{ per digit}$$

Depreciation is treated as an expense, and for each period it will be charged to the profit and loss account. The accumulated depreciation is added together to form a provision for depreciation which is then deducted from the cost price of the fixed asset it represents in the balance sheet.

	Digits	Depreciation charge (£)	Accumulated depreciation (£)
Year 1	3 × 2000	6000	6 000
Year 2	2 × 2000	4000	10 000
Year 3	1 × 2000	2000	12 000

Conclusion

The emphasis in this chapter has been on providing readers with an understanding of the process of financial accounting. It should thus help readers to answer questions such as:

- What is accounting?
- Why does it exist?
- Are accounts necessary?
- What do accounting statements mean?
- How do stock levels and inflation affect accounts?

This chapter has aimed to provide readers with an understanding of the format, presentation and meaning of a set of final accounts and of the standards that relate to these areas.

Questions

Short-answer questions

1. Name three groups of people interested in financial information about a company.
2. List the differences between the respective roles of financial and managerial accountants.
3. How would an increase in interest rates affect the shareholders in a highly geared company? (*Source*: AEB)
4. Describe two concepts that underlie financial accounts.
5. Use an example to describe the process of double-entry bookkeeping.
6. State three items that might appear as current liabilities in the balance sheet of a company. (*Source*: AEB)
7. What is meant by the term 'goodwill'?
8. Name two ways in which a company might appropriate its profits. (*Source*: AEB)
9. The directors of a company recommend a dividend on their £1 ordinary shares of 8 per cent. How much would a company pay to an investor holding 100 shares if the current market price were £1.20 each? (*Source*: AEB)
10. Explain the meaning of the expression 'a highly geared company'.
11. Sales at cost divided by average stock:
    (a) What is the name of this ratio?
    (b) What information does it provide? (*Source*: AEB)

12. Name two dangers of using ratio analysis.
13. Why is a cash flow statement a useful further analysis of the position of a company?
14. Name two advantages of keeping accounts under the historical cost convention.
15. Briefly explain what is meant by current purchasing power.
16. Using a numerical example, show the influence of stock valuations on profits.
17. What is meant by 'the lower of cost or net realizable value?'
18. Explain the differences between FIFO and LIFO.
19. What is the residual value of an asset?
20. Choose one technique of depreciation and explain how it works.

Essays

1. Company financial statements are used by a variety of individuals and institutions for a variety of purposes. Specify six different types of users of financial statements and in each case describe the aspects of performance in which they would be interested.
2. (a) State three items that might appear as current liabilities in the balance sheet of a company.
   (b) Define the terms 'dividend per share' and 'earnings per share' and explain the difference between them. (*Source*: AEB)
3. To what extent would ratio analysis enable you to draw meaningful conclusions about the performance of different public companies? (*Source*: AEB)
4. State the reasons why companies prepare financial statements and accounts. Comment on their usefulness. (*Source*: AEB)
5. Explain how cash flow statements operate. Why are cash flow statements a useful further analysis of a company's position?
6. Is inflation accounting necessary? Comment on the differences between current purchasing power and current cost accounting.
7. Explain what is meant by the valuation of stocks at the lower of cost or net realizable value. How does this relate to the consistency concept?
8. 'In our opinion the financial statements give a true and fair view of the state of affairs of the Company and Group at ———————————— and of the profit and cash flows of the Group for the year then ended and have been prepared in accordance with the Companies Act 1985.' Explain what this statement means. Why do accountants make such a statement?
9. Explain why many assets are depreciated. Comment on two techniques for calculating depreciation.
10. What are accounting standards? With specific reference to one standard, explain why they are necessary.

Data response questions

1   Cumbrian Food Processors Limited

The summarized balance sheets of Cumbrian Food Processors Limited at the end of consecutive financial years were as shown in Fig. 15.16.

Summarized Balance Sheets as at 31 July

1993				1994	
£'000	£'000			£'000	£'000
		FIXED ASSETS (at written down values)			
32		Premises		35	
105		Plant and equipment		170	
31	168	Motor vehicles		75	280
		CURRENT ASSETS			
64		Stock		173	
48		Debtors		55	
48		Bank		18	
160				246	
		Less CURRENT LIABILITIES			
73		Creditors		141	
22		Proposed dividends		32	
95				173	
	65	Working capital			73
	233	Net assets employed			353
		Financed by:			
200		Ordinary share capital		200	
33	233	Reserves		53	253
		Shareholders' funds			
		Loan capital: 7% debentures			100
	233				353

Figure 15.16

Calculate for each of the two years, the following:

1. Current assets/current liabilities
2. Quick assets/current liabilities
3. Gearing ratio
4. A funds flow statement

Make brief comments on the figures you calculate and mention some possible reasons for the differences between the years.

2   Fisher's Furniture Ltd

Fisher's Furniture Ltd is a small furniture retailer whose accounts for the year ending 30 April are given in Fig. 15.17.

	£		£	
Shareholder's funds		*Fixed assets*		
Share capital	100 000	Land & Buildings		120 000
Reserves	30 000	Van	12 500	
		Depreciation	(2 500)	10 000
Long term liabilities				
Loans	60 000	*Current assets*		
		Stock		85 000
Current liabilities		Debtors		8 000
Creditors	24 000	Cash		3 500
Provision for tax	12 500			
	226 500			226 500

Figure 15.17

1. Explain what you understand by the following terms which appear in the balance sheet in Fig. 15.17:
    (a)   Shareholders' funds.
    (b)   Long-term liabilities.
2. During the year ending 30 April 1987, the following transactions took place.
    £240 000 of goods were bought.
    £300 000 of goods were sold; these were originally bought by Fisher's for £195 000.
    £220 000 was paid to suppliers.
    £7500 was paid on average each month to cover wages, the running expenses of the shop and van, and interest on the loan.
    £12 500 was paid for last year's tax.
    £2500 allowance was made for depreciation on the van.
    All profits are retained within the firm and tax is chargeable on them at the rate of 50%. Debtors have risen by £2000.
    (a)   Calculate the profit made for the year ending 30 April 1987 and the cash in hand at this date.
    (b)   Draw up a balance sheet for the year ending 30 April 1987.
3. Explain how the following assets that appear in the balance sheet have been valued and identify alternative methods that could have been used.
    (a)   The van (which was purchased on 1 May 1985 and was expected to have a five-year life).
    (b)   Stock.
4. What else is legally required (other than the balance sheet and profit and loss account) to appear in all published accounts? (*Source*: University of Cambridge Local Examinations Syndicate)

3   LIFO/FIFO

Table 15.2 shows details of the movements in the stock level of a product which is purchased for resale.

Table 15.2

Date	Purchases (units) (£)	Purchase price per unit (£)	Issues (units) (£)	Balance (units) (£)
1991				
1 June balance	—	—	—	300
8 August	200	8.00	—	500
15 September	—	—	500	—
17 September	500	8.25	—	500
1992				
5 January	—	—	100	400
8 January	—	—	200	200
16 March	200	8.75	—	400
31 May	—	—	200	200

1. Explain the meaning of the following terms:
    (a)   FIFO.
    (b)   LIFO.
2. Using the available information, calculate the value of the closing stock on 31 May 1992.
    (a)   if the method of valuation is FIFO.
    (b)   if the method of valuation is LIFO. (*Source*: adapted from AEB)

4   Time-wise Ltd

Read the information and answer the questions that follow.

Time-wise Ltd, a subsidiary of a major computer manufacturer, makes only one product—an electronic, pocket-sized, personal planner. This product is distinctive and is enjoying rapid sales growth with little competition at present. However, competition is expected to increase during the next year. The parent company sets one overriding objective for its subsidiary: a net profit-to-sales ratio of 10 per cent or better. The next stage in the growth of Time-wise is under consideration. The statement shown in Fig. 15.18 has been prepared by Time-wise Ltd for the year 1 June 1991 to 31 May 1992.

For the year 1 June 1992 to 31 May 1993, a 20 per cent increase in sales volume is planned. The following decisions have been taken by the Board:

(a) Because competitors are entering the market, the sales price will be lowered to £19 per unit. Production overheads will remain unchanged.

	£	£
Sales revenue (80 000 units @ £20 each)		1 600 000
Direct costs	800 000	
Production overheads	300 000	1 100 000
Gross profit		500 000
Marketing & sales overheads:		
Sales persons' salaries	80 000	
Sales administration	40 000	
Advertising & sales promotion	80 000	
Marketing research	20 000	
	220 000	
Administration overheads	100 000	320 000
Net profit		180 000
Net profit to sales ratio = 11.25%		

Figure 15.18

(b) Advertising and sales promotion expenditure will be increased by 20 per cent.

(c) An additional sales person will be employed: salary costs will increase by £14 000 per annum.

(d) An assistant sales administration manager will be employed at an additional cost of £14 000 per annum.

(e) The level of administration costs will be kept at the same proportion of gross profit as before.

1. What is meant by the term 'overheads'?

2. Calculate the net profit-to-sales ratio for the planned sales period 1 June 1992 to 31 May 1993. Show all your workings.

3. Discuss whether the Board's decisions are appropriate at this stage in their product's life-cycle.

Suggested reading

Black, G., *Accounting Standards*. Longman, 1987.
Randall, H., *Business Accounting 1* (NVQ 3). DP Publications, 1993.
Wood, F., *Business Accounting*, 15th edn. Pitman, 1989.

16

Finance and decision-making

In all organizations money comes in and then flows out. From time to time managers might pose questions such as:

- Can we afford X?
- Are we going to be able to pay our workforce this month?
- We seem to be profitable and we have plenty of work—why do we never have any money?
- If we borrow money to buy a new machine, can we meet the repayments?

To answer such questions and to make the right critical decisions, an organization has to engage in financial planning.

Financial planning

Financial planning involves defining objectives and then developing ways of achieving them. To be able to do this, a financial manager must have a realistic understanding of what is happening and what is likely to happen within the organization; for example, when is money going to come in, what is it needed for, and would it be possible to use some of it for expansion and development? In the 'money-go-round' (Fig. 16.1), capital and sales revenue come into a business, but is there enough left over, after paying all of the costs, for expansion and development?

We can appreciate the importance of financial planning by considering a report prepared by the Society of Practitioners of Insolvency during the recession of the late 1980s–early 1990s, which produced statistics to show why business failed. As you can see from Fig. 16.2, the biggest single cause of business failure was financial problems, which accounted for 36 per cent of business failures: 20 per cent because of cash flow problems, 5 per cent because of loss of finance when lenders in the market became cautious about who they lent to, and 11 per cent because of bad debts when businesses failed to pay their bills.

To help with the provision of finance and the making of financial decisions, many organizations turn to financial markets. The price paid in these markets for using money is the *interest rate*. A number of factors influence this rate. For example, if the demand for funds increases and the supply remains unchanged, then interest rates are likely to rise. Conversely, if the demand for loan capital is low in comparison with the availability of funds, interest rates are likely to fall.

476

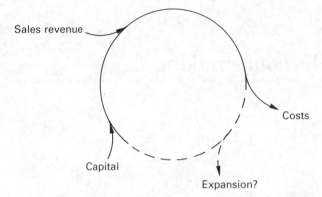

Figure 16.1 The money-go-round.

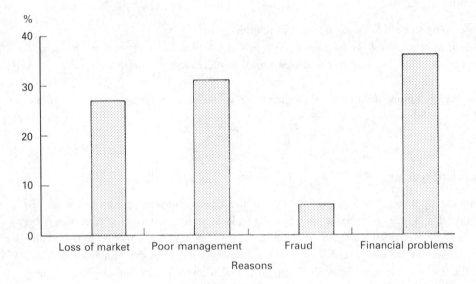

Figure 16.2 Causes of business failure.

Governments also have a strong influence on financial markets; they can use their position as borrowers to influence interest rates by increasing or decreasing their own demand for finance. In doing so they may seek to push up (or pull down) interest rates to further economic policies.

The market for finance is a complex arrangement involving banks, unit trust companies, stockbrokers, investment and venture capital companies, pension funds, assurance companies and many more. Each of these acts as an intermediary by accepting savings and channelling them to businesses through short-term money markets or long-term capital markets. Savers have a wide range of investment possibilities and each of these bears a different degree of risk. One person may opt for risk capital in the form of company shares where the return is the dividend earned by each share, while another may place funds with a bank which passes them on to businesses as loans or overdrafts.

A business's financial possibilities are not limited to the availability of loans or the expansion of share capital; retained profits are a major source of funds for many organizations, while others try to maximize the benefits from trade credit.

Sources of finance

A business organization has to take into account many factors before deciding how to satisfy its financial requirements (Fig. 16.3). For example, decisions about finance may determine the type of business structure an organization takes. Another important factor is the length or period over which finance may be required. Although short-term finance is more expensive, it is also more flexible and this benefit would offset the lower cost of long-term funds which might not be fully employed owing to fluctuations in business activity. Many companies expand by using short-term finance and then later replace it with long-term finance through a *funding* operation. Funding raises long-term funds to pay off the short-term finance so that further short-term finance is then available to help the business expand again.

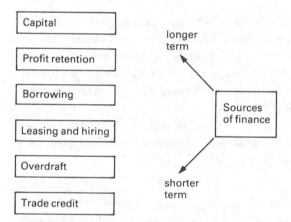

Figure 16.3 Sources of finance.

NB: In Chapter 15 we looked at how gearing compares long-term capital provided by shares with that provided by loans and saw how this reflected both the degree of risk and the allocation of profits.

Risk capital

Sole traders

A sole trader proprietorship is easy to set up and is the most common form of business ownership. Although sole traders have considerable flexibility, much of their finance will often come from personal sources and additional sums may be difficult to raise. Many sole traders seek to expand by taking in partners and thus increasing their business capital.

Partnerships

Partnerships provide further opportunities for expansion and are particularly suitable for professions where large amounts of capital are not required. However, limitations exist on the number of partners, and this can restrict capital-raising opportunities.

Companies

In order to achieve the benefits of limited liability and to extend capital-raising opportunities, many partnerships eventually opt for corporate status with the issue of shares. The company comprises a group of people who unite together to form a separate legal entity. This legal 'personality' provides the company with perpetual succession and continuity. As we have seen, companies can be either private or public.

A *private limited company* is one that restricts the rights of members to transfer their shares and limits the ability of the public to subscribe for its shares. Membership of the Unlisted Securities Market (USM) is often seen as a halfway stage between a small company and a fully listed company on the Stock Exchange. The USM was created in 1980 by the Stock Exchange and has enabled many smaller companies to become public and to raise finance for expansion before progressing to a full Stock Exchange listing.

A fully listed *public company* on the Stock Exchange has almost limitless opportunities to raise fresh capital from the market as long as it abides by its rules. For example, a public company has a number of methods open to it for the issue of shares:

1. It can create a *public issue by prospectus*. An issuing house will organize the issue by compiling a prospectus, accompanied by an advertisement and an invitation to buy shares. This can be an expensive method, and up to 7 per cent of the money raised by the issue can go to meet the costs.
2. An *offer for sale* exists where a public company issues shares directly to an issuing house which then offers them for sale at a fixed price. This is also an expensive method and is best used when the size of the issue is too small to need a public issue by prospectus.
3. A *rights issue* is a cheaper method, whereby existing shareholders are offered further shares at an advantageous price.
4. A *placing* avoids the expense of going to the market by placing shares with a number of investors through an intermediary. Since this method avoids the market, the Stock Exchange keeps a close eye on these transactions.
5. With an *offer by tender*, an offer is made to the public but the company states a minimum price below which shares will not be offered. Buyers then have to indicate the price they are willing to offer for shares.

Ordinary shares

Most capital is normally raised through the issue of ordinary shares. An ordinary share is a fixed unit of ownership giving the holder the opportunity to share in the profits or losses. Ordinary shares carry voting rights at shareholders' meetings. Shareholders elect the board and can sanction the level of dividends proposed. *Authorized capital* is the amount of share capital a company is empowered by its shareholders to issue. *Issued capital* is the nominal amount of share capital issued to shareholders.

Deferred shares

Another class of shares is deferred shares or *'founders' shares*. These are issued to the originators of the business and sometimes carry enhanced voting rights so that a small group of people can maintain control of a family business.

Preference shares

A less flexible class of share is the preference share. Owners of these shares are not, strictly speaking, owners of the company, and their exact rights will be set out in the company articles of association. Holders of these shares have preferential rights to receive dividends if profits exist and, in the event of a company winding up, will receive the face value of their shares before the ordinary shareholders are paid; however, dividends on preference shares are limited to a fixed percentage of par value.

Some companies issue *cumulative preference shares* and this avoids the difficulty of having to pay preference shareholders if profits are too small; the holder of a cumulative preference share will receive arrears of dividends accumulated from the past in later years. With *redeemable preference shares* the company can buy back the shares from the shareholders; redemption can be made from profits or reserves or it may be financed by a fresh issue of shares. *Participating preference shareholders* receive dividends above the fixed rate when ordinary shareholders have been paid if the company has done well in a particular year.

Case Study 1—Floating on the Stock Exchange

(a) Devro, the sausage skin maker, is about to be floated on the Stock Exchange. It will have an initial market capitalization of £224 million. The company will get £77 million of new money in the issue and it will use this injection to repay debt and to redeem preference shares. After the floatation Devro will be left with borrowings of £17 million, 50 per cent of net assets.

Questions

1. Why do companies float on the Stock Exchange?
2. Explain what is meant by the term 'redeem preference shares'.
3. What is the importance of the ratio of borrowings to net assets?

Case Study 2—Raising a rights issue

London-based Asda Property Holdings is raising £16 million from shareholders to help build up its property portfolio. The company stated that commercial property prices were beginning to rise again and that there were attractive opportunities for making selective acquisitions. The two-for-five cash call at 75p a share will initially reduce the group's net borrowings from £70 million to about £55 million, but borrowings are expected to rise again as more properties are bought. The rights issue was accompanied by a pledge from the company that it would maintain at least a 2.1p dividend this year.

Questions

1. Explain what is meant by 'rights issue'?
2. The example refers to a 'two-for-five cash call': what does this mean?
3. Why might the issue of large numbers of shares affect the size of dividends?
4. If you were in the position of a shareholder, what would be (a) one advantage and (b) one disadvantage of being offered a rights issue?

Advantages and disadvantages of risk capital

There are many benefits of using risk capital instead of alternative sources of finance, including the following:

1. If the business has had a bad year, the company is under no legal obligation to shareholders.
2. Unlike loans, whereby the principal has to be returned at the end of a period on a contracted date, the company does not have to pay the share capital back.
3. Interest on loan capital is an overhead which reduces profits, whereas share capital does not create overheads.

However, there are several disadvantages of issuing risk capital. These include:

1. It can be expensive to issue shares.
2. Companies have to undergo the rigorous financial requirements of the Stock Exchange to be listed, and then demands for shares are subject to the uncertainties of the market-place.
3. The creation of more shareholders may dilute the influence of the founders of the company and affect their ability to make decisions.

Venture capital

Another form of capital for businesses is venture capital. Venture capital companies provide finance in return for an equity shareholding in the company and an element of control. 3i is the largest venture capital company of this type in this field. In recent years the law has changed to allow companies to buy back their capital if certain safeguards have been met.

Profit retention

One of the most important sources of finance for businesses are profits that have been ploughed back. Initially, profits are subject to corporation tax, payable to the Department of Inland Revenue. Then a proportion of what is left is allocated to shareholders as dividends. The directors will recommend how much profit should be distributed in this way. The board needs to satisfy shareholders while at the same time ensuring that sufficient funds are available for reinvestment (Fig. 16.4). Directors do not want shareholders to express dissatisfaction at the annual general meeting or to sell their shares and thus cause share prices to fall so that under-valuation leaves the business vulnerable to takeover. The profits retained in the business will be shown in the balance sheet as reserves, and the funds represented by these reserves will be spread among the assets.

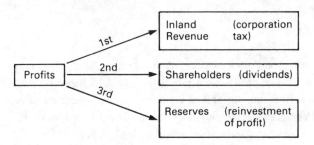

Figure 16.4 Order of profit allocation.

Borrowing

Borrowing is considered an acceptable feature of commercial activity. The charge for borrowing is interest, and a crucial element in calculating the interest charge is the amount of *risk* involved with the loan. For example, longer-term loans tend to carry higher rates, as will loans made to small businesses with an unproven track record. In order to obtain a loan, an organization needs to use its business plan to convince its financial backers of the viability of its propositions. Many financial institutions involved with lending activities will try to provide a package of lending facilities to match the specific requirements of each borrower.

Banks

Although loans can come from a variety of sources, the main source is the banks. Banks offer a range of types of loans for businesses, including the following:

1. *Business starter loans* These are designed to help new businesses or businesses that have been operating for less than 12 months. The loans range from £1000 to £15 000 and carry a

fixed rate of interest. They are usually repayable over a term between one and ten years. (NB: Secured loans tend to be at a lower rate of interest.)

2. *Business development loans* These loans are for business development and expansion. They can be for virtually any purpose and usually come with fixed interest rates and fixed monthly payments. Loans can range from £2000 to £250 000 and be repayable from anything between one and 20 years.

3. *Franchise finance* Banks can specifically tailor business loans to aid with the purchase and running of franchises.

4. *Small firms loans guarantee scheme* This is a service offered by banks and supported by a guarantee by the DTI for businesses that do not have a proven track record. The government guarantees a proportion of the loan up to £100 000 over two to seven years.

Banks usually offer a range of loan protection schemes to cover situations such as accident or sickness which might affect the ability of a businessperson to make regular repayments.

Debentures

Large, publicly quoted organizations may borrow money by issuing debentures. A debenture is an acknowledgement of a debt made to a company for a fixed rate of interest which specifies the terms of repayment at the end of a period. It is therefore a long-term loan which is transferable on the Stock Exchange. A debenture holder is not a shareholder but a creditor. This means that interest payments are an expense to the company and are allowable against profits.

Although holding debentures is much less risky than holding shares, their value in the market-place will vary according to interest rates. For example, a debenture that pays a 10 per cent rate of interest will be worth 10/8 or 1.25 per cent of its face value when interest rates are 8 per cent; if interest rates rise to 15 per cent it would only be worth 10/15 or 0.66 of its face value. Thus, if interest rates rise the value of the loan falls and vice versa.

An important source of finance for many businesses is the availability of government grants, 'soft loans' and subsidies. Government help may come from the EC as well as from central and local government and can be provided by a variety of different agencies. For example:

1. The *Enterprise Allowance Scheme (EAS)* provides an allowance for people starting a new business of £40 per week for up to 40 weeks.

2. *Development agency loans* for 'desirable' businesses are available in a location where there is high unemployment.

3. The *British Technology Group (BTG)* may offer finance to companies wanting to develop new products and processes.

4. *Regional selective assistance* may provide grants for capital investment projects within development and intermediate areas. It also provides access to loans from the *European Investment Bank (EIB)* and from the *European Coal and Steel Community (ECSC)* for projects that create jobs in areas suffering from job losses in the coal and steel industries.

Lenders will usually seek to minimize the risks of lending. For example, when providing finance for a limited company, it is conceivable that the lender will demand a *personal guarantee* of repayment from the main shareholder. This effectively removes that shareholder's liability and puts him or her in a similar position to a partner or sole trader. Lenders frequently ask for *security* or *collateral* against a loan. In this way loans are secured against assets so that if the business starts to flounder the lender will have priority over other creditors and the receipts from the sale of these secured assets can be used to repay the loan. For example, a commercial mortgage enables businesses of all types to acquire freehold and leasehold premises and provides the lender with a good title on default. It is possible for lenders to insist upon *covenants* or *conditions* to restrict the activities of businesses being lent money.

Advantages and disadvantages of loan capital

The benefits of using loan capital are as follows:

1. In relation to raising funds through share issue, it is cheap.
2. Inflation will benefit the borrower because the value of the interest payments will diminish; the loan and the interest will be worth less in real terms.
3. Interest payments are a company expense and appear in the profit and loss account before corporation tax is assessed.

The dangers of using loan capital are:

1. Any loan charge must be paid irrespective of business performance.
2. A highly geared company would reduce its ability to allocate profits to shareholders.
3. Excessive loan capital may affect a business's flexibility. Repayments will have to be met at certain times and these dates might not match incomes from sales. Covenants, guarantees, etc., could affect decision-making.

Case Study—What is the bank manager going to look for?

When applying for a loan, a bank manager will wish to view a *business plan* as this will show what the business is, the resources and expertise at its disposal and its proposed developments.

At the first meeting the bank manager will ask: 'What is the money required for?' It might be needed for working capital or to purchase fixed assets. The bank will expect the lender to provide evidence that the money really is needed for a specific purpose and that it will be spent as indicated.

The bank manager will also wish to know *how much* is needed, *for how long* it is required, and *how it is to be paid back*. How much could depend upon the amount put into the business by the owner. Assessing the cost of fixed assets is usually fairly straightforward; however, anticipating working capital requirements will require a detailed estimate of cash flows. Projecting how long finance is needed for will require detailed projections of costs and sales taking into account all eventualities. Paying money back should take into account the cost of borrowing the money and the use of realistic cash flow projections.

In deciding whether or not to grant the loan, the bank manager will use certain principles of lending which can best be remembered by using the mnemonic IPARTS. This stands for:

- Integrity
- Purpose
- Amount
- Repayment
- Term
- Security

Customer *integrity* is an important consideration in determining whether or not a customer is going to honour a debt. The bank will not wish to resort to legal action to recover the loan. The past history of the customer will therefore be very important.

The bank will wish to know the *purpose* of the loan and how it is to be used. It will also wish to know whether the *amount* requested is the right amount; for example, will the customer require more, or has he or she asked for too much?

Repayments are an important consideration in lending. Given customer projections of cash flow, is the firm going to be able to meet the repayments? The period over which the loan is required will be an important consideration of risk. The longer the *term*, the larger the interest repayments; however 'long term' means higher risks and a greater likelihood of something going wrong.

Finally, *security* will provide some form of insurance against default by the customer. The bank will then have an asset that it can sell in order to recover the loan.

Whatever the business proposition, there is always a level of uncertainty. Those wishing to borrow money have to show a level of personal financial commitment to the business process and to use their business plans to predict carefully the chances of a business succeeding.

Questions

1. Explain why a bank manager will wish to examine a business plan. In your answer, identify at least four areas that should be included in the plan.
2. Risk is always an important feature of lending money. Name two factors that would indicate some degree of risk.
3. What measures might a bank take to reduce the risks of lending?
4. Obtain a copy of a bank loan application form and comment briefly on the information it requires.

Leasing and hiring

Major banks have links with finance houses which provide a variety of schemes enabling customers to receive goods and make payments over time. Goods on *hire purchase* remain the property of the finance company until the customer has made all of the payments, whereas other *credit purchasing* schemes enable the goods to belong to the customer from the first payment.

Another way in which a company can gain the use of an asset without having to pay for it is through *leasing*. The lessee uses the asset and makes regular payments to the lessor, who owns it. An operating lease is for a small amount, and a capital or finance lease is for a large item over an extended period. As the asset does not belong to the lessee, it will not appear in the balance sheet.

The procedure for leasing is for a company to choose the equipment it requires which is then purchased by the leasing company. A contract determines the rent payable and the conditions, e.g. options to purchase, maintenance agreements, etc.

The benefits of leasing are that:

1. It enables a business to have complete use of an asset without having to use risk or loan capital to finance it.
2. Leasing payments are an expense and are charged to the profit and loss account before tax is assessed.
3. Leasing enables business to change their equipment more often and thereby to keep up to date with modern technology.
4. Tax allowances can be claimed by the lessor and be filtered through to the lessee in lower lease payments.

Although leasing enables the lessee to manage expenditure more easily, the lessee does not own the equipment. If income falters, lease payments may impose a considerable burden on a business; furthermore, loans cannot be secured on assets that are leased.

Overdrafts

An overdraft is the most frequently used form of short-term bank finance and is used to ease cash flow problems. Arrangements are made between the customer and the bank to include an agreed limit on an account beyond which the customer will not draw. Interest is calculated on the level of the overdraft on a daily basis. Often a bank will make a special charge for arranging an overdraft and committing the bank's money, whether the withdrawal facilities are used or not. After an agreed period, the bank will examine the account and make a decision about whether to revise or reinstate the limit.

Whereas the account of a personal customer will show a regular input of income per month and a regular pattern of expenditure (see Fig. 16.5(a)), this does not happen with a business customer who is dependent upon debtors paying their bills. As a result, it is easy to understand why business customers often slip into an overdraft situation (see Fig. 16.5(b)) and need this flexible form of short-term finance.

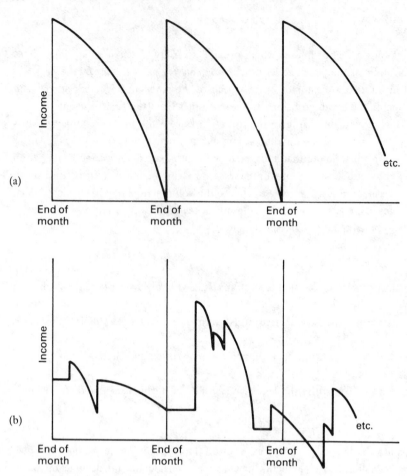

Figure 16.5 (a) Personal account, (b) Business account.

In order to overcome this problem, a bank might offer an organization the use of its *factoring* service. Trade debts can be tied up for periods extending beyond three months. A factoring company offers an immediate payment against these debtors (normally 80 per cent) and the rest when the debt is paid. In this way, the firm improves its liquidity with immediate funds and ensures that its assets are not tied up in debtors. The factoring company takes away the burden of running the sales ledger and the problem of collecting payments. It charges interest on the sum advanced as well as administration charges.

Trade credit

A useful form of credit for all businesses is the use of trade credit provided by suppliers. This is often governed by the type of industry and by the relationship between the purchaser and the supplier. Although no rate of interest is attached to trade credit, cash discounts are forfeited if payments are not promptly met. Another danger is that businesses that try to maximize the use of credit periods might find that their reputations tend to suffer.

Case Study—Credit indemnity

One of the problems of providing trade credit is that customers may fail to meet their commitments and become 'bad debts'. Look at the details about 'Infocheck' credit insurance provided in Fig. 16.6 and then answer the questions that follow.

Questions

1. What is the purpose of taking out credit insurance?
2. What benefits arise from taking out such a policy?
3. Describe what is meant by each of the following:

- Working capital
- Protracted default
- Debtor cover
- Profit margin
- Security
- Information databases
- Whole turnover
- Credit sales

4. How could credit indemnity help an organization to improve its cash flow?

Forecasting financial requirements

Whereas cash is a liquid asset owned by a business which enables it to buy goods and services, profit is a surplus arising from trading. It is therefore possible for a business to be selling goods at a higher price than they cost and to be making a profit but, if creditors have not been paid, for it nevertheless to be having cash flow problems. A business must look carefully at its flow of cash to ensure that the use of its most liquid resource is economically utilized. For example, if a business holds too much cash it could be sacrificing profits, and if it holds too little it could run out.

The opportunity cost of holding too much cash would be the interest that could otherwise be earned. If interest rates are high, businesses will be sacrificing income by holding cash and would prefer to hold the lowest possible cash balances so that they can earn interest from the rest. In times of inflation, businesses will wish to hold higher levels of cash in order to finance the increasing price of transactions.

Cash flow

A careful assessment of the availability of liquid funds is essential for the smooth running of any company. With cash planning or budgeting, the accountant will forecast the flows of cash into and

WHAT IS CREDIT INSURANCE?

Most companies that supply goods and or services probably also offer some form of credit to their customers. Credit insurance protects a company's financial stability by reimbursing losses incurred when customers to whom credit has been supplied, fail in their payment commitments, usually through insolvency or protracted default.

The trend towards more customers taking full advantage of the credit facilities you may offer inevitably exposes your company to the possibility of bad debt losses. The subsequent effect on working capital and net profits can be extremely damaging and could result in the eventual liquidation of the leading party.

HOW DOES CREDIT INSURANCE AFFECT YOU?

CREDIT INSURANCE WILL:

■ **Protect working capital (and net profits) by minimizing the effect of bad debt**

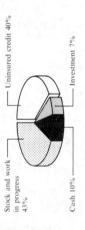

Assuming a profit margin of 10% and a bad debt of £10 000, new sales totalling £100 000 will be required to maintain parity.

■ **Protect your profit margin and provide a sound base from which to expand business and sales**

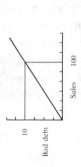

With sales debtor cover your profit forecast will be maintained.

■ **Protect the company's current assets represented by credit sales (frequently this can be up to 40%)**

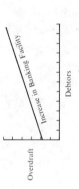

Uninsured credit 40%
Stock and work in progress 43%
Investment 7%
Cash 10%

■ **Provide added security to the bank manager**

Increase in Banking Facility
Overdraft
Debtors

Normal overdraft facilities provide 40-50% of your debtor balance. With up to 100% debtor cover through credit insurance your bank or alternative finance could increase to 80% of debtors (see 'Finance-Check' leaflet).

WHAT ARE THE DISTINCTIVE FEATURES OF INFOCHECK CREDIT INSURANCE?

Infocheck provide an integrated approach to credit insurance by linking the underwriter, the broker and the client with the largest UK business information database in the world. By working closely with AMA Underwriting Agencies Ltd. we have developed tailor-made online credit insurance policies that can provide your company with the cover it needs. Policies available include:

■ WHOLE TURNOVER
■ CATASTROPHE
■ SPECIFIC RISK
■ MANAGED POLICY

offering:

■ UP TO 100% INDEMNITY COVER
■ COVER ON GOODS SOLD AND DELIVERED AGAINST INSOLVENCY AND PROTRACTED DEFAULT
■ A 'MADE TO MEASURE' COST WITH COMPETITIVE PREMIUMS CALCULATED AGAINST INSURABLE TURNOVER ONLY
■ THE FIRST ONLINE CREDIT INSURANCE POLICY PROVIDING AN INSTANT CREDIT UNDERWRITING DECISION ON MORE THAN 420 000 UK LIMITED COMPANIES
■ CONSTANT MONITORING AND INFORMATION UPDATE ON COMPANIES COVERED
■ 15 20% NO CLAIM BONUS
■ LOW-COST ADMINISTRATION
■ SIMPLE CLAIMS PROCEDURE WITH NEGOTIATION AND SETTLEMENT
■ AN ONLINE UNDERWRITER ON YOUR DESK

CREDIT INSURANCE FOR THE SMALLER BUSINESS

'Cover-Check' launched late 1992 provides the alternative solution for the smaller business that has an insurable turnover of up to £2m. It is flexible and cost-effective, offering a flat rate premium which is not linked to the company's turnover.

DO YOU HAVE AN OPTION?

Insolvency was responsible for over 62 000 company failures in 1992. An upturn from the recession is predicted: as a consequence there will be an increase in the growth rate as the economy revs up. Unhappily, however, insolvency will claim more victims from companies struggling to meet the increase in demand for sales.

YOUR NEXT STEP

To find out more about Infocheck's full range of insurance products please complete and return the tear-off slip and let our insurance services help you towards safeguarding your profits vital for your company's growth.

Figure 16.6 'Infocheck' Credit Insurance leaflet.

out of the company's bank account so that any excess of payments over receipts can be highlighted and action taken to overcome the shortfall; for example, overdraft facilities can be arranged well in advance so that funds are available when required.

In order to prepare a cash budget, the accountant needs to know what receipts and payments are likely to take place in the future and exactly when they will occur. It is important to determine the length of lead time between incurring an expense and paying for it as well as the time lag between making a sale and collecting the money from debtors. The art of successful cash budgeting is to be able to calculate accurately receipts and expenditures. For example, goods might be bought in January and used in May; these goods could then be sold in May and the money received in August. This clearly refers to the principle of the cash cycle shown in the previous chapter.

Example

A cash budget for the six months ended 31 December 1994 can be drafted from the following information:

1. Cash balance on 1 July 1994: £4500.
2. Sales are £15 per unit and cash is received three months after the sale. For the period in question, the sale of units is:

1994										1995	
Mar	Apr	May	Jun	Jul	Aug	Sept	Oct	Nov	Dec	Jan	Feb
60	60	75	90	55	140	130	150	150	160	170	150

3. Production in units is:

1994										1995	
Mar	Apr	May	Jun	Jul	Aug	Sept	Oct	Nov	Dec	Jan	Feb
40	50	80	70	80	130	130	150	145	160	170	160

4. Raw materials cost £4 per unit and these are paid for two months *before* being used for production.
5. Direct labour at £5 per unit is paid in the same month as the unit produced.
6. Other variable expenses are £4 per unit: 50 per cent of the cost is paid in the same month as production while the other 50 per cent is paid for in the month *after* production.
7. Fixed expenses of £50 are paid monthly.

Receipts

						£
July	60	(April)	×	15	=	900
August	75	(May)	×	15	=	1125
September	90	(June)	×	15	=	1350
October	55	(July)	×	15	=	825
November	140	(Aug.)	×	15	=	2100
December	130	(Sept.)	×	15	=	1950

Payments

July

						£
Raw materials	130	(Sept.)	×	4	=	520
Direct labour	80	(July)	×	5	=	400
Variable expenses	80	(July)	×	2	=	160
	70	(June)	×	2	=	140
Fixed expenses						50
						£1270

August

						£
Raw materials	150	(Oct.)	×	4	=	600
Direct labour	130	(Aug.)	×	5	=	650
Variable expenses	130	(Aug.)	×	2	=	260
	80	(July)	×	2	=	160
Fixed expenses				=		50
						£1720

September

						£
Raw materials	145	(Nov.)	×	4	=	580
Direct labour	130	(Sept.)	×	5	=	650
Variable expenses	130	(Sept.)	×	2	=	260
	130	(Aug.)	×	2	=	260
Fixed expenses				=		50
						£1800

October

						£
Raw materials	160	(Dec.)	×	4	=	640
Direct labour	150	(Oct.)	×	5	=	750
Variable expenses	150	(Oct.)	×	2	=	300
	130	(Sept.)	×	2	=	260
Fixed expenses				=		50
						£2000

November

Raw materials	170	(Jan.)	×	4	=	£ 680
Direct labour	145	(Nov.)	×	5	=	725
Variable expenses	145	(Nov.)	×	2	=	290
	150	(Oct.)	×	2	=	300
Fixed expenses					=	50
						£2045

December

Raw materials	160	(Feb.)	×	4	=	£ 640
Direct labour	160	(Dec.)	×	5	=	800
Variable expenses	160	(Dec.)	×	2	=	320
	145	(Nov.)	×	2	=	290
Fixed expenses					=	50
						£2100

The cash budget shown in Fig. 16.7 indicates that, although the cash balance will fall over the following six months from £4500 to £1815, no overdraft facilities will be required.

	Jul £	Aug £	Sep £	Oct £	Nov £	Dec £
RECEIPTS						
Sales	900	1125	1350	825	2100	1950
Total receipts	900	1125	1350	825	2100	1950
PAYMENTS						
Raw materials	520	600	580	640	680	640
Direct labour	400	650	650	750	725	800
Variable expenses	300	420	520	560	590	610
Fixed expenses	50	50	50	50	50	50
Total payments	1270	1720	1800	2000	2045	2100
Cash balance	4500	4130	3535	3085	1910	1965
add Receipts	900	1125	1350	825	2100	1950
	5400	5255	4885	3910	4010	3915
less Payments	1270	1720	1800	2000	2045	2100
Balance carried forward	4130	3535	3085	1910	1965	1815

Figure 16.7 Cash budget.

Managing working capital

Working capital is the difference between current assets and current liabilities. Current assets are either in the form of cash or in a form that can soon lead to cash, and current liabilities will soon have to be paid for with cash. In the previous chapter we indicated that a prudent ratio of current assets to current liabilities is considered to be 2:1 although most businesses operate with a slightly lower ratio than this. It is now more commonly thought that a satisfactory working capital ratio will depend upon the company concerned, the type of business operation, stock levels and other factors.

Working capital is often considered to be the portion of capital that 'oils the wheels' of business. Funds employed in fixed assets are concerned with producing goods and services. Working capital provides stocks from which the fixed assets may produce. It allows the salesforce to offer trade credit and create debtors. Firms with insufficient working capital are in a financial straitjacket. They lack the funds to buy stocks, and to produce and create debtors. In these circumstances providers of finance may well call a meeting of creditors and appoint a liquidator. Clearly, a business must always have adequate short-term funds to ensure the continuation of its activities.

The operating cycle expresses the connection between working capital and movements of cash. It can measure the period of time between:

- The purchase of raw materials and the receipt of cash from debtors
- The time when cash is paid out for raw materials and the time when cash is received from sales (see Fig. 16.8).

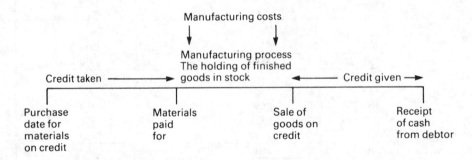

Figure 16.8 Managing the credit cycle.

Example

A firm buys raw materials on two months' credit and holds them in stock for half a month before issuing them to the production department from which they emerge as finished goods. These are held on average for one and a half months before sale. Debtors take three months to pay. The cash cycle would be:

	Months
Raw materials credit from suppliers	(2)
Turnover of stock of raw materials	0.5
Turnover of stock of finished goods	1.5
Debtors' payment period	3.0
Cash cycle	3.0 months

Not only does this cycle show the time ingredient; it also shows that income from debtors should be more than enough to cover any manufacturing costs and overheads encountered.

The dangers of insufficient working capital are clear to see:

1. A company with limited working capital will not be able to buy in bulk and could miss out on opportunities to gain trade discounts.
2. Cash discounts will be lost as the business will avoid paying creditors until the last possible opportunity.
3. It will become more difficult to offer extensive credit facilities to customers. By shortening the credit period, customers may well go to alternative suppliers.
4. The business will be unable to innovate. Limited finances will hinder its ability to develop new products or improve production techniques.
5. The business's financial reputation as a good payer may be lost.
6. Creditors may well take action. As capital becomes squeezed, a business will be forced to finance its activities by overdrafts and trade credit. A point could well be reached where its future is dependent upon the actions of creditors.
7. Overtrading can take place. This would involve financing a large volume of production with inadequate working capital, often from short-term loans. This can lead to a complete imbalance of the working capital ratio.

Ratio analysis enables a check to be made on a company's liquidity. Those ratios of particular use in assessing working capital are:

- Current or working capital ratio
- Acid-test ratio
- Debt collection period
- Period of credit taken from suppliers

⌕ Case Study—Dinsdale Electronics Ltd

Dinsdale's managing director (MD) is constantly worried about the company's cash flow position and its effects on decision-making and innovation. Although profits have been fair, the company's market share has been falling. The following have been extracted from the company's accounts:

Current ratio	=	0.8
Quick ratio	=	0.5
Debt collection period	=	73 days
Period of credit from suppliers	=	45 days

Questions

1. What sort of problems could Dinsdale's MD be experiencing?
2. Advise Dinsdale's MD on how to improve the company's working capital position.
3. It has been said that profits are not as important as cash flow. How valid is a statement of this kind?

Accountants will constantly review an organization's asset structure to ensure that resources are utilized efficiently. Depending on their review, it might be necessary to increase working capital. This might take place in a number of ways:

1. Reducing the period between the time cash is paid out for raw materials and the time cash is received from sales will provide funds for regeneration. Although the improved efficiency of the cash cycle will help working capital, however, it might be unpopular with creditors.
2. Fixed assets such as land and buildings might not be fully utilized, or space might be used for unprofitable purposes. Space could be rented, sold or allowed to house a more profitable operation so that cash flow could be improved. A business's cash flow might be improved by selling assets and leasing them back, although this can commit the firm to heavy leasing fees.
3. A company could review its stock levels to see if these could be the subject of economy measures. If the stock of raw materials is divided by the average weekly issue, the number of week's raw materials held in stock can be calculated. Some companies attempt to maximize liquidity by using a 'just-in-time' approach so as to hold the minimum stocks possible. Although this might save on expenses associated with running a large store and looking after stocks, the company might lose out on trade discounts and be susceptible to inconsistent supplies.
4. Many businesses employ a credit controller to economize on debtors. A credit controller will vet new customers and set them a credit limit, ensure that credit limits are not exceeded and encourage debtors to pay on time. Credit controllers are often caught in a conflict with the sales department, whose staff wish them to extend credit limits, and the accounts department, who want debtors to pay quickly and so increase their working capital.
5. As we have seen, cash budgeting can be used as an important control mechanism to predict the effects of future transactions on the cash balance of a company. Cash budgeting can help a company to take actions to ensure that cash is available when required.

6. A number of short-term solutions are available to increase working capital. Companies might extend their overdraft or bring in a factoring company. It might be possible to delay the payment of bills, although this obviously displeases creditors.

Accountants will ensure that the solution adopted will use the capital employed more efficiently.

Case Study—Why do the numbers sometimes fail to add up?

The economic recession of the late 1980s and early 1990s claimed some notable scalps. During 1991 business failures were at their highest for many years. The early signs of business failure tended to appear long before a business crashed. Initially profits would start to fall, levels of gearing would start to increase and then losses would start to appear. The beginning of the end would occur when trading in shares was suspended.

Liquidation would occur when it was considered that a company could no longer pay its debts. This was ordered by a court, usually by a creditor. Frequently this would be followed up by *receivership*, whereby independent accountants would supervise the sale of the business. Sometimes, while struggling to survive and meet the demands of creditors, a *white knight* would appear on the scene to launch a rescue bid and save the company from extinction.

Why did so many companies fail during this period? Clearly, the recession affected the business environment, but liquidators' reports frequently referred to 'weak financial management' as the main shortcoming. The importance of effective cash management was highlighted again and again in booklets, starter-packs and guides. For example:

1. 'Finance . . . is where your numbers have to stand up and be counted.' (Price Waterhouse)
2. 'Many businesses measure their trading success mainly in terms of the bottom line, but the banker is far more concerned by the cash-flow that trading generates.' (Ernst & Young)
3. 'Many businesses fail to make profits or to have enough cash at the right time, because the management has not planned ahead.' (National Westminster)
4. 'The big question in cash-flow is: What would happen if . . .?' (Barclays)

Although similar messages were made in more than 1700 books and information sources, it seemed slow to penetrate. One senior manager at accountants Buchler Phillips pointed out that 'weakness in company management and the information available to it' was a common theme running through reviews carried out for lenders. This manager identified the following five principal components within this theme:

1. Most companies that suffer financial difficulties are victims of inadequate and insufficient management information with particular emphasis on up-to-date cash flow information.

2. Cash flows are often prepared at the start of a business period and not updated or reviewed again until the end of the period. This defeats the object of cash flow.

3. Cash flows are often optimistic and fail to provide for contingencies such as bad debts.

4. Management fails to ignore the quality of debtors and values them at absolute value rather than at their likely recoverability.

5. Companies are often brought down by moving to speculative projects which are away from their core business. Such projects frequently drain finances at the expense of more profitable areas of the business.

The main reason why so many companies have ignored cash management is that it imposes restrictions on the range of available options that businesses can choose. Despite this, the lesson to be learnt is that 'cash is king', and has to be if businesses wish to develop in a way that does not see them leaping from one crisis to another.

Questions

1. What is the difference between liquidity and receivership?
2. Describe in your own words why cash flow is often considered to be more important than profits by so many different accountants and business advisors.
3. Why do so many businesses ignore cash flow?
4. Why should cash flow forecasts be constantly updated?
5. What is meant by the term 'quality of debtors'?

Investment decisions and the appraisal of capital

Investment involves the immediate risk of funds in the hope of securing returns later. There are often more investment proposals than the necessary finance to back them. It is therefore important to be able to compare projects in order to assess the degree of risk. A good decision will provide a high return, while a poor decision may result in few benefits. Managers must try to make decisions that maximize returns and provide shareholders with the best possible investment.

Entrepreneurs use their creative and imaginative skills to look for investment opportunities. In the early stages they will gather information in order to appraise alternatives. When decisions involve non-financial aspects—for example the image of a business—this can be difficult. The decision-making process will be concerned primarily with weighing up the benefits against the costs. Once the decision has been made, projects can be put into action and their results monitored.

The primary objective of any investment decision is to obtain a return on the investment that is greater than the initial outlay of capital. Three important criteria determining that outlay will be: the sum invested, its returns, and the length of time the project is expected to last.

In the following paragraphs we will look at:

- Accounting rate of return (ARR) method
- Payback method
- Discounted cash flow (DCF)—net present value
- Discounted cash flow (DCF)—internal rate of return

Accounting rate of return (ARR) method

This method is concerned simply with expressing profitability as an average *rate of return* on an investment. It is generally considered to be a quick and convenient guide for assessing the profitability of alternative projects. Profit is expressed as an *average* over the life of the project, and capital is considered to be the initial outlay or the capital invested. It is therefore calculated by dividing the average annual profit by the initial investment:

$$\text{ARR} = \frac{\text{Average annual profit}}{\text{Initial investment}} \times 100$$

For example, if we had two projects we could select an alternative as shown in Table 16.1. Project A provides an accounting rate of return of 20 per cent and project B, an accounting rate of return of 25 per cent. Using this form of appraisal, project B would be a better investment.

The accounting rate of return method can be criticized for being based upon book values and therefore failing to take heed of changing price levels. It also fails to consider the timings of cash receipts.

Table 16.1

	Project A £	Project B £
Initial cost	− 10 000	− 20 000
Year 1 cash receipts	+ 4 000	+ 9 000
Year 2 cash receipts	+ 5 000	+ 9 000
Year 3 cash receipts	+ 5 000	+ 12 000
Year 4 cash receipts	+ 4 000	+ 10 000
Total cash receipts	+ 18 000	+ 40 000
Profit over four years	+ 8 000	+ 20 000
Average annual profit	+ 2 000	+ 5 000
Initial investment	10 000	20 000
	20%	25%

Payback method

The purpose of this method is to establish how quickly the investment cost can be repaid. The shorter the payback period, the better the project. Using this method, for example, if we had two investment possibilities that both cost £15 000, we could select an alternative as shown in Table

Table 16.2

	Project A £	Project B £
Initial cost	− 15 000	− 15 000
Year 1 cash receipts	+ 3 000	+ 1 000
Year 2 cash receipts	+ 3 000	+ 3 000
Year 3 cash receipts	+ 4 000	+ 3 000
Year 4 cash receipts	+ 5 000	+ 3 000
Year 5 cash receipts	+ 3 000	+ 5 000

16.2. Project A repays the initial cost by the end of year 4, whereas project B does not repay until the end of year 5. Using the payback method, we would choose project A.

The essential feature of the payback form of capital appraisal is that it takes timing into consideration, and the early return of funds could be of primary importance to firms with liquidity problems. For businesses where capital equipment is constantly being changed, it can provide a rough guide to the extent of a risk.

The main criticism of the payback method is that it does not take into account cash flows (see Table 16.3). The payback method does not differentiate between project A and project B because both methods pay back in three years. In the same way, this method ignores cash receipts expected after the payback period. No attention is given to subsequent years. It does not, therefore, take into account the profitability of the two alternatives.

Table 16.3

	Project A £	Project B £
Initial cost	− 15 000	− 15 000
Year 1 cash receipts	+ 5 000	+ 1 000
Year 2 cash receipts	+ 5 000	+ 2 000
Year 3 cash receipts	+ 5 000	+ 12 000

Not only does the payback method fail to account for the timing of cash flows, it also fails to relate the value of future returns with immediate investments. In money terms, an investment made today should have a higher value in the future. Discounted cash flow relates the expected value of future cash receipts and expenditures to a common date.

DCF (net present value)

This method of weighing up investment decisions leans heavily on the theory of opportunity cost. Before managers commit a company to an investment decision, the benefits of which will be reaped over a number of years, the real value of future returns needs to be assessed. Because the value of money alters with time, it is helpful to look at future flows in terms of their present value.

Interest payments compensate for:

- Cost of time (not having the money available now)
- Cost of inflation (price rises erode the real value of money)
- Risk of investment

The interest rate gives a guide to the future value of investment. Alternatively, the current value of investment can be compared with what it was worth in the past.

If an investor has £1000 in a bank account where it is earning 10 per cent interest, the balance will stand at £1100 at the end of the first year. By compounding this annually,

- At the end of year 2 it will be worth £1210 (£1100 + £110)
- At the end of year 3 it will be worth £1331 (£1210 + £121); etc.

At the end of this time the investor can say that £1331 was worth £1000 three years earlier.

This can be shown the other way round; i.e. what would £1000 now have been worth three years ago at a 10 per cent rate of interest?

$$\frac{£1000}{£1331} \times £1000 = £751.3$$

Two years ago?

$$\frac{£1000}{£1210} \times £1000 = £826.4$$

One year ago?

$$\frac{£1000}{£1100} \times £1000 = £909.1$$

Thus, assuming a constant rate of interest of 10 per cent, £1000 now was worth £751.30 three years ago, and will be worth £1331 in three years' time. The time element has been taken into account. DCF tables are available relating rates of interest to a period of time in years (see Table 16.4).

Looking at the net surplus returns for two projects that have an initial capital investment of £200 000 (Tables 16.5 and 16.6), it is clear that project A is the project to opt for as, at today's value, returns will be higher. If net present value comes out at less than the original investment, it is not worth considering the project at all.

The clear advantage of the net present value method is that it takes into account the time element of money and also is easy to calculate. The dangers of depending upon it are that both interest rates and cash flows are subject to uncertainty.

Table 16.4 DCF tables from 1 per cent to 10 per cent over six years

Future years	% rate of discount									
	1	2	3	4	5	6	7	8	9	10
1	0.990	0.980	0.971	0.962	0.952	0.943	0.935	0.926	0.917	0.909
2	0.980	0.961	0.943	0.925	0.907	0.890	0.873	0.857	0.842	0.826
3	0.971	0.942	0.915	0.889	0.864	0.840	0.816	0.794	0.772	0.751
4	0.961	0.924	0.888	0.855	0.823	0.792	0.763	0.735	0.708	0.683
5	0.951	0.906	0.863	0.822	0.784	0.747	0.713	0.681	0.650	0.621
6	0.942	0.888	0.837	0.790	0.746	0.705	0.666	0.630	0.596	0.564

Table 16.5

	Project A £	Project B £
Earnings year 1	100 000	80 000
Earnings year 2	110 000	100 000
Earnings year 3	100 000	100 000
Earnings year 4	80 000	100 000
Earnings year 5	20 000	30 000
Total return	410 000	410 000

Table 16.6 Discounted cash flow at a rate of interest of 10 per cent

Year	Project A			Project B		
	Earnings £	NPV* £	Discount factor	Earnings £	NPV* £	
0		200 000			200 000	
1	100 000	90 000	0.909	80 000	72 720	
2	110 000	90 860	0.826	100 000	82 600	
3	100 000	75 100	0.751	100 000	75 100	
4	80 000	54 640	0.683	100 000	68 300	
5	20 000	12 420	0.621	30 000	18 630	
		£323 920			£317 350	

*NPV = net present value

Example

Sutton Coldfield PLC is considering two alternative projects to develop its profitability. Until recently the company has always appraised projects on the basis that any investment should pay back within four years. After extensive discussions at board level, it has been decided to use a DCF method of project appraisal (net present value) with a target rate of return of 10 per cent.

Project A   This involves setting up a production line to fully automate the productive process. It will cost £120 000 and provide a saving of £30 000 each year for the first six years.

Project B   This involves spending £100 000 on a prolonged advertising campaign. Evidence suggests that this will increase net revenues by:

	£
Year 1	20 000
Year 2	30 000
Year 3	30 000
Year 4	40 000
Year 5	10 000
Year 6	10 000

Both projects are to be evaluated using both the payback and DCF (net present value) methods.

For *project A*, as the initial investment is £120 000 and the annual saving is £30 000, the investment will be paid back in four years. This only just meets the criterion that the payback period should be reached within four years (Table 16.7). Clearly, the returns are greater than the initial investment, and the project provides a net present value of £10 620 with a discount factor of 10 per cent.

Table 16.7   Project A: DCF (net present value)

Year	Earnings £	DCF (NPV) £	Discount factor
0	120 000		
1	30 000	27 270	0.909
2	30 000	24 780	0.826
3	30 000	22 530	0.751
4	30 000	20 490	0.683
5	30 000	18 630	0.621
6	30 000	16 920	0.564
		£130 620	

For *project B*, the initial investment of £100 000 can be paid back in three and a half years. This is an improvement on the payback period for project A. The returns are, again, greater than the investment and provide a net present value of £4660 (Table 16.8).

We are now left with a problem. Project B is clearly preferable under the payback method because it pays back in three and a half years in comparison to project A's four years. Project A brings in a net present value of £10 620 whereas project B brings in a net present value of £4660. Whereas project B has been favoured by the payback method because it has a better cash flow earlier in its life, it could be argued that, taking into account real values by using DCF, project A would be more profitable.

Table 16.8 Project B: DCF (net present value)

Year	Earnings £	DCF (NPV) £	Discount factor
0	<u>100 000</u>		
1	20 000	18 180	0.909
2	30 000	24 780	0.826
3	30 000	22 530	0.751
4	40 000	27 320	0.683
5	10 000	6 210	0.621
6	10 000	<u>5 640</u>	0.564
		£104 660	

DCF (internal rate of return)

This method aims to find out the average return of an investment throughout its lifespan. This 'internal rate of return' is then compared with the criteria for the project to see if it is worth while. This method is therefore concerned with percentage returns on investment, and *not* with cash figures.

$$
\begin{array}{ll}
 & £ \\
\text{Year 0} & -\ 20\ 000 \\
\text{Year 1} & +\ 8\ 000 \\
\text{Year 2} & +\ 5\ 000 \\
\text{Year 3} & +\ 5\ 000 \\
\text{Year 4} & \underline{+\ 5\ 000} \\
 & £23\ 000
\end{array}
$$

We can try to find the internal rate of return by trial and error. At 10 per cent it would be:

$$
\begin{array}{lll}
-20\ 000 & +\ 8000 \times 0.909 = & 7\ 272 \\
 & +\ 5000 \times 0.826 = & 4\ 130 \\
 & +\ 5000 \times 0.751 = & 3\ 755 \\
 & +\ 5000 \times 0.683 = & \underline{3\ 415} \\
 & & 18\ 572
\end{array}
$$

$$
-20\ 000 \quad +\ 18\ 572 \quad\quad = \underline{-1\ 428}
$$

The return is clearly not 10 per cent, and so we need to try a lower rate. At 6 per cent it would be:

$$
\begin{array}{lll}
-20\ 000 & +\ 8000 \times 0.943 = & 7\ 544 \\
 & +\ 5000 \times 0.890 = & 4\ 450 \\
 & +\ 5000 \times 0.840 = & 4\ 200 \\
 & +\ 5000 \times 0.792 = & \underline{3\ 960} \\
 & & 20\ 154
\end{array}
$$

$$
-20\ 000 \quad +\ 20\ 154 \quad\quad = \underline{154}
$$

We have shown that the internal rate of return lies between 6 and 10 per cent. To obtain the exact internal rate of return, we:

1. Take the lower rate (6).
2. Add to it the difference between the two interest rates (4) multiplied by the difference at the lower rate (154), divided by the total difference between the two rates (1582):

$$6 + \frac{(4 \times 154)}{1582} = 6.39\%$$

As long as the firm can borrow money at a rate lower than 6.39 per cent, it will find the project worth while. The internal rate of return does not aim to obtain a cash figure but seeks a percentage rate, so that returns can be expressed as a percentage of investment cost.

Cost–benefit analysis

By their very nature, investment decisions not only affect the well-being of a particular organization, but also have implications for the community in which the organization is based. Our analysis of investment decisions and capital appraisal only considered the benefits accruing to a particular organization. Cost–benefit analysis takes the process further and considers the wider and longer-term social implications of investment proposals.

Commercial enterprise is about the creation of wealth. It provides employment and incomes for a variety of groups and, in doing so, improves living standards. Its *private costs* are the costs to the enterprise arising from engaging in a particular activity, e.g. building and running a factory. Its *private benefits* are the income derived from engaging in this new activity, e.g. the revenue from the new factory. This organization will have created *social benefits* within the community, such as jobs and sports grounds. However, there are some bad effects. These are *social costs*—pollution, dereliction, noise, etc. External costs that go beyond the management of the internal affairs of the firm are sometimes known as *spillover effects* or *externalities*.

Cost–benefit techniques were developed after the Second World War to help analyse complex investment decisions in a developing industrial nation. They take into account a balance of both social and financial criteria in order to aid decision-making. For example, the benefits of building a supermarket would be employment, improved facilities, increased rates for the local authority, etc., whereas the costs would be traffic congestion, adverse effects on other businesses, etc. These benefits and costs would have to be considered and weighed against one another by local authorities.

Cost–benefit analysis attempts to look objectively at all of the aspects of a decision-making process and to express those values in monetary terms so that some level of measurement can take place. Costs and benefits are therefore given a common unit of account for each year of the project's expected life. The net social benefit is obtained by subtracting a particular year's social cost from the same year's social benefit.

Cost–benefit analysis aims to measure not just the quantifiable private costs and benefits of an investment decision but also the surplus of social benefit over social cost. It must therefore be a more complete analysis, as it measures both cost and benefits to members of the community. Techniques are more appropriate when a large investment takes place which has significant spillover effects.

⌀ Case Study—Northfield Tannery Ltd

Northfield Tannery is in the process of acquiring a site that could be developed to provide a new factory at Wolverditch. The company is hoping to develop a compact new unit and then, over a five-year period, to move all of its operations over from Bridgemoor. Although residents in Wolverditch are unhappy about the prospect of increased traffic noise and water pollution, they concede that the moving of the tannery to the town and the subsequent creation of jobs would provide a number of benefits. Alternative uses for the land could be for a new supermarket, though the town already has three, or a multi-storey car park. Local fishermen have lobbied councillors over the possible effects on the local river. Conservationists in the town argue that residents' needs could best be served by creating a park or municipal golf course.

Questions

1. Identify the
   (a) private costs
   (b) private benefits
   (c) social costs
   (d) social benefits
   of building a tannery in Wolverditch.
2. Why are social considerations thought to be important?
3. Should chartered accountants involve themselves in social accounting? Provide an explanation with your answer.

Questions

Short-answer questions

1. Why are interest rates known as the cost of using money?
2. Provide an example of the use of funding.
3. Explain the workings of a cumulative preference share.
4. Name two dangers of using risk capital.
5. Name two ways in which a company might appropriate its profits. (*Source*: AEB)
6. How does a debenture work?
7. Give two reasons why a business may sell a debt to a factor. (*Source*: AEB)
8. What percentage of its face value will a 10 per cent debenture be worth when the rate of interest is 6 per cent?

9. What is meant by a personal guarantee?
10. What is meant by the term 'venture capital'?
11. Name two internal sources of capital.(*Source*: AEB)
12. Give three situations which may cause a cash flow forecast to be incorrect. (*Source*: AEB)
13. How would an increase in interest rates affect the shareholders in a highly geared company? (*Source*: AEB)
14. A company wishes to install a new machine. Give four methods of financing the purchase. (*Source*: AEB)
15. Name two benefits of leasing.
16. Why will businesses wish to hold cash in times of inflation?
17. Briefly explain why working capital 'oils the wheels' of business.
18. Name two dangers of insufficient working capital.
19. In your own words, explain the meaning of the term 'discounted cash flow'.
20. Distinguish between social costs and private costs.

Essays

1. What are the quantitative techniques of investment appraisal? Assess the extent to which they should be used by firms to plan future capital investment. (*Source*: AEB)
2. The following is an extract from the balance sheet of a public limited company:

	£
Ordinary shares	
Authorized 800 000 at £1 each	800 000
Issued and fully paid 700 000 at £1 each	700 000
Long-term borrowing	
Debentures 10 per cent (2010)	300 000
Capital employed	£1 000 000

The company now wishes to raise an additional £500 000 to finance the development of a new product. Assess the implications of the relevant alternative sources of finance. (*Source*: AEB)
3. How is it possible for a profitable firm to run out of cash, or for a cash-rich firm to be unprofitable?
4. Consider the view that a firm's growth imposes so many strains, of both an internal and external nature, that ultimate failure is inevitable. (*Source*: AEB)
5. Discuss the considerations that influence a firm in deciding between growth by internal or external expansion. (*Source*: Oxford)
6. (a) What do you understand by the term 'gearing', and how might it be measured?
    (b) How might a finance house use gearing ratios when considering an application from a medium-sized manufacturing company for a loan of £5 000 000 for expansion purposes?
    (c) What alternative sources of funds might the firm examine? (*Source*: Cambridge)

7. Compare the benefits of using risk capital with the benefits of using loan capital.

8. Leasing is a way a company can gain the use of an asset without having to buy it. Why has leasing become an increasingly popular way of acquiring fixed assets?

9. (a) What factors would a firm have to consider before acquiring an item of capital equipment?

   (b) How would these change if the item was expected to last only three years instead of ten? (*Source*: AEB)

10. Cash budgeting is an important technique for forecasting a company's financial needs and will influence the management of working capital. Discuss.

Data response questions

1 Delta Machine Tools Limited

Delta Machine Tools Limited is a well established light engineering company involved in the manufacture of specialist parts for the motor industry. It is listed on the Stock Exchange. A large proportion of its products are manufactured for the more expensive type of motor car such as Mercedes, BMW and Volvo and involves exporting to Germany and Scandinavia.

The company uses fairly traditional machinery, produces its product parts in medium-size batches, and assembles the final products. It operates at 90 per cent average capacity. Peaks are coped with by overtime in the evenings and weekends. The work-force is 30 per cent skilled and 70 per cent semi-skilled. Trade-union membership is 100 per cent and is split between two craft unions and one general worker union.

A number of new products have been developed to the tested prototype stage and the commercial prospects for them are good. It is estimated that in five years these products will account for 30 per cent of the company's sales. The effect will be to broaden the company's product range, and the market for existing products will not be affected.

The development work was not cheap and the company faces a serious cash flow problem over the next two to three years while bringing the new products into production.

The managing director has decided to raise the finance to deal with the situation as follows:

- Increase product prices   20%
- Bank borrowing   40%
- Internal savings mainly through labour lay-offs   40%

1. (a) Evaluate the managing director's solutions.
   (b) Suggest, giving reasons, other means whereby management might solve its cash flow problem. (*Source*: Oxford)

2 Business failures in the UK

Read the extract and answer the questions that follow.

24,000 business failures last year

THE deepening recession killed off a record 24 442 businesses in England and Wales in 1990, and the problem is likely to get worse before it improves.

The figure, which covers businesses being declared bankrupt or going into liquidation, easily beats the previous high of 21 682, recorded in 1984, according to Dun & Bradstreet, the business information company.

Last year's 34.6 per cent increase in the number of business failures compared with 1989 was also the highest annual rise on record.

The south of England was the worst affected area of the country, with the southwest region showing the biggest increase of all, a rise of 70.2 per cent. The smallest increase was in Wales, which saw only a 17.3 per cent rise in liquidations and bankruptcies.

London and the southeast recorded a 35.2 per cent increase.

Philip Mellor, marketing manager at Dun & Bradstreet, said, 'It is very disturbing that the level of business failures is now nearly twice as high as it was 10 years ago.'

'All the signs are that for the foreseeable future, the situation will get worse rather than improve,' he added.

'The 1990s have not started well for new businesses. The more new businesses there are, sadly, the greater the rate of failure. Many companies are not applying basic procedures to safeguard their cash flow.'

(*Source*: adapted from *The Times*, 2 January 1991)

1. What is meant by 'recession' in line 1?
2. Sketch a diagram that shows the comparison, between regions, of increases in business failures.
3. Why do some firms experience cash flow problems?
4. Outline two ways in which a business might ease cash flow problems, and state one drawback of each.
5. Describe three ways in which the failure of a small business might affect the owner's business position. (*Source*: AEB)

3 Stable finance

In some ways the problems had started with the milk quotas imposed by the European Community in 1987 to prevent the over-supply of milk, but William Provender reckoned the quotas were simply the final straw. In his opinion the difficulties had started much earlier—on the death of his father in 1979, when he and his brother Benjamin had inherited the 120-acre Home Farm. William and Benjamin had disagreed about the way to run it almost from the first moment. William was keen to continue the family tradition in farming, but Benjamin was far more interested and increasingly involved with the antiques trade. The land at Home Farm was used to produce arable crops, although the soil was really too wet to guarantee acceptable levels of profit. Indeed, from 1980 onwards profits steadily declined. This was partly due to geographical factors, but it was also a result of the different personalities of William and Benjamin.

William and Benjamin Provender

Although the two brothers got on well enough, their different interests meant that making decisions about the future of Home Farm was both difficult and extremely lengthy. William wanted to move into dairy farming, which was highly profitable given the price support then on offer from the European Community, and which in any case suited the farm's geography. Benjamin, on the other hand, argued for staying with arable production, which they both knew and understood. Any change would only delay his desire to move into the antiques business full-time. In the end, however, the declining profitability of arable production, and the attractiveness of the dairy option, persuaded Benjamin that it was the right move. Unfortunately, their delay in making the decision had a profound effect.

Dairy farming

The change-over involved the construction of a calving shed and a milking parlour. This was completed by 1987, but it required a considerable outlay, resulting in a shortage of capital to purchase a dairy herd. Consequently the farm was not producing milk at a critical moment: the time when the EC decided to limit milk production by the introduction of quotas. The new system meant that each farm was allowed to produce a certain amount of milk—its *quota*—based on existing levels of production. Zero output, as in the Provender's case, meant no quota, and, although it was possible to buy a quota from another farmer who did not need it, this was very expensive and therefore not an option for the Provenders.

The Crisis of 1993

Having missed the chance of a milk quota, the brothers continued to farm as before, but profitability went into serious decline, and the long-term view for arable farming looked bleak as the European Community continued its reform of the Common Agricultural Policy. Added to this was the brothers' quite different approaches to farming. By 1993 it was necessary to look at alternatives.

Plans for the future

William and Benjamin decided that there were three practical alternatives which they should investigate:

- *Project 1: Keep Home Farm, but convert it to organic production* The advantage of going organic was the price premium that could be earned on the farm's output. In order to qualify, however, the farm would need to use no artificial fertilizers on the fields for three years. During that time output would fall, and prices would remain low as at present. Given the small scale of the farm, there was some doubt that it would be able to sustain both brothers even when the price premium was earned. In any event, there was no guarantee that the premium would last indefinitely. There might also be the possibility of a 'set-aside' payment which the European Community was making to farmers who did not use all their land for production, but again, such a payment could not be guaranteed.

- *Project 2: Change the farm into a small working unit using animals that would have been kept on an English farm in the past, and open it to paying visitors*   This option attracted both brothers. William could continue to run the farm as at present, while introducing new breeds for tourists to enjoy. The visitors would in effect subsidize the farm's output so that it would not have to be so efficient in terms of output as it would otherwise need to be. Benjamin liked the idea because he felt he could use his knowledge of the antiques trade to acquire old farming implements. There were, however, marketing considerations; the reaction of neighbours, especially to the increased traffic and the problems of parking; and they would have to make alterations to the farm's outbuildings.

- *Project 3: Develop the farm into a livery and riding stable*   The farm's location, within an hour of London, made it an ideal spot for well-off commuters. The countryside was pretty, and many people kept horses or ponies. Consequently a large and ever growing number of farms in the area had turned over to livery stables. These stables looked after the animals for the owners for a set fee each week. As an extension of the livery, many also offered riding, either in the form of lessons and/or 'hacks'—rides into the countryside. The brothers were not that knowledgeable about horses, but they knew Lucy Girth, who was. Lucy had recently been forced to leave another local stable and was looking for work. Stable lads or girls would also be needed, but there were opportunities to employ them at very cheap rates under government training schemes. There would have to be a considerable capital outlay for the horses and ponies, and for the provision of loose boxes. In addition, the fields would require new fencing to reduce their size. There were marketing implications as well, although at present demand appeared to outstrip supply.

Table 16.9   Financial information

	Capital outlay		
	Project 1	Project 2	Project 3
Net cash flow	£37 000	£40 000	£106 000
Year 1	£8 000	£22 000	£59 000
Year 2	£8 000	£22 000	£59 000
Year 3	£8 000	£22 000	£59 000
Year 4	£12 000	£22 000	£59 000
Year 5	£12 000	£22 000	£59 000

Having considered the financial information presented in Table 16.9, both brothers realized that changes had to be made, but they feared that, not only might their current information be imperfect, their predictions for the future were also fraught with uncertainties. The days of the gentleman farmer were well and truly over . . .

1. Explain why, in supermarkets, organic produce costs more than non-organic produce.

2. Apart from financial considerations, what factors would the brothers have to take into account if they chose project 3?

Discount values (NPV of £1)

Year	10%
1	0.9091
2	0.8264
3	0.7513
4	0.6830
5	0.6209

(b) Study Fig. 16.9. What do you understand by the term 'internal rate of return'?
(c) What does Fig. 16.9 tell you about project 1?

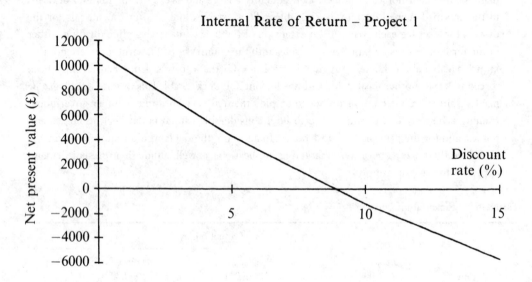

Figure 16.9 Internal rate of return, project 1. (*Source*: AEB)

(d) Assuming that the projects return a positive cash flow equally throughout the year, apply the payback method to all three projects, and on these calculations decide which is the best.
(e) Identify one advantage and one disadvantage of the payback method.
(f) Name one other method of investment appraisal apart from payback, discounted cash flow and internal rate of return.

4. Explain the impact of good motivation on organizations. Use examples from the Home Farm survey wherever appropriate to illustrate your answer. (*Source*: AEB)

4 Comparing investment projects

Consider the following data on two investment projects:

	Project A £	Project B £
Initial capital expenditure	60 000	60 000
Profits year 1	20 000	15 000
Profits year 2	20 000	20 000
Profits year 3	18 000	20 000
Profits year 4	20 000	23 000

The cost of capital is 10 per cent.

Using the percentage rates of discount from Table 16.4:

1. Calculate the payback period, the net present value and the internal rate of return for each project.
2. Comment on the merits of each of these methods.
3. Explain which project you would recommend.

Suggested reading

Bangs, D., *Controlling Cash Flow*. Kogan Page, 1989.
Chadwick, L., *Accounting & Finance in Practice*. Stanley Thornes, 1990.
Hines, T., *Foundation Accounting*. Checkmate Arnold, 1987.
Lines, D., *Controlling Business Finance*. Longman, 1993.

17

The management of costs

Almost all business activities involve some element of cost, and most managers have to deal with costs on a day-to-day basis. Costs are fundamental, from the early development of business plans through to the controlling and monitoring of expenditure. Costing techniques help managers to work out what they should be doing and to develop measures that help them to control their activities. Cost accounting and the use of costing techniques also provide a useful source of information for management accountants, who use information from costs to try to guide their organization in a particular direction in order to achieve objectives (Fig. 17.1).

Information about costs will help to:

1. Create short-term, medium-term and long-term plans.
2. Control the organization's activities.
3. Decide between alternative strategies.
4. Appraise performance at strategic, departmental and operational levels.

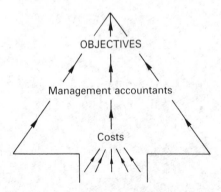

Figure 17.1 Using costs to achieve objectives.

Management accounting therefore involves collecting data and processing them so that decisions to control operations can be more efficient (see Fig. 17.2).

Cost accounting and the knowledge of costing techniques provide access to important sources of data for management accountants. They will use their knowledge of costs to predict future events. In doing so they will try to anticipate changes in taxation, interest rates, actions of

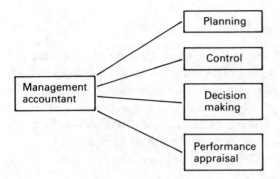

Figure 17.2 The role of the management accountant.

competitors and markets and so on. They will also look at past events, and at information recorded about these events, in order to guide future decision-making.

Over the past 20 years the nature of industry has changed dramatically. Information technology has revolutionized the ways in which information is being provided. Managers have to be adaptable to changing disciplines so that they can provide the right information when required. In order to do this they must be constantly aware of new concepts, principles and techniques designed to help them meet their objectives.

Costs

Even in everyday language, the word 'cost' has several meanings. The cost of items we purchase is something we think about daily; for us it is a money sacrifice we have to make for goods or services that we require. Cost also infers a form of measurement, and we automatically attach value to many products we see. It can be an unwelcome word, particularly if we come across hidden costs which we had not anticipated having to pay. Organizations frequently refer to calculating the cost of an event or an activity, and managers might talk about *costing an activity*. Within this context, they are using a knowledge of costs together with a knowledge of revenues to determine whether or not something they are planning will ultimately reap the rewards they desire.

Nearly all business activities involve some sort of cost. A good knowledge of costs and their influences is fundamental in assessing the profitability of alternatives, as profits are only a reflection of income over these costs. Costs from the past, which have already been incurred, should provide a guide to costs in the future; however, they have to be critically examined, discussed and often adjusted to be of use to the accountant for predicting future profitability. At a later stage accountants will make informed comparisons between actual events and standards that have been set.

$\mathcal{P}$ Case Study—The cost of the Tunnel

The Channel Tunnel finally opened one year later than planned and at a cost of around £10 billion, which is more than double the original estimate. Eurotunnel frequently had to turn to banks and shareholders for help, and there have been many compensation claims against the British and French governments and their national railways; these relate to inadequate infrastructure on the UK side linking the tunnel to the rail network, late entry into service of through trains, excessive costs imposed on Eurotunnel by the intergovernment safety commission, and alleged unfair subsidies for rival ferry and airline operators.

In June 1993 Eurotunnel again had to seek help from shareholders. Shareholders were also told that there was no end in sight to the £1.3 billion dispute between Eurotunnel and TML concerning *cost overruns*. Furthermore, Eurotunnel is in dispute with the consortium building its passenger shuttle trains.

André Bénard, the Eurotunnel chairman, also told shareholders that Eurotunnel was examining ways of bringing new partners into the project. This might involve bankers agreeing to swap debt for equity, and part of the eventual settlement with TML could include Eurotunnel shares.

Questions

1. How important is it for an organization to forecast the future cost of a project?
2. Why do you think that Eurotunnel's forecasts were so wildly inaccurate?
3. What factors indicated above had they not taken into consideration?
4. Why might 'cost overruns' make it difficult for managers to control the project?
5. To what extent does the Channel Tunnel project point towards a lack of planning? Provide an explanation with your answer.

Types of cost

There are a number of ways in which costs can be classified.

Fixed costs

These are costs that do not increase as output increases. Fixed costs do not change over a range of output even though output within that range will vary (see Fig. 17.3). For example, if a factory has the capacity to do so, it might increase its production from 10 000 to 15 000 units; but its overheads such as rent, rates and heating bills would still be the same as they were when the factory was producing only 10 000 units.

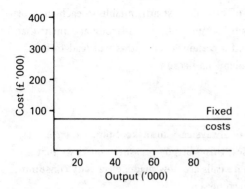

Figure 17.3 Fixed costs.

Economists say that fixed costs are costs that do not vary with output in a given period, but that in the longer term they will vary; for example, if the company needed to increase its production of units further it might have to build another factory, buy new machines and incur new overheads.

Average fixed costs

Average fixed costs represent the percentage of total fixed costs incurred by each product. As output rises, the level of average fixed costs will fall. This figure is arrived at by dividing total fixed costs by output. For example, if fixed costs are £100 000 and output is 2000 units, average fixed costs will be £50 per unit. If production increases to 4000 units, average fixed costs will fall to £25 per unit.

Variable costs

Variable costs are those that increase as output increases, because more of these factors need to be employed as input to increase output (see Fig. 17.4). For example, if you produce more goods you may need more raw materials, more production line workers, more power, etc.

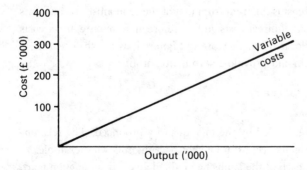

Figure 17.4 Variable costs.

Average variable costs represent the average level of variable cost attributable to each item of output. This is found by dividing total variable costs by output. There is a strong argument that average variable costs rise when capacity goes beyond a certain level as this will lead to break-downs, inefficiencies, overcrowding, managerial problems and so on.

Semi-variable costs

The distinction between fixed and variable costs is not always easy to make. Some expenses may be considered to be semi-variable. If output increases, this will put pressures on costs that are relatively fixed. The telephone bill might go up as more calls are now made; electricity consumption in the office may go up as staff put in more overtime; etc.

Direct costs (prime costs)

These are costs that can be attributed directly to the product whose costs are being assessed. For example, it might be possible to say that 10 per cent of a particular product cost is the direct labour cost of producing it, 15 per cent might be the cost of its direct materials, and so on. It tends to be easier to identify variable costs with direct costs as they vary more directly with output. Fixed costs are more difficult to allocate to the production cost of particular commodities.

Indirect costs

These costs cannot be identified with the production of specific commodities. They will probably include costs attributable to all departments, e.g. costs of cleaning, and the salaries of salespeople and management.

Marginal costs

In economics the marginal cost is the cost of producing one more unit of output; e.g., the marginal cost of producing the 100th unit of output is the extra cost of manufacturing the 100th unit after having already made 99. It is therefore the total cost of making the first 100 minus the total cost of making the first 99.

An accountant's definition of marginal cost is different from that of the economist. Accountants recognize the problems of trying to allocate indirect costs and therefore allocate only direct costs to a product. Indirect costs are left unallocated but they are not ignored; as we shall see, there must be a sufficient income to cover them and provide a surplus for profits.

Average costs

Average cost is quite simply the total cost divided by the total quantity produced. The relationship of the marginal concept to the average concept can be shown in the following example.

If a farmer normally receives £100 for each of the lambs he or she delivers to an auction mart, then a revenue of £110 per lamb will push the average up and £90 per lamb will push the average down. Therefore the marginal return will affect the average return, as at the top price the average will increase and at the bottom price it will decrease.

In a similar way, if average costs are rising marginal costs will be above average costs, and when average costs are falling the marginal costs will be below them.

With a small output marginal costs per unit tend to be high, but in the long run, as output increases costs fall owing to economies of scale or the advantages of being large, such as being able to obtain discounts for bulk purchases, preferential interest rates and the like.

As firms move beyond an ideal size, they begin to develop diseconomies of scale and to incur the disadvantages of being too large—poor morale, long chains of command, etc. At this point marginal costs will start to rise.

♀ Case Study—Taylour Coats PLC

Taylour Coats manufactures high-class country jackets. Business has developed well over recent years, particularly in their export markets to the United States, where English country clothing has become increasingly popular.

The company is managed and owned by Manjit Gill, the Managing Director, and Rosemary Williams, who supervises the operations. They own a factory unit on a trading estate in Gosforth and employ 20 full-time employees: a foreman, 15 machine operators who cut out the materials for the part-time workers, and 4 dispatchers. The part-time workers are employed as subcontractors, using their own sewing machines at home to make up the jackets from the cut-out pieces that have been sent to them.

The foreman is paid £400 per week, the machine operators £230 per week and the dispatchers £180 per week. The part-timers are paid £10 for each jacket they make up.

Other business costs include:

- Electricity at £100 per week
- Rent and rates at £500 per week
- Loan repayments, including interest at £200 per week
- Other fixed costs at £120 per week
- Directors' salaries for Manjit and Rosemary of £600 per week each
- Direct material costs for each jacket of £5

The existing capacity for Taylour Coats is 400 jackets per week. If it needs to produce more than this, it has to pay higher rates to cover overtime put in by part-time workers, which results in an increase in part-time rates from £10 for each jacket to £15 up to a maximum capacity of 500 jackets. At present jackets are priced at £35 and Taylour has a consistent weekly turnover of 350 jackets.

Taylour has been approached by two American chain stores who have tested samples and wish to purchase some jackets on a regular basis. Austin Stores Inc. wishes to purchase 100 jackets per week and is willing to pay £28 per jacket. NMAUSA wishes to purchase 50 jackets per week and is willing to pay £32 per jacket.

As a personal friend of the directors and an adviser to the business, these figures have been left with you for further analysis.

Questions

1. Construct a table to show the fixed, variable and total weekly costs at each 50 units of production up to a maximum of 500 jackets.
2. Present the fixed, variable and total costs in a graphical form for the week.
3. Calculate the profit the company is generating at its present level of sales of 350 jackets per week.
4. Advise the directors as to whether they should accept:
   (a) the Austin Stores order;
   (b) the NMAUSA order;
   (c) both;
   (d) neither.
   Support your answer with figures and explanations.

Budgetary control

Budgetary control is the technique of looking at a business's future in order to anticipate what is going to happen and then trying to make it happen. It is considered to be a system of responsibility accounting because it puts an onus on budgeted areas to perform in a way that has been outlined for them. Its success will depend upon the quality of information provided.

Businesses that do not budget may be pleased or upset when presented with their final annual accounts. This method of management is uncertain and undisciplined. In order to compete more efficiently, it is not feasible for management to wait for the results of an audit to see how they have performed. Budgeting enables the financial manager to develop an understanding of how the company is likely to perform in the future. Budgets can cover almost every aspect of business activity, from production, cash and overheads to labour, purchases, debtors and creditors. Information drawn from these budgets can then be used to forecast the final accounts for the end of the following year.

We all budget to a greater or lesser extent. Our short-term budget might relate to how we are going to get through the coming week and do all of the things that we want to do. Our slightly longer-term budget might involve being able to afford Christmas presents in two months' time. Our longest-term budget could involve the planning necessary to afford the car tax, MOT and motor insurance which all fall due ten months from now. In the same way, businesses try to see far into the future. Although a detailed budget is prepared only for the year ahead, it can be part of a five-year plan. The problem is that, the further one looks into the future, the more difficult it is to see accurately.

Companies often appoint a budget controller whose job is to co-ordinate budgetary activities. The budgeting team will consist of representatives from various areas of activity within the

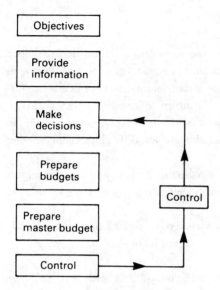

Figure 17.5 The budgetary process.

company. This team should be involved in every stage of the following process (see also Fig. 17.5):

1. *Consider objectives*   All decisions should enable a firm to work towards achieving its objectives, e.g. profit-maximizing, improving product quality, increasing output.
2. *Provide information*   Managers often look at figures from the past so that budgets are based on the results of the previous year. Zero-based budgeting is a technique that starts each year afresh so the performance of the whole organization is re-appraised. A clear knowledge of the likely performance of the industry in general and the political and economic climate is likely to help.
3. *Make decisions*   Forward planning and co-ordination of departmental activities will inevitably present a need to make decisions such as how much to spend on advertising, whether to put off the purchase of capital equipment, etc.
4. *Prepare budgets*   Detailed budgets are then prepared for all of the necessary areas of business activity.
5. *Prepare a master budget*   Various budgets can be linked together to produce a master budget which will show a forecast set of final accounts.
6. *Control*   Even though a plan is outlined in the form of a budget, this does not necessarily mean that it will take place as planned. Managers try to use budgets as a guide to achieve certain results. If there is a difference between actual performance and budgeted performance at the end of a year, action can be taken. Variance analysis is used to analyse the difference between the two. Feedback from variance analysis can affect decision-making in subsequent years.

The benefits of a budgetary system are:

1. Every year the business is reviewed and this gives members of the various departments a better understanding of the working of the organization as a whole. Often by participating in the budgetary process they feel that their experience is contributing to policy decisions. The process also provides targets and highlights areas of concern.
2. Budgeting increases co-operation between departments and lowers departmental barriers. In this way members of one department can become aware of the difficulties facing another department.
3. By being involved in the budgetary process, non-accountants become aware of the importance of costs. Their increasing awareness will probably encourage them to work harder to meet budgeted targets.
4. Budgeting will encourage those who participate in the exercise to think more about profitability and about their role in helping the company to reach its objectives.

There are, however, some inherent dangers, particularly if the budgetary system is rigid. These could be:

1. If actual results are considerably different from the budgeted targets, the budget can lose its significance as a means of control. Whereas a *fixed budget* is unable to adapt to changes, a *flexible budget* will recognize changes in the behaviour of its variables and can be amended each control period in line with changing activities.
2. Following a budget too rigidly can restrict a business's activities. For example, if the budget for entertainment has been exceeded and subsequent visiting customers are not treated with the usual hospitality, orders may be lost; on the other hand, if a manager realized towards the end of the year that the department had underspent, it is quite possible that he or she might go on a spending spree.
3. If senior management decides to impose its budget on departments or middle managers, they are likely to pay little attention to it and make no effort to ensure it succeeds.

The main objective of budgetary control is for management to survey the future and for managers to exercise some control over future events. By doing this they can develop an insight into areas of concern and take action to avoid any problems.

Preparing budgets

In the last chapter we prepared a cash budget so that we could forecast cash flow over a period of time. We will now examine all of the budgets necessary to produce a master budget or a forecasted set of final accounts.

Altron Limited's balance sheet at the end of its second year of operations is shown in Fig. 17.6. The company's accountant, Andrew Baxter, has been asked to set up a budgetary system to forecast the next six months' activities. As budgetary controller, he has met representatives from

Altron Limited balance sheet as at 30 April 1993

	£	£	£ Net book value
FIXED ASSETS			
Premises			90 000
Plant and machinery			105 000
Office equipment			9 000
Motor vehicles			50 000
			254 000
CURRENT ASSETS			
Stocks: finished goods			
(2000 units)		26 000	
Raw materials		2 000	
Debtors		87 000	
Bank		4 000	
		119 000	
less CURRENT LIABILITIES			
Creditors for fixed expenses	3 000		
Creditors for raw materials			
(March 28 500 and April 25 500)	54 000	57 000	
Net current assets			62 000
Assets employed			316 000
Financed by:			
Share capital			
Ordinary shares			250 000
Preference shares			46 000
Reserves			20 000
Capital employed			316 000

Figure 17.6 Altron Limited: balance sheet.

various departments and discussed details at length before putting together budgetary estimates. Their plans for the six months ending 31 October 1993 are as follows:

1. After lengthy consultations, a sales price of £15.00 per unit has been agreed. By carefully analysing the market, the sales figures are expected to be:

	May	June	July	Aug	Sept	Oct
No. of units	6500	7750	8000	8200	8550	9000

All of the sales are on credit, and debtors usually pay their outstanding balances one month after they have bought the goods.

2. In order to satisfy production requirements, it has been agreed that the purchases of raw materials will be:

	May	Jun	July	Aug	Sept	Oct
	£23 700	£24 300	£24 500	£27 500	£28 250	£24 750

All raw materials are bought on credit, and the creditors for raw materials will be paid two months after purchase.

3. It has been decided that production will be 8000 units per month for May to August and 9000 units per month for September and October.

4. Production costs will be (per unit):

	£
Direct materials	3.00
Direct labour	4.00
Variable overheads	6.00
	13.00

Direct labour and the variable overheads will be paid for in the same month as the units are produced.

5. Fixed expenses average £3000 per month and these are always paid one month in arrears.

Andrew Baxter intends to produce:

- A sales forecast
- A raw materials budget showing figures for each month
- A production budget showing figures for each month (in units)
- A production cost budget showing figures for each month
- A statement showing total debtors and creditors at the end of October
- A cash budget
- A forecast operating statement (trading and profit and loss account) for the six months ended 31 October 1993
- A forecast balance sheet as at 31 October 1993

Sales forecast

The *sales forecast* is found by multiplying the selling price of £15.00 by the number of units for each month. In May the value of sales is expected to be £97 500, in June £116 250, July £120 000, August £123 000, September £128 250 and October £135 000. The total sales figure for the six months is £720 000. Debtors pay one month after having bought the goods, so the debtors from the balance sheet in April will pay in May, May debtors will pay in June, etc. When Andrew produces his cash budget, these will be entered as receipts.

Raw materials budget

The raw materials budget (Fig. 17.7) ensures that there is always an availability of resources moving on to production and that levels do not dwindle or run out. Decisions about minimum stock levels will have been taken beforehand. The raw materials budget involves adding purchases to the opening stocks of raw materials for each month and then deducting those used in production each month.

Raw materials budget

	May £	June £	July £	Aug. £	Sept. £	Oct. £
Opening stock	2 000	1 700	2 000	2 500	6 000	7 250
add Purchases	23 700	24 300	24 500	27 500	28 250	24 750
	25 700	26 000	26 500	30 000	34 250	32 000
less Materials used in production*	24 000	24 000	24 000	24 000	27 000	27 000
Closing stock of raw materials	1 700	2 000	2 500	6 000	7 250	5 000

*Production is 8000 units from May to August and 9000 units in September and October. Production costs for raw or direct materials are £3 per unit. Production will therefore use up £24 000 of materials from May to August and £27 000 of materials in September and October.

Figure 17.7 Altron Limited: raw materials budget.

It must be remembered that creditors for raw materials are paid two months after purchase. This means that those for March (see balance sheet) will be paid in May, those from April in June, etc. In the cash budget these will be payments.

Production budget

There is a clear link between the production budget (Fig. 17.8) and sales. Closing stocks of finished goods are also an important issue, and the directors of Altron Limited will need to ensure that the company can respond readily to increasing orders if this becomes necessary. The production budget is normally produced in units.

Production budget (in units)

	May	June	July	Aug.	Sept.	Oct.
Opening stock of finished goods	2 000	3 500	3 750	3 750	3 550	4 000
add Production	8 000	8 000	8 000	8 000	9 000	9 000
	10 000	11 500	11 750	11 750	12 550	13 000
less Sales	6 500	7 750	8 000	8 200	8 550	9 000
Closing stock of finished goods	3 500	3 750	3 750	3 550	4 000	4 000

Figure 17.8 Altron Limited: production budget (in units).

The opening stock of finished goods is added to the anticipated production levels for each month and then the monthly sales are deducted. The closing stock of finished goods is therefore 4000 units. As stocks are valued at cost price, the value of the closing stock of finished goods to be transferred to the balance sheet will be:

$$4000 \text{ units} \times £13 \text{ production cost} = £52\ 000$$

Production cost budget

The production cost budget (Fig. 17.9) supplies the costs of production on a month-by-month basis and produces the total cost of goods completed, which can then be transferred to the trading section of the forecast operating statement. It involves multiplying the unit production cost of direct materials, direct labour and direct overheads by the number of units produced month by month.

Production cost budget

	8000 units per month				9000 units per month		
	May £	June £	July £	Aug. £	Sept. £	Oct. £	Total £
Materials cost	24 000	24 000	24 000	24 000	27 000	27 000	150 000
Labour cost	32 000	32 000	32 000	32 000	36 000	36 000	200 000
Overhead cost (variable)	48 000	48 000	48 000	48 000	54 000	54 000	300 000
	104 000	104 000	104 000	104 000	117 000	117 000	650 000

Figure 17.9 Altron Limited: production cost budget.

Total debtors and creditors

Andrew now works out the debtors' figure for the end of October. As debtors pay their outstanding balances one month after they have bought goods, the debtors' figure for the end of October will be the sales figure for September of £128 250. He knows that creditors for raw materials are paid two months after purchase; the creditors' figure will therefore be made up of September's and October's purchases of raw materials of £28 250 and £24 750, totalling £53 000.

Cash budget

Andrew now has sufficient information to work out his cash budget (see Fig. 17.10):

Receipts

	£
May (April's debtors)	87 000
June (May's debtors)	97 500
July (etc.)	116 250
August	120 000
September	123 000
October	128 250

Payments

May		£
Raw materials (March)	=	28 500
Direct labour 8000 × 4	=	32 000
Variable overheads 8000 × 6	=	48 000
Fixed expenses	=	3 000
		£111 500

June		£
Raw materials (April)	=	25 500
Direct labour 8000 × 4	=	32 000
Variable overheads 8000 × 6	=	48 000
Fixed expenses	=	3 000
		£108 500

July		£
Raw materials (May)	=	23 700
Direct labour 8000 × 4	=	32 000
Variable overheads 8000 × 6	=	48 000
Fixed expenses	=	3 000
		£106 700

August		£
Raw materials (June)	=	24 300
Direct labour 8000 × 4	=	32 000
Variable overheads 8000 × 6	=	48 000
Fixed expenses	=	3 000
		£107 300

	September	£
Raw materials (July)	=	24 500
Direct labour 9000 × 4	=	36 000
Variable overheads 9000 × 6	=	54 000
Fixed expenses	=	3 000
		£117 500

	October	£
Raw materials (August)	=	27 500
Direct labour 9000 × 4	=	36 000
Variable overheads 9000 × 6	=	54 000
Fixed expenses	=	3 000
		£120 500

Cash budget

	May £	June £	July £	Aug. £	Sept. £	Oct. £
CASH BALANCE	4 000	(20 500)	(31 500)	(21 950)	(9 250)	(3 750)
add Receipts	87 000	97 500	116 250	120 000	123 000	128 250
	91 000	77 000	84 750	98 050	113 750	124 500
less Payments	111 500	108 500	106 700	107 300	117 500	120 500
Balance carried forward	(20 500)	(31 500)	(21 950)	(9 250)	(3 750)	4 000

Figure 17.10 Altron Limited: cash budget.

Master budget

Now that all of the sectional budgets have been completed, Andrew is in a position to provide a master budget in the form of a *forecast operating statement* (Fig. 17.11) and a *forecast balance sheet* (Fig. 17.12).

Forecast operating statement for the six months ended 31/10/93

	£	£
Sales		720 000
less Cost of sales		
Opening stock of finished goods	26 000	
add Cost of goods supplied	650 000	
	676 000	
less Closing stock of finished goods	52 000	624 000
Gross profit		96 000
less Overheads		
Fixed expenses		18 000
Net profit		78 000

NB: For the purpose of this example, we have assumed no taxation and no payment of dividends.

Figure 17.11 Altron Limited: master budget.

Forecast balance sheet as at 31/10/93

	£	£	Net book value £
FIXED ASSETS			
Premises			90 000
Plant and machinery			105 000
Office equipment			9 000
Motor vehicles			50 000
			254 000
CURRENT ASSETS			
Stocks: finished goods (4000 units)		52 000	
Raw materials		5 000	
Debtors		135 000	
Bank		4 000	
		196 000	
less CURRENT LIABILITIES			
Creditors for fixed expenses	3 000		
Creditors for raw materials (Sept: 28 250 + Oct: 24 750)	53 000	56 000	
Net current assets			140 000
Assets employed			394 000
Financed by:			
Share capital:			
Ordinary shares			250 000
Preference shares			46 000
Reserves (20 000 + retained profit)			98 000
Capital employed			£394 000

Figure 17.12 Altron Limited: forecast balance sheet.

Information from the sectional budgets and the master budget can now be fed back to departments. The budgetary system has co-ordinated revenue and expenditure areas and organized them into an overall plan.

⌕ Case Study—Widget Supply Limited

You have recently been appointed to the board of Widget Supply Limited, a company based in Hessle near Hull which has successfully supplied widgets to light engineering companies for the past 30 years.

The present managing director has recently succeeded his father who had held the position over many years. In the past the only financial information available to management has been half-yearly profit and loss accounts and balance sheets. These have always been presented on traditional lines. In your role as company accountant, you feel that management could improve decision-making within an improved control structure and you suggest that budgeting will go a long way to providing the solution.

Questions

1. What steps would you take to initiate a budgetary system?
2. What problems are you likely to encounter and how might these problems be overcome?
3. Which budget statements would you suggest?
4. How will information be displayed in these statements?
5. How will this information improve the quality of decisions?

Variance analysis

As the budget period gets under way, departmental co-ordinators will follow its progress and, by exercising close control over their areas, will try to ensure its success.

They could break the year down into monthly accounting periods so that, as the year progresses, the actual figures can be compared with budgeted figures and the difference of variance analysed. If actual figures are more than budgeted figures, there will be:

- An adverse expenditure variance
- A favourable sales variance

If actual figures are less than budgeted figures, there will be:

- A favourable expenditure variance
- An adverse sales variance

Variance analysis detects problems and enables managers to take prompt action to try to improve efficiency and profitability. For example, there could be a sudden upturn in the raw materials budget; this might be due to:

- Increased wastage
- Inefficiency by operators
- Materials damaged in transit
- Inefficient buying
- Increasing raw material costs

The list is inexhaustive. The variance has indicated a problem; managers can now use their experience to find the cause.

If variations persist and actual and budgeted figures differ dramatically, the budget will lose its relevance, unless flexible budgets have taken into account these variations.

Case Study—Beatties Wool Limited

The report reproduced in Fig. 17.13 was extracted from a production department at Beatties.

Cost variance report (Department: Dyes; Month: June)

	Actual £	Budget £	Variance £
Direct labour	12 000	12 000	0
Indirect labour			
Clerical	450	400	+50
Supervision	1 200	1 200	0
Overtime	300	100	+200
Repairs and maintenance	500	200	+300
Power	700	1 000	−300
Total budget	15 150	14 900	+250

(Actual) production: 40 000 units
(Budgeted) production: 38 000 units
Production variance: +2 000 units

Figure 17.13 Cost variance report.

Questions

1. Comment briefly on the cost variance report.
2. In what ways does a report of this kind help management to control the business?
3. How might a report be an investigative tool?
4. What would have happened to variances if the actual amount produced was 50 per cent higher than expected?

Standard costing

Standard costing is a system of costing that can take place only where a system of budgetary control exists, as it works hand in hand with such a system. It provides a method of assessing efficiency by comparing an advance estimate of cost with actual costs. Variance analysis enables differences to be highlighted and presented in a tabular form so that management can see from this breakdown why standard and actual costs have differed. Investigations reveal the causes of the variations.

Costing

Whereas the financial accountant analyses historical costs in order to produce financial statements, the management accountant tries to obtain information that will help current decisions to be made and plans to be established Two major areas of concern for any manufacturing company are:

- The cost of manufacturing each product
- The cost of running each department

For example, management accountants will want to know which products are profitable and which are not. They will also want to know which departments are uneconomic and too expensive to run. Savings might be made if certain departmental activities were contracted out. Costing provides information enabling decisions of this magnitude to be taken.

Establishing *cost centres*, which allow each section or product to be costed separately, enables costs to be attributed to a particular product or a particular department. These are convenient units from which accounting information can be extracted. However, there are sometimes problems. Allocating direct costs such as raw materials is relatively easy, but how do you allocate canteen costs, maintenance costs, insurance and so on? The apportionment of costs needs to be carefully considered.

There are two contrasting methods of determining the ways in which a product's cost is prepared.

Absorption costing

This method incorporates full costs into a product's manufacture; all costs are absorbed into the cost of a product. The absorption unit cost is calculated by dividing total costs (both fixed and variable) by total production in order to obtain a unit cost. In order to price the product, a profit percentage is added to the cost to obtain a selling price.

For example, Safe Products Limited manufacture one particular type of cooker guard. Over a particular year it intends to manufacture and sell 20 000 units. It looks for a 20 per cent profit on sales, and its fixed costs are £40 000 and variable costs are £80 000.

The absorption unit cost is found by adding together fixed and variable costs to calculate total cost:

	£
Fixed costs	40 000
Variable costs	80 000
Total cost	= £120 000

This is then divided by the number produced in order to obtain the unit cost:

$$\frac{120\,000}{20\,000} = £6 \text{ per unit}$$

The profit is to be 20 per cent on sales. This means that £6 will reflect 80 per cent of the selling price. In order to determine the selling price, we perform the following calculation:

$$£6 \times \frac{100}{80} = £7.50$$

The selling price necessary to obtain a 20 per cent profit on sales from costs of £6.00 is £7.50.

Marginal costing

Marginal costing takes into account all of the problems involved in allocating fixed costs. Here only the variable costs are allocated to each product. The difference between the variable costs and the selling price is known as the *contribution*. By manufacturing and selling enough units to produce a total contribution in excess of fixed overheads, a business will make a profit.

In the case of Safe Products Limited, assuming a similar selling price of £7.50, the contribution will be the selling price of £7.50 less the variable costs of £4.00, or £3.50.

The variable cost per unit is found by dividing the total variable costs by the total number of units:

$$\frac{\text{Total variable costs}}{\text{Total number of units}} = \frac{£80\,000}{£20\,000} = £4.00$$

The company will aim to sell a sufficient number of products at £7.50 to pay off fixed overheads and then provide a surplus. If 20 000 units are sold:

At 20 000 units	Absorption costing £	Marginal costing £
Sales (£7.50 × 20 000)	150 000	150 000
less Absorption cost (20 000 × 6)	120 000	
less Marginal cost (20 000 × 4)		80 000
Contribution		70 000
less Fixed cost		40 000
Net Profit	£30 000	£30 000

Using both costing methods, if production is increased to 30 000 units the following figures apply:

	Absorption costing £	Marginal costing £
At 30 000 units		
Sales (£7.50 × 30 000)	225 000	225 000
less Absorption cost (30 000 × 6)	180 000	
less Marginal cost (30 000 × 4)		120 000
Contribution		105 000
less Fixed cost		40 000
Net Profit	£45 000	£65 000

With absorption costing, the unit of fixed expenses at this level of production is not £40 000 at a unit cost of £2.00 (£40 000 divided by 20 000 units), but £40 000 divided by 30 000 units or £1.33. Absorption costing has therefore overstated the overhead if production goes beyond an anticipated level.

Marginal costing, and the principle of costing the variable costing and providing a contribution to cover fixed costs, can be developed further in break-even analysis.

Break-even analysis

Break-even is the unique point at which a business makes no profit and no loss. If sales are beyond the break-even point profits are made, and if they are below the break-even point losses are made. In marginal costing break-even is at the point at which the contribution equals the fixed costs.

To calculate the break-even point:

1. Calculate the unit contribution (selling price less variable costs).
2. Divide the fixed overhead costs by unit contribution. For Safe Products Limited:

$$\frac{\text{Fixed overhead costs}}{\text{Contribution per unit}} = \frac{£40\,000}{£3.50} = 11\,429 \text{ units (to nearest unit)}$$

The sales value can be calculated by multiplying the 11 429 by the selling price:

$$11\,429 \text{ units} \times 7.50 = £85\,717.50$$

Safe Products Limited has covered costs and broken even with a sales value of £85 717.50. Anything in excess of this will provide the company with profits.

If Safe Products Limited has a profit target, this technique can be used to calculate the number of units that need to be sold and the value of sales required to achieve that target. For example, if the company aims for £20 000 profit, then, by adding this £20 000 to the fixed costs and dividing by the contribution, we will arrive at the number of units that need to be sold to meet this target:

$$\frac{\pounds40\,000\,(\text{fixed costs}) + \pounds20\,000\,(\text{profit target})}{\pounds3.50\,(\text{contribution})} = 17\,143\text{ units (to nearest unit)}$$

That is, 17 143 units (to nearest unit) need to be sold to achieve that target with a sales value of

$$17\,143 \times \pounds7.50 = \pounds128\,572.50$$

Break-even charts

Information such as this could be obtained quickly from a graphical representation of marginal costing techniques in the form of a break-even chart. This will show the position at which a business will break even and the extent to which it will make profits or losses at various levels of activity.

A break-even chart (see Fig. 17.14) is constructed as follows on p. 534:

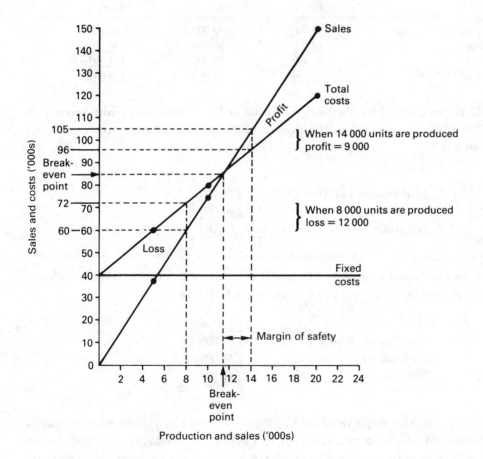

Figure 17.14 Break-even chart.

1. *Label the horizontal axis* for units of production and sales.
2. *Label the vertical axis* to represent the value of sales and costs.
3. *Plot fixed costs*   Fixed costs will remain at the same level over all levels of production and will be plotted by a straight line parallel to the horizontal axis.
4. *Plot variable costs*   These are shown rising from where the fixed-cost line touches the vertical axis. The variable cost line will therefore also represent total costs. It is plotted by calculating total costs at two or three random levels of production.
5. *Plot sales*   These are plotted by taking two or three random levels of turnover. This curve will rise from the intersection of the two axes.

The break-even point will be where the total cost and sales lines intersect. The area to the left of the break-even point between the sales and total cost curve represents losses, and the area to the right of the break-even point between the sales and total cost curves represents profits.

| | 5000 units | 10 000 units | 20 000 units |
	£	£	£
Variable cost = £4 per unit	20 000	40 000	80 000
Fixed costs	40 000	40 000	40 000
Total cost	60 000	80 000	120 000
Sales = £7.50 per unit	37 500	75 000	150 000

Figure 17.14 graphically shows the break-even point of 11 429 units with a sales 'revenue' of £87 717.50. If sales are at 14 000 units, we can see that profit (the difference between sales and total costs) is at:

Contribution: 14 000 × £3.50   = £49 000
less Fixed costs   £40 000
Net profit   £9 000

This is known as the *margin of safety*. The margin of safety is the difference between a selected level of output and the break-even point. If sales are at 8000 units:

Contribution: 8000 × £3.50   =   £28 000
less Fixed costs   £40 000
Net loss   £12 000

The break-even chart is a simple visual tool enabling managers to anticipate the effects of changes in production and sales upon the profitability of a business. It emphasizes the importance of earning revenue to make profits and particularly helps those who are unused to interpreting accounting information.

₽ Case Study—Uncle John's cottage

Your Uncle John, a local farmer, has come to you for some advice. He is considering the future use of a recently vacated tied cottage on his farm as a holiday cottage.

The property has been allowed to deteriorate over the years and it is obvious that considerable internal improvements will be necessary before the cottage can be used as a holiday let. The house is, however, full of character with extensive views over North Yorkshire, extending to the Pennines on a clear day. There is easy access to Teesside, Northallerton and Thirsk.

The accommodation comprises:

- Upstairs: three double bedrooms, large bathroom/toilet
- Downstairs: large kitchen/diner, large lounge with open hearth and french window into the garden

The legal aspects of letting the cottage have been cleared, and all that remains is for the cottage to be renovated and furnished.

The following quotation for renovation has been received:

	£
Complete redecoration	1895
Refit bathroom and kitchen	2800
Central heating	2200
Wash basins in bedrooms	200

The quotation has been supplied by Penine Rose Builders, a fairly large local firm with a reputation for doing work of a reasonable quality.

Your uncle decides to fit the cottage out with basic items of reasonable quality and some durable furniture. These cost:

	£
Furniture and fittings	3000
Kitchen equipment and household items	750

The finance for the renovation and for the purchase of the furnishings and fittings is obtained by means of a five-year bank loan with a fixed annual interest rate of 10 per cent payable each calendar month, and based upon the original sum. The loan principal is to be paid in five equal instalments.

Your uncle anticipates the following costs:

Fixed costs
- Annual loan repayment
- Annual interest on loan
- Council tax: £215 per half year
- Water rates: £80 per half year
- Insurance: £150 per annum
- Electricity: £17.50 per quarter

Variable costs
- Cleaner: £3 per hour for 5 hours per week
- Electricity and heating: £5 per week

The suggested scale of charges is as follows:

April–September: £170 per week
October–March: £110 per week

Questions

1. How many weeks would it take for Uncle John to break even in:
   (a) the summer season?
   (b) the winter season?
2. If variable costs and rental prices both increase by 10 per cent in the second year, what would the new break-even point be? (Your answer should be supported by the appropriate break-even chart.)

The latter part of the Safe Products example (pages 531–534) shows the effects on profit of changing selling prices. For example, Safe Products Limited might want to reduce the selling price to £7.00, and its market information indicates that it could expect to sell 10 per cent more at this price. It is hoped that this will improve profitability.

1. At 14 000 units and a price of £7.50, profits are £9000.
2. If the price falls to £7.00, the company expects to sell 10 per cent more at this price.

Sales will therefore be 15 400 × £7.00 =	£107 800
less Variable costs 15 400 × £4.00 =	£61 600
Contribution =	£46 200
less Fixed costs =	£40 000
Net profit =	£6 200

Clearly, dropping the price by 50p to gain the 10 per cent extra sales that would be generated would not increase profitability.

Limitations of break-even analysis

Marginal costing is often felt to present an oversimplification of business behaviour. It reduces business to an equation: how to generate enough contribution to cover fixed costs and provide a surplus for profit. Its limitations are:

1. It can be argued that, in reality, fixed costs are likely to change at different activity levels and that a stepped fixed-cost line would be a more accurate representation.
2. The business might be restricted by a limiting factor restricting its ability to break even or meet a profit target, such as lack of space, shortage of labour, shortage of orders.
3. Variable costs and sales are unlikely to be linear. Discounts, special contracts and overtime payments mean that the total cost line should really be a curve.
4. Break-even charts depict short-term relationships and forecasts and are therefore unrealistic where the time scale covers several years.
5. Break-even analysis is dependent upon the accuracy of forecasts made about costs and revenues. Changes in the market and in the cost of raw materials could affect the success of the technique.

The usefulness of accounting in supporting decision-making

An essential function of management is to make decisions, and decisions have to be made whenever there are alternative courses of action (Fig. 17.15). The main problem of any accounting system is that information reflects *data* from the past and present and enables only *predictions* to be made about the future. Time pressures can often be imposed on managers which constrain their ability to collate sufficient information. Also, the information extracted from the accounting system may prove to be unmanageably detailed. The problems can be numerous. Many decisions will require information not only from the accounting system, but also about external factors such as:

- Current tax rates
- Current state of the economy
- Market value of shares, if listed
- The state of the market
- Goodwill and corporate reputation
- Industrial relations

Clearly, nothing can be forecast with absolute certainty. No matter what research takes place, and however competent the accounting team, business involves taking risks.

Although accounting information has reduced the unpredictability, it will never eliminate it, and there will always be a need for human judgement.

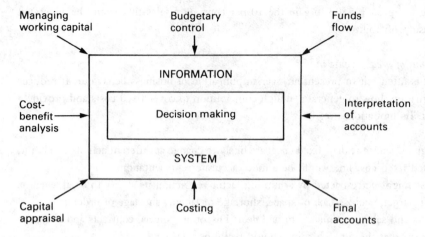

Figure 17.15 Accounting as a decision-making system.

Questions

Short-answer questions

1. Why do fixed costs become less significant over a larger output?
2. Give two examples of variable costs.
3. State an example of a semi-variable cost and explain why such a cost might be semi-variable.
4. Why are fixed costs more difficult to allocate to departmental or product costs?
5. What is the significance of marginal costing for the accountant, and how does the accountant's definition differ from that made by an economist?
6. Explain the relationship between average cost and marginal cost.
7. Why do businesses budget?
8. Name two dangers of a budgetary system.
9. Why would a budgetary controller need to estimate when debtors will pay?
10. What is the purpose of a raw materials budget, and what is its connection with the production budget?
11. What makes up a master budget?
12. Explain what is meant by the term 'adverse expenditure variance'.
13. Name two types of decisions influenced by costing.
14. What is a cost centre?
15. Define what is meant by absorption costing.
16. What is the significance of the term 'contribution'?
17. What happens if sales are lower than the break-even point?
18. How is the break-even point calculated?
19. Name two criticisms of break-even analysis.
20. What three factors external to an accounting system might affect the quality of decision-making?

Essays

1. In the light of advances in the development of management information systems, why are so many decisions made under conditions of inadequate information?
2. Explain why break-even analysis is an important management tool. What are the dangers of relying too heavily on this technique?
3. As a production manager for a firm that manufactures clogs, you have been asked to make a presentation to a group of staff next week and you decide to use a break-even chart to represent your profitability. You obtain the following figures:

   (a) Variable costs are £5 per unit.
   (b) Clogs are to be sold at £7.50 each.
   (c) Fixed overheads are £140 000 per annum.
   (d) Sales are expected to be 60 000 units.

   Write out a speech explaining your technique. Draw a chart to show how large a profit or loss you are likely to be making.

   You would like to show the group the effects of a drop in price on the market. If you drop the price to £7.00, there will be no increase in variable costs per unit or overall fixed costs and your marketing team has told you that orders would increase by 28 000 units. Show how this would affect your profitability.
4. What are the dangers of imposing a rigid budgetary system? Using an example, explain why variance analysis would be useful for managers.
5. Compare the role of the management accountant with that of the financial accountant. In your analysis comment on situations where their respective roles are (a) similar and (b) dissimilar.
6. Comment on the various ways in which costs are generally classified. Using an example, show how a knowledge of costs, together with revenues, might help a manager with the decision-making process.
7. Budgets help managers to survey the future. What are the benefits of setting up a system of budgetary control?
8. Compare and contrast a system of absorption costing with that of marginal costing.
9. Describe how and why different types of cost vary with different levels of output.
10. Explain the objective of budgetary planning and control systems. Outline the duties of a budget committee.

Data response questions

1 A single-product company

The following information relates to a company that produces a single product:

Direct labour per unit	£11
Direct materials per unit	£6

Variable overheads per unit	£3
Fixed costs	£200 000
Selling price per unit	£30

1. Explain the term 'break-even'.
2. Using these figures, produce a chart to show the minimum number of units that must be sold for the company to break even.
3. Market research has indicated potential sales for the coming period of 30 000 units at the current price, or 37 500 units if the selling price were lowered to £28 per unit. Which strategy would you advise the company to adopt and why?
4. Outline the factors that *any* business should take into consideration before using break-even analysis as a basis for decision-making. (*Source*: AEB)

2   Watcher Ltd

Study the information and answer the questions that follow.

Watcher Ltd is a small firm that manufactures high-quality pillow cases, duvet covers and fitted sheets. Solely on the basis of the figures given in Table 17.1, the board of directors has decided to discontinue producing duvet covers and not to replace them with any other product. This will leave production capacity unused, and fixed costs unaltered.

Table 17.1

	Pillow cases		Duvet covers		Fitted sheets		Total	
	£	£	£	£	£	£	£	£
Income								
Sales income		100 000		120 000		70 000		290 000
Direct costs								
Direct materials	30 000		40 000		20 000		90 000	
Direct labour	35 000		50 000		25 000		110 000	
Overheads								
Variable overheads	10 000		12 000		7 500		29 500	
Fixed overheads	15 000		21 400		10 700		47 100	
Total costs		90 000		123 400		63 200		276 600
Profit (loss)		10 000		(3 400)		6 800		13 400

(Show any appropriate calculations.)
1. Explain to the board the implications of its decision to discontinue the production of duvet covers:
   (a) in the short term.
   (b) in the long term.

2. The directors decide *not* to discontinue duvet covers production. Outline two other options that may be available to them.

3. One of the directors suggests that there should be a more structured decision-making process. What might be the key elements of such a process? (*Source*: AEB)

3   Coley Ltd

Coley Ltd is an engineering firm. It is the largest supplier of a particular tool in a market where, at a standard price of £500, there is very little competition. The home market is reaching saturation point, but Coley Ltd is not yet working at full capacity. Present output is 1500 units, while full capacity is 2500 units.

An order for 500 units has been received from an Italian firm on condition that the tools can be delivered to their factory, all expenses paid, at a price of £400 each.

Coley Ltd's present cost structures are:

		£
Materials	⎫	120
Direct labour	⎬ per unit	100
Variable overheads	⎭	60
Fixed overheads		300 000

However, to these must be added the costs associated with exporting to Italy. A sum of £20 000 is thought to be ample to cover this order.

The company's first reaction was to reject the order on the basis that it meant a loss of £70 per unit, while at present sales produced £20 profit per unit. However, further consideration of the financial and commercial aspects of the deal swung the decision in favour of accepting the order.

1. Use appropriate financial calculations to demonstrate whether the decision to accept the order was justified. Show all your workings.
2. Discuss three other reasons for accepting the order.
3. Explain two problems that might be encountered if the order is accepted.   (*Source*: AEB)

4   Peter Bean's shop

Peter Bean intends to open up a shop on 1 January 1994 into which he is to invest £80 000 as capital which is to be placed into a business bank account. His plans are:

(a) In January 1994 he will buy premises for £45 000, shop fittings for £4000 and a motor van for £6000.
(b) He will employ a sales assistant who will receive a monthly salary of £500, payable at the end of each month.
(c) The following goods are to be bought:

	Jan.	Feb.	Mar.	April	May	June
(units)	450	500	550	550	800	800

(d)   Units will cost £15 from January to March inclusive and £19 from April to July. Suppliers are to be paid in the month of supply.

(e)   Sales are anticipated as follows:

	Jan.	Feb.	Mar.	April	May	June
(units)	400	450	500	500	720	750

(f)   Units are sold for £30 each. One half of sales are to be for cash and the other half on credit. Customers are expected to pay the month after they have bought the goods.

(i)   Peter is to take £900 per month as drawings.

(ii)   Fixed expenses are estimated at £600 per month.

(iii) Stock at the end of June is to be valued on a FIFO basis.

Prepare:

1.   A cash budget showing the balance at the end of each month.
2.   A budgeted profit or operating statement for the six months.
3.   A budgeted balance sheet as at 30 June 1994.

Comment on the performance of the business.

Suggested reading

Bendry, M., Hussey, R. and West, C., *Accounting and Finance for Business Studies*, 2nd edn. D. P. Publications, 1992.

Fardon, M. and Cox, D., *Finance*. Osborne Books, 1990.

Giles, R. A., *Foundation in Business Accounting*. Stanley Thornes, 1991.

18

Recruitment and the role of personnel

From the personnel point of view, the purpose of recruitment is to buy in and retain the best available human resources to meet a company's needs. It is therefore important to be clear about:

- What the job entails
- What qualities are required to do the job
- What incentives are required to attract and motivate the right employees

There are a number of stages that can be used to describe and set out the nature of particular jobs. Readers should note that the pattern depicted in Fig. 18.1 is most likely to relate to the creation of new jobs rather than to the recruitment for existing jobs.

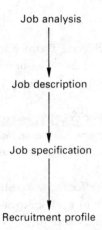

Figure 18.1 The nature of particular jobs.

Job analysis

Job analysis is the process of examining jobs in order to identify the key requirements of each job. A number of important questions need to be explored:

- What tasks have to be performed?
- What skills and qualities are required to perform these tasks?
- How can these skills be acquired?

Job analysis is used in order to:

1. Choose employees either from the ranks of existing staff (*redeployment*) of from the recruitment of new staff.
2. Set out the training requirements of a particular job.
3. Provide information that will help in decision-making about the type of equipment and materials to be employed with the job.
4. Identify and profile the experiences of employees in their work tasks (information that can be used as evidence for staff development and promotion).
5. Identify areas of risk and danger at work.
6. Help in setting rates of pay for job tasks.

Job analysis can be conducted by direct observation of employees at work, by information obtained from interviewing job holders or by referring to documents such as training manuals. Information can be gleaned directly from the person carrying out a task and/or from his or her supervisory staff.

Some large organizations specifically employ 'job analysts'. In most companies, however, job analysis is expected to be part of the general skills of a training or personnel officer.

Three different areas of job analysis can be identified:

1. *Task analysis* involves the study of a particular task which is aimed at achieving a particular objective or end-product. For example, a particular employee may have the task of ensuring that all the assemblers in an electronics factory are supplied with a steady flow of components.
2. *Activity analysis* is the study of the elements involved in a given task. For example, one of the activities involved in circulating components in the electronics factory may be taking them down from the shelves in the stock room. Activities can be subdivided into physical (e.g. lifting, sorting) and mental (e.g. exercising judgement).
3. *Skills analysis* is the study of the ability needed to carry out a given task effectively. A wide range of skills may be identified such as the ability to work in groups, to work independently, to perform manual operations, to make calculations, to communicate, to follow written instructions and many more.

Case Study—Carrying out a skills audit and involving the firm's employees

In preparing for the challenges of the 1990s, Rowntree Mackintosh set up a joint skills audit of the company's 850 workers. The skills audit was set up to look at:

- Employees' existing skill levels
- Employee needs
- New technology

One of the main aims of the exercise was to prepare for multi-skilling within the company. *Multi-skilling* means moving away from the old single-skilling of the past when workers in a plant performed only one task. Multi-skilling involves training workers to develop a broad range of skills and competencies related to work operations. Rowntree believes that multi-skilling is most likely to be successful when employees are involved in the process.

The audit related to all the Rowntree sites including York, Halifax, Newcastle-upon-Tyne and Norwich. The scheme involved all the unions represented in Rowntree plants.

Questions

1. What do you understand by the term 'multi-skilling'?
2. Why is multi-skilling essential in an industrial world of new technologies?
3. What are the potential benefits and drawbacks of multi-skilling for a confectionery manufacturer?
4. What is a skills audit?
5. How do you think that doing a skills audit will help Rowntree to introduce multi-skilling?
6. How do you think that the audit may be improved by involving management and employees in the process of carrying it out?
7. Are there any potential drawbacks from having a joint initiative?

Job analysis is not an easy task. There are a number of major difficulties to be overcome. It can be a very slow process, and the outside observer will not always be fully aware of what is going on. This is particularly true of jobs that require both mental and physical skills, because it is difficult to appreciate what is going on in the mind of the skilled operative. Individuals will often develop styles of work that suit their own particular aptitudes and may not be appropriate for other employees. When you ask a person to describe a particular job, he or she may miss out important steps which have come to be taken for granted.

Job description

A job description will set out how a particular employee is to fit into the organization. It will therefore need to set out:

- The title of the job
- To whom the employee is responsible
- For whom the employee is responsible
- A simple description of the role and duties of the employee within the organization

A job description could be used as a job indicator for job applicants. Alternatively, it could be used as a guideline for an employee and/or line manager as to his or her role and responsibility within the organization. (It is not, however, a contract of employment.)

Job specification

A job specification goes beyond a mere description; in addition, it highlights the mental and physical attributes required of the job holder. For example, a job specification for a trainee manager's post in a retail store included the following:

> Managers at all levels would be expected to show responsibility. The company is looking for people who are tough and talented. They should have a flair for business, know how to sell, and to work in a team.

Job analysis, description and specification can all provide useful information to a business in addition to serving as recruitment instruments. Another use is for staff appraisal, which is a means of monitoring staff performance and is a feature of promotion in modern companies. In some companies, employees and their immediate line managers discuss personal goals and targets for the coming time period (e.g. the next six months); the appraisal will then involve a review of employees' performances during the previous six months, and the setting of new targets. Job details can serve as a useful basis for establishing dialogue and targets. Job descriptions can be used as reference points for arbitrating in disputes as to 'who does what' in a business. Job analysis can serve as a useful tool for establishing performance standards.

Job requisition (recruitment profiles)

The person responsible for interviewing and recruiting is not always the person with a specialist knowledge of the job in question. For example, the personnel department may be given the responsibility of recruiting staff for all the functional areas within a company. Personnel will therefore ask for a recruitment profile giving the nature of the skills required, the type of person sought and a description of the job. The *job requisition* will therefore provide the specialist knowledge required to enable personnel to recruit the appropriate individuals. Job requisitions are also used to give advertising agencies and specialist recruitment companies more information from which to create recruitment advertisements. (A business might employ a specialist recruitment firm to carry out a national recruitment campaign.)

Case Study—Sony's recruitment drive

Study the journal article in Fig. 18.2 before answering the questions that follow.

ELECTRONICS GIANT ON THE HUNT FOR TECHNICAL STAFF

Sony seeks specialist skills for Welsh plant

An intensive recruitment drive will accompany electronics giant, Sony's £36m investment at its plant in Bridgend, South Wales.

Sony's industrial relations executive, Alun Jones, said that a tough, hectic two months lie ahead for the five-strong recruitment team.

The company plans to have 300 extra engineers and managers working at Bridgend by May next year. Staff recruited need six to 12 months' training in Japan and the US to acquire the necessary technical skills for Sony's new technology.

Specialist high-tech skills are vital to Sony's ambitious expansion plans. Before the investment was finalised, Sony carried out detailed research to make sure it could recruit people with the necessary skills from the area.

But the search promises to be difficult. Jones pointed out

Sony: investing £36m

that there is a worldwide shortage of electronic and engineering staff as every industry relies on them.

Sony's investment will expand its 1,500 workforce by one-fifth and it hopes to recruit an initial 34 who will be partly responsible for the recruitment of lower level staff.

No campaign budget has

been set by Sony management and bosses are still assessing the best recruitment channels. They are looking at university and polytechnic research laboratories throughout Europe. They are targetting regions such as the West Midlands, Manchester, Southampton and Glasgow, where they suspect there are significant numbers of the people they need. It wants staff who are highly qualified in state-of-the-art automated manufacturing and surface-coating technology.

Sony recognises that these skills are unusual as its recent campaign for similar people only attracted 30 responses. The company may be forced to train up lower level people if it cannot find enough people with at least two years' experience.

The Welsh Development Agency welcomed Sony's expansion.

Figure 18.2 Job analysis at Sony. (*Source*: *Personnel Today*, February/March 1989)

Questions

1. How might Sony have had to carry out job analysis in preparing plans to recruit 300 extra engineers and managers at Bridgend?

2. Lay out a job description for an imaginary new job at the Bridgend plant.
3. How would a job specification differ from the description you have just drawn up?
4. What problems does the article suggest Sony is likely to have in its recruitment drive?
5. What suggestions would you put forward for dealing with these problems?
6. Why do you think that the Welsh Development Agency has welcomed Sony's expansion?

The challenge of the 1990s

A pressing problem for most companies as we move through the 1990s is that of recruiting employees in sufficient numbers and with the required skills. The Department of Employment White Paper, *Training for Employment* (1989), warned:

> 1990 seems likely to bring radical change to the industrial economy. In looking to the future, three areas of change have profound implications for employment and training:

- The number of people who are available for work
- The structure of employment
- The nature of available jobs

It is perhaps the first of these predicted changes that could have the most serious implications for the recruitment sector. The White Paper states that, while in the decade up to 1986 the population of working age in Britain grew by almost 2 million, between 1986 and 1990 that figure will have slowed to fewer than 500 000.

On top of that, the White Paper predicts: 'the number of 16- to 19-year-olds in the population is projected to fall substantially from a peak of 3.7 million in 1983 to less than 2.6 million in 1994.' In simple terms, the number of young people available for jobs will fall dramatically. At the time the Manpower Services Commission said that those figures clearly showed that fundamental changes will have to be made in the way companies develop their workforces. Businesses that today make older workers with older skills redundant in favour of new blood with new skills will be forced by the shortages to retrain. This presents a major challenge to the whole concept of recruitment.

The expansion of the service sector has favoured the growth of jobs traditionally performed by females. Women have come to dominate support and personal service occupations. At the same time, with the development of new technologies a number of occupations have been moving away from single-skilling to multi-skilling and towards the rise of the technician.

A business concept that has been growing in importance has been that of the 'flexible workforce' (part-time, temporary and self-employed), which now comprises over one-third of all employment. This sector, again, is dominated by women (two-thirds of all flexible workers), particularly in hotels and catering, distribution, repairs and professional and business sevices.

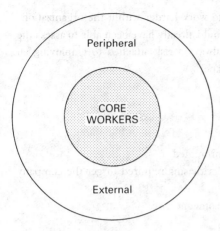

Figure 18.3 The flexible firm.

The notion of the 'flexible firm' has become very popular in management theory (Fig. 18.3). It distinguishes between:

- Core workers (multi-skilled, full-time, enjoying good pay, conditions and benefits)
- Peripheral workers (short-term, temporary, part-time and receiving less favourable pay, conditions and benefits)
- External workers who are not employees of the firm (agency temps, workers in contracted-out services and the self-employed)

The flexible firm will cut its labour costs to a minimum by limiting core workers, relative to peripheral and external workers.

Avenues for recruitment

Recruiting individuals to fill particular posts within a business can be done:

- Internally, by recruiting within the firm
- Externally, by recruiting people from outside

Internal recruitment

The advantages of recruiting from within are that:

1. Considerable savings can be made. Individuals with inside knowledge of how a business operates will need shorter periods of training and time for 'fitting in'.
2. The organization is unlikely to be 'disrupted' by someone who is used to working with others in the firm.

3. Internal promotion acts as an incentive to all staff to work harder within the organization.
4. From the firm's point of view, the personnel staff should already have been able to assess the strengths and weaknesses of an insider. There is always a risk attached to employing an outsider who may prove to be desirable only 'on paper'.

The disadvantages of recruiting from within are that:

1. You will have to replace the person that has been promoted.
2. An insider may be less likely to make the essential criticisms required to get the company working more effectively.
3. Promotion of one person in a company may upset someone else.

External recruitment

In the United Kingdom, the most common way of finding a job is by directly contacting a firm or place of employment; sometimes people apply for a job as a result of a personal contact such as a relative already working for a firm. But there are other channels (Fig. 18.4).

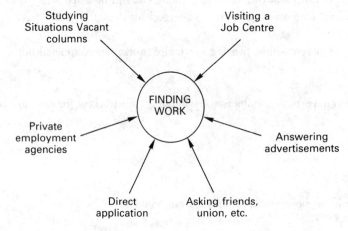

Figure 18.4 Where to go to find a job.

Recruiting through newspaper and magazine advertisements

Newspaper advertisements are an obvious place to scout for jobs. A good newspaper advert gives a substantial amount of information. Personnel managers place adverts in the most suitable medium. Jobs demanding limited skills can often be advertised locally, whereas jobs requiring specialist skills need to be advertised in specialist papers and journals. Advertisements for marketing specialists, for example, may be placed in *Marketing Week* or in the recruitment section of the *Sunday Times*.

When recruiting labour, therefore, the personnel manager will do the following:

1. Target the recruiting campaign at the most suitable audience.
2. Advertise in the most cost-effective way (e.g. the cheapest method possible to get to the right sort of people).

To ensure that a newspaper advert gets the right response, it will be necessary to make at least some of the following points clear:

- Where the job is
- How much the job pays
- What qualifications are required to do the job
- What the job involves
- What fringe benefits are available
- How to go about applying for the job

The personnel manager will then sift through the replies, looking for applications from candidates that seem to have the required qualities.

Jobcentres

The Department of Employment is responsible for the running of Jobcentres, which can be found in a prominent position in major towns. The Jobcentres run window displays of available jobs in the area, and people seeking work are encouraged to come in and look at the other cards with details of job vacancies which are on open display. The Jobcentre staff will arrange appointments for job-hunters to meet personnel staff at the relevant firm for an interview.

Private employment agencies

There is a wide range of private employment agencies that help businesses to recruit staff. Fields in which these agencies are particularly common are secretarial work, high-technology areas, nursing and casual work.

A business looking for staff will approach an agency, which will either undertake to interview applicants itself or will send suitable applicants to the firm to be interviewed.

The agency will take a commission on the salary of the worker. In the case of secretarial staff, wages may often be paid by the employing firm to the agency which will then pay the worker (after deducting its commission).

○ Case Study—Recruitment for a new Tesco superstore in Dover

```
┌─────────────────────────────────┐
│  SUPERSTORE FEATURES            │
│  ────────────────────           │
│  □ Petrol station.              │
│  □ Instore bakery.              │
│  □ Market stalls, one of Tesco's│
│    innovations.                 │
│  □ Health and beauty sections   │
│    with special lighting.       │
│  □ Toy section.                 │
│  □ Special trolleys for disabled│
│    people.                      │
│  □ Checkouts with electronic    │
│    points of sale (EPOS).       │
│  □ Possible introduction of     │
│    crèches.                     │
└─────────────────────────────────┘
```

Figure 18.5 Features of the new Tesco superstore.

The Tesco success story began during the First World War, when young Jack Cohen began trading from a barrow in Hackney, East London. By 1950, Cohen was the first in the United Kingdom to open a supermarket, which he had seen in the United States.

Decades later, Tesco is among the top retailers, with an annual turnover of £4.5 billion (Fig. 18.5). Competition is tough and recruitment has to be highly co-ordinated. More than 100 superstores have opened in the past ten years and Tesco now employs 72 000 staff.

Pat Lennon, Tesco's retail personnel director, explains that the process of opening a superstore varies considerably from area to area: 'Every time we open a store, it is a one-off recruitment exercise which needs to be localized with in-depth research into potential customers and employees.'

One of the more recent recruitment exercises was at Dover's new superstore, which opened at the end of June 1988. Tesco had to recruit 470 staff, from check-out operators to departmental supervisors.

The recruitment schedule began 12 months before the store opened (Fig. 18.6). Staff managers and store manager were recruited internally and initial research was carried out into the Dover area. Three months later, Tesco met with advertising agency Charles Barker to discuss the campaign.

Barker's research department then looked at potential competitors for staff at Dover's superstore. Salaries in the area were noted along with the available transport, housing and Job Centres. Research was carried out into the type of people likely to work in the store and the percentage of unemployed.

RECRUITMENT SCHEDULE

Countdown 12 months before store opens:

1. Recruit senior management.
2. Initial research into area.
3. Advertising agency researches media and area.
4. Advertising agency presents campaign package.
5. Recruitment centre opens.
6. Advertisements for supervisory staff appear.
7. Advertisements for general staff go out.
8. Store opens.

Figure 18.6 Stages in preparing for recruitment at Tesco.

Meanwhile, Charles Barker's media department was looking at local media, including daily and weekly newspapers and local radio. Tesco advertises in the local press rather than national newspapers when recruiting its retail staff.

After about three weeks of collecting the necessary data, the agency put together a package for Tesco which included a suggested budget. This was presented to one of Tesco's six regional personnel managers. After a series of internal advertisements, the Dover campaign was launched.

Tesco always sets up a recruitment office either in offices above the local shopping centre or at the local Job Centre. Job Centres are not used often, however, because, although free, they are rarely large enough. In Dover a terraced house in the middle of the town was used. This recruitment centre was kitted out in red with colour posters and red arrows.

The budget for the recruitment campaign was set at about £35 000 and slightly less than that was spent. Out of 470 staff, only 30 vacancies were left, after the initial recruitment drive. The first advertisement did not specify job vacancies but invited people to go along to the centre. In this way, Tesco attracted about 200 applicants before even opening the recruitment centre.

Charles Barker designed four advertisements for the Dover campaign which appeared in the main local newspapers. The campaign used mono (black and white) advertisements with occasional (spot) red. White space was used creatively with crisp outlines so as to show up on the busy newspaper pages. Tesco's personnel department wanted straightforward advertisements. They felt that the benefits and the salary offered were the key ingredients.

Tesco's advertising campaign emphasized that the Dover superstore would be opening for 12 Sundays until 18 September. This meant an extra day's work for staff and was popular with applicants.

Supervisory and skilled vacancies were advertised 19 weeks before the store opened and general vacancies were advertised 13 weeks before. Charles Barker monitored the budget weekly, and reported to Tesco.

Tesco's Dover campaign received a good response, but if it had not the agency would have been able to draw on ideas in the original package. A contingency plan would have been put into effect immediately, perhaps with radio commercials or leaflet drops.

(*Source*: adapted from *Personnel Today*)

Questions

1. Why was it necessary for Tesco to carry out research before opening up its Dover store? (A detailed answer is required to this question.)
2. Why do you think that Tesco hired an agency to carry out the research work rather than doing it itself?
3. From the evidence given in the article, would you consider the research and subsequent recruitment exercise to have been effective?
4. What do you think would be the major problems faced by Tesco in the recruitment exercise? What measures could have been taken to encounter these problems?
5. What do you consider to be the major strengths and weaknesses of the job advertisement as illustrated in Fig. 18.5?
6. Are there any improvements you would have liked to make to the job advert?
7. If you were going to open up a new superstore in your local town, what are the key labour recruitment questions you would need to answer? List 15 questions.

The work of the personnel department

Personnel is a key function in all but the smallest business units. Traditionally, personnel is associated with the 'employment procession' of recruitment—selection—induction—training—transfers—termination of employment (see Fig. 18.7).

However, in a modern business organization personnel is also responsible for 'appraisal', which is a key part of monitoring and helping an employee to develop a clear career path (see below page 563), and for the administration of disciplinary procedures; for workplace bargaining with unions; developing and supervising payment systems for employees; supervising health and safety; equal opportunities and many other areas related to employment (Fig. 18.8).

In some companies employing as many as 100 workers, you will find a lone personnel manager working him- or herself to the bone. In contrast, in some larger modern companies you will find personnel departments comprising a range of specialists housed in an extensive suite of offices.

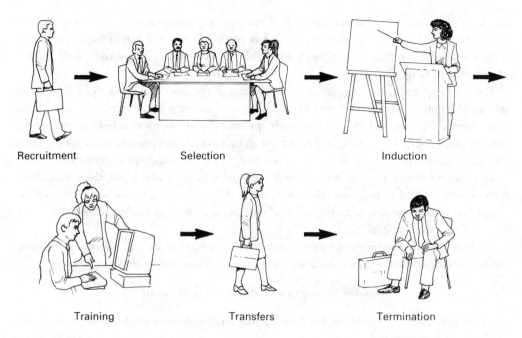

Figure 18.7 The employment procession.

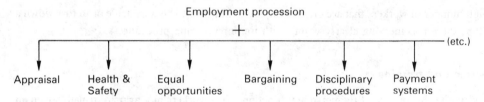

Figure 18.8 The work of personnel.

Recruitment and selection

We have already dealt with recruitment at length earlier in the chapter. Recruitment involves job analysis, description and specification. Selection involves procedures to identify the most appropriate candidate to fill each post. An effective selection procedure will therefore take into consideration the following:

- Keeping the costs of selection down
- Making sure that the requisite skills and qualities have been specified, and developing a process for identifying them in candidates
- Making sure that the candidate selected will want the job, and will stay with the company

Keeping the costs of selection down will involve such factors as holding the interviews in a location that is accessible to the interviewing panel and to those being interviewed; ensuring that the interviewing panel has available to it all the necessary documentation, such as application forms, that should be studied before the interviews take place; and that a short-list is made up of suitable candidates, so that the interviews do not have to take place a second time, with new job advertisements being placed.

The skills required should have been identified through the process of job analysis, description and specification. It is important then to devise ways of testing whether candidates meet these requirements. One way of doing this is to study applicants' application forms and to interview the most suitable people. Some employers go further and give applicants aptitude tests, putting them through a number of 'real-life' situations to see how they cope with given business situations.

To gauge whether applicants will stay with the firm, it is important to ask them about their future intentions, and to familiarize them with the working environment into which they will be placed. There is no point in attracting a first-class candidate only to find that he or she does not like the firm's working conditions.

It is important to monitor the job selection process continually to see how effective it is. Ratios can be a useful method of appraising a selection process. These may include:

Number of interviews : number of offers made

The most effective ratios would involve the minimization of interviews relative to offers made that fill the posts as required:

Number starting work : number of suitable employees

If a high number of workers that are offered employment prove to be unsuitable or to turn down a job offer, there is something clearly wrong with the interviewing procedure.

Induction and training

This is another major area of the personnel function. New workers in a firm are usually given an induction programme in which they meet other workers and are shown the skills they must learn. Generally the first few days at work will simply involve observation, with an experienced worker showing the 'new hand' the ropes. Many large firms have detailed training schemes which are conducted on an 'in-house' basis; this is particularly true of larger public companies such as banks and insurance companies. In conjunction with this, staff may be encouraged to attend college courses to learn new skills and get new qualifications. Training thus takes place in the following ways:

- On the job—learning through experience at work
- Off the job—learning through attending courses

Promotion within a firm depends on acquiring qualifications to do a more advanced job; in banking, for instance, staff are expected to pass banking examinations. At the same time, a candidate for promotion must show a flair for the job. It is the responsibility of the training department within a business to make sure that staff with the right skills are coming up through the firm or being recruited from outside.

As well as sending staff to local colleges and universities the firm may use a government-run training centre. These are run by the Training Commission and provide specialist training all over the country.

The business might also contribute to a national training scheme such as the Youth Training Scheme, whereby the government subsidizes the firm to employ and train school-leavers.

Case Study—Management training at 'Do It All'

Do-It-All train their assistant managers using a performance-related scheme. Training is concentrated on the first six months after a new assistant manager has been appointed. The aim of the training package is to monitor and test the assistant manager's understanding of his or her role and to test their understanding and skills in the job.

The job of assistant manager consists of a range of responsibilities, from ordering the stock to making sure it is presented well. Assistant managers are responsible for interviewing job applicants, training staff and following the company's procedures.

The trainers of the new assistant managers have broken every element of the job into testable parts. Within six months of being appointed, the assistant manager will attend a one-week assessment at college. Management on First Assessment (MOFA) tests all systems of work and skills against criteria that have been laid down.

To establish these criteria, a number of experienced assistant managers were put through the same tests to produce benchmarks. Only when new assistant managers reach those benchmarks can they be said to be relatively competent.

On completion of MOFA, each assistant store manager is interviewed by tutors and Do-It-All managers. The assistant manager's performance in each of the areas is discussed at length, particularly those in which he or she is under-performing, which will then be focused on in further training.

To meet the needs of further training, a variety of training responses have been devised. In some cases suitable courses in specific skill areas like interviewing are available at the college; other managers may simply need to re-read the operations manual.

Most managers will use open learning packages to study topics like budgets, target-setting and security.

Alongside such training methods, the assistant store manager will be supported throughout the programme by his or her store manager, who will have received notification of those training needs identified by MOFA. Consequently, the store manager can ensure that the trainee gets whatever extra practice is required.

Questions

1. In what ways does an assistant manager's training at Do-It-All involve
   (a) on-the-job training?
   (b) off-the-job training?

2. How does Do-It-All diagnose weaknesses in an assistant manager's performance? How does this diagnosis assist such managers to improve their performance?
3. What would you consider to be the main costs and benefits to Do-It-All of the training package?
4. What would you consider to be the main costs and benefits to Do-It-All assistant managers of the scheme?
5. How could you evaluate the effectiveness of the scheme?

Transfers and termination of employment

The personnel department has a responsibility for negotiating the smooth *transfer* of employees between departments. This may be necessary if employees are not able to 'get on', or if it is felt necessary to give an employee a 'change'.

Termination of employment may be the result of a number of factors including retirement, dismissal and redundancy.

When employees *retire* after a long period of service to a business, they will need some form of recognition for their service. Companies such as the John Lewis Partnership keep in regular contact with retired employees, and arrange regular reunions.

The procedure for *dismissal* must follow strict legal guidelines. When a new worker is taken on, he or she must be given a written contract of employment within 13 weeks of starting the job. Under the Contract of Employment Act 1972, the written contract must include the following:

- Title of the job
- Date the job starts
- Hours of work
- Rate and method of pay
- Holiday arrangements
- Period of notice that must be given
- Pension scheme arrangements
- Rights concerning trade unions
- The organization's discipline rules

The personnel manager will agree on a date with the employee for work to start, and the contract of employment becomes binding from this date. The period of notice that an employee must be given when being dismissed is stated in the contract, which is a legal document.

Over the years, an elaborate system for the dismissal of staff has developed as a result of the large number of cases that have come before industrial tribunals or other courts. The heart of the matter lies in the difference between what is termed 'fair dismissal' and what the court regards as 'unfair dismissal'.

'Fair dismissal' can take place when grounds can be shown such as:

- Wilful destruction of company property
- Sexual or racial harassment
- Continuous bad timekeeping
- A negative attitude at work
- Inability to do the job
- Sleeping on the job

In some cases, e.g. bad timekeeping, employees would normally receive written warnings and suspensions before dismissal.

'Unfair dismissal' includes:

1. *Pregnancy*   You can be sacked only if you are unable to do your job properly, e.g. stack shelves.
2. *Race*   A worker cannot be sacked on grounds of race.
3. *Homosexuality*   If a worker is a homosexual there is no reason why he or she should be sacked unless it can be proved that it affects his or her standard of work.
4. *Union membership*   An employer cannot sack a worker for belonging to a trade union.
5. *Criminal record*   If an employer does not find out about an employee's criminal record until some time after employing him or her, the employer cannot sack the worker on these grounds unless it was a very relevant crime, e.g. a cashier who has a record of stealing the petty cash.

Redundancy occurs when a business or firm closes down, when part of a business closes down, or when particular types of workers are no longer required. It will usually be the responsibility of personnel to supervise and administer the redundancy procedures.

Health and Safety

The personnel department will also normally be concerned with health and safety at work. There are thousands of pages of legal regulations covering this aspect of employment. Some firms go so far as to employ a specialist health and safety department. Unions are also particularly concerned with this issue. The main laws concerned with health and safety are described below.

The Health and Safety at Work Act 1974 (HSWA)

This Act covers all persons at work except domestic servants in private households. Sets of regulations under the Act deal with different kinds of work in different places of work. All those receiving training or work experience in the workplace are covered by the Act.

The Act establishes a responsibility of both employers and employees to provide safe conditions at work. The employer's duty is to ensure, as far as is reasonably practical, 'the health, safety and welfare at work of all employees'. This general responsibility includes health and safety in relation to:

- The provision and maintenance of plant and systems of work
- Arrangements for use, handling, storage and transport of articles and substances
- Maintenance of the place of work and access to and egress from it
- The working environment

It includes the duty to provide:

- Adequate welfare facilities
- Necessary information, instruction, training and supervision

Also, the employer must consult with union safety representatives if there are any. A notice containing the requirements of the Act must be displayed.

An employer must prepare a written statement of policy with respect to the health and safety at work of employees, and show it to an inspector if required.

An employer must show similar responsibilities to non-employees, such as visitors in a college or school party, who need to be given information and instruction about health and safety requirements.

The employee's duty is to take reasonable care to ensure both his or her own safety and the safety of others who may be affected by what he or she does or does not do.

Employers or employees who do not abide by these rules can be punished in a court of law.

An example of an area covered by the Act is the use of protective guards for cutting machines such as food-slicing machines and industrial presses. Accidents can occur if the guards are faulty or if they are moved.

The Act lays down training standards for workers in potentially hazardous occupations. Generally the workplace must be designed in such a way as to minimize the risk of accidents.

The Act is backed up by a Health and Safety Executive which includes representatives of employers, employees and local authorities. Health and safety inspectors are appointed with responsibility for making sure that the law is being observed.

Not only must the safety officer be aware of general laws, but there are also specific laws and codes relating to specific industries. For example, there are laws relating to miners, workers in the explosives industry and in textiles. Many industries also set out their own safety regulations. A firm's personnel officer will normally attend conferences and refresher courses on safety as a regular feature of his or her work.

The Factories Act 1961

Until it is replaced by regulations under the HSWA, this Act remains important. It covers most businesses that use mechanical machinery and therefore includes a wide range of premises including garages, printing works, building sites and engineering works. A factory is a place where people are employed in manual labour (work done mainly by hand) in any process for, or incidental to, the making, repairing, altering, cleaning, adapting for sale or demolition of any article.

The Act sets out that:

1. Adequate toilet and washing facilities must be provided.
2. The inside of buildings must be properly heated and ventilated.
3. Floors must not have slippery surfaces.
4. Machinery such as presses must have fenced screens to prevent serious injury.
5. Fire escapes must be provided and kept in good order. Fire doors should not be locked or obstructed.

The Offices, Shops and Railways Premises Act 1963

Most of this Act's provisions are similar to those covered by the Factories Act. The Act is applied in office and shop conditions.

Examples of requirements are that:

1. Temperatures must not fall below 16°C (60.8° F) in places where people work for any length of time.
2. There must be adequate supplies of fresh or purified air.
3. Toilet and washing facilities must be adequate for the number of employees and kept in a clean state. There must be running hot and cold water with soap and clean towels.
4. Suitable lighting must be provided wherever people walk or work.
5. The minimum amount of space for each person is 12 square metres of floor space.

Reporting of Injuries, Diseases and Dangerous Occurrences Regulations 1985 (RIDDOR)

Injuries that result from accidents at work where an employee is incapacitated for three or more days must be reported to the authorities within seven days. Injuries involving fatalities must be notified immediately by the most practical means, e.g. by phone. Listed diseases must also be reported.

Control of Substances Hazardous to Health Regulations 1988 (COSHH)

Employers must carry out an assessment of work tasks that are likely to create risks for the health and safety of employees. Following on from the assessment, decisions need to be made on how to prevent or limit risks of exposure to such substances.

Workers dealing with dangerous substances should be given appropriate information and training. Measures taken under COSHH need to be continually monitored.

Substances covered by the act cover all substances potentially harmful to health, whether in solid or liquid form or in the form of a gas or vapour.

Noise at Work Regulation 1989

Employers have an obligation to reduce the risk of hearing damage to employees to the lowest level practical. The employer has an obligation to make sure that, when the sound reaches or exceeds a set level, ear protectors are worn.

Other regulations

Other regulations cover the use of electricity in the workplace, the provision of first aid facilities and training, fire precautions and other important areas.

Enforcement of the laws is principally by the Health and Safety Executive backed up by local authority inspections. Inspectors have substantial powers, including the right to enter premises, to obtain information and to take possession of articles and substances. Offending organizations can be taken to court and given substantial fines as well as prison sentences.

Negligence at common law

An employee can claim for damages from an employer's negligence if the employer fails 'to abide by the duty of care to the employee so that the employee suffers injury or damage to health'.

The employer has a duty of reasonable care for the safety of employees, and this responsibility extends to when he or she sends employees to the premises of third parties. Negligence occurs when there is a breach in the duty of care which applies to:

- Safe premises
- A safe system of work
- Safe plant, equipment and tools
- Safe fellow workers

The European Dimension of Health and Safety

Health and safety is an important part of the Single European Act which lays emphasis on providing safe working conditions in all member-states. The emphasis is on harmonizing working conditions. In addition, new Directives have been established about the technical requirements and safety standards for specific products.

A manufacturer needs to show that products are produced to European standards. This should involve:

1. A manufacturer's declaration backed up by test results
2. A certificate of standard from an independent body
3. The provision of test results by the independent body

The Directives include such areas as:

- Toy safety
- Gas appliances
- Personal protective equipment
- Machinery safety including mobile machinery and lifting equipment

Equal opportunities

Businesses have a legal obligation to provide equal opportunities at work. In addition, many enlightened employers provide their own codes of conduct which go beyond the bare essentials of statutory obligations. For example, Littlewoods have produced their own code of practice. 'Littlewoods Equal Opportunities Code of Practice' is a 21-page booklet covering policy on the company's recruitment and advertising; selection processes; training; career development; job satisfaction; terms and conditions; part-time employment; responsibilities of managers and supervisors; ethnic minorities and religious beliefs; and employees with domestic responsibilities. It states that no job applicant or employee should receive less favourable treatment on grounds of gender, marital status, social class, colour, race, ethnic origin, creed or disability, or be disadvantaged by conditions or requirements that cannot be shown to be relevant to performance.

The company's aspirations, at least so far as employees are concerned, are backed up by an equal opportunities internal appeals procedure to be 'invoked in cases of alleged sexual or racial harassment'. Where this process fails to resolve a problem, the employee can then use the company's formal grievance procedure.

The administration and implementation of equal opportunities policies often rests with personnel.

Bargaining

Bargaining over wages and conditions at work, at plant or office level is usually the responsibility of personnel. During a typical week the personnel manager may meet representatives from all of the major unions involved in a business to discuss conditions and working practice.

Appraisal

Most large organizations have well established procedures for collecting and recording information about how personnel are evaluated. These are called 'appraisal schemes' and will normally be implemented by the personnel function. They are mainly used for white-collar staff, managers and technical staff. The appraisal scheme will require individual post holders to collect and record, in a set way, the impressions they have gained of each subordinate in their charge.

Use of an appraisal scheme enables an organization to:

1. Make the best use of personnel by locating areas of strengths and weaknesses in job performance, perhaps identifying training and other employee needs.

2. Help the individual being evaluated to record his or her perceptions of the host organization and to contribute to outlining the individual's own career path within the organization.

The appraisal interview

An organization needs to make time available for well organized and structured appraisal interviews to take place. The appraisor will need to be trained in the appraisal process. The appraisor and the appraisee may use a structured form containing such questions as:

- What were your most important objectives/achievements during the last year?
- What were/are your major problems?
- What do you consider to be your main objectives during the coming year?
- In your present post, how do you feel you could improve your current contribution to the work-team?
- What action might be taken to bring about this improvement?

You can see from the structure of the questions that the appraisal interviews gives the appraisee an opportunity to talk about his or her aspirations and to set targets. If these are carefully listened to, then individuals may gain the essential motivation that is required in an effective team. The person being appraised will feel that the company at least knows what his or her hopes and plans are.

The person who conducts the interview in many cases will be one organizational level removed from the person being appraised; i.e. it may be the interviewee's line manager's line manager. This may help to prevent any workplace antagonisms or mistrust from creeping into the process.

Prior to the interview, the appraisee will fill in an appraisal form and send a copy to the appraisor. The two parties then conduct the appraisal using the form as the basis for discussion. Both parties sign the document stating that they are in agreement regarding the objectives, recommendations and actions to be taken.

Where an organization is operating clear company-wide objectives (i.e. management by objectives; see page 2), then precise and quantifiable targets may be required from each individual.

A skilled appraisor would do many of the following:

1. Agree on feasible objectives and targets with the appraisee.
2. Emphasize targets and goals rather than criticize performance.
3. Evaluate previous performance by reference to specific cases and examples rather than generalities.
4. Make a point of taking an individual's criticism of the organization seriously rather than trying to 'sweep it under the carpet'.
5. Focus the interview on real job behaviour and performance.

Other functions of personnel

Personnel may also take under its umbrella the design and conduct of disciplinary procedures, and the organization of the payment system for wages and salaries.

In addition, personnel will have a welfare function. This will involve the provision of social facilities and activities; lighting, heating and ventilation; canteen facilities; Christmas activities; complaints at work and many other related areas.

Questions

Short-answer questions

1. What key questions need to be answered in job analysis?
2. Explain the terms
   (a) task analysis.
   (b) activity analysis.
   (c) skills analysis.
3. Carry out a skills audit of the members of your class. What problems would you have if you wanted to set up a cake manufacturing company employing the members of your class?
4. Write a job description for a job with which you are familiar.
5. What is a job specification? Write out a job specification for a business studies teacher.
6. What is the purpose of a job requisition?
7. What are the advantages and disadvantages of internal recruitment?
8. What is the purpose of a Job Centre?
9. What is meant by staff 'appraisal'?
10. Describe the stages in the 'employment procession'.
11. What is the difference between 'on-the-job' and 'off-the-job' training?
12. What details are normally included in a contract of employment?
13. Give three examples of 'fair' and three examples of 'unfair' dismissal.
14. Give a simple definition of redundancy.
15. What details should be included in an 'equal opportunities' code of practice?
16. What arguments would you put forward for having a specialist health and safety department in a large company?
17. What do you think would be the best method of recruiting part-time secretarial staff for a large company in London?
18. Why is it important to make job applicants aware of the conditions in which they will be working?
19. How can ratios be used to monitor the effectiveness of a selection process?
20. What do you understand by the term 'job induction'?

Essays

1. Personnel is the most vital of all company functions because it deals with the human resource. Discuss this statement.

2. Why is it important for a business to devise an effective 'equal opportunities' policy?
3. What are the most important stages involved in recruiting and selecting skilled managers?
4. Why is a detailed knowledge of health and safety regulations important to business?
5. What are the most important steps in interviewing candidates for a job?
6. The best method of recruitment is not always the cheapest. Discuss this view.
7. In what situations should a company employ the services of recruitment agencies?
8. How can personnel help and support the other functions of a company? Illustrate your answer with examples.
9. What are the essential qualities of a 'good' personnel manager?
10. All management posts require an understanding of 'personnel'. Discuss this statement.

Data response questions

1   Job descriptions and job specifications

Read the information and answer the questions that follow.

A job description

Job title:	Office services supervisor
Department:	Administration
Main purpose of job:	To ensure the provision of efficient typing, reprographic and switchboard services to company personnel
Scope of job:	Responsible to: administration manager
	Responsible for: five staff; equipment to value of £300 000

Main duties:

(a) To allocate suitable personnel to switchboard, telex, offset printer and photocopiers, as required.
(b) To ensure the provision and maintenance of an accurate and efficient typing and reprographic service.
(c) To ensure the maintenance and upkeep of equipment.
(d) To collate control information on departmental costs, etc.
(e) To order stationery, reprographic chemicals and other materials, recording use and maintaining suitable stock levels.
(f) To train and assist in selection of new staff.

A job specification

Seven-point plan

Essential	Desirable
Physical make-up	
Good health record	Pleasant appearance,
Acceptable bearing and	bearing and speech
speech	
Attainments	
GCSE English language	GCSE maths or
Ability to type, and to	equivalent
operate office machines	RSA II typing
Experience of general	Experience of using sim-
office work	ple statistical information
	and experience of staff
	supervision
General intelligence	
Above average.	
Special aptitudes	
Reasonable manual	
dexterity	
Facility with figures	
Interests	
	Social activities
Disposition	
Persuasive and	Good degree of accept-
influential	ability, dependability and
Self-reliant	self-reliance
	Steady under pressure
Circumstances	
No special circumstances	

(*Source*: adapted from *Recruitment and Selection*, ACAS)

1. Using examples given in the data, distinguish between a job description and a job specification.
2. How might a company recruit for this post?
3. What factors might be important in the conduct of an interview?
4. The firm has appointed someone to fill the post without interview: what information might they have used in making their selection?
5. Outline four pieces of legislation that might be taken into account during the recruitment and selection process. (*Source:* AEB)

2   Literacy skills 'lacked by 6 million adults'

One in seven 21-year-olds are below the standard of most 8-year-olds in reading and writing, and one in five performs less well than a 9-year-old in maths, a survey carried out for the Adult Literacy and Basic Skills Unit revealed in June 1993.

As part of the test, 1650 men and women from a group born in one week in 1970 were given a 30-minute assessment. When they were shown an advertisement for 'The Firm, appearing at the Birmingham National Exhibition Centre', 5 per cent could not even say where the concert was taking place.

Scores for maths were worse than those in English: 40 per cent could not work out how many pound coins to give a shopkeeper to pay for four items costing £1.40, £7.15, £3.86 and 79p. Overall, 35 per cent were below the level of most 13-year-olds. However, 15 per cent scored full marks on reading and writing and 25 per cent on numbers.

The director of the research pointed out that the results broadly backed up previous research and indicated that 6 million people in Britain lack the literacy skills they need, though only about 1 per cent of the population is illiterate. The survey showed that problems are passed from one generation to another: 61 per cent of 10-year-olds with low reading and writing scores had parents in the same category. Men in this group were three times as likely to be unemployed.

1. What sampling techniques were used in the survey outlined?
2. Do you think that the results of the survey indicate that business organizations are likely to have problems in recruiting labour with basic skills required in the workplace?
3. How could a business organization make sure that the people it recruits have the essential skills required to perform particular jobs?
4. How can a business make sure that the people it recruits are given the opportunity to develop the skills and knowledge required in a dynamic business environment?
5. How can 'appraisal' contribute to
   (a)   the personal development and career structure of people at work?
   (b)   the development of the business organization so that it effectively meets business objectives?
6. (a)   Who is responsible for the development of literacy skills in young people?
   (b)   How can literacy skills be improved?
   (c)   What are the resource implications of your answer to (b)?

3   Job recruitment in the motor trade

Study the article in Fig. 18.9 and answer the following questions.

Driving the job message home

Job description and salary are the most important items to be included in an advertisement for the motor trade. Job description was the most important to 25 per cent of survey respondents and salary to 22 per cent. Other significant factors are job title (13 per cent), location (11 per cent) and employers name (11 per cent).

The *Motor Trader* Employment Survey looks at how, when and why staff in the motor trade move jobs. It covers senior management and skilled jobs.

Over two-thirds of staff in the sector look at job advertisements even when they are not actively looking for a job.

According to the survey, the local press is the main information source. It is used by 44 per cent of staff looking for a job. It was used by 32 per cent when they were last looking for a job. The trade press follows in second place, used by 17 per cent of staff in this sector when they last looked for a job.

But the trade press and local papers are almost equally popular as the best source in which to look for a job.

Less than half of the respondents, 43 per cent were willing to move home for a new job. But distance was of little consequence. Of those prepared to move, 62 per cent would move more than 200 miles.

Of those prepared to move 28 per cent would move to the South West. The South East and East Anglia follow in popularity.

Figure 18.9 Features of a 'good' job advertisement. (*Source*: *Personnel Today*, September 1989)

1. What does the article indicate are the best methods of placing job advertisements for senior managers and skilled employees in the motor trade?
2. What features do members of the motor trade particularly look for in job advertisements?
3. Design a job advertisement for a car sales manager. Study existing adverts for reference. How is your advertisement more effective than existing ones?

Suggested reading

Breakwell, G. M., *Interviewing*. Routledge, 1990.
Cole, G. A., *Personnel Management*, 2nd edn. D. P. Publications, 1988.
Lanz, K., *Employing and Managing People*. Pitman, 1991.

19

The experience of working life

What any one individual experiences in the course of his or her working life depends on a complex mix of factors, including:

- The individual
- The group
- The nature of the work
- The organization of the business

For the *individual*, this experience is highly subjective. One's 'personality' is the result of a multitude of elements of heredity and environment. For the purposes of business studies at 'A' level, you will need to be aware that every individual has his or her own needs and requirements, and that these will need to be considered within the constraints of organizational needs. Research into stress at work consistently finds that the way individuals are treated constitutes the main feature of their job satisfaction.

Work is important for the feelings of self-worth it gives as well as for being a way of earning a living. As the American writer Studs Terkel suggests in his book *Working*, 'It is about a search, too, for daily meaning as well as daily bread, for recognition as well as cash, for astonishment rather than torpor; in short, for a sort of life rather than a Monday-through-Friday sort of dying.'

Many people spend considerable amounts of their working lives operating in *groups*. They will interact with others in formal and in informal settings. Formal groups are those that are set up for a particular purpose, with a set pattern of operation, with set targets and goals. Individuals will have set roles and positions within a formal group, e.g. works manager, supervisor. Informal groups exist on a casual basis involving loose arrangements. People frequently engage in informal relations at work with the people they work with. The quality of these relationships will influence an individual's attitude to work.

The *nature of the work* will be an important determinant of the quality of working life. However, there is no simple pattern of 'good' and 'bad' jobs, 'dull' and 'rewarding' ones. An individual's evaluation of a job will be influenced by other factors such as personality, and by one's degree of sociability and team-spiritedness.

The *organization of the business* and the style of management and leadership is an important influence in the experience of work. Rank Xerox, for example, recognizes the importance of praising and acknowledging individuals within the organization. A recognition programme has therefore been introduced in its personnel department. It is called 'You Deserve an X Today' (X being a positive letter at Xerox). Anyone in the department, whether an executive or not, can give an X certificate (redeemable for $25) to anyone else for 'excellent support, excellent attendance, extra work or excellent co-operation'. This means that any member of the organization can reward any other colleague for a quality contribution.

Human needs and work

People have a wide range of attitudes towards work. Many people see work simply as a means of earning money; others find that work is tremendously rewarding. Attitudes to work often depend on how much opportunity individuals are given to express their skills and talents. Some work is alienating because people are treated like part of the machinery; they are expected to do very boring and repetitive work, without any responsibility. Some work is fulfilling because individuals are given a lot of freedom, and the opportunity to be creative.

Conditions of work are also important. Some modern workplaces are air conditioned, brightly decorated and with a pleasant working atmosphere. Others are stifling in summer and freezing in winter; the premises are decrepit and personal relationships are discouraged. Pay can be used as an incentive to encourage people to work harder, but it cannot help them to enjoy their work.

Some of the things different people might look for in a job include:

- A good rate of pay
- Good opportunities for promotion
- Long breaks and holidays
- Prestige
- The opportunity to combine work and family life
- Job security
- Friendship with workmates
- Opportunities to be creative
- A degree of independence
- Responsibility

Generally, satisfaction will be greatest for individuals who have the greatest freedom to choose a job, and this will be those who have had the opportunity to acquire the most widely accepted range of qualifications and skills. Most jobs have some disadvantages, but workers will enjoy work if these disadvantages can be minimized.

The ingredients of a 'good job'

It would be very difficult to agree on the 'commonly accepted' ingredients of a good job. One person likes the freedom to work when and how she wants, another feels secure only when there is someone there telling him what to do; one person likes variety and change, another wants a good steady job. There are an infinite number of variations on this theme.

Job satisfaction results from a complex mix of factors, including:

- The individual employee
- The work
- The nature of the business
- The rewards
- The working environment

Individual employees bring their attitudes into the workplace, and these attitudes are also shaped by the workplace. Some employees come to work looking for challenge and excitement and place little emphasis on monetary rewards; others might see work as a means to enjoying a good life outside of the workplace and will not be too bothered about the nature of the work provided the pay is high.

The social researchers Goldthorpe and Lockwood studied workers in three firms which used a range of different technologies in production. Their sample of 250 men included assembly-line workers at the Vauxhall car company; machine operators, machine setters and skilled maintenance workers at the Skefko Ball Bearing Company; and process workers and skilled maintenance workers at Laporte Chemicals. Goldthorpe and Lockwood found that skilled workers had a greater level of enjoyment in their work than did the routine machinists and assemblers. However, they also found that the level of technology made very little difference to employees' attitudes to work and to their behaviour. In particular, they found that all workers had what they defined as an 'instrumental approach' to work. Work was seen as a means (an instrument) to earn wages high enough to enable the individual to enjoy life outside the workplace. Work therefore was seen as a means to an end, enabling a wider range of consumer goods to be bought and more leisure to be enjoyed. Goldthorpe and Lockwood felt that these attitudes to work resulted from the employees' attitudes to life in general, which were formed outside of the workplace.

The nature of the work performed will inevitably influence employees' perceptions of the pleasure involved. At one end of the spectrum will be the job that involves endless repetition of a simple and tedious operation, where there are only a few seconds in which to perform the task before it has to be repeated. Employees will get little sense of achievement from producing a very small part of an end-product which they may never see. There may be very little time for conversation with workmates because of noise and the urgency to perform the next operation.

At the other extreme, there will be jobs involving personal involvement and individual contributions to production methods. These jobs may require high levels of training and expertise and will give the employee prestige as well as meaning to his or her working life.

Dorothy Wedderburn and Rosemary Crompton investigated work attitudes in a large chemical plant in northeast England which they called 'Seagrass'. They found that 'different attitudes and behaviour *within* the work situation could be manifested by different groups of workers largely in response to the differences in the prevailing technologies and control systems.' For example, the process workers in the plant (which was mainly automated) found their jobs interesting, and felt that they had enough scope to try out their own ideas and sufficient freedom to organize their own work tasks. In contrast, workers in the machine shop felt that their work was boring and gave them little freedom to organize their own work tasks. Attitudes produced by the job situation tended to be reflected in attitudes to supervisors; workers who found their jobs interesting and enjoyable tended to have a favourable view of their supervisors, while employees who found work boring tended to resent supervision.

While finding that within the work situation attitudes were influenced by technology, Wedderburn and Crompton went on to conclude that workers still had an instrumental general attitude towards work itself. For example, in the assessment of their jobs the Seagrass workers listed four major considerations: 'the level of pay, the security of the job, the good welfare benefits and the good working conditions'. 'Job interest' was regarded as relatively less important.

The nature of the business organization is also of importance. Some organizations try and create an atmosphere of employee involvement; for example, Toshiba UK holds a daily five-minute communication meeting between workers and management. Organizations that directly involve employees in decision-making help to foster a feeling of shared involvement in the success or failure of the enterprise. Some organizations such as co-operatives deliberately set out to share the decision-making process. In contrast, large companies based on hierarchical procedures can foster feelings of alienation.

The way in which employment is rewarded is another factor in determining attitudes to work. Some methods of payment, such as by piece-rate (where employees are paid according to the number of items produced), can add to a feeling of alienation (e.g. workers rushing to produce given targets in order to increase pay). In the past ten years there has been a dramatic rise in the number of British companies introducing incentive schemes to motivate staff. The range of incentives offered by companies are diverse, ranging from school fees, pensions, executive cars and private telephones to merit awards, life assurance bonuses and profit-sharing schemes.

The working environment covers a range of factors, including lighting, heating, ventilation, the state of furnishing and equipment and recreation facilities. For example, recent reports have pointed out some of the dangers of the high-tech office; reports indicate that typists and computer operators nationwide are suffering from increasing problems caused by repetitive strain injury (RSI). Fast keyboard work can lead to the overuse of muscles, making it impossible to sleep, work or do ordinary household tasks.

Individual needs in the workplace

What do people need to give them a general feeling of well-being? If you put this question to a number of individuals you would come up with a wide range of differing answers. For example, in a recent article for the *Independent* newspaper Koo Stark (a former girlfriend of Prince Andrew) wrote: 'In my view, privacy is as necessary to human happiness as eating or sleeping. If you are deprived of your privacy you cannot eat or sleep and you become ill. You cannot breathe, you distrust every flicker of light in case it is the glint of a long lens. You are deprived of a basic human need.'

Not only do perceptions of needs vary from one individual to another, but they also vary over time and in different circumstances.

We shall now consider the views of a number of sociologists concerning individual needs in the workplace.

Maslow

Abraham Maslow (1970) suggested that, although it is difficult, if not impossible, to analyse individual needs, it is possible to develop a *hierarchical picture of needs*, split into five broad categories (Fig. 19.1).

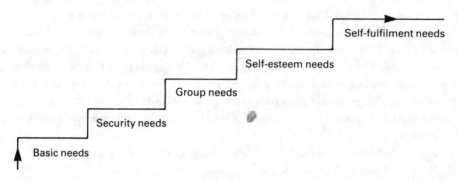

Figure 19.1 Abraham Maslow's 'hierarchy of needs'.

Basic needs are for reasonable standards of food, shelter and clothing and those other items that are considered the norm to meet the needs of the body and for physical survival. This base level of need will typically be met in modern industrial society by the exchange of labour for a wage packet or salary.

Security needs are also concerned with physical survival. In the context of the workplace, these needs could include physical safety, security of employment, adequate rest periods, pension and sick schemes and protection from arbitrary actions.

Group needs are concerned with an individual's need for love and affection. Within groups there are always some people who are strong enough and happy to keep apart; however, the majority of people want to feel that they belong to a group. In small and medium-sized organizations (up to 200 people) it is relatively easy to give each member of the group a feeling of belonging. However, in large organizations individuals can lose their group identity, becoming just another number, a face in the crowd. As we shall see later in this chapter, there are ways of dealing with this problem, for example by putting groups of workers into smaller work units with a common productive interest.

Self-esteem needs are based on an individual's desire for self-respect and the respect of others. Employees have a need to be recognized as individuals of some importance, to receive praise for their work and to have their efforts noticed.

Maslow placed *self-fulfilment* at the top of his hierarchy of needs. Self-fulfilment is concerned with full personal development and individual creativity. In order to meet this need, it is important for individuals to be able to use their talents and abilities fully.

Maslow argued that individuals first have to have their lower-level needs met; however, if they are not to experience frustration it is also important for their higher-level needs to be met. Frustrated employees are likely either to develop a 'couldn't care less' approach or to become antagonistic to working life. Maslow felt that in modern industrial settings, if employees are to feel a greater commitment to work and to become more effective workers, it is necessary to meet these higher-level needs. Self-fulfilment at work creates the 'complete' employee, the person who enjoys work and feels a direct involvement in it.

Herzberg

The research work of Herzberg in many ways complements the findings of Maslow. Herzberg argued that different factors in the work situation act in different ways to motivate people to work well or badly. He drew a distinction between what he called 'hygiene' factors (which potentially could act as *dissatisfiers*) and motivating factors or *satisfiers*.

Herzberg set out nine dissatisfiers:

- Autocratic or arbitrary company policy and administration
- Low pay
- Poor working conditions
- Antagonistic relationships between different levels in the hierarchy
- Unfriendly relationships within the hierarchy
- Unfair management and supervisory practices
- Unfair treatment of employees
- Feelings of inadequacy
- Impossibility of growth and development

Herzberg suggested that if these factors did not reach an acceptable standard it could lead to employee dissatisfaction, which might be expressed by absenteeism, poor levels of output, resistance to change, obstruction and/or other negative work practices.

In contrast, Herzberg pointed to five motivating factors, which he referred to as *satisfiers*, which can increase the motivation to work better and harder.

- Recognition of effort and performance
- The nature of the job itself—does it provide the employee with the appropriate degree of challenge?
- Sense of achievement
- Assumption of responsibility
- Opportunity for promotion and improvement

On the basis of his research, Herzberg went on to suggest that jobs could be given more meaning if they incorporated elements of responsibility and a more creative use of abilities and opportunities, enabling employees to feel a sense of achievement.

Vroom

An alternative way of looking at motivation is presented in Vroom's *expectancy theory*. This theory puts forward the notion that the key ingredients in motivation are:

- An individual's wants
- His or her estimation of the likelihood of meeting these wants

An individual's wants at work may include promotion, a high salary, a particular job, a company car and so on. Vroom used the measure *valency* to describe the level of a particular want, which can be placed on a scale of High to Low. However, if high valency for a particular target is going to act as a motivator, the individual concerned must believe that the target is attainable. For motivation to be high, it is essential that employees feel they can achieve their goals at work. For example, an individual who wants to work up to the position in which he or she is entitled to run a company car, or manage a department at work, must believe that this goal will be met in the course of time. The implications of the theory are that working life should offer opportunities for the goals of employees to be met, and at the same time provide clear evidence that these targets *are* attainable.

Vroom sets out a diagram showing that valence and expectancy are the two key ingredients in motivation. The × sign indicates the multiplier effect created by the interaction of valence and expectancy:

$$(\text{Valence} \times \text{Expectancy}) \rightarrow \text{Motivation} \rightarrow \text{Action} \rightarrow \text{Results} \rightarrow \text{Satisfaction}$$

Schein

Theories related to motivation are all based on assumptions about the underlying nature of people. Schein has classified these assumptions under three main headings:

1. *Socio-economic drives*   The assumption here is that people are driven by material urges alone. Satisfaction can be created by meeting these basic needs in the workplace.
2. *Social drives*   Here the assumption is that people have a basic need to feel part of a group, and to be accepted.
3. *Complex drives*   A much broader perspective of motivation is that people are driven by a host of different factors which change over time and in different circumstances.

Schein believes that simplistic explanations of motivation should be avoided.

McGregor

The traditional theory of management as set out by Fayol is based on the assumption that the organization is controlled and directed by management. Certain other basic assumptions are made in traditional theory, which Douglas McGregor characterizes as 'Theory X' (Fig. 19.2). These are:

1. The average person has an inherent dislike of work and will avoid it if possible. So management needs to emphasize productivity, incentive schemes and a fair day's work, and to denounce restrictions on output.
2. Because people naturally dislike work, most people must be coerced, controlled, directed and/or threatened with punishment to get them to work towards business objectives.
3. The average person likes to be directed, wishes to avoid responsibility, has little ambition and above all seeks security.

Against this view of human motivation and its implications for management of an organization, McGregor proposed an alternative 'Theory Y' (Fig. 19.2). The underlying emphasis here is on 'integration' to replace direction and control. The assumptions about human motivation of Theory Y are:

1. Physical and mental effort in work is as natural as play or rest. The ordinary person does not dislike work: it all depends on the conditions under which work takes place—it can be enjoyable or not.
2. External control is not the only way to get people to work. If they are committed to objectives, then they will be motivated to work towards achieving them.
3. The most significant reward that will motivate people to work is the satisfaction of an individual's self-actualization needs. This can be the result of working towards an organization's objectives.

Figure 19.2 Mr Theory X and Mrs Theory Y.

4. The average human being learns, when given the opportunity, to accept—and, more importantly, to seek—responsibility.
5. Many people can contribute to a business's objectives when given the chance.
6. Currently the potentialities of the average person are not being fully used.

McGregor sees the potential to make organizations far more effective by unleashing the people that work for them. Organizations need to see themselves as interacting groups of people enjoying 'supportive relationships' with each other. Ideally, members of an organization will see its objectives as being personally significant to them.

Taylorism

Over the years, many different approaches to work organization have been employed. Frederick Taylor, writing at the beginning of the century, spelled out his *principles of scientific management*.

According to Taylor, there is 'one best way' of carrying out any work task; it is the job of management to find out this method by using scientific principles. For example, various tools should be tested to find the most effective ones for a particular job; rest periods of different lengths and frequency should be tried to discover the relationship between rest and productivity; the various movements involved in a task should be studied to find the least time-consuming and tiring way of doing it. In this way, scientific managers should experiment with the various components of work tasks to produce the best methods. Employees would then be carefully matched with work tasks according to their aptitudes. Instructions set down by management for the performance of tasks would then be followed to the letter. The workforce and the machinery could thus be seen as one and the same. It would then be possible to provide incentives, usually in the form of high wages, to encourage employees to identify with these scientifically devised procedures. Employers would be able to maximize profits, and employees to maximize wages.

Taylor's work is based heavily on the assumption that high wages are the key motivator.

Human relations

Taylor's scientific management approach can be contrasted with the human relations school of thought. Elton Mayo and a team of researchers from the Harvard Business School carried out a series of experiments from 1927 to 1932 at the Western Electric Company in Chicago. Initially Mayo had taken on board some of the assumptions of the scientific management school, believing that physical conditions in the working environment, the aptitudes of workers and financial incentives were the key ingredients in motivation. To this end, Mayo had experimented with different levels of heating, lighting, lengths and frequencies of rest periods and other variables. However, the results of the experiments were inconclusive; for example, Mayo and his team were surprised to find that wide variations in the level of lighting had little or no effect on output.

During the course of the experiments, Mayo found that the productivity of the group studied kept climbing, irrespective of various changes. Mayo came to the conclusion that, as a result of the experiment, a great deal of attention had been given to the group and members of the group had come to feel much closer ties with each other. Mayo felt that this was the important factor, and his work led to an appreciation of the importance of the informal group in industry.

The Hawthorne studies moved the emphasis from the individual worker to the worker as a member of a social group. Mayo suggested that managers should establish and maintain a sense of group purpose in industry. A famous example of this is the Volvo car assembly plant, where the traditional assembly line has been scrapped and small teams of workers build virtually the whole car. Not only do the workers build up a sense of group solidarity, but also they are able to identify with the production process from start to finish.

Peters and Waterman

Within an organization, it is management's role to ensure that objectives are delegated and communicated clearly, from the highest management level through the management chain, ensuring that each manager within the chain knows clearly his or her individual role and objective.

To do this effectively requires shared values and the commitment of the whole organization. Thomas Peters and Robert Waterman set out in their book, *In Search of Excellence*, what they refer to as the 'McKinsey 7-S framework'. Shared values are at the heart of a successful operation; without them things can start to disintegrate.

On the basis of this framework of seven interdependent aspects of organizing (Fig. 19.3), i.e.:

- Structure
- Strategy
- Systems (and procedures)
- Style (of management)

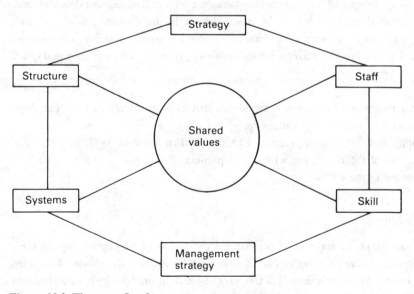

Figure 19.3 The seven Ss of success.

- Skills (corporate strengths)
- Staff (people)
- Shared values (culture)

They set out eight attributes which are characteristics of 'excellent' innovative US companies.

1. *A bias towards action* These organizations have a 'can do' and 'let's try' approach. People within these firms are enterprising. Managers get out of their offices and keep in touch informally with what is happening throughout the organization. At Hewlett Packard this is referred to as MBWA (Management By Wandering Around).

2. *Keeping close to the customer* These US companies have an obsession with the customer. They are market-led and are concerned to find out the real needs and wants of customers.

3. *Autonomy and entrepreneurship* Innovative companies foster many leaders and innovators at all levels of the organization.

4. *Productivity through people* 'Excellent' companies treat the ordinary members of their organizations as the basic source of quality and productivity gains. Such organizations are opposed to an 'us and them' approach.

5. *Hands-on, value-driven* Those at the top of such an organization need to work hard to maintain the values of the company in a very public hands-on way. Senior managers are renowned for getting involved in the actual processes (design, selling, etc.), thus publicly demonstrating their commitment to high standards.

6. *'Stick to the knitting'* These companies don't move into areas they don't know anything about; they concentrate on what they can do best, and move on one manageable step at a time.

7. *Simple form, lean staff* 'Excellent' firms have a simple clear structure, with only the necessary number of people being employed in each function.

8. *Simultaneous loose–tight properties* These companies are both centralized and decentralized. Independent decision-making tends to be pushed down to the divisions, to the product development team and to the shop-floor. However, some key aspects of the organization are controlled from the centre, e.g. quality, reliability, action, regular communication and quick feedback.

One conclusion that Peters and Waterman came to was that in nearly every case an 'excellent' organization was associated with strong leadership.

(It is worth noting that Peters and Waterman produced their book in 1982; in 1993 they revealed that a number of the companies which they pinpointed for their 'excellence', such as IBM, had fallen behind in the 1990s.)

Hammer and Champy

Michael Hammer and James Champy have popularized the notion of 're-engineering' in their influential book, *Re-engineering the Corporation: A Manifesto for Business Revolution*. This term applies to the massive, fundamental upheaval of the ways in which businesses organize themselves as part of a process of continuous change. During a period of recession the concept came to be associated with 'downsizing', with fewer more highly qualified people doing more complex work. It is not just at the lower end of the workforce that the changes are felt. Managers' lives are probably altered more dramatically. Workers take over many aspects of management, the manager moving from a supervisory role to a more strategic one.

This 'collapse of skills' means that highly paid senior managers have to get their heads back into the business and create the operating models that give the company its distinct quality. For example, these could be based on features such as customer satisfaction or innovation. The return to focusing on the business is in marked contrast to the traditional approach of managers moving steadily away from the work as they are promoted.

$\mathcal{P}$ Case Study—Highlighting a lack of shared values at BCL Cellophane

A shrinking market and growing competition prompted BCL Cellophane in Bridgewater to review its culture.

Managing director Ken Vickers says: 'Cellophane manufacture is a complex chemical process, but it is a very traditional business.' He admits it had a conventional approach to management. 'It was very much a top-down, blame-culture,' he says. The company, a division of Courtaulds Yarns, recognized it had to change or it would be out of business within five years.

Its problems stemmed not from marketing and distribution but from inadequacies in its manufacturing. Management concluded that the route to increasing productivity lay in improving teamwork, breaking down the mistrust between management and work-force and developing a common approach to solving the problems.

It invited the Coverdale Organization to initiate a training programme to tackle the problem under its business results scheme. The scheme means that paying for the training is directly linked to the improvement in the performance of the business as a result of the training.

The Coverdale approach is geared to developing teamwork concentrating on using training techniques to explore the effects particular behaviour has on working in teams. It also established a common approach to tackling problems, planning ahead and seeing plans through.

The programme began with an initial diagnosis of the company's problems. Specific, measurable, project aims were set. These were then cascaded down to precise targets even at individual shift level (see Fig. 19.4). A monitoring process was set up next to log and measure progress, and the training programme began.

The factory management had identified the target. It wanted to reduce factory waste from 17.45 per cent to 15 per cent by March.

This translated down to specific goals within the company.

Managing director Vickers explains that it was important that any training exercise should be more than 'just a quick fix'. 'We had to make a permanent change to the culture and attitudes; to the way we were running the organization. We wanted to weave into the fabric of the business,' he says.

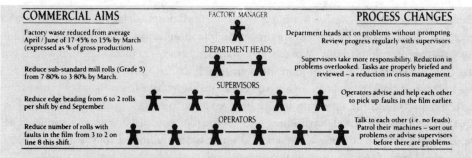

Figure 19.4 Changing behaviour in the manufacturing plant was achieved by addressing very specific problems and setting clearly identified goals.

Vickers explains that the market for Cellophane has grown very tough, declining at a rate of 12 per cent a year. There are nine companies, all vying for larger shares of this smaller market. Survival depends on more efficient manufacturing.

According to Vickers, the company suffered because there were no shared values, and very little contact between sales and the shop-floor. One of the key changes brought in by Coverdale was taking people of all disciplines and training them together. 'The shopfloor began to see that sales people were human and had problems too,' explains Vickers. But the most important aspect was behavioural changes. 'You do not change attitudes unless you change the behaviour of management,' he says.

So training began at the top and the re-setting of precise goals began there too. 'Managers were struggling because they did not have direction; they did not have the vision,' explains Vickers.

Coverdale's training programme was tightly linked to changes in the structure of BCL and driven by top management. In parallel, and in part through the training, improvements were being made to the internal organization.

'We had to flatten the management structure,' explains Vickers. 'There were eight or nine levels of management. But the company management had recognized that productivity depended on sharing responsibility for production with the workforce, if it could not trust its workforce then it could not succeed. One of the important ways of developing that was through common training, which taught common methods.'

A mark of the success of the project was that barely a year into the programme there was a major programme of redundancy at the Bridgewater plant. Forty per cent of the workforce had to be made redundant and yet production had still to be pushed up even higher.

Efforts were made to do this as quickly as possible and without disruption. The company found others jobs for all those who wanted them. At the same time the relentless drive to push up production carried on and it lifted output from 25 to 35 tonnes per man per year. Part of the reason for this was, explains Vickers, 'the atmosphere that emerged. People were no longer resistant to change; they were seeking it.'

Coverdale is still working with BCL 'It takes longer than you think,' insists Vickers. But it is important to him that the training be seen right through to the point at which he is satisfied it is changing the roots of the business.

Get it right first, he suggests, and then bolting on to other kinds of training, or making changes, becomes easier because the base is solid.

(*Source:* Helena Sturridge, *Personnel Today*, 1968)

Questions

1. What circumstances led BCL Cellophane to review its culture?
2. What evidence is given in the article that before the review there was a lack of shared values at BCL Cellophane?
3. What weaknesses in company organizational structure existed before the review?
4. What changes in training procedures were introduced by Coverdale?
5. In what ways can the commercial aims of BCL Cellophane and process changes be seen to go hand in hand?
6. Why was it felt to be essential to change management attitudes?

Non-monetary techniques of motivating employees

There are a number of possible ways of motivating workers apart from pay. These usually involve an increase in one or all of the following:

- Variety of work
- Responsibility
- Recognition
- Sense of working as a team

1. *Job enrichment* involves giving employees an increase in responsibility/and or recognition. The aim of job enrichment is to make employees feel that their contribution has been upgraded so that it is more highly appreciated. Ways of doing this vary from an employee being given a new title, to an extension of the perks associated with a particular job.
2. *Job enlargement* involves giving employees a greater range of responsibilities. An employee who feels that a job is going 'stale', and as a result is losing interest in it, may feel rejuvenated when asked to take on additional tasks. For example, an employee who has been used to handling routine mail and answering telephone calls may gain fresh motivation if she takes on the additional responsibility of meeting clients and taking them out to dinner as part of the public relations function.
3. *Employee participation* in decision-making can be a great motivator. The flattened organogram in which decisions can be made at all levels of an organization helps employees to feel

important and valued for their contribution to the decision-making process. Effective employee participation goes beyond the factory floor suggestion box to actually giving a wider number of people the responsibility for making decisions. The flattening out of the organizational chart has become particularly possible in organizations that employ modern information systems so that communication links are better and information is more readily available.

4. *Quality circles* are particularly important motivators in the 1990s. Although quality circles are a fairly recent arrival on the British industrial scene, they have proved to be a very popular innovation. By the end of 1985 there were estimated to be between 400 and 500 quality circles operating in British manufacturing companies and between 30 and 40 in services.

    Quality circles in Britain are typically made up of small groups of seven or eight people who voluntarily meet on a regular basis to identify, investigate, analyse and resolve quality-related matters or other work-related arrangements using problem-solving techniques. Members tend to be from the same work area or to do similar work.

    Quality circles are about participation, teamwork, job satisfaction, self-esteem and organizational commitment as well as resolving work and quality-related problems. They have been particularly effective in Japanese industry and have been a cornerstone in creating group loyalty coupled with high productivity. However, there have been reservations about the introduction of quality circles in Britain; in many cases they have not worked because support has not been maintained from the top. For quality circles to be effective, the culture of an organization has got to be based on participation. Quality circles are not effective in autocratic environments. Circle members quickly become frustrated when their suggestions are ignored.

○ Case Study—Changing employment relations at British Rail

British Rail seems to have been chugging along the same line for some time. But according to the new director of personnel development, Steven Colloff, a dramatic culture change is about to take place, with customer service right at the top of the list of priorities.

Staff training is to be improved, better communications are planned with staff, a performance review is to be brought in for supervisors and promotion at all levels is to be speeded up.

The first step in the culture change was taken with an attitude survey, the results of which have just become available. A random sample of 7000 staff were invited to fill in a questionnaire on what they thought about BR's customers, communication within the company, training, career development and job satisfaction. All the points raised by staff members are now being considered. 'The name of the game is to move BR towards a more enterprising customer-orientated and result-based culture', says Colloff.

Colloff was encouraged by the high level of response to the survey: about 40 per cent returned the questionnaire. Most of the respondents said they believed their job to be worth while and liked working for the railway. 'There is a built-in loyalty to BR. We don't have the problem some companies have of convincing staff their job is worth while. But we do need to make sure staff are getting the promotion and recognition they deserve,' says Colloff. A new post has been created—employment development manager, responsible for identifying the potential in employees.

Although railway employees like working for BR and most want to stay in the company, the survey highlights a belief among staff that their capabilities are not being fully utilized: 80 per cent said promotion should be decided on merit rather than length of service, and 85 per cent wanted more opportunities to be selected and trained for better paid jobs.

'Promotion will be related more to performance instead of staff waiting years to fill a dead man's shoes. We particularly need to improve the opportunities for high-performing employees. We must bring in young managers and rapidly give them responsibility instead of waiting until they are past peak performance. To do this, we must identify potential early on.'

Colloff has urgent plans to improve training in supervisory and management skills. A 'leadership 500' programme for BR's top managers is being set up, the first part of which will be delivered at the end of November. The group will consider how to achieve quality management and how to identify the key values laid down at a recent top-level conference. These values include making the customer Number 1 and involving employees to a larger extent.

From the programme will come action policies which, says Colloff, will have to be incorporated into the whole infrastructure of the company. 'I believe the greatest mistake a company can make is to make changes from bottom to top. All that happens is that you get all these motivated employees knocking on managers' doors with ideas that then get rejected.'

Colloff has also introduced performance reviews for supervisors. When asked whether staff take notice of such a scheme when no financial incentives were offered, he replied: 'Our staff are more interested in basic rates of pay than performance-related pay, so long as they are recognized for their capabilities.'

The survey, however, reveals that employees in operations and engineering find that their present payment system offers very little incentive to do a better job.

Colloff explains that supervisors' and managers' attitudes need to be changed: 'We are trying to inculcate more of a "can do" attitude into our managers. There is vast scope for introducing the new culture of "tell me the problem and I'll do something about it" instead of "tell me the problem and I'll tell you why I can't do anything about it".'

To bring about the culture change, smaller identified units are needed in place of remote bureaucracy. Colloff says that he aims to make performance review non-threatening and creative, claiming that it is a process that should not produce conflict if carried out properly. Most workers, according to the survey, feel that their bosses are slow to praise or criticize their performance.

In fact, a large majority of staff say their management does not make any real effort to communicate with them. Only 30 per cent have a boss who holds a regular meeting to keep the staff informed. Employees want to know more about the outlook for their own area or function, including investment plans and actions to improve quality or service. *Railnews* was rated much higher than managers as a good source of information.

A majority of staff do not feel that the top management's direction is right for BR or that management understands the problems faced by staff at work. Staff perceived their boss's priority to be doing the job properly and keeping costs down; customer service is seen as the last thing on the agenda.

But the staff themselves believe that customers' views are important, and 50 per cent think that their jobs have an impact on the quality of service to customers. Customer relations training appears to be helping.

(*Source: Personnel Today*, November 1988)

Questions

1. What do you understand by the term 'culture change'?
2. Why do you think British Rail felt that it needed a culture change?
3. Why do you think British Rail got such a high response from the questionnaires it sent out to its employees? Do you think that the results from the questionnaire would be likely to be representative of all British Rail staff?
4. Why has British Rail employed an employment development manager? Do you think that this is a good idea?
5. Do you think that the notion of promotion related to performance is likely to serve as a good motivator? What drawbacks can you see to such a scheme?
6. How does British Rail hope to change 'the whole infrastructure of the company'? Evaluate BR's policies for making these changes.
7. What suggestions would you put forward to British Rail to help improve employee motivation?

Work and pay

Pay can be seen as a way of 'compensation' or 'rewarding' employees for work done. There are many different types of job, and there are many reasons why people receive different levels of payment.

Wages and salaries

Many organizations draw a distinction between those employees who are paid in the form of wages and those who receive a salary. There are a number of differences between wages and salaries, including the following:

1. Wages are normally expressed as an hourly rate, wheras salaries are expressed as an annual figure.

2. Wages are normally paid a week in arrears (i.e. the wage you earned at the end of one week would be for that week's work), whereas salaries are paid at the end of the month.

3. Salaries are normally paid on the basis of an annual rate divided by 12; a salary would thus be expressed in terms of an annual figure. Wages are calculated in several different ways including piece-rate and time rates (see below).

4. In many organizations the package of benefits available to an employee is different for salaried and waged employees.

5. Salaries are typically paid automatically into an employee's bank account by credit transfer; wages are paid either in cash or by credit transfer.

Fees

Fees represent an alternative system of payment to wages and salaries. In the United Kingdom today they are becoming increasingly commonly used as employees are hired indirectly to carry out a service contract for a business. The fee is payment for work done, but the employee is not taken directly on to the firm's payroll. A fee may be paid for a short-term contract, e.g. to a photographer helping to make a film about a company, or on a longer-term basis, e.g. regular fees to a financial consultant. Fees may be paid on the basis of the time worked, the quantity of output produced, the completion of a particular contract or on some other basis.

Objectives of systems of payment

Payment systems are usually arrived at as a result of a process of collective bargaining. In setting out the objectives of such a system, we therefore need to explore the aims and purposes of both management and trade unions.

Management's objectives

1. The pay system needs to be effective in recruiting the right quantity and quality of labour.

2. The pay system needs to be effective in retaining labour over the required level of time. It is expensive to have to keep placing new recruitment adverts with the media, and to keep having to train new employees.

3. The pay system needs to be effective in keeping unit labour costs as low as possible. The unit labour cost is the proportion of output cost that can be attributed to labour. Keeping labour costs low is one of the key factors to being competitive in local, national and international markets.

4. The pay system can also be seen as one of the key ingredients in motivation. Careful thought needs to be applied to structuring pay systems in a way that encourages motivation and performance.

5. The pay system should be aimed at maximizing output per unit of factor of production employed—i.e. maximizing productivity.

6. The pay system should be designed in such a way as to effectively incorporate fringe benefits.

Trade unions' objectives

1. The pay system should maximize the growth of trade union members' real earnings.
2. The pay system should be combined with working practices that best suit trade union members' needs—including considerations of fatigue, boredom, safety and other matters.
3. Wage considerations should be balanced with those of hours worked, breaks and holidays.
4. The pay system should offer the best long-term benefits for trade union members; these may be tied in with notions of competitiveness.
5. Pay systems that are unpopular with their members, e.g. systems based on unattainable bonus targets, should be replaced.

Clearly, different groups within an organization will have different perceptions of what makes an effective system of payment. What works in one company, or for one type of production, may clearly be inappropriate in another. What is needed is a system that creates the 'best fit' given the type of company, types of employee, technologies used, time available for production, state of the market and other relevant factors.

Calculating pay

The amount paid for a normal working week is referred to as a 'basic' wage or salary. Many employees receive other benefits in addition to their basic wage, in either a money or a non-money form. The main ways of calculating pay are outlined below. Sometimes elements of these methods are combined.

Flat rate

This is a set rate of weekly or monthly pay, based on a set number of hours. This system is easy to calculate and administer but it does not provide an incentive to work harder.

Time rate

Under this scheme, the worker receives a set rate per hour. Any hours worked above a set number are paid at an 'overtime' rate.

Piece-rate

This system is sometimes used in the textile and electronics industries, among others. Payment is made for each item produced that meets a given quality standard. The advantage of such a scheme is that it encourages effort. However, it is not suitable for jobs that require time and care. Also, the output of many jobs such as service occupations is impossible to measure.

Bonus

A bonus is paid as an added encouragement to employees. It can be paid out of additional profits earned by the employer as a result of the employee's effort and hard work. Bonuses may also be used as an incentive to workers at times when they might be inclined to slacken effort, e.g. at Christmas and summer holiday times.

Commission

This is a payment made as a percentage of the sales a salesperson has made.

Output-related payment schemes

Output-related schemes are the most common method used to reward manual workers. Most schemes involve an element of time rates plus additional bonus or other incentive rate.

Standards are set in many ways, varying from casual assessments to detailed work study. Work study involves: (a) method study, and (b) work measurement.

Method study sets out to determine what is the most effective way of carrying out particular tasks.

Work measurement takes place in three stages:

1. The time taken to perform a task is measured.
2. The effort of an individual worker or work-group is rated.
3. The work carried out is assessed and compared with the standard rate.

A standard allowable time or price is set according to the first two stages. The worker's pay is then determined according to success at the third stage.

Variations in output-related schemes

There are many variations of such schemes, for example according to individual or group performance, the time period covered (day/week/month), etc. There are several variations in schemes relating earnings to changes in performance (see Fig. 19.5).

The type of output-related scheme used will be determined by the required objective; for example, do you want to encourage workers to beat a set standard? Do you want to encourage learners? Do you want to prevent too high a performance being achieved? Here are the alternatives:

1. *Straight proportional* Earnings and performance vary in the same proportion.
2. *Geared* The rate of change of earnings (although constant) is greater than the rate of change of performance.
3. *Stabilized* The change of earnings is less than the change in performance.

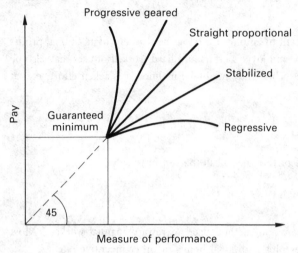

Figure 19.5 Variations in output-related schemes.

These three schemes can be represented by a straight line (they are linear relationships); i.e., the bonus rate does not vary with performance.

4. *Progressive*   The rate of change of earnings gradually changes with performance.
5. *Regressive*   The rate of change of earnings gradually falls with performance.

These two schemes are non-linear; the bonus rate varies with performance.

Profit-sharing

During the 1980s there were substantial increases in profit-based methods of pay. There are two main schemes:

1. *Cash-based systems*   A bonus in cash is paid on profits.
2. *Share-based systems*   Employees receive a profit bonus in the form of shares, or are given incentives to acquire shares in the business. In this way, cash flow is not affected; at the same time, employees are given a stake in the ownership of the enterprise.

A survey carried out in the mid-1980s found that as many as 65 per cent of companies operated at least one type of profit-related scheme. The Conservative government encouraged profit-sharing schemes by giving tax incentives to employers and employees who adopted such schemes. The government had the twin aim of creating both an enterprise culture and a share-owning democracy.

However, recent evidence suggests that such schemes have had only limited success; in 1992, the proportion of adults owning shares in their companies was only 4 per cent. Explanations of why such schemes have had a limited success include:

1. *Failure to consult employees* in decisions about whether to adopt or participate in such schemes.
2. *Lack of trust by employees* that employers will run such schemes to their benefit.
3. *Unequal status and outcomes* In recent years many jobs have become less secure, and there are widespread inequalities in earnings. Profit-related schemes are seen to do little to reduce worsening conditions.
4. *Lack of institutional support* Top management support for such schemes has been perceived to have been lukewarm and detached from the interests of ordinary employees.

Performance-related pay

In recent years the emphasis has shifted towards performance-related pay in both the public and private sectors. Such schemes are based on performance appraisal techniques and have been adopted in a wide range of occupations, from the police force to university staff, insurance and banking. Evidence indicates that up to three-quarters of all employers are now using some form of performance appraisal to set pay levels.

Managerial jobs are most affected by performance-related pay. Today managers' performances are increasingly assessed against working objectives. Individual objectives can be set by reference to company goals. An individual may be set broad objectives known as 'accountabilities'. Shorter-term goals may be attached to each objective. Scoring systems are then worked out to assess performance against objectives, and these distinguish levels of attainment, e.g. high/medium/low.

One way of rewarding performance is to give a bonus if certain targets are met. Another method is to give a progression of increments when targets are met; each year the individual will continue up an incremental ladder (see Fig. 19.6). A third common method is a salary range

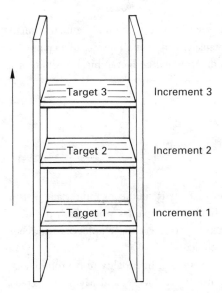

Figure 19.6 Performance-related pay—meeting the targets.

scheme. Here, a 'rate for the job' is set against a mid-point of a salary range; for example, in a salary range of £20 000–£25 000 the mid-point would be £22 500. The salary would then depend on one's performance against the 'rate for the job'. If you equalled the rate for the job you would receive £22 500; if you exceeded the rate for the job you might receive, say, 110 per cent of £22 500; and so on.

While performance-related pay has become increasingly popular, there have been a number of criticisms of its implementation:

1. Not enough emphasis has been placed on employee development. Too much emphasis has been placed on performance as a way of calculating pay and rewards.
2. Performance objectives have often been too vague.
3. Subjective elements of performance-related pay give rise to criticisms of favouritism; e.g. 'Why has that person's performance been graded in that way when we all know that she is a waster and the boss's favourite?'
4. Complex schemes are often misunderstood by employees.
5. The scheme tends to benefit 'high flyers' who do not stay long in an organization.
6. Teamwork can be fractured when some individuals are rewarded and others are not.
7. Trade unions are often resistant to such schemes.

Running an effective payroll department

The wage bill in most companies constitutes a sizeable chunk of total overhead costs. Effective control of the cash necessary for the payment of wages is the payroll manager's most important task.

To be effective, it is vital that the payroll manager is seen as part of the middle management structure, and in some companies as part of the senior management team. The size of a company, together with the frequency of payment to employees, determines the hierarchical position of a wages department.

A host of tasks face the payroll manager.

Security

The most inefficient method of payment is payment in cash. It is time-consuming, and it is a security risk to every individual who uses the system. In those companies where cash payment continues, the payroll and personnel managers should try to convert the employees to accept direct payment into a bank or building society of their choice.

Payroll managers must pay close attention to the security and confidentiality of payroll details. These include not just details of salaries and wages, but also the deduction and payment of court orders, etc.

Training

Training staff in modern methods of payrolling is essential. Important areas for training might include controlling the conversion from manual systems to computer systems, and assisting in the design and the implementation of any changes.

Communication

Lines of communication with other departments must be effective, particularly with personnel (if it is separate), accounts and production control. Wages departments generate the payroll based on information supplied by others, usually personnel, the Inland Revenue, the Department of Health and Social Security and/or managerial staff.

Sick pay

Payroll departments must apply, strictly, the rules and regulations regarding statutory sick pay (SSP) and statutory maternity pay (SMP). (SSP are payments made if a worker is sick on normal working days; SMP applies in a similar way to maternity). Both articles of legislation are complicated and difficult to operate. These laws make it essential for the records maintained by the wages and personnel departments to be checked against each other on a regular basis.

Deductions

The payroll department must ensure that Pay As You Earn (PAYE) and national insurance contributions are deducted from pay. Such deductions must be passed to the Collector of Taxes by the middle of the following month.

Accounting

The payroll department must supply the accounts department with the details of payments, deductions and net pay so that these can be entered in the books of accounts and a bank reconciliation can be completed.

Benefits

An increasing burden on the payroll manager is the annual disclosure, to the Inland Revenue, of perks that have been provided by the company to certain employees; these include company cars and fuel, beneficial loans, free medical treatment and free holidays. By law, these must be disclosed to the Inland Revenue to enable the inspector of taxes to determine the tax due on such benefits.

Computerization of wages

In large firms, much of the work on wages is done by computers. This involves the calculation of wages, the printing of wage slips and the production of payment instructions to the bank. Data relating to the time an employee works are picked up by computer from magnetic tape, enabling the continuous recording of wages. Computers are able to handle a lot of work quickly and accurately.

One danger of using computers to calculate and record wages is the risk of losing information if something should happen to the wages program or disk. Therefore, firms will normally keep at least two 'back-up' copies of a disk, which will be continually updated, at least once each day.

Women at work

The Equal Pay Act 1970 aimed to eliminate discrimination on grounds of sex in relation to pay, overtime, piecework rates and holiday entitlements. The Act gave all female employees the right to treatment equal to that given to male employees in the same employment who are doing the same or 'broadly similar' work. This Act was amended in 1984 to include equal pay for work of equal value.

The Sex Discrimination Act 1975 made sex discrimination unlawful in employment training and related matters. This Act was updated in 1986 to remove restrictions on women's hours of work which had prevented them from taking on manufacturing jobs involving shift or night work.

The main problems for women as a group at work have been low pay and a concentration in low-paid occupations. Economic expansion in the United Kingdom from the 1950s onwards has created more and more jobs for women. There has been a growth particularly in the proportion of married women at work, so that over half now work.

Women have been finding work in hard times because of the nature of the work they do, i.e. part-time low-paid work. In Belgium, Denmark, West Germany and Britain women do over 80 per cent of all part-time jobs. The growing service industries are the main employers of part-time workers.

Part-time workers are especially low-paid, but this is not the only reason for women's generally low pay. Another factor is that men's earnings are boosted by shift work, overtime and productivity deals. Such payments make up a quarter of men's earnings and only one-seventh of women's. The 1986 amendment to the Sex Discrimination Act may help to alleviate this discrepancy.

Major problems for women are that they tend to work in industries where unions are weak and because of family commitments are often unable to work overtime. Women are concentrated in a very narrow range of occupations: catering, cleaning, hairdressing, bar work and other services occupy over half of all women manual workers, and office work employs a large proportion of female non-manual workers. The 1984 amendment to the Equal Pay Act, which allows for job evaluation to see if work is of equal value, is regarded as an important change.

The effect of the passing of the Equal Pay Act and the Sex Discrimination Act was to raise women's pay to 75 per cent of men's; however, by 1984 it had fallen back to 59 per cent of men's earnings in non-manual work and to 61.5 per cent in manual work.

Figure 19.7 shows that inequality between the sexes is greater in Britain than in nearly all other EC countries. In 1993, almost half the women at work in Britain—4.6 million—were in part-time jobs. Huge numbers of these, and a large percentage of their colleagues in full-time work, were, by any standards, low-paid. They got £3.08 an hour to work behind a British Home Stores till, and less than £2.50 to clean or £3.57 to be a checkout assistant at Sainsbury's—a company that in 1992 announced record annual profits of £733 million.

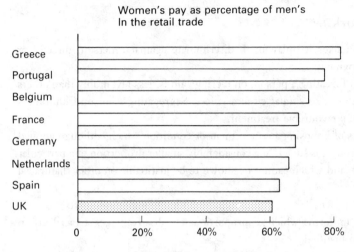

Figure 19.7 Women's pay as percentage of men's in the retail trade, 1992 (*Source*: Eurostat.)

A feature in the United Kingdom in recent years is that women now have more qualifications than ever before, which should lead to an advancement in their earnings. Women with better qualifications can choose from a wider range of careers. Women now own a quarter of all American small businesses. Whereas women graduates of the 1960s tended to go into a small number of occupations (often teaching), more of the female graduates of the 1990s are going into medicine, law, banking, insurance and accounting, among other areas. Half of UK medical school graduates are now women. Between the mid-1970s and the mid-1990s, the proportion of women members of the Chartered Insurance Institute rose from 4 to over 20 per cent. However, in the early 1990s women accounted for only 27 per cent of managers and only 1 per cent of top managers. There is a significantly lower percentage of women employees in managerial jobs in Britain than in Germany, France, the United States, Canada and Australia.

One explanation for the lack of women's career progression in the United Kingdom is that they may be less mobile than men. More generally, management may be seen to require certain 'male' characteristics, such as aggression and drive. The stereotypical female is sometimes assumed to lack these qualities. It is argued that women are 'socialized' into female attitudes and behaviour, which discourage them and others from seeing them as ideal managers.

Today, there is increasing pressure to change personnel practices, by introducing provision for child care and extended periods of paternity as well as maternity leave. Social stereotypes are changing, if at all very slowly.

It is the fastest growing industries that are taking the most women into their senior ranks, e.g. the information industry (including public relations, computer services, and the press), financial services, tourism and design. Those parts of the economy where women are rarest—upper and middle management in medium-sized and larger companies, especially in manufacturing—are generally those that are now entering into relative decline.

Ethnic minorities at work

The Race Relations Act 1976 makes it unlawful to discriminate against a person, directly or indirectly, in the field of employment.

Direct discrimination consists of treating a person, on racial grounds, less favourably than others are, or would be, treated in the same or similar circumstances. Segregating a person from others on racial grounds constitutes less favourable treatment.

Indirect discrimination consists of imposing a requirement or condition which, although applied equally to persons of all racial groups, is such that a considerably smaller proportion of a particular racial group can comply with it, and which cannot be shown to be justifiable on other than racial grounds. Examples are:

1. A rule about clothing or uniforms which disproportionately disadvantages a racial group (e.g. Sikhs) and cannot be justified.
2. Requirement of higher language standards than are needed for safe and effective performance of the job.

The Commission for Racial Equality has produced a code of practice for the elimination of racial discrimination and the promotion of equality of opportunity in employment. This code aims to give practical guidance which will help employers, trade unions, employment agencies and employees to understand not only the provisions of the Race Relations Act and its implications, but also how best they can implement policies to eliminate racial discrimination and to enhance equality of opportunity. The code covers a variety of areas including recruitment, training and appraisal.

Ethnic minorities tend to be concentrated in a range of relatively low-paid occupations compared with the national average, such as health, catering and cleaning.

Job-sharing

Job-sharing has become an increasingly important part of modern business life. It is likely to become ever more important as employers face recruitment difficulties in the 1990s.

A survey carried out by Industrial Relations Services (an independent research organization) in 1989 of 37 organizations offering job-sharing schemes showed that the majority found that the advantages of job-sharing outweighed the problems.

The main advantages cited by employers were:

- Being able to retain skilled employees
- Easing recruitment problems
- Opening up career paths for women with children
- Increased flexibility of cover for peak periods, holidays and sickness
- High motivation among sharers

The survey speculated that the high motivation is perhaps due to sharers wishing to prove that the arrangements work. The sharers were able to combine a wider level of experience and ability in a job, bounce ideas off each other and develop different aspects of the work.

Working fewer hours, job-sharers tended to bring more enthusiasm to the job, according to personnel managers. They start their part of the week or day fresher, when a full-timer might be winding down.

Disadvantages mentioned by employers included the possibility of extra recruitment and administration expenses, worries about a lack of continuity, and concern that personnel might be left with half a job to fill.

Sharers used log books, special desk filing systems, telephone conversations and overlapping work periods to keep in touch. Concern about being left with a half a job does not appear to have been borne out in practice, the survey revealed.

Questions

Short-answer questions

1. What are the most important factors influencing how an individual feels about his or her work?
2. Why does 'job satisfaction' vary from one individual to another?
3. Describe Maslow's hierarchy of needs.
4. In what ways can large organizations be 'alienating'?
5. Draw a distinction between 'dissatisfiers' and 'satisfiers' in a working environment with which you are familiar (perhaps a workplace where you have had a part time job).
6. Outline Vroom's expectancy theory.
7. What are the assumptions on which most theories of motivation are based?
8. List the seven Ss of business success. Why do shared values need to lie at the heart of a successful business?
9. Explain how a process of (a) job enrichment and (b) job enlargement could be used to improve a job with which you are familiar. What would be the main costs to the company implementing the scheme? What would be the main benefits
    (a) to the company?
    (b) to the employee?
    Would it be worth while?
10. What is a quality circle? How could it improve employee motivation?

11. What is the difference between a wage and a salary?

12. What are fees (as a form of reward)?

13. What would be the main advantages and disadvantages of piece-rate payment in a factory making bridal wear?

14. What additional rewards might a factory operative earn on top of basic pay?

15. Why might the government want to encourage profit-related pay schemes?

16. Is performance-related pay a fair method of payment?

17. What was the main purpose of the Equal Pay Act? Has it been effective?

18. What are the main types of work carried out by women? What are the main features of these types of work?

19. What were the main provisions of the Race Relations Act 1976 in the field of employment?

20. What is meant by
    (a) direct discrimination
    (b) indirect discrimination?

Essays

1. What are the essential human needs that must be met if work is to be carried out willingly?

2. What is the relationship between technology and job satisfaction?

3. What do you understand by 'pleasant working conditions'? How can management create such conditions?

4. 'Scientific management' is the best way to get results from the human resource. Discuss this statement.

5. What methods are available to motivate employees other than pay?

6. Why is it important to define your objectives when drawing up a payment structure?

7. Outline the main responsibilities of a payroll manager. How does the payroll department need to relate to other functions?

8. What are the main problems encountered by women at work? How can these difficulties be reduced or removed?

9. The prospects for women at work are better than those for men in the 1990s. Discuss.

10. How important is the human resource to effective production?

Data response questions

1   The 100 best companies to work for

After two years of meticulous research, financial writer Bob Reynolds put together a guide to the modern British workplace in his book, *The 100 Best Companies to Work For in the UK*. Reynolds listed his best five companies as Hallmark Cards, Nissan, United Biscuits, Glaxo and Mars.

The following extracts are made up of short interviews with an employee at Hallmark Cards and an employee at Nissan.

Employee: Moira MacKechnie, age 50
Job: Compensation and benefits manager, Europe
History: Joined the company 12 years ago as a secretary and was quickly promoted into management

I joined Hallmark in my late thirties when my three children were all capable of looking after themselves. I never wanted a career, but Hallmark offered me the chance to get involved. I became secretary to the European managing director and after six months I was asked to set up a personnel department in Henley.

I am now responsible for reviewing reward packages. As a manager I get free private health insurance for myself and my family, and I drive a company Ford Sapphire Ghia. There is a non-contributory pension scheme for all, and there is no separate directors' dining room. Everyone gets the same holiday entitlement, from MD to junior salesman.

Also, anyone who has been here a year gets an extra day off on their birthday. Until recently, they all received a large card signed by everybody, but now the company is so big that's proved unmanageable.

I was the first secretary to move into management. Although Hallmark is a great place for women to work—an increasing number are in senior management positions—there is no bias towards us. It is more a case of everyone being treated equally. All 'Hallmarkers' are on first-name terms and there is an open-door management policy. When we moved into this building three-and-a-half years ago many of us were involved in its design and planning. All of us who helped were given a plaque recording our contribution.

Every year we have a staff dinner and dance which is free to staff while their guests pay a nominal sum. And if you want to study, the company will pay half the cost and if the course leads to a qualification then they pay all costs.

But, perhaps most importantly, if you have a problem or a crisis at home then the company is absolutely wonderful. Just after I joined I had a phone call to say my youngest had been knocked over by a bus. They sent me straight home and told me not to come back until I was ready. If you are loyal to the company you can expect every consideration and support back.

Employee: Grahame Fyfe, 28
Job: Team leader, manufacturing staff
History: Joined Nissan almost three years ago and was trained in Japan
Salary: £10,532–£12,169 (on shifts)

I've been in the motor trade ever since I left school at 16 but never in manufacturing. I joined Nissan in March 1986, when 32 of us started on the same day. I was one of the first to be trained in Japan.

I've already progressed to being a team leader, responsible for 10 men, and the next step is supervisor. If I felt I was going to be stuck at one level for the rest of my life, I would look elsewhere. But I know there's a chance to get on here.

The benefits are incredible compared to garage work. It's more secure, there's a private health scheme, there's a pension, it's clean and it's much better paid! It's a totally different environment from one where you're lying out in the open on your back most of the day.

The lads here are very happy, and few people leave. We're especially pleased with our latest pay increase. Negotiations happen every two years through the Company Council, a body elected by the employees.

It definitely feels like working in a team, because everybody realizes that we all rely on each other. If you've got a few people who want to go absent it destroys the team and people can't have their holidays and you can't rotate people.

The management are very approachable. There's never a problem and they work with you. On the shop-floor you're as likely to see a manager standing behind you as you are one of your mates. They're really interested in what's going on.

This is the best place I've ever worked in. If I'm standing in the pub people will come up and ask if I can get them application forms. When people read in the papers about the benefits at Nissan they can't believe it.

1. What features of employment at Hallmark and Nissan that are mentioned in the extracts are likely to create motivation in employees?
2. Why do you think that these companies are able to offer such favourable conditions?
3. In what ways do good human relations at work help firms to be more competitive?
4. Which practices highlighted in the extracts could be adopted by other British companies?
5. Is it possible for all companies to implement the sorts of practices highlighted by the Hallmark and Nissan cases?

2 Coventry Brown's productivity deal

Read the extract and answer the questions that follow.

Manufacturer opens door to modern practices

A Midlands manufacturing firm has agreed the most wide ranging productivity deal of recent years in the engineering industry.

The agreement will allow it to update working practices among 9,000 manual workers at three Midlands plants.

Managing director Bill Hayden described the Coventry Brown's Lane assembly plant, the firm's biggest, as among the worst he had seen outside the Soviet Union.

Workers will receive a 12.5 per cent pay rise this year and 7 per cent or inflation next November.

Four per cent of this year's deal covers the end of antiquated practices such as the production quota system.

This allowed line workers to go home after producing a specified number of units. Now they will work full shifts, doing other jobs if necessary.

The working week will also be reduced by an hour to 38 hours next November and to 37 in November 1992, adding pressure to other Midlands engineering firms to follow suit.

A pilot scheme brings in group leaders for teamworking. The group leader will receive an allowance and will back up salaried supervisors.

Line workers will take over responsibility for simple maintenance and to improve quality control.

The agreement contains a commitment to accept on-going changes including the improvement of processes, quality and skills levels. Quality improvement groups are part of this.

The firm is also giving its workers a direct incentive to reduce unofficial stoppages, with a bonus of £26 a week for good behaviour.

Although the rises will fuel fears of inflation, plus demands in other companies, the firm can argue that productivity improvements pay for its 4 per cent.

The changes are part of a business plan to boost production. It wants to triple output to 150,000 units a year over the next 10 years.

(*Source:* adapted from *Personnel Today*)

1. What is meant by 'productivity' (line 3)?
2. Explain how 'productivity improvements pay for its 4 per cent' (penultimate paragraph).
3. Identify in the agreement:
   (a) two features that may reduce worker dissatisfaction.
   (b) two features that may lead to worker motivation.
4. Explain how the features you have identified in question 3 relate to Herzberg's theory of motivation.
5. Discuss one reason why improved job satisfaction may not result in improved productivity.

(Source: AEB)

3   Problems with profit-related pay

Profit-related pay (PRP) was heralded in the 1980s as a miracle cure for many of the British economy's problems. It would help to lower unemployment for a given rate of inflation by making pay more flexible, its supporters claimed.

In the middle of 1993 the Inland Revenue announced that 1 167 400 people were on 4615 officially recognized schemes. The number of participants took off after the Chancellor of the Exchequer doubled the tax relief on PRP in 1991, allowing employees to receive up to £4000 or 20 per cent of their salaries tax-free. As the schemes became more popular, so too did the cost of tax relief—to £400 million in 1993.

However, the evidence of benefits to offset these costs is limited. PRP is said to soothe industrial conflict by giving both workers and shareholders an interest in profitability, thus boosting productivity and effort. It is also supposed to reduce job turnover, because workers' remuneration falls automatically as profits fall, reducing the need to cut costs through redundancy.

However, the evidence is shaky. Firms with poor industrial relations are reluctant to try PRP because it gives the unions something else to object to. The most effective firms with happy, productive workers are the most likely to join. A number of companies, indeed, may simply be using PRP to reduce their tax bills.

The benefit to job mobility and employment is also doubtful, as workers may demand that a fall in the profit payout be compensated for by a rise in basic pay.

The best that can be said with confidence is the PRP hands public money to efficient companies.

1. What are the main arguments put forward for PRP?
2. Why might companies be keen to adopt PRP?
3. Why might companies be reluctant to try PRP?
4. Who benefits from PRP?
5. Who loses out from PRP?
6. Is PRP a good thing for the economy?

Suggested reading

Huczynski, D. and Buchanan, D., *Organisation Behaviour*. Prentice-Hall, 1991.
Philip, T., *Making Performance Appraisal Work*. McGraw-Hill, 1990.
Winfield, I., *People in Business*. Heinemann, 1990.

20

Trade unions

What is a trade union?

Trade unions are made up of groups of employees who have joined together in an organization to further their common interests. These employees may have in common a skill, a trade, an industry, an employer or an occupation. Trade unions are formed, financed and run by their members, and a number of unions have existed for over a century.

Trade unions in a changing environment

Like other organizations in the business world, trade unions in the last decade of the twentieth century have had to adapt to a rapidly changing environment in order to survive.

Some of the important changes in the external environment include:

1. The development of new jobs and skills requiring greater flexibility of working practices and attitudes.
2. The growing importance of women in the working population.
3. The growth of part-time jobs.
4. The hiving off of non-core service functions and the contracting out by large businesses to smaller organizations (the development of the 'flexible firm').
5. The growing affluence of many employees.
6. The growth of the service sector of the economy at the expense of manufacturing.
7. The development of new business practices related to human resource management.

These changes and others have demanded wide-scale changes in union practice. In the late 1970s there were 12 million trade union members; in the mid-1990s there are nearer 9 million. With prodding from the Trades Union Council, unions have begun to develop new strategies for attracting members and updating their image.

Decline in trade union density

Trade union density is a statistic showing actual trade union membership as a percentage of potential union membership. Since 1979 this figure has declined from over 50 per cent to less than 39 per cent at the beginning of 1992 (Table 20.1).

Table 20.1   Trade union membership and density in the UK, 1979–1991 (at the year end)

	Trade union membership ('000)	Potential membership ('000)	Trade union density (%)
1979	13 289	23 244	57.2
1980	12 947	22 409	57.8
1981	12 106	21 602	56.0
1982	11 593	21 126	54.9
1983	11 236	21 170	53.1
1984	10 994	21 464	51.2
1985	10 821	21 633	50.0
1986	10 539	21 718	48.5
1987	10 475	22 035	47.5
1988	10 376	22 496	46.1
1989	10 158	22 832	44.5
1990	9 947	22 652	43.9
1991	9 479	21 884	43.3

 Task

Draw a line graph to plot the decline in trade union membership and the decline in union density shown in Table 20.1.

Rising employment in the 1980s was experienced mainly in the service industry, where unions tend to be weak. The recession in the early 1990s made it difficult for unions to win back members as the numbers of people in employment fell. Many of the largest unions have continued to lose members in the 1980s. As a result, there have been a number of mergers, which has led to the formation of some very large unions. For example, the GMB (General, Municipal, Boilermakers and Allied Trade Union) was created in the early 1980s, and a series of mergers between print unions created the GPMU (Table 20.2) in 1991.

Unions in traditional manufacturing industries such as the National Union of Miners (NUM) in coal mining and steel (the ISTC) now have memberships of less than 50 000. The engineering industry (AEU) union lost 10 per cent of its members in 1991. Public service unions have declined in numbers with cut-backs in the public sector (e.g. the decline of health service unions National Union of Public Employees (NUPE) and Confederation of Health Service Employees (COHSE)).

Responding to a changing environment

Today the trade union movement is facing the challenge of a rapidly changing world of work. Many of the old jobs are disappearing, to be replaced by jobs requiring new skills and working practices. Increasingly, employers are seeking 'single-union deals' with only one union operating in an industrial unit. The dominance of the blue-collar workers (i.e. manual operatives) has been whittled away by the decline of manufacturing and the rise of white-collar services (i.e. people

Table 20.2   Change in membership of the 20 largest trade unions affiliated to the Trades Union Congress, 1979–1990

Union	Members in 1990	% increase or decrease, 1979–90
Transport & General Workers Union (TGWU)	1 223 891	−41.3
General, Municipal, Boilermakers & Allied Trade Union (GMB)	933 425	−3.5
National & Local Government Officers' Association (NALGO)	744 453	−1.2
Amalgamated Engineering Union (AEU)	702 228	−45.9
Manufacturing, Science and Finance Union (MSF)	653 000	−5.6
National Union of Public Employees (NUPE)	578 992	−16.3
Electrical, Electronic, Telecommunications & Plumbing Union (EETPU) (expelled from TUC)	366 630	−12.7
Union of Shop, Distributive, & Allied Workers	361 789	−23.0
Union of Construction Allied Trades and Technicians	207 232	−40.4
Confederation of Health Service Employees	203 511	−4.5
Union of Communication Workers	201 200	−1.1
Banking Insurance & Finance Union	171 101	+28.1
National Union of Teachers (NUT)	169 007	−32.1
Society of Graphical & Allied Trades 82 (SOGAT 82)	165 635	−19.5
National Communications Union	154 783	+23.1
National Graphical Association (1982)	122 834	+10.1
Civil & Public Services Association	122 677	−45.2
National Association of Schoolmasters/Union of Women Teachers (NAS/UWT)	119 816	−1.8
National Union of Rail, Maritime & Transport Workers	118 000	−26.4
National Union of Civil and Public Servants	113 488	−34.4
Institution of Professionals Managers & Specialists	91 713	−10.2

who work with paper and pen). With 52 per cent of the total population now women, the percentage of male unionists is falling consistently. In 1980 the number of men in full-time and part-time employment exceeded the number of women by more than 45 per cent—13.1 million against 9.4 million; by mid-1993 the balance of the sexes was almost equal—10.7 million men in work against 10.1 million women. This trend is likely to continue. The number of women at work already exceeds the number of men in 11 regions, including Cornwall, Essex, Merseyside, Mid-Glamorgan and Lothian (Fig. 20.1).

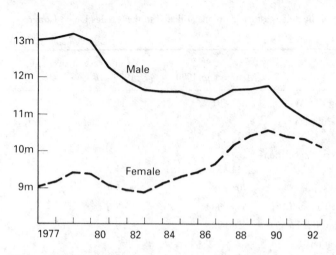

Figure 20.1 Workers in employment, UK, 1977–1992. (*Source*: Department of Employment)

A growth in skilled jobs has led to more people being considered in the A/B/C1 social groups. Higher incomes have enabled more people to buy their own houses and to purchase shares in publicly listed companies. All these factors have helped to change people's attitudes towards trade unions, and have led to changes in the relative size and importance of various trade union groups.

An indication of these dramatic changes was illustrated in a recent report from the Henley Centre for Forecasting, which cited the following example. The Centre predicted that by the end of the 1990s there will be over 700 000 electronics engineers in Britain. More than half will be women. Salaries for this group of workers will be on average 30 per cent higher than those for similar workers in the late 1980s, for working a maximum 35 hours a week. They will have the money to enjoy seven weeks' holiday a year, at least one of which will be spent abroad. When they are at home, each family will have the use of two cars. Unemployment will not be much of a worry, and they are unlikely to want to become members of a traditional trade union. They will be attracted not by ideas of solidarity and collective action but by pensions, investment advice and fitness clubs.

Throughout the 1960s and 1970s, the numbers of employees who were members of trade unions continued to grow. During the 1980s, however, when the adoption of new technology in industry greatly increased, this trend was reversed.

Unions have not been seen as a natural part of some of the key growth industries and services. In response, a number of trade unions have become increasingly 'image'-conscious and have adopted modern marketing techniques such as advertising and opinion research to influence public opinion. For example, the General, Municipal, Boilermakers and Allied Trade Union spent £35 000 on hiring the Jenkins design group, which had worked for W. H. Smith and Next, to help improve its image. A number of changes were made, including shortening the initials of the union to the 'GMB' and replacing its motto from 'Unity is Strength' to the softer 'Working Together'. Other unions, including the Transport and General Workers, followed the GMB's lead. The TGWU launched a 'Link-Up' exercise to recruit part-timers, women and ethnic groups. The campaign started with a large rally at Wembley costing £500 000.

Recruitment adverts were broadcast on the radio and co-ordinated literature and videos were produced to show the benefits of membership.

Unions are also realizing that they have to provide better services. The Electricians' Union led the way with a range of services and benefits, including free legal advice and attractive insurance and pension schemes.

Another way in which trade unions have responded to a changing environment is by merger. Most of the major trade unions have been involved in merger discussions during the late 1980s (e.g. the AEU with the EETPU, and NUPE with NALGO). At the root of the merger talks was the loss of members and the resulting sharply lower incomes, coupled with what was regarded as changes in the law pertaining to trade unions in an anti-union way, all of which magnified the appeal of the economies of scale to be gained from merger. The result of these mergers was to create at least five mega-unions with memberships of over 750 000. Large unions have more resources, enabling them to offer more benefits and services.

Trade unions have also adapted to a rapidly changing economic environment by allowing and encouraging more flexible working practices. A report published by ACAS in 1987 revealed that Britain now has a more flexible workforce, and decades of demarcation between skilled and unskilled workers are being swept away. The survey painted a picture of rapid change in the way the country is working, particularly with respect to manufacturing companies, where there is a growing tendency for production workers to do routine maintenance, normally the preserve of skilled craft workers.

The increasing use of new technologies also means that the demarcation lines between manual, technical and clerical workers are fast disappearing. More people work flexi-time and part-time, and companies are increasingly turning to contract or temporary staff rather than hiring full-time employees. The ACAS report confirmed the growing move away from companies with big payrolls to those employing fewer people directly and relying on contractors or part-time employees to carry out 'peripheral' work.

A further important development in trade union practice has been in the willingness to strike 'single-union deals' with companies. Britain has tended to have a more complicated union structure than some of its major competitors at a plant level. It is not unknown for a UK car plant to have ten or more separate unions individually negotiating with management; deals regarding pay and conditions are struck at different times of the year, and management has to negotiate with separate groups of employee representatives. This process can waste a lot of time and effort and lead to continual instability. Increasingly, unions are coming to accept the principle of having a single union operating within a plant.

Trade unions have also been active in creating better opportunities for women at work. Amid warnings of an increasing shortfall in teenage labour, market forces look set to bolster women's position at work as employers compete to recruit and retain their labour.

Possible strategies

In recent years six possible strategies have been identified for the trade unions:

1. *Work for a Labour government and the legislation that it would create to support trade unions* However, in 1992 the Labour Party was defeated for the fourth successive time.

In 1993 the Labour Party in some measure distanced itself from the influence of the larger unions in order to encourage a more democratic membership structure. In turn, a number of influential unionists have spoken in favour of constructive talks about such things as industrial strategy with the government 'of the day'.

2. *Merger unions*   For example, in July 1993 NALGO, NUPE and COHSE formed UNISON a union of 1.5 million members. Merger or absorption is often seen as a route to survival as well as to increased influence.

3. *Recruit new members in the fastest growing industries*   Women workers (who now represent one-third of all union members) are a popular target for many unions. The GMB, for example, has reserved 10 out of 40 places on its National Executive Committee for women.

4. *Improve services to members*   In recent years blue-collar unions have set the pace, with advisory and financial services in insurance, savings and share ownership, as well as private health insurance.

5. *Change trade union purposes*   There is debate among trade unions about their primary purposes. One view, put forward by the *new realists*, is that the primary purpose of trade unions is to further the needs and interests of their members in terms of pay and conditions, seeking to get the best deal for them. This view is supported by unions made up largely of core workers whose jobs are guaranteed.

   An alternative view is put forward by the *new traditionalists*, which tend to represent groupings of peripheral and part-time workers. These unions concentrate on wider social issues such as a community-based approach to women's issues, the needs of the disabled and other disadvantaged groups. The GMB talks about extending its membership to the new 'servant class', such as people on low incomes in low status jobs.

6. *Develop firm links with the European Community*   A number of trade unionists see EC membership as providing a real opportunity for developing the strength and influence of unions through the Social Charter and resultant Social Chapter of the Maastricht Treaty (see below page 619).

Industrial relations

Industrial relations is concerned with communication between the representatives of employers and the representatives of employees (Fig. 20.2).

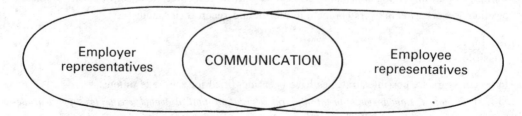

Figure 20.2 Industrial relations.

Successful industrial relations involves striking a balance of interests. From the employer's point of view, industrial relations is about having the right to manage—the ability to plan for the future so that the company can continue to be a success, to make profits for its shareholders and to keep its employees motivated. From the employee's point of view, industrial relations is about securing the best possible living standards for trade union members.

Day-to-day industrial relations

On a daily basis, the main industrial relations bargaining usually takes place between the personnel department and a shop stewards' committee. Normally they would meet regularly once a week and thrash out issues such as:

- Pay
- Bonuses
- The working environment
- Disputes
- Work schedules
- Grievances
- Health and safety at work
- Hours
- Production targets

Major industrial relations issues

In addition to local bargaining, which is concerned with small-scale industrial relations, larger issues may be thrashed out on an industry-wide scale. Wages for state employees, for example, are usually agreed upon at an annual pay award. The parties involved will normally be the central executive of a union and employers' leaders.

Trade union structure

This varies in different industries, but a typical form is shown in Fig. 20.3. Groups of workers are members of a branch. They choose branch officials to represent them. The branches also choose members to represent them at a regional committee. Regional groups then choose representatives to go to an annual conference. The annual conference makes decisions relating to the industry and chooses a full-time body of officials known as the national executive. The top official in the union is the president.

A good example of union industrial structure is in the National Union of Mineworkers (NUM). The local branch is based on the colliery, the unit of operation in mining; and the branch personnel deal with the day-to-day problems, disputes, grievances and many minor issues that can arise. Shop stewards as such are not found in the mining industry. The branch is based

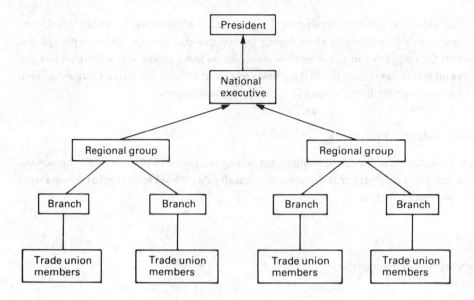

Figure 20.3 A typical union structure.

on the pit and includes in its membership all manual and craft grades. The branch officers undertake the duties allotted to shop stewards in other industries. (Factories in many trades are traditionally divided into 'shops', e.g. the cutting shop, the sewing shop. Each shop chooses at least one steward to represent it in the workplace. The leading shop steward is called the *convenor*, and is responsible for calling together and organizing meetings of stewards.) There is a single line of communication, from the branch up through the area coalfield office to the national centre, and similarly from centre to branch.

Unofficial trade union structure

While much trade union activity takes place on a day-to-day basis through the official union structure as described above, we should not ignore unofficial union activity. This takes place when members carry out actions not approved by the union, for example when local stewards call out workers in a lightning strike. In fact, in the United Kingdom most industrial action is unofficial but only short-lived. This was particularly true in the late 1970s in industries like car manufacture, in which shop stewards had a lot of local influence. Union funds cannot be used for unofficial action, because it is not officially approved.

Unofficial action will generally take place if local unionists feel that the national union is out of touch with their feelings or if they want to take prompt action.

Types of trade union

Trade unions are typically organized into four main categories:
- Craft unions

- Industrial unions
- General unions
- White-collar unions

However, many unions do not fit easily into a particular class; often they have characteristics common to more than one class.

Craft unions

The earliest type of union in this country was the craft union. These unions were made up of highly skilled craft workers in a particular trade. Often these groups were mutual benefit societies before the welfare state came into being. Subscriptions could be quite high, and in return the union would provide sick pay, unemployment pay, a pension and other benefits. These unions are less important in the United Kingdom today. Their membership is relatively small.

Industrial unions

Industrial unionism is common in many European countries, notably West Germany. The economy is divided up into industrial sectors, and workers in each sector belong to the industrial union for that sector. The National Union of Mineworkers at one time was often quoted as an example of an industrial union. However, in the 1950s a rival union, the Union of Democratic Mineworkers, was formed, and on top of this there are smaller unions such as the pit deputies' union, NACODS. In many areas of industry today, there is a tendency for new 'super-unions' to take in groups of workers from several industries.

The advantage of an industrial union is that it caters for all workers in an industry whatever their job. Negotiation with employers is greatly simplified and all workers are united in their efforts.

General unions

These include some of the largest unions in the United Kingdom today. They recruit workers from several industries and include semi-skilled and unskilled workers. A particular advantage of this form of union is that it gives strength to workers who have little power on their own and enables them to belong to a well-funded and organized body.

An example of the creation of a general union occurred in 1988 with the formation of what was then Britain's third largest union. The white-collar and supervisors' unions Association of Scientific and Technical Managerial Staff (ASTMS) and the manufacturing union Technical and Supervisory Staff (TASS) joined together to form the Manufacturing Science and Finance Union (MSF). The leaders of the two merging unions put forward their case in the following way: 'We can now tackle even more effectively the problems our members face...our objective is to work for a well rewarded, well trained, and highly skilled membership throughout the whole range of industries and services covered by MSF.'

White-collar unions

White-collar workers are those who carry out non-manual work. The term 'white-collar' is used to distinguish them from 'blue-collar' employees, who carry out manual operations and would traditionally be associated with blue overalls. Examples of white-collar employees are office workers and bank clerks.

White-collar unions have seen the biggest increase in membership in the late twentieth century. As more people have become involved in office and administrative work, and as these groups have become more prepared to join unions, their ranks have swelled. Examples of white-collar unions include the teachers' unions such as the National Union of Teachers and the civil servants union, the Civil and Public Servants Association.

The negotiation process

The first stage of union communication with management prior to industrial action should be through the negotiation process. Ramsumair Singh exemplifies the process of negotiation in diagrammatic form (see Fig. 20.4). He points out that in negotiations, managements and unions tend to choose positions that favour their own interests. The starting-point in a wage dispute would be the union's initial demand (UID) and the management's initial offer (MIO). One party is unlikely to be able to persuade the other to accept its starting position; therefore there has to be a movement towards a central, compromise position. There is, however, a limit to this process, which can be called the break-point or fall-back point. Neither party is prepared to go beyond its own break-point. In Fig. 20.4 the management's break-point (MBP) overlaps with the union's break-point (UBP). There is therefore a zone of agreement in which a settlement can be made. The point at which the final settlement is made (point X) depends on the bargaining strength and skill of the two parties.

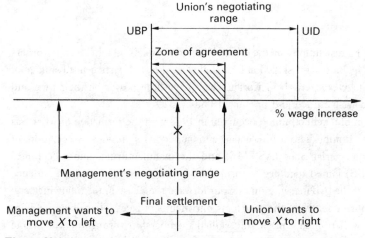

Figure 20.4 A zone of agreement in bargaining.

Problems occur if there is no zone of agreement. Parties may then become involved in industrial action to push forward their claims (see below).

Forms of union action

There are a number of types of action that trade unionists can use to put pressure on employers. A distinction needs to be made between individual and unorganized actions on the part of employees against management, and organized or group sanctions against them. In unorganized conflict employees will respond in individual ways, using strategies that seem right at the time, with little planning. Organized conflict, in contrast, is far more likely to form part of a conscious strategy to change the situation that is seen as the cause of discontent.

Unorganized industrial action can take the form of high labour turnover, bad time-keeping and high levels of absenteeism. It may also occur in the form of slackness by individuals, poor performance, deliberate time-wasting and similar practices. Other evidence of discontent will be revealed in complaints, friction, an ignoring of rules and apathy. Trade unions can take a number of forms of organized industrial action, including the following:

1. *Picketing*   *Primary picketing* is legal. This involves members of a union that is on strike standing outside a firm's entrance and trying to persuade other workers not to cross the picket line. *Secondary picketing* is not legal. This involves workers who are on strike from one firm trying to dissuade workers at a firm not involved with the strike from going to work. Secondary picketing is resorted to by trade unionists trying to spread the impact of their action.
2. *Withdrawal of goodwill*   Workers become obstructive about things that require co-operation.
3. *Go-slow*   Workers take their time over the work they are doing.
4. *Work-to-rule*   Workers stick strictly to the book of rules relating to their particular job in order to reduce efficiency. For instance, railway workers may check that every carriage door is firmly closed at each station.
5. *Ban on overtime*   Workers refuse to work more than the hours laid out in their contract of employment.
6. *Official strike*   Workers cease work with the authority of the union.
7. *Unofficial strike*   A group of workers ceases work without the official approval of the union.
8. *Sit-in*   Occasionally workers may occupy a factory. Similarly, if a factory has been threatened with closure, the workers may remain at work operating a *work-in*, whereby they refuse to stop work.
9. *Blacking*   Members of a firm refuse to handle particular materials or work with particular machinery.

Forms of employer action

Employers and management can use a number of sanctions against employees. These may take the form of uncoordinated and individual actions, or organized and collective actions.

Uncoordinated, individual actions may include close supervision of working activity, tight works discipline, discriminatory employment practices against certain employees, lay-offs, demotions and the unofficial speeding up of work processes or job tasks.

Organized and collective sanctions include the withdrawal of overtime, mass suspensions, changing of work standards without negotiation, lock-outs, the closing down of enterprises and the removal of workplace equipment.

The Trades Union Congress (TUC)

This is the annual meeting of the trade union movement. All the major trade unions are members of the TUC and send a number of delegates to the conference depending on the size of their membership. The annual congress takes place in September every year at seaside resorts like Scarborough and Blackpool, where there is a lot of hotel space after the holiday season is finished and where large conference halls are available.

The conference lasts for a week and during this time a number of motions and issues are debated. It is a false conception to assume that the TUC is concerned simply with wages. The congress discusses matters as far-ranging as education, the health service, privatization, AIDS and the environment.

The TUC appoints full-time officials including a president and vice-president, and it has its own substantial headquarters. The TUC is an important organization because it reflects the general feelings of the trade union movement. It is particularly active in the field of negotiation in industrial disputes. It offers advice and assistance to unions with problems and tries to iron out difficulties that arise between unions. It also acts as a pressure group, trying to influence government and employers on a wide range of issues.

Despite its importance, the TUC is often regarded as having very little power. Individual unions are not bound by its decisions, and the only threat it can use is to expel a union from membership.

Professional associations

Many workers belong to a professional association. These organizations do many of the same things as trade unions but are not registered as trade unions. They tend to cover better-paid white-collar workers. An example is the British Medical Association which is the body that negotiates on behalf of doctors. Professional associations also try to establish standards for members and to insist on a high level of competence for membership.

Employers' organizations

Like trade unions, employers' organizations fulfil a wide range of functions but the main one is collective bargaining. Faced by large and powerful trade unions, small employers would be at a disadvantage if they had to stand alone. An employers' association may bargain on behalf of all firms in an industry. Other functions of employers' organizations include:

- Pooling ideas and funds for industrial research
- Collectively setting up training centres
- Discussing common interests such as the threat of foreign competition
- Providing a collective voice to raise industry-wide problems with government and other bodies

The Confederation of British Industry (CBI)

Britain's mouthpiece for the business community is the CBI. It exists primarily to voice the views of its members and ensure that government of whatever political complexion—and society as a whole—understand both the needs of British business and the contribution it makes to the well-being of the nation.

The CBI is acknowledged to be Britain's business voice, and as such is widely consulted by government, the civil service and the media. But it is not solely concerned with major national issues; an important part of its task is to represent business interests at local level. It is also directly involved in providing essential information and research services for its members.

CBI members come from every sector of UK business, including:

- More than 250,000 public and private companies—half of them smaller firms with fewer than 200 employees—and most of the nationalized industries
- More than 200 trade associations, employers' organizations and commercial associations

The organization

The main elements of the organization are:

1. The CBI's ruling Council, chaired by the CBI president, which sets policy.
2. Some 30 standing committees, 13 regional councils and a Smaller Firms Council contributing to policy-making.
3. The CBI permanent staff, headed by the director-general, based at Centrepoint in London, in the UK regions and at the CBI's own Brussels office.
4. The National Conference and the President's Committee, advising on major issues and overall CBI strategy.

Who belongs to the CBI?

Membership of the CBI is corporate—organizations and companies are members, not the individuals nominated to represent them. Well over 10 million people are employed by companies associated with the CBI, either directly or indirectly through trade organizations or chambers of commerce.

   CBI membership is extensive and almost exactly matches the profile of business in the United Kingdom—from manufacturing to retailing, from agriculture to construction, from computers to finance, from transport to consultancy.

The president

The president is the CBI's chief office bearer. Elected by the CBI membership, he or she normally serves for two years. The president chairs the monthly CBI Council meeting and the annual National Conference. He or she also leads delegations to see government ministers.

The director-general

The director-general is the CBI's chief executive. He or she is appointed by the president of the day with the approval of CBI Council and regularly puts across the business view on radio and TV and in the press. The director-general heads the permanent staff who carry out the bulk of the day-to-day running of the CBI, preparing policy and negotiating with ministers and their civil servants.

Whom does the CBI seek to influence?

The short answer is, anyone who, in turn, can influence how business performs—at Westminster, in Whitehall and the UK regions, around Europe and beyond—within the trade union movement and the general public.

Westminster and Whitehall

The well publicized meetings that the CBI has with ministers and as a member of 'Neddy' (National Economic Development Council) indicate the central role the CBI plays in national affairs, but they are only a small part of its work.

   The CBI seeks to influence government policy-making at an early stage in its development; to be continually aware of the thinking of ministers, the research arms of political parties, back-bench MPs and civil servants, in order to ensure that its views are put forward at the best possible opportunity. It is a lobbying process that continues as government policy is published and Bills pass through Parliament.

In the UK regions

The CBI has 13 regional offices which seek to influence local decision-making procedures.

Europe and '1992'

The CBI has played a prominent part in influencing the process of completing the Single European Market. CBI experts have followed Community developments for many years. The CBI is consulted by the European Commission as the voice of British industry. It is permanently represented in Brussels, where it opened an office even before Britain joined the Community.

Trade unions and the CBI

Although the CBI and TUC may put forward opposing views on a number of issues, a constructive working relationship is maintained both directly and through joint membership of such national bodies as Neddy, ACAS and the Health and Safety Commission.

The public

As part of the process of explaining business needs and concerns, CBI policies and views need to be put to the public at large as well as to official bodies.

Who decides CBI policy?

CBI policy is decided by CBI members—firms large and small throughout the country. The policy work has two aspects. In the long term, the aim is to make a constructive contribution to attitudes and forward thinking on issues affecting business. In the short term, the CBI has to be equipped to react quickly and positively to any proposals by government, or others, that have a bearing on industry and commerce.

More than 2500 people are involved in the CBI policy-making process.

Governing body

The CBI's governing body is its Council, chaired by the president. Proposals must be approved by the Council before they can become official CBI policy. Council membership is made up of leading national officials as well as representatives of employer, trade and commercial organizations, the public sector, the 13 CBI regional councils and people drawn from member-companies of all sizes and activities.

The CBI's standing committees cover every aspect of business life and are responsible for most of the detailed work on policy-making.

The government and industrial relations

Government has passed laws on a wide range of issues relating to industrial relations, which are dealt with in greater detail in other parts of the book. The main areas include the following:

- Health and safety at work
- Discrimination
- Training
- Employment of the disabled
- Employment of young workers
- Dismissal and redundancy
- Pay
- Industrial action
- Restriction in the workplace

Establishing negotiating procedures

It is in the interests of managers and employees to establish a clear set of workable negotiating procedures. A negotiating procedure sets out a framework in which parties can establish terms and conditions of employment.

This framework will cover four main elements:

1. The area (which may be geographical, occupational grouping, etc.) in which the union's representatives' role is acknowledged. Where several unions are involved this may clarify the 'territory' of each; for example, 'This agreement covers industrial relations between Sunny Bakeries plc and the Bakery Union, ...'
2. Those issues that will be subject to negotiation, such as wages and salaries, conditions at work and union recognition.
3. The steps by which agreement will be sought; for example, 'In the first instance a meeting will be organized between the personnel managers of individual plants and the divisional officer of the trade union.'
4. The steps to be taken when there is a failure to agree; for example, the matter may be put before an outside negotiating body such as ACAS (see below).

The Advisory, Conciliation and Arbitration Service (ACAS)

This body was set up by the government in 1974 in order to improve industrial relations. ACAS is managed by a council of nine members: three chosen by the TUC, three chosen by the CBI and three who are independent.

In an industrial dispute in which there is deadlock, the parties may ask ACAS to help. Sometimes they may allow ACAS to look at the issue and come up with a solution that is 'binding'; at other times ACAS might simply be asked to make recommendations.

Conciliation takes the form of attempts to persuade the parties to reach, by negotiation, a settlement of their dispute.

Arbitration takes the form of an award made after the arbitrator has heard the cases of the parties involved in the dispute. In general, arbitration is more appropriate to *disputes of rights* (i.e. disputes over the interpretation of an existing agreement) than to *disputes of interest* (disputes over new terms and conditions of employment). In the former case the arbitrator can simply clarify existing rules; but with disputes of interest the two sides may be reluctant to trust the proposal of new ideas or fundamental changes to an outsider.

The media and public tend to view ACAS as ambulance chasers and firefighters in situations of conflict. Although this sort of emergency repair work is a critical part of the work of ACAS, it is only a small part of the overall workload. ACAS deals with over 20 new collective disputes a week (1993 figures).

The greater part of the work of ACAS involves individual grievances. Each year in the 1990s ACAS has had to deal with over 50 000 cases of individual arbitration. Individual disputes involve a variety of cases including unfair dismissal and sex discrimination applications. ACAS has a legal obligation to try and resolve individual grievances before they reach industrial tribunals. Most individual cases will be resolved either through conciliation or because the complaint is dropped. Nine out of ten disputes involving ACAS are settled before industrial action is taken.

The rest of ACAS's resources are dedicated to advisory work involving both unions and employers, including surveys, projects, training activities and advisory visits.

The Social Chapter of the Maastricht agreement

The President of the EC, Jacques Delors, was instrumental in creating the Social Charter as part of EC policy. The Social Charter was proposed to offset 'social dumping' within a completely free Single Market.

'Social dumping' refers to a situation in a free market where there are no minimum employment rights (e.g. minimum wages, limits to hours that can be worked, etc.); this would mean that some EC member-states could take advantage of their relatively low-wage status and their 'softer' employment laws at the expense of, say, Germany, France or other EC countries that have tighter employment laws, minimum wages, etc. The argument is that countries that did not adopt the employment regulations of the Social Chapter would be able to produce cheaper goods by offering poorer conditions to employees. Some people feel that this would lead to exploitation of the weaker members of society, who are in a poor bargaining position.

The Social Chapter—the source of the recent crisis over the Maastricht Treaty—provides for the adoption of minimum Community-wide requirements for the protection of workers' health and safety. It would also establish the principle of equal pay for women and men for work of equal value. The agreement, signed by 11 member-states (excluding Britain), follows the Social Charter, which led to measures such as the working time Directive with a proposal for a 48-hour week, to which Britain objected.

The 11 member-states that signed the agreement said that their objectives under the Chapter were the promotion of employment, improved living and working conditions, proper social protection, the establishment of a dialogue between management and labour and the development of human resources with a view to lasting high employment. The British opposed the Chapter on the grounds that it would allow working conditions to be decided at Community level and would add unacceptable costs to business.

The Social Chapter provides for co-operation on: improvement of the working environment to protect health and safety, working conditions, information and consultation of employees, equality between men and women with regard to labour market opportunities and treatment at work, and the integration of people excluded from the labour market, e.g. the disabled. The European Council of Ministers, working largely by majority voting, would be able to adopt Directives on minimum requirements for gradual implementation.

Questions

Short-answer questions

1. Identify the following trade unions:

   - TGWU
   - GMB
   - NALGO
   - BIFU
   - NUM
   - IPMS
   - NUT
   - COHSE
   - NURMTW
   - EETPU

   What sorts of people would belong to each of these unions?
2. What is the difference in view about the purpose of trade unions put forward by
   (a) new realists?
   (b) new traditionalists?
3. Who are the core workers in an organization?
4. What is industrial relations?
5. What are the main issues covered by industrial relations?
6. Draw a diagram to illustrate the structure of a trade union.
7. How does the unofficial structure of a union differ from the official structure?
8. What is unofficial action?
9. What are the essential differences between (a) craft, (b) general and (c) white-collar unions?
10. How are unions financed?
11. What is the 'zone of agreement' in a pay bargaining process?
12. What is the difference between primary and secondary picketing?
13. What actions can a union take to further its case in a dispute?

14. What actions can employers take?
15. What are the three main functions of the TUC?
16. What is a professional association? Give two examples.
17. Explain what is involved in
    (a) conciliation?
    (b) arbitration?
18. What are
    (a) disputes of rights?
    (b) disputes of interest?
19. What is the concern of the Social Chapter of the Maastricht agreement?
20. Why is the UK government opposed to the Social Chapter?

Essays

1. What is a trade union? Explain the main functions of trade unions.
2. What factors have changed in recent years in the external environment in which unions operate? How have these changes affected trade unions?
3. How have unions responded to changes in their external environment in the 1990s?
4. Explain five main issues covered by industrial relations.
5. How is a union organized? Who has power within the union?
6. Name five major forms of union action. What factors are likely to influence the success of such actions?
7. Compare and contrast trade unions with professional associations.
8. Why is it essential to build and clarify negotiating procedures within organizations?
9. How can outside bodies help industrial relations to run smoothly?
10. What are the main arguments for and against the adoption of the Social Chapter of the Maastricht Treaty by the United Kingdom?

Data response questions

1 Industrialist calls on unions to join forces

In June 1993 Neil Johnson, secretary-general of the Engineering Employers' Federation, which represents 5000 companies, addressed the annual congress of the GMB.

In his address he argued that professional politicians had been letting industry down for a long time. 'They really don't know much about industry. They really don't care much about industry. And they certainly don't understand that our time-scales are different from theirs', he commented. He added: 'It's time to take off our dinosaur suits and to start talking real business.'

Mr Johnson argued that there was an urgent need for a clear and sustained industrial policy. He went on to say: 'The problem is that a long-term industrial strategy for prosperity is not a glamorous thing...A long-term industrial strategy does not produce profits tomorrow. Nor does it win votes tomorrow.' He concluded by saying that there was a need for all the main parties to agree on a mutual policy.

1. Explain the following in the context of the above paragraphs:
    (a) GMB
    (b) Employer's federation
    (c) Industry
    (d) Annual congress
2. Which groups does Neil Johnson identify as having a responsibility for British industry?
3. What sorts of strategy does Johnson imply may provide the way forward for British industry?
4. Why is Johnson critical of government?
5. What do you think Johnson means when he says that:
    (a) 'It's time to take off our dinosaur suits'?
    (b) 'A long-term industrial strategy for prosperity is not a glamorous thing'?

2   Union action at the TSB

In January 1993, TSB managers were forced to turn away customers when hundreds of branches were closed by a strike. Staff agreed a 24-hour walkout over 1000 planned redundancies and the shutting of more than 600 of the bank's 1400 branches. The strike was called by the Banking, Insurance and Finance Union.

All 120 branches of TSB in Merseyside closed, 130 out of 150 in Manchester, 51 out of 67 in the North West, about 80 out of 140 in Yorkshire and Humberside and 40 out of 80 in Nottingham.

The cuts include more than 300 compulsory redundancies. The jobs were part of a cost-cutting reorganization that involved merging the management of TSB's banking and insurance businesses. The TSB had already cut 5000 other jobs in the early 1990s.

Union officials hoped that the action would persuade the TSB to return to negotiations and at least avoid compulsory redundancies.

1. What is the issue involved in this case?
2. What indication is given that there may be a zone of agreement between the two sides?
3. Why has the union resorted to industrial action?
4. What action has the union taken? What alternative steps might it have taken?
5. What risks are the two sides taking in resorting to industrial action?
6. How might (a) conciliation and (b) arbitration have been used in this case?
7. What factors are likely to determine the outcome of the dispute?
8. Carry out some research to find out what the most recent outcomes of the dispute have been.

Suggested reading

Gospel, H. F., *British Industrial Relations*, 2nd edn. Routledge, 1993.
Green, G. D., *Industrial Relations*, 3rd edn. Pitman, 1991.
Towers, B., *A Handbook of Industrial Relations Practice*. Kogan Page, 1992.

21

Communication

At the heart of all organizations is the need for effective communication. Communication is the passing on of ideas and information. In business it is essential to have good clear channels of communication. The contact may be between people, organizations or places and can be in a number of forms including speech, writing, data communication, actions and gestures. As communication probably takes up the largest proportion of managers' and administrators' time, the building and developing of communication skills must be viewed as a vital managerial requirement.

Case Study—Creating the 'hybrid manager'

One feature of business in recent years has been the development by managers of broad-based skills outside their traditional area of expertise. The British Computer Society, among others, recently called for information technology (IT) professionals to spend time and effort extending their business skills into other areas. They refer to people able to do this as 'hybrid managers'. In making this pronouncement they have recognized that, although the role of a technical specialist is necessary, managers of the future must have a greater diversity of skills. These skills can be divided into five groups.

1. *Information management skills* involve a broad understanding of information as a strategic resource and the ability to be able to use information to develop decision-making needs.
2. *Financial skills* are essential for any senior manager, and the use of such skills plays an effective part in reducing risk and maximizing the ability to achieve objectives.
3. *Marketing skills* are another key area and involve being able to contribute to satisfying customer needs and developing business strategies.
4. *General management skills* involve problem-solving, decision-making, motivation and delegation.
5. Last, but not least, hybrid managers must have good *communication skills*. Hybrid managers must be able to communicate effectively in both spoken and written form and should not seek to blame other people for their lack of understanding. They should be good listeners and should seek to influence not through domination and

authority, but through intelligence and reasoning. Communication is also the crux of human relations, and if hybrid managers want to develop effective and creative interdisciplinary teams, they will need to be the best communicators.

Questions

1. What is a hybrid manager?
2. What are the benefits of being a hybrid manager?
3. Create an example to show why information management skills are important for managers.
4. Explain why good communication skills would improve a manager's ability to deal with day-to-day human relations problems.

We all have to communicate. Effective communication requires not only the development of the basic skills of speaking, listening, reading and writing, but also an awareness and an understanding of the subject, the audience and the environment.

For communication to be successful, not only must information be transmitted, but it must be fully received and understood. Listening and reading skills are therefore just as important as speaking and writing skills.

The passage of information can be seen as a flow from the sender to the receiver (see Fig. 21.1). Communication problems are known as *noise* and may lead to a message not being adequately communicated; they may include:

1. *Situations where the language is not properly understood*   This may occur if the language is too technical or if the receiver comes from a different background from the sender.
2. *Situations in which the receiver does not want to listen to the content of the message*   In these situations the message has to be redesigned to appeal to the receiver.
3. *The use of a poor channel of communication*   Effective communication will be hampered if the means of passing the message is poor.
4. *Too many steps in the message*   If there are too many stages in the message, or if it is too complicated, it may not be properly understood.
5. *Message badly set out or ambiguous*
6. *The competing environment*   Background activities or interference from other activities in the working environment may interfere with the message, particularly if it is long or complicated and requires concentration by the receiver.
7. *Cultural differences*   Our cultural backgrounds and differences may influence how we interpret the message.

 Task

What other barriers to communication could you add to these?

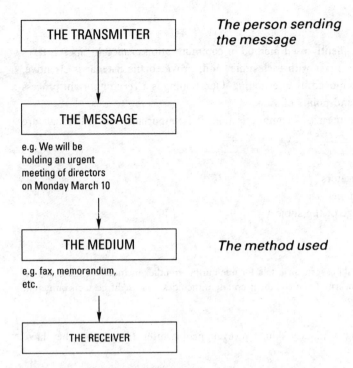

Figure 21.1 The flow of information from sender to receiver.

The basic communication skills

The five basic communication skills are:

- Listening
- Speaking
- Reading
- Writing
- Using information technology

Figure 21.2 shows the order in which the first four basic communication skills are learned, the degree to which they are used and the extent to which they are taught. Listening is the communication skill that is used most but taught least.

	Listening	Speaking	Reading	Writing
Learned	1st	2nd	3rd	4th
Used	Most (45%)	Next most (30%)	Next least (16%)	Least (9%)
Taught	Least	Next least	Next most	Most

Figure 21.2 The use of basic communication skills. (*Source*: Engineering Careers Information Service)

Speaking and listening

In most businesses, the most frequently used method of communication is speech. Speech takes place between people in direct contact with each other, and, provided the listener is attentive, ambiguity in discussion can be removed by questioning. Questioning is a very important process because it can clarify meanings and points of view.

For speech to be an effective means of communication, it is important that individuals are aware of:

- Their own role as communicators
- The receptiveness of the listener
- The listener's own knowledge of the subject

 Task

Form small groups and, taking it in turn, talk for one minute to other members of the group on any area of interest or concern. Then comment on any difficulties you might have encountered.

We tend to assume that listening is an easy skill. However, people often forget what they have heard. Listening involves:

- Physically hearing the message
- Interpreting the message
- Evaluating the message, which entails deciding how to use the information
- Reacting to the message

It is therefore hardly surprising that many verbal messages are quickly forgotten, misunderstood or not followed up. As a result, it is particularly important, after a meeting involving a lot of verbal discussion, that conclusions, recommendations and plans for further action are written down and circulated.

 Task

In the same groups formed above, starting with the statement 'When I went shopping, I . . .' each member of the group should in turn add a piece of information. Continue to go around the group without taking any notes. How much information can you remember? Were other members of the group easy to listen to? Was the exercise affected by any noise? How would taking notes have transformed the exercise?

Writing and reading

Written communication varies from the very simple to the very complex. Written communications tend to be used in situations where:

1. The receiver of the information is remote from the sender.
2. Information is highly complex, requiring extensive study.
3. Information needs to be referred to over a period of time.

The written word in some circumstances can be open to ambiguity if the receiver is not immediately able to question the sender. For this reason, even informal notes need to be accurate, clear in their meaning and easy to read. Documentation systems are widely used in industry to reduce elements of ambiguity; very often, drawings and sketches are used to support the written text.

Some forms of written communication are more easily read than others. The target audience and the nature of the information are important factors in deciding how to present data.

Information technology

The revolution in information technology has completely transformed the way in which people and organizations handle the availability, processing and distribution of information. The result is that the quality of information is much improved; it can be accessed more quickly and sent more effectively and, by improving the quality of decision-making, can create a competitive advantage for the firm.

Body language

It is possible for some messages to be transmitted without the use of the spoken or written word. Non-verbal communication or body language can be used either on its own or to reinforce the spoken word. Physical gestures and facial expressions can often say as much as a written or spoken message. Being able to observe such signs is an important communication skill.

 Task

Make a list of physical gestures and facial expressions and comment briefly on what each might communicate.

Case Study—Communicating the wrong image

An image is what people and organizations project about themselves for others to receive. We all project an image of some kind by our actions, gestures, clothes, speech, the people we mix with and by our possessions. Image is important. It communicates a message which helps others to make a more informed judgement. Good images are often created by good external communications and will help a firm's performance, whereas bad images may hurt companies whatever their performance.

For example, Gerald Ratner's notorious comments on the quality of his merchandise certainly took the shine off his business. In the early days Ratner kept a high profile in the press and was featured in many of the glossies. But in recent years the man whose PR and communication skills had been admired by many had become a liability for his company. A new low point was reached when he gave the infamous speech in which he pointed out that one of his cheap jewellery products cost less than a Marks and Spencer prawn sandwich and then followed this up by describing another of his products as 'crap'. Communicating the wrong image in this way cost his company dearly.

Questions

1. Explain why organizations should be concerned about their image.
2. Why did Gerald Ratner's comments damage his business?
3. Working in groups, identify an organization with a very good image and an organization with a poor image. Identify the communications from each organization that might have influenced your judgements.

Feedback

Most messages generate some form of response, or feedback (see Fig. 21.3). Some responses may be verbal while others might require a written answer. Feedback will indicate how a message has been interpreted and whether the information has been understood.

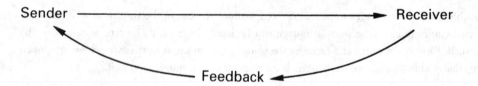

Figure 21.3 Feedback from a message.

Internal communications

Internal communications are communications within an organization. They may flow:

- Downwards from higher to lower levels
- Upwards from lower to higher levels
- Horizontally between people and departments at the same level
- Multi-directionally

 Task

Identify and comment on the internal communications systems in either the place you work or the place you attend.

Verbal communications

Verbal communications involve the transmission of information by word of mouth. For many people at work this involves *face-to-face* exchanges for the purpose of relaying messages, providing advice, personal discussion, analysis, giving instructions and guidance, etc. Face-to-face contact creates a less formal relationship, enables communicators to get to know each other and allows for instantaneous feedback. The main disadvantage of face-to-face contact, however, is that it can be a time-consuming exercise which usually provides no permanent record of the discussion. It can also lack precision and create misunderstandings.

Verbal communications are important in *meetings*. Meetings are held to deal with many issues and areas of concern. They provide an opportunity for staff to pool their experience and knowledge to contribute to a range of areas.

Perhaps the most frequently used form of verbal communication, after face-to-face contact, is through use of the *telephone*. Telephones are used for both internal and external communications. With the use of a telephone an enquiry can be resolved in the shortest possible period of time and in many systems a number of users can converse at the same time.

Written communications

Written communications are used within an organization to convey information and ideas to others. They may also be used to confirm important verbal messages.

Memos

One of the most frequently used forms of internal written communication is the memo. The word 'memorandum' derives from the Latin *memorare*, which means 'a thing to be remembered'. Today memos have a wider business use than just as a memory aid. They are used to communicate information, instructions and enquiries and are the internal equivalents of the letter (see Fig. 21.4). As they are internal, there are one or two minor differences. An organization's name does not normally appear on a memo for internal use, and it is not necessary to have a salutation or a complimentary close. Memos should be kept as short as possible and should deal with only one item. They will frequently be distributed to more than one person. Most organizations will provide memo pads of headed message forms.

The style of memorandum may vary considerably. Instructions from senior management will probably be written in relatively impersonal language, whereas a quickly scribbled message to a close colleague may be written in conversational English. It will therefore be necessary to be more cautious when writing memos up the ladder, rather than down. It is important to take account of people's sensitivities and of the position you hold.

 Task

Imagine that you are a school or college administrator. Write a short memorandum to be circulated to all heads of department, asking them to supply you with their budget estimates and proposals for the forthcoming year.

```
MEMO
To: All Staff
From: CB & WS
Date: 25.06.90

Safety Reports

Please refer to the section on 'Safety Procedures' on pages 81 to 84
of the Staff Handbook. Please refer also to the copy of the letter
showing how to fill in a safety report.

Reports are to be dated June 1990.

Reports are to be signed by the member of the staff with the
appropriate initials and surname: eg C.H. Clarke.

1st July-Reports to Section Head.
10th July-Reports to Department Head.
17th July-Reports to Safety Inspector.
```

Figure 21.4 Example of a memorandum.

Reports

Reports are another form of internal written communication. A report is simply a written communication from someone who has collected and studied some facts to a person who has asked for the report because he or she requires it for a particular purpose. A report will often either contribute towards or form the basis for a decision. Reports may be used as follows:

1. To supply information for legal purposes, e.g. as a result of an incident or accident, or to be presented to shareholders.
2. To present the results of some research and to recommend some form of action.
3. To assess the possibility of some form of change of policy.

A well written report will be concise and will not contain anything the reader does not need to know. It should be clear and logically arranged, but at the same time should not exclude anything that the reader requires. Reports may be written as short informal reports or as formal reports set according to a particular pattern.

Informal reports might be written on a report form or on a memo. They will contain:

- Title
- Introduction
- Body of report (complete with findings)
- Recommendations
- Action required

A more usual structure of a long *formal report* will look like this:

- Title page (name of organization, name and post of writer, subject)
- Table of contents/index
- Terms of reference (explaining the reason for the report)
- Procedure (how the task was completed)
- Findings
- Conclusion (summary of findings)
- Recommendations
- Signature of writer and date

In preparing a report, considerations have to be made concerning aspects such as language style, circulation list, presentation of cover and binding, and confidentiality.

Agenda and minutes

Before a meeting takes place, an agenda will list the items of business to be discussed and the order in which they will be taken. Minutes are a detailed record of a meeting and are often used as a form of internal communication. They are often placed on noticeboards or sent to key people to inform them of decisions that have taken place. Minutes of a meeting must be presented in a clear and unambiguous way. They require concise sentence construction with accurate spelling, punctuation and layout (see Fig. 21.5).

Notices and house publications

Notices are another common form of written communication within the organization. They can be placed in prominent positions and used to publicize any changes in policy, dates to be remembered, events taking place, functions, etc.

House magazines, journals and company newspapers can also be a useful way of communicating policies, information, events and activities to employees. They are a particularly useful form of internal communication in large organizations.

```
┌─────────────────────────────────────────────────────────────┐
│              Midtown Junior Chamber of Commerce               │
│                                                               │
│                          Minutes                              │
│  of the meeting of members of the Junior Chamber held at 7.30 p.m. on │
│  Thursday 10th July, 1990 at the Angel and Royal.             │
│  Present K. Thompson (Chair)                                  │
│          P. Bridle                                            │
│          H. O'Neill                                           │
│          M. Khan                                              │
│          E. Obeng                                             │
│          D. Lee                                               │
│  1.  Apologies for absence                                    │
│      Received from B. Cribb, I. Cottee and T. Wells.          │
│  2.  Minutes of previous meeting                              │
│      The minutes of the previous meeting held on              │
│      Thursday 12th June, 1990, were accepted as an            │
│      accurate record of the meeting.                          │
│  3.  Sponsored walk                                           │
│      . . . etc.                                               │
└─────────────────────────────────────────────────────────────┘
```

Figure 21.5 A layout of minutes.

⌀ Case Study—Hawker Siddeley News

The *Hawker Siddeley World* recently won the 1991 Public Relations Award for the best internal publication. It contained a strong cocktail of visually led features as well as human drama and business stories. Aimed at some 43 000 shop-floor and office employees from more than 80 autonomous engineering companies, the editorial staff fulfilled the objective of creating a features magazine that links Hawker Siddeley's diverse worldwide companies and cultures.

The magazine's stories have been wide-ranging, covering everything from power stations in guerilla-filled Colombian swamplands to the changing economy of Belfast.

Internal market research showed that seven out of ten employees describe the magazine as 'good' or 'excellent'. The budget per issue is £5000 on photos, £4000 on travel and £3500 on production, with printing costing £17 500 for 50 000 copies and distribution costing £5000.

Questions

1. Examine the benefits of a good house magazine.

2. What sort of stories should appear in house magazines, and why would such stories be of interest for employees?

3. House magazines such as the *Hawker Siddeley World* can, as illustrated, involve a considerable investment. Comment on the arguments for and against making such an investment.

External communications

External communications are concerned with how an organization is viewed by others. They encompass all of the actions that emanate from an organization. Every organization has a public face which conveys a message that influences those who have dealings with it, from customers and shareholders to suppliers, competitors, governments and communities. The positive image that can be projected through external communications helps to create a better external environment for the organization. The successful manipulation of this *public relations* function will help to convince others that the organization is worth dealing with and might provide it with a considerable competitive and strategic advantage.

Verbal communications

The most frequently used form of external verbal communication is the *telephone*. A telephone call may be the first point of contact an outsider has with an organization, and if a bad impression is created through the first call, this may be difficult to correct.

From time to time it may be necessary to have a *face-to-face* exchange with somebody from outside the organization. In many administrative posts employees are constantly in situations where they are meeting customers, members of the public, suppliers, visitors, candidates for jobs and so on. Dealing with people on a day-to-day basis requires many special skills.

 Task

Identify and then comment on the necessary skills that people who meet regularly with others from outside their organization should ideally have.

Written communications

Business letters

The business letter is still the most widely used form of external communication. It provides a written record and can be used to send almost any type of information. A well written business letter may convey a favourable impression of an organization. Its greatest benefit is its reasonable cost. Business letters are usually typed on headed A4 or A5 paper. Fully blocked layout is the most common form of display (see Fig. 21.6).

McGraw-Hill Book Company Europe

Shoppenhangers Road
Maidenhead, Berkshire, England SL6 2QL
Telephone Maidenhead (0628) 23432
Cables MCGRAWHILL MAIDENHEAD Telex 848484
Faxes (0628) 770224 *Editorial, Marketing, Financial*
35895 *Customer Services* 777342 *Export, Distribution*
777891 *Production, Credit Control*

Our ref: MN/JW

15 June 199-

Mr P Wilde
Marketing Manager
Thompson House Publishers
Beaverbrook Broadway
Birmingham
West Midlands
B3 2JB

Dear Mr Wilde

Thank you for sending me the photographs we requested so quickly.
They match the requirements of the manuscript perfectly and will
help to enhance the copy.

At some stage in the near future we must arrange a meeting and
discuss our future specialist photographic needs.

Could you please send us a copy of your new photographic brochure
when it is released.

Yours sincerely

Mark Newton
Editorial Assistant

McGraw-Hill International (UK) Ltd.   Registered no. 64070 England   Registered office: as above

Figure 21.6 An open-punctuated fully blocked business letter.

Letters should be presented in a logical sequence and written in a style that lacks ambiguity. They should be concise and yet not leave out any relevant information. A typical business letter will contain the following features:

- Heading or letterhead
- Reference, enabling the letter to be filed and later traced
- Date
- Inside address of the recipient
- Salutation ('Dear . . .')
- Subject heading
- Body of the letter
- Complimentary close ('Yours sincerely, . . .')

Any enclosure will be noted by the letters 'Enc(s)'.

There is a convention about the pairings of salutation and complimentary close. 'Dear Sir/Madam' should be paired with 'Yours faithfully' and 'Dear Mr/Mrs' should be paired with 'Yours sincerely'.

Fax and e-mail

Another form of written external communication, and one that has experienced massive expansion over recent years, is the use of *facsimile* ('*fax*') machines to send information electronically over telephone lines.

 Task

Make a list of the benefits of using fax machines.

Another alternative to writing letters is to use *electronic mail*. The 'mail-box' is a computer terminal linked to the telephone network; it can put messages into the system and store messages that have been sent through the system. Every user has a password to allow him or her to use the system. A message can be sent to several mail-boxes at once, so the system can be used for internal memos in a company with several branches. The message will be stored in a terminal's memory until the mail-box is 'opened'.

There are now a number of subscriber-based electronic mail services such as Telecom Gold. To use such a system, a subscriber sends a message using the telephone line. The advantage over ordinary mail is speed and low cost.

Other forms of external written communications

Advertising is a form of external communication. At the heart of advertising lies the need to understand how consumers will respond to both advertising copy and visual images. The effectiveness of an advertising campaign goes beyond the sale of products.

An *annual report* is a form of external communication produced by all limited companies. In addition to information required by the Companies Acts, many will also contain a range of non-financial information covering areas such as operations, business strategies, social and environmental objectives, etc.

ρ Case Study—The Well Informed Customer

Setting the agenda

The purpose of my keynote address is to urge the Conference to focus on the wishes of the ultimate customer and to rate real-time travel information as highly as train reliability. Our success criteria must be **The Well Informed Customer** in the 1990s.

It is a significant fact that Network SouthEast customers not only rate information at times of disruption above the availability of a seat and journey time, but they even rate it only one per cent lower than train reliability.

The implication is that customers will forgive the occasional disruption to a complex rail system but they will *not* forgive being left in the dark. This is certainly borne out by the daily post bag.

British Rail is currently undertaking a major reorganization which presents the opportunity to direct resources to managing this vital area of customer need. It will firmly separate the responsibility for Operations from Retail.

Retail will embrace everything that is customer service whether it be the telephone enquiry, ticketing, the train announcer, the indicator systems or the on-train services. I do hope that the information industry is ready for the acceleration that this new focus is going to bring.

The customers' priorities

Network SouthEast has developed sophisticated market research which allows us to identify the customers' top priorities. It confirms that the craving for real-time information is on a level with reliability:

	Customer priority (%)
● Reliable train	95
● Information in disruption	94
● Clean train	94
● Seat	91
● Departure information	91
● Journey speed	90
● Telephone enquiry service	82

Customer satisfaction levels are measured every three months by individual route and they reveal that only 71% of customers are fully satisfied with information at times of disruption.

As a result of this research, Network SouthEast has developed an initiative for **The Well Informed Customer** and I would like to share with you the opportunities for making this a real breakthrough for customers and the UK industries.

Figure 21.7 Extract from an address given by C. E. W. Green, managing director of Network SouthEast.

The extract reproduced in Fig. 21.7 formed part of an address to the Institution of Electrical Engineers (Power Division) Conference by C. E. W. Green, managing director of Network SouthEast.

Questions

Imagine that you have been asked to join a team that has been designated the task of developing ideas and following through many aspects highlighted by the agenda. Work in groups to answer the following:

1. Customers clearly rated the need for information in times of disruption very highly. Explain why they might have done so.
2. Discuss and then outline your proposals for providing customers with better information.
3. The cost of such a communication exercise may be very high. Is it possible to justify such a cost? Discuss.

Magazines, *publicity literature* and *educational services* can provide strong informed links between organizations and their various publics. *Corporate videotapes*, although they constitute a visual rather than a written resource, have become an increasingly popular way of providing interested parties with information about an organization's activities. *Visits*, *open days*, *exhibitions* and *demonstrations* can also be effectively used to generate interest, provide information and improve people's understanding and perception of an organization's activities.

Processing information

Presenting information in such a way that your message is clear and easy to read is never a simple process. The transmitter of a message will try to present material that he or she understands in a way in which recipients will also understand it. However, it is unlikely that material can be transmitted from one person's understanding to that of another intact. The current belief is that knowledge has to be reconstructed as it passes from one person to another. What an individual already knows and understands controls how he or she interprets, processes and even stores new information. Since individuals' backgrounds differ and their stores of knowledge and understanding vary, so will their development of new understandings differ.

We can illustrate this point by a few simple examples. A motorist who is also a supporter of Aberdeen FC could pass a sign for Pitrodie (a village in Angus) and easily read it as Pittodrie (the home of his or her football team). A set of numbers would mean little to most people, but might indicate a telephone number to some or even a birthday date.

It is not surprising, therefore, that misunderstandings frequently take place in the communication of information. You will have experienced times in your life when you have said something and it has been taken 'the wrong way'. The clear lessons to be learnt from the problems of constructing meanings are:

1. When communicating information, you should give the recipient an opportunity to 'kick around' the idea and ask questions.
2. When receiving information, you should not always take it at what you presume is its face value—try to find out more about what is being communicated to you by asking questions.

Using information systems

Today, people use phrases such as 'the information society' or 'the wired society' to refer to the way in which the revolution in information technology is transforming our lives. This is nowhere more true than in the business environment.

A modern business system can be seen as consisting of three sub-systems:

1. The *management* sub-system is concerned with all the people and activities involved in planning, controlling and decision-making.
2. The *operations* sub-system is concerned with all the activities, material flows and people directly involved with performing the primary function of the organization, e.g. manufacturing operations.
3. The *information* sub-system is made up of the people, machines, ideas and activities that are concerned with gathering and processing data in order to meet the formal requirements of an organization for information. They may include the way in which information is collected, stored, handled, exchanged and utilized for accounting purposes, monitoring stocks, or a range of other interrelated functions.

Information systems are based on the use of data. Data can be handled in simple ways, e.g. recording transactions by quill in a ledger. However, in modern business organizations the computer has become the most important tool for producing information from data. A number of standard operations are required to produce this information, and they can be applied to any form of information system:

1. *Capturing data* involves recording data generated by an event or occurrence, e.g. from invoices, sales slips, meters, counters.
2. *Verifying data* refers to checking that data have been recorded/captured accurately, e.g. checking that an instrument is working correctly, or cross-checking someone else's recording procedures.
3. *Classifying data* entails putting different types of data into appropriate sections; for example, the sales of a company could be sorted into the different departments that made the sales.
4. *Sorting data* refers to the placing of data elements into a specified order; for example, an inventory file could be sorted into money value order, into code number order, etc.

5. *Summarizing data* can be used to aggregate data. One way this can be done is to total up various figures, e.g. sales, or to draw up balancing figures for a balance sheet. Alternatively, it could be used to reduce data logically to a common form, e.g. by producing a list of all employees that were working on the night shift for a particular day.
6. *Calculating using data* involves computing various figures in a mathematical sense, e.g. by adding, subtracting, dividing. For example, wages of employees can be calculated by multiplying hours worked by the wage rate and then subtracting necessary deductions.
7. *Storing data* involves transferring data to the appropriate medium, e.g. floppy disk, microfilm.
8. *Retrieving data* involves calling them up from the place of storage.
9. *Reproducing data* is the process of transferring the same data from one medium to another. At a simple level this could involve photocopying material, or calling up data from one screen to another as with Stock Exchange dealing.
10. *Communicating* refers to the transfer of data from one place to another. This can take place at any stage of the data processing cycle. The ultimate aim of information processing is to provide information for the final consumer.

 Task

Identify the tools of information technology in either the place you attend or the place you work. Comment briefly on the function of each, and indicate which of the above operations they perform.

Information technology as an aid to effective communication

The success of a business enterprise depends in large measure on the efficient and accurate production of goods and services that meet customer requirements. We can add to this that the survival of any medium- or large-sized company also depends on the rapid and accurate processing and distribution of information. This process is increasingly being carried out by using new technology, principally computers.

What features of modern business life make computer aided communication so important?

1. The scale of many large organizations makes it impossible for every individual to meet face-to-face.
2. Many organizations are geographically spread out, but require communication links between interrelated plants and offices.
3. Modern business decision-making frequently requires up-to-date information drawn from a variety of business functions; e.g. the marketing department may need sales figures from sales, costings from accounts, etc.
4. Competition between firms is more fierce; it is almost impossible for a company to find a market area that is not extremely competitive. (This is particularly true with the opening up of the Single Market.)

5. The rate of change of industrial development has increased. Firms must therefore be quicker in responding to factors such as technological change, market forces and better competition.

ρ Case Study—The development of global communication links at Ford

The Ford Motor Company has recently spent $77 million to create a massive database which can be accessed from any of 17 000 terminals worldwide, with a maximum response time of 4 seconds.

The system, called WERS (Worldwide Engineering Release System), links Ford's hundreds of sites across the world to a database which holds all the engineering information about parts for all cars that the company makes—Thunderbirds, Mustangs, Escorts and many more. Ford believes that this system will give the company at least a two-year lead over its competitors.

WERS has been set up to replace six formerly separate systems which were difficult to link up. The new system will link up 20 000 engineers and designers for Ford in Europe, the United States, South America, Australia and East Anglia.

The advantage of having all the information centralized and accessible worldwide is that manufacture can be switched to available capacity; and designers need not be in the same factory, site or even country as the engineers or assemblers.

The system is capable of handling 500 000 queries daily. One of the key features of the design was speed. This is why the system has been built to respond to queries within 4 seconds.

Questions

1. Who will benefit from Ford's new Worldwide Engineering Release System? How will they benefit?
2. In what ways will the new system help to make Ford more competitive?
3. Why is it important to an organization like Ford to use such a high-powered communications system?
4. How do you expect other major manufacturers to respond to WERS?
5. How will Ford be able to evaluate the effectiveness of WERS?

Information technology skills

Most people today use some form of information technology (IT) at work. In order to be able to do so, they may have had to develop:

- General skills for the use of IT for a range of applications
- Specialist skills for the development of specialist technology software and systems

General IT skills are useful for all employees who come across information technology and its application in their working environment. For example:

1. Managers can use information technology as an aid for decision-making.
2. Technicians, maintenance and craft workers need to deal with IT components in plants, machinery and vehicles.
3. Clerical workers have to be familiar with a variety of word processing, spreadsheet, database and similar applications.
4. Professionals frequently use specialist IT applications to improve the efficiency of their work—e.g. accountants, architects, etc.

Specialist users of IT make up about 1 per cent of the working population (approximately 250 000 people). These people are in the IT professions. Despite the recession, the numbers in this area have grown by about 20 per cent since 1985. This is one of the fastest growing job sectors in the country.

Using computers

Not long ago, most people were frightened by the prospect of using a computer. The machines appeared to be so complex that they could be used by only a few people; they came with rather daunting manuals and seemed to stop co-operating at the most inconvenient of times. Modern computers have become much more consumer-orientated, and much more thought has gone into making them more user-friendly and suitable for the needs of different organizations.

A major breakthrough in modern computers came with the development of *graphical user interfaces* (GUIs, or 'gooies'). GUIs are designed to make the technology easier to understand and use, and in doing so they are literally changing the face of computers. A GUI presents the user with a series of small pictures called *icons* which represent the various options it is possible to use. A *mouse* is used to move an arrow around the screen and select the appropriate icon for the desired action. At the press of a key, the screen then redraws itself to show the next set of options. If the user has selected word processing, for example, the screen will change to provide a second series of options, and each option chosen will lead to a further set of options (Fig. 21.8).

Windowing systems go one stage further, giving the same type of graphical interface but allowing the user to carry out several tasks simultaneously. For example, you could be writing a document in the word processing window while carrying out some other function at the same time.

Word processing

Word processors are used for manipulating text. They display information on a screen and record on a memory the text that is typed in on a keyboard. Most word processors can:

1. Insert text on to a screen while the existing text moves along to create the necessary space.
2. Move blocks of text from one place to another.

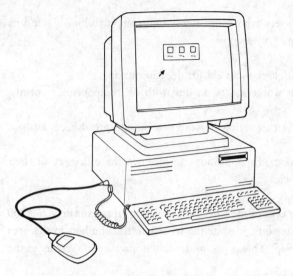

Figure 21.8 Using icons to select an option.

3. Space the text to fill a whole line.
4. Search for a word or phrase and replace it with another word or phrase.
5. Add a 'header' or 'footer' (a piece of text printed either at the top or the bottom of the page).

More sophisticated features available on some word processors include:

1. Different printing styles (e.g. italics, or underlined text) can be shown on screen either as different colours or as they could appear when printed. This is referred to as WYSIWIG (pronounced 'wizzywig'), which stands for 'what you see is what you get'.
2. The text can be written in more than one column, as in newspapers.
3. Graphics can be built into the text.
4. A number of similar letters can be produced, with information added, from a database, on each letter. For example, if a company has a database of suppliers and wishes to contact local ones, the database can be used to select all suppliers who are situated in the same town; the word processor can then print a letter to each supplier selected, adding personal information, such as the name and address of the firm, to the letter.
5. A spell check can be included. This checks all the text against an inbuilt dictionary facility and points out any words that it does not recognize.

🔍 Case Study—Word processing a series of similar letters

A fashion house, Novelty Fashions, regularly deals with a large number of enquiries from prospective customers. It responds to these enquiries by sending out standard letters, containing a number of set paragraphs. The required text has been entered on to a disk and paragraphs are called up as appropriate. The set paragraphs are listed below, along with the relevant index number used to call the paragraph.

Paragraph of text	Index no.
Thank you for your letter expressing an interest in our range of fashion clothes.	e1
Further to our recent telephone conversation in which you expressed an interest in our range of fashion clothes,	e2
Further to our recent meeting at which you expressed an interest in our range of fashion clothes,	e3
we have pleasure in forwarding to you our most recent catalogue and an order form for our goods.	o1
we are able to offer the following terms: 5 per cent 28 days.	t1
we are able to offer the following terms: 8 per cent 28 days.	t2
Yours sincerely Novelty Fashions	
Sales Director	x1

Questions

1. (a) Load a word processing package into a computer and prepare it to receive text.

   (b) Enter a letter heading for Novelty Fashions, using a fictional address. Enter the complete set of paragraphs. Save on the disk.

   (c) Produce six letters:

   (i) to High Street Fashions, High Street, Grantham, offering 5 per cent, 28 days, in response to a phone call.

   (ii) to Black on Black, Castlegate, Aberdeen, offering 5 per cent, 28 days, in response to a personal meeting.

   (iii) to Today Fashion, High Street, Portrush, offering 8 per cent, 28 days, in response to phone call.

   (iv) to Shorties, Claire Avenue, Dawlish, offering 8 per cent, 28 days, in response to a letter.

   (v) to Miss Elspeth, Donald Road, Barnsley, offering 8 per cent, 28 days, in response to a personal meeting.

   (vi) to New Fashion, High Street, Brighton, offering 5 per cent, 28 days, in response to a letter.

2. What would be the advantages to Novelty Fashions of word processing its letters in this way?
3. What constraints would there be to Novelty Fashion's ability to word process its letters?
4. What would be the disadvantages to Novelty Fashions of word processing letters?
5. What considerations should a firm bear in mind in deciding whether or not to word process its letters?

Desk top publishing

Desk top publishing (DTP) has been an important spin-off from developments in word processing and computer graphics.

DTP programs make it possible to produce pages of well illustrated text. No longer do pamphlets and other short publications have to be sent out to the printers. Large, medium and even some small firms can save a lot of money by developing their own in-house DTP facility.

Desk top packages offer a range of different character designs (typefaces), the freedom to adjust the space between characters and lines, the ability to place a diagram or picture on a page and a number of other important editing functions. DTP programs can be used to produce newsletters, training manuals and advertisements. Newspapers can also be produced in this way at a fraction of the cost.

Databases

A database is a store of facts that can be called upon to provide up-to-date information. It may be used, for instance, in a bank or building society to store information on the state of all accounts. Data (information) are fed into the base in a clear form. For instance, a firm could store information about the firms it supplies credit to; if it had a record for the account of Yeaman's Stores, it would store the information in a number of 'fields', such as address, value of goods bought, payments and balance of account. Then, if Mrs Yeaman rings up asking for the state of her account, the firm can simply order the computer to find the balance on Yeaman's account.

Under the provisions of the Data Protection Act, companies wishing to store personal information on a computer must register with the (government-appointed) Data Protection Officer, and indicate the type of data that is being stored and the use they wish to make of these data. Any individual has the right to request (on payment of a small fee) details of any information held about him or her by any organization, and to require any mistakes to be corrected.

Any work with a database needs careful planning. For example, if you were undertaking an investigation and intended to use a database, you would have to ask yourself:

- What questions do I want to ask?
- What information needs to be collected to answer the questions?

When using a database it is important to be consistent. For example, if entering 'name' you have to decide whether you mean first or second name; if you use 'gender'; you have to decide whether you will use man/woman or male/female; etc. When information is extracted from a database it can be presented in a variety of forms, including pie charts and bar charts. A database can be a particularly useful tool for collating the results of a piece of research.

 Task

Undertake a piece of consumer research. Collate the information, enter it into a database and use graphics to display the information.

Spreadsheets

A spreadsheet is a table of numbers which can be organized and altered on a computer. It can be used for making forecasts and undertaking calculations. They are frequently used in financial forecasting; for example, a firm may make a forecast of all the money that will come in and go out over the next 12 months. The person using the spreadsheet can alter the inputs to calculate the effect, for example, of lowering a cost. The computer will automatically recalculate the columns to cater for the lower cost and will show the influence on profits for each month as well as on the total profit figure. In this way a business manager can quickly carry out calculations to show the effects of minor changes.

A spreadsheet program is essentially a very large grid of 'cells,' which contain text, numbers or formulae, and are used for numerical problems where a large number of figures are calculated (see Fig. 21.9). The number in any one cell can be calculated from the numbers in any other cell (or combination of cells) using the spreadsheet to perform the calculations. If any one number is changed the result on all the other cells is seen immediately, thus saving long calculations.

The spreadsheet is usually used as a financial tool, but is also used by engineers, scientists and any others who have to deal with a range of figures on a regular basis. Most spreadsheets have the ability to produce graphics from the data.

	Jan	Feb	Mar	Apr	May	Jun	Jul	Aug	Sep	Oct	Nov	Dec
REVENUE	200	200	300	400	400	400	500	500	500	500	500	500
COSTS												
Heat	20	20	20	20	20	20	20	20	20	20	20	20
Fuel	20	20	20	20	20	20	20	20	20	20	20	20
Labour	50	50	60	70	70	70	80	80	80	80	80	80
Materials	50	50	60	70	70	70	80	80	80	80	80	80
TOTAL COSTS	140	140	160	180	180	180	200	200	200	200	200	200
PROFIT	60	60	140	220	220	220	300	300	300	300	300	300
TOTAL PROFITS: 2720												

Figure 21.9 Layout of a spreadsheet.

Task

Prepare a simple cash budget and put the figures into a spreadsheet. When the spreadsheet is completed you can experiment with some 'what-if' situations:

- What if your receipts increase by 10 per cent in the first month?
- What if payments increased by 30 per cent in the second month?

Calculate the effects of both of these.

Further IT applications

Project planning

Project planning packages can be used to plan and monitor projects consisting of a number of stages or 'activities'.

Initially the activities will be defined, and an estimation made of the time required for each activity. The interrelationship between activities then needs to be specified. The computer can then calculate the total time required to undertake the project, and will indicate the way in which activities should be completed, in order to prevent delays. A simple example could involve the building of a new factory. The activities and times required may be:

1.	Prepare the land and build the foundations	30 days
2.	Build the walls	30 days
3.	Build the roof	15 days
4.	Install the machinery and equipment	30 days
5.	Equip the offices	20 days

Activity 1 must be carried out first, followed by 2 and 3. Activities 4 and 5 can, however, be carried out simultaneously. The total project can therefore be carried out within 105 days, i.e. 30 + 30 + 15 + 30 (rather than 125 days, if stage 5 had waited for the completion of stage 4) (see Fig. 21.10).

The program would also inform project planners that stage 5 is not 'critical'; i.e. it could start late or take a few days longer than planned without delaying the total project. Such information is a useful aid to decision-making because it helps project managers to work out priorities. Most versions of the program can also help to plan the use of resources on activities, to record costs and to produce a variety of reports.

In a real project many thousands of activities will need to be co-ordinated, and project planning packages can be very useful in cutting down time, costs and waste.

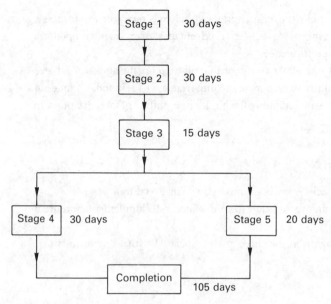

Figure 21.10 Planning the building of a new factory.

🔍 Case Study—Benefiting from IT

In large organizations today, almost every junior, middle and senior manager will have a PC on his or her desk. Their machine will probably be networked locally with the machines of colleagues. Some will have a modem installed to enable public electronic mail services and databases to be accessed. But, what are the benefits of such investment?

There are generally accepted to be three broadly achievable goals associated with IT investment:

- To improve productivity
- To increase flexibility
- To gain competitive advantage

Productivity gains are probably the most obvious benefit. In many industries, for example banking, the use of IT has dramatically cut down on the use of manpower and dramatically increased the productivity of those still in employment. IBM claims that, for every $1 invested internally in IT, organizations will make a $4 improvement in return.

The second achievable goal is *increased flexibility*. It is frequently argued that IT can improve an organization's responsiveness to its customers. For example, if an organization wants a custom-built product, IT will cut the lead time and enable customer needs to be satisfied more quickly. At Swan Hunter it is possible to order a warship and, with the help of a computer simulation, to 'walk around' the ship before it is even built.

Finally, both of the above help the organization to achieve *competitive advantage*. Electronic systems enable organizations to derive advantages over their competitors and improve overall business performance.

As a result of these benefits, the effective use of IT will help organizations to achieve their overall objectives. The failure to recognize the importance of IT in today's modern and competitive environment will undoubtedly hinder the ability of organizations to reach a successful outcome.

Questions

1. Explain why PCs have become such an important managerial tool.
2. What are the benefits to an organization from the successful implementation of an IT strategy?
3. Use an example to comment on the three goals associated with IT investment.

Expert systems

Expert systems (ESs) are the first commercial products of research into artificial intelligence. ESs are computer programs that embody some of the knowledge of human experts, knowledge that even those experts have until now found difficult to formulate and communicate.

An ES has two distinct elements, a 'knowledge base' and an 'inference engine'. The 'knowledge base' consists of all human knowledge that it is possible to collect on a particular subject. The area of knowledge an ES covers may be narrow, but expert systems aspire to quite comprehensive knowledge in those fields. It may be difficult to collect the information from human experts who often think of their expertise as irreducible to rule—though the real difficulty may be that human experts have paid inadequate attention to formulating and communicating their knowledge and the rules according to which their minds work. But, because they use knowledge gathered from many different human experts, ES may be more knowledgeable than any single human being.

The 'inference engine' is simply a collection of the rules that manipulate the knowledge in the ES. For example, one of the rules might be: If runny nose then cold or excessive stimulation or allergy, where 'runny nose', 'cold', 'excessive stimulation' and 'allergy' are all terms that would need to be in the knowledge base.

There are two essentials for an ES to function properly: the knowledge base should be kept entirely separate from the rules manipulating that knowledge (the inference engine), and the knowledge should be represented uniformly. These two principles allow additional pieces of knowledge (new discoveries about medical diagnosis, for example) to be added to an expert system without changing the system itself. When small changes are made, it is not necessary to edit and recompile relevant parts of a program by human agency, as it would be in the case of an ordinary computer-based program. Nor, indeed, is it necessary to have every full stop and comma in place: ES can operate on the basis of approximate commands or information.

Another thing that differentiates ES from an ordinary computer-based system is that an ES will be able to work out new rules for its own guidance on the basis of its existing knowledge and its inference engine. And, as it gathers new knowledge from the outside world, it can use this to modify its inference engine too.

The only difficulty with an ES, at present, is that of enabling it to keep up with advances in knowledge, especially as some of these may necessitate human intervention to change the rules in the inference engine.

Already, ES can be used by people to get specialist advice on subjects such as where to drill for oil, coal or other natural resources and how to diagnose and treat disease.

 Task

Make a list of other uses to which an expert system may be put.

Accessing remote databases

A number of large computer databases have been set up for specialist use, covering rapidly changing areas such as the law in relation to business activity, information on companies, international stock exchanges and foreign currency markets.

For a fee, companies can call up and do a search for specific topics. Searches can specify a combination of factors; for example, an enquiry could be carried out to assemble information on 'chemical fertilizer suppliers', 'employing more than 100 workers', in 'Birmingham'. Up-to-date information can be readily accessed. Prestel is an example of such a database. Prestel gives users access to a range of computer-held information. The information is set out in 'pages'. A page is a screenful of information, and the pages are organized into groups.

In addition to getting information from the Prestel service, business people can input their own information and use the service for sending messages. Prestel can be used to make hotel reservations and holiday bookings. Orders can be fed into the system and company personnel can use the system to keep in touch with their offices.

While many of the pages of Prestel are accessible to all users, it is also possible for a firm to arrange to use private pages available only to members of the firm.

Networking

When an organization uses a number of personal computers, it is possible to link the system so that information can be shared. This has been particularly important in the late twentieth century and makes it possible for teams of workers to combine far more frequently and effectively. It also makes it possible for specialists to access information quickly from other company departments.

Rather than continually swopping data using floppy disks, it is possible to connect the machines together using a local area network (LAN). This consists of a mixture of hardware and software which enables data to be transferred between the machines. There are two basic ways of using a local area network:

1. Computers use their own programs and their own data, but can exchange data when necessary.

2. The program and data are held on one machine, called a 'file server', and the others act as 'terminals', updating the data on the 'file server'.

Homeworking

A number of forecasters have predicted that by the mid-1990s many commuters will be travelling to work only three days a week. It is likely that 'teleworking' will be an important contributory factor to this trend. 'Teleworking' involves working from home with the tools of information technology—mainly, a network of personal computers and databases, backed up by fax or other transmission systems.

The availability of information technology is changing the nature of office work. More and more tasks are skill- and knowledge-based 'thinkwork' which, although at present carried out in centralized offices, does not need to be. Groups of specialists will still be able to work as a team, even if they are separated by large distances. Employers will be able to tap into their workforce in any part of the country. This may create more employment for skilled women with young families, and for others for whom commuting is an inconvenience.

Production control

An awareness of the importance of production control systems is essential. MRP is used to describe both *materials requirements planning* and *manufacturing resource planning* (sometimes referred to as MRP II)—two activities that stand at the centre of modern manufacturing control philosophy.

The functions of MRP are invariably embodied in a sophisticated multi-user computer system which is usually the starting-point for the development of computer integrated manufacture (CIM) (see page 422). CIM is a must for all major manufacturers that have any serious intentions of surviving into the twenty-first century.

A materials requirement planning system is one that contains information on all the items that make up a firm's products, all the items currently in stock, and the requirements for finished products. It can calculate the total requirements for all items that the firm uses, work out when they are needed and tell the production control and purchasing departments to order them. This process would not be possible on a personal computer.

A manufacturing resource planning system extends this process by incorporating items such as cost information, the automatic scheduling of parts on the shop-floor, the monitoring of purchase orders, etc. The whole company is thus able to use the same set of data. Installing such a program and learning how to use it can take over two years, and is expensive. The benefits to a company in terms of integration of company functions, time-saving and cost-cutting can be enormous, however.

For the majority of manufacturing companies, MRP is the central management system. Surveys have shown that at the end of the 1980s over half of all UK manufacturers had an MRP system installed, and the numbers are increasing.

MRP was originally developed in the United States during the 1960s and 1970s around the prevalent technology of the day—the batch mainframe. In the 1970s the original MRP system was developed into a 'closed-loop' MRP II manufacturing philosophy consisting of a computerized database of parts, work-in-progress, finished goods and material requirements. Details on production lead time and relationships between parts are also held so that the computer can calculate the best way to meet the master production schedule, a plan based on forecasts and orders. Because MRP systems hold details on stock levels at every stage, it is possible to push goods through the manufacturing process according to a carefully drawn up plan. The term 'closed loop' means that adjustments can be made when new information arises.

Software and hardware suppliers were quick to jump on the MRP bandwagon, and they, as much as anyone else, have been responsible for promoting the MRP philosophy. There are probably more than 100 packages available in the United Kingdom alone, most of these linked closely to accounting systems.

 Task

Explain how MRP could help a manufacturer to gain and develop a competitive advantage.

Modern information systems in large organizations

Every organization must have some form of system for storing, processing and communicating information. In its simplest form this will consist of filing cabinets, an in-and-out tray and a telephone. Today, however, to have an information system that works effectively, it is necessary to organize all the required data in such a manner that it can be readily recorded, stored, processed, retrieved and communicated by a variety of users.

An information system converts raw data into either a finished report or an input for a further stage in the information processing cycle.

The dominant form of information processing in modern organizations is computer-based. A computer system alone is not an information system, however: it is simply a tool that can improve the effectiveness of an information system.

Case Study—Shaping organizations with information

Managing information efficiently is a key area in most organizations. For example, changing the availability of information might result in some form of disruption, or it could change the basis on which employees communicate with one another. Information is clearly one of an organization's most valuable assets, and the need to gather, record, organize and act upon information efficiently is, therefore, a very important factor.

Information systems and information technology are tools that enable companies to utilize information effectively. Introducing an information system may require considerable change in the flow of information into an organization to ensure that the information gets to the right employees, in the form they require, at the right time. In order to maximize the benefits to be derived from introducing an information system, it may be necessary to make structural changes to the organization. These may include providing flatter structures, and moving away from highly functional hierarchies and bureaucratic structures towards multi-disciplinary teams. Many business writers call this sort of organization a *transformed business*.

In a transformed business, people involved in particular processes are given more freedom to make decisions and have more information at their fingertips. The business processes are handled by teams of people from different functions working together to achieve the aims of the organization. Groups working together in a team share information, and computer terminals of different specialists are linked so that information is available to all. The great benefit of this is that team-work is more enriching and satisfying. Work flows are also simplified, as a job stays with a team instead of passing from department to department. Teams have greater responsibility for their own destiny and this increases their overall business awareness. Such a situation can improve an organization's flexibility and allow it to respond more quickly to its customers needs.

Questions

1. What is an information system?
2. What might happen if an organization managed information badly?
3. Why might it be necessary to make structural changes to an organization before introducing an information system?
4. What is a transformed business?
5. Outline the benefits of a transformed business.

Systems analysis

Before introducing computers to an information system, it is necessary to carry out a process of systems analysis to investigate the ways in which computers can benefit the system.

Systems development is a procedure used to design and develop an information system. The systems analyst will look at an organizational system as a co-ordinated whole and will examine the ways in which the parts of the organization need to fit together and support each other. The systems analyst will then attempt to integrate within the organization and its needs a multi-level, cross-functional and timely flow of information. The information system will then (it is hoped) serve the needs of both the management sub-system and the operating sub-system.

A good illustration of a modern computer-based information system is that operated by the commercial banks to handle customer information. A business or private customer may have several accounts with a bank: a current account, savings account, mortgage account, loan account, etc. Using a customer information system, it is possible to cross-reference such accounts easily so that the bank can quickly call up a statement of a customer's total activity even though the customer may be dealing with several departments of the bank. Such information makes it possible for a bank to develop a more detailed picture of its customers, to provide a better service for them, to provide up-to-date information and to market readily new services to existing customers.

Retailers are able to use computer-based information systems to access and use information related to a variety of functions. This is particularly useful when information related to individual items can be recorded at point of sale. Detailed information can then be accessed and processed in relation to stock levels, prices, turnover, demand and many other important variables.

Designing an information system

Systems design involves the preparation and planning of an information system by drawings, sketches and plans. It is concerned with deciding how a system should be developed.

The form of design will depend upon a number of factors:

1. The *resources available* to an organization will clearly constrain the type of system planned. The five basic resources of any organization are machines, material, money, methods and people. Quite clearly, there would be no point in designing an expensive information system for a company that had little money to spare.
2. The *information requirements of users* are an important design factor. Systems design clearly needs to be coupled with an understanding of who needs what information and in what form.
3. The *user's ability to use information provided and to operate the system* will need to be considered. The designer will have to make the system as user-friendly as possible. This will involve the reduction of jargon and technical language to a bare minimum. Other such features that can be built into a system include speed of communication, to prevent the frustration of waiting.
4. The *requirements for the system* are another important element of design. The designer needs to be clear of what is expected of the system, e.g.
   (a) Cost
   (b) Performance
   (c) Reliability
   (d) Flexibility
   (e) Expected life-cycle
5. The *use to which data operations will be put* is also an important design feature. As we have seen, a number of important operations can be carried out on data: capturing, verifying, classifying, arranging, summarizing, calculating, storing, retrieving, reproducing and communicating. Systems analysis will reveal information such as the order in which these operations need to be carried out in particular operations, e.g. building up a series of personal accounts. This information will need to be carried forward into systems design. The designer will then use a number of *design tools* such as flow charts, and decision tables (see Chapter 9) to help with the design of the information system.

Systems evaluation

The systems designer will come up with various alternative plans for implementation. Some of these suggestions will be set out as *imperatives*, i.e. features of design that must be adhered to whatever the final system. In addition, the designer will suggest a number of *desirable features*, which are optional.

It will then be necessary to find suppliers who are willing and able to provide the required computer equipment to meet the design needs. This might involve finding suppliers who can provide the equipment that has the 'best fit' with the desired system in terms of criteria such as cost, reliability, maintainability and other factors. Other considerations will be the ability to extend a system to account for future growth, and the overall level of support from the supplier, e.g. in the form of training and maintenance. These and other factors will need to be weighed up before a final decision is made.

Questions

Short-answer questions

1. What is meant by communication? Give four examples of different types of communication. (Explain, with reference to your work on communication, why different students are likely to give different types of answer to this question.)
2. Outline the possible stages involved in the passage of a message from a transmitter to a receiver.
3. Set out a simple memo for members of your class warning them to prepare themselves for a forthcoming examination.
4. Why is it unlikely that information can be transmitted intact from one person to another?
5. Explain how a mouse works.
6. For what purpose might an individual use spreadsheets? How do spreadsheets facilitate business decision-making?
7. What sort of records may be kept on a bank's database? What fields might records be sorted into?
8. Outline three applications of desk top publishing for a medium-sized furniture wholesaler.
9. How might a project planning package help
    (a) a building company constructing a new housing estate?
    (b) a large fashion company producing consignments of shirts, trousers and dresses?
10. What are expert systems?
11. What advantages does electronic mail have over the postal service?
12. Explain why homeworking has expanded over recent years.
13. What is the purpose of
    (a) systems analysis?
    (b) systems design?
    (c) systems evaluation?
14. What are the key considerations of systems design?
15. List the factors that might impede the communication of a message.
16. What is meant by feedback and why might it be useful?
17. Outline the structure for an informal report.
18. List the various parts of a business letter.

19. What are the benefits of graphical user interfaces?
20. Explain how use of a system such as Prestel could benefit a large organization.

Essays

1. Effective communication is vital to the success of any organization. Discuss.
2. Outline the stages that may be involved in preparing a new information system.
3. Information technology strategies can be effective only if their formulation involves a genuinely two-handed affair with senior management and systems specialists contributing equally. Discuss.
4. How important are production control systems to modern industry?
5. Have computer-based information systems removed the need for traditional communication links?
6. Examine the link, if any, between good communications and employee motivation.
7. Discuss the importance to a modern organization of
   (a) databases.
   (b) word processing facilities.
   (c) spreadsheets.
8. What forms of internal communication are used in an organization with which you are familiar? How could such communication systems be improved?
9. How would you set up a database to record
   (a) the hobbies and interests of members of your class?
   (b) part-time work carried out by members of your class?
10. Examine the difference between internal and external communications.

Data response questions

1 CIM technology development

Study Fig. 21.11 illustrating the development of computer integrated manufacture and answer the questions that follow.

1. What is meant by
   (a) computer aided design?
   (b) 'just in time'?
   (c) robots?
   (d) manufacturing resource planning?
   (e) expert systems?
2. How can (a) 'just in time' and (b) expert systems help a business to reduce costs and raise productivity?
3. What factors are likely to constrain the ability and willingness of companies to use the available technology?
4. Which of the technology developments listed in the figure do you regard to be most important? Explain your reasoning.

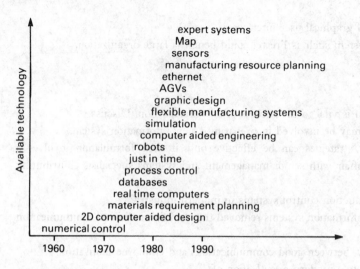

Figure 21.11 CIM technology development.

5. Which of the CIM technology developments highlighted in the figure would you regard to be essential to large manufacturing companies wishing to survive into the twenty-first century? Explain your answer.
6. What new developments can be added to the figure?

2 Domestic Appliances Limited

Domestic Appliances Limited makes an almost complete range of the larger electric domestic appliances (washing machines, refrigerators, spin dryers, tumble driers, dishwashers, food mixers, cookers) in four widely separated plants. The largest plant, which is situated in Scotland, manufactures washing machines, spin driers and dishwashers.

Many of these products have a large number of common parts; for example, the heating units on the Twin Tub de Luxe, the Dadomatics and the Washorinses are identical. Most of the components are manufactured internally in the part machining and fabrication shops except for a few standard items such as the bearings, which are purchased from specialist suppliers.

Final assembly is done on four lines as indicated in Table 21.1. Changeovers are scheduled for the items on a given line in order to obtain the desired product mix; usually at least three shifts are worked on each item before a changeover.

Before final assembly, however, many sub-assemblies are built up (e.g. the heating unit). In general, individual components are manufactured and put into part stores and these are issued against 'kitting lists' to make a batch of sub-assemblies which are again returned to stores and may be issued against a further kitting list to form a 'higher-level' assembly which is returned to stores to await final assembly. As many as six levels may be identified for some assemblies and four including raw material is common (see Fig. 21.12).

Although the sub-assemblies that go into the final assembly of an item may not be identical, many of the *components* of the sub-assemblies are common. For example, the heater unit for the

Table 21.1

Appliance	Model	Production line usually used
Washing machines	Dad Twin Tub	Line 1
	Dad Twin Tub de Luxe	
	Dad 707B (Single Tub)	
	Dadomatic	Line 2
	Dadomatic de Luxe	
	Dad Progomatic	
Spin driers	Dadospin B526	Line 3
	Dadospin B526 de Luxe	
	Spinmatic	
Dishwashers	Washorinse	Line 4
	Washorinse 741	
	Washup (portable)	

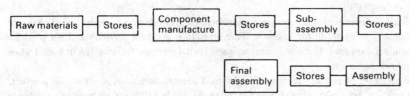

Figure 21.12 Materials flow in Domestic Appliances Limited.

Progomatic has identical components to that of the Dadomatic except for the heating coil, the insulator and a switching unit, which are all slightly larger, and the addition of two other components not used elsewhere.

The component and sub-assembly stores, besides supplying the needs of the assembly lines, also supply spares stores, but the requirement is usually for sub-assemblies such as the complete heater unit. However, two service centres operate rebuild lines, and these usually place orders for components rather than assemblies.

Orders for components and sub-assemblies are based on a periodic review system with a critical level and re-order quantity rule based on past usage of the particular item.

The management of the company has been very concerned about the amount of capital tied up in inventory and has recently installed a large computer system (run on the company computer adjacent to the washer plant) which records movements, locations and levels of all inventories.

1. Outline ways in which the new computer system will enable manufacturing and other processes to be carried out more effectively by Domestic Appliances Limited.
2. Outline further possibilities using computer applications within the company.
3. Explain how these will benefit the company.
4. How might the company benefit from 'just in time'?

3   Technological advances in the retail sector

Read the following extract from an article by Nick Kerridge, general sales manager of Omron Systems UK Ltd, and answer the questions that follow.

The major shift in technology over the last ten years has been from simple electronic cash registers (ECRs) to sophisticated computer-based electronic point-of-sale (EPoS) systems which offer a wealth of management information. ECRs were themselves a major advance, offering improved accuracy and security. They still have a valuable role to play: it is possible to use them to look at patterns of sales in some detail—what is sold and when. Offering flexible and convenient opening hours is something the independent retailer has to do—but it may be worth looking at what is actually sold late at night, for example, and now an ECR can help do that.

With the availability of increasingly powerful microprocessors, no one needs reminding how fast technology has developed. Undoubtedly, the banks and the big supermarket chains have been a major influence driving retail technology, and in establishing the standards which are key to moving the retail community forward. Customer expectations have changed almost as fast as the technology, and that has put pressure on the independents, who must offer the same facilities to compete.

But, while the banks have a clear interest in cashless trading, from the retailer's point of view nothing is as fast and convenient as cash, and a lot of development effort has gone into making sure that transactions are as fast as possible, without sacrificing security. That picture is changing now, with SWITCH and electronic funds transfer (EFT).

Quite rightly, most independent retailers are underwhelmed by technology alone—what they are interested in is what it is going to do for business. That attitude is good for retailing and it's good for suppliers. Too much, too soon leads to disillusionment; but it is vital that new facilities can be added when there is a real benefit in doing so.

The widespread adoption of product identification by food manufacturers—now almost all products have the familiar European Article Number (EAN) bar code—has made EPoS and its benefits available to even the smallest independent. Scanning bar codes is a highly accurate and virtually effortless way of collecting sophisticated management information on what's sold and when. Weights and measures-approved interfaces for scales pull produce into the same system. That information is useful to the individual outlet; aggregated for a group of outlets it can become even more valuable, which is why the partnerships between wholesalers and independent groups is so important. In fact, these partnerships can be seen as the new prime movers in retail technology, particularly in the area of electronic data interchange (EDI).

Keys to future developments

EFT and EDI are the keys to future developments. From the point of view of service, the idea of streamlining transactions to a card swipe—EFT—is highly attractive. However, it has to be backed with excellent security, for example regularly updated hot-card lists, facilities for authorisation for above-the-floor-limit transactions.

EDI cuts paperwork and the chance of errors by sending pre-formatted data between business partners. That is clearly of enormous benefit to wholesalers, and can help cut the administrative overheads for the individual retailer. Moving to EDI requires special software, but the major element is agreement and commitment between everyone in a particular trading community. Once in place, EDI helps cut paper-work dramatically: it is possible to re-order automatically using EDI, but facilities are available to review and edit orders. It's easier to do that than explain to the system why, for example, the sudden demand for chocolate eggs won't be sustained after Easter!

Retaining flexibility

The last decade has shown that the independent retailer must retain flexibility in the use of technology. Retailers can grow from stand-alone to networked systems, adding new facilities as and when they feel it appropriate, in the confidence that they will remain in the mainstream of technological and legislative developments.

And the future? As the community of technology users grows, the benefits of scale will certainly increase. But at the same time, there's a continuing and major role for technology in helping independent retailers play to their individual strengths. Store design and the positioning of products is one area to be explored: an EPoS system can provide prompt, accurate feedback on the impact of any changes. There is also discussion currently about credit card holders having to carry laser pictures of themselves as confirmation of identity.

Appropriate technology

AF Blakemore is one of the eight UK Spar wholesalers and is responsible for the Meridian Guild area. The area covers 300-plus stores in mid to north Wales, the Midlands and Humberside. The group's activities, which contributed to a turnover of around £230 million last year, also include cash-and-carry outlets, catering and shopfitting; it is a sophisticated user of technology, including computer-aided design (CAD) techniques for store design.

Involvement with retail technology goes back around ten years, when the company put dumb terminals into all the stores in its area for order entry. That was primarily for the wholesaler's benefit—orders went straight into the central computers, rather than having to be transcribed. 'It wasn't until 1988 that we started to migrate selected stores to true EPoS—picking up information as part of the sales transaction', said Jim Knowles, IT manager for AF Blakemore. That move had had to wait on the widespread adoption of bar coding. 'Over the next two years, systems were installed in 14 stores; in the first six months of 1991 another 13 went in, and we're now averaging one a week.'

Appropriate technology

That's an aggressive roll-out programme, but it's based on proven technology and established techniques. Jim Knowles certainly doesn't advocate technology for its own sake. 'The Spar group is highly aware of technology, but it wants technology that is appropriate. It's important to keep your eyes open for advances but, equally, you have to ask what those advances are going to do for the business. Successful implementations of technology have to be driven by wholesaler, retailer and supplier all working in partnership. They can't simply be imposed.'

Under AF Blakemore's implementation programme, the smaller stores are being offered the Omron RS3510, a low-cost entry point to scanning. Larger stores have a choice of systems, including the 'build as you need' Omron RS5500, a modular system which offers the retailer a range of scanners, scale interface, card reader, etc., to be added as and when required. Both systems leave the way open to add electronic funds transfer (EFT) again, when the retailer is ready.

Jim Knowles identifies two key areas where this technology is already helping the independent retailer.

It helps make the business more efficient. 'Retailers are there to run a business, and any technology has to help them do that—it is never an end in itself. We can now update retailers' price files automatically, in line with individual store pricing policies; scanning has effectively eliminated price errors at point of sale; control of stock levels, and monitoring of slow and fast movers are automated—it all helps to save time on

Figure 21.13 The TEC EPoS stock control system.

administration, speed customer throughput, and help keep stocks (and the money tied up in them) at the optimum level.'

Customer throughput may be increased, but the technology should also help to provide a better service. 'As far as customer service is concerned, we're well down the road, with scanners, itemised till receipts, and so on. These create a better image for the store, and a faster and more accurate service. There are small refinements to be made, but basically we're at the stage when we can start to concentrate on other areas.'

Real synergy

One of those areas is managerial control. There's a real synergy in the partnerships between the wholesaler and the retail group—every new scanner installed benefits the whole group, because it means more information is being picked up at point of sale. And the larger the sample of information to be analysed, the more accurate the results. Interpeting the information is not simple, as Jim Knowles points out. 'You need to be careful when looking at generic products, for example: to get useful information, you may have to combine figures for variants within a group.'

He sees this type of analysis as very much part of the support wholesalers should be offering their groups: 'Individually, yes, the retailer does stand to gain from using a scanner. But those gains are multiplied if he is only one of a larger group of retailers generating information at the point of sale.'

What about EFT? 'That's certainly the next step. We're looking to have an EFT solution in place around the middle of this year. It needs careful co-ordination and liaison with everyone concerned—the technology suppliers, the banks, the consolidation bureaux.' That's an attractive prospect for retailers, for whom it must seem that the wheel has come full circle, with EFT offering the prospect of the healthy cash flow that cash itself provides.

(Source: Independent Grocer)

1. What sort of management information could an EPoS system supply?
2. How would such information improve the way in which retailers manage their organizations?
3. What are the benefits of EAN and bar codes?

4. Examine the dangers of electronic funds transfer and using a card swipe.
5. If you were a retailer and were considering updating and further developing the technology in your organization, what considerations would be of importance to you, and what sorts of processes would you undertake before making any investment?

4   Developing your own IT needs

Examine your own IT skills and then try to identify your IT needs using the checklist below. Having developed your profile, discuss with your tutor how you could improve your IT skills.

Indicate by ticking the appropriate box what, in your opinion, is your *level of experience* with the skills mentioned:

1. I am experienced at this.
2. I have some experience of this.
3. I have no experience of this.

Indicate by ticking the appropriate box what, in your opinion, is your *level of success* with the skills mentioned:

1. I am successful at this.
2. I am reasonably successful at this.
3. I have rarely been successful at this.

	Experience			Success		
	1	2	3	1	2	3
Using a microcomputer						
Using a word processor						
Using a painting package						
Using a DTP						
Using a spreadsheet						
Using a printer						
Using a database						
Using a plotter						
Using a colour printer						

Other experiences (specify)

Suggested reading

Gondran, M., *An Introduction to Expert Systems*. McGraw-Hill, 1986.
Gremillion, L. and Pyburn, P., *Computers and Information Systems in Business*. McGraw-Hill, 1988.
Pepperell, D., *Communication Skills: A Thematic Approach*. Stanley Thornes, 1988.
Stafford, C. E., *People in Business*. Cambridge University Press, 1991.

22
The influence of the economy on organizations

The economic system in which business organizations operate exerts an extremely powerful influence on their success or failure. It is a system made up of many parts, each of which is dependent on changes made in other parts of the system. National economic systems are in turn part of an international system, in which changes of great magnitude frequently occur. The economic system is also intertwined with other systems—environmental, technological, political, social, legal and cultural. The informed business decision-maker needs to be outward-looking to be constantly aware of forces and developments in a rapidly changing world.

National income

The national economic system produces thousands of different outputs in many interlinked markets.

The link between consumers and producers in the national economy is shown in Fig. 22.1. Individuals offer their services as factors of production and by working, letting land, investing and being enterprising receive wages, rent, interest and profits. They are then able to buy goods or services from producers with these incomes.

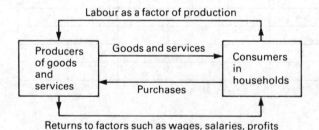

Figure 22.1 A simple economic model.

National income is made up of the total flow of the goods and services produced by factors of production in a particular time period. When national income rises we talk about economic growth taking place in the system. This can lead to improved standards of living.

Figures measuring national income can be used to assess living standards. They can also be broken down to show changes in the structure of the economy and to provide comparisons with other countries.

Measuring income generation

The national income accounts provide three methods of measuring income generation in a country.

The income approach

This involves counting up all the incomes received by citizens in a time period; e.g.

> Incomes from employment and self-employment
> + Interest
> + Business profits
> + Rents

The output method

This method counts up the value of outputs made by industries in an economy. It involves summing the values added by each industry. For example, if the steel industry buys in £100 million worth of inputs from other industries and sells £200 million worth of outputs to other industries, then it will have added value to the economy of £100 million:

$$£200 \text{ m outputs} - £100 \text{ m inputs} = £100 \text{ m value added}$$

In calculating national output, the following method is used:

> Value added by all primary industries
> + Value added by all secondary industries
> + Value added by all tertiary industries

The expenditure approach

This method measures all final expenditures on goods and services. It is important that only final expenditures are counted (to avoid what is called double-counting). If I buy a sandwich it is a final expenditure, likewise a litre of petrol; if a school buys chalk and exercise books those are final expenditures. However, if a business buys raw materials this is not a final expenditure, because the raw materials will go into *making something else*. These raw materials would not be counted under the final expenditure method (unless they are stockpiled for use in another year).

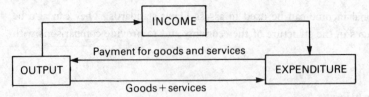

NATIONAL OUTPUT = NATIONAL INCOME = NATIONAL EXPENDITURE

Figure 22.2 Identity of income, output and expenditure.

In a simple economic model (see fig. 22.2) we expect the three methods of calculating national income to produce the same result—because when goods are produced, the factors of production that make the goods receive all the income from making goods in factor rewards; if they spend all the money they receive, it will then return to the producers of the output that households buy.

Equilibrium

An equilibrium state is one in which there is balance; i.e.. there is no tendency to change.

An equilibrium level of income for a country is one that does not change from one period to another. If all goods and services are bought and all incomes are spent, a country will be in equilibrium. A disturbance in the equilibrium position will occur if income, expenditure, or output increases or decreases for some reason.

In simple economics, we talk about a *withdrawal* from the circular flow when money is taken out; we talk about an *injection* when fresh money is put into the system.

We must now look at what happens when injections or leakages disturb the existing circular flow.

Injections and withdrawals in the economy

Much of our understanding of the complicated forces that govern the working of the UK economy is drawn from the work of John Maynard Keynes.

Keynes argued that demand and supply analysis could be applied when examining the whole economy. Until then, economists had argued that the economy would sort itself out and that full employment was the natural state of affairs. These economists believed that if demand in the economy increased then producers would respond with increased supply; if demand fell then supply would fall. If supply fell workers would be laid off. These workers would seek new jobs. Because the supply of labour would be increased, wages would fall. With cheaper labour employers would take on more people until full employment returned. The economists prior to Keynes were known as the *classical economists*. They believed that the economy, if left alone by government, was a self-righting system in which prices would restore full employment after a temporary period of recession.

Keynesian economics

Keynes, however, disagreed with the classical economists. He believed that full employment was not a natural state of affairs. He argued that the supply of goods in the economy and the demand for goods were determined by different groups of people. There was no guarantee that full employment would occur. The economy was therefore likely to go through periods of upturn and downturn. In some circumstances the economy could get stuck in a long period of depression, as in the 1930s.

Keynes showed that the level of output and the employment of resources depended upon:

- Total demand for goods and services in the economy (*aggregate demand*)
- Total supply of goods and services in the economy (*aggregate supply*)

As with supply curves for individual products, the aggregate supply curve slopes upwards from the bottom left as the economy increases its output towards higher prices (Fig. 22.3). But there will always be a limit to supply, and this is at the point where the factors of production are fully employed. At the full-employment point the supply curve will be vertical (given the current state of technology). The aggregate demand curve will slope downwards from the top left because as prices fall total demand for goods and services will increase.

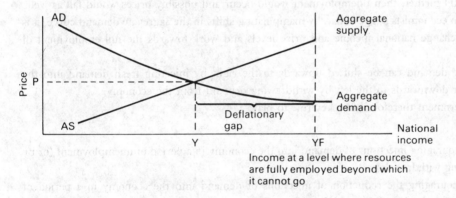

Figure 22.3 The deflationary gap.

The actual level of national income at any time will be established at the point where the aggregate demand curve intersects the aggregate supply curve. However, this will rarely be at full employment.

The difference between the *equilibrium national income* (where AD cuts AS) and the *full-employment* point shows the extent to which it is possible to expand national income to reduce the unemployment of resources. The difference between equilibrium national income and full employment is known as the *deflationary gap*.

However, it is also possible to have situations in which resources are already fully employed. Increases in aggregate demand cannot then be met by increases in output. Instead, increased demand will be met by increased prices.

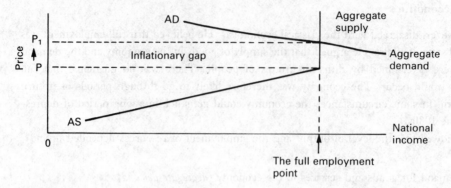

Figure 22.4 The inflationary gap.

In Fig. 22.4 we can see that prices would be at P if aggregate demand were equal to aggregate supply at the full-employment point. However, because there is *excess demand* in the economy, prices are pushed up to P₁. We call this excess demand the *inflationary gap*.

If demand decreased we might fall back to the full-employment point with no inflation. If it decreased still further, then unemployment would occur and possibly prices would fall as well.

Keynesian economists suggest that, by manipulating shifts in the aggregate demand curve, it is possible to change national income and price levels and work towards the full employment of resources.

Aggregate demand can be shifted upwards to the right by injecting fresh demand into the economy, or downwards to the left by withdrawing demand from the economy.

The government therefore has a key role to play:

1. By encouraging injections of demand into the economy in a period of unemployment (or by reducing withdrawals).
2. By encouraging the reduction of injections of demand into the economy in a period of inflation (or by increasing withdrawals).

A complex model of the economy

Figure 22.5 illustrates a more complex circular flow model indicating injections and withdrawals from the circular flow.

Injections into the circular flow of income include:

- Government expenditure (G)
- Investment (I)
- Exports (X)

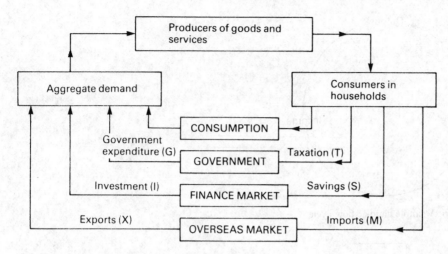

Figure 22.5 A complex circular flow model of the economy.

Withdrawals from the circular flow of income include:

- Taxation (T)
- Savings (S)
- Imports (M)

If an equilibrium state is to exist in the economy so that there is no tendency for national income to change from one period to the next, then withdrawals need to equal injections:

$$\text{Injections} = \text{Withdrawals}$$
$$G + I + X = T + S + M$$

Let us now look at the components of the circular flow in greater detail.

Output, income and expenditure

Firms produce goods. They pay incomes to the factors of production that made those goods. These factor rewards are received by people who live in households. Households then spend their incomes buying all the goods that have been produced (Fig. 22.6).

A major component of this circular flow is *consumer spending*. For example, an imaginary household receives an income of £1000 a month (mainly in the form of wages, with some interest, some rent and a little bit of profit). Quite understandably, they will consume nearly all of this income on housing, food, clothes, petrol, entertainment, etc. If they were to spend *all* of their income on consumer goods, we would have a very simple circular flow model (Fig. 22.7). However, as we have seen in the more complex model, we need to examine injections into and leakages from this circular flow.

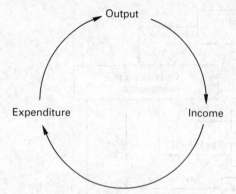

Figure 22.6 A simple circular flow cycle.

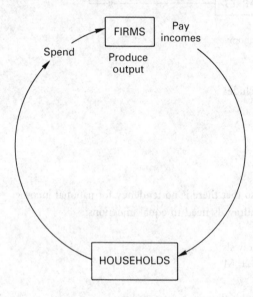

Figure 22.7 A simple circular flow model: all income spent.

Injections

Government

In Chapter 4 we saw that the government plays a role in the economy in order to limit some of the defects of the market system by providing the following:

1. *Public goods and services* These are goods or services of which the consumption by one person does not reduce the amount that is available for use by others. Public goods include police protection, defence, streetlighting, etc. As it is almost impossible to exclude anyone from using these goods and services, it would be virtually impossible for them to be provided by the private sector.

2. *Merit goods*   These benefit the person who directly consumes them as well as other members of society. By having a well educated population, individuals benefit and so does society. A new traffic system will mean that people can get to work more quickly and will also reduce congestion. These benefits are *externalities*, and governments will encourage their consumption by subsidizing them or providing them free of charge.

3. *Monopolies*   Governments in the past have been concerned about the provision of certain necessities by the private sector. They were worried about the possibility that private operators would charge high prices and exploit consumers. By supplying services through a government-owned corporation, they were able to set minimum standards, provide a national network, reduce average costs and gain benefits from economies of scale.

4. *Income redistribution*   A vast proportion of government expenditure consists of transferring payments towards low-income households. Payments of this kind include pensions, allowances, social security and unemployment benefits.

Successive privatizations and a movement away from emphasis on the public sector have been a key feature of the 1980s and 1990s.

Investment

Investment refers to additions to the capital stock of the economy such as new factories, machinery and roads. It will include anything that adds to the physical stock of wealth. Investment or capital goods are not immediately consumed; their purpose is to facilitate the production of further goods which are for consumption.

Exports

Exports are goods and services sold abroad, in return for which there is a flow of money into the circular flow.

Withdrawals

Savings

Many people save a portion of their income rather than spending it. Over recent years the main savers have been the household and business sectors. Savings tend to depend on the level of a household's current income or likely future income. They are also influenced by interest rates.

Saving and dis-saving can be illustrated by means of a savings function diagram (Fig. 22.8). This shows that at low levels of income dis-saving will occur, while at higher levels of income saving becomes possible. This is as true for individual households (an individual's savings function) as it is for a national economy (national savings function).

Taxes

Taxation helps to finance government activity. *Fiscal policy* is used by the government to alter the relationship between its spending and the taxes it imposes to meet particular objectives (see Fig. 22.9). For example, in a period of unemployment the government may want to spend more than it collects in taxes to pump extra aggregate demand into the economy; whereas in a period of

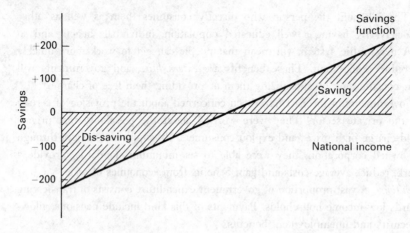

Figure 22.8 A simple savings function.

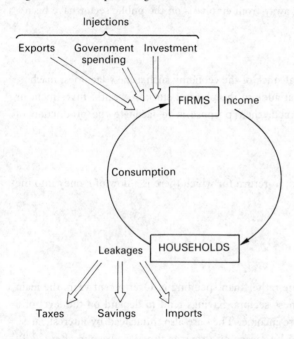

Figure 22.9 Withdrawals and injections.

inflation it may want to suck excess demand out of the economy by spending less than it takes in taxes. The government will adopt different budgetary strategies in different situations:

- Surplus budget: Expenditure less than tax revenue
- Deficit budget: Expenditure greater than tax revenue
- Balanced budget: Expenditure equal to tax revenue

Taxation results in a withdrawal from the circular flow.

In addition to raising money through taxes, the government can borrow money for long periods (through the capital market) and short periods (through the money market).

Direct taxes are levied on income or earnings and are paid to the Department of Inland Revenue. They include:

- Taxes on income such as income tax
- Taxes on profits such as corporation tax
- Taxes on capital such as inheritance tax

Indirect taxes are levied on expenditure as part of a payment for goods and services. They are called indirect because it is the retailer (or other middle person) who pays the tax charged to the government, rather than the consumer paying the tax directly.

Value added tax (VAT) is levied on selling prices and is calculated at each stage of production. *Customs duties* are levied on certain goods coming into the country and *excise duties* are levied on other goods to gain revenue for the government. We are affected in many ways by licences, car taxes and stamp duties.

Direct taxes are more likely to be *progressive*, i.e. to take proportionately larger amounts away from the rich in order to reduce extreme inequalities in wealth or income. However, it is often argued that progressive taxes discourage effort and hard work (see Fig. 22.10).

Many indirect taxes are said to be *regressive* in that they take a larger percentage of the income of the lower paid. The cost of a television licence will probably take a significantly larger proportion of an old age pensioner's income than that of a business executive. An important advantage of indirect taxes (from the government's point of view) is that they are 'hidden'; i.e. people are often unaware that they are paying them.

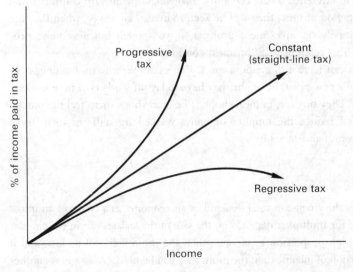

Figure 22.10 Types of taxes.

Imports

Imports are goods and services that enter a country. Money is withdrawn from the circular flow to pay for imports.

Playing with the variables

Keynes argued that it was possible to interfere with the economic system to help the market to operate more effectively. In a situation where demand is insufficient to create full employment, there are a number of options available:

1. Encourage consumers to spend more, e.g. by giving them more money in their pockets and by reducing incentives to save, e.g. by lowering interest rates.
2. Encourage investment, e.g. by giving tax incentives to businesses to invest more, or by lowering interest rates so that money becomes cheaper to borrow.
3. Increases the government's own expenditure, particularly on projects that will create jobs.
4. Encourage exports, e.g. by subsidizing them.
5. Discourage savings, perhaps by offering lower interest rates on government saving schemes.
6. Lower direct and indirect taxes.
7. Discourage imports, perhaps by putting restrictions on them.

Demand-side economics

Keynes concentrated on the demand-side policies as a means to influence the economy. In particular, he emphasized that investment demand is quite volatile and is the key to understanding the need for government interference in the economy. If business people are confident that the economy will boom for a period of time, they will be keen to invest. However, when they are gloomy they will cut back heavily on investment projects. If you watch business news programmes you will frequently hear references to 'business confidence'.

Changes in demand factors can have a dramatic impact. For example, when a building contractor loses a contract to build a new plant, he or she may have to lay off workers. These workers then forgo their wage packets. They buy less in local shops. The local shops then 'feel the pinch'. They buy in fewer stocks and reduce the number of hours worked by staff. In turn, these shopworkers have smaller incomes and *they* buy less.

The multiplier effect

The multiplier effect measures the change in total demand in an economy as a result of an initial change in demand. The size of the multiplier depends on the size of the leakages from the circular flow. If leakages constitute a high proportion of income, then the multiplier will be low, and if leakages make up a low proportion of income then the multiplier will be high. (*Leakages* is another name for withdrawals.) The multiplier can be measured mathematically in the following way:

$$\text{Multiplier} = \frac{1}{\text{Marginal propensity to leak}}$$

The *marginal propensity to leak* (MPL) is the fraction of extra income earned by the average person that is leaked from the circular flow; for example, if my income increases by £1, how much of that income will I withdraw from the circular flow? The marginal propensity to leak is obtained by adding together the marginal propensity to save, the marginal propensity to be taxed and the marginal propensity to buy imports.

This sounds complicated but it is not. For example, if the typical citizen saves one-quarter of his or her extra income, is taxed one-eighth of his or her marginal income and spends one-eighth of marginal income on imports, then the marginal propensity to leak in the economy is one-half. The formula is:

$$\text{Multiplier} = \frac{1}{\text{MPL}} = \frac{1}{\frac{1}{2}} = 2$$

The multiplier is a useful tool because it enables us to calculate the effect of an initial change in demand. For example, it will indicate to government: 'if you increase your own spending by £x then the total effect on the economy once the multiplier has worked through will be £y.'

The accelerator

The accelerator is another simple but useful tool. It shows us that, even if consumer demand falls by just a little, this may have a much larger consequential effect on the machinery and capital goods industries.

One way of classifying industry is into companies that produce capital goods and those that produce consumer goods (see Fig. 22.11). Consumer goods producers buy machinery from the capital goods industries. And each year they will need to replace machinery that is wearing out; for example, they may replace 10 per cent of their machinery on a regular basis each year. Now if the economy is in a slump they may not buy any new machinery at all. Just imagine the effect if all consumer goods producers did the same thing: there would be little demand for capital goods; the capital goods industry would have a massive downturn in orders; many capital goods companies would be crippled. We can therefore say that a relatively small downturn in orders for consumer goods will have a vastly accelerated effect on capital goods companies.

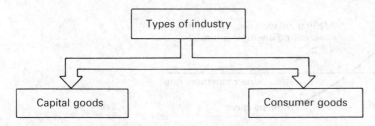

Figure 22.11 Classification of industry.

It is not surprising, therefore, that capital goods producers look carefully at the economic forecasts of booms and slumps. When they are gloomy they will start to make cutbacks, and these cutbacks may be multiplied into a slump in consumption which feeds back into an accelerated slump in investment. The accelerator and multiplier effects therefore work together.

The impact of demand

Our demand-side analysis so far has shown the tremendous power of demand to influence the fortunes of the economy, and hence of business organizations. Falling demand leads to recession, unemployment and wasted resources. On the other hand, excess demand can lead to rising prices and inflation. Rising investment can have a multiplier effect on expenditure. The same is true of increases in exports, government spending and/or, indeed, an increase in consumer spending. If demand rises and supply is not able to expand at the same rate, then inflation will result.

Most economists recognize that there is a trade-off between unemployment and inflation. If the government is worried about inflation, then it will need to dampen down demand. It can do this by, for example, raising interest rates to reduce borrowing, and cutting back its own spending. This will lead to a slow-down in the economy and to unemployment. If the government feels that the unemployment level is unacceptably high, then it can increase demand, perhaps by lowering interest rates and increasing its own spending.

The Phillips curve

This is an attempt to show a statistical relationship between unemployment and inflation. When inflation is rising unemployment is falling, and when unemployment is rising inflation is falling. Today the notion of the Phillips curve is sometimes used to describe this trade-off (see Fig. 22.12). However, it is clear that the position of the Phillips curve moves from one period to the next (and also that at times the two variables can move together in the same direction).

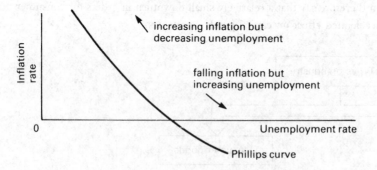

Figure 22.12 The Phillips curve.

Supply-side economics

During the 1980s there was a big switch in economic policy away from demand-side towards supply-side theories. While demand management had worked very well from 1945 until the 1970s, the policy eventually ran into trouble.

After the war most governments used Keynesian policies (i.e. the ideas of Keynes) in managing their economies. To counteract unemployment, the government would use its own spending to pump up demand in the economy. However, a major fault of this policy was that outdated industries were artificially supported. Inefficient units, instead of being cut out, continued to survive on government subsidies. This meant that the United Kingdom was losing its competitive edge in world markets.

The supply of goods (i.e. output) in the economy rose very slowly in the 1960s and 1970s. Because supply was rising slowly, an increase in demand led to both rising prices and an increased reliance on foreign imports. Too many imports led to a growth in the national debt, and the government was then forced to cut back on spending to reduce imports. Britain experienced *stagflation*—a stagnant economy that was not growing, coupled with inflation. Demand management did not seem to be working.

The cure was thought to lie in some new policies that the Conservative government began to introduce in 1979. Those policies concentrated on increasing supply rather than demand. A whole host of measures were introduced to get supply going. These included:

1. Reducing income tax to encourage people to work harder and for longer hours.
2. Reducing benefits to those out of work.
3. Reducing subsidies to loss-making industries.
4. Privatizing previously nationalized industries.
5. Reducing the size of the civil service.
6. Reducing government spending.
7. Passing laws to reduce trade union powers.
8. Taking measures against monopolies and restrictive practices.
9. Encouraging competition among groups such as solicitors, opticians and even in the health service and schools.
10. Emphasizing the importance of education and training, e.g. through a national curriculum that focused on areas such as numeracy and literacy for all children; improving the status of vocational qualifications, e.g. vocational A-levels.
11. Doing away with minimum wage laws.

The emphasis in these policies was on using supply as the means to drive the economy forward.

Balancing expenditure and revenue

Any form of government—whether at local, national or European level—needs to raise money in order to carry out its expenditure policies. Many supply-side economists feel that, the smaller the role the government plays in the economy, the more efficient the system is likely to be. Moreover, they point out that the larger the part that government plays in running things, the more employees it will need to carry out purely administrative tasks; for example, in 1993 the Scottish Office—which looks after the interests of 5 million people—employed over 6240 officials. On a wider front, we are used to hearing criticisms of the bureaucracy of the European Community at Brussels.

From 1994 the British government will announce its plans for expenditure and revenue-raising both at the same time (in the autumn).

The major sources of UK government revenue for 1993/4 are shown in Table 22.1

Table 22.1   UK government revenue, 1993

	£bn
Income tax	57.5
VAT	39.9
National insurance	39.1
Corporate tax	14.6
Petrol/derv	11.8
Tobacco	6.6
Drinks	5.5
Vehicle excise duty	3.7
Stamp duty	1.7
Inheritance tax	1.3
Betting and gaming	1.1
Capital gains tax	1.0

Taxation affects businesses in that taxes such as VAT add to costs of production. Also, corporation tax is charged on business profits. The administration of taxes, e.g. the paperwork involved, is another cost. However, businesses also clearly benefit from all the services that government provides, for example roads for transport links, the law courts to regulate business activity, refuse collection to take away waste.

Supporting strategic planning

In recent years there has been a groundswell of opinion that the government should intervene in the economy in a strategic way. Today, as we have seen in earlier chapters, the emphasis in business life is on flexibility and strategic planning.

Strategic planning refers to a firm's plan of action based on a comparison of its strengths and weaknesses with those of its competitors. Whereas central planning involves extrapolating past trends into the future, strategic planning seeks new ways to develop competitive advantage in an environment of change. Strategy involves increasing an organization's efficiency or strength relative to those of its competitors. Competitive advantage replaces profit maximization as the goal of the business enterprise. Profit maximization focuses on price competition; competitive advantage involves price competition, but also marketing ability, product engineering, creative flair, basic research, quality, technology, leadership and service. Corporate planning therefore needs to be built into all the layers of an organization.

On an international basis, countries are trading in a highly competitive world market. Competitiveness is given a spur by competition between firms within a country. However, there is also scope for the government to encourage groups of firms in an industrial sector to work together to create international competitiveness.

In Japan the Ministry of International Trade and Industry (MITI) works closely with industry to develop a strategy for the development of industrial sectors. MITI decided to establish industries that require an intensive employment of capital and technology, such as steel, oil refining, petrochemicals, motor cars, aircraft, industrial machinery of all sorts and electronics, including electronic computers. Working closely with industry, MITI outlined plans for developing the contours of industrial policy and enterprise strategies.

These policies have been very successful. Japanese government agencies such as MITI and the Economic Planning Agency intervene in the market to promote strategic planning at the enterprise, sector and sub-sector levels in order to promote international competitiveness. Individual firms pursuing product competition are backed by an institutional infrastructure that helps with the refinement, testing and co-ordination of the firms' strategic plans and shares the costs of technology development and international market promotion.

In the mid-1990s there has been an increasing emphasis in the United Kingdom on the role of the government as a partner in the process of industrial development. These sentiments are reflected in a book written by Michael Heseltine (*Where There's a Will*), who in 1993 was the Minister for Industry:

> The capitalist economies with which we have to compete do not operate on the theory held in Britain that the government is an onlooker in the industrial game or at best a referee. In most of these countries, there are partnerships between the government and the industrial world.
>
> France and Germany share with Japan the sense of national purpose which so many observers note in our competitors but do not find in Britain. This purpose is based on partnership.
>
> In many of the high-technology fields, the role of the government is the manifestation of French will. . . . We would not have a major civil airframe manufacturing capability in Europe today if it were not for France. We would not have a launcher capability in the space field but for France . . . .
>
> It is not intervention that is wrong in the modern world: it is unavoidable. What was wrong before was the subsidising of losses and the cosiness and lack of professionalism associated with that. Intervention and featherbedding are not the same thing. The trick is to distinguish between them.
>
> The evidence is that there will be continuing development and growth in, for instance, aerospace, robotics, telecommunications and biotechnology. These are all areas which Britain's competitor governments are supporting. Government and industry in Britain must talk together about what markets exist, could be created or are under threat.

Unemployment and inflation

We have already seen that there is usually a trade-off between unemployment and inflation. Part of government policy-making involves deciding what economic objectives to give priority to; for example:

- Should we focus on the growth of national income?
- Should we seek to reduce unemployment?
- Should our priority be to keep inflation down?
- Should we try to redistribute income and wealth?
- Should we emphasize increasing exports and limiting imports?

After the Second World War all political parties committed themselves to working towards keeping unemployment down. In recent years, however, the Conservative government has emphasized controlling inflation as a key policy target.

Unemployment

Although unemployment refers to the fact that factors of production generally are not being fully utilized to produce goods and services, we tend to focus on the unemployment of *labour*.

Unemployment exists where people are willing and able to work but are unable to find work. Figures are obtained from a monthly count of those registered as unemployed and claiming benefit at offices throughout the country and are expressed as a percentage of the working population. In Britain during the 1950s and early 1960s the numbers unemployed were around 300 000, which was less than 2 per cent of the workforce. This era was described as one of full employment, as the unemployment figures were at about the lowest that could be achieved, given that some people are always *frictionally unemployed*, i.e. between jobs, whether voluntarily or not, and waiting for work to crop up. Unemployment rose gradually during the 1960s, increased steadily during the 1970s and doubled during the early 1980s before falling back. In the early 1990s unemployment moved up towards 3 million but began to decline again in 1993.

We have already considered *de-industrialization* as a major cause of unemployment (see page 56).

Areas in which certain types of industry were concentrated geographically, and which were therefore dependent on these industries, felt the harsh realities of unemployment more than any others. The term *structural unemployment* refers to unemployment resulting from major changes in the structure of demand for particular product sectors.

A major cause of unemployment on a national scale is the booms and slumps in the world economy. The UK experiences a series of regular cycles of boom and slump. *Cyclical unemployment* arises during periods in which there is a downturn in demand on a national scale.

Another cause of unemployment is the development of new technology, both within organizations and within wider industrial sectors. We use the term *technological unemployment* to describe this situation. The fear of new technology has led a number of trade unions to resist changes in working practice.

Sometimes industries are overstaffed. It is possible to argue that some labour is *underemployed*; a major criticism of Eastern European countries is that ten people are doing jobs that could be done by five.

The causes of unemployment can be divided into demand- and supply-side factors. A lack of demand for goods and services reduces economic activity and contributes to recession. Whereas increasing spending through injections into the economy would work towards solving any demand deficiency, the Conservative government has preferred to use monetary policy (see below page 683) with a tight fiscal stance and has given the control of inflation a higher priority than reducing unemployment. On the supply side, the working population has increased during the 1990s and, inevitably, unemployment has risen, reflecting its increasing size.

Inflation

Inflation occurs where the general price level is persistently moving upwards. (An alternative definition used by monetarists is 'Too much money chasing too few goods.')

Creeping inflation is a condition experienced by most developed countries since 1945, whereby continued but not excessive rises have taken place in average price levels. If people's expectations are based on the past, when inflation rates were low, then increases in the inflation rate will be unforeseen but low; however, as inflation rates increase, consumers will start to anticipate higher increases and will adjust their behaviour accordingly. If inflation then really begins to accelerate and dramatic rises in prices take place, at hundreds or thousands of per cent, the resulting condition is said to be that of *galloping* or *hyperinflation*.

In the United Kingdom prior to the 1970s high rates of inflation were linked with low rates of unemployment and vice versa. Then during the 1970s, as this trade-off disappeared, *stagflation* developed, and high rates existed side-by-side with high unemployment.

There are three general causes of inflation.

Demand-pull inflation

'Demand-pull' refers to a situation in which aggregate demand persistently exceeds aggregate supply and prices are constantly being pulled upwards. In Fig. 22.13 you can see that an economy can initially increase output without price rises. There then follows a zone in which both price and output rise along the aggregate supply curve. Finally, the aggregate supply curve is represented by a vertical line whereby it is impossible to increase output further and only prices will rise.

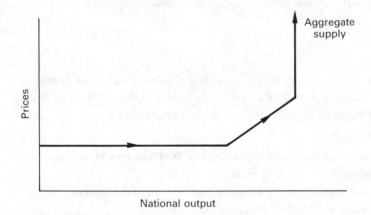

Figure 22.13 The aggregate supply curve.

Under demand-pull inflation the aggregate demand curve moves upwards and to the right, and this leads to an increase in price rises. Demand-pull inflation occurs when supply in the economy responds poorly to increases in demand (see Fig. 22.14). (Hence the emphasis in supply-side economics is to extend the range over which the aggregate supply curve represents rising real output.)

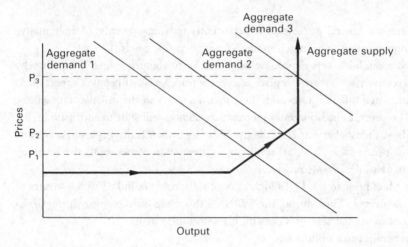

Figure 22.14 Demand-pull inflation.

Cost-push inflation

Cost-push inflation occurs where rising costs provide better rewards to the factors of production which then leads to rising prices. *The wage–price spiral* is the most dangerous feature of this type of inflation; increasing prices will cause increases in wage demands from employees, and if these do not match increases in productivity will lead to a further rise in costs and therefore prices, and then further rises in wage demands, and so on. Many attribute the rises in inflation rates in the 1970s largely to increasing oil prices and inflationary pay settlements.

Monetarism

Monetarists argue that increases in the money supply are a cause of inflation and that inflation can be brought under control by reducing the rate of growth of the money supply. Milton Friedman, the most famous advocate of monetarism, lists what he calls five simple truths:

1. Inflation arises from a more rapid increase in the quantity of money than of output.
2. Governments can determine the quantity of money.
3. A slower rate of increase in the quantity of money is the only cure for inflation.
4. Inflation develops over years and can only be cured over years.
5. Side-effects are unavoidable.

The effects of inflation

Inflation has a number of effects which are significant to business organizations.

The distribution of income

Inflation influences different types of income groups in different ways. Those who lose tend to have fixed incomes in money terms, while those who gain tend to have commission-based incomes related to sales values. Inflation tends to encourage borrowing, as loans are repaid in money that is now worth less while those who lend are concerned about whether it is worth their while to do so. Debtors therefore gain and creditors lose. Those whose bargaining power is strong are able to ensure that their salaries keep up or move ahead of inflation, while those with weaker bargaining power tend to see their salaries fall behind.

Expectations

If inflation persists it will distort expectations. A society used to inflation will try to stay ahead of prices by anticipating price rises, and this can lead to a wage–price spiral.

Investment

Inflation can disrupt a firm's investment plans as it finds itself in a situation in which it is difficult to predict expenditure, incomes and interest rates. Interest rates will tend to be high as a result of government policies and also so that those who lend can earn a real rate of interest, and this discourages investment. The falling value of money may encourage spending rather than saving/lending and so may reduce funds for investment.

External effects

If other countries are not experiencing similar high rates of inflation and there is not a compensating adjustment in foreign exchange rates, home-produced goods will be more expensive to foreign buyers and this will dampen export sales. At the same time, imports will be more competitive with home-produced goods and this could lead to balance of payments difficulties (see page 686).

The monetary system

The success of a country's economic system depends on its monetary system. Money is often likened to the oil that helps the wheels of industry and commerce to run smoothly.

Early developments

When early man began to develop skills, and to specialize, a limited form of trading using *barter* was developed, whereby goods and services were exchanged for other goods and services. Although barter enabled surpluses to be traded, however, it was often difficult to find someone with what you wanted who wanted what you had to offer. There were also problems in deciding on exchange rates and on how to give change. What was required was a form of money that would be generally acceptable to all members of society. This money needed to perform the following functions:

1. *A medium of exchange*   Everyone would have to be willing to accept money as a form of payment.
2. *A unit of account*   The value of items would have to be measurable in money units; e.g. one biro = 10p, one sports car = £20 000, etc.
3. *A store of value*   It would have to be possible to store wealth in the form of money for future use.
4. *A standard for deferred payments*   Money would need to enable debts to be built up in one period and paid off in another, so that a trader could sell goods on credit, issue an IOU and expect payment at a later date.

Over the centuries in various parts of the world, a wide variety of different commodities have been used as money, including sharks' teeth, cowrie shells and precious stones. Some were more successful than others. As well as being generally acceptable, money needs to be scarce enough to be valuable. At the same time, it needs to be easily recognizable. Salt is capable of divisibility, but lacks durability. Stones cannot be carried around.

Precious metals have many of the properties required of a money form. Gold and silver are easily recognizable, scarce and hence valuable. They have use value as expensive ornaments and jewellery. They can be shaped and divided. For these reasons, precious metals came to be used as a form of money in many parts of the world. In the United Kingdom the goldsmiths played an increasingly prominent part in handling money from the seventeenth century onwards. Gold and silver was increasingly deposited with goldsmiths for safekeeping in their strongrooms and vaults. Depositors were issued with receipts called 'promissory notes', enabling them to reclaim quantities of gold and silver on demand. These receipts were themselves often used as a form of payment. Instead of paying for valuable items in gold and silver, the promissory notes could simply change hands. If I wanted to buy an acre of land from Mr Smith, I could simply sign on the back of a note to say that it now belonged to Mr Smith.

Goldsmiths soon began to issue bankers' notes for set amounts, e.g. £10, £20. These were the first bank notes.

As only a fixed proportion of the gold left in the vaults was ever used, goldsmiths started to lend some of it out. They had become bankers, and were the forerunners of the *retail banks* which are today one-stop financial supermarkets providing a wide range of services.

The Bank of England

The Bank of England was founded in 1694 because William III was short of money to finance the war against France. In return for a Royal Charter, the Bank of England lent him the money. From this early privileged position, the Bank went on to play a central part in our financial system. As a result of successive Bank Charter Acts protecting the position of the Bank, it finally became the sole issuer of notes in 1928.

Because the smooth running of the financial system is so vital to the economy, it is important for the Bank of England to closely supervise and monitor the operation of financial institutions. Confidence in the financial system is imperative. Since the Banking Act 1987, the Bank of England now supervises all deposit-taking institutions, and the name 'Bank' is restricted to authorized institutions with a capital of £5 million or more.

A major role of the Bank of England is to advise the Treasury on the various *monetary policies* necessary to steer the economy in a particular direction and to suggest ways in which this can be done.

Monetary policies are policies designed to influence one or a combination of the following:

- The supply of money
- The demand for money
- The price of money

Money supply is measured by a number of different aggregates or totals. Each of these represents a different level of liquidity. (*Liquidity* means the ease with which assets can be converted into money.) Many economists believe that there is a direct link between the quantity of money in the economy and the level of spending that occurs: in simple terms, the more money in existence, the greater the level of spending. If the spending power in the economy increases faster than the quantity of goods available to be bought, then prices will be pushed up. The problem, however, is finding a definition of money that gives an accurate measure of spending power.

The government frequently changes the way it measures the money supply—you will read about M0, M1, M2, M3, M4, M5 and many others. Some definitions, such as M0, concentrate on highly liquid assets such as notes and coins, money in bank tills and other bank assets which are very close to being immediate cash. Other definitions, such as M5, include highly liquid assets but also less liquid ones such as National Savings certificates, which can be turned in for cash but only after a fixed period of time.

The Bank of England is active in the following three areas in its pursuit of government monetary policies.

Bank lending

It can restrict bank lending to suit economic conditions by influencing interest rates. Higher rates lead to a squeeze on credit and a fall in bank lending, and lower rates lead to an increase in bank lending. A sudden rise in interest rates can cause severe embarrassment to businesses that have borrowed money. They may find it increasingly difficult to meet interest rate payments, resulting in cash flow problems. In the 1990s a number of commercial banks have been severely criticized for being too harsh on businesses.

In the early 1990s the government increased interest rates quite strongly in an attempt to damp down on spending in the economy and thereby cut back on inflationary pressures. This policy had an effect on mortgages and the housing market in the following way:

1. People with mortgages suffered a reduction in their spending power through having to pay more interest.
2. With house prices no longer rising overall, personal wealth rose only very slowly. People were thus not able to use their rising house prices as an asset against which to increase their borrowing.
3. With house prices under pressure, housing sales slumped. This depressed spending on household durables such as carpets, curtains, cookers and fridges.

In 1993 inflation fell to just a few per cent. The government therefore allowed interest rates to fall. Borrowing then became more attractive and saving less attractive. This encouraged a recovery of the economy.

Funding

The gilt-edged market provides the bulk of money that government borrows. *Gilt-edged* stocks are fixed-term government securities that pay regular interest. By selling gilt-edged securities to the non-bank private sector, the Bank of England reduces the impact of the public sector borrowing requirement (PSBR) on the money supply by soaking up funds in the markets.

Exchange rates

Exchange rates are the link between the domestic economy and the rest of the world. They are important when considering monetary conditions such as inflation and interest rates. The Bank of England supervises exchange rates and carries out government policies by buying pounds if sterling is weak and selling pounds if sterling is too strong.

Discount houses

Discount houses are unique to the British banking system and have a key role to play in helping the Bank of England to exercise monetary controls over the economy.

The traditional function of discount houses has been to discount bills of exchange. As a result of trade and communication difficulties in the eighteenth century, bills of exchange developed as a method of payment. Often, however, the merchants who accepted these as a form of post-dated payment needed funds more immediately. They took them to brokers who exchanged them for the value of the bill, less a discount for the service. Such brokers became known as discount houses, and today they still discount commercial bills of exchange to provide organizations with short-term funds.

Discount houses occupy an important link in the banking system by enabling commercial banks to place short-term deposits with them so that they can earn interest for periods varying between overnight (termed as being 'on call') and 14 days. This money is used to underwrite the weekly Treasury bill tender. Discount houses have an arrangement with the government to buy up any Treasury bills that are not purchased by other banks and private investors so that the government can always cover its borrowing requirement. In this way, discount houses engage in the relatively precarious activity of borrowing short and lending long. If discount houses cannot renew loans to balance their books at the end of each day, they can approach the Bank of England as lender of last resort or try to sell some of their Treasury bills on the open market. (As lender of last resort, the Bank of England is providing funds to pay for its own Treasury bills!) Because the sale of Treasury bills is underwritten, the government has a greater certainty of reducing liquidity and soaking up funds when desired.

An important aspect of these open-market operations is that they enable the government, through the Bank of England and the discount market, to influence *interest rates*. The discount to the face value of bills bought and sold has an implied interest rate. Interest rates on bills traded have an influence on other market rates such as the London Inter-Bank Offered Rate (LIBOR), and these influence Bank base rate. Since October 1988 the Bank of England has been prepared to deal with institutions other than discount houses if they meet certain standards.

Other types of bank and market

A large number of other institutions and markets perform the role of bringing together buyers and sellers of money. These *parallel markets* are a recent development and provide short-term funds for a variety of specialized intermediaries. Their services include arranging for loans between banks and between companies, the transaction of fixed-term bank deposits known as certificates of deposit (CDs) and the raising of loans by local authorities.

Firms needing foreign currency to pay for goods and services, as well as individuals going abroad, require currency, and this is obtainable on the *foreign exchange market*. Through the London International Financial Futures Exchange, finance can be purchased today for payment at a fixed price on a future date.

Merchant banks are prominent institutions in the City of London. Although their traditional role is that of accepting bills of exchange and providing assurances that they will be paid, today they also engage in money markets, provide finance for companies, deal in bullion and arrange for shares to be underwritten.

London now has around 500 *foreign banks*, British banks with *overseas head offices* and a number of *consortium banks* made up of interests from different banking institutions.

Deregulation in the form of the Big Bang has led to more competition in securities in the market-place, and successive privatizations and the subsequent publicity have led to an increasing awareness of the respective roles of *life assurance companies*, *pension funds*, *unit trusts* and *building societies*.

International trade

No country today can provide all of the resources necessary to fully develop its economic potential and satisfy the needs of its population. By virtue of its geographical situation, Britain has historically been a major trading nation. International trade has enabled it to gain from the advantages of specialization by exchanging its surplus goods for surpluses produced by other countries so that its inhabitants can prosper from lower prices and higher living standards.

Although this is important, however, international trade does increase interdependence between nations and can pose a threat to economic stability. This did not matter during the colonial period, but today the benefits of international trade must be offset against losses in employment in domestic industries and it can lead to arguments for protectionism.

Balance of payments

International trade involves making payments overseas for goods and services received and receiving payments for goods and services supplied (Fig. 22.15). At the same time, capital movements will have taken place between countries. The balance of payments is a statistical device used to record both a country's international trade and its movements of capital over a particular time period. Balance of payments accounts always balance as they are based on a double-entry format so that for every plus item there will always be a corresponding minus one.

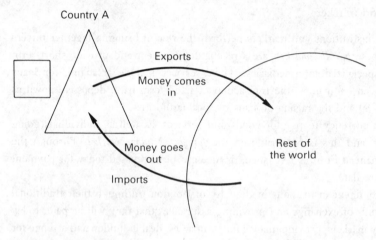

Figure 22.15 International trade.

In recent years the method of presenting balance of payments accounts has changed as there is less of a need to highlight changes in reserves. Today the broad classification of transactions are:

1. *The current account*   The current account comprises the *visible balance*, which is sometimes referred to as the 'balance of trade', and the invisible balance. The visible balance is the difference between the sale of exported goods from the United Kingdom and the purchase of imported goods to the United Kingdom. As Britain depends on raw materials and foodstuffs, it usually runs a deficit on visibles; although a surplus developed from 1980 to 1982 because of North Sea oil and gas, it soon disappeared because of the glut in the supply of oil and increased import penetration. The *invisible balance* consists of services. Income earned from selling services abroad is known as invisible exports, and when we buy services from overseas we are creating invisible imports. Invisibles include the interest, profits and dividends earned as a result of investments overseas, the selling of financial services such as

banking and insurance overseas, transfers by private individuals, and transfers by governments for areas such as overseas aid and embassies as well as tourism:

Visible exports	500	Invisible exports	400	Total exports	900
Visible imports	650	Invisible imports	200	Total imports	850
Visible balance	−150	Invisible balance	+200	Current balance	+50

2. *Changes in UK external assets and liabilities*   This aspect involves capital movements by individuals, firms and governments. Assets purchased abroad by UK residents are considered to be an outflow of capital and are given a negative sign; this would include any increases in gold and foreign currency reserves. Investment by foreigners in the United Kingdom are considered to be liabilities and are shown by a plus sign.

Case Study—When 'Made in Europe' isn't

A small Nissan car factory, built just four years ago in Northern England, is posing two big questions: How much is an argument about the 'local content' of its cars being used to create a Fortress Europe against foreign manufacturers? And can the Japanese help bring manufacturing's next generation to Europe?

Mrs Margaret Thatcher may excoriate the EC bureaucracy in Brussels, but sometimes she needs its help. Lord Young has asked the European Commission to intervene in a dispute with France over the export of Nissan Bluebird cars from the Japanese car maker's plant in England. France says it will treat these cars as Japanese until less than 20% of the value of the car comes from components imported from Japan; Britain argues that a car with less than 40% imported components (i.e. 60% 'local content') should be considered European. The outcome of this dispute will shape both Europe's post-1992 trade policy and the type of foreign investment it attracts.

Though Nissan says it will reduce imported components to less than 20% of a Bluebird's value by 1990, the present local content of 70% sits uneasily between the British and French positions. France now counts each Bluebird against 'voluntary' import quotas which allow Japanese cars 3% of France's car market, with Nissan's share just under 1%. For the distributor of Nissan cars in France, M. Jean-Pierre Richard, delays in delivery from overstretched French car makers provide a prime opportunity for him to expand—if only the government will let him. There are no hard and fast rules for local content in the EC because imported goods and components, with duty paid in the country where they first enter the Community, are thereafter supposed to be treated like local products. But recent Community practice in disputes involving local content has tended to use a 60% yardstick for determining when something is European-made.

(*Source: The Economist*)

Questions

1. Why are the French expressing concern about the local content of Nissan cars?
2. Comment on the position of Nissan with regard to
    (a) visible imports.

(b) visible exports.

(c) invisible imports.

(d) invisible exports.

3. Briefly outline the main arguments to this dispute.

4. Why is resolving it so important?

5. Explain whether your sympathies lie with the British or the French in this particular instance.

Each year countries experience either a deficit or a surplus on their balance of payments. Whereas surpluses provide an injection into the economic system, deficits provide a leakage from the circular flow. Serious problems develop if the balance of payments is in fundamental disequilibrium with persistently large deficits or surpluses over a number of years. Persistent surpluses create inflationary pressures if inflows of reserves are not prevented from raising the money supply, and they will mean that the currency is undervalued. A persistent deficit will probably be more serious, as it will exhaust official reserves, reduce its ability to borrow, cause a downward fall in the exchange rate and have serious implications for a country's stability.

Exchange rates

Whenever international trade takes place, there is a need for foreign exchange by at least one of the parties to the transaction. The foreign exchange market is a global market providing the mechanism for the buying and selling of foreign currencies. A country's foreign exchange rate is the price at which its own currency exchanges for that of others. Every currency has many rates to reflect all other traded currencies—the rate of sterling against the dollar, the yen, the Deutschmark and so on.

In the foreign exchange market, buyers and sellers can come together and set prices according to supply and demand. In theory, this provides an automatic mechanism for keeping the balance of payments in equilibrium. For example, with an adverse balance of payments, the exchange rate would fall, enabling exports to become cheaper and more competitive and imports to become more expensive. This will change the imbalance and cause the deficit to subside. If the government does not intervene and allows its currency to find its value, it will not be necessary to use up foreign exchange reserves to support its value.

In practice, however, this does not tend to work. Falling exchange rates increase the price of imports, and if a country is dependent on these this can cause severe inflationary pressures. In effect, it would be importing cost-push inflation. The costs of home manufacturers would then rise, so the increasing competitiveness resulting from a fall in the exchange rate will have been offset by the imported inflation. For this reason, governments seldom allow exchange rates to be determined solely by the forces of supply and demand. If currencies threaten to vary too much, authorities intervene to manage the float and ensure that variations do not harm economic objectives. As we will see later, when managing the float governments have to look for alternative measures to overcome balance of payments disequilibrium, and using high interest rates or imposing tariffs and quotas can be harmful to economic growth and world trade.

Economic and Monetary Union (EMU)

In 1978, member-states of the EC agreed to establish an Exchange Rate Mechanism (ERM), designed to limit fluctuations in the currencies of members who choose to join it. The system is sometimes known as the 'Snake in the Tunnel' because currencies in the system must keep between an upper and lower limit against a basket of other currencies (Fig. 22.16).

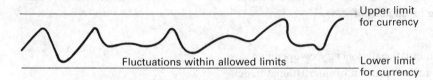

Figure 22.16 The Snake in the tunnel.

The early stages of EMU are intended to develop closer co-operation on economic and monetary policy. In the final stage, national governments and central banks will no longer set interest and exchange rate policies for individual countries; instead, there will be a single interest rate policy and exchange rates will be locked together. Eventually there will be a single currency for all countries that move to the final stage.

Britain is not committed to moving to a single currency. The United Kingdom negotiated a *special protocol* to the Maastricht Treaty which means that the UK government and Parliament will decide not just when to join a single currency, but whether to join at all. Nor does Britain have to be a member of the ERM.

At the final stage of EMU, a new European central bank will take decisions on interest rates. Its objective will be to achieve price stability. It will be independent of governments, but required to report regularly to the European Parliament, the Council of Ministers and the European Council.

For the most part, other economic policies will be the responsibility of national governments; but the Council of Ministers can make recommendations on member-states' economic policies. In the final stage, for example, it could also insist that a government reduced its borrowing if the Council, taking account of all the circumstances, thought this too high. Each country can continue to produce its own notes and coins. So if Britain decides to move to stage 3, the Queen's portrait will still appear on UK notes and coins.

Having one currency would make it easier to do business throughout the EC. There would be no bank charges for changing money and no risks arising from fluctuating exchange rates. It would also be easier and cheaper for travellers. But there would be disadvantages, too. A single set of interest rates, over which national parliaments had no influence, might well not be right for every participating country at any one time. If a country were to join the EMU before its economy was ready, unemployment could rise steeply. This would result in pressures for financial transfers from other member-states.

International co-operation

International Monetary Fund

After the financial crash in the United States in 1929, followed by the European financial crisis and the abolition of the Gold Standard, countries retreated into nationalistic economic policies and erected protectionist barriers. This just worsened the effects of the depression as economic advantages from specialization were lost. However, during this period views were changing about economic co-operation across international barriers, and although the Second World War hindered development, a conference of the major Western allied nations was held at Bretton Woods in the United States in 1944 with a brief to tackle the problem of international economic relationships. An agreement at this meeting established the International Monetary Fund (IMF), with the broad aims of

- Providing international monetary co-operation
- Encouraging the expansion of international trade
- Encouraging exchange rate stability
- Making resources available from a fund for members needing to correct balance of payments problems

Today members of the IMF include nearly every nation in the world. In the 1990s the IMF has played a major role in providing support for Eastern Europe and enabling developing countries to raise finance for capital expansion and reconstruction programmes based on the servicing of loans.

The International Bank for Reconstruction and Development (World Bank)

This was set up as an affiliate organization to the IMF in 1946 to make loans to war-shattered countries. In time, it increasingly took on the role of supporting development. However, leaders of this bank became heavily involved in politics in the late 1980s and early 1990s, as a result of which a number of Western nations have been reluctant to provide it with funds.

Organization for Economic Co-operation and Development (OECD)

This was set up in 1947 also to administer postwar aid. It too has now turned its attention towards helping the poorer countries of the world.

General Agreement on Tariffs and Trade (GATT)

This has been an ongoing conference of trade ministers of countries attempting to reduce protectionist restrictions on trade. The Uruguay Round established the 'most favoured nation' principle, under which member-states agreed to limit trade restrictions on all countries to the level affecting their most favoured trading partners.

The GATT has a tremendous potential to create free trade in the world. However, in the 1990s there have been extensive disputes between the EC and the United States, particularly over support to agriculture.

EC CAP

The Common Agricultural Policy (CAP) is a prominent and severely criticized feature of the EC. Its aims have been to increase agricultural productivity, to ensure that reasonable prices are charged, to provide a fair standard of living for the agricultural community and to stabilize markets and supplies. Prices are supported by imposing a levy on imports and by holding up market prices for products and buying them if prices fall too low. These stocks are intended to be released if prices rise beyond certain levels. However, in practice this has led to the build-up of surpluses and to resources being wasted.

Questions

Short-answer questions

1. Why is opportunity cost an important aspect for understanding decision-making processes?
2. Name two differences between an economy geared to the free market and one in which central intervention takes place. Comment briefly on the type of economy you would prefer to live in.
3. What is a monetary policy?
4. Name two functions of discount houses.
5. Why is an 'equitable distribution of income' an objective of government policy?
6. Name two injections and two withdrawals from the circular flow of income.
7. What is meant by an equilibrium level of income?
8. What is the difference between a public good and a merit good?
9. Contrast the workings of a budget deficit and a budget surplus.
10. Name two causes of unemployment.
11. Distinguish between stagflation and creeping inflation.
12. List four undesirable effects of inflation.
13. Explain why countries trade overseas.
14. Provide two examples of a visible and two examples of an invisible.
15. Describe the danger of falling exchange rates on a country dependent upon imports.
16. Give one economic argument in favour of and one economic argument against UK membership of the EC. (*Source*: AEB)
17. Name two policies designed to influence employment.
18. What relationship did the Phillips curve identify?
19. Name two advantages and two disadvantages of privatization.
20. Provide two strategies available to a government to create domestic deflation.

Essays

1. 'Most internationally traded products compete more on quality than on price. Exchange rate fluctuations are relevant only in that they alter individual importers' and exporters' profit margins.' Comment on this statement and explain the relationship between exchange rates and profit margins. (*Source*: AEB)

2. Analyse the strategies available to a firm to enable it to survive a period of recession in its home market. (*Source*: AEB)

3. Why are some governments of Western industrialized countries reconsidering the introduction of protectionist trade policies? What are the main arguments for and against such policies? (*Source*: Oxford)

4. There is a major revaluation (+20 per cent) of the UK exchange rate. Discuss:
   (a) the effect on the UK.
   (b) the implications for a manufacturing firm which assembles bought-in components to make its product and exports half its output. (Before revaluation profit margins were equal for home and overseas orders.) (*Source*: Oxford)

5. Examine the evidence that Britain has a problem with current industrial performance. Discuss the extent to which industrial management should take the blame. Comment on the methods available to the government to increase the country's industrial performance. (*Source*: Oxford)

6. With reference to at least two criteria, discuss the recent performance of the UK economy.

7. Contrast monetarist strategies with those used for demand management and comment on their usefulness for dealing with inflation.

8. Assess the respective roles of the Bank of England, discount houses and merchant banks within the financial system.

9. What is meant by cyclical unemployment? With reference to the multiplier and accelerator, examine the role of investment on the trade cycle.

10. Explain why governments intervene in the economy and comment on their need to 'trade off' priorities in order to move towards their macroeconomic objectives.

Data response questions

1 Labour market indicators

Study the data in Fig. 22.17 and answer the questions which follow.

1. Explain the possible effects of *both* the changes in the Retail Price Index (Fig. 22.17(a)) and the changes in average earnings (Fig. 22.17(b)) on sales of domestically produced consumer goods.

2. Using the data in Fig. 22.17(c), discuss whether the changes since May 1991 are likely to make the goods of UK manufacturers more competitive or less competitive with imported goods.

3. Outline *three* ways in which a manufacturing business might increase output whilst reducing the number of people they employ.

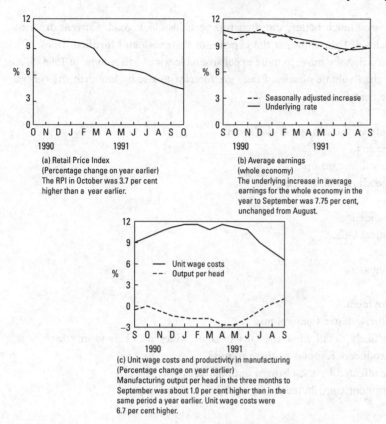

(a) Retail Price Index
(Percentage change on year earlier)
The RPI in October was 3.7 per cent
higher than a year earlier.

(b) Average earnings
(whole economy)
The underlying increase in average
earnings for the whole economy in the
year to September was 7.75 per cent,
unchanged from August.

(c) Unit wage costs and productivity in manufacturing
(Percentage change on year earlier)
Manufacturing output per head in the three months to
September was about 1.0 per cent higher than in the
same period a year earlier. Unit wage costs were
6.7 per cent higher.

Figure 22.17 labour market indicators (*Source*: *Employment News*, January 1992, Issue No. 203)

2   Trends in beer and wine sales

A consumer spending forecast produced by Staniland Hall in June 1993 predicted that beer and spirits sales would continue their decline while cider, wine and perry sales would increase.

The business forecasters predicted that in 1994 consumer spending would decrease and real incomes would not go up. Any recovery in the housing market would be likely to flatten out in 1994–5 when mortgage rates are likely to increase. Consumer confidence had increased in the spring of 1993 but was not as high as it had been in the spring of 1992.

Using figures released by the Central Statistical Office, the forecasters reported that spending had risen by 2.1 per cent from its most depressed point in the first quarter of 1992, but this was expected to slow in the second half of 1993 and would be even less in the first half of 1994.

Factors that would affect this included an increasing squeeze on pay, a rise in inflation, the persisting debt burden of consumers, and tax increases likely to occur in 1994.

All these factors add up to bad news for the beer market. The recession in the early 1990s, the impact of the Council Tax on the high-spending young adult sector, higher prices and more concern about drinking and driving have all combined to hit beer sales.

It is suggested that the consumption of beer is related to its price relative to prices in general, and also to the level of male unemployment.

Wine and cider have fared much better, and their prospects also look good. Current drinking trends will benefit the sales of light wines, at the expense of vermouth and fortified wines.

Staniland Hall suggested that the move to more expensive table wines will resume in 1994–5, so spending will rise faster than volume of sales. Prices are forecast to rise by less than the general rate of inflation over the next five years.

1. Explain the following in the context of the above:
   (a) Business forecaster.
   (b) 'Real incomes will not go up.'
   (c) 'Consumer spending will decrease.'
   (d) Mortgage rates.
   (e) Consumer confidence.
   (f) Central Statistical Office.
   (g) Squeeze on pay.
   (h) Average earnings.
   (i) Recession.
   (j)* Male unemployment.
   (k) 'Spending will rise faster than volume.'
2. Why are beer sales likely to fall while the sales of some wines are likely to increase?
3. How might beer producers respond to these trends?
4. Who is likely to be affected by the changes outlined above?
5. How has the government contributed to the changes outlined above?

3   Second thoughts on Sweden

Sweden, the archetypal corporatist state, has won a standing ovation for its switch to supply-side economics.

Polite applause is more in order

In 1991 central government income tax was no longer levied on 90 per cent of the wage-earning population in Sweden; they now have to pay only a local government income tax of roughly 30 per cent. The better off still pay both sorts of income tax, but their top marginal rate has been reduced from 72 to 60 per cent.

The Swedish government has also reduced all controls on foreign exchange and has scrapped all bilateral agreements restricting the import of clothing and textiles. As part of its GATT commitment, Sweden has also scaled down its protection against farm imports.

1. What are supply-side measures?
2. How can the reduction of income taxes be seen as a supply-side measure? What would be the advantages of such a policy?
3. What are bilateral agreements in trade?
4. How can the reduction of protection against farm imports be (a) harmful to and (b) beneficial to an economy and to members of that economy?
5. What is GATT? What does GATT set out to achieve?

4   UK government policy and performance

Some economic statistics

(i)   *Unemployment*   The seasonally adjusted figure for April 1993 showed a fall of 1400 to a total of 2 939 600 which represents 10.5 per cent of the workforce.

(ii)   *Inflation*   1.9 per cent for March 1993 (3.5 per cent, taking mortgages out of the basket); a further fall in April to the lowest level for many years.

(iii)   *Interest rate*   A base rate of 6 per cent and a mortgage rate of around 8 per cent.

(iv)   *Exchange rate*   The United Kingdom was taken out of the Exchange Rate Mechanism and current exchange rates are £1 = DM2.5, \$1.55.

(v)   *Others*
   - Poll tax replaced by council tax
   - Problems over the Maastricht Treaty and internal disagreements
   - Teachers dissatisfied over testing
   - Police dissatisfied over contract changes
   - VAT announced on electricity and gas
   - Privatization of British Rail proposed
   - Privatization of other areas such as police records, production of economic statistics, student grant and loan allocations

1. Look at points (i)–(v) above and grade them with one of the following performance measures: (a) Excellent; (b) Good; (c) Satisfactory; (d) Must do better.

2. In your opinion, has John Major's government been successful in tackling the economy's problems? If not, how do you think the problems should have been handled?

3. Has the government overlooked any areas where you think they should have invested more time and money?

4. Are you satisfied with the performance of John Major's administration?

Suggested reading

Beardshaw, J., *Economics: A Student's Guide*, 3rd edn. Pitman, 1992.
Griffiths, A. and Wall, S., *Applied Economics*, 5th edn. Longman, 1993.
Harbury, C. and Lipsey, R., *An Introduction to the UK Economy*, 4th edn. Basil Blackwell, 1993.

23

The consequences of business

Society is made up of a large number of individuals, groups and institutions, each with its own aims and views about the way in which scarce resources should be used. Because business activity is such an important part of social relations it will often be the subject of conflicts of interest. For example, a town may want a company to build a new factory because of the extra employment it will bring; the trouble is that green fields have to be built on and the extra lorries will add to traffic in the area.

In the following case study we can see that frequently controversy exists not only about what an organization produces, but how it produces, and the attention that is given to the vital area of 'quality'.

Case Study—Inquiry after water protests

Water watchdogs yesterday called for a full public inquiry after foul-tasting tapwater prompted thousands of complaints from across the Harrogate district. The switchboard at Yorkshire Water was jammed as anxious customers demanded an explanation for water which both smelled and tasted of chemicals.

Yorkshire Water claimed the problem was caused by vegetable matter washed into the water supply by heavy rain over the Easter weekend and reacting with chlorine. And, yesterday afternoon, the company said it has identified and rectified the fault.

But the recently privatised industry's own watchdog organisation, the Office of Water Services (OFWAT), pointed out [that] Yorkshire Water's policy states [that] an alternative source of drinking water should be made available to customers affected by 'interrupted' water supplies after five hours.

Chair Mrs Diane Scott said she believed Yorkshire Water had acted correctly in identifying and rectifying the problem. But she added: 'Some customers may have been supplied with undrinkable water for up to 24 hours. I consider this is unreasonable and alternative supplies should have been arranged. I would also like to see a thorough investigation being made into this incident, with the results made public.'

The Drinking Water Inspectorate in London confirmed it had been alerted to the problem and a spokesperson said the organisation would monitor the situation.

On the map [Fig. 23.1], the thinner arrowed lines represent pipelines from reservoirs around the district which carry untreated water to the Harlow Hill Water Treatment Works on the edge of Harrogate. The thicker lines represent pipelines carrying treated water to the consumer. The problems are said to have arisen as water contaminated

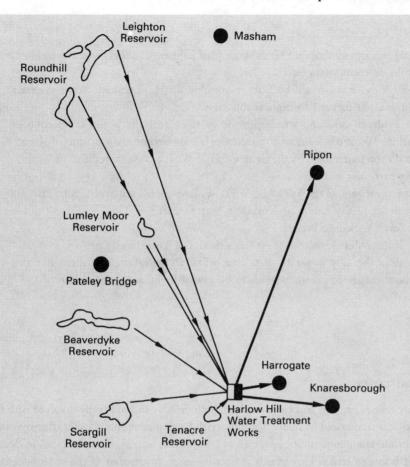

Figure 23.1 Map showing water supply on edge of Harrogate.

with vegetable matter arrived at Harlow Hill for treatment.

However, many Harrogate residents remained reluctant to use tapwater, and on Wednesday [14 April] supermarket shelves were quickly emptied of bottled waters. Some residents were planning to bill Yorkshire Water for their purchases.

Mr Denis Walton, of Beckwith Crescent, said he thought it was only reasonable the company should pay. 'My water rates bill is about £45 a quarter and I'll be sending my receipt to them for a refund.'

Hotel owner Mr Julian Bennett of Franklin Road, Harrogate, said he spent yesterday morning apologising to guests at breakfast. 'It not only smells bad, it tastes bad. It's shocking. But I assured my customers the water in Harrogate was usually first class.'

At Betty's Restaurant the staff were told to warn customers before they chose from the menu that the water had a strong chemical taste. 'We had a few complaints and had to explain it was the water and not our tea or coffee', said the restaurant manager.

Yorkshire Water yesterday apologised for any inconvenience to its customers. But a spokesperson added: 'However, in this instance, there is no evidence of any failure on Yorkshire Water's part.'

(*Source: Harrogate Advertiser*, 16 April 1993)

Questions

1. Outline at least two different views about what happened in this particular incident. Why do different views exist?
2. In your view, who should be held responsible for this incident? What evidence would you put forward to support this view?
3. What evidence does the article provide to show that the action or inaction of Yorkshire Water has a spillover effect which goes beyond its provision of water?
4. What do you understand by the term 'quality'? What are the ingredients of 'quality' in this particular instance?
5. What is your view of the Yorkshire Water spokesperson's statement that: 'There is no evidence of any failure on Yorkshire Water's part'?
6. Who owns Yorkshire Water?
7. How is the public protected from the activities of Yorkshire Water?
8. How does the case illustrate that, even when an unfortunate incident like this occurs, there are still some benefits to be gained by business organizations?

Benefits and costs

Business activity creates benefits and costs for those both directly and indirectly involved with the business. Today it is recognized by many that industrial development only socially effective can if it takes into consideration community losses as well as profits. Society as a whole has to decide what balance it wants to strike. How much pollution—even destruction of the environment—should we accept? Heavier lorries are more cost-effective in moving goods—how heavy is too heavy? More factories and better roads can mean more jobs—but the price can be the loss of more farmland.

We therefore need to look at the social benefits and the social costs of business activity to get a clearer picture of net benefits.

1. *Private benefits* are all the benefits accruing to an individual or group as a result of a particular activity, e.g. the profits from a business that are earned by the shareholders, the wages earned by employees.
2. *Private costs* are all the costs to an individual or group resulting from a particular activity, e.g. the cost to a sole trader of building and running a cinema.
3. *Social benefits* are the private benefits plus all the beneficial effects for other members of the community resulting from a particular activity, e.g. the entertainment value received by cinema-goers, and the wages earned by the projectionist, cashier and ice cream seller.
4. *Social costs* are the private costs plus all the detrimental effects for other members of the community, e.g. the extra traffic congestion, parking problems and litter left in the street by cinema-goers.

Wealth creation

Wealth is the sum total of all the ingredients we have come to value as necessary for our material well-being. Comfortable houses, efficient transport, hospitals, health care and education to enable us achieve our full potential—all these contribute to well-being. So everyone concerned in providing them is also helping to create our 'wealth'. We all depend on each other to create a wealthy society.

Income and wealth

An important distinction must be made between income and wealth. Income is a *flow*, which is created by an individual, group or country in a given period. For example, Citizen Average may earn an income of £15 000 in a year and Somewhereland may have a national income of £10 million in 1990. (National income is the sum of all the individual incomes.)

In contrast, wealth is a *stock*, i.e. a sum of valuables that exist at a given moment of time which were owned by individuals, groups or countries. For example, on 31 March, 1995 Citizen Average may own wealth valued at £200 000 which is made up of property, money, stocks and shares, paintings and other valuables. The total wealth of Somewhereland at that date may be calculated at hundreds of millions of pounds and in addition to personal wealth will include business wealth in the form of buildings and equipment, and public wealth in the form of public hospitals, schools, parks and other state-owned services; in addition, we should not forget *human wealth*, in the form of the skills and aptitudes of people which have been enhanced by education and training.

It is very difficult to measure wealth, because it is often hard to ascribe a monetary value to such items as human capital. In addition, as new wealth is created, some of the old wealth deteriorates in the form of depreciation. Calculations of depreciation values are highly subjective.

Many people involved in business and industry see its fundamental importance as the creation of wealth. Industry provides all the goods and services that we need. Almost everything that we see around us has been produced by industry—our clothes, homes, means of transport, our living environment and even much of our food.

Product development

Industry reacts to people's changing wants and produces the products that consumers are prepared to buy. Sometimes industry creates new demands for products by developing new products and then introducing them to the market. However, product development needs to go hand in hand with marketing activities. Some new products are in advance of their time. Innovators develop these goods or services before introducing them to the wider public. For instance, the mass market did not know that it wanted the microwave oven. The product had first to be invented, then tested, test-marketed and researched. Finally, it was launched to a wide audience. Eventually it became a huge success.

Product development involves a considerable risk. Many new ideas never get beyond the drawing board, while others flop after being on the market for only a few weeks. In recent years a number of new newspapers have been launched. Some, like the *London Daily News*, went under within a few months; some, like *Today*, managed to survive after significant changes in strategy; others, like the *Independent*, have gone from strength to strength.

In May 1989, when the first edition of this textbook was published, *The European* newspaper was launched with a £10 million promotional budget and a projected initial circulation of 5–6 million. At the time we asked readers of the book to gauge whether or not the product would prove to be a success. The paper has been through some difficult times since then. At one time it was not expected to survive after the death of its former owner Robert Maxwell. However, it continues to sell. In 1989 we said that the success of the paper would depend in part on whether the people of Europe consider themselves Europeans, and on whether advertisers could be persuaded to place adverts in it. Recent evidence does indicate an increase in support for the notion of a European Community (Fig. 23.2)—so perhaps there are still opportunities for *The European* to exploit at a time when the sales of many British newspapers are in decline.

Modern products are often highly complex and may be assembled thousands of miles apart. Parts of motor vehicles, for example, are built in many different plants before being finally assembled. Workers often have only a very limited knowledge of what they are producing. In a similar way, consumers may have only a sketchy idea of how products are made and distributed.

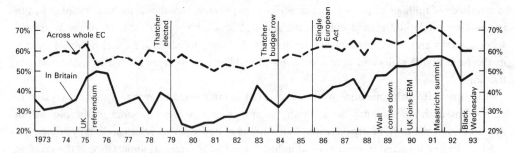

Figure 23.2 Support for EC membership.

The benefits of industrial activity

Industry brings together productive resources to produce wealth. In so doing it produces the following major benefits:

1. *Industry provides employment.* Millions of people are employed in industry and commerce. Some of them are doing enjoyable, creative work while others are in boring, unimaginative environments where work is a burden rather than a pleasure.
2. *Industry creates income.* The factors of production that produce goods earn factor incomes. Shareholders receive profits, landlords receive rent, lenders receive interest, workers receive wages, and so on.
3. *Industry creates products.* Value is added at each stage of production. For example, bringing petrol to the final consumer involves the addition of value at several stages—extracting oil from the geological reserves, refining and storing oil, transporting the fuel, and providing the petrol to consumers in an easy-to-handle form.

4. *Industry improves living standards.* Materially, most people are better off today than ever before. Figure 23.3, for example, shows that real household disposable income has risen considerably between 1971 and 1990. The loaf of sliced white bread that could be paid for with 9 minutes work in 1971 required only 5 minutes' work in 1991.

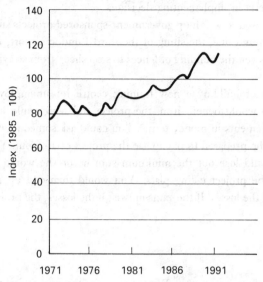

Figure 23.3 Real household disposable income (for a married couple, with husband only working), 1971–1991.

5. *Industry makes it possible for people to enjoy more leisure.* Because of industrial growth and the resulting technological innovations, people have more free time on their hands. Hospitals, schools, museums and many welfare functions which we have come to take for granted are all supported by the wealth created by businesses in the public and private sectors of the economy.

The costs of business activity

When a firm produces something, it has to bear in mind a number of *internal costs:*

- Production costs
- Marketing costs
- Financial costs
- Administration costs

In addition to these, there are *external costs*, which are costs that go beyond the balance sheet of the firm. These are sometimes known as externalities or spillover costs:

$$\text{Externalities} = \text{Social costs} - \text{private costs}$$

An individual business will be more interested in weighing up decisions in terms of private profits and losses than in accounting for externalities. However, when a firm applies to the planning authorities or other governmental bodies for permission to put into effect a business decision, the wider social implications will be an important consideration.

Society benefits if resources are used in a socially effective way. It is particularly important for government agencies to employ social criteria in implementing decisions.

Cost–benefit analysis has frequently been used to weigh up government-sponsored projects such as the building of a new London Underground line, the siting of the third London airport, the subsidizing of firms in depressed regions—even the building of fences to stop sheep from straying into the streets of Merthyr Tydfil.

In carrying out a cost–benefit analysis of building a new training centre for unemployed workers, you would need to find out who would benefit from the project and who would lose out. You would then have to make measurements in money terms. You could ask someone who would benefit how much he or she would be prepared to pay to see the project carried out. You would then have to ask someone who would lose out the minimum sum he or she would be prepared to accept as compensation for the project taking place. You would then add up the monetary values put on all the gains and all the losses. If the gains outweigh the losses, the project passes the test: it is worth going ahead.

Pollution

The most obvious social cost of business activity is pollution. We can compare the private and the social perspectives of pollution by taking the example of a chemical firm that uses a nearby river as a convenient dumping ground for untreated waste products.

If we assume that a firm sets out to maximize profits, then it will carry on expanding output so long as the revenue from selling one extra unit is greater than the cost of producing that extra unit. The technical term used to describe an extra unit is *marginal unit*. Let us also assume that the firm is faced with the schedule in Table 23.1, showing the cost and revenue from producing different levels of output. Given this schedule, the firm will produce 4 tons of chemical in the given period: the surplus of revenue over cost from producing the first ton would be £6, from the second ton £5 and the third ton £3.

Table 23.1

Amount of chemical produced (tons)	Price per ton (marginal revenue) £	Cost to firm of producing an extra ton (marginal cost) £
1	40	34
2	40	35
3	40	37
4	40	40
5	40	44

However, if we are to take account of social factors, let us assume that the pollution kills a large proportion of the fish population of the river and that this seriously affects the business of a commercial fishery downstream. In order to further simplify our example, we will also assume that the only way of reducing the pollution is to cut back on chemical production. (In the real world, of course, the firm could invest in pollution control equipment.)

We can now draw up a new table which includes the cost of the pollution. The second column in Table 23.2 shows the price the firm could get for each ton given existing market conditions. The third column shows that it is more costly to produce larger outputs than smaller outputs, reflecting the fact that the firm has to bring into use older units of machinery to produce the larger quantities. The fourth column shows the damage to the downstream fishery's business resulting from the dumping of each extra ton of waste. The last column shows the combined cost to the chemical firm and the fishery of producing extra units of output. If we assume that no one else is affected by the pollution, this final column will represent the marginal cost to society of additional units produced.

Table 23.2

Amount of chemical produced (tons) (£) (1)	Price per ton (£) (2)	Cost to firm of producing an extra ton (£) (3)	Pollution damage to fishery of an extra ton of production (£) (4)	Social cost of producing an extra ton (£) (5)
1	40	34	3	37
2	40	35	3	38
3	40	37	3	40
4	40	40	3	43
5	40	44	3	47

If we now look at the table, we can see that the most socially efficient output will be 3 tons, rather than the 4 tons that would have been the case if we considered only the chemical firm. The benefits to society can be measured by the price that consumers of chemicals are prepared to pay for each ton. These must then be weighed up against the private costs and externalities incurred in chemical production. At the end of the day we still have pollution, but society will have traded off the benefits of chemical production against the social costs of chemical production.

Water pollution

It has been standard practice for a long time for industry to locate by canals, rivers and seas. Industries such as paper production, chemicals and breweries not only use water in the manufacturing process, but also pour out their effluent into rivers and the sea. Perhaps the most notorious example of this type of activity is the dispersal of waste products from the nuclear fuels industry. We have purification and filtration plants where water is treated, but it is difficult to eliminate the effects of industrial chemicals which destroy water life.

In Hungary, France, West Germany and other European countries, firms are charged heavily for causing water pollution. This puts great pressure on the firms to clean up their production processes.

Of course, one problem of checking on water pollution levels in order to tax firms that pollute is the cost of administering the system. In Britain we tend to prosecute firms that break water safety laws; fines can be imposed and imprisonment ordered in serious cases.

Air pollution

This has been dramatically illustrated by several events in the mid-1980s. In December 1984, there was a leak of poisonous gas from a Union Carbide plant at Bhopal in India. More than 2000 people died and at least 10 times this number suffered from breathing and eye complaints. The Carbide plant was part of an American multinational producing pesticides to spray on crops. Subsequent investigations have led to a questioning of safety standards at the plant.

Perhaps even more dramatic was the nuclear disaster at Chernobyl in 1986. Here we have an example of a growing centrally planned economy trying to promote the use of new power sources rapidly. Again, the safety standards of the nuclear reactor were highly questionable. As a result of the incident, wide tracts of land have been made uninhabitable and a cloud of nuclear waste was carried airborne across northern Europe. The reindeer herds of the Laplanders were declared inedible for several years, threatening the ruin of the whole Lap economy. Livestock of Welsh hill farmers also had to be banned from sale in the market-place because of heavy contamination.

Emissions from UK factory chimneys and power stations are recognized as major sources of the 'acid rain' that results in the destruction of forests and pollution of lakes in Scandinavia and Germany. Acid rain can be described as pollution, both solid and liquid, resulting when emissions of sulphur dioxide, nitrogen oxides and ozones undergo chemical changes in the atmosphere. Reaction of these gases with moisture in the air causes sulphuric and nitric acids to precipitate along with particles of sulphur. A special characteristic of acid rain is its ability to travel thousands of miles from the point of emission, and the United Kingdom is estimated to export about half of its sulphur dioxide to the rest of Europe. In West Germany half of the Black Forest has been designated a 'total damage area'. Forests are an essential part of the ecosystem and are important for commercial and recreational purposes. They provide employment—1.4 million jobs in the EC alone—and are converted to wood pulp to help meet a growing demand for paper and packaging. Damage thereby inflicted on them has to be taken seriously.

Dereliction

If we consider the decision to build a new mine, or to drill for oil or natural gas, we can see that this might destroy areas of natural beauty in a non-reversible way. Furthermore, when the extraction business pulls out of an area, the effects can be worse; for not only do jobs disappear, but the community is also left with derelict land which is unpleasant to look at and sometimes dangerous. These dangerous remains include disused railway tunnels, mine shafts, quarries, coal tips and old buildings. Generally it has been left to imaginative local councils to redevelop the areas as parks, boating lakes and sites for new industry.

Traffic congestion

The growing pace of modern business life has put enormous pressures on our road networks. In 1986 the M25 orbital road around London was opened. By the time it was made fully operational it was inadequate to meet the need for a circular road. It has been described as the longest traffic jam in Europe.

Motor vehicles cause accidents, pour out noxious fumes and are noisy. One way of calculating the cost of modern roads is to compare house prices near a large road with those of similar housing that is placed further away from the road in the same locality.

Long-term waste

British Nuclear Fuels PLC reprocesses nuclear waste at its plant in Sellafield. This waste is collected from Britain's second-generation power stations. A report produced in 1986 shows that, if these power stations were shut down immediately, it would take 10 years to reprocess the existing spent fuel.

Highly radioactive spent nuclear fuel is transported by road or rail in nuclear waste 'flasks'. The resulting waste is then either dumped in the sea or buried in stores underground. It is argued that in this way we are storing up problems for the future.

Noise

This is another external effect of business. Concorde is a great flag-flyer for British airways. It is also a considerable nuisance for those citizens who live close to its take-off and departure points. Noise from road and rail traffic (see Fig. 23.4) can also be a considerable nuisance to householders.

In the United Kingdom, noise nuisance is controlled through by-laws passed by local authorities covering a wide range of matters from noisy animals and fireworks to radios and televisions. People can be prosecuted for continually making noise. In the same way, the activities of businesses and construction firms are controlled, and certain areas may be designated by the local authority as Noise Abatement Zones.

Food additives

In modern society, presentation and value for money are part of the marketing package of many foodstuffs. Artificial colourings and flavourings are used as well as synthetic ingredients. The medical profession has pointed out the dangerous side-effects of additives, particularly with regard to, e.g. hyperactivity in children.

Insufficient testing of products

In order to capitalize on market leadership, some firms have put products on the market without sufficient background testing. A classic example of this was the production by the Distillers Company of thalidomide, a drug used by women to reduce the effects of morning sickness in pregnancy. An unforeseen side-effect resulted in the birth of many badly deformed babies.

Measures to control pollution

⌕ Case Study—'Toilets of Shame'

In January 1989 the government of Singapore launched a campaign against the 'truly ugly Singaporean', a public menace whose 'filthy habits' had become 'a terrible embarrassment and a prime complaint by tourists', according to Chia Mia Chiang, head of the Environmental Health Department.

In a series of stories labelled 'Toilets of Shame', the *Straits Times* set out to reveal the extent of the problem. A journalist-turned-toilet cleaner found that 80 per cent of his fellow citizens did not flush the toilet.

During the past ten years, Singapore's government has held numerous educational campaigns aimed at improving toilet habits. In the middle of 1988 it announced that anybody caught failing to flush a lavatory or urinal would be fined 200 Singapore dollars (£57); anybody caught urinating or defecating on 'the floors and sinks' of public toilets would be fined 1000 Singapore dollars.

For those urinating in the lifts of government-owned apartment blocks, sophisticated detection techniques have been employed. Some lifts have been fitted with urine detectors that jam lifts, at the same time activating a hidden camera to film offenders in the act. Environment officials are considering extending them to all areas where there are 'serious urination problems'.

Questions

1. Identify two distinct policies outlined in the article which have been employed by the government of Singapore to deal with 'filthy habits'.
2. What do you see as the major advantages and disadvantages of each method?
3. What alternative methods could you suggest? State your reasons to support particular measures.
4. Why do you think that the government involved itself with this issue?
5. What lessons learned from this case study can be applied to business practice?

Dirty toilet facilities and a lack of care for other people's property are all too common a feature of life in the United Kingdom. They are issues over which many people have strong views, and areas in which it is felt that offenders should be held responsible in some way. But what about the wider issue of environmental pollution by wealth-creating activities? How should we control the costs of such activities?

⌀ Case Study—Many freshwater fish 'in danger of extinction'

More than one-fifth of all species of freshwater fish in Britain face extinction and many others will become threatened unless urgent action is taken, according to a government-funded survey.

Several species have already died out this century, but the immediate concern should be for those rare and threatened species still in existence, fish biologists Peter Maitland and Alex Lyle said.

Their research, backed by the government's Nature Conservancy Council, showed that British native freshwater species face a number of problems.

Rivers and lakes have become repositories for enormous amounts of waste, ranging from toxic industrial chemicals to agricultural slurries and herbicides to domestic sewage.

Acid rain has been washed into water courses, and as a result fish can no longer survive in many rivers, especially those in the industrial and heavily populated lowland areas. Many rivers were devoid of oxygen and comprised a lethal cocktail of industrial chemicals, the biologists said.

(*Source: The Independent*, January 1989)

Questions

1. Is the pollution of rivers a problem?
2. Why?
3. Who is it a problem for?
4. Who is responsible for river pollution?
5. What should be done about river pollution?
6. Who should be responsible for dealing with the problem?
7. Who should pay for the implementation of policies for dealing with the problem?

Government intervention to deal with the problems of pollution can take any of five forms:

1. The purpose of *education* is to make individuals and groups more aware of the real costs of business activity and to bring home the possible long-term effects.
2. *State provision* would involve the state taking over activities that generate pollution and operating them in such a way as to produce levels of output that are the most socially effective and fair. Such a policy might involve quite an extensive programme of nationalization, and would run against the trend of privatization in the 1980s and early 1990s.
3. In the real world, *regulation* is the most common form of controlling pollution. Most countries have regulations governing the disposal of waste, restrictions on smoke emissions and rules about motor vehicle exhaust fumes. Given sufficient information, the government would be in a position to control waste-creating activities effectively. Unfortunately, the information to hand is at the best imperfect and subject to debate. Powerful producers' groups provide convincing statistics and other information to prove that their activities do not need control, while consumers' groups provide a strong lobby producing alternative statistics. In such a climate it is difficult for governments to know what types of business activity to regulate and to what extent. This is particularly true in a competitive global economy.
4. An alternative way of controlling pollution-creating activity is through *taxation*. Taxes can be levied either on the quantity of a product produced by a business, or on the quantity of effluent produced. Taxation makes it possible to control the output of such firms. However, in order to tax firms according to the social costs they create, there needs to be some way of measuring these costs. At best, such measures can be only rough and ready, but they create an important principle, i.e. that of penalizing polluters in proportion to the harm they create.
5. A final measure is to provide a *subsidy* to businesses in order to persuade them to reduce the pollution they cause. A firm that causes pollution could be subsidized for each unit of quantity by which it reduces its output. The firm would then consider the loss of the subsidy to be a cost of production for each additional unit of output that it produced. As with taxes, the government would need to know the social cost of each additional unit of output produced.

John Day and David Hodgson set out a table to compare taxes and standards as means of controlling the creation of sulphur dioxide, which as we have seen is an important ingredient in acid rain (Table 23.3). They point out that currently sulphur dioxide emissions are controlled internationally by pollution enforcement agencies setting standards that polluters ought not to breach. The use of taxes has long been discussed as a possibly more efficient way of controlling pollution.

The authors go on to conclude that, given existing information, there is no single measure that can conclusively be pointed to as the best for dealing with sulphur dioxide emissions, and the same conclusion applies to the general control of pollution.

Table 23.3 Sulphur dioxide control: taxes versus standards

Taxes	Standards
The cost of continuous monitoring of total emissions to assess how much tax is to be paid, is high.	Continuous monitoring is not necessary. Standards can specify some maximum limit not to be breached and can be monitored by spot checks at sample sites.
Law and enforcement can be aided by the monitor providing a cumulative record that can be checked. It is less susceptible to coercion.	Enforcement can be lax if it is too informal, with firms and enforcement agencies having too 'cosy' a relationship.
Firms are encouraged to seek new pollution control technologies to cut their tax bills.	This method provides little incentive to reduce sulphur emissions at source. Firms may think they have the right to pollute to the maximum standard set.
Setting the same rate of tax on sulphur emissions irrespective of where they occur is inefficient. Varying the tax rate is more efficient but is impractical to administer.	It is administratively easier to use.
It is difficult to take account of different meteorological conditions.	It can be used to restrict emissions under certain meteorological conditions or on days when pollution has already built up to danger levels.

Case Study—Minimizing the costs of pollution

This case study looks at decision-making about how many resources should be allocated to pollution control.

Figure 23.5 illustrates three hypothetical cost curves for water pollution. The horizontal axis measures different quantities of pollution control, while the vertical axis represents costs in monetary terms. Curve A shows that the greater the level of control over water pollution, the less will be the costs of damage to society caused by water pollution. Curve B shows that the greater the level of pollution control, the greater will be the cost of implementing the control policy. Curve C results from combining curves A and B to give the aggregate cost of damage and control with different levels of pollution control.

Questions

1. What types of cost might be incorporated in curve A? Give at least six examples.
2. What types of cost might be incorporated in curve B? Give at least six examples.
3. Explain: the shape of curve C, the position of curve C relative to curves A and B.
4. What would be the optimum level of pollution control? Explain your answer.
5. In your opinion, what would be the 'best' level of pollution control?
6. Why might decisions to control water pollution in the real world be more difficult to implement than theory suggests?

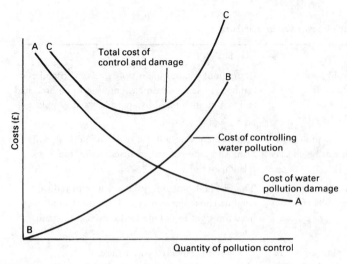

Figure 23.5 The cost of controlling pollution.

○ Case Study—Pollution control in the chemical industry

Britain's chemical industry spent more than £1 billion on the environment in 1992, which represents about 3 per cent of the industry's £29.9 billion turnover.

The chemical industry was the first British sector to publish its spending and environmental emissions statistics (Fig. 23.6). Between 1990 and 1992 capital expenditure on the environment increased substantially. As a proportion of total capital spending, it rose from 8 to 14 per cent. Environmental operating costs rose from £646 million to £727 million.

Discharges of 'red list' substances—a list of 23 groups of chemicals defined by the government as being unwelcome in aqueous waste—fell 40 per cent.

The industry's energy consumption fell 19 per cent between 1967 and 1990, although production increased 112 per cent. Energy consumption per unit of output fell 61.6 per cent.

Environmental indices created for the 114 sites between 1990 and 1992 showed that 84 had improved their performance while 30 had deteriorated. Friends of the Earth called for the industry to publish complete records of all toxic emissions. A spokesman for Friends of the Earth stated that the industry is generally improving, but has a long way to go.

Questions

1. What do you understand by the following:
    (a) turnover?
    (b) environmental emissions figures?

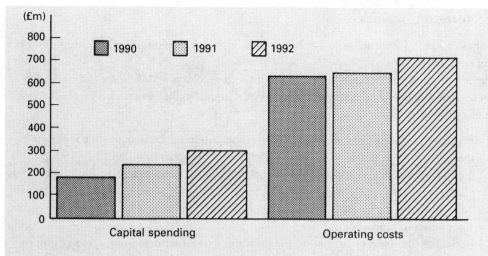

How much pollution has been discharged?

	No. of sites	1990 (tonnes)	1991 (tonnes)	1992 (tonnes)	1990–92 Change (tonnes)
Chemicals dangerous in water	37	403	334	243	−40%

Figure 23.6 Chemical industry's estimated spending on environment protection.

    (c)   capital expenditure on the environment?
    (d)   environmental operating costs?
    (e)   energy consumption?
    (f)   Friends of the Earth?
2. Why do you think that the chemical industry has been monitoring its environmental spending and emissions?
3. What has been happening to the impact of the chemical industry on the environment?
4. What measures could be used to limit environmental emissions?
5. Why is it in the interests of the chemical industry to carry out environmental audits?
6. What evidence does the case provide that environmental concern is increasing in the chemical industry?

Pressures on business

Businesses have to operate against a background in which they are faced by many different competing interests.

Internally, the business needs to make a profit for shareholders and the shareholders need to be kept content with the way the business is being run. Externally, the business has to contend with a number of pressures:

1. Perhaps the biggest pressure is actually to sell its products. Consumers do not have to buy them.
2. The business is under pressure from its competitors. Competition is often a spur to business efficiency.
3. The government and other regulatory bodies exert pressures on businesses to produce within certain standards.
4. Businesses also have to respond to the pressures exerted by organized 'pressure groups'.

Types of pressure group

Pressure groups do not fall readily into categories. Some groups are highly organized, with paid officials, set subscriptions and planned meetings—these groups may last for many years. Others may be 'three-day wonders', set up on the spur of the moment, lacking any real structure and vanishing as quickly as they arose.

Two main types of pressure group are commonly recognized:

1. *Protection groups*   These are set up to fight a specific issue such as danger on a local road caused by construction traffic building a local airport; in other words, people or groups are protecting their interests against an outside threat. Other examples would include a parents' protection group set up to fight the threatened closure of their local school, or rail commuters objecting to the closure of a threatened train service. A protest meeting will usually be called at which tactics will be planned. For example, a group of commuters protesting against the threatened cut of an early morning train from Grantham to Kings Cross decided to back up their case by occupying all the toilets on the train, and by pulling emergency communication cords.
2. *Promotional pressure groups*   These are more formal groups which are sometimes highly organized and fight campaigns on a wide range of issues. Examples include Greenpeace and Friends of the Earth. Such organizations have clearly defined long-term objectives related to environmental concern, and their sustained pressure on such issues as the environment has helped to create a radically new perspective to that which existed even 20 years ago. They campaign on a range of topics using measures that vary from madcap adventurist stunts (climbing up Nelson's column to hang slogans, colliding with very much larger shipping vessels) to sustained high-profile media advertising campaigns.

   Promotional pressure groups for environmental concern could chart their success in the large number of businesses that have begun to line themselves up behind the green campaign. For example, in November 1988 Varta introduced a 'green' range of batteries;

the following week Ever Ready responded, claiming that it was taking the green issue 'several steps further'. In early 1989 Ever Ready marketed a battery in its Silver Seal line (the top selling chloride battery in the United Kingdom) which was mercury- and cadmium-free, using the colour green in its packaging. The development of a mercury-free battery gave Ever Ready a major advantage over its major UK competitor Duracell.

Businesses also find that from time to time political parties exert strong opposition to some of their activities, such as their record of paying low wages, or supplying components of socially undesirable products. In 1992 a number of British and German companies were strongly criticized for supplying components to the Iraqi 'supergun' project.

Consumer pressure groups

A well-known and powerful consumer group is the Consumers' Association, which produces the magazine *Which?* The group is funded by subscriptions from members who buy the magazine. The Association uses its funds to test a wide variety of products on which it then produces reports in its monthly magazine. It also produces books on consumer-related matters.

The influence of the Consumers' Association goes beyond its publication of *Which?* because its reports are frequently reported in the national press. Consumer programmes also get a fair amount of time on national television, the most famous being Esther Rantzen's *That's Life*. Typical media coverage involves the investigation of complaints, and the comparison of goods and services.

Nationalized industries also have consumers' councils, examples of which are the Post Office Users' National Council for the Post Office and the Central Transport Consultative Committee for British Rail. The government has made provision for the continuation of these groups when these industries are privatized, e.g. the Office of Water Services (OFWAT).

Consumer boycotts

Consumers are sometimes organized into groups to stop buying certain products. In 1986 Barclays Bank sold off its South African subsidiary. Throughout the 1970s and 1980s, opponents of apartheid had put pressure on Barclays customers to use other banks. It is arguable that this sort of pressure finally helped to influence the bank's decision to sell.

In a similar way, Animal Rights campaigners were encouraging customers to boycott Boots in 1993 because of the way it used mice in drugs testing. Figure 23.7 shows an extract taken from one of their leaflets.

At the same time as they are trying to draw the public's attention to companies that they believe to be cruel to animals, animal rights groups also try to publicize businesses that are not cruel. For example, the 'Choose Cruelty-Free' campaign was launched in 1987 in order to highlight the suffering of animals for cosmetics testing and production. Most importantly, it was also aimed at offering the consumer a choice in the products that could be purchased. A list was drawn up and publicized of companies that had not tested their ingredients or finished products on animals in the previous five years.

ANIMAL TESTING OF BOOTS DRUG BRUFEN

Mice were injected with a substance, carrageenan, to induce pain and swelling; Brufen was then given and the effects noted. Not satisfied with this, the unfortunate mice were placed on hot plates, and 'writhing tests' with and without Brufen were conducted. Dogs were addicted to morphine and then deprived of the drug until withdrawal symptoms became apparent. Brufen was then administered to see if the symptoms were eliminated. Standard tests were carried out on dogs, rats, mice and monkeys. The lucky ones at the top dosing levels died quickly; others endured gut damage and ulceration before being put to death.

(*Source: Brufen Clinical and Technical Review*, the Boots Company Limited)

Please write for further information if you would like to know more about how Boots use many thousands of animals in experiments every year, or how they have used the courts to silence opposition. More about a healthy approach to life which does not involve prescription drugs, cruelty to animals, or human suffering, is available from the address on this leaflet.

TAKE THE FIRST STEP NOW
DON'T CONTRIBUTE TO CRUELTY – DON'T BUY THEIR PRODUCTS

DON'T BOTHER WITH BOOTS

✄ ···

Please send me further information about Boots, and how I can help stop animal cruelty

Name_____

Address_____

_____ Donation_____

NOTTINGHAM ANIMAL RIGHTS CONFEDERATION
180 Mansfield Road, Nottingham

Figure 23.7 Part of a leaflet produced by an animal rights group.

As an extension of these activities, sabotage has been used as an extreme form of protest against some forms of industrial production. For example, just before Christmas 1988, fire bombs were placed in several department stores that sell furs. The bombs were placed by the Animal Liberation Front, and one store in Plymouth was gutted, causing millions of pounds worth of damage, as well as the threat of job losses. Within the area of animal experimentation in the food, chemical and drugs industries, there are several animal rights protest groups (each with its own way of protesting), including the Animal Liberation Front and the National Anti-Vivisection Society.

Quite clearly, this can cause adverse publicity for businesses operating in this area and raise operating costs. Animals have been freed and premises attacked, and businesses have had to spend money on the employment of security, such as the specialist security firm Control Risks, which specializes in risk assessment and kidnap negotiations.

Local lobbying

There are many reasons why local residents may want to put pressure on a business to change its operations, including:

- Traffic danger
- Emission of fumes
- Emission of fluids
- Litter and noise
- Safety hazards such as tips, pits, etc.
- Threats to local employment

Normally, a pressure group will develop out of protest meetings and letters to the press. The group will then try to encourage the firm to change its policy, or will put pressure on local authorities to force the firm to change its policy. The issue may be taken further, with letters to the local Member of Parliament and attempts to interest national groups in supporting a campaign. At the highest level, local issues may come before the notice of Parliament, the national press and the courts of appeal. For example, disquiet over the safety of nuclear power stations has frequently developed from a local to a national issue.

Enlightened firms will try not to antagonize local feelings, which brings adverse publicity for the business.

Other organized pressure groups

Sometimes groups operate in a highly organized way to influence public opinion. They will try to get a wide number of people to accept their views in order to exert pressure on the business community. Trade unions use this method of persuasion quite often. Teachers, seamen and post office workers have used national advertising to try to win support from the public and from political parties for their cause. Picketing and industrial action are other ways of trying to put pressure on businesses.

The employers' organization, the CBI, and the unions' organization, the TUC, also exert influence. An example of this was a report published by the TUC in March 1993 and circulated to businesses, trying to encourage safe practices at work. Other promotional groups, such as the Campaign for Lead-free Petrol and the anti-smoking lobby, use similar techniques.

Sometimes groups use less peaceful methods to impress their views on the public. Demonstrations, protest marches and sit-ins often lead to publicity on television and in the press.

If a pressure group can gain the support of a political party, this will give it greater weight and influence because it will now have the implicit support of a large section of the electorate. It will also have reason to believe that, should that party form the next government, its aims will be realized in some measure.

Business responses to pressure groups

There are a number of ways in which businesses can respond to pressure groups:

1. They can ignore them, using the argument that consumers can choose whether to buy the product, and in the meantime can make sure that production takes place within the bounds of legal requirements.
2. They can run a counter-campaign to win public support. This is the policy that has been used by British Nuclear Fuels PLC. 'Come to Sellafield. Look around the place. See for yourself how safe it is.' This, loosely paraphrased, was the message of a multi-million-pound advertising campaign that was commissioned by BNF. The campaign appeared on television as well as in newspapers.
3. They can take advice from consumers in order to compromise and win public support in this way.

ρ Case Study—'Are Greens good for you?'

Today 'green consumerism' is being taken seriously.

Retailers have to ascertain the efficiency and cost of new green products, perhaps trading off maximum profits against a good reputation for greenness. For example, organic fruit and vegetables account for under 5 per cent of Safeway's sales in that area, but the company has persisted in giving it valuable shelf space and has given [away] lunch boxes and salad packs of such produce [during] trial periods. In Tesco the number of stores selling organic produce has been upped from an initial 8 to roughly 30. The selected stores tend to be in residential areas where shoppers are more likely to be able to afford an extra 10p–15p per pound for organics.

Biodegradable packaging is viewed favourably. Off-licence chain Victoria Wine and Safeway won plaudits at a recent Design Council exhibition for offering recycled paper bags at the checkout in favour of plastic bags.

Tesco (now one of the largest independent petrol retailers in the country) has decided that all its 80 outlets that sell petrol will stock unleaded petrol by the summer of 1989. Currently, however, a store manager can complain that the one unleaded petrol pump provides a much smaller return than a four-star pump—it's a game for the long term, but at least motorists will know [of] one outlet for unleaded.

The supermarkets also have the problem of supply and demand. The market for green products has heretofore not been big enough. It is unlikely that it could cope with a sudden surge in demand. Tesco reckons that if 1 per cent of its fruit and vegetables were to be organic, demand would outstrip supply. As devotees of BBC Radio's *The Archers* will know, it takes a farm two years from starting out on organic production before its goods can be labelled as organic by the Soil Association. This process adds a further hiccup in the supply chain. Standards have to be doubly exacting as organic produce can be more susceptible to disease.

There is also a time lag between consumer and manufacturer awareness. The CFC debate crept up on people. Many manufacturers thought that it would remain a fringe issue.

'Increasingly, the greenness of a product will have to be considered within the production, the packaging and the marketing efforts', says Sheila Moorcroft, a market research analyst looking into future social trends. 'If one product is less environmentally sound than another, then people will choose the better. And, for manufacturers, it will be cheaper in the long run to avoid environmental controversy.'

'Companies must think about their vulnerabilities', Moorcroft adds. 'They may see this as negative, but benefits can come out. Companies must ask: what are the risks in our products and/or our production? Where are there alternative possible solutions? If there are no alternatives, how do we respond? And what are our communications strategies as a contingency arrangement?'

'Manufacturers must assess their existing product. Is the target audience one that is likely to be concerned about environmental issues? Is it environmentally friendly, and can problems be ironed out or modified?' She warns about a headlong rush into greenness. 'You have got to be sensible and commercial. Do not assume that being green is essential. In some areas it could be irrelevant. In other areas, such as health care or food products, there could be significant competitive advantage to be gained.'

'Green consumerism is making an impact on exports to other European countries,' she adds, 'and it will grow to be a major influence. And if European manufacturers already have environmentally friendly products, then they may begin to make inroads over here. It is vital that indigenous manufacturers seize on the opportunities in the UK market.'

There are hoops through which any manufacturer must jump before gaining that competitive edge, and they are not just in the adapting of the manufacturing process. There are matters of labelling and legislation. Already phrases such as 'ozone-friendly' and 'cruelty-free' are appearing on products. The Soil Association has its recognised stamp for approved organic produce. There is a danger that the consumer will simply be blinded and confused by the profusion of claims and symbols.

One of the trickiest aspects is reading and anticipating which issues will be picked up by the consumer.

The CFC battle has been fought—aerosol manufacturers and fast food chains, highlighted as the principal commercial culprits in the depletion of the ozone layer, have changed their ways.

The environmental pressure groups are switching their attention. Motor manufacturers Ford and Peugeot have been at the end of stinging attacks over policies relating to cleaner engines. There are also likely to be major changes in the detergents market; phosphates, bleaches and enzymes—ingredients in washing powders and the like—are all under scrutiny.

(*Source: The Director*, January 1989)

Questions

1. Choose any one environmental issue mentioned in the case study and explain how it might bring pressure to be applied to manufacturing processes.

2. In what ways does environmental concern put pressure on retailers both from a demand and a supply side?

3. What questions might a manufacturer wish to explore before altering production to meet demands from the environmental lobby? Illustrate your answer by exploring the issue of the use of chemical fertilizers in agriculture.

4. What factors might discourage farmers from changing to organic farming?

5. In what type of product areas is 'greenness' most likely to give a competitive edge?

6. What are the costs and benefits to (a) manufacturers and (b) consumers of the reduction in the use of CFC gases?
7. How do pressure groups operate to create an environmental concern? Examine the strategy used by a particular environmental pressure group, e.g. Greenpeace: how effective are they?
8. What is meant in the case study by the statement, 'You have got to be sensible and commercial.' Do you agree with this statement?

Employment and unemployment

Another consequence of business is the creation and destruction of employment. There are more people working in the United Kingdom today than ever before as a consequence of the rise in population. Business has continually to expand to take on extra people. At the same time, the sorts of skills required are constantly changing. Almost 70 per cent of the employed and self-employed in Britain now work in services.

The latest 1987–95 forecasts from the Institute for Employment Research and other sources suggest the following employment trends:

1. Strong growth in numbers in all professional occupations took place between 1987 and 1990; demand for information technology specialists was likely to be very buoyant, especially for software and networking skills.
2. Managers, engineers, technologists and other professionals are expected to make up a greater proportion of the workforce in engineering and other production industries.
3. Technological change, including use of new materials, components and manufacturing processes, pointed to the importance of keeping engineers and technologists up to date.
4. Management jobs were expected to grow, reflecting growth in the number of small firms.
5. In the service sector, an extra 800 000 jobs were forecast in hotels and catering by 1995, 600 000 jobs in business services also by 1995, and 150 000 in distribution by 1992. Growth was expected to be concentrated within small firms, and many of these jobs were likely to be part-time.
6. Engineering craft occupations were likely to contract, reflecting automation. In many manufacturing companies existing engineering craft skills were being upgraded or broadened to support more flexible working and the wider use of new computer-controlled equipment.
7. Fewer jobs were expected at operative level across manufacturing industry.
8. Strong growth was anticipated in demand for construction workers at all levels. There was concern that existing reported shortages at craft level could worsen, particularly as few young people will be available for initial training in the 1990s.

At the same time, many jobs have been lost in agriculture and mining. The manufacturing base of the United Kingdom has been steadily declining for a long time. In the 1950s exports of manufactures were three times bigger than imports. Today we import more manufactured goods than we export. Some of the factors that have been used to account for this deterioration include low quality and an over-concentration of low-value products which many other countries now also produce.

Unemployment can be seen as a consequence of the failure of business to keep up to date. In a survey of products developed in the latter half of the twentieth century, Japan's Ministry of International Trade and Industry (MITI) found that Britons were responsible for 52 per cent of what were termed 'revolutionary' ideas; the Americans came up with 22 per cent, while the Japanese produced only 6 per cent. But when it came to product development, this order was reversed. A number of UK commentators have pointed out that industry is not spending enough on research and development to bring new products and processes to the market.

A contrasting view of modern unemployment is that it is a consequence of new technologies. A recent report by the West German Kommerzbank estimated that every robot employed in industry today replaces on average three workers, and that by the early 1990s the second generation of 'intelligent' robots will each have replaced between five and ten workers in certain assembly jobs. In the service sector too, job losses are being felt; CHAPS, a new automated way of clearing cheques in the City of London, has already made the activities of 8000 messengers unnecessary. Whether information technology will create more jobs than it causes to be lost is subject to debate. If the microchip revolution makes us more competitive, we should actually create more jobs than we lose, particularly as we move into the open market of the European Community.

We can thus see that the relationship between business development and unemployment is a complicated one. What is clear is that in the UK today a higher level of skill is required in workers. In the early 1980s, for every 100 unemployed general labourers there was one job vacancy, whereas for every 100 unemployed electronic engineers there were 87 vacancies. As a rule of thumb, higher levels of skill are being required in both factories and offices, and people are expected to have a wider range of skills.

A further problem is that regional imbalance is a consequence of the way business locates in profitable areas and later abandons these areas if locational advantages decline. Firms might choose locations in East Anglia and the South East on the basis of private costs and benefits. However, the greatest benefits to society might be reaped from locating in an unemployment blackspot like central Scotland, South Wales, the North East, the North West or Northern Ireland. (This argument could be contested by the view that the highest level of net benefit will be achieved by allowing areas with the greatest advantage to expand, while ineffective labour and other resources are shaken out of less effective areas.)

For much of the 1980s, school-leavers formed the age group with the highest rate of unemployment, although this trend is being put into reverse by demographic changes. Other groups that have been particularly hard-hit are older workers and those in racial minority groups.

Business and communities

Centres of population develop around work. As these centres become established, a community comes into being. Very strong communities develop where people share similar jobs, working together and experiencing similar life-styles. Mining communities, farming communities and sea fishing communities, for example, are well known for the strong bonds that tie people together.

In modern societies people tend to travel further to get work and to change work more frequently, and modern housing estates are characterized by people doing a wide range of different jobs. Inevitably, this tends to reduce the bonds that hold people together.

Conservation

Modern business depends on the use of non-renewable resources, particularly in the use of energy. Modern technology is particularly dependent on three main fossil fuels: oil, coal and natural gas. Together they account for over 90 per cent of the world's energy supplies.

A non-renewable resource is one of which only a limited stock exists (not necessarily totally discovered) on the planet and of which no new stock is being created. Some commentators are very worried about the way in which non-renewable resources are being used up. D. H. Meadows and his associates, in their book *The Limits to Growth*, argued that, if resources continue to be used up in the way they are being used today, then within the next hundred years a crisis will occur because certain resources are limited, namely:

- Arable land
- Coal
- Oil
- Aluminium
- Copper
- Iron
- Other minerals

In the follow-up book, *Beyond the Limits to Growth*, published in 1991, the authors argued that in many ways we are already living beyond these limits. Modern economies need to learn to pull back. The authors used systems theory to show that there are only limited resources that provide inputs to the global economy. At the same time, waste products are an output that goes into a 'sink'; and if the sink fills up too quickly it will begin to overflow and to have a negative effect on existing resources. At the Earth Summit in Rio in 1992 a number of these issues were addressed. For example, Britain is now committed to stabilizing its annual emissions of carbon dioxide at their 1990 level by the year 2000. However, there are disagreements about how this will be done. Some people want to impose the targets by government regulation, while others think that it can be achieved through the market.

In 1990 UK emissions stood at 160 million tons and this rose marginally to 161 million tons in 1991. However, in 1992 emissions fell to 156 million tons (mainly as a result of the recession, mild weather and a switch from coal-fired to nuclear electricity). Some people feel that advanced industrial nations should cut back their carbon dioxide emissions far more severely (perhaps by up to 100 per cent by the year 2000) if we are going to avoid fundamentally altering the Earth's climate while meeting the needs of Third World countries. Production of carbon dioxide depends very much on the growth path that advanced nations choose to take. High growth leads to high production of wastes and effluents, including carbon dioxide (see Fig. 23.8).

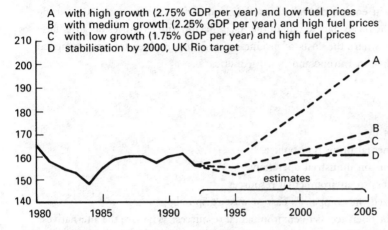

A   with high growth (2.75% GDP per year) and low fuel prices
B   with medium growth (2.25% GDP per year) and high fuel prices
C   with low growth (1.75% GDP per year) and high fuel prices
D   stabilisation by 2000, UK Rio target

Figure 23.8 Britain's CO_2 emissions (million tons of carbon).

A number of EC countries have been putting pressure on Britain to impose a Europe-wide carbon and energy tax. However, the Conservative government would prefer policies to be determined by national governments and has opted for the imposition of VAT on power and tax rises on petrol.

Case Study—The creation of wastes in Asian economies

As urban industries expanded in Asia, they created wastes that could not be adequately absorbed in the air, water and soil around the cities. Most governments were reluctant to impose restrictions on industrial operations or to raise the costs of their operation in any way that would make them less competitive. In other words, households and businesses were given 'open access' to environmental resources.

Because governments were unwilling to penalize industries for polluting the environment or to tax them sufficiently to cover the costs of cleaning up, they externalized the costs of waste disposal and subsidized production techniques that emitted hazardous substances.

The results have been predictable. In South Korea industry is producing more than 733 000 tons of hazardous waste annually and is increasing its output by more than 20 per cent a year. In Malaysia metal and chemical industries have been discharging untreated wastes into public waterways and coastal waters near to large cities. At least 42 rivers in Malaysia have been declared 'dead'.

China's coal, which is publicly subsidized and widely used by state industries for much of their production, has an average ash content of 27 per cent and a sulphur content of as much as 5 per cent, which explains in part the high level of respiratory disorders in major Chinese cities.

Asian economic development policies have been designed to encourage foreign direct investment, and have been successful in attracting foreign multinationals. Many multinational companies in environmentally hazardous industries such as petroleum, crude oil, pesticides and chemicals have set up in the Asian Pacific Rim countries because these are known as places where the costs of production and the penalties for environmental pollution are less than in Europe and North America.

Questions

1. What is meant by
   (a) environmental protection policies?
   (b) restrictions on industrial operations?
   (c) open access to environmental resources?
   (d) externalized the company's cost of waste disposal?
2. Should there be open access to environmental resources? What are the alternatives?
3. Should companies be allowed to externalize the costs of waste disposal? What are the alternatives?
4. Why and how does government 'subsidize' productive activity?
5. Why have governments encouraged multinationals to operate in their countries?
6. Why do multinationals set up in Asian countries?
7. What problems are caused by having foreign multinationals in Asian countries?

The Environmental Protection Act 1990

This Act created two new systems for regulation industrial pollution in the United Kingdom.

Integrated pollution control (IPC) will apply to more than 5000 existing industrial processes with the largest pollution potential, and will regulate all their releases to land, water and air. It will be enforced by an Inspectorate of Pollution.

The second system to be enforced will cover 27 000 *complex processes* and will control only their emissions to air. Under both systems, operators will have to employ the 'best available techniques not entailing excessive costs' to minimize releases of the most polluting substances, and to 'render harmless' all releases from their processes.

IPC extends the sorts of control previously applied only to air pollutants to all the wastes—gases, solids and liquids—generated by organizations. The new Inspectorate will ensure that the least environmentally damaging solution overall—the *best practicable environmental option*, or BPEO—is chosen to deal with these.

Green audits

In 1986 a new environmental law was passed in the United States. It did not require organizations to fix anything, install anything or clean up anything; all it obliged them to do was submit, to the Environmental Protection Agency, an annual list of the quantities of hazardous chemicals they had released into the environment. The Agency would publish the information in a Toxics Release Inventory. The aim was to create a massive shift in power away from government and industrial regulation and towards the public.

Local communities in the United States are now able to knock on companies' doors armed with detailed information about what is being put into their air and water. Environmental groups have found the inventory a valuable campaigning resource. In industry, senior management and other employees have started asking pointed questions about why such large amounts of costly raw materials and valuable products are being thrown away. Many businesses have been able to set up new strategies for saving waste and cutting down on pollution.

In Britain there is growing pressure for environmental auditing. The Environmental Protection Act has paved the way for further registers on industrial pollution, waste disposal sites, contaminated land and so on.

Some of the 'green' investment funds have joined environmentalists in arguing for compulsory audits which provide information on companies' raw material and energy consumption as well as pollution. The TUC has urged its members to demand green audits in workplace negotiations.

Leading oil and chemical companies have been running auditing programmes since the 1970s. These are generally intended to show up weaknesses in environmental management systems and breaches in internal standards. Companies also like to take an audit of another company's environmental legacy before considering a merger. The findings of such audits are intended for management's eyes, rather than the public's.

In 1990 the European Commission produced a draft idea to enforce environmental audits on companies in a number of leading sectors. However, the Commission is now expected to suggest only a voluntary scheme.

The Eco-industrial Revolution

Corporate strategy involves planning ways of securing a competitive edge in the market-place. Today a company's environmental performance will be increasingly central to its competitiveness and survival.

The term 'eco-industrial revolution' was first given prominence by a group of Asian industrialists in 1991. The eco-industrial revolution is concerned with ways of developing competitive strategies which take as their foundation the need to derive a key part of their competitive advantage from their superior environmental performance.

Matthew Kiernan, in *The Age of Eco-strategy*, has identified four main keystones that businesses will need to adopt to develop this competitive advantage:

1. A shift towards an economy of long-term investment and capital appreciation rather than short-term profits. (If we continue to concentrate on the short term, we will no longer have a long term to contemplate.)

2. A shift away from an opportunistic economy to one based on opportunity. Such an economy would be sensitive to the interdependence between economy and ecology; priority would be given to a wide access to markets, credit, appropriate technology and training.

3. A shift towards an economy of conservation and re-consumption, with incentives to integrate environmental values into everyday business practice. This would involve a recycling, remanufacturing and repair economy, in which the developing world could actually enjoy a number of comparative advantages.

4. A shift to a culture of savings, away from a culture dominated by immediate consumption.

Ethical behaviour in business

In addition to informing us about highly successful business activities, the media also bring to our attention questionable activities. For example, we hear about *insider trading* (i.e. people with advance information about company performance, arising from their privileged position working for the company, buying and selling shares to make unfair capital gains), about executives of companies using company money to their own ends and purposes, about bribery and corruption, testing products on animals, trade taking place with inhumane governments and so on.

As a result of this attention, we are becoming increasingly aware of the influence of ethical and moral values on business decisions. Views about what is or is not ethical vary considerably, and this chapter has already covered a number of ethical issues in its analysis of the consequences of business activity.

A recent *Which?* report found that 63 per cent of respondents to one of their surveys were concerned about the activities of companies they might invest in. Business ethics is clearly an area of growing concern. As with the environment, a modern organization can gain a competitive edge by developing ethics-based strategies.

Ethics concerns the moral principles or rules of conduct that are generally accepted by most members of a society. It constitutes a guide to what should or should not be done, and involves what one believes to be right and what one considers to be wrong. From an early age, parents, religions and society in general provide us with moral guidelines to help us to learn and form our ethical beliefs. Many ethical principles are reinforced in our legal system and thus provide a constraint to business activities, but others are not. In areas not covered by law, pressure groups are often formed to put forward their case.

Ethics is a problem for business. Everybody thinks it is important, but few seem to know what to do about it. A study by Integrity Works, a business ethics consultancy, and Ashridge Management Consultancy in 1993 looked at the views of non-executive directors. This group was chosen because it is in a good position to shape and guide corporate values.

Forty-three per cent of directors questioned said that their organizations had codes of ethics; 'ethics awareness training' takes place in 13 per cent of companies, and ethics audits in 8 per cent. However, the majority of companies (61 per cent) were said to use discipline rather than audits and codes of practice to create ethical practices.

Half of the people questioned said that ethical standards in business had improved during the previous ten years, but a fifth said that their companies had never had formal discussions about the issue, and a quarter said that there was no means of ensuring ethical behaviour in the company. Forty-two per cent of directors felt that the general public sees business in general as being 'quite ethical', while 25 per cent felt that the public views business as 'quite unethical'!

To develop an effective ethical strategy, companies need to identify the ethical requirements of being in business and to see how they currently fall short of these standards. They will then need to ensure that ethical standards are articulated, monitored and enforced in the organization. An ethics index could be developed to monitor performance over time.

The costs of developing an ethical approach are likely to be far less than the costs of carrying on with no awareness of ethical issues and imperatives. Evidence indicates that the stance of the chief executive and senior managers in a company is essential in developing effective strategy.

Case Study—Bangers Sausages Ltd

Bangers Sausages Ltd is a small sausage factory employing 30 people situated in the heart of an area of high unemployment. The company is doing well and looking to expand, which will probably mean moving away from its existing location.

Express your views on each of the following problems facing the board of directors:

1. Whether to move away from the area of high unemployment in order to obtain cost advantages.
2. Whether to make the sausage more healthy by reducing the fat content and pushing up prices.
3. Whether to purchase an incinerator for waste products that only just meets the necessary health and safety requirements for waste disposal, or to consider an alternative form of disposal.
4. Whether to promote the company as an equal opportunities employer.

A frequently debated aspect of business ethics refers to a company's actions where there is no law or where the law is unclear. For example, if there is no law forbidding a particular action, should a company pursue that particular course if it is ethically dubious? There is an example of an American corporation which discovered that it was more cost-effective to pay compensation to injured employees than to invest in research to improve safety.

Today business ethics is at the forefront of the industrial debate. We are concerned about living in a better society, and if this society is to materialize many people believe that ethics must play an important role.

Questions

Short-answer questions

1. A derelict piece of land in an inner-city area of high unemployment can be used:
   (i)   to build a leisure centre;
   (ii) to build a hypermarket;
   (iii) to build an industrial estate.
   The local planning committee decides to allow the land to be used for the development of the leisure centre.
   (a) List five private costs and five private benefits for the developer.
   (b) List five further costs and benefits to the local community.

2. Explain the difference between wealth and income. Illustrate your answers with examples of
   (a) private and national wealth.
   (b) private and national income.

3. How would value be added in the production of furniture? How would it be possible to increase the existing levels of value added at each stage?

4. List five major types of pollution. What measures could be taken to (a) prevent and (b) reduce one of these forms of pollution?

5. How could taxes be used as a weapon to control pollution?

6. What are the main types of pressure group? Outline the main aims of one pressure group.

7. Give an example of a nationalized industry consumer council. What is its purpose?

8. What is meant by (a) renewable and (b) non-renewable resources? Give five examples of each.

9. What is meant by conservation? Describe three measures that can be employed by society to conserve a particular resource.

10. What is the purpose of cost–benefit analysis?

11. What are the costs and benefits of installing a new piece of equipment in your school or college?

12. What are the costs and benefits to (a) you personally and (b) society of your journey into school or college?

13. Make a list of the externalities of some of your social activities.

14. Table 23.4 illustrates the costs and revenues of producing additional units of a product. The firm in question produces chemicals. Some of the effluent is discharged into a local river at a social cost of £2 per ton. Assuming that the firm is a profit-maximizer,
   (a) how much output would the firm produce if it did not have to pay for social costs?
   (b) how much output would the firm produce if it was made to pay for social costs?

15. What problems would be involved in making producers of acid rain responsible for the damage it causes?

16. In what ways can business be seen as being responsible for the creation of unemployment?

17. What are the major benefits of industrial activity for society?

18. What sorts of risk are attached to business activity?

19. Give an example of problems caused by the insufficient testing of products.

Table 23.4

Output (tons)	Revenue per additional ton produced (£)	Cost per additional ton produced (£)	Pollution damage per additional ton produced (£)
1	20	10	2
2	20	12	2
3	20	14	2
4	20	16	2
5	20	18	2
6	20	20	2
7	20	22	2
8	20	24	2

20. What is meant by the term 'recycling'? In what circumstances is 'recycling' economically viable?

Essays

1. Suppose that a new urban motorway is to be built around the centre of a large city. This centre contains both commercial development and housing for low- to middle-income families. They will be affected by the motorway.
   (a) List the costs and benefits of such a proposal.
   (b) How will the desirability of this project differ as to the following groups:
      (i) private motorists?
      (ii) commercial vehicle operators?
      (iii) shoppers?
      (iv) local residents?
2. Imagine that you live in a semi-rural community that has been worried by the presence of a large chemical factory and its emission of toxic fumes, which local farmers have suggested are causing diseases in cattle. Local people are also worried about the possible long-term effects on human health. You have been approached by various residents to help set up a local pressure group and fight a campaign against the firm in question. What typically are the problems such a group might face, and how might you try to overcome them?
3. To what extent should a government legislate to control business activity? (*Source:* AEB)
4. With reference to a local company, investigate the costs and benefits of installing a new piece of machinery.
5. Should business be made accountable to the local community?
6. We face a world 'more polluted, less stable ecologically, more vulnerable to disruption than ever before'. What sorts of measures need to be taken to deal with this situation?
7. Compare and contrast the effectiveness of different measures for dealing with the problem of pollution.

8. What is cost–benefit analysis? Examine the strength and weaknesses of such a method of analysing and evaluating business projects.

9. Is it possible to carry out the process of 'wealth creation' to the benefit of all members of a society?

10. Why is it more difficult to control pollution from several international sources than from a single-nation source? What are the implications of this in the case of the destruction of the ozone layer?

Data response questions

1   Dioxin outlawed by manufacturers in search for safer nappies

At the beginning of 1989, the disposable nappy industry launched a clean-up campaign to outlaw [the] dioxins added to the paper wadding filler by traditional chlorine bleaching. It was feared that these substances were being transferred to babies' skins.

The UK nappy maker Peaudouce and its rival Procter and Gamble both announced that their fillers are being produced without the chlorine bleach process.

The Ministry of Agriculture is investigating dioxin contamination of food from bleached-paper wrappers. In early 1989 the pressure group Women's Environmental Network began lobbying for all sanitary and other soft tissue products to be made without chlorine bleaching.

Peaudouce signalled its change to a lightly bleached filler with harmless hydrogen peroxide as an environmentally friendly gesture to stop water pollution by toxic organochlorides, which are coming under increasingly strict government control, at its Swedish pulp mills. This new process also doubles the number of nappies obtained from each tree felled. A spokesperson for Peaudouce said that the new process reduced dioxins, a by-product of incineration and chemical processing in the pulp, to scarcely detectable levels. The product now contains less dioxin. It is not dioxin-free. The company believe that there is no evidence that dioxins in nappy fillings are a danger. They cling tightly to the cellulose and are not likely to be given off by a product designed to absorb.

The Women's Environmental Network have welcomed the modified nappy, but added that dioxins are absorbed by fat and grease, making baby lotions a possible transmitter from the nappy to the skin.

The risk attached to the main dioxin, TCDD, is contentious. The US Environmental Protection Agency called it the most potent cancer-agent in animals it had tested, and studies have linked low concentrations—which the chemical industry says are harmless—to human cancers and birth defects.

(*Source: The Independent*, January 1989)

1. List three groups mentioned in the extract with different interests in the production of disposable nappies. Outline the particular interest of each group and explain what you think that their perspectives are likely to be.

2. What are the costs and benefits to a disposable nappy producer of outside pressures?

3. What are the costs and benefits to consumers of disposable nappies of outside pressures?

4. Is it necessary to have governmental regulation of the production of disposable nappies?

5. Why do you think that manufacturers have not totally removed dioxins from paper nappies? Is this a desirable state of affairs?

2   A local pollution incident

This question is based on an incident that happened in 1975 and all figures quoted are actual. This exercise can be used either as a written case study or as a role-playing exercise; students could then be given only the factual information and arrive at their own verdict.

The parties involved

- Regional Water Authority (RWA) prosecutor
- Solicitor acting for the firm
- Magistrates; chairman of the Panel and two others
- Managing director of XYZ Cloth Scourers
- Day shift foreman of XYZ Cloth Scourers

N.B.   Cloth scouring is the process by which dirt and grease that collects on the cloth as it is woven is removed.

Other interested parties are a representative of the local anglers and one could introduce local conservationists and the local government officer responsible for tourism. The latter two did not appear in the original case but the area concerned, in the South Pennines, does now try to market its scenic attractions. These centre around a not unpleasant mix of open countryside and working towns along with close proximity to the Peak National Park.

The background

The stream involved is classified as Class 1.

Class 1 water has high amenity value, is a potable water supply and will support game fish, e.g. trout. Class 2 is potable after treatment, has moderate amenity value and will support coarse fish. Class 3 is polluted to the extent that fish are absent or only sporadically present. Class 4 waters are grossly polluted and likely to cause a nuisance.

In 1976 the water quality in the RWA area was approximately:

Class 1 82%
Class 2 6%
Class 3 4%
Class 4 8%

The RWA has a policy of maintaining the quality of those water-courses at present in Class 1 and 2 whilst improving those in Class 3 and eliminating all Class 4 watercourses. At the time, the area was subject to drought conditions and this aggravated the effect of the pollutant.

The incident

Rather than risk damage to an export order worth £10 000, the textile firm deliberately contaminated an adjacent fresh water stream.

The results

One hundred trout between three and ten inches in length were killed by the waste material which had the approximate strength of untreated sewage. The effluent was discharged for three hours and affected a one-and-a-quarter-mile length of the stream. The visual effect of the pollutant was apparent for two to three days afterwards.

The firm's decision

The firm normally disposed of this waste into the sewer by means of an electrically driven pump. A fault had developed in the starter for the motor that drove the pump and so had rendered it inoperative. Rather than risk damage to the cloth loaded on the machine, the firm turned on a valve to allow the effluent to go directly into the stream. This occurred over the period 7.30 to 10.30 that day. The initial decision was taken by the foreman but was backed by managers at both the senior level and at the top of the firm. The firm normally carried spares for the pump and the motor but it did not have a spare starter in stock.

The solicitor for the firm pointed out that, whilst there was no excuse, one could perhaps understand their actions given the nature and value of the order. The firm had from the outset admitted exactly what had happened.

The firm's individual action

Arrangements were being made after the incident:

- to install an alternative pump at a cost of £700
- to restock the water with trout at a cost of £25

The magistrate's Court decision

A fine of £500 was imposed on the firm for the two charges of poisoning the water, at that time the maximum fine possible. The Court also awarded costs of £50.

(*Source: Economics Journal*, March 1987)

1. Did the firm make the right decision?
2. In the end, has anybody really suffered?
3. Would we have a different view of this incident if seen as:
   (a) a single incident?
   (b) part of a wider policy towards the reduction of pollution over the RWA catchment area?

3   Morality in business

1. Why is the reputation for honesty, integrity and fair dealing in the City beyond price?
2. Consider whether it is fair to go ahead with a particular action if the law does not forbid it.
3. What is the danger of 'my word is my bond' becoming 'catch me if you can'?
4. Present your views of the implications for society if moral and ethical standards begin to slip.

The new morality of business that says 'catch me if you can'

William Rees-Mogg on the significance of the Queen's warning to the City

Even goldfish find it hard to live in a goldfish bowl; it can be no easier for the Royal Family. The glass bowl of personal publicity in which they live is bathed in the arc lights of television. They are given too little room to breathe freely; in particular the younger members of the Royal Family are allowed little freedom to be young. Those who are trained for this life find it, I suspect, difficult enough. Those who marry into it must find it virtually unbearable. Most of the publicity is trivial, and some of it is malicious.

The tabloid Press is beginning to hint that there is a problem for the Royal Family, but if so it is of their own making. Too much publicity is damaging; drivelling publicity is absolutely. *The Sun*, in particular, is quasi-republican, an attitude which strangely contradicts its fervent nationalism.

This false publicity, which all the members of the Royal Family must resent, is matched by a widespread failure to report the serious business which they conduct so unobtrusively and on the whole so well.

Last Wednesday, for instance, the Queen lunched with the Lord Mayor of London to celebrate the 800th anniversary of the mayoralty. She took the occasion to make a thoughtful and serious speech. Read with any care it contained a serious warning, and to warn is one of the duties of a constitutional monarch. It was only quoted a couple of times in any newspaper; I heard about it by chance, and obtained a copy of the full speech from the Press Secretary.

What the Queen said was this: "The 30,000 people who come to work (in the City) are reaping the benefits of the reputation for honesty, integrity and fair-dealing which has been created by generations of their predecessors. That sort of reputation is beyond price . . . Free and open markets may be the key to financial success, but if they are to operate fairly and honestly, someone has to write the rules and to see that they are rigidly enforced . . . Rules and structures may be important, but much more important are the unwritten rules and the will to abide by them. In the end it is the loyalty and good sense of the citizens themselves that makes the whole system work."

It is the natural custom of the Queen to couch her warnings in language which will be acceptable to her audience. She is not entitled to be deliberately shocking and aggressive. Not for her the Edwina Currie approach. Perhaps for that reason most of the newspapers missed the significance of what she was saying.

Yet she was taking the occasion to address the issue of City ethics, and was warning the City of the danger that ethical standards might be slipping, or might have slipped. However politely it was put, it was a tough message to a Guildhall audience.

It is a message which has multiple warheads. First, there is the significance that it is the Queen who is saying it. She is not a City journalist, nor is she the Governor of the Bank of England. The Queen would only be raising the question in this way if she had become convinced that the supposed decline in City ethics was not merely a technical question but a national one.

The second warhead is the reminder that the City's business has been built on generations of trust. Trust is slowly won, but quickly lost. The City inherits a vast credit from its ancestors, not only in its business, but in the standards they created. Of course the old City had its rogues, but it was founded on partnership, on unlimited liability and on a code of personal honour. Its credit was earned by good faith.

The third warhead is the statement that regulation must be enforced "rigidly". It is an interesting word. The Queen is not, I think, implying that there ought to be a more bureaucratic type of regulation, of the Securities and Investments Board kind. She is saying that people must not be allowed to bend the rules. That is surely right. When one reads the Companies Acts, one realises that each clause has historically been written to prevent a particular abuse. If the clauses can be bent, the abuses can creep back through the gap — just as the abolition of the old Section 54 has again made it lawful for companies to be bought with their own money.

The biggest warhead came last. What worries people about the City is the suspicion that it will only obey written rules, that it has lost its sense of "unwritten rules and the will to abide by them".

The Queen is attacking a very common view of modern business ethics, that if the law does not forbid an action, it is fair to go ahead. This can be taken to justify all sorts of business malpractice and bad faith, false markets, oppression of the weak, meanness of spirit, dishonouring of assurances. "My word is my bond" becomes "Catch me if you can."

In fact, the City's business cannot be successfully conducted without an ethic which goes wider and deeper than the law can require. The basis of sound finance is not merely keeping inside the statutes, but honesty and honour.

After all, the City's whole existence depends on the acceptance of fiduciary responsibility; that involves an attitude not of bare legality but of the utmost striving to fulfil a trust. Such an attitude is all the more important because no businessman can guarantee always to succeed, or that all his investments will prosper.

The issue, of course, goes much wider than the City. There is a dual basis for every occupation. There is indeed the discipline of the bottom line. Every business has to be profitable if it is to survive and expand. Newspapers must win circulation. Politicians can keep power only if they win votes. Teachers must help their students to pass examinations; doctors must cure their patients when that is possible. The Royal Family must retain the loyalty of the nation.

Yet always there is a moral as well as a practical standard to be met, and the moral standard is also a condition of survival. The City will gradually wither away if it ceases to be seen as a trustworthy manager of other people's funds. Businesses which do not meet their moral commitment to their customers lose them. Newspapers cannot afford to be despised. Politicians who become cynical about the gullibility of the electorate — and electorates can be gullible — lose elections.

The Queen is right about the City — and her warning needs to be taken — but she is also giving a broader warning about national life. That needs to be taken as well.

Figure 23.9 Leader article on business ethics (*Source: The Independent*)

731

Suggested reading

Crafts, N., *Can De-Industrialisation Seriously Damage Your Wealth?* Anforme, 1993.
Le Grand, J. and Robinson, R., *The Economics of Social Problems* Macmillan, 1984.
Dransfield, R., Yeomans, B., Wales, J. *The Limits to Growth*, Nuffield Project/Longman 95.

24
Business studies in practice

Business and industrial studies is an area that attempts to link life after school with life at school and therefore provide a more practical academic experience for students whether they wish to go into higher education, the public sector or the private sector. Although preparation can be immense and can provide a real challenge to students, the rewards can be enormous. We have tried to emphasize throughout the text that business studies is a dynamic area, and to make the subject relate to real activities through the persistent use of case studies. By doing so we hope that we have provided:

1. An understanding of the main forces underlying change in the business world.
2. An understanding of many of the problems that businesses face.
3. Opportunities for students to practise basic problem-solving skills.
4. An understanding of factors governing business decision-making.

The purpose of this final chapter is first to place emphasis on the interdependent nature of the business world by providing a number of case studies that link in various parts of the subject so that it can be seen as a whole. Looking at case studies covering specific areas of the syllabus is useful, but does not show how business problems interrelate. The final part of this book, 'Linking business studies: Notes for teachers', provides useful suggestions and sources of information which can be used for reference by both student and teacher, together with ideas for activities to enhance courses.

Case Study 1—Micro Tech PLC

Micro Tech PLC is a progressive and very profitable UK engineering company producing high-technology equipment for the aerospace industry. Its biggest customer is the military, which takes over 80 per cent, by value, of Micro Tech's products.

An important factor in the firm's success is its ability to modify quickly its standard products and to meet a customer's special needs. It can do this by virtue of a very competent design department well-equipped with up-to-date computer-aided design (CAD) facilities.

The company employs over 500 skilled and well-trained personnel in the manufacturing processes in which it is engaged. Labour turnover is very high and there are plenty of alternative employment opportunities for Micro Tech's employees. Replacement and recruitment are a headache to the company, and the performance of the personnel department is beginning to assume a position of key importance in the company's operations. The company is facing growing competition from a number of American firms, and there is evidence of government support for these companies. At the same time, there has been a change of UK government and the new Chancellor is clearly concerned to make savings and cut back on government expenditure. This is bound to affect the economic environment in which Micro Tech is operating.

Increased overseas competition and the new UK government's expected austerity measures were the main subjects of Micro Tech's last board meeting. The board decided that the company must diversify its range of products and extend its market opportunities. Such a policy would involve the company in a significant re-equipment programme and there is considerable doubt concerning the company's capacity to finance such an investment programme from within its own resources.

Questions

1. As Micro Tech's personnel manager, how would you set about tackling the company's labour turnover and recruitment problems?
2. Identify the characteristics of the CAD that make the facilities so important for the particular needs of Micro Tech.
3. What are the main mechanisms available to the UK government to shape the environment within which companies such as Micro Tech operate?
4. What financial alternatives are available to the board which might facilitate a capital investment programme and allow Micro Tech to diversify its range of products?
5. On what basis might Micro Tech choose among these alternatives? Make your assumptions clear.

(*Source*: Oxford)

Case Study 2—An organization chart

The organization chart in Fig. 24.1 is typical of the organizational approach adopted in many light engineering companies. Study it and answer the following questions.

Questions

1. Discuss the problems that might arise from such an organizational structure and suggest an alternative, giving reasons for the changes.

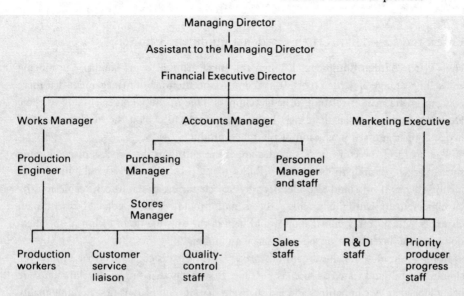

Figure 24.1 Organization chart of an engineering company.

2. The managing director (MD) has been summoned to attend a senior management meeting at the parent company. The meeting will be concerned with evaluating the factors materially affecting the group's long-term efficiency. The detailed programme lays great stress on the technique of value engineering. Accordingly, the MD writes a memo to his works manager requesting a reminder of the main points on no more than one side of A4.

   Assume that you are the works manager: produce the work called for by the managing director.

3. The purchasing manager is preparing a briefing for the induction of some new members of staff about to join his department. He decides to include in his brief the main objectives of the purchasing department and the major operations with which it is involved. Assume that you are the purchasing manager: produce a skeleton draft of the purchasing objectives and operations you would wish to cover in your briefing to the new staff.

4. The company is going through a major exercise of revising and rewriting its job descriptions. Outline the main responsibilities that you would expect to see covered in the production engineer's job description. Base the job description on the alternative structure you devised in question 1.

(Source: Oxford)

Case Study 3—High Garth Garden Equipment Limited

High Garth Garden Equipment Limited is a small manufacturing company producing and selling a range of garden tools. It has come to the attention of management that there is a gap in the market relating to hedge clippers. One of the younger employees, Jane Dean, has suggested that there may be an opportunity to exploit the need for a rotary hedge clipper and sell it as a top of the range product.

The board of directors finds the idea appealing and is in the process of conducting some market research to assess the viability of the idea. Not only would the survey identify demand, it would also identify physical characteristics and features desired by customers, help with the pricing process and provide a knowledge of distribution channels. Much of this information would help in the drawing up of technical specifications and the installation of the necessary equipment.

In the event of going ahead with this project, the board is concerned that a prototype should be built and tested as soon as possible. It suspects that similar developments are being looked at by competitors and is also aware that, its company is first to put a quality product on to the market, current factory capacity may have to be expanded. In addition, the board is looking at the best means of promoting and advertising the product.

The sales and production team have made an initial estimate of sales for the first year which is independent of the market survey. They suggest a range of between 600 and 1000 units. The sales director expects that, if the new product were made, the selling price per unit would be £100 and the variable distribution cost would be £3 per unit. The production manager estimates the material cost to be £27 per unit, and that each hedge clipper will require six hours' labour. Factory workers receive a basic wage of £5 per hour. New machinery will have to be purchased costing £5000. This is expected to last five years with no scrap value. Fixed factory overheads per annum would be as follows:

Rent and rates	£2000
Heat and light	£1000
Insurance	£ 100
General expenses	£3900

The company secretary anticipates that extra paperwork will require a part-time clerical worker at £2000 per annum.

Apart from the variable distribution cost, the only selling cost relating to this product will be advertising. There are two possibilities. One is a local campaign, the total cost of which would be £10 000, and the other is a combined national and local campaign which would cost £20 000.

Though wary about investing too much too soon on this product, High Garth Garden Equipment Limited is confident of a bright future for rotary hedge clippers.

Questions

1. As High Garth Garden Equipment Limited is likely to be involved in producing only one type of hedge clipper, explain why producing the top of the range model would be an example of concentrated marketing.

2. Briefly advise on the most appropriate and cost-effective strategies for collecting information on this type of product.

3. Explain why quantitative analysis is used to interpret data from market research and suggest two possible methods of presenting consumer data from research conducted in the market for rotary hedge clippers.

4. Comment briefly upon the advisability of expanding factory capacity during a period of rising interest rates.

5. Suggest how an effective advertising campaign capable of reaching the right target group for rotary hedge clippers could be cheap in relation to the extra sales made.

6. Comment on
   (a) the dangers of putting an insufficiently tested product on the market.
   (b) the social costs and benefits of expanding current factory capacity.

7. Management would like to know the budgeted outcomes of sales of 600 units and 1000 units when the advertising costs are:
   (a) £10 000.
   (b) £20 000.

   In case the projected figures are not realized, management would also like to know the break-even point with regard to sales at each level of advertising. Prepare this information for management use.

Case Study 4—Boscom Limited

Two years ago Peter Roberts, a married man of 43 with two children, suddenly found himself faced with the prospect of redundancy. For the past 15 years he had worked for Schultz, a large multinational firm manufacturing electrical components for the 'white goods' industry. Peter had originally been employed as a design draughtsman and was now production manager. Schultz had made the decision to trim its UK operations and to concentrate its main activities on its more profitable operations in Germany, where the emphasis was on the manufacture of electrical components for cars.

Schultz was placed in the embarrassing position of letting down long-standing customers, selling off UK assets and dismissing the workforce. It circulated its employees accordingly.

Peter was an enterprising person and saw this as an opportunity to grasp at something he had always wanted to do and start up a business of his own. He made an approach to a number of employees at Schultz whom he trusted and whose skills he respected and they put together a plan to set up in business on their own. They approached Schultz's senior management and presented it with their scheme, which involved taking over existing customer contracts and buying the firm's machinery and equipment.

They argued that, although Schultz had found this area of its operations unprofitable, a smaller firm with fewer overheads and more efficient use of labour and equipment could be successful. Schultz was delighted to be given a workable solution to its problems, and not only sold the machinery to the men at a reasonable price, but co-operated with them throughout the transfer of ownership.

Boscom Limited was set up as a private limited company in a small factory unit within 300 yards of the old premises. Although on a significantly smaller scale than the previous organization, it employs over half of the previous workforce. During its first year it had difficulty managing its working capital mainly because of an excessive debt collection period, but, using the payback method, all of the formation expenses will have been paid by the end of year 3. The quality of electrical components has been improved and, over recent months, export houses have contacted Boscom and suggested that there is a market for these types of electrical component in the Middle East. Peter and his colleagues anticipate considerable growth in the market over the next few years, and with careful planning their future seems bright.

Questions

1. Explain why a large multinational organization such as Schultz might have wished to trim its UK operations and why a smaller organization might be able to make existing UK operations more profitable.
2. Consider the advantages to Boscom Limited of joining the Unlisted Securities Market and critically examine the methods through which the company could achieve growth.
3. Describe the likely objectives Boscom could use to assess its own performance.
4. Consider how growth for Boscom Limited could
    (a) affect the career prospects of staff.
    (b) affect working conditions.
5. If Boscom Limited decides to diversify in order to expand, outline the sequence of events you could envisage to lead to the successful launching of an alternative product.
6. Discuss the effects of high interest rates and an overvalued pound on Boscom's export competitiveness.
7. Point out the dangers of insufficient working capital. How might Boscom Limited reduce the period of the cash cycle?
8. Explain why the payback method is often criticized as a method of investment appraisal, and comment upon the benefits of alternative methods.
9. Explain why quality control is not just a system designed to improve quality but is designed to do so at a cost-effective level.
10. As Boscom Limited gets larger, outline the benefits they would achieve by moving from batch to flow production.

Case Study 5—Powervanes Plc

Powervanes is a subsidiary of a major international engineering company based in the English Midlands. It currently manufactures only one product, the Powervane 2000.

One Tuesday morning the managing director of Powervanes finds the following memos on his desk:

POWERVANES PLC
INTERNAL MEMORANDUM

TO: Managing Director   FROM: Percy Knell, Personnel Director
DATE: 4 November 1991   REF: SW/PK/63/2
SUBJECT: Industrial Relations

I had Bill Brookes in again today. On the whole he's a pretty reasonable bloke, but he says the operatives are getting fed up with conditions on the shop-floor. He says we're breaking the Health & Safety at Work Act because everything's so crowded and mucky. I don't agree with him on that point, but certainly all is not well. We've got to be a bit careful because there's no lack of jobs in the area, and recruitment is getting more and more difficult. I thought you'd like to be informed of what's going on. I can keep a lid on it for now, but for how long I'm not too sure. I know it's great to be working at full capacity like we were last year, but it does impose strains, as I'm sure you're aware.

INTERNAL MEMORANDUM

TO: Managing Director   FROM: Ivor Labcote, Research Director
DATE: 6 November 1991   REF: LP/IL/97/4
SUBJECT: Powervane 2000 Replacement

We have run into a number of technical difficulties with the Powervane 3000, and revised European standards on exhaust emissions could involve some modifications. We are currently testing three prototypes to examine their performances. It is therefore difficult to provide you with an exact date for launch, but I would not expect it to be less than eighteen months.

INTERNAL MEMORANDUM

TO: Managing Director   **FROM:** Posie Wales, Marketing Director
DATE: 7 November 1991   **REF:** FS/PW/32/4
SUBJECT: Projected Sales Figures

In reply to your recent memo, limited market research undertaken by my area sales managers and their teams reveals the following information:

Selling price	Projected annual sales for 1992
£4.80	600 000
£4.90	550 000
£5.00	510 000
£5.25	525 000
£5.50	470 000

Last year's sales, as you know, were 500 000 at an average selling price of £5.00
The competitive position is tightening, and there is a rumour in the industry that Transones have a new model about to hit the market. If this is so, the above figures would certainly have to be revised. My department is naturally concerned since the Powervane 2000 has always had a technical edge over the competition.

INTERNAL MEMORANDUM

TO: Managing Director   **FROM:** Hans Onit, Product Engineering
DATE: 7 November 1991   **REF:** LM/HO/47/3
SUBJECT: New Plant Feasibility Study

As requested, we have undertaken a survey of our present plant. By altering its layout, and buying new German machine tools, capacity could be increased to 600 000 units. We could shed some labour, we estimate 10 operatives, and with increased efficiency we could reduce variable costs to £1.50 per unit. Fixed overheads would rise to £700 000 per annum. There would be some disruption to present production, but the changes could be completed within one year.

We should perhaps consider a greenfield site. There are a number which look interesting — particularly in Northern Ireland.

INTERNAL MEMORANDUM

TO: Managing Director   FROM: I. Watch, Work Study Dept.
DATE: 8 November 1991   REF: SL/IW/39/4
SUBJECT: Cost Breakdown

At last year's level of production, variable costs were £2.00 per unit, and our fixed costs were £600 000 per year. We could increase production by up to 10% using overtime, in which case costs would rise to £2.10 variable, and by £10 000 p.a. fixed.

I hope this information suits your requirements. You will appreciate that it is necessarily only approximate.

Questions

1. (a) What is the current break-even output for the Powervane 2000?
   (b) What was the level of gross profit last year?
2. (a) Draw and label a diagram to illustrate the concept of the product life cycle.
   (b) Mark the position where you think the Powervane 2000 is currently and briefly explain why you have placed it there.
3. Clearly stating any assumptions that you make, and supporting your arguments with numerical calculations wherever possible, outline the advantages and disadvantages of the following alternative courses of action:
   (a) Using the present plant and increasing output by 10%.
   (b) Increasing production to 600 000 units per annum.
   (c) Moving to a greenfield site in Northern Ireland.
4. Using the information contained in all of the memos, as well as your answers to 3 above, explain what strategies you would employ in the company over the next 18 months if you were the managing director.

(Source: AEB)

Case Study 6—Clean up the world

Reckitt & Colman is aiming to clean up the world. Although already a major global force with sales of £1.9 billion, by the year 2000 it plans to be the world's leading producer of household products (apart from the main detergent manufacturers).

John Honey, R & C's household and toiletries general manager, says that 'this is probably the most aggressive period I have known.' In his opinion, markets are now beginning to move fast and he feels that if Reckitts are going to lead the market they must move faster. This is certainly the case at R & C. They have set the ball rolling on a mammoth campaign to heighten awareness of well-known products and to launch others.

In 1993 R & C pushed the household sector from several fronts and each drive was backed by a well-planned campaign. One of its biggest successes is in the air freshener market. John Honey claims that 'Haze Aroma Jar now outsells the SC Johnson equivalent by two to one.' It was launched in August 1991. As a complement, R & C has launched the Haze Aroma Plug—an air freshener activated when plugged into a wall socket, as a competitor to the Johnson Glade Plug-ins. Honey believes that the Aroma Plug will take the market by storm. It has a number of new features to rival the SCJ product, such as an adjustable aroma control which allows three settings.

The Down to Earth green range of products was relaunched in April. R & C now have about 65 per cent of the green brand market which is worth about £20 million. John Honey feels that 'people are interested in buying environmentally friendly products provided they do not have to pay a premium and the cleaning performance comes close to the brand leaders'. He believes that the Down to Earth range meets these criteria. Multi-media advertising for this range starts in July with a £1 million spend.

Old favourite Mr Sheen polish will also be back on TV from July 1993 through a £600 000 campaign. Ten years ago it only had a 10 per cent share of the market and now it is 32 per cent with Pledge as the main competitor.

Another major launch for this year is the Dettox room spray. Honey has confidence in the product because, 'Unlike most air fresheners, this does not just cover up odours but destroys them in the air.' R & C also plan to launch the Immac Body Care Collection in 1993. This includes Body Conditioning Milk, Moisturising Satin Mousse, Body Toning Gel and Invigorating Body Scrub. Advertisements will run through to September and cost £1 million. Deepfresh is another relaunch under the Dettol banner using new packaging and graphics.

The R & C assault on the household market comes at a time when many industry commentators are questioning the durability of brands in the face of own-label products. John Honey feels that R & C are 'offering something that own label brand cannot directly match—brand assurance, brand quality and innovation'.

Questions

1. What is Reckitt & Coleman's objective?
2. If markets are moving faster than ever, what is the implication for product life-cycles?
3. Reckitt & Colman has launched the Haze Aroma Plug as a line extension to the Haze Aroma Jar.
   (a) Comment upon the idea of an aroma plug.
   (b) Describe the various stages a product goes through before its launch.
   (c) By referring to accounting information, principles and practices, discuss the sort of information an accountant may prepare before a product launch.
4. What is meant by 'multi-media' advertising?

5. Identify three criteria for measuring the success of a brand such as Mr Sheen.

6. Using the Dettox room spray as an example, explain what is meant by a differential advantage.

7. What is meant by
   (a) brand assurance?
   (b) global force?
   (c) innovation?
   (d) relaunch?

⌕ Case Study 7—The Eye-case

For all their advantages, contact lenses have a number of drawbacks. The earliest lenses were large and uncomfortable to wear, and prone to scratching. Soft lenses were a huge technical and marketing breakthrough, but they too have problems. They do not allow the eyes to 'breathe' and so they cannot be worn all the time; dust and other air particles build up on the lenses; and natural secretions cause protein deposits which have to be cleaned off. Soft lenses are also relatively expensive because of the technical problems involved. They have to be manufactured to a high level of accuracy in an absolutely sterile environment.

Opticon UK Ltd manufactures and sells both lenses and peripherals directly to retailers. 'Peripherals' is the collective name used to describe the family of solutions needed by lens-wearers: 'Eyeclean', the solution for soaking the lenses, 'Eyeneut', the cleansing agent, and 'Eyeprot', the protein remover.

Opticon has a large research and development department, constantly seeking to find ways of overcoming consumer resistance to contact-lens-wearing. In June 1991 a directors' meeting was addressed by the company's head of research and development, Ms May Opia:

> 'As you all know, one of our biggest problems is with peripherals. The lens wearer has to take the lenses out every night, clean them by hand, place them in a chemical for a period of time, and then put them in a soaking solution. Once a week wearers also have to remove the protein deposits. All this activity is both time-consuming and expensive, and a lot of people simply can't be bothered. So they just take the lenses out and place them in the soaking solution. As a result the lenses don't last as long as they should—which in a way is good for us—but now we've got the Department of Health breathing down our necks. They say that there may be a harmful long-term effect on the nation's eyes which will eventually be a cost on the National Health Service.
>
> 'Well, I've got good news. We've developed a solution which cleans, sterilizes and removes protein deposits in one go. We call it Eyewash, and we reckon we can manufacture it for only 50% more than the cost of our standard soaking fluid.'

There was a buzz of excitement around the room, but then the finance director spoke:

'That sounds great, May, but let's have a close look at the figures before we go overboard on this. Currently the breakdown of our peripherals' market is as follows.'

He rose from his seat and placed figures and charts so the meeting could study the facts pertaining to 1990 (Table 24.1 and Fig. 24.2). He continued:

'Clearly we are going to have to revise our figures if Eyewash is introduced. It seems to me that we could have problems if my rough estimates are correct. What do you think, Stig?'

Table 24.1

	Eyeclean	Eyeneut	Eyeprot
Recommended retail price (per litre)	£24	£16	£24
Sales ('000 litres)	100	70	10
Overheads allocated to peripherals: £300 000			

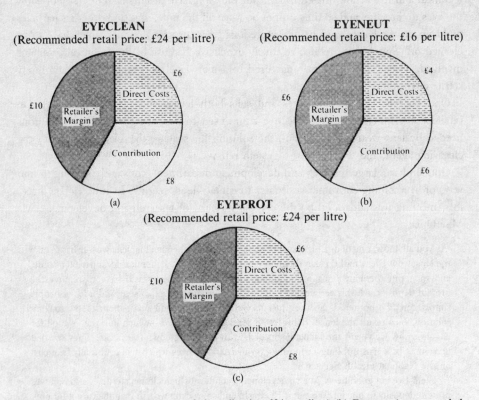

Figure 24.2 (a) Eyeclean (recommended retail price £24 per litre) (b) Eyeneut (recommended retail price £16 per litre) (c) Eyeprot (recommended retail price £24 per litre).

The marketing director, Mr Matism, thought for a moment, and then replied:

'As you all know, we are in a pretty competitive market, but the manufacturers have all been skimming it for some time now. There are really only three producers in the market, and we all more or less agree not to upset things too much. The other two companies are both American, but we're a bit concerned that Yeuxo, the French firm, and Eyetize of Milan might try to elbow their way in, come 1992. Our research indicates that the peripherals market is price-elastic, but it's complicated by the connection with the price of the lenses themselves, on which, as you know, we make very little profit.

'As far as Eyewash is concerned, I think it's a winner, but only if we can offload some of our current production elsewhere; and I don't mean Europe, which I think we have got to regard as a part of our domestic market now. I think it's high time we thought about selling to the Third World. Our preliminary market research indicates that sales of our existing peripherals will fall by 80 per cent if we introduce Eyewash. But on the other hand, we reckon it will sell more by volume than Eyeclean did, although the exact volume will clearly depend on the retail price. We would want to work on the assumption, however, that Eyewash's contribution to profits and fixed overheads was at least the same as Eyeclean's.'

The meeting was quiet for a moment, and then the production director spoke:

'We've also got to think about the production implications in all this. We may be able to modify our facilities at our existing plant, but then we might end up with unused capacity of both capital and labour. What will we do with that?'

At this point the managing director stepped in.

'Hang on a minute, everyone; I think we should focus on one thing at a time.'

Questions

1. (a) Briefly explain why Opticon is not concerned about the low level of profit made on the manufacture of their contact lenses.
   (b) Explain what is meant by the 'market is price-elastic' (lines 45–6).
   (c) If the price elasticity of demand for Eyeclean is 1.5, what would be the effect on sales of a price reduction to £21.60?
2. Assuming that all the predictions in the case study turn out to be correct, what level of sales will Eyewash have to achieve in order to generate the same contribution as Eyeclean? Make all your workings clear, and state any assumptions that you make.
3. Outline and evaluate the non-financial factors that Opticon should take into account before deciding on the production of Eyewash.
4. What do you think are the issues raised, for a company like Opticon, by the marketing director's comments: 'As far as Eyewash is concerned, I think it's a winner, but only if we can offload some of our current production elsewhere; and I don't mean Europe, which I think we have got to regard as a part of our domestic market now. I think it's high time we thought about selling to the Third World?'

(*Source*: AEB)

Case Study 8—Business at the close of the twentieth century

Business at the close of the twentieth century will be without boundaries because of the globalization of economies, technologies and communications.

Geographic boundaries have been removed with the restructuring of Eastern Europe and the former Soviet Union. Mergers, acquisitions and joint ventures will be replaced by fluid international partnerships with companies in other countries and other industries. Strategic alliances will become more standard practice as product life-cycles shorten and the need to reach markets quickly becomes more important.

Technological changes will also have a significant impact on global business. Products will become more intelligent as chips are built into more consumer goods. Smart cards will become commonplace. Multimedia interactivity will blend with virtual reality and artificial intelligence.

Business meetings will be called in an instant and held internationally as communications bridge time zones and language barriers. Many managers will spend part of the day at home and part dealing with an office across the globe.

The sheer volume of information and the immediacy with which it is available will lead to a flattening of the levels of management so that there will be decline in the need for middle managers. More individuals will be involved in the decision-making process and will take responsibility for their decisions. International work-teams will develop new projects.

Corporate growth will be measured not just in profitability as businesses become the platform for social change. Solutions to issues such as health care will increasingly become the responsibility of the corporation. The company may also subsidize other facilities, such as child care and elder care. Education will become an international process, with companies forming strategic alliances with universities offering both management and community courses. They will also become increasingly involved with world issues.

For managers of the future, change will be a daily process and innovation will be the mechanism for dealing with such change.

The above case was developed from a series of articles appearing in business journals. It represents a range of views about business at the close of the twentieth century.

Questions

1. Using a multinational business as an example, explain the term 'global market-place'. Why will more companies operate in such a market-place over the next few years?
2. Comment on the implications for a marketer of:
    (a) shorter product life cycles.
    (b) the need to reach markets more quickly.

3. Describe what is meant by:
   (a) multimedia activity.
   (b) virtual reality.
   (c) artificial intelligence.
   How will they affect (i) consumers and (ii) producers?
4. Comment on the benefits of managers being able to work from home. Explain how they will be able to deal with offices across the globe at the same time.
5. Explain what is meant by 'flattening of the levels of management'. How might this affect the ways in which an organization operates?
6. Describe how the business objectives of organization of the future might change.

Suggested reading

Edge, A. G., and Coleman, D. R., *The Guide to Case Analysis and Reporting*, 3rd edn. System Logistics, 1986.
Marcouse, I. with Lines, D., *Business Case Studies*. Longman, 1992.
Needham, D. and Dransfield, R., *On Target*. MBA Publishing, 1990.
Needham, D. and Dransfield, R., *Business Studies A-Level Workbook*. McGraw-Hill, 1993.

Linking business studies: Notes for teachers

Perhaps the best form of link for any business studies course is one built up with a local organization which allows *regular student visits* and is also happy to provide *work experience* placements. Both project (e.g. as required by Cambridge) and written case-study (e.g. as required by Oxford) requirements of certain examining boards can be met when students establish contacts on work placements and therefore have both the stimulation and close contact with a company, so that they can research and develop ideas at first hand. We have deliberately avoided suggesting project titles, because to do so would have taken away the creative element of students choosing titles that (a) meet their own needs and (b) are relative to the organization with which they have contact. Creative investigation may be related to something that has recently happened, a problem that needs to be analysed or a change within or external to a business, or it may be based on the future. Comprehensive advice on the preparation of practical projects and their requirements is provided for students by the respective examination boards.

One way in which young people can learn about a particular line of work is through *work shadowing*. This involves a student 'keeping in step' with an employee, observing the tasks performed and learning about the employee's role. In this way the employee acts as a 'work guide' and the student attempts to place himself or herself in the employee's shoes in order to see the world of work through an employee's eyes. Work shadowing is therefore different from work experience, in which a student is given a job of his or her own to do. The 'helping-out' a student provides while work shadowing is a way of helping the student to understand the employee's work.

Another area of link, and one that is almost as good as first-hand experience, is to invite *visiting speakers* into school or college. Though it is always possible to use your contacts or the speaker services of organizations such as the Banking Information Service, it is often better to integrate visits into a comprehensive programme so that it becomes a course covering a spread of areas. Understanding Industry does this by inviting senior speakers from the world of business and industry to visit schools to talk about a variety of carefully identified business areas such as human relations, marketing and management. Visits involve eight sessions and, though it is more common to organize sessions on a weekly basis, a particularly exciting format is to condense all of the UI speakers for a course into a two-day conference. UI therefore aims to:

- Provide 16–19-year-old students staying on in education with a better understanding of industry and commerce.

- Operate in the school/college timetable
- Work with teachers and lecturers to develop UI as a curriculum resource
- Involve business people in their local schools and colleges as part of a managed programme

Through its eight-part courses, Understanding Industry demonstrates to those staying on in education—the future opinion formers and business leaders—how a company operates, and why successful companies are so necessary for the creation of the nation's wealth. As a resource to support a business studies course, it is useful to have the opportunity to ask pertinent questions of people who have both specialized and become successful in their particular field.

A particularly popular activity, which enables students to appreciate the difficulties involved in integrating the decision-making process as well as the hard work necessary to succeed in business, is to set up some form of *mini-company*. There are a variety of kits on the market, and on a number of occasions in recent years there have been sponsored competitions designed to encourage students to produce a business plan and then to go through the motions of setting up a company. Young Enterprise is an organization providing the mechanism by which schools and colleges can set up their own business. Their literature states that:

> Young Enterprise offers a truly exciting opportunity to students aged 15–19. We provide a 'Company Kit' which includes all the paperwork and guidance needed to set up a business. This practical business education helps students to recognise and develop their skills and abilities and helps bridge the gap between school and work. The student can get a better understanding of how a business works and how wealth is created in what amounts to a real business situation. Students will find this opportunity invaluable when it comes to choosing their own career and understanding how work and the business world can be fun. The Young Enterprise company kit involves real money, real products developed by the students and, with the aid of business advisors, will help the students to realise marketing, sales, management and hopefully profit. The results achieved and the business experience gained will be the property of the students alone and relate to their learning needs in school and for life.

The real benefit of Young Enterprise and the setting up of mini-companies is the creation of the ability to put ideas into action to see if they work and to develop practical business skills in real situations.

Another useful form of simulation is that of the *business game*. One of the first of these was, of course, Monopoly, in which the combination of dice and strategy determined success. The benefit of business games is that they provide experiments which enable business behaviour to be better understood. Students develop strategies and build up their problem-solving skills, often with an element of competition, and tend to enjoy doing so. Business games vary considerably in nature. Some are just macroeconomic models; others involve a broad spectrum of interacting business areas such as marketing, purchasing, finance and so on; and many appear as computer models.

Games have several advantages:

1. They provide an alternative approach to fulfil learning objectives.
2. They provide a vehicle for assessment.
3. They provide an opportunity to use alternative resources such as computers.

4. They can enable group work to take place.
5. They are often suprisingly easy to use.

It is important that with business games teachers carefully brief students beforehand so that they understand the purpose of the exercise and have a good idea of both the principles and the rules involved. It is just as essential that students are debriefed after the game so that they can identify the principles covered. Games are not a substitute for teaching but they do provide a valuable additional technique of putting over principles. It is always useful to try and test a game beforehand to ensure that potential problems are taken into account.

Wherever possible, try to bring *written materials* into the classroom. Companies publish a tremendous range of information, much of which is for educational purposes. Understanding British Industry produces a directory of teaching materials from industry and commerce which can be used in the classroom. Written materials from companies can add a realistic element to classroom discussion and can often be used as a base for the writing of case studies.

Finally, business studies is an area of constant change. By its very nature, it is topical and covers events that appear on a daily basis on both business and headline pages in newspapers, on radio and television, and weekly in magazines such as *The Economist*. Keeping up to date with events and using recently published materials enables students to use real-world examples in their work and to apply theories to actual situations.

Making this subject practical helps to create realism, generate interest, encourage discussion and ultimately provide a better understanding.

Index